Managing Global Busines

MANAGING GLOBAL BUSINESS

Michael Wynn-Williams

 palgrave

First published 2016 by
PALGRAVE

Palgrave in the UK is an imprint of Macmillan Publishers Limited, registered in England, company number 785998, of 4 Crinan Street, London, N1 9XW.

Palgrave Macmillan in the US is a division of St Martin's Press LLC, 175 Fifth Avenue, New York, NY 10010.

Palgrave is a global imprint of the above companies and is represented throughout the world.

Palgrave® and Macmillan® are registered trademarks in the United States, the United Kingdom, Europe and other countries.

ISBN 978–1–137–34825–8 paperback

This book is printed on paper suitable for recycling and made from fully managed and sustained forest sources. Logging, pulping and manufacturing processes are expected to conform to the environmental regulations of the country of origin.

A catalogue record for this book is available from the British Library.

A catalog record for this book is available from the Library of Congress.

Printed in China

Short Contents

Contents

List of Figures

List of Tables

Introduction

You might think that if there is one business that can be accused of over-supply it is the business of producing business textbooks. With slight variations in their titles they are all written from the same point of view: academics presenting theories on how to be successful in business. So what makes this textbook any different?

Well, for starters this book has been written by someone who gained broad experience in international business before taking the academic path. Over my professional life I have gained first-hand knowledge ranging from consulting with multinationals to dealing with customers face-to-face. It was on this foundation that I was then able to take the next step of joining academia. This book, then, attempts to show how theories of global management have value only when they are rooted in the real world of business.

CATCHING UP WITH HISTORY

To be frank, management theories lag behind practice by some distance. For example, one of the oldest firms in the world that is still trading is the Japanese temple constructor, Kongo Gumi. It was a family-owned enterprise from 578AD until 2006, when it finally succumbed to the financial misfortunes of the bubble economy and was absorbed into the Takamatsu construction empire. Kongo Gumi still operates even after its 1428 years of independence came to an end. Contrast that heritage with the oldest theories of the firm: appearing in the early years of the twentieth century, one key theorist was Ronald Coase and his 1937 theory. It was a ground-breaking piece of academic work but Kong Gumi had already happily survived for 1359 years without Coase's help.

As a consequence we need to acknowledge the weight of history whenever we argue for a new management theory. Whatever the latest theory may espouse we can be pretty sure that there will be a manager, somewhere in history, who has put it into practice quite unschooled in its principles. In my own life I recall just such an occasion when an experienced manager summarily dismissed a new theory as little more than, as the old adage has it, money for old rope.

The manager I have in mind was a family friend, a respected member of the local business community, and he was in heated conversation with his son. The boy was one of those children who collected enthusiasms and his latest obsession was with the new-fangled concept of just-in-time (JIT) deliveries. He was probably no more than fourteen years old, but he was fascinated by the idea of supplies arriving at the factory gates the minute, even the very second, they were required on the assembly line. Just as all boys seem to be infatuated by the superlatives of supersonic speeds, warships and racing cars, so this lad was entranced by the high-wire balancing act of an industry acting at the very limits of economic efficiency.

His father was not so impressed. He had heard this kind of talk before, only without the dangerous sounding 'just-in-time' epithet. It was not that he was cynical but that he could see little that was really new. As he angrily retorted to his son, minimising stock and scheduling deliveries to the last possible moment had been standard features of business since time immemorial. A modern printing firm would only order paper and ink for the time when it was needed, a medieval blacksmith would hold only what raw iron was immediately required. For any business to store more stock than was necessary meant tying up funds that could be used elsewhere and this, at all times in history, has been an action that would harm the competitive health of the company.

FUSING PRACTICE AND THEORY

Never mind the youthful enthusiasm of that excitable young lad, I was no older myself and deeply impressionable. Except that my own interest was in the father's defence of the pragmatics of standard management practice in the face of the celebrity of the latest headline-grabbing management theory. The point the father was making was that the theory was an observation of established practice repackaged as a new approach to be sold back to managers. I do not share quite such a negative view these days and would argue that the purpose of academic learning is to distil years, centuries even, of experience into sets of principles that can be far more rapidly learned by the neophyte manager. The alternative would be for each manager to go through the exhaustive process of reinventing the wheel time after time, which would be hugely wasteful.

If we are to bring theory and practice together into a mutually beneficial relationship then we must first abandon the pretence that one side has the advantage over the other. This book takes this line of healthy scepticism. Management studies is not a science made up of provable theories; it is not about questions and answers. Instead, it is about problems and solutions. Just as business is made up of an infinite variety of challenges, so managers meet them with an infinite variety of possible strategies. You could even argue that this is the thrill of being a manager: knowing that you have just as much chance of devising the best way forward as anyone else.

The best managers like to think of themselves, in their most private thoughts, as swashbucklers. In more sober terminology we call them entrepreneurs but they are, all the same, out for the thrills of business as much as they are after the treasure of financial returns. They will use whatever tools come to hand for only as long as they are useful. This book presents those tools, shows how to use them and treats them all with the disrespect they deserve. If any management theories were perfect they would have made perfect millionaires of all of us by now.

CHAPTER STRUCTURE

The book is made up of eighteen standalone chapters. It is not structured like a novel; there is no requirement to start at the beginning and finish at the end. It is perfectly possible to dip in and out of the book at will, according to one's needs. For ease of reference, though, the chapters are grouped into seven themes as follows:

PART I – Global possibilities (Chapters 1–2)

It is on the back of internationalising markets that the multinational enterprise (MNE) has ridden to the centre stage. In Chapter 1 we will look at how international trade has been with us since the earliest commercial enterprises, developing rapidly in recent decades as we have taken the ultimate step of globalisation, that being the integration of businesses across worldwide locations. Chapter 2 takes a deeper look at how business can exploit the opportunities of globalisation to grow their operations.

PART II – Global markets (Chapters 3–6)

Risk is an indelible feature of all business, balanced by the rate of financial return that can compensate for the danger. Chapters 3 and 4 will define the nature of international risk, how it can be assessed and what this means for the MNE as it positions itself in unfamiliar overseas markets. Chapter 5 presents the routes into the chosen market and Chapter 6 follows this up with the marketing options.

PART III – Global locations (Chapters 7–9)

How the company supplies its overseas markets defines its status as an MNE. The first step is usually to access the traditional channels of international trade, exporting and importing, these topics being discussed in Chapter 7. The greatest commitment, foreign direct investment (FDI), is covered in Chapter 8 when the MNE gets its boots on the ground with a local operation over which it has direct managerial control. Chapter 9 will then take a close look at the network of international suppliers that sustain the MNE.

PART IV – Global strategies, alliances and structures (Chapters 10–12)

For an organisation that started with only a domestic market to serve, globalisation can put its structure under severe strain. Chapter 10 considers the strategic implications of its global reach. Chapter 11 discusses the temptations of taking the fast track route by forming alliances, as well as the dangers of hitching corporate fortunes to an erstwhile rival. Of course, it is unlikely that the organisation's original domestic structure will be up to the job of coping with global operations and so Chapter 12 lays out the options for restructuring.

PART V – Global regulations and finance (Chapters 13–15)

Despite the liberating effect on MNEs of free trade there is no escaping the necessity for controlling the wilder excesses. In Chapter 13 we will look at the global regulatory frameworks that attempt to maintain some sense of order. Chapter 14 then considers the minutiae of running global operations by evaluating the challenges of financial accounting across borders. Chapter 15 builds on this by exploring sources of new funding, including novel financial solutions offered by the explosion in social media.

PART VI – Global management of people (Chapters 16–18)

The bedrock of any firm is the workforce, and for an MNE this is still true, only more complicated. Chapter 16 introduces us to the many characteristics of international cultures that both challenge and invigorate the MNE. Chapter 17 shows how these global human resources can be managed to enhance competitive advantages. Finally, Chapter 18 reminds us that all people who have any connection with the MNE are deserving of respect. It is the job of the global manager to devise appropriate strategies that allow the MNE to take its proper place in human society.

Throughout each chapter we will treat every academic approach with the irreverence it deserves. This book is not a hagiography of business theory; the value of each is measured only by the extent it is useful to the manager seeking to learn from it. Included are test cases taken from around the world, which may, or may not, support the theories being presented. It is only then, when the theory has been re-forged in the heat of experience, that the global manager can develop unique and competitive solutions to the ever-occurring problems thrown up by global business.

Part I Global Possibilities

International trade has existed almost since the historic day a group of humans joined together into a community, planted a flag into the ground and proclaimed 'this land is our land'. Whatever nationalistic pride might have bound them together it would not have taken them long to realise that their much disparaged neighbours, gathered under their own flag and working their own land, were not as stupid as they looked. Indeed, there were some things they were actually pretty good at. Thus was international trade born.

Although the development of international trade is an integral part of the human story, it was centuries before anyone really began to understand what advantages it brought. The fundamental mis-understanding seems to be that trade has been viewed as a budgetary issue: if you bought nice stuff from your neighbour it brought pleasure to your life but it made your neighbour richer. It would be preferable, then, to sell to your neighbours and enrich yourself on their money. That, at least, is the theory behind mercantilism with its drive to minimise imports and maximise exports. Back in the medieval days, nations found they could source bargain-price commodity imports by invading new lands and stealing the raw materials. Royal treasuries were filled to bursting with shiny, but essentially useless, gold while colonies received little in exchange but iron shackles.

The Renaissance brought a new wave of thinkers, intellectuals who believed that trade could be an exchange that benefited both parties. Adam Smith argued that countries could trade in those goods where they had an absolute advantage, exchanging their surpluses with trading partners to their mutual benefit. This took trade out of the grasping hands of the imperialists and put it into the hands of the merchants. International trade did not have to be governed by muskets but could be allowed to flourish where it would. However, with theory still lagging far behind business practice, even absolute advantage was only a partial explanation of why the exchanges took place. If a country enjoyed no absolute advantage then it was assumed to be doomed to eternal poverty, a result that was fortunately not reflected in reality.

It was David Ricardo who put forward a theory of trade that finally revealed how all countries, rich and poor, can benefit from their exchanges. They do this by identifying their own internal compara-tive advantage, which is the economic activity that they are better at than anything else. It is of little consequence that there may be other countries that enjoy even greater advantages in that activity; as long as those countries have another comparative advantage of their own they will prefer to focus their resources on that. A rich country may have absolute advantages across the economic spectrum but because it will gain more from shifting resources to its comparative advantages it will still need to trade with the poorer country.

Although comparative advantage trade theory still does not quite capture all the subtleties and appar-ent contradictions of international trade, it does show how entrepreneurs anywhere in the world can push trade forward. Indeed, in the latter half of the twentieth century it reached such dizzy heights that the very structure of businesses began to change. Originally, internationalisation meant that firms imported raw materials and simple components, incorporating them into high-value products for return export. The new era of globalisation was not just an extreme form of internationalisation; it was a whole new way of doing business. Firms created overseas branches that would conduct their own high value work, leading to a cross-flow of ideas and product innovations. This was a mutually beneficial exchange that mirrored the advantages of international trade. This new kind of interdependence gave rise to a new breed of business: the multinational enterprise (MNE).

It seems to be accepted without question that these MNEs are the most powerful commercial forces on the planet. They have even been accused of being able to act with complete indifference to the government of the country within which they operate. Such suspicion may be more the paranoia of conspiracy lovers than actual fact, but there is no doubting that most self-respecting companies harbour ambitions to grow internationally. Theorists like Ansoff suggest how the senior managers can choose to plunge straight into the deep end with the existing product range or else develop the market so that it becomes accepting of the products in the future. Product adaptation is another option, but if none of these options appeal then the company can diversify itself into the new market with new products.

Tempting though these international opportunities are, sometimes commercial caution is the better part of management valour. These international adventures are always high risk, but it still takes a brave manager to argue against growth. The promise of increased sales seems to offer higher profits, but this is not necessarily the case. The product may have to be adapted beyond recognition, marketing campaigns instigated and new production facilities created. The end result may be a company that is weighed down by additional costs that wipe out the increased revenues. A successful company, therefore, is one that never forgets the fundamental purpose of all commercial enterprises:

To deliver maximum value to the customer at minimum cost to the enterprise.

1 Globalisation and the New International Environment

Chapter Objectives

By the end of this chapter, you should have a better idea of globalisation and how this has made a real impact on modern business. We will look at the following topics:

- The first glimmers of international business and how this process of internationalisation is so different from globalisation.
- Attempts to generate theories of international trade even if trade itself seemed to expand without their help.
- How globalisation serves the interests of developed economies more than it does those of emerging economies.
- The myths surrounding the balance of payments.
- What globalisation means for managers and employability.

THE HISTORIC ROOTS OF GLOBALISATION

In Lake Mälaren near the Swedish capital of Stockholm lies the unremarkable island of Helgö. Apart from its pleasant location and the pretty eighteenth-century Kaggeholm Castle, it might be thought that there is nothing there to detain an ambitious student of global management. Yet the island symbolises, not how much the world of business has changed over the centuries, but how little the underlying principles have remained constant. In 1954 an archaeological dig on the island turned up three remarkable Viking possessions: an Indian Buddha statuette, a sacred Irish crozier and an Egyptian scoop (Waller, 1982). The statuette and the scoop are of sixth-century origin, making the eighth-century crozier, an ornamental bishop's crook, almost disappointingly modern by comparison.

Each of the items is exquisite by any standard, but the staggering fact is that together they had travelled over 16,000km to reach their Scandinavian destination. These journeys would have been completed at a time when Vikings were marauding through Europe, Egypt was under Byzantine rule and India was made up of medieval states. Long-distance trade would have taken many months to complete, but essentially this is the same process in which modern international trade operates. Simply, there are specialist producers in distant locations who are able to trade with each other to mutual advantage. It is not known what the Viking buyers were able to exchange for the artefacts, but it was most likely to have been plunder that they had amassed from their numerous raids through Europe.

While the fundamentals of trade may have remained surprisingly constant, there are areas where changes have taken place. The speed that goods can be shipped is certainly faster, reduced to mere hours if they are transported by air. It is also possible to be in direct contact with the originator of the good. If the shirt you wear says it is from India, it would be quite feasible to research its entire supply chain. The great leap forward that international trade represents, then, is not how we can profit from it, we have always done that, but how we can co-ordinate and control it to our advantage. This is where the science of business management steps in, many eons after the benefits of trade were first experienced.

FROM INTERNATIONALISATION TO GLOBALISATION

Current experience suggests that the pace of international trade has been accelerating, particularly in the past few decades. It has also been spreading to the extent that it can be said with some confidence that no country in the world is now isolated from its influence. Yet even in the past 150 years, the process of international connectedness has not been an inexorable march towards total economic integration but has been a series of advances and retreats. The emergence of the United States as a major economic power in the mid-nineteenth century proved to be a major draw for immigration and capital investment which only served to stoke the furnace of economic expansion even further. The spirit of optimism was then undermined by the financial disasters after World War I and the reversal away from free trade towards the kinds of protectionist policies that are so stubborn to remove (Hirst and Thompson, 2002).

It is because the isolationist doctrine of holding back imports with a protectionist wall of tariff and non-tariff obstacles is mutually destructive that, post-World War II, global economic institutions have been created to unjam the mechanisms of free trade. Chief among them is the **World Trade Organisation (WTO)**, but even it has struggled to liberalise trade. There is still a visceral faith in the idea that exports are good, imports are bad. As we shall see, whatever the intuitive attraction of this one-sided trade doctrine its obstinate blindness to the enlightenment of free trade will continue to suppress trade and hold back global economic development.

International trade being entrenched in human existence over so many centuries means that any theories that seek to explain it are guilty of ex-post rationalisation. Nevertheless, we need their insights if we are to combat the ever-present tendencies for countries to give in to the temptation to safeguard their industries by protecting them from international competition. When international managers know the theories behind trade then they will understand why they should embrace globalisation.

MERCANTILISM AND THE ZERO-SUM GAME

The earliest attempt to structure our understanding of international trade resulted in the theory of **mercantilism**. Unlike most theories, this has no single inventor and it is instead an approach that emerged over a century or so. Some of the blame is attached to Adam Smith, although he never used the word. Instead, Smith referred to a mercantile system and the necessity for balancing the nation's accounts favourably. Indeed, mercantilism is less a theory of trade and more a rationale for nation building, one that confuses money and wealth as part of a policy for securing a nation's status within the world's flow of trade (Harris, 2004).

It is not difficult to see why this is so since mercantilism has a strong intuitive basis. You can imme-diately see this even today when you ask a group of people the simple question, 'which is better for your national economy, exports or imports?' Invariably you will find that the vast majority of people will opt for exports. The simple logic of the argument is that if your country is selling more than it is buying, then it must be growing richer. It is what is known as a zero-sum game, meaning that there are absolute limits on what can be gained, and so it is better to grab what you can at the expense of your neighbour. In fact, this is quite wrong; both exports and imports are important: it is trade between the two that brings the most benefits. The key point is that international trade brings mutual benefits, even for the most disadvantaged nations.

Nevertheless, there are certain short-term attractions to the mercantilist approach. It can result in the rapid expansion of particular industries as they gain access to the wider international market. The industrial emphasis is on retaining the skills that add maximum value, which is where the profits lie. Mercantilist policies sanction imports of commodities to feed the domestic industry while imports of rival finished goods are suppressed. The rest of the world, then, is seen as a source of raw material and a market for finished goods. Since countries in the rest of the world have their own economic development agendas for a mercantilist policy to be fully implemented it implies suppression of rival industries in those countries. Inevitably, this created the shameful urge to build empires and thereby control the flow of trade. In response, poorer countries are forced to mount their own trade barriers because their exports face obstacles put up by wealthier countries (Looi Kee et al., 2009).

 ## CASE STUDY: SPAIN AND THE GOLDEN BANKRUPTCY

The association between mercantilism and the worst aspects of imperialism are most obvious if we go back to the sixteenth century. This was a time when Spain, for example, was expanding its empire and amassing wealth in the form of gold, not all of it earned through fair trade. In Spain this gold was as good as currency, with the effect that the economy was awash with cash. According to monetarist economic theories, the excess cash was chasing the same quantity of goods in the market, with the result that prices climbed and inflation raged.

Those engaged in the mercantilist trade continued to accumulate gold; therefore, they could afford to keep pace with inflation, but for poorer people with no gold the higher prices were intolerable. So while the rich were lavishing gold leaf on religious patronage, the poor in Spain were starving. Corruption is an integral feature of mercantilism and another example of how economic resources can be misallocated. One of the reasons Spain lost the sea battle against England in 1588 was that the Spanish armada was poorly maintained and the sailors were severely malnourished.

It was not only Spain, the mother country, that suffered from its mercantilist policies; the colonies did too. Their nascent economies were tightly controlled in order to maintain their status as suppliers of raw materials to the value-adding industries of the mother country. It could be argued that Spain's colonies were handicapped by this legacy even after they had won their independence.

Point of consideration: If Spain had focused instead on developing its colonies economically rather than using them for cheap commodity imports, how would Spain's own economic development have been different?

Source: Mahoney (2010)

NEO-MERCANTILISM IN THE MODERN WORLD

You might well wonder about the point of the history lesson. The fact of the matter is that there is still a strong popular belief in the mercantilist approach. It is particularly tempting for developing countries since it encourages the expansion of export-oriented industries, bringing them up to global standards of scale and technology. With gold now replaced by national currencies, the effects on the economy of amassing wealth are no longer so immediate. Nevertheless, the impact is still just as pernicious and this approach is known as **neo-mercantilism**.

Under neo-mercantilism the medium of exchange becomes money. Unlike gold, money can generally only be spent in the country of origin. The principle is still the same, a beggar-thy-neighbour zero-sum game where both sides ultimately suffer. Self-sufficiency and exports are emphasised over imports, while overseas capital investments are restricted. Countries may profess to operate liberal economies but most will protect domestic industries to a degree. As with traditional mercantilism, there is a strong political emphasis on nation building even if that means that the welfare of the domestic population is a lower priority. Rather, goods are sold to overseas consumers who then feel the welfare benefits of the competitive prices, while at home consumers are denied access to imports.

The main beneficiaries, as before, are those that are involved in the export-oriented industry, with the effect that income inequality widens between the rich and the poor. For a developing country this period may be considered part of its growing pains: a few getting rich on the new industries while the rest of the economy gradually catches up. Kröger (2012) argues that Brazil's support of national industrial champions is another example of neo-mercantilism.

In the long term the bias towards exporting creates its own problems. Domestic consumers are not served by the new industries and they have poor access to imported goods. Even if they could find the imported goods they would find that the low value of their currency made imports relatively expensive. Usually, the currency of an exporting nation rises in value as international customers seek it out in order to purchase the goods, but the exporting government works to suppress the value of the currency. It does this by hording foreign currency in its reserves, thereby reducing the amounts of that currency in circulation and therefore raising its value.

MANAGEMENT SPOTLIGHT: NEO-MERCANTILISM FOR MODERN MANAGERS

Neo-mercantilist policies restrict the range of strategies open to business managers. They will find that the government will support strategies that substitute for imports or use basic imports, usually commodities, in value-adding processes. The government is therefore looking for businesses that:

- Reduce the nation's payments for imports
- Improve the national skills base
- Earn foreign exchange through exports.

This is a national strategy that is often employed by developing nations that are looking to accelerate their economic progress, or developed nations that wish to promote a key industry. For developing nations that lack the skill base the shortest route to economic development is to invite **multinational enterprises (MNEs)** from overseas to invest. The MNEs are willing to engage in **foreign direct investment (FDI)** because although it may be substituting imports they are the imports of rival MNEs. The local government's worry will be that the national skills base is not being expanded by the MNE, so joint ventures are often made compulsory in order to encourage knowledge transfer from the MNE.

Managers will find that whether they work for a local corporation or the incoming MNE, the business strategy needs to be closely aligned with the national strategy. This implies those that can deliver high-value content:

- Electronics
- Fashion clothing
- Complex consumer goods
- Import substitution of high-value goods, e.g. cars, aircraft, trains, defence goods
- National champions upon which other industries depend, e.g. steel production, construction.

Many other industries will be on the losing end of this national trade policy bargain. These include:

- Low-value exports, e.g. commodities
- Domestic agricultural goods
- Importers of high-value components.

There will be some latitude in these policies, such as where high-value imports are necessary for a given type of production to go ahead, but going against government strategy invariably involves overcoming numerous bureaucratic hurdles.

Point of consideration: How closely should managers work with politicians in formulating trade policies? Is it better to work within a framework imposed by government rather than attempt to influence the decision making?

ABSOLUTE ADVANTAGE THEORY

The mercantilist approach to trade is simple to understand and can accelerate the economic progress of a developing country during its formative years. However, the zero-sum game assumes that the global economy as a whole is not expanding. In essence, the world's economy is considered to be static and it is only by exporting that a country can gain a greater share of the wealth.

Adam Smith, the famous economist, challenged this negative advancement, arguing that human wealth was not dependent on gold but rather goods and services (Harris, 2004). If a country has an absolute advantage then it is able to produce a particular good with the lowest input of all its trading partners. This means it is the most efficient.

 MYTH BUSTER: CHAMPAGNE AND CONTRIVED ABSOLUTE ADVANTAGE

It might be thought that France holds an absolute advantage in the production of Champagne. Certainly, by reputation it is the very monarch of wines, thanks to the excellent growing conditions that the country enjoys for the grapes, such as Pinot noir. Yet it is not unique in this, and other countries have the potential to produce rival wines of the same type, even the UK with its decidedly uncooperative climate. The French, though, have created a unique advantage that no competitor can replicate: they have registered the Champagne name so that it is legally restricted to only those white sparkling wines from the Champagne district of France, much to the chagrin of the wine-making village of Champagne in Switzerland.

This is known as Protected Designation of Origin (PDO), a European Union (EU) ruling on where named products can claim a geographical link. In a sense this ensures that France has an absolute advantage in the production of Champagne in perpetuity. Not only have other wine-growing regions sought protection for their particular products, the same approach has created absolute advantages for Greece in the production of feta cheese, as well as many products in other countries.

There is no doubt that PDO is a restriction on free trade. Other EU schemes include Protected Geographical Indication (PGI), where at least one process takes place in the named location, and Traditional Speciality Guaranteed (TSG), which refers to the character of the product or a process.

Point of consideration: What are the advantages and disadvantages to the consumer of PDO?

Source: European Commission PDO-PGI-TSG, 2014

Adam Smith realised that two trading nations could achieve mutual gains by expanding the total amount of trade, not just taking shares of some fixed global amount. They do this by focusing on those activities where they have an absolute advantage and trading with nations that have complementary absolute advantages. Since both are working at their most efficient then the consumer should benefit through falling prices.

If we take the United States and Canada as examples, both countries have forests for timber and open grasslands for growing wheat. It is clear, though, that the vast forests of Canada indicate an absolute advantage in timber, while the United States would hold an absolute advantage in wheat. Smith would measure these advantages in terms of the labour input, which we illustrate in Table 1.1.

To make the calculations easier, let's assume that equal amounts of timber and wheat are needed by each country. So, from the example above, for the two countries to provide a tonne of each product domestically for their own consumption would require a total of ten units of labour. However, if the countries focus their efforts where they have the advantage, producing one tonne for domestic consumption and one tonne for export to their trading partner, then the total labour input comes to eight units. This breaks down into six units of labour for timber production in Canada, and two units of labour for wheat in the United States. In this imaginary case, international trade saves two units of labour, which can then be employed elsewhere in the economy. In this way, trade is a positive-sum game that leads to an overall economic expansion.

Table 1.1 *US and Canadian absolute advantages*

Country	Product	Labour input per tonne
US	Timber	4
	Wheat	1
Canada	Timber	3
	Wheat	2

In practice, the theory of absolute advantage fails to explain the complexity of international trade. If a country has an absolute advantage over all its trading partners, then the theory states that it should focus all its energies on the production of that one product and import everything else it needs. You do not have to be a geography expert to realise that the Canadian economy is engaged in far more than simple timber production.

COMPARATIVE ADVANTAGE THEORIES

David Ricardo set down the foundation of the modern approach to international trade with his theory of **comparative advantage**. Roy Ruffin (2002) asserts that it is one of the most important economic theories devised.

In the theory of comparative advantage, attention is now focused on the internal economy of a country. Perhaps a little confusingly, the comparison being made is not between two countries but is between two economic activities being conducted within the country. So, a comparative advantage is the activity that the country is more efficient at than any other activity it might be engaged in. In relation to a potential trading partner, the country may be less efficient at producing both goods but there is one that it is least worst at; in this it has a comparative advantage. This is illustrated in Table 1.2 for trade between the United States and Mexico, this time for the computer software industry and textiles.

Table 1.2 *US and Mexican comparative advantages*

Country	Product	Labour
US	Computer Software	3
	Textiles	6
Mexico	Computer Software	10
	Textiles	7

Table 1.2 is an example of how the United States might have absolute advantages in production of both computer software and textiles, though it is clearly best at computer software. The strong position in both industries invites a mercantilist response from the United States to produce both products and Mexico will be obliged to import both products.

As before, if we assume both countries want equal amounts of each product, then concentrating all production in the United States will involve labour input of 18 units. The only way Mexico could maintain its industry would be by refusing to trade with the United States, perhaps by applying punitive tariffs that price US goods out of its market. You can think of this as taking Mexico's cost disadvantage and adding it to the price of the imported US goods. The total labour input by both countries after the trade restrictions have been put in place would be 26 units. Since the total labour input has risen, both countries are worse off.

HECKSCHER–OHLIN THEORY

When the Ricardian theory of comparative advantage was first proposed the industrial revolution had barely started. It was therefore fair to assume that the only production factor of any note was labour and that this was not mobile across national borders. This view became outdated once investments in machinery began to change the commercial landscape.

The work of **Eli Heckscher** contributed to **Bertil Ohlin's** publication in 1933 of his theory on a two factor explanation for trade, adding capital to labour in the scenario of two countries deciding how to produce two distinct products (Baldwin, 2008). This is known as the Heckscher–Ohlin (HO) **factor endowment model** since the country is seen to have capital and labour as inherent qualities, almost as if it was born with them. This is most obvious with a country with a large population where we can readily accept that it must be well endowed with labour resources. Capital is less easy to define. However, it includes those factors that are part of the production process but are not consumed by it, so are distinct from raw materials. Infrastructure, institutions and banking would be examples of capital endowment.

As in all business and theoretical models, the HO model simplifies its view of the world by making a long list of assumptions. It is not that these assumed factors of production are seen as irrelevant, only that their inclusion would complicate the calculations unnecessarily and obscure our view of the two critical factors, labour and capital.

HECKSCHER–OHLIN ASSUMPTIONS

1. Capital mobility: capital is available freely within the country, but cannot be transferred to other countries.
2. Labour mobility: labour can move freely within the country, but cannot migrate to other countries.
3. Technology: countries enjoy the same access to technology, so their choice of production depends on labour and capital. The two commodities under consideration use unrelated technologies.
4. Law of one price applies: a commodity sells for the same price in all markets, unaffected by trade barriers, tariffs and transportation costs.
5. Constant returns to scale: as production expands there is no additional advantage found in the scale of output, which would then affect costs and prices.
6. Perfect competition: established producers can be challenged by new rivals at any time.

As you look through the assumptions you can probably argue with each and every one of them – just another one of the joys of studying economics for business! Nevertheless, the theory should provide sufficient illumination for us to understand the basic mechanisms of international trade.

The HO model, quite reasonably, states that a country that is abundantly endowed with one factor will use it intensively because the cost will be cheaper. Again, labour is the factor that illustrates this best because we understand that a country that has a relatively large population should have lower labour costs. We understand this because of simple supply and demand: if supply exceeds demand then the price of the supply must fall. The capital factor is less readily identified but the same principle applies: where capital is readily available it will be cheaper, most likely expressed in the form of interest rates.

If we explore this theory with two countries, let us say the United States and China, we can fairly claim that the United States is capital abundant and China is labour abundant. Trade allows them to specialise in their production system where they have the comparative advantage. As they develop their industries their intensive factor will gradually become scarcer, with the natural consequence that the other factor becomes relatively abundant. So as the United States exploits its capital the demand will begin to outstrip supply, raising its price (i.e. higher interest rates) and labour prices will start to look more attractive.

The same dynamic change will take place in China, except related to the abundant factor input of labour. As factories take on more workers labour prices will rise and it will be capital that becomes more attractive. This sets the two countries on a convergent path until eventually the costs will meet and factor price equalisation will have been achieved. This is the **factor equalisation theory (FET)**. At this point no more gains from trade can be made and volumes between the two countries stabilise (Markusen and Venables, 2000).

HO MODEL IN PRACTICE

The trading destination implied by the HO model, that countries will specialise in their comparative advantage up to the point where factor prices have equalised, is readily testable. **Wassily Leontief** took the wise decision to use the United States as his subject. Since the United States was a capital-intensive country, and of course still is, the prediction was that it would export capital-intensive goods and import labour-intensive goods. The contrary discovery that in fact it does the opposite became known as the **Leontief Paradox** (Dietzenbacher and Lahr, 2004).

Any number of attempts have been made to explain the paradox, few of them entirely satisfactorily. Leontief argued that US labour was three times more productive than that of other countries, so it should be multiplied by three to make a proper comparison. Casas and Choi (1984) found that in the year that Leontief conducted his study, 1947, the United States was not in the trade balance situation that the HO model demands but was instead in a trade surplus. Thus when a country is export oriented it will export all goods, even those where it does not necessarily have a comparative advantage. This helps to explain why China is currently an exporter of capital, thereby placing it in the Leontief Paradox.

NEW TRADE THEORY

The **New Trade Theory (NTT)**, advocated by such luminaries as Paul Krugman (Findlay et al., 2002), does not directly contradict the HO model but tries to take a more pragmatic view of how industries might gain some dominance in a country, drawing in national factors of production from other potential candidates. As each country has different industries, there is a reason for international trade. For example, if a country has a very large industry in which there are substantial **economies of scale** then that country will hold a cost advantage over rivals. Not only will other countries want to trade with it to benefit from the lower costs but the specialisation that country has chosen means that it will then need to trade for what it is not producing. Thus trade is based on reciprocal demand.

There are a number of reasons why a country might end up specialising, each with varying levels of predictability. A government may have anointed an industry as a national champion, such as financial services in the tax havens scattered around the world. There may also be a very large domestic market where new technologies can be launched and achieve economies of scale before overseas markets are invaded. This would certainly explain why the United States has come to dominate so many new industries and why the EU was formed to create a European market of comparable power.

MANAGEMENT SPOTLIGHT: COMPARATIVE ADVANTAGE AND INTERNATIONAL MANAGEMENT

Although the mercantilist approach to trade is economically misguided over the long term it is quite clear in its intentions. Clarity is always the friend of business since it allows planning to be conducted in an atmosphere of reasonably predictable conditions. A major reason why mercantilism can help a developing country rapidly industrialise is that managers can be reasonably sure of the sort of industry to be in, what to produce and who to sell it to.

Comparative advantage and all the international trade theories derived from it are much more difficult for international managers to use in business planning. The assumptions are useful in developing the theories but few managers would recognise them on the ground. Most industries enjoy increasing returns to scale, so there is an incentive in growing a company ahead of rivals in pursuit of economies of scale. The government may also support this expansion with financial aid and training programmes to improve the skills base. Alternatively, the government may not have the political will or the resources to help.

As a consequence, the principles of comparative advantage are not so readily incorporated into management decision making. For MNEs there are company-specific strategies that include analysis of the economic conditions of locations around the world, not the theoretical ruminations on how those conditions came about.

With each company taking a different line on international trade no business consensus emerges except by industry. The advantages for the shipbuilding industry lie in economies of scale and government support to smooth demand fluctuations so, according to the NTT approach, shipbuilding centres can enjoy strong international sales. Textiles, on the other hand, are manufactured labour-intensively so it is the HO model that reigns. As industries seem to be governed by different theories of trade we find that government policy can be short-term and lack coherence. A predictable outcome of this is that rates of internationalisation and globalisation tend to be specific to the industry, and even the company on occasion.

Point of consideration: Would it be better for MNEs if all countries had the same policies on international trade?

INTERNATIONAL TRADE THEORIES AND GLOBALISATION

If the theories seem to be having trouble keeping up with developments in the real world of international trade, then globalisation has thrown everything up in the air. The list of assumptions that made the HO model manageable now seems hopelessly out of date. Capital and labour is increasingly mobile across the globe and while technology can be made available to consumers in all markets, companies will restrict access to their proprietary technologies using laws concerning **intellectual property rights (IPR)**.

The HO model made the assumption that no country enjoyed a technological advantage. This was not because it was true but because it was not considered a core factor of trade, so it was simpler to exclude it from the calculations. This is difficult to justify when countries like China are exporting vast quantities of technical goods, such as computers and mobile phones. Michael Posner (1961) argued that when a country makes a technological advance it gains a new comparative advantage in the product and so exports it. This continues until such time that the competitor countries are able to replicate the technology and close the so-called imitation gap. It is in this sense that technological differences are not a core feature of international trade, because they are specific to firms. The largest technological firms can become globalised even when their home countries, or compatriot businesses, are not.

It is this firm-specific feature of trade that marks out the shift from internationalisation to globalisation. **Internationalisation** is based on the kind of trade we are familiar with, the swapping of raw materials and finished goods at some agreed rate of exchange. Typically, industrialised countries import raw materials from less developed countries and in return supply them with manufactured goods. The high value-added work is in the manufacturing so the less developed countries have to trade high volumes of raw material for given quantities of manufactured goods. As a consequence, industrialised nations tend to be wealthier than nations that supply raw materials. If we return to our opening example, the three ancient artefacts found in Helgö, Sweden, it is likely that these high-crafted objects were traded for agricultural goods or plunder. This kind of trading relationship has persisted into the modern era and is often seen as an oppressive force on the economic growth of developing countries. It is therefore the basis of drives to bring industrialisation to the developing world.

Globalisation is more than just an accelerated version of internationalisation. Globalisation involves an integration of functions so that industries in different countries work with each other to produce the final product. It is no longer possible to characterise one country as the raw material supplier and the other as the manufacturer; they are now integrated into a complex network of suppliers and producers. Of course, those countries that are abundant in commodities will continue to be the chief sources of raw materials, but they can also participate in the value-added work as well.

 ## CASE STUDY – AUSTRALIA THE GLOBALISED

Australia exemplifies the emergence of globalisation; figures for 2011–2012 from the Department of Foreign Affairs and Trade (DFAT, 2015) showed that 62.8% of its exports were made up of primary goods, with minerals and foods making up 81% of that figure. Of its imports, around 55% is made up of manufactured goods. Even from these figures, inflated by high demand for its commodities, it is clear that the country is far from simply trading raw materials for imports of manufactured goods. Indeed, it is both an importer of primary products (around 18% of total imports) and an exporter of manufactured goods (around 13% of total exports). There is also significant import substitution, with passenger vehicles comprising 5.1% of all imports even as the domestic industry supplies almost a quarter of local demand (FCAI, 2012).

Point of consideration: If Australia is rich in raw materials as well as having a vibrant manufacturing industry, why should the country bother to trade at all when it appears to be self-sufficient?

Sources: DFAT, 2015; FCAI, 2012

The international trade picture becomes so complicated with globalisation that an altogether new approach is called for. This should ignore the national perspective and instead focus on industries and even companies.

MICHAEL PORTER'S DIAMOND MODEL

As international boundaries become porous and open to trade, it makes less sense to quantify a country's in-built advantages. Globalisation shows us that it is possible to acquire resources on the open market as and when they are needed. It is no longer necessary to trade only for the finished goods, as countries may hold advantages in just part of the production process. If we think of a single product being made up of a number of different components, each sourced from unrelated industries, it is possible for different countries to make contributions to the final product according to their strength in those supplier industries.

Michael Porter (1998) devised the Diamond Model of Competitive Advantage in an attempt to explain a nation's position in terms of its competitive strength in a particular industry. The model encompasses the different factors that drive the competitiveness: not only the factors with which the country was originally endowed but also the historical factors that have helped to build a dominant position. Many of the factors that had to be assumed away by the HO model, but in the age of globalisation have come back to prominence, can be included in the Diamond Model. We can therefore see how a country can develop a highly competitive industry based on the interplay of various stimulating factors.

Interestingly, some factors that would once have been considered inherent to the national advantage, such as labour, in a globalised market can instead be bought in from outside. In this way the model takes account of the seismic shift taking place in migration and the mobility of labour. The four main factors then interact with each other dynamically:

1. **Factor conditions** – we are already familiar with this concept since we have considered it before in the HO model. We can therefore include the availability of natural resources, capital and labour. Porter, though, goes much further and includes the kind of factor condition development that occurs in the modern world. So, labour is not just a passive resource to be used according to its availability; it can also be improved through investments in education and training. New knowledge-based industries, such as the software and electronics companies in Silicon Valley, show how high educational standards can stimulate a fundamentally labour-intensive industry when the nation itself is said to be capital abundant.
2. **Demand conditions** – the model recognises that the characteristics of the market have a significant impact on the viability and strength of a given industry. The UK has a very powerful pharmaceutical industry, much of which can be attributed to the British National Health Service, which operates in near-monopsony conditions. Pharmaceutical companies can enjoy stable and profitable relations with the NHS, which then encourage high levels of business investment.
3. **Firm strategy, structure and rivalry** – over a period of time an industry will mature to a point where the domestic players are in continual and habitual competition. It is not that they are acting and reacting to each other's moves in the market; the sense of competition is raised to a level where they have almost established a culture or a system of competition. If we look at the fashion houses in Paris we see an industry that is shaped by the sense of rivalry that not only maintains the pace of innovation but also creates very high entry barriers to new firms.
4. **Related and supporting industries** – the model includes other industries to show that the links between them help to raise the competitive stature of the industry. This includes the networks of suppliers that are technically members of other industries, but their own competitive dominance is highly supportive. The shipping insurance industry is dominated by Lloyd's, the London insurance market. Surrounded by the huge London financial services industry it is clear that Lloyd's can draw on the local skills and experience. There is also an historical advantage, dating from an age when British merchant shipping was a world force that was insured through the Lloyd's market.

The Diamond Model eschews the definition of a nation, with its arbitrary boundaries, and focuses on specific industries with their constituent firms. The trading advantage is therefore measured in competitive power, either to repel imports or to penetrate foreign markets. The comparative advantage is held by the industry cluster, not the country as a whole. When we say that the United States has a comparative advantage in aircraft production we are really referring to the industry in its current industrial centres, such as Redmond, Washington, and Fort Worth, Texas. The Diamond Model shows that it would make little sense to establish a new firm in a state like Idaho where there is no supporting industry.

Although Porter's Diamond Model is intended only for evaluating domestic industries, it can be stretched to include aspects of globalisation. This is important when we consider that firms do not operate within a single geographic location but draw on resources around the world. We might want to consider how the international market can broaden demand to allow the industry to achieve economies of scale. Both the Swiss and Japanese watch industries have grown far beyond their domestic strongholds and count the entire world as their markets.

GLOBALISATION AND DEVELOPING ECONOMIES

All the trade theories, bar one, extol the virtues of international trade for the purposes of enriching both sides in any deal. Even the exception to this rule, mercantilism, with its promotion of domestic industry over foreign industry, is simply being self-centred; it has no interest in whether the trade partner is better off or not.

By allowing countries, and therefore industries and companies, to specialise in their strengths, the advantages are not only compounded through learning effects and economies of scale, consumers also benefit from access to better products at lower prices. A natural consequence of this focus on national strength is that the country will also have to relinquish those industries where it is weak and so import the products and services instead. This adjustment period, when companies are wound up and industries disappear, can be difficult for the public to stomach, so there are often cultural and political obstacles to the formation of perfectly free trade. Nevertheless, the mutual benefits of globalisation for all involved are feeding through at a sufficient pace for the basics of international free trade to be broadly accepted.

However, this may not be the case in many developing economies. Many economists, most notably Joseph Stiglitz (2002), argued that the liberalisation of trade was being foisted on developing economies before they were ready for it. While developed economies had created their national and government institutions centuries before globalisation, and so were able to respond to it in an organised fashion, developing countries had no way of accommodating the vast changes being forced on them. Without a strategic approach the apparent advantages of incoming investment were frittered away on domestic corruption and the enrichment of foreign multinational enterprises (MNEs).

These problems were exacerbated by supranational institutions, such as the **International Monetary Fund (IMF)**, which supported the imposition of market structures that were seen to be effective in developed economies that had the institutions to contain them. The market structures being imposed on developing economies included liberalisation of financial services and the privatisation of strategic industries. Such dramatic prising open of markets was viewed as an open invitation to MNEs to exploit the weak and vulnerable economies.

Not only could globalisation suppress the economic growth of developing nations, it could even lead to them being worse off. Jagdish Bhagwati (1958) demonstrated that when a developing country is the location for a large export operation, not only may the rest of the economy lose out on any possible economic benefits but it may actually be worse off. This is due to the distorting effect the operation has on the country's terms of trade. This has been called **immiserising growth** and it is a phenomenon that is considered to be unfair on the poorer countries because the richer countries have centuries of economic development underpinning their advantage.

Although the weight of argument is still in favour of international trade, it is the suffering of poorer nations at the margin that has led to attempts to defend them from the worst effects of globalisation. For example, the **WTO** allows developing economies to use tariffs as trade barriers to defend their new-born, **infant industries**. This is quite distinct from that enemy of free trade, **protectionism**. The WTO allows infant industries to be defended for only a limited period until such time that they should be able to stand up for themselves against the global competition, at which point the permitted tariffs should be dropped. In contrast, protectionism is the use of trade barriers to defend domestic industries for the long term, despite the fact that they may already be strong enough to withstand exposure to globalisation.

Protectionism is not only seen as being contrary to the tenets of free trade, it is also counterproductive. Safe from the full competitive forces of globalisation, managers are under much less pressure to develop the business. Instead of honing their management skills and innovating, managers have little incentive to progress. The result can be a depressing amalgam of inefficient production, high costs, low quality and poor product design. This can become so entrenched that if at some point the government is obliged to remove its protectionist policies the pampered industrial champions simply collapse in the face of the global competition.

ANTI-GLOBALISATION REBELLION

Globalisation is often believed to benefit only large MNEs, which, due to their economic importance, are able to wield undue economic influence. This influence is considered to be most pernicious when it comes to developing nations, which are obliged to accept the conditions imposed by the MNE or risk losing the promised investment. It is argued that these MNEs can play one developing country off against the other, driving down conditions of employment and hording any economic benefits. This is perceived to imbue the MNEs with a power that exceeds that of the sovereign government and its citizens. A social movement has emerged in, often violent, rebellion against the power of MNEs, a movement that has become known as anti-globalisation.

The rebellion against globalisation can often become chaotic, obscuring the rational argument. Noam Chomsky (2002) has attempted to return the conflict to that of a reasoned debate, pointing out that it is not globalisation *per se* that is so objectionable but rather the kind of economic globalisation that has diminished the power of self-determination of ordinary people. Other forms of globalisation, such as internationally agreed human rights standards, represent international integration of a form that should be welcomed.

On the basis of Chomsky's criticism, we can see that 'anti-globalisation' is not an accurate term since it describes the resistance against abuse of economic power, not globalisation in its broadest sense. Nevertheless, it is the term that is now accepted for the overall protest movement. Neither is anti-globalisation a new argument: misgivings about large corporations have a long history, including the concerns about monopoly powers. We are therefore familiar with the various rules and regulations that are put in place to corral the larger corporations before they become too dominant, and the anti-globalisation critique taking this same argument to the international level.

Although the focus of anti-globalisation is economic the movement is fragmented across a number of organisations. For example, the anti-capitalists have directed their ire against the global institutions of the IMF, World Bank and WTO. Although there may be some justification in pointing out that these institutions are founded on Western concepts of economic progress through capitalism and free trade, it seems that the protest movement's fundamental grievance is against those institutions as symbols of political power. The protests staged in Seattle during the WTO summit in 1999, the so-called Battle of

Seattle, comprised a wide spectrum of participant groups such as trade unions, environmentalists and anarchists (Gillham and Marx, 2000). Although ultimately ineffectual, these protests around the world underline the irony of the globalised anti-globalisation movement.

Given the disparity of forces ranged against globalisation it is probably inevitable that they will fail in their purpose of diminishing the power of big business. Supporters of globalisation point out that no matter how wealthy a corporation might be, and some are richer than the poorest countries, their income is always dependent on political co-operation. Even if the benefits to a developing country of allowing an MNE to invest are marginal, as the economy progresses on a broad front the influence of that one MNE will proportionately weaken as other MNEs enter the market.

Perhaps the best example of a state that has developed economically on the back of globalisation, all the while maintaining a strong political framework, is Singapore. For Hobson and Ramesh (2002) the city state represents a happy middle ground between the structuralist theory of an omnipotent globalisation and the agentic-centric argument that states are agents that can control the institutions of globalisation to their own designs. The authors call this new view a structurationist approach, an awkward sounding phrase that denotes Singapore's success at both benefiting from globalisation and its institutions while also participating in how globalisation is continually shaped. It is because globalisation is dynamic by nature that it keeps one step ahead of its detractors.

COUNTING TRADE

The huge volumes of international trade cannot go uncounted. Governments, and their electorates, like to know whether they are making money off the rest of the world or, heaven forbid, the rest of the world is making money off them. This is not as easy to assess as one might imagine since trade volumes can fluctuate wildly year-by-year and even more so month-by-month. This can affect countries that export big ticket items that have high value in comparison with the total national trade volume. Finland, for example, may book the value of a number of ship exports one month that give a false indication of rising trade in its favour; the next month the figures might show the reverse. Other countries can labour under persistent trade deficits as they import more than they export year after year, alarming the electorate but apparently to no ill effect on the economy.

TRADE AND THE MYTHICAL BALANCE OF PAYMENTS PROBLEM

As we saw earlier, the mercantilist approach to trade, where the government encourages exports and discourages imports, has long been superseded in the text books by much more effective theories, yet it still clings to life in the political and business worlds. Mercantilism has some practical value to developing countries that are building up their economies under the menacing shadow of established industries in developed countries. Once developing economies are up to speed they can switch to a free-trade approach, where it is the exchange of goods and services that brings the greatest mutual benefit. We should not just blame politicians for stoking the mercantilist argument in order to gain popular support; some of the responsibility also lies with those that give that popular support, the people of the country.

At the heart of the matter is something that is often known as the balance of payments problem. You might want to ask yourself the following question: 'what does it mean if the balance of payments does not balance?' Actually, it is a trick question because the only possible answer is this: 'you have not done the calculations correctly'. By definition, the balance of payments must always balance so a loss made in one area is made up in another. The balance of payments shows that an export strategy may seem to lead to gains being made, but it is inevitably balanced by losses elsewhere. We can see this if we look at the components of the equation:

Current Account + Capital and Financial Account (+ Balancing Item) = 0

The balance of payments expresses all the financial transactions that a country has made with all other countries of the world. Since these transactions form many different types of payment they are allocated to different categories. Not all institutions use exactly the same categories but there is enough commonality to ensure sufficient consistency. Historically, the **IMF** had used a set of definitions peculiar to itself, which was the source of some confusion, but it has now consolidated its definition into just two major categories: the first is the current account; the second is the capital and financial account (IMF, 2012). The new definitions bring the IMF into harmony with the **System of National Accounts (SNA)**.

The **current account** is the one that tends to get the media excited as it measures the trading record of the country with regard to goods and services. If a country holds a competitive advantage in these two areas, then it is likely that its exports of goods and services will exceed its imports and it will want to boast of having a trade surplus. Also included in the current account are income from overseas, in the form of wages, and transfers, such as insurance payments but excluding capital transfers such as ownership changes.

It might be useful to think of the national current account as being analogous to an individual's personal current account at a bank, and indeed this is why it has become such a useful political device. Just as your own account receives your wages and pays your bills, you feel richer if you have a surplus at the end of the year. Politicians play on this analogy for political gain by suggesting that a current account surplus in trade means the country is richer.

The **capital and financial account** is the other side of the story that either spoils, or restores, the impression given by the current account. In the IMF definition, the capital and financial account provides information on the investment position of the country. It is not concerned with the flows of money but with transfers of ownership and flows of investment funds. This account is less easy to understand than the current account because it does not really fit our homely personal spending analogy. Instead, we need to understand that any result from the current account must be balanced by an equal and opposite result from the capital and financial account.

The reason why national accounting is different to personal accounting is because a country is identified with its own currency. It is the same when several countries share a single currency, although it does complicate the picture somewhat. Taking the one country view, the currency it releases can only be spent within its borders, where the currency has legal tender status. Outside its borders it may be acceptable but only at the discretion of the receiver and for the reasons that the money will eventually find its way back to its home country where it can be legally spent. The money can only be created and spent within its home country. This means that when a country spends its money on imports, that money is not lost but must return to it in some form.

The money returns because the exporting country is earning money but in the form of a foreign currency. One use of the money is to buy goods from the trading partner, creating reciprocal trade. Another route is to invest in the importing country, buying property or lending it money. These funds are measured in the capital account. In this way, whatever money is spent on imports in the current account must either return through reciprocal trade shown the current account or through investment shown in the capital account. Either way, the money must return and the balance of payments must sum to zero.

TRADE AND THE FOREIGN CURRENCY PROBLEM

When the current account is in balance, two countries, A and B, are paying each other in their own currencies. When Country A pays for imports from Country B the money is used by Country B to pay for imports from Country A. Neither country is accumulating the other's money and each national currency is finding its way back home through the current account. In the case where there is a trade imbalance, foreign currency will begin to accumulate in the country that is doing more exporting than importing. The imbalance is addressed in the capital and financial accounts for both countries.

It is the balancing act by the capital and financial account that demonstrates there is no particular advantage to being a mercantilist, export-oriented country. The exports are being paid for in the currency of the importing country, the only currency that it has authority over. While it may seem obvious to simply state that this money can be exchanged for that of the exporting country, this can only be done if there is a complementary trader who wants to buy that currency. So the problem of two currencies is not solved; it is only being shifted onto someone else.

When an exporting country is running a current account surplus it will accumulate the foreign currency that it is receiving in payment. Even if it does nothing with it, the funds will build up in its foreign currency accounts, which then show up in the capital and financial account. More curiously, the funds can be lent back to the country of origin. The importing country then uses them to purchase yet more goods. The exporting country is perpetuating its export drive by becoming a creditor country lending back currencies to the importers so that they can carry on importing.

This strategy means that the exporting nation is effectively taking production responsibilities away from the importing nation, promoting its own industrial development at the expense of its importing partners. Conversely, though, the market in the importing nation benefits from cheaper foreign goods, while consumers in the exporting nation are denied. Furthermore, foreign currency reserves can grow out of control. Table 1.3 shows the accumulation of foreign currency reserves, how they relate to the total output of the economy (% of gross domestic product, GDP) and the current account position. The table provides the figures for the top four biggest hoarders of foreign currency, as well as the United States and India for reasons of comparison.

From the table we can see that the top three holders of foreign currency, China, Japan and Russia, confirm our suspicions that they are doing this as part of their export drive. This view is further supported by the United States, which holds low quantities of foreign reserves relative to its gross domestic product, while also running the largest current account deficit in the world. At the same time, India

Table 1.3 *Foreign currency reserves and the current account – 2014*

Country	Reserves (US$billions)	Reserves/GDP %	Current Account
China	3948.1	39.4	224.3
Japan	1282.8	26.5	57.2
Russia	472.3	22.6	44.9
Switzerland	548.9	79.1	68.8
India	311.9	15.6	–47.5
US	143.5	0.8	–391.1

Sources: IMF (estimates), 2014; Bank of Korea, 2014

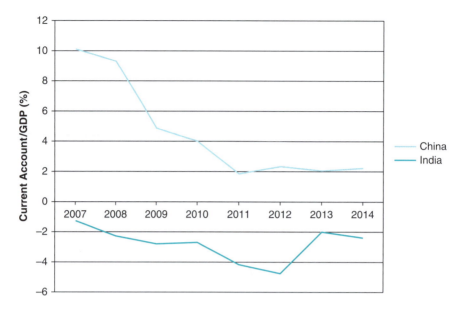

Figure 1.1 *China and India Current Account/GDP 2007–2011*

Source: IMF (estimates), 2014

stands out as a contrarian, with strong reserves and a current account deficit. Indeed, Figure 1.1 shows how India compares with China on trading strategies as the two great developing economies make their rapid advances.

Although the two countries are well known to be exhibiting impressive rates of growth in GDP, sometimes exceeding 10% per annum, they are funding themselves in contrasting ways. China is using a mercantilist approach, exporting to drive the growth of its industries and providing importing countries with much of the financial credit. In contrast, India is a debtor nation using overseas credit to invest in its economic development. There are pros and cons to both approaches, but China will have to undergo a challenging economic restructuring when it needs to shift out of its mercantilist policies. This will then impact on the managers of companies that operate in or with China.

MYTH BUSTER: GREECE AND THE EUROZONE BALANCE OF PAYMENTS PROBLEM

Some might argue that Greece's problems within the Eurozone have been brought on by itself. Certainly, Greece has been suffering a litany of financial problems recently, but at the bottom of it all is a balance of payments crisis.

Before it joined the single European currency, the euro, Greece would have paid for its imported goods in its own currency, the drachma. If you imagine a situation where it was buying goods from China, paying in its own currency would have left the Chinese holding drachmas. There is only one place in the world where this money can be spent, namely Greece, so China would have been obliged to buy goods from Greece. How much it wanted those Greek goods would have effectively decided the exchange rate between the two currencies. As a result, China would have spent its drachmas buying a variety of goods from Greece, including manufactured goods.

Once Greece had joined the euro it would have paid for its imports from China as before, but this time using euros. China is now free to pay for goods made anywhere in Europe, not just Greece. When it comes to manufactured goods Germany holds a substantial competitive advantage and so has attracted the Chinese buyers. Where Greece was previously able to compete with Germany on price by devaluing its currency, now that they share the same currency Greece must compete by way of an internal devaluation in the form of wage reductions.

Point of consideration: If Greece were to leave the Eurozone but stay in the EU, how would this impact on Germany?

Source: Chen et al., 2013

THE EVOLUTION OF INTERNATIONAL BUSINESS WITH TRADE POLICY

Governments interfere in their nation's trade to differing degrees, with consequent implications for domestic businesses. In neo-mercantilist countries, like China, it is important for a company to become an exporter because that is the most buoyant sector of the economy. At the same time, the strategy brings with it a number of challenges. Any foreign earnings must be exchanged with the government at the official rate, which then determines the profitability of any transactions. The government may also choose to nominate certain industries for special attention, which can help them to grow but may also force them into consolidation or joint ventures. For example, the automotive companies in China require government licences to build new plants, and this policy pushes growing companies to acquire smaller companies for their production rights when they wish to expand their output.

In economies that are structured around free trade and the principles of comparative advantage, firms enjoy greater liberty for pursuing the opportunities that they perceive. We have seen that the Heckscher–Ohlin theory suggests that companies dependent on factors of production that are abundant in the country will expand to make use of those factors, with a clear potential to export. However, the Leontief Paradox has shown that the opposite can be the case, with the United States famously exporting from labour-intensive industries when capital is the abundant factor. The **gravity equation theory** of trade suggests that the practicalities of economic dominance and geographic proximity are the main drivers of trade (Chaney, 2013).

There is empirical support for the gravity equation but it seems to have little to say about Free Trade Agreements (FTAs), which can occur between countries in close proximity or geographically separated. However, research by Baier and Bergstrand (2007) found emphatic evidence that FTAs do have a very positive impact on trade if the gravity equation calculations are adjusted accordingly. This seems to tie in with Michael Porter's Diamond Model, which argues that trade is not national or international but occurs between industrial clusters. These clusters give economic 'mass' to the gravity equation. The purpose of the FTA, then, is to render the concept of nationhood irrelevant in the process of removing the trade barriers and allowing clusters to develop links.

The problem for developing countries is that they do not yet have those industrial clusters, and so they are in a poor position to trade. They can do this, though, through mercantilist trade policies to build up their economic strength even at the expense of the rest of the world. During this period the infant industries can enjoy the support of the WTO and World Bank. Once the industrial clusters have matured, the country can enter into FTAs and join the movement towards global free trade.

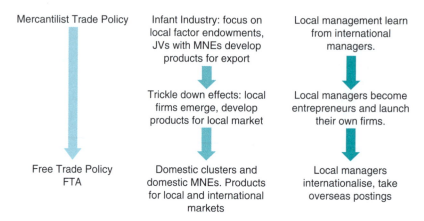

Figure 1.2 *Evolution of trade policy, industry and management*

For international business this evolution of the trading position from protectionism to free trade represents a destabilising shift in its environment. For this reason managers need to be prepared to develop their corporations in step with the evolving trade policy. Figure 1.2 illustrates how industries, and the corporations that comprise them, should adapt in step with trade policy guided by increasingly experienced managers.

RAISING EMPLOYABILITY: THE GLOBAL MANAGEMENT STUDENT

Matters of international trade seem to be aggregated far above individual businesses and outside the influence of managers. Yet trade comprises the same business–customer relationships as exist in domestic commerce, only greatly more complicated by the acts of transacting across borders. This does not mean that the international manager is a different breed of professional, but they do need to be operationally sharper and more sophisticated. This requires education, training and experience.

Taking education first, it is common these days for managers to have a degree in business. There is a myriad of these courses around, including international business, business psychology, business law and so on. Kim et al. (2002) found that students were certainly focused on their future careers, rather than the reputation of the institution. This was all the more so as the degree specialisation narrowed; accounting students, for example, placed the highest emphasis on the employability their degree would provide. Students of general management were the least convinced of the direct applicability of the degree, although this may reflect their own lack of conviction and subsequent choice of the broadest degree topic. Across all topics, though, the perception of the business degree being a direct step towards a business career underlined the importance of offering related extracurricular activities like work experience and internships.

The career focus of business students may be laudable, but they may be specialising unnecessarily early in their lives. Other degree topics can provide, somewhat counter-intuitively, the same basic skills. One of the most surprising is a degree in music. It may appear to be the very antithesis of the kind of commercial ambition that seems to characterise the business world, but music is nevertheless a highly disciplined practice. While a mediocre business student can bluff their way through assignments, the music student is compelled to identify and fix problems as they occur, or risk being publicly exposed.

Indeed, one university in the UK found that its music graduates were amongst the most employable in the jobs market, including business management (University of Nottingham, 2015).

At graduation, students like to think their education ends there. It does not. All businesses operate in a dynamic environment and this is all the more true of those operating internationally. Training that is made available within the organisation should be embraced at all opportunities. If it is not available then the ambitious manager should seek the training elsewhere. Ultimately, this can involve returning to college for a formal course. There is a wide variety of postgraduate courses to choose from but most likely it will be a Masters of Business Administration (MBA), given that in countries like the United States it is the most popular graduate degree. Yet the promises of higher financial rewards flowing from the higher value degree are not always supported by the evidence. The course may aim to compress experiential learning into the academic timetable, but the success of a business depends on human passion, not textbooks (Hann, 2014).

Yet all this education pales into insignificance behind the most important managerial asset of all: experience. Whatever impression textbooks may give, even this one, the true business skills are learnt in the execution, not the academic exercise. It is therefore crucial that anyone with a plan to succeed in international business acknowledges that first that they must embrace opportunities to experience international business for real.

THE STORY SO FAR: THE BIRTH OF GLOBAL BUSINESS

There is nothing new about the attraction of people trading with each other; indeed, trade is probably a basic human characteristic. It took a long time for theorists to wake up to it, though, and the early obsession with mercantilism, with its short-sighted protection of domestic industry, did more harm than good. Some countries still benefit from mercantilist principles in the short term but over the long term comparative advantage encourages trade that can benefit all sides. Starting from internationalisation, importing raw materials and exporting high value manufactured goods, we have progressed to full globalisation. This means a complex global web of importing and exporting with corporate operations integrated worldwide. Yet despite the theory of an economic promised land some developing countries appear to have become victims of international trade. Even if they are not exactly getting poorer they are certainly not getting richer very fast.

For international managers globalisation offers a massive expansion in business opportunities. There are new markets to sell to and greater varieties of suppliers to source from. All businesses can then specialise in their strengths, giving rise to learning benefits and the cost advantages of economies of scale. There are also greater risks, and international managers need to sharpen their skills as they compete with the best of their peers around the world. It is not just a global business; it is global management as well.

 WEB SUPPORT

1. 'The Silk Road: Connecting the ancient world through trade'. A video from TedEd with a rapid fire historical review of trade routes from ancient times to the present day. Consider carefully, though, whether ancient trade is simply the slower equivalent of modern globalisation.
   www.youtube.com/watch?v=vn3e37VWc0k

2. 'What was mercantilism?' A fascinating article from *The Economist* putting mercantilism into perspective. Includes a handy reading list for those who want to dig deeper.

    www.economist.com/blogs/freeexchange/2013/08/economic-history

3. 'Rigged rules and double standards: Trade, globalisation and the fight against poverty'. A 2002 report from the international charity Oxfam with an excoriating critique of rich countries and how they, according to some, manipulate the rules of trade to their advantage. Available in various languages.

    www.policy-practice.oxfam.org.uk/publications/rigged-rules-and-double-standards-trade-globalisation-and-the-fight-against-pov-112391

Project Topics

1. How would Porter's Diamond Model explain the Leontief Paradox?
2. To what extent do you think that Switzerland enjoys an absolute advantage in watchmaking?
3. What are the limits to growth in China's foreign currency reserves? What will happen if the reserves are allowed to continue expanding unchecked?
4. If the world 'rebalances', meaning that each country becomes more self-sufficient in manufacturing, services and agriculture, do you think this will reverse globalisation? Will the world be better or worse off?
5. As a management consultant, if you were asked by a developing government to advise on promoting economic growth, which theory or theories of international trade would you find most useful?

CASE STUDY – SWITZERLAND AND THE INTERNATIONAL WATCH INDUSTRY

Watchmaking is literally and figuratively globalisation in miniature. Boasting mechanisms of exquisite ingenuity, watches are also dependent on the industrialisation of their national economies for technological progress. In the pre-industrial medieval era, clocks were massive pieces of ironmongery, each part hammered into shape in the blacksmith's forge. Their sheer scale demanded robust structures to house them, such as church towers and civic buildings. Clock mechanisms known as verge and foliot were an advance over the ancient water clocks, but they were hopelessly unreliable by today's digital standards and could not be shrunk to the size of a watch.

It was in Britain that the first practical, and reliable, watches began to appear. With scientific progress being made in all areas the country had luminaries such as Robert Hooke, the seventeenth-century polymath, who developed the delicate hairspring. This powered the steady oscillations of the balance wheel, the watch equivalent of the clock's swinging pendulum. The supply of innovations received its impetus from the Royal Navy, which demanded accurate timepieces in order to safely navigate around the British Empire. Building on the work of John Harrison and Thomas Tompion, the British watchmaking industry came to global dominance in the eighteenth century, with Coventry emerging as the centre of gravity for production.

Britain, though, failed to embrace the logic of factory production and its promises of economies of scale. The United States, with its vast domestic market, was a zealot for mass production even in the nineteenth century, and watchmaking factories brought the global focus across to their side of the Atlantic. Yet even as American brands stole the mantle from the British craftsmen the Swiss were waiting for their opportunity. Although it is a small country, it has long been wealthy and politically stable. Its position at the heart of Europe also meant it could learn from French watch designers, famed for their innovation but never for their industrial levels of output. Then in the twentieth century the Swiss learnt from the US companies how to manufacture efficiently. From then on the world belonged to the Swiss watch brands.

To be a little more precise, what the Swiss owned was the world of mechanical watches. Even the finest chronometers, the pinnacle of the watchmaker's art, can only manage to be accurate within a few seconds a day. True accuracy needed a technological innovation and it came in the form of a tiny vibrating crystal: quartz. Passing a current through this minuscule piece of rock induced it to oscillate at an entirely reliable 8192 Hz. This could be harnessed as an electronic timekeeping device in place of the mechanical balance wheel. The Swiss industry was well aware of the technological possibilities of quartz but it was the manufacturers in the Far East that understood the production and marketing potential. By the 1970s the Quartz Crisis had the Swiss industry reeling, as rates of production rocketed on the other side of the world.

This should have spelt the exit of the Swiss from watchmaking and the death of noble brands like Omega, Rolex and Patek Philippe. Figures from the Federation of the Swiss Watchmaking Industry (FH, 2015) confirm that global production is dominated by China, from where 669 million units were exported in 2014. In comparison, Switzerland exported a miserly 28.6 million. Money, though, tells another story. The Swiss earned US$24.3 billion, or around US$803 per watch, while all those Chinese exports earned just US$5.3 billion, representing approximately US$4 per watch. Clearly the Swiss watchmaking industry is far from dead.

International trade theories like the HO model would not have anticipated the international fame achieved by watchmakers in Switzerland. It is a labour-intensive process, yet the country is not labour abundant; indeed, it is home to a banking sector with international standing. Porter's Diamond includes additional factors that help us to see the complete picture. Labour may not be especially abundant in the country but it is well educated, useful for a skilled craft like watchmaking.

These skills have long been present throughout Swiss industry, so the watchmaking industry can rely on supplies of components that match the high product standards. Many of these are exported as sub-assembly ebauches, basic watch mechanisms that are then included in the models of non-Swiss manufacturers. Furthermore, there is international input into the Swiss watch designs, such as British master watchmaker George Daniels and his co-axial escapement for Omega. The famous Swiss brands may like to portray themselves as survivors of an ancient tradition, but in reality they form an industrial cluster with global impact.

Point of consideration: Theories of international trade tend to identify national strengths and assume that this will drive the exports. Yet we often find that countries develop leadership in unexpected industries. Think about how India, for example, has found a comparative advantage in the development of computer software and suggest which international trade theory might have predicted it. Can you use that theory to predict a future comparative advantage for a country of your choice?

Sources: Glasmeier, 2000; Sobel, 2007; FH, 2015

? MULTIPLE CHOICE QUESTIONS

1. The Silk Road is the ancestor to modern globalisation because:
   a. It specialised in the transport of silk.
   b. It was a network of routes for the international exchange of goods.
   c. It eventually became a hard surface highway for modern cars and trucks.

2. Why is mercantilism still practised by some developing countries?
   a. They can use the short-term export advantages to establish their new industries.
   b. They have not yet learnt about the advantages of Porter's Diamond Model.
   c. They have no absolute advantages.

3. Does Greece enjoy an absolute advantage in feta cheese?
   a. No, feta cheese can be made anywhere.
   b. Yes, all feta cheese comes from Greece because no one else can make it as well as they do.
   c. Not quite; feta cheese can be made anywhere in the world to the same quality, it just cannot be called feta because the name is protected.

4. Germany is a top exporter because it has a comparative advantage in what industry?
   a. Cars.
   b. Banking.
   c. Olive oil.

5. Which is better, to export or to import?
   a. Import; it provides access to a global range of products at various specifications and prices.
   b. Export; it brings cash into the country and so increases national wealth.
   c. Both; it is trade that permits access to imported global products while allowing the country to specialise in its comparative advantage for exports.

6. Which theory best explains American exports of rice?
   a. Absolute advantage; the United States is better at growing rice than any other country.
   b. Comparative advantage; the United States is better at growing rice than it is at any other economic activity.
   c. No theory does; it is the Leontief Paradox.

7. Why is Japan a large exporter of cameras?
   a. Michael Porter's Diamond Model shows that a supporting industrial cluster has evolved in the country.
   b. The Japanese people have small, nimble hands that are suited to the production of small, complex products.
   c. The Japanese are very skilled at innovating in high technology.

8. Does the WTO ever permit protectionism?
   a. No, the WTO stands for free trade.
   b. Yes, when a developing nation is nurturing an infant industry.
   c. Yes, when a wealthy country has a long-established industry employing many people.

9. How can exporting countries prevent damaging rises in the value of their currencies?
   a. They reduce the circulation of their own currency.
   b. They raise domestic interest rates.
   c. They accumulate foreign currencies in their reserves.

10. How does India sustain its long-term deficit in the balance of trade?
    a. It borrows money from its trading partners.
    b. It allows the value of its currency to rise.
    c. It invests in overseas operations.

Answers
1b, 2a, 3c, 4a, 5c, 6c, 7a, 8b, 9c, 10a

REFERENCES

Baier S L and Bergstrand J H (2007) 'Do free trade agreements actually increase members' international trade?' *Journal of International Economics,* 71 (1), pp. 72–95

Baldwin R E (2008) 'The development and testing of Heckscher-Ohlin trade models: a review from MIT Press' www.mitpress.mit.edu/sites/default/files/titles/content/9780262026567_sch_0001.pdf accessed 20 August 2015

Bhagwati J (1958) 'Immiserizing growth: a geometrical note' *The Review of Economic Studies*, 25 (June), pp. 201–205

Bank of Korea (2014) 'Foreign Currency Reserves (June 2014)' from www.bok.or.kr/contents/total/eng/boardView.action?boardBean.brdid=14072&boardBean.rnum=88&menuNaviId=634&board Bean.menuid=634&boardBean.cPage=9&boardBean.categorycd=0&boardBean.sdt=&boardBean.edt=&boardBean.searchColumn=&boardBean.searchValue= accessed 5 July 2014

Casas F R and Choi E K (1985) 'The Leontief Paradox: continued or resolved?' *Journal of Political Economy*, 93 (3) (Jun., 1985), pp. 610–615

Chaney T (2013) 'The gravity equation in international trade: An explanation (No. w19285)'. National Bureau of Economic Research from www.nber.org/papers/w19285.pdf accessed 21 August 2015

Chen R, Milesi-Ferretti G M and Tressel T (2013) 'External imbalances in the Eurozone' *Economic Policy,* 28 (73), pp. 101–142

Chomsky N (2002) 'A world without war? Reflections on globalization and antiglobalization' *Canadian Journal of Development Studies/Revue canadienne d'études du développement,* 23 (3), pp. 493–511

DFAT (Department for Foreign Affairs and Trade)(2015) Composition of Trade 2014-2015 published December 2015 available from www.dfat.gov.au/about-us/publications/Documents/cot-fy-2014-15.pdf

Dietzenbacher E and Lahr M L (Eds.) (2004) *Wassily Leontief and input-output economics*. Cambridge: Cambridge University Press

European Commission PDO-PGI-TSG (2014) 'Geographical indications and traditional specialities' available from www.ec.europa.eu/agriculture/quality/schemes/index_en.htm accessed 20 June 2014

FCAI (Federal Chamber of Automotive Industries)(2012) Key Facts (7 September 2012) from FCAI website www.fcai.com.au/key accessed 18 March 2013

FH (2015) 'The Swiss and world watchmaking industry in 2014' from Federation of the Swiss Watch Industry FH www.fhs.ch/file/59/Watchmaking_2014.pdf accessed 1 June 2015

Findlay R, Jonung L and Lundahl M (Eds.) (2002) *Bertil Ohlin, a centennial celebration (1899-1999).* Cambridge and London: MIT Press, 2002

Gillham P F and Marx G T (2000) 'Complexity and irony in policing and protesting: The World Trade Organization in Seattle' *Social Justice,* pp. 212–236

Glasmeier A (2000) *Manufacturing time: Global competition in the watch industry, 1795-2000.* Guilford, NY: Guilford Press

Hann C (2014) 'To MBA or not to MBA' *Entrepreneur,* Oct2014, 42 (10), pp. 79–83

Harris J G (2004) *Sick economies: Drama, mercantilism, and disease in Shakespeare's England.* Philadelphia, PA: University of Pennsylvania Press

Hirst P and Thompson G (2002) 'The future of globalization' *Cooperation and Conflict* 37 (3) (2002), pp. 247–265

Hobson J M and Ramesh M (2002) 'Globalisation makes of states what states make of it: Between agency and structure in the state/globalisation debate' in *New Political Economy* 7 (1) (2002), pp. 5–22

IMF (2012) *Balance of payments manual* from www.imf.org/external/pubs/ft/bopman/bopman.pdf accessed 13 November 2014

IMF (2014) *World Economic Database: October 2014* edition from www.imf.org/external/pubs/ft/weo/2014/02/weodata/index.aspx accessed 13 November 2014

Kim D, Markham F S and Cangelosi J D (2002) 'Why students pursue the business degree: a comparison of business majors across universities' *Journal of Education for Business,* 78 (1), pp. 28–32

Kröger M (2012) 'Neo-mercantilist capitalism and post-2008 cleavages in economic decision-making power in Brazil' *Third World Quarterly* 33 (5) (2012), pp. 887–901

Lang M, Mahoney J and vom Hau M (2006) 'Colonialism and development: a comparative analysis of Spanish and British colonies' *American Journal of Sociology* 111 (5) (March 2006), pp. 1412–1462

Looi Kee H, Nicita A and Olarreaga M (2009) 'Estimating trade restrictiveness indices' *The Economic Journal* 119 (534), pp. 172–199

Mahoney J (2010) *Colonialism and postcolonial development: Spanish America in comparative perspective.* Cambridge: Cambridge University Press

Markusen J R and Venables A J (2000) 'The theory of endowment, intra-industry and multi-national trade' *Journal of International Economics* 52 (2), pp. 209–234

Porter M E (1998) *The competitive advantage of nations.* Basingstoke: Macmillan

Posner M V (1961) 'International trade and technical change' *Oxford Economic Papers,* New Series, 13 (3) (Oct., 1961), pp. 323–341

Ruffin R (2002) 'David Ricardo's discovery of comparative advantage' *History of Political Economy* 34 (4), pp. 727–748

Sobel D (2007) *Longitude: The true story of a lone genius who solved the greatest scientific problem of his time.* Bloomsbury: London

Stiglitz J E (2002) *Globalization and its discontents.* New York: WW Norton & Company

University of Nottingham (2015) *Department of music: graduate profiles* from www.nottingham.ac.uk/music/prospective/careers/alumni/intro.aspx accessed 2 June 2015

Waller J (1982) 'Swedish contacts with the Eastern Baltic in the pre-Viking and early Viking Ages: the evidence from Helgö' *Journal of Baltic Studies* 13 (3), pp. 256–266

2 International Growth and Diversification

Chapter Objectives

This chapter will look at that *sine qua non* of business success: growth. It is not always as simple as it seems and there must be a robust argument for growing the business. The rationale for it may involve the existing products and resources, or growth could take the company into a whole new industry. The canny manager may even conclude that stability, not growth, is the logical way forward. Sometimes, just occasionally, contraction and extinction is the only sensible option. In this chapter, we will consider the different perspectives on growth:

- How growth is not synonymous with success; there have to be reasons for growing the business.
- The ways in which a manager must assess the growth potential in the product, market and the company.
- Investigate diversification as a growth strategy and who it really benefits.
- How a powerful new breed of conglomerate emerged in South-East Asia.

LIKE GROWTH FOR SUCCESS

We all like to assume that growth is a sign of a healthy company. How could it not be? If the company is growing then surely it must be doing something well and more customers are being converted to its product offerings. When the growth is international then this is taken as the greatest stamp of approval of all. Yet growth can actually become dangerous as its stock market value outstrips its underlying worth and the company is unable to deliver on the expectations, leading to its own destruction. The purpose of the management team, then, is to ensure that the company is delivering value, not growth *per se* (Jensen, 2005). On this basis there are a number of reasons why a company might decide that caution is the better part of valour; that consolidating and stabilising are the recommended strategies for continuing to deliver value.

REASONS NOT TO GROW

The business world is full of risk. Expansion is risky, contraction is risky, even just standing still is risky. Whatever the direction the company is going in it should be the result of assiduous business planning and the appropriate strategy. Although, as Jensen (2005) argues, most managers are programmed to look for growth, there are occasions when the company needs to hold fast on its expansionary ambitions. In a declining market this may actually count as relative growth when constant sales are maintained by enlarged market shares at the expense of departing rivals.

These are a number of reasons why a company might decide to eschew further growth:

1. **Saturated market** – when a product has been fully diffused through a market then everyone who wants one already has one. The product will be a mature one with little prospect of any dramatic technological advances to develop the market. Most demand will be for replacement, and the only market growth will come through exogenous factors such as population growth or rising purchasing power. Growth opportunities for companies exist but only at the expense of other companies. There is likely to be a great deal of price competition, with the main advantages being with those companies that can access economies of scale. Smaller companies tend to compete with products that are highly differentiated, even if the underlying technology is nothing new. In the 1990s the emergence of the internet seemed to offer limitless growth and start-ups pursued GBF (get big fast) strategies only to discover the market had become overcrowded, leading to the bursting of the so-called **dot.com bubble** (Oliva et al., 2003).

2. **Growth available offers poor financial returns** – this is common in mature markets where the technology and the product features are stable. This leaves price as one of the few competitive levers and as a consequence profit margins fall to a minimum sustainable level. To grow in a market like this means being even more competitive than rivals on price, reducing profit margins to a negligible or even negative level. Only very large MNEs, or government backed organisations, would pursue growth in such a punishing environment as a way of taking future dominance of the market. If successful, prices can then be subsequently raised. In any case, there may be attractions in the stability of a mature market, such as one made up of older consumers, that companies may erroneously neglect when they perceive a lack of volume growth instead of opportunities for adding value (Birtwistle and Tsim, 2005).

3. There is **uncertainty over the future direction of the market** – at the birth of a new technology it is difficult to know what shape the market will take. It is therefore impossible to know what kinds of production volumes should be planned. Some new technologies can take years to reach the market as commercial exploitation is tentative at the start. A current example would be self-driving cars, which are feasible using existing technology but actual market demand is unknown.

4. The company's **competitive position is founded on the talents of just one person** or a limited team of people – for some corporations the founder and Chief Executive Officer (CEO) remains the beating heart of the enterprise, guiding the corporate strategy on 'gut feeling'. This should not happen when a business is run on rational principles, but sometimes, like a sports team structured around a star player, the CEO's dominance suppresses the development of the rest of the management team. When the CEO leaves the rest of the team are paralysed by indecision and are unable to grow the company. These 'superstar' CEOs may appear charismatic but there are many examples where they have betrayed the faith put in them (Khurana, 2002).

    If the competitive advantages of the company are embodied in one person, or a small team of people, then growth can lead to a collapse in product quality. This is often the case where creativity is paramount, from Michelin-starred chefs to film directors, and attempts to expand their output by franchising their names can lead to a dilution of their product quality.

5. The company has achieved **economies of scale** – perhaps the most awkward reason for not growing, because expansion would mean the company becoming less efficient. Economies of scale do not relate only to manufacturing plants but they provide a readily understandable example. When a company is experiencing the cost benefits of economies of scale then it must have the right plant size. To expand from this while retaining the same cost benefits the company must build another, identical plant. This will result in a doubling of output. Expansion is risky at the best of times, but a doubling of output will be an extreme test of the company's ability to market its products. Rather

than expose itself in this way the company may take an intermediary step, such as a joint venture or a small plant that can be readily expanded. Not only manufacturing but also service industry companies suffer the same dilemma when deciding how to grow teams that are working at their most efficient.

6. The company has **no experience of overseas markets** – fear of the unknown should have no place in a rational business decision-making process, yet it can still be a drag on companies exploring overseas opportunities. They can overcome this by hiring new managers who have that expertise, or working with the government to make contacts in new markets. Leonidou (2004) suggests two external resources: government policy makers who can ease the company's internationalisation and educators who can embolden the management team with the relevant knowledge.

7. Company is **too small to grow** – an apparent paradox: a company that needs to grow but is too small to take the risk. When smaller companies grow they are making the greatest proportional risk of all. It may well find that it only has the management skills for its current position in the market and to grow means taking on new staff of unknown capabilities. International expansion is even riskier since it means getting to grips with a whole new clutch of unknowns, from the culture to the peculiarities of the local market demand.

Corporate contraction is a more contentious issue, as it can look on the surface like a failure of management. Let us see the circumstances under which shrinkage is the only option:

1. The **market is in decline** – when the market is shrinking then the company needs to enter a controlled descent, eventually being wound up altogether, or it needs to reinvent itself as a new kind of business. Many large corporations have brands and acronyms that betray their previous lives in other industries. National Cash Register started in 1884 in the United States manufacturing mechanical cash registers, or tills. It is now known as NCR and is a major producer of electronic products, particularly for use in automated processes.

2. **Legislation** – companies may get legislated into decline due to government intervention. There are many examples of arms manufacturers that have been forced to cut back on production due to peace and security agreements made at the national level, or due to a reduction in government spending. More recently, environmental concerns have put pressure on companies to cease operations, or at least radically modify how they operate. Almost all Japan's whaling fleets have gone out of business due to the lobbying of anti-whaling organisations.

 ## MYTH BUSTER – NO END TO CARBON PAPER

It seems that the extinction of paper is perpetually just around the corner, thanks to the dominance of computers. In the days before computers and personal printers the only practical way to make copies of documents was to slip a sheet of carbon paper under the document to be copied. Whatever was then written on the document was then transferred to a piece of paper beneath. The ease of printing, or scanning, documents has consigned the technique to history, or it should have.

There are still a few companies around the world manufacturing carbon paper. In fact it is not carbon but a kind of wax, and pressing on it with a sharp implement, like a pen, or striking it with a typewriter key, will press the wax onto another sheet of paper. Placed between two sheets of paper, whatever is written on the top sheet will be transferred, via the carbon paper, to the bottom sheet. The bottom sheet is known as the carbon copy and two of these, plus the original, are usually the maximum number.

There is just one company in the UK hanging on in what is left of the market, York Haven Ltd. It has been in decline for over 40 years but is still in operation. Where it once had four factories and fifty employees producing up to 100 tonnes of carbon paper per month it now has one factory, three employees and output of 1 tonne per month.

Despite having a virtual monopoly of the UK market the company lacks the market power of a conventional monopoly. There are a number of substitute goods that could take the place of carbon paper. Nevertheless, there is enough demand remaining and the company's overheads are low due to the basic, even antique, production technology. For most people the term carbon copy lives on only as the CC initials in an email, but properly managed there are still reasonable returns to be made from this fading technology.

Point of consideration: Should York Haven Ltd invest in new manufacturing technology that allows higher rates of production and a lower cost per unit at that output level? What alternatives are there to growth for the company?

Source: BBC (2013)

REASONS FOR GROWTH

Given all these uncertainties and impediments to growth, it is hardly surprising that some conservatively minded managers may prefer to stay safely within the confines of the familiar. Equally, though, there are many incentives, and indeed compulsions, for growth:

1. **Market growth potential may attract new competitors** – if the market is expanding fast enough for rival companies to become interested then the result will be heightened competition with resultant pressures on costs and prices. Growth in an expanding market is therefore a defensive strategy to prevent rivals gaining a commercially viable market presence.
2. The company holds a **competitive advantage** that has not been fully exploited – a simple growth strategy of following market demand. However, the only certain demand is that which has been translated into sales, the rest is speculation or hype. If a company has a highly differentiated product then it may prefer to maintain constant levels of production secured by a long waiting list of orders. The length of the waiting list may fluctuate over time but as long as it exists the company can make long-term plans for stability.
3. **Economies of scale** have not been achieved – the first company to expand to the point where it experiences economies of scale will hold cost advantages that no competitor can beat, at least not with the same production system. To an extent the kind of output necessary for economies of scale is theoretical, based on the limits of the production technology. In practice, production processes are highly complex systems, so their ultimate configuration tends to be arrived at through trial and error as much as by theoretical analysis. Consequently, most companies in the industry will be looking for growth opportunities in the belief that it may lead to a drop in unit costs of production and a cost advantage for them.

4. The **product is generic** and can be sold in any market – the least risky international growth strategy since demand in new markets can be broadly anticipated. It is particularly helpful if the product requires little or no modification for each new market. The growth strategy then becomes internationalisation by default and the management team can steadily gain experience of overseas business practices in preparation for a more serious test later. The problem is that generic products tend to sell on price, so there is a danger of being swept out of an overseas market by a cheaper rival. To combat this it would be vital to use the additional overseas sales to target cost savings from economies of scale.

5. The **cost of sales is low** compared to the overhead costs – capital-intensive production methods have high fixed costs and relatively low variable costs. In the short-term any new sales should cover the variable costs without difficulty, the rest of the sales revenue contributing towards the fixed costs. The company is therefore motivated to find these additional sales as a tactical measure. The long-term strategy must be to have sales volume that covers both fixed and variable costs, which may take the company in the direction of growth for economies of scale or stability, depending on the state of the market.

6. The **domestic market is saturated** but there are overseas opportunities – we have seen that market saturation can be a reason not to grow, but only if the stagnation is in that one market. Growth can then be found in new markets but only if those markets offer one of the expansion opportunities listed above.

7. The **management team has skills** that can be readily applied to a growing operation – one of the more contentious reasons for corporate growth since it can become tangled up in principal-agent problems and moral hazard. If management incentives are tied to growth then they will push for growth for its own sake. This can be despite the absence of any of the above objective reasons for growth. This can create a boom–bust business model of rapid expansion, high management pay-outs, followed by painful corporate consolidation and restructuring as a new management team is forced to bring the corporation back to a sustainable size. If the growth incentives remain in place this position becomes the launch pad for another cycle of boom followed by bust.

   A less cynical view of management allows for the fact that their skills can be applied to a growing organisation without diluting their effectiveness. This is a way of realising economies of management where the decisions of a talented manager can be applied as much to a small enterprise as a large one. This is the logic that underpins the growth of conglomerates, the senior management team using their financial skills to identify investment opportunities based on their analysis of the data. The approach is less suited to those that like to micro-manage and can become lost in the minutiae of the business operations.

We can see that the choice of contraction, stability or growth is not down to whether the management are the cautious, risk-averse types rather than dynamic, macho risk takers since the appropriate strategy depends on the circumstances. In Table 2.1, the management decision is linked to market, company or external conditions and the range of strategic options.

Growth does not have to be in the form of expanding sales of the existing product line or services. The corporation as a whole can grow by developing new product lines, entering new industries or expanding through **mergers and acquisitions (M&A)**. This includes diversification, a kind of defensive growth that is intended to stabilise revenues across the corporation and exploit economies in management by having the same management team make decisions for a larger number of operations.

Table 2.1 *Management strategic options for the contraction, stability or growth decision*

Environment	Condition	Contraction	Stability	Growth
Market	Saturated		Low risk: defensive position to hold market share	High risk: dependent on new innovation
	Shrinking	Low risk: accept the inevitable and manage the decline	Medium risk: maintain sales volumes by expanding market share	High risk: raise production volumes to reduce unit cost and compete on price. Opportunities for mergers and acquisitions
	Uncertainty		Wait and see strategy	
	Growth			Raise volumes by maintaining market share
	Generic product	Low risk: exit strategy when new entrants hold unassailable cost advantage	Low risk: maintain market share. Long-term high risk of new entrants	Medium risk: expand market share as a barrier to new entrants
	Overseas growth			Maintain domestic market share and seek additional overseas sales
	Poor financial returns	Low risk: implement exit strategy	Low risk: maintain current volumes	High risk: grow production to reduce unit costs
Company specific	Dominant individual(s)	Low risk: when individual leaves assume they are irreplaceable and manage the decline	Low risk: consolidate market position after individual leaves	Low risk: Individual as source of competitive advantage
High risk: difficult to maintain growth when individual leaves
	Competitive advantage		Low risk: defend a well-defined market niche	Medium risk: exploit the advantage. However, limits are unknown
	Economies of scale		Low risk: hold position if market demand is low	Medium risk: grow to size with scale benefits
High risk: further growth after scale has been reached
	Small company	Low risk: develop an exit strategy, or agree to be acquired	Medium risk: defend a market niche with a differentiated product	High risk: takes the company into unchartered territory in all areas
	Management skill		Low risk: management accepts its limitations	Medium risk: exploit economies of management through mergers and acquisitions
High risk: management believes its own hype and expands company beyond their capabilities
	Government involvement	Legislation outlaws process or product	Government defends the company as part of national industrial strategy	Government subsidises growth

MANAGEMENT SPOTLIGHT: "SUPERSTAR" MANAGERS

CEOs occasionally enjoy the kind of celebrity status usually accorded to stars of film and music. Perhaps they are even more deserving of the fame given that they provide jobs for the unemployed and wealth for investors. As Khurana (2002) points out, these 'superstar' managers need to demonstrate more than mere talent and experience but also that mystical quality of charisma. Some of the most famous business leaders in the world have had this attribute, from Henry Ford to Bill Gates, though it does not appear to be a characteristic that can be used to identify these managers at the start of their careers.

This can be dangerous: if charisma is a quality that is perceived only after success has been recognised then it is not a reason for hiring senior managers. Yet this does not seem to inhibit shareholders from accepting the appointment of CEOs who display these larger-than-life characteristics. The emergence of the superstar CEO may be related to increasing numbers of ordinary investors who have little understanding of the metrics of business and so are more dependent on judging the style of the leadership. Frequent appearances in the media must also carry some of the blame. Lee Iacocca of Chrysler came to public prominence thanks to his personal appearances in TV commercials; he was, though, already a highly decorated business leader.

In fact, some of the most successful CEOs have little charisma, despite frequent appearances in the media. Warren Buffet and Bill Gates are both high profile yet they have never enjoyed the semi-divine status of luminaries such as Steve Jobs. There are also cases of charismatic CEOs whose luck has run out, leaving investors to rue the day they fell for their charms. Bernard Madoff, chairman of Madoff Securities and perpetrator of the biggest Ponzi scheme in history, may stand out as the most extreme example, but he is not alone in exposing how unsophisticated many investors can be in choosing their leaders (Smith, 2010).

On the international stage it might be expected that investors would exhibit a more sober evaluation of their senior management teams. Less likely to be known for their media exploits, such CEOs should be chosen on their track records. When in 2006 Steve Ballmer, one of the earliest Microsoft employees, was granted full control of the company from Bill Gates, he was seen as a safe pair of hands. Although he was responsible for increasing the financial returns he was less skilled at exploiting the burgeoning technical innovations coming onto the scene. He was replaced in 2014 by Satya Nadella, a native of India who had gained his early professional experience with Sun Microsystems. He did not join Microsoft until 1992. According to Forbes ranking system, the retired Bill Gates is counted as the seventh most powerful person in the world, while Nadella only makes it to number sixty-four. Whatever Nadella's undoubted qualities as the leader of a hugely profitable MNE, apparently charisma is not seen as a necessary attribute (Forbes, 2014).

Point of consideration: How important is charisma for leading a global corporation and how can an individual obtain it?

Sources: Forbes, 2014; Khurana, 2002; Smith, 2010

ANSOFF'S GROWTH STRATEGIES

Growth is not entirely about the market but also what the company has in its product arsenal to exploit the new opportunities and the company's own risk analysis. In 1965 Ansoff set out four possible strategies for a company to grow and arrayed them in a matrix format. Two of the strategies were related to the market, one to the product and the final one to the overall risk management strategy of the company. The matrix is shown in Table 2.2, adapted from Ansoff's 1965 publication:

Table 2.2 *Ansoff's Matrix*

		Products	
		Existing Products	New Products
Markets	Existing Markets	Market Penetration	Product Development
	New Markets	Market Development	Diversification

Source: Based on Ansoff, 1965

Ansoff's assertion was that the market- and product-related strategies were based on the existing capabilities of the company, at least to a degree. If we first look at the product side of the matrix we can see that a product may be an existing one, or newly developed. For the new product, as long as its market is an existing one and well understood then the company is still largely operating in familiar territory.

It is important to emphasise with the market that we are not considering them at the international or national level. Instead, it is the market as defined by the product itself. For example, vehicles sell into two broad markets, passenger and commercial. Passenger vehicles are generally cars, while commercial vehicles comprise trucks and vans for carrying goods. From the company's point of view, it may have an established presence in the market or be entering it for the first time, but as long as the new market is being explored with an existing product then the company is not entirely stepping out into the unknown.

If the company launches a new product into a new market then the situation is entirely unfamiliar. Ansoff's contention is that this is too risky to be rational unless the move is part of a wider push for diversification. We can think of diversification as a portal into a whole new range of possible strategies that take the company into a completely new league, as opposed to those strategies that are based on some existing familiarity and therefore almost seem to write themselves.

Leaving diversification aside for the moment, from Ansoff's Matrix we can see there are three iterations of product and market, which contain at least some familiar ground for the company involved. Each of these then implies a related strategy:

- **Existing Product, Existing Market** – the company is starting from an established position, so in order to grow it must dig deeper into the market with a penetration strategy. It can achieve this by selling more products to its existing customers or by conquest sales that take sales away from the competition.

  Telecommunications companies will employ both these strategies, either bundling established services so that customers buy the entire product range or taking sales of each other by offering introductory deals.
- **Existing Product, New Market** – the company has a firmly established product but believes its unique features can find competitive advantages in other markets if they are carefully developed. Remember that the market is defined by the product, so a new market is not necessarily an overseas one but could be a parallel market at home. As a new market, the product will probably undergo some mild adaptation.

  It is a curious fact that the most popular personal vehicle in the United States is the Ford F150 truck, essentially a commercial vehicle that is used for private duties. To meet the demand of the passenger vehicle market the F150 has been gentrified with luxuries like leather seats, electric windows, etc., but it remains fundamentally a truck (Ford, 2014). There are a few examples of passenger cars, particularly station wagons, being converted to commercial duties. In both cases, the company needs to manage the expectations of the market to get it to accept the product.

- **New Product, Existing Market** – the company develops a new product but experience with the market means that it can anticipate demand with some accuracy. Many e-commerce companies have become adept at this as the internet is a very flexible platform.

Amazon sells into a broad market of consumers who are internet savvy, so it is relatively easy for the company to add new product lines (Amazon, 2014).

Although each of Ansoff's strategies appears to be distinct, the fact that the definition of new market and new product is rather subtle can make identification of the strategy an inexact science. In some ways, this is the problem of trying to impose a simple matrix structure on a subtle and dynamic business environment (Morrison and Wensley, 1991). Take the truck-as-car Ford F150 in the United States as an example: the reason the vehicle is so popular is that it not only carries people in the cab but it can also carry goods on the flat-bed in the rear. It is the fact that the vehicle can straddle two markets simultaneously that makes it so appealing. If we then accept the vehicle market as one single market, particularly at this price point and usage, then Ansoff's distinction disappears.

Equally, it is difficult to find examples of products that are new under Ansoff's definition that cannot also be dismissed as variations or updates of existing products. As Ansoff states, the new product should adhere to the same 'mission' and it is often challenging to see how it can do this unless it is essentially the same kind of product. Reinterpreting the telecommunications example, service providers will bundle together internet, telephone and television into packages to suit the consumer's own personal desires, but from the company's technical point of view there is little to differentiate the services. So when the company introduces the ability to watch the latest movie releases on television, is this a new product, a new market or both? Some consumer might argue that it is neither since movies can already be viewed on television, just not quite so soon after their public release. All the customer is doing is switching provider.

 ## CASE STUDY: AMAZON SEND THE SAME LETTER SINCE 1997

Amazon first appeared in 1994 as an online book retailer. Within a short period it had very quickly expanded its operations into other product offerings, initially with music CDs and then into products of almost every description. Yet since 1997 the company CEO, Jeffrey Bezos, has been sending a copy of the same letter to shareholders along with the annual report. He does this as a reminder that the company's basic purpose remains unchanged, which is to deliver maximum value to the customers. One might argue this is only what all companies should do, but in the case of Amazon there is an inherent flexibility that permits the company to continually evolve its product offerings and tap into new markets without changing the fundamentals of the business. At the heart of this strategy is the internet revolution that the company has so comprehensively embraced. It is almost as if the internet and Amazon have merged into each other so wide is the scope of the company's activities.

Perhaps, though, Amazon has created the illusion of a dynamic, fluid enterprise when all it is actually doing is riding the internet wave. From a website perspective there is nothing to distinguish between a washing-machine and a bag of marbles. Even from a logistical point of view there is little difference between the two products: both can be transported and stored using existing systems. For those products that Amazon does not itself sell it is simply a matter of adding a link on the website to a supplier who can provide the product. Amazon's clever trick is to charge for a service that the consumer could search for themselves free of charge on any internet search engine.

Has Amazon ever offered a genuinely new product, as opposed to an internet link to a company that is doing so? Is Amazon simply a shop window displaying the full wonders of the internet? In 2007, the company revealed the Kindle, a device for reading books on a pocket-size electronic screen. The company had set up the team that designed the device, so it can fairly claim to be the developer. Although the Kindle was conceptually new, Amazon was an experienced seller of books to people who were familiar with internet shopping. Not quite a step into the unknown, then, as the company was staying within the same basic mission of selling books, albeit virtual ones. Ansoff would therefore allocate the strategy to the 'new product, existing market' category.

Points of consideration: To what extent could other companies that we normally think of as dynamic, such as Apple or Google, send the same letter to shareholders year after year? How stable are their business fundamentals? When would that letter have to be changed to account for shifts in the underlying business model?

Source: Amazon, 2014

DIVERSIFICATION

If Ansoff's strategies for new products and markets seem rather mild, more like extensions of existing practices than anything genuinely novel, then diversification is a strategy at the other extreme. In this the company is stepping outside its familiar territory; you might call it a move beyond its comfort zone.

DIVERSIFICATION FOR RISK REDUCTION

It is easy to confuse the terms of diversification (Reed and Luffman, 1986). Growth and diversification often occur together, but they are not the same thing. As we saw at the beginning of the chapter, there are many reasons why a company would want to grow. These can vary from reaching for economies of scale to exploiting some unique and firm specific advantage. The end result will be increased output and, hopefully, increased profit levels, although embarrassingly sometimes the profits do not grow as fast as output.

Diversification is a strategy focused on risk reduction (Greenspan, 2008). This may not be related to particular projects but rather to the company as a whole. Indeed, diversification may involve taking on new, additional risks, but if they can be used to balance other risks then overall risk for the company will fall. Figure 2.1 shows how two projects with synchronous business cycles can increase the overall risk. By taking on Project 2 the company has grown, and when revenues are positive the two projects sum to create a revenue bonanza for the company. However, when the business cycle turns down, the combined revenue slump puts the company into a far worse position than when it just had the one project. By having two projects with similar revenue fluctuations overall company risk has been heightened. **Synchronous growth** means that the good times may be brilliant, but the bad times could threaten the very existence of the company.

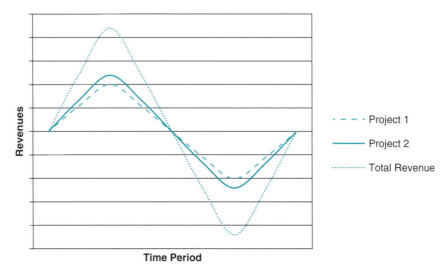

Figure 2.1 *Synchronous growth*

In Figure 2.2, we see what happens to revenues when the business cycles are **asynchronous**; as one project falls to the bottom of its cycle it is balanced by the other reaching its peak. The result is stable total revenues over the time period.

The revenue profile for each project is the same but because they are out of phase the total revenues have been smoothed out. Since only projects that are unrelated can have opposing business cycles, the company must have diversified into activities where it did not previously operate. If it has done this with the same product range then it must have moved into a new market with opposing demand. A company in the construction sector might want to have a parallel presence in the home improvement market.

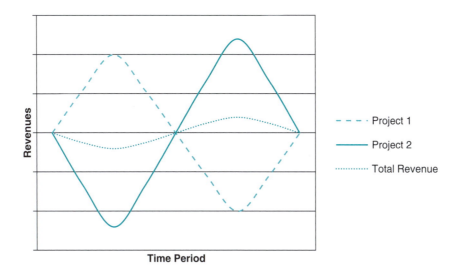

Figure 2.2 *Asynchronous growth*

This is because new house construction tends to do well when the economy is vibrant, but in a recession consumers prefer instead to improve the houses they are already in. Over the complete business cycle total revenues should be reasonably stable.

We might conclude from this that asynchronous growth is a diversification strategy that reduces risk for the company, but this is not quite the case. Granted, it does not suffer the worst of the slowdown, but then again it misses out on the revenue bonanza when the times are good. In the short term the company can appear stable, but in the long term it looks stagnant. Over the complete business cycle, then, asynchronous diversification has no effect on revenue or company risk.

We might think that it is the company's owners, the **shareholders**, who benefit from the short-term stability. It is a sad fact with shareholders that they have limited lifespans and so often have to take a short-term view. For such mortals, the promise of a revenue bonanza at some point in the future is of little interest if they are not going to be around to enjoy it. They would therefore consider an investment that promised steady revenues as being lower risk than one that fluctuated wildly. Yet if shareholders wanted to smooth out their share of company revenues, which they earn in the form of dividends, then they could have made the investment in the opposing project themselves. They did not need the company's management to do it for them. Furthermore, the company itself may not benefit either.

This begs the question as to who might actually be benefiting from the **asynchronous diversification** of business cycles. If we consider a hypothetical oil company we might get some idea. At some point in the distant future, the world's oil wells will run dry and the oil companies will go out of business. To counter this inevitable demise, many such companies have explored alternative power sources, such as solar panels. The idea is that as oil sales dwindle the slack will be taken up by rising sales of solar panels. But who gains from this? Shareholders are ambivalent since they can invest in solar panel companies themselves if they want to. Oil company workers receive no benefits since solar panels are an unrelated technology and they would still lose their jobs. The only people to gain would be the oil company senior managers who can transfer their generic management skills to the expanding solar panel company. In other words, asynchronous diversification reduces **management risk**, not company risk (Del Brio et al., 2011).

This may be a little unfair on the managers. While it is true that shareholders can decide on investments for themselves, generally they trust to the better skills and experience of professional managers to do it for them. They might surmise that if the senior executives of their oil company are running the show particularly effectively, then they are probably going to be just as adept at running a solar panel company. We can extend this and trust to those executives to run multiple businesses, none of which are operationally related but which all benefit from the managerial talents of the senior executives. This kind of group is a **conglomerate**.

 ## MYTH BUSTER – TOYOTA BUILDS MORE THAN CARS

Toyota is famous as one of the largest and most successful car manufacturers in the world. It was formed as an off-shoot of the Toyoda Automatic Loom Works and is now a major constituent part of the Toyota conglomeration of companies. The various member companies are not owned by a holding company but instead have shares in each other alongside other shareholders. This is the style of the Japanese *keiretsu*, although in Toyota's case there is no bank at the centre of the web.

An unusual feature of Toyota Motor is that it has a home building division, Toyota Housing. This business unit is not another member of the group, it is under the complete control and ownership of Toyota Motor. The houses are prefabricated, meaning that they are manufactured in a plant and then transported in sections for final assembly on site. The precise reasons why the housing business was started are not clear, but it seems that it was on the whim of senior management, perhaps in the belief that Toyota's skill in efficient car production could equally be applied to prefabricated housing. In reality, there is no evidence of synergy between the car and housing operations.

Points of consideration: What is the purpose of this style of diversification? Who is benefiting from it?

Source: Toyota, 2014

UNRELATED DIVERSIFICATION – CONGLOMERATES

The most diversified form of company is one that has structured itself as a **conglomerate**. This is often known as **unrelated diversification** because the different business units have no operational connection. The rationale for such a strategy is rather ephemeral and there is not much theoretical or empirical support (Laeven and Levine, 2007). Of course, supporting evidence should never stop a good business strategy and there are a number of conglomerates that have secured their place amongst the industry leaders. The following list of conglomerates includes a sample, far from complete, of their business interests:

- Virgin Group – airline, train company, bank
- GE – aviation, finance, healthcare
- Sony – consumer electronics, music publishing, film production.

As previously discussed, the lack of rational support for conglomerates is due to the fact that shareholders are free to diversify their investments themselves. The senior managers seem to be the only ones to benefit directly from the diversification, as they can hold onto their jobs in a stable holding group even as business cycles wreak havoc on individual business units. This view is based on the assumption that shareholders and managers have access to the same information and have the same ability to analyse it, but it is only their intentions that differ.

In reality, managers are professionals who spend their time honing their corporate skills, while shareholders have much more limited resources in picking investment winners. In effect, the shareholders employ the managers to research and select investments on their behalf. If we look again at the three conglomerates given above, a common feature is the strong leadership by a single visionary. The Virgin Group is led by Sir Richard Branson, who has long been a poster-boy for dynamic entrepreneurial leadership. GE was for many years presided over by Jack Welch, seen by some as the exemplar of the American management style. In Japan, Sony was commanded by Akio Morita, co-founder and chairman until 1994.

A name that could be added to the list is that of Warren Buffet, chairman and CEO of Berkshire Hathaway. The company has an interesting structure because it takes the concept of a conglomerate run by a cadre of professional managers one step further. Berkshire Hathaway originated as a textile manufacturer with Buffet buying control in 1964, apparently to spite the president, Seabury Stanton (O'Loughlin, 2002). A few years later Buffet used the company as a springboard to obtaining other companies using purely financial analysis. Berkshire Hathaway could therefore be considered as a hybrid form of conglomerate and investment fund. Strictly speaking, an investment fund is not a conglomerate because, like individual shareholders, the fund managers have little or no operational involvement in the companies they own.

JAPANESE AND SOUTH KOREAN CONGLOMERATES

In South-East Asia a curious form of conglomerate has emerged. Early Japanese industrialisation was driven by the creation of *zaibatsu*, groups of companies held together by controlling families. There were four such groups and their names are still familiar to us: Sumitomo, Mitsui, Yasuda and Mitsubishi. They were later joined by similar groups as the Japanese economy expanded in the twentieth century. The great advantage of these groups was that they were able to operate with their own internal markets, supporting each other as they progressed. Conglomerates also benefit from internal markets but not to the same extent. The zaibatsu carried such economic weight that their progress was synonymous with national advancement, and so political influence was an inevitable consequence. It is for this reason that the groups were forcibly broken up at the end of World War II at the behest of the occupying Allied powers.

However, the zaibatsu then reformed as *keiretsu*, a linked system of companies centred on the financial control of a bank rather than a family. The groups are held together by the members having cross shareholdings in each other, with the bank being the dominant partner. Western business are often envious of the way that Japanese companies can work together, apparently in an atmosphere of trust, but these relationships are enforced by cross-ownership ties. These ties can be so extensive they act as a de facto barrier to entry for Western businesses (Port, 1994).

South Korea has industrialised with a similar pattern to the Japanese zaibatsu, based on groups called *chaebol* (Kim, 2006). These were formed after the Korean War as powerful families were selected by the government to be recipients of business aid and access to foreign technologies. Amongst the more famous names were Hyundai and Samsung, although some of the groups have more recently been broken up. The Hyundai name, for example, is still associated with construction, shipbuilding and car production but no longer as part of a single group. Samsung only has a minority interest in the car company that bears its name.

KEIRETSU LESSONS FOR THE EMERGING ECONOMIES

The influence that the zaibatsu and chaebol had in accelerating economic development is significant, yet it is remarkable that the approach has not been used in other developing nations to spur development. The South-East Asian model of conglomerate, unlike the products, seems resistant to export.

The customary approach in developing countries is for the government to become directly involved in selecting and supporting a particular industry, a national champion, in the belief that it will become a beacon for economic development. Part of this is the trickle-down effect, where technologies at the national champion, most likely created with substantial foreign assistance, somehow permeate into the wider economy via businesses that are connected to the national champion.

With a zaibatsu or chaebol the trickle-down is much more focused, as the partner firms push each other to develop the specific technologies that are needed within the group. It is an attractive economic strategy but one that would be open to wide-scale corruption. It is perhaps for this reason that the South East Asian style of conglomerate is almost always based around a family. The reputational capital invested by each family member far outweighs the personal financial gains from accepting bribes. If this is so then the zaibatsu/chaebol structure will remain a strictly cultural phenomenon.

An approximation of the South-East Asian model might be to centre the conglomerate on a foreign MNE but surround it with local satellite firms. This is contrary to other approaches to economic development by foreign direction investment (FDI), where the MNE is at liberty to form business ties in the locality as it sees fit, even inviting suppliers from its own country to join it. Where the government imposes conditions it is on the MNE itself, such as the way China obliges MNEs to join local companies in joint ventures (JV). The knowledge transfer then passes horizontally across the JV.

A possible alternative would be for the MNE to have free rein with its own investment but to be required to take equity positions in local firms. With money committed to these firms, like in a keiretsu or chaebol, it is in the interests of the MNE to form lasting and stable partnerships with these firms. It creates the kind of mutual dependency and quasi-internal market of the South-East Asian model that would render corruption pointless. After all, there is little reason to bribe a company of which you are already a part owner.

 ## CASE STUDY – THE COLUMBIAN KEIRETSU

Columbia may have found a way to transplant the concept of the Japanese keiretsu conglomerate structure to an emerging economy. Located in the Antioquia Department in the north-western part of the country, the Grupo Empresarial Antioqueño (GEA) comprises 125 separate companies structured as three main groups. At the head of each group is a dominant company: Nutresa, a food company, Argos, an energy producer, and Sutra, a financial services group. Sutra is also the majority owner of Bancolumbia, the largest commercial bank in the country. GEA is held together by a network of crossholdings in the keiretsu style.

The group, known as the Sindicato Antioqueño, was originally formed as a defence against hostile takeovers from other Columbian companies and even powerful local drug lords. In a region renowned for business acumen the group is a way of protecting the most famous enterprises in the region, held together by a culture of innovation and austerity. There is no overall headquarters building and no main board. When the three main company CEOs meet they do so informally and as equals.

GEA has grown to directly employ 100,000 workers and contributes over 6% of national GDP. This has brought economic stability and growth to the region, progress that could never have been possible when the drug lords held sway. With so much regional and national success, the group is beginning to look outside Colombia at international expansion.

Point of consideration: If GEA is a keiretsu with a specific Columbian character, how should a keiretsu look in a developing economy in Africa?

Source: Financial Times, 2014

RELATED DIVERSIFICATION

Stopping short of the highly controlled zaibatsu/chaebol structure, there are company groups that are structured around business units that work together, engaging in related diversification. In this way they are similar to the more recent Japanese keiretsu form. It is quite distinct from the conglomerate made up of unrelated business units, where the superior skills of the management are the only *raison d'être* for bringing the diversified firms together. As we have seen, in a conglomerate the asynchronous business cycles are mainly effective in diversifying management risk rather than investment risk.

In related diversification the business cycles of the various business units must be synchronising to a degree because they are in the same line of work. The company is extending its existing competencies and developing organically. Like the zaibatsu/chaebol structure this may be suited to developing-nation companies as circumstances force them to look to internal resources (Kazmi, 2008).

As long ago argued by Ansoff (1957), the connections between them take one of two forms:

- Vertical – upstream component suppliers or downstream clients, distributers and consumers.
- Horizontal – parallel operations that sell into the same market as the company's products but are technically different.

Vertical diversification takes us into complex questions about whether the company should source components in the market or make them itself. This is the **make-or-buy** predicament that faces almost all companies. It was first observed by Ronald Coase (1937) and it continues to be a fundamental structuring force in all businesses. It involves the **vertical integration**, forward or backward, with sales outlets or suppliers in order to reduce the transaction costs of making deals with them in the market.

There are advantages to sourcing components in the market, such as obtaining the best price and being able to take advantage of technical developments as suppliers make them available. There are also a number of disadvantages, such as suppliers selling important innovations to rival companies that can afford to pay higher prices. The vertical relationship between a company and its suppliers is therefore one that can suffer intolerable levels of risk, particular at times when technical development is occurring at a fast pace. It is quite common, for example, for fashion houses to manufacture their collections in their own workshops. **Backward vertical integration** of this type ensures reliable supplies and prevents rivals gaining intelligence on the new look.

Vertical diversification is not only upstream but also downstream. The reasons for this are the same, to ensure reliable sales outlets and to secure innovations in a rapidly changing environment. **Forward vertical integration** is observed in high technology firms like Sony and Apple which have dedicated sales outlets.

Horizontal diversification involves operations that are within the company's existing range of competencies but send it off at a slight tangent to the established strategy. This should be contrasted with a conglomerate which can wander into entirely new industrial sectors in search of a financial investment opportunity. Where a conglomerate can only find synergy in management, horizontal diversification looks for synergies across the product ranges. Chanel is a French fashion house that was founded in 1909 as a designer of *haute couture*, literally high dressmaking. In 1921 the company released the famous N°5 perfume (Marber and Wellen, 2007). Although the production process has no common ground with dressmaking, it is still clearly high fashion and the company's twin activities found synergy in the market by providing mutual support. In the minds of consumers, the perfume and the 'little black dress' are inextricably linked, and the profile of the brand has been raised exponentially.

CASE STUDY – VERTICAL DIVERSIFICATION AT GM

A famous case in the United States concerned the car maker GM and its most important supplier, Fisher Body (Klein 1988). In those days car manufacturers produced the engines and vehicle platforms (a rigid chassis, or frame) and outsourced body production to suppliers. These bodies were made from wood and fabric, a labour intensive process that had barely changed since the era of the horse and cart. From the 1930s a new body production process emerged, developed by Edward Budd and Joseph Ledwinka (Nieuwenhuis and Wells, 2012), that made bodies from sheet steel and did away with the need for the rigid frame. To fabricate the steel bodies, powerful presses were needed and although expensive they could be operated at high rates of production to offset the cost. The era of mass production was born.

The problem for GM was that it was heavily dependent on Fisher for supplies of these bodies. At any time Fisher could have decided to switch to another car manufacturer that offered a more profitable deal. In fact, the problem was not of price but reliability of supply; GM needed Fisher to build a dedicated body plant in the vicinity of its own car assembly plant, but Fisher was not prepared to make the necessary investment. The only solution was for GM to buy Fisher and direct the body plant investment itself. It is now only the smallest of car manufacturers that still outsource body production.

Point of consideration: The dilemma in which GM found itself has been repeated over the subsequent decades. These days fuel cell technology has been suggested as a replacement for fossil fuel engines and could secure the long-term future of the industry, although that is far from certain. Do you think GM should contract with an independent fuel cell research company or internalise the research?

Sources: Klein, 1988; Nieuwenhuis and Wells, 2012

INTERNATIONAL DIVERSIFICATION

Geographic diversification brings with it the same possibilities that are experienced by domestic companies: exploitation of firm-specific assets, economies of scale and scope, learning effects and the reduction of transaction costs, amongst others. In addition to these, international diversification brings opportunities for exploiting location-specific advantages.

In a study of Japanese companies Lu and Beamish (2004) found that the benefits to the organisation waxed and waned with internationalisation. In other words, during the early and mature stages in the internationalisation of the company the benefits were scarce: in the beginning the senior management team lacked sufficient experience and in the later stage the higher costs of co-ordinating an internationally spread organisation partly negated the gains. It was only during the middle period, where the management had gained the appropriate experience but the team had not yet grown to unwieldy proportions, that the international diversification was at its most efficient.

While the corporate benefits of international diversification are largely inconclusive there is evidence that the strategy is often driven by intangible influences. For example, Tihanyi et al. (2000) found that it is the demographic profile of the senior management that tends to push the company towards diversifying overseas. In essence, the most successful firms had a senior management team that was young, highly educated and experienced overseas. Other studies have suggested the benefits might come from product innovation, extending the corporate structure into overseas locations to source new developments with minimal transaction costs. Jeong (2003) found that US companies certainly benefited in this way, but it was not true of Chinese firms. This could be due to the political environment within which they operate, or perhaps because US firms have more dynamic new product development strategies.

Research that culminates in hard conclusions on international diversification, though, is becoming harder to achieve. Globalisation has meant that few firms can claim to be isolated from international networks, so even if they are not structurally diversified overseas they can still derive many of the benefits. Hitt et al. (2006) suggest that it has become almost impossible to identify a universal set of rules for international diversification since it has become too heterogeneous for analysis. If that is so, then international diversification strategies are more firm-specific than previously thought, and management teams have to look to their own unique decision making capabilities rather than an accepted industry-wide approach.

FAILURE OF DIVERSIFICATION

Diversification is directed at risk reduction, but it often does this by taking on new risks as part of a broader growth strategy. This apparent contradiction is explained by the way the new risk offsets existing risks. In a conglomerate, the new risk simply needs to have an opposing business cycle for the overall financial risk for the group to be reduced. This is despite the fact that the individual risk for each business unit remains untouched. In related diversification, risk to the group is reduced by enhancing security of supplies, sales and intellectual property.

When growth and diversification are so closely linked it can be difficult to apportion blame when the enterprise fails. By their nature, internationally diversified groups are under multiple national jurisdictions and this adds another complicating factor. Like any strategy, diversification has its own advantages and disadvantages and these are listed in Table 2.3:

Table 2.3 *Advantages and disadvantages of diversification*

Advantages	Disadvantages
Spreads risk	Resources get spread too thinly
Exploits managerial experience	Subjective decision-making
Exploits corporate advantages	Dilution of corporate culture
Opportunity to experiment with strategy	Strategic friction within the group
Company attains dominant position in the market	Attracts anti-trust legislation; becomes a takeover and break-up target

At the planning stage, managers can sketch out some possible causes of diversification failure based on the original strategic purpose, as shown in Table 2.4:

Table 2.4 *Diversification failure*

Diversification Purpose	Reason for failure
Conglomerate – unrelated diversification	Global recession mean all business cycles turn down at the same time
Vertical diversification – reliable supplies	Alternative suppliers develop new technology; larger suppliers offer cheaper prices
Vertical diversification – sales outlet control	Consumers prefer wider choice of independent retailers; poor responsiveness to local market conditions
Horizontal diversification – new product or service	New product cannibalises sales from existing products; company has no experience with the new product; poor synergy between the products

MANAGEMENT SPOTLIGHT: EXPERTISE IN DIVERSIFICATION

Warren Buffet, the famous fund manager, is reputed to have said 'Wide diversification is only required when investors do not understand what they are doing.' This should not be taken as a criticism of diversification, at least for investors who have neither the time nor the business talent to discover new opportunities. Professional managers, though, are employed to make the right investment decisions and so should only diversify when the company is likely to make a financial gain. They should engage in a rational decision-making process, like the one recommended by Costas Markides (1997). He provides a sequence of questions that a CEO should ask themselves before embarking on a diversification strategy:

1. **What can I do better than any of my competitors in existing markets?**
   It is tempting to diversify the company along the lines of its current activities, but this could lead to strategic overstretch. Rather, the company should identify where it has an advantage with further potential and take that to its logical conclusion. If the company has a highly dynamic management, then conglomeration could be a possible route forward.
2. **What strategic assets do I need in order to succeed in the new markets?**
   Markides asserts that a company should have 100% of the assets necessary to make the diversification strategy work. When GM diversified into car body production it knew that it could take all of Fisher Body's production output.
3. **Can we catch up or leapfrog competitors at their own game?**
   If the company is lacking any strategic assets then it must consider whether it can obtain them externally. This may involve acquiring another company.
4. **Will diversification break up existing strategic assets that need to be kept together?**
   The process of diversification involves some transfer of assets. If the asset is managerial skill then there is a danger that the company strength is based on a team spirit that would be lost if the managers were given new responsibilities.
5. **Will we simply be another player in the market or will we emerge as a winner?**
   Strategies can often be replicated by the competition. When this happens the advantages of diversification will prove short-lived.
6. **What can our company learn by diversifying, and are we sufficiently organised to learn it?**
   Diversification plunges the company into a new, dynamic situation, and to exploit the synergies the company must be ready to learn.

As Markides concludes, the possibilities of diversification should motivate a company to look beyond its own boundaries with imagination but not fantasy. Too many diversification strategies have come apart simply because the management team has allowed their ideas to run away with themselves.

Point of consideration: What additional questions should a CEO ask of themselves when looking at international diversification?

Source: Markides, 1997

RAISING EMPLOYABILITY: GROWING MANAGEMENT SKILLS

One of the great business secrets is that managers have little to do once a new project is up and running. It could even be argued that the best managers should make themselves redundant when day-to-day operations are effectively self-sustaining. Managers are therefore fated to be on an eternal hunt for new opportunities, and corporate growth is the main provider. To put it bluntly, growth makes work for managers.

This creates an element of moral hazard in that managers will grow the firm for their professional gain rather than the interests of the company. More interested in making a name for themselves, they dramatically improve their employability while the company comes off second best. Only at the extreme do managers render themselves unemployable: the senior management team at the US telecommunications giant Enron being one of the most infamous examples (Gordon, 2002).

A company can have a closer involvement in shaping its future management team by recruiting them straight out of university. In particular, they can offer graduate training schemes. Available only to the top university graduates, these schemes provide a mix of vocational training and experience that would be unavailable on a postgraduate programme.

Some MNEs also offer international graduate schemes specifically intended to nurture a new breed of internationally minded managers. The training will cover all the main corporate functions (finance, human resources, management information systems, etc.) with the added incentive of international travel. The multinational pharmaceutical firm GSK offers a Future Leaders programme to recent graduates (GSK, 2015), but only the highest achieving students need apply. While recruitment is highly competitive, retention can become a significant problem. Although the training schemes are customised to the corporation they provide so much valuable management experience in a short space of time that the graduate's employability is vastly improved.

Diversification can restore levels of management retention by offering opportunities in new industries without the risks of leaving the company for a new employer. Conglomerates and private equity firms trade on their abilities to apply management skills in a wide variety of businesses. Less well known is the way companies can engage in strategically irrelevant but high-profile activities as a form of internal incentive. For example, Mercedes-Benz has maintained a huge presence in Formula 1 motor racing for decades. There are, of course, the supposed trickle-down engineering benefits for the road cars, but, in fact, the Formula 1 team is a standalone organisation that has almost nothing to do with the company's mainstream operations. The real advantage of sharing a brand with such a high-profile racing outfit is that it helps to attract and retain the best engineers for the road car business, avoiding the inconvenience of having to offer them more money.

THE STORY SO FAR: GROWTH FOR GROWTH'S SAKE

We expect successful businesses to grow but this has to be based on meticulous analysis and a solid strategic purpose. Still, it takes a brave manager to eschew a growth strategy. The pressure is on for managers to exploit existing strengths within the company and the product range to conquer new market opportunities, thereby expanding the company organically. An alternative is to make a sudden step up in size by acquiring or merging with a competitor. When the acquisition takes the firm outside its established industry position then diversification is the aim and a conglomerate structure is the result. With suspicions that diversification serves the needs of the management rather than the corporation, they have fallen out of fashion in many countries. However, a special breed of conglomerate in South-East Asia continues to dominate and may hold clues to new approaches for progress in developing economies.

WEB SUPPORT

1. For those with superspy James Bond delusions, there are some curious management training opportunities with the security services. The National Security Agency in the United States is surprisingly sensible; try the UK's MI5 espionage agency if you dream of being issued with an Aston Martin.

   www.nsa.gov/careers/opportunities_4_u/students/graduate/
   www.mi5.gov.uk/careers/graduate-careers.aspx

2. Milk is one of life's staples but the extraordinary range of products that are based on its pure white goodness opens the door to corporate related diversification almost without limits. The French company Danone is a prime example of how to successfully diversify; think about how much further the strategy can be taken.

   www.danone.com/en/

3. Excellent guide from the state government of Queensland, Australia, on the pros and cons of growth. Also provides information on growth strategies, including exports.

   www.business.qld.gov.au/business/business-improvement/ways-grow-business/
   growing-quickly

Project Topics

1. Research a company that is currently fast growing. At what point would you argue that further growth would be too risky and instead the company needs to stabilise?
2. Department stores have been historic features of many city retail areas but are now threatened by online shopping. If you were the owner of a department store, how would you manage its decline?
3. It has long been said that letter writing is losing out to emails and that the postal service is a dying industry. What kind of diversification strategy would you devise for a postal service?

 CASE STUDY – HYPERCOMPETITION IN THE JAPANESE BEER MARKET

When it comes to Japanese drinks sales in the 1980s it is difficult to avoid making bad jokes about the market being saturated in beer. The truth was that growth opportunities had ground to a halt, and the market had stagnated around an oligopoly made up of Kirin, Sapporo, Suntory and Asahi. Forty years before, Asahi had a third of the market, almost equal with Kirin and Sapporo. By 1985 the dominant player was Kirin, with 61.4% of the market, followed by Sapporo with 19.7%, Suntory on a climbing trend to 9.9% and Asahi in long-term descent to 9.0%, considered to be below break-even.

At this rate of decline Asahi was on course to market irrelevance within a couple of decades. The Japanese government discouraged price competition as it wanted to protect its tax revenue stream from beer sales. In this business environment conquest sales would be made through advertising, while profits were earned through economies of scale, two areas where the giant Kirin held an advantage. Even a brief period of wild innovation in packaging did little to shake up the market.

In the early 1980s, Japanese consumers started to demand greater variety, a need that was satisfied by short production runs of niche beers. However, consumers remained loyal to their chosen brands and total market shares enjoyed little growth. Asahi was getting desperate; it had to undertake a full-frontal attack on Kirin.

Researchers at Asahi believed that Japanese tastes were shifting towards richer tasting food and drink. The company conducted the largest test in industry history and discovered that consumers were looking for both rich taste and dryness, a combination that had been considered contradictory. Asahi concocted such a beer and launched it in 1986, enjoying a 12% increase in sales.

Emboldened by the success, and perceiving a continuing market shift towards dryness, Asahi launched the Super Dry beer in 1987. It quickly overtook all other beers in the market and demand was so high that the company had to forbid its own employees from buying it in order to supply customers. In 1989 Asahi could claim 24.3% of the total market, with 20% of the market dominated by Super Dry alone.

Asahi's almost miraculous resurgence touched off a period of hypercompetition with radical corporate restructuring and product development. As the industry started to cool off in the 1990s it was further destabilised by the rise in popularity of niche beers, a trend seen in many other countries at the same time. By then, though, Asahi's position in the market seemed to be safe.

Points of consideration: Do you think that Asahi should have acted earlier in launching Super Dry? Do you think Super Dry was a high-risk strategy?

Source: Craig (1996)

? MULTIPLE CHOICE QUESTIONS

1. Growth is good for a company when:
   a. It brings in additional profits.
   b. It results in a higher profit per unit sold.
   c. It results in higher sales.

2. On which occasions should a company <u>not</u> pursue growth?
   a. When it means building additional, small-scale plants.
   b. When it means that the company needs to focus on a narrower range of products.
   c. When new management teams need to be hired.

3. When should a company seek to shrink its operations?
   a. The market is in terminal decline.
   b. The economy is in a recession.
   c. Overseas markets have existing local producers.

4. For which corporation would Ansoff recommend diversification?
   a. A dairy company launches a new cheese in its domestic market.
   b. A hotel operator starts a nursing home for old people in a new market.
   c. A European construction company builds a skyscraper in Nairobi.

5. Who benefits most from diversification?
   a. The managers, as it reduces the risk of losing their jobs.
   b. Shareholders, as it increases their income.
   c. Consumers because it increases competition in the market.

6. Asynchronous diversification is preferred because:
   a. It heightens revenues during the boom years.
   b. It minimises revenues during sales downturns.
   c. It smooths out total corporate revenues over the business cycle.

7. Conglomerates are examples of related diversification.
   a. True
   b. False

8. Conglomerates are a tool of economic development.
   a. True – *chaebol* and *keiretsu* have shown how they create an internal, vertical market that can kick-start national economic development.
   b. False – they concentrate power in the hands of an elite and encourage political corruption.

9. Diversification strategies ultimately fail because:
   a. They waste scarce resources.
   b. Shareholders can diversify their own investment portfolios.
   c. In business, specialisation is a key source of competitive advantage.

10. Does corporate growth improve human resource (HR) recruitment of managers?
    a. Yes – it provides new opportunities for career development.
    b. No – managers need to do the same jobs more efficiently.
    c. Probably – it depends on the nature of the growth. International growth with new products will always attract more management talent than domestic growth with existing products.

Answers
1b, 2a, 3a, 4b, 5a, 6c, 7b, 8a, 9c, 10c

REFERENCES

Amazon (2014) '2013 Annual Report' from phx.corporate-ir.net/phoenix.zhtml?c=97664&p=irol-reportsannual accessed 12 July 2014

Ansoff H I (1965) 'Strategies for diversification' in *Harvard Business Review, Sep/Oct57*, 35(5), pp. 113–124

Ansoff H I (1965) *Corporate strategy*. New York: McGraw-Hill Book Co.

BBC (2013) Inside the UK's last carbon paper factory from 15 May 2013 www.bbc.co.uk/news/magazine-22525310 accessed 9 July 2014

Birtwistle G and Tsim C (2005) 'Consumer purchasing behaviour: an investigation of the UK mature women's clothing market' *Journal of Consumer Behaviour*, 4(6), pp. 453–464

Coase R H (1937) 'The nature of the firm' *Economica*, New Series, 4(16) (Nov., 1937), pp. 386–405

Craig (1996) 'The Japanese Beer Wars: initiating and responding to hypercompetition in new product development' *Organization Science,* 7(3), Special Issue Part 1 of 2: Hypercompetition (May–Jun., 1996), pp. 302–321

Del Brio E B, Maia-Ramires E L and De Miguel A (2011) 'Ownership structure and diversification in a scenario of weak shareholder protection' *Applied Economics. 11/20/2011,* 43(29), pp. 4537–4547

Financial Times (2014) 'Colombia's Sindicato Antioqueño has become a force for the country's good' *Financial Times* 23 March 2014 by Andres Schipani from www.ft.com/cms/s/0/3b95966a-a61b-11e3-8a2a-00144feab7de.html#axzz3QOhD94wz accessed 31 January 2014

Forbes (2014) The world's most powerful people from www.forbes.com/powerful-people/ accessed 24 August 2015

Ford (2014) The Future of Tough: All New F150 from www.ford.com/trucks/f150/2015/ accessed 12 July 2014

Hitt M A, Tihanyi L, Miller T and Connelly B (2006) 'International diversification: antecedents, outcomes, and moderators' *Journal of Management,* 32(6), pp. 831–867

Gordon J N (2002) 'What Enron means for the management and control of the modern business corporation: some initial reflections' *The University of Chicago Law Review,* pp. 1233–1250

Greenspan A (2008) 'We will never have a perfect model of risk' *Financial Times,* 17 March 2008, p. 9

GSK (2015) Graduates: future leaders programme from www.uk.gsk.com/en-gb/careers/graduates/ accessed 2 June 2015

Jensen M C (2005) 'Agency costs of overvalued equity' *Financial Management,* 34(1) (Spring, 2005), pp. 5–19

Jeong I (2003) 'A cross-national study of the relationship between international diversification and new product performance' *International Marketing Review,* 20(4), pp. 353–376

Kazmi A (2008) 'A proposed framework for strategy implementation in the Indian context' *Management Decision,* 46(10), pp. 1564–1581

Khurana R (2002) 'The curse of the superstar CEO' *Harvard business review,* 80(9), pp. 60–67

Kim E (2006) 'The impact of family ownership and capital structures on productivity performance of Korean manufacturing firms: corporate governance and the "chaebol problem"' *Journal of the Japanese & International Economies,* 20(2), pp. 209–233

Klein B (1988) 'Vertical integration as organizational ownership: the Fisher Body-General Motors relationship revisited' *Journal of Law, Economics, & Organization,* 4(1) (Spring, 1988), pp. 199–213

Laeven L and Levine R (2007) 'Is there a diversification discount in financial conglomerates?' *Journal of Financial Economics,* 85(2), August 2007, pp. 331–367

Leonidou L C (2004) 'An analysis of the barriers hindering small business export development' *Journal of Small Business Management,* 42(3), pp. 279–302

Lu J W and Beamish P W (2004) 'International diversification and firm performance: the S-curve hypothesis' *Academy of Management Journal,* 47(4), pp. 598–609

Marber A and Wellen P M (2007) 'Developing products with soul: the marketing strategy of Chanel in Japan' in *Marketing Management Journal,* 17(1), pp. 198–207

Markides C (1997) 'To diversify or not to diversify' *Harvard Business Review.* Nov/Dec97, 75(6), pp. 93–99

Morrison A and Wensley R (1991) 'Boxing up or boxed in?: a short history of the Boston Consulting Group share/growth matrix' *Journal of Marketing Management.* April 1991, 7(2), pp. 105–129

Nieuwenhuis P and Wells P (2012) 'Transition failure: understanding continuity in the automotive industry' *Technological Forecasting and Social Change,* 79(9), November 2012, pp. 1681–1692

Oliva R, Sterman J D and Giese M (2003) 'Limits to growth in the new economy: exploring the "get big fast" strategy' in e-commerce' *System Dynamics Review,* 19(2), pp. 83–117

O'Loughlin J (2002) *The real Warren Buffet.* London: Nicolas Brealey Publishing

Port K L (1994) 'The case for teaching Japanese law at American law schools' *DePaul Law Review,* 43, p. 643

Reed R and Luffman G A (1986) 'Diversification: the growing confusion' *Strategic Management Journal.* Jan/Feb1986, 7(1), pp. 29–33

Smith F (2010) 'Madoff Ponzi scheme exposes the myth of the sophisticated investor' *Baltimore Law Review,* 40, p. 215

Tihanyi L, Ellstrand A E, Daily C M and Dalton D R (2000) 'Composition of the top management team and firm international diversification' in *Journal of Management,* 26(6), pp. 1157–1177

Toyota (2014) Toyota Housing Corporation from www.toyota-global.com/company/history_of_toyota/75years/data/business/housing/toyotahome.html accessed 12 July 2014

Part II Global Markets

From the secure familiarity of the home market the allure of global markets can be difficult for managers to resist. Promises of untapped demand, first-mover advantage and the prestige of beating rivals to the punch are all temptations for the ambitious manager. Yet the move into new markets carries risks and opportunities unlike those originally experienced in the home market. Here, the company began life with the simultaneous launch of product, production, marketing and management.

Not so with international markets. From its established home base the company can cherry-pick not only the most attractive overseas markets but often also the products with which to enter the market and how the entry should be best conducted. Where the founding of the company meant tackling the risks as they were, with international markets the management has the luxury of being able to analyse and control the risks. If the risk is too high then the management can just walk away from the opportunity.

Risk is an inherent component of business management. It could be argued that success at business is simply success at managing risk. Perhaps this is why success has become synonymous with the stereotypical macho manager: one who treats high risk ventures as a kind of sport. This is completely incorrect. Real managers calculate the risk and look for the appropriate rate of return on the investment that compensates for that risk. There is no place in management for thrill seekers.

Risk analysis must take in the full spectrum of threats. The most secure investments are those calculated to have the lowest associated risks and so a low rate of return can be tolerated. High risks are equally acceptable, but only if the rate of return is suitably high as well. It doesn't matter if the company is selling waffles in a war zone, ice creams in Iceland or bicycles in Beijing, the risk and the return must always be matched.

Even uncertainty, which is incalculable and beyond the far end of the risk spectrum, can be brought under control by the canny entrepreneur. If the uncertainty can be converted into a calculable risk, or high risk converted to low risk, all without reducing the expected rate of return, then high profits are assured. Entrepreneurs make their money by being extreme risk managers, not extreme risk takers.

Once the risks attached to the political, economic or other factors have been taken into account then risk specific to the product's position in the market must be considered. Profitability is the long-term aim and Michael Porter's Five Forces Model looks at attractiveness of the market by highlighting the commercial pressures on profit. These include the way suppliers and consumers squeeze costs and prices, as well as the competition from alternative products and substitutes.

Into this competitive maelstrom the company must find a gap in the market for its product. Dividing the market up into segments and niches can help to expose unexplored areas but they bring with them their own problems. It might even be argued that vacant parts of the market are not risks but uncertainties, the total lack of information about them rendering risk calculation impossible. Hardly surprising, then, that companies generally prefer to deal with the devil they know in the established segments.

Much of this cautious attitude is due to the imperatives that drive the search for international markets in the first place. These obligations are not about the desire to earn higher profits from attractive new markets but about minimising costs and taking the fight to rival firms. If a production system is underused, or too small for economies of scale, then the additional overseas sales can bring efficiencies in production. On a more positive note, a new product may be so innovative that it would be foolish not to place it in markets across the world and earn the profits it deserves before rival products emerge. Of course, if the company is one of those late arrivals then the imperative is to enter markets in an attempt to contain the rival's advance.

Whatever the pressures, at least the manner of market entry can be controlled by the management. There can be a tentative first dip of the toe with a single product or a full-blown assault on the market with the entire product range. Even if local production is necessary there are varying degrees of commitment, from licensing a local enterprise to building a wholly owned plant as part of a foreign direct investment (FDI) strategy.

Once the market has been chosen and the mode of entry selected the real fight for market share can begin. This means getting to grips with marketing, a business activity that in the international arena requires a degree of self-discipline. While it might seem that local market characteristics demand a custom campaign with a suitably adapted product, any change brings with it unwelcome additional costs. The four Ps of the marketing mix can help, but local marketing is always constrained by the global strategy. The pinnacle of international marketing is easing that tension between local demand and the corporate strategy, which demands the management skills of a master tactician.

3 International Risk Analysis

Chapter Objectives

You might say that risk represents the very essence of the business: the entrepreneur putting their idea into the market to see if anyone will like it. If they do like it, then the entrepreneur can make a handsome return; if not, then there are no returns and the business collapses. In this chapter, we will be looking at a number of topics related to risk:

- The nature of risk and its relationship to uncertainty.
- How risk is related to the rate of return, normal profit and what it means to be risk averse.
- Risk analysis for developing economies.
- Currency exchange rate risk for international business.
- Technological risk in a fast changing world.

BUSINESS AND RISK

Risk is an integral part of doing business; indeed we might argue that it is the single most important feature. Risk simply tells us that few things in life are guaranteed. Those things that we like to think are guaranteed, such as the water we drink, we take for granted and assume we have free access. But for those of us who live in industrial cities or arid regions of the world we realise that even for this most basic of elements there is a degree of risk attached. This risk can take many different forms, including the cleanliness of the water itself and the dependability of its supply. When we pay for drinking water we are essentially paying for a business to assume the associated risk. The company takes on the problem of sourcing a reliable supply of clean water and charges us accordingly.

We can also view risk as the business perspective on the relationship with paying customers that is forged in the market place. Although the law of supply and demand shows how sellers and buyers can negotiate their way to a mutually agreed price, there are limits below which the seller cannot go, at least in the long term. A sustainable business does not simply cover its immediate costs, those that are known for certain, it also needs to keep an eye on possible future changes in the business environment. Returning to our clean water example, a supplier would need to be able to account for any conceivable future developments, such as burst pipes or drought conditions, which would have an impact on the business. A company that underestimates these risks could enjoy a short period where it was able to compete in the market with low prices but as soon as any expensive problems reared up it would rapidly go out of business. It is therefore important to note two defining features of risk:

1. Risk does not refer to precisely predictable events but those that can be reasonably expected to occur at some point in the future.

2. The company can adjust the desired rate of return, and consequently its pricing strategy, to account for the level of risk it believes it is facing.

Risk is therefore an event that can be included in our business calculations so that it can be covered by the appropriate rate of return: a high risk simply means that we require a high rate of return.

Despite the posturing of tough-talking business people there is nothing macho about taking on a high risk as long as it is correctly matched with an appropriately high rate of return. When confronted by two rates of return that are the same, a company will rationally choose the one with the lower risk attached to it. In this sense all companies are risk averse. Of course, the secret for a highly successful enterprise is to find a way of lowering the risk for itself while enjoying the benefits of the relatively high rates of return demanded by its competitors.

THE NATURE OF RISK

Risk and uncertainty

Frank Knight was one of the first to distinguish risk from uncertainty, and there have been many reprints of his seminal work, 'Risk, Uncertainty and Profit' (Knight, 2012).The two concepts of risk and uncertainty are easy to confuse. They are often used interchangeably in daily life but in business, at least, there is a broad agreement on the distinction. Figure 3.1 shows how risk and uncertainty are related to each other, along with the kinds of return we would need on our investment for it to be sustainable.

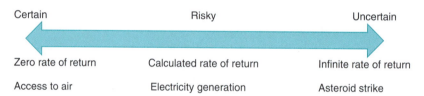

Figure 3.1 *Risk and uncertainty continuum*

We can see that risk exists as a continuum, from absolute certainty of no risk to the complete uncertainty of random events. In business, the lowest risk investment would be government **bonds** since it is highly unlikely that a government would **default** on its repayments, although it does happen from time to time. At the other end of the risk continuum are the high-risk industries such as those in technology or oil exploration. Whether an investor is risk averse or not is irrelevant, all that matters is that the **rate of return** is appropriate for the risk being taken on. The stock market is a good place to see how the return on equity for different companies changes according to the perceived risk, and this is illustrated by Table 3.1 for one randomly chosen day in 2014 on the New York financial markets.

The table shows that the chances of the US government defaulting on its debt are extremely low to non-existent. Depositing cash with the Ally Bank is also low risk, given that there are no account fees and the money can be withdrawn at any moment, but then the yield is not high either. Moving into the equity markets the yield jumps in recognition of the fact that the value of the investment is subject to market sentiment and can change at a moment's notice. Of the three organisations shown, the pharmaceutical company is seen as the safest bet relatively speaking; people will always need medicines but there is no guarantee that Pfizer will continue to develop successful new drugs in the future.

Table 3.1 *Perceived risk and yield 2014*

Industry Sector	Institution	Perceived Risk	Yield (%)
Government Bonds	US 6 month	Extreme low risk	0.03
Cash Deposit	Ally Bank	Very low risk	0.87
Oil Production – equity	Total SA	Medium	4.6
Pharmaceutical – equity	Pfizer	Medium	3.5
Telecommunications – equity	AT&T	High	5.2

Source: Yahoo! Finance (2014)

In Figure 3.1, we can see that the risk has been identified to some extent and so the required yield on the investment is determined. Uncertain events cannot be calculated because the risk, and consequently the appropriate rate of return, cannot be determined. In practice, though, instances of pure uncertainties are hard to find. Even classic examples, such as earthquakes and asteroid strikes, are not quite as uncertain as they might appear. While specific earthquake occurrences are unpredictable, from historical records we can gain some idea of where they are likely to occur and with what frequency. An insurance company will use this data when calculating the kinds of premiums it should charge its customers. By spreading the risk across a number of regions the insurance company reduces the chance that it will have to pay out to large numbers of its customers at one particular time.

 ## MYTH BUSTER – TOKYO WAITS FOR THE BIG ONE … OR NOT

Japan is unlucky enough to find itself in one of the most earthquake-prone regions in the world. In 1923 Tokyo and neighbouring Yokohama were subjected to a seismic shock measuring 7.9Mw, which was the highest that Japan had suffered to date. The cataclysm laid waste to 45% of structures in the capital and up to 90% in the port city of Yokohama. Tragically, it occurred in the middle of the day as meals were being prepared, the shock sending hot stoves flying and setting fire to the fragile wooden houses. The resultant fire storm ripped through the two cities and culminated in the deaths of over 110,000 people, including over 2000 ethnic Koreans murdered by mobs seeking scapegoats for the disaster. The economic cost was immense at around ¥6.5 billion, or four times the annual budget (Schencking, 2008). Tokyo's tram system was torn apart and the city could not afford to replace it. With no significant domestic automotive industry the American giants Ford and GM were able to capitalise on the disaster and dominate the Japanese vehicle market.

While earthquakes are said to be unpredictable, many believe that Tokyo is long overdue another violent quake. They occur in the region around every 24 years and The Earthquake Research Institute at the University of Tokyo is reported to be putting the chances of a magnitude 7.0 quake before 2016 at 70%. This time round, though, the country will be much better prepared. Modern commercial buildings are both fire- and quake-resistant, which should preserve lives and reduce the impact on the economy. Nevertheless, the Great Hanshin earthquake struck the cities of Osaka and Kobe in the early hours of 17 January 1995, killing over 6000 people and causing damage estimated at ¥10 trillion, equivalent to 2.5% of Japan's GDP.

Point of consideration: If you were a manager of an insurance company in Japan, how could you make the premiums on earthquake insurance affordable to customers in Tokyo?

Source: Schencking (2008)

THE MYTH OF RISK AVERSION

There is no such thing as **risk aversion** *per se*, it is about **risk appetite** and finding the rate of return that matches it. To put it another way, investment is about risk management, not risk aversion.

One might be tempted to simply opt for the investment with the highest rate of return, but this is also the one with the highest risk attached to it. In which case, an investor with a nervous disposition might want to play it safe and choose a low-risk investment, but this will earn only low returns. In practice, the two scenarios might involve the same investor, the only difference being their appetite for risk in a given situation. Their strategy could be to stratify their investments, starting with a bedrock of low-risk/low-yield investments for long-term security followed by high-risk/high-yield investments to make speculative gains.

The appetite for risk depends on a number of factors, and it is for this reason that it is nonsense to characterise an investor as risk averse or not. For example, gamblers are clearly not risk averse since they love the thrill of attempting to beat the odds, but it would be a foolish investor who gambled in the same way with the mortgage on their house. A sane gambler plays only with spare cash, they are no more wasting money than they would if spending money on a leisure activity. To gamble with life savings is more a sign of an addiction that needs medical treatment than one of macho grit.

Similarly, it is incorrect to characterise a company or a manager as a risk taker; it depends on the nature of the investment. When faced with a high-risk high-return investment opportunity, a manager would ask themselves the following **risk-investment** questions:

1. If the investment fails, will it threaten the future viability of the company?
2. Will the investment add value to the core competency of the company?
3. Do we have a unique ability to reduce the overall risk of this investment?

A manager who embraces high risk is simply an investor who is able to answer the first question with a clear 'no', meaning that they have surplus funds for a speculative investment and thus a high tolerance for risk. This is the 'bet-the-farm' decision, whether to risk everything on the new opportunity. If the future of the company is not threatened by the failure of the investment then the company-specific risk is actually low, despite the risk inherent in the venture.

If the answer to the first question is that the company's very existence is on the line then the company should proceed to the second question: the investment can go ahead if it is a vital contributor to the company's core competency. In other words, the venture is inherently risky but to not take the opportunity would be even riskier. We can think of this as the company pushing ahead of the competition before the competition does. Aircraft manufacturers regularly make massive investments in new product development but that is the nature of their industry.

For the final of our three questions, the company would need to know if it has the ability to reduce the risk of the project in a way that competitors cannot easily replicate. The inherent risk of the project has not changed, but if the company can enjoy a lower overall risk than the competition then it can snatch a competitive advantage. Management of the company-specific risk means being able to tolerate rates of return that would frighten off rivals where they perceive a higher risk to themselves.

Let's try the decision process for one high-risk high-return project, that of building a theme park, as three very different organisations view the investment (see Table 3.2). In this hypothetical situation two of the firms you will know, Disney and Exxon, but alongside them is an imaginary firm with only a local presence.

Table 3.2 *Project risk and company-specific risk for a theme park*

Investment Decision	Disney Corporation	Exxon	Local Engineering Firm
Bet the farm?	No – Disney is a very large corporation	No – Exxon is a very large corporation	Yes – the investment would destroy the firm if it failed
Core competency?	Yes – theme parks are a major Disney business	No – Exxon is in the oil industry, not leisure	No – engineering has few connections with leisure
Ability to reduce the risk?	Yes – Disney has many years of experience	Possibly – there may be some managerial synergies	No
Appetite for the risk	Strong	Medium	Low
Nature of the investment	Strategic	Diversification	Speculation

We can see from Table 3.2 that the same investment, with the same risks and rates of returns, appeals to different companies based on their circumstances. For Disney, a large corporation that can readily absorb the losses, it is a core part of what the company does and it has built up enough experience to reduce the risk specific to itself. The investment would therefore be part of its existing strategy.

Exxon could also absorb any losses, and although it has no activities in the leisure industry we would expect its professional managers to be able to transfer some of their skills to another business. The corporation might look at theme parks as a way of diversifying its exposure to the varying fortunes of the oil industry.

Finally, the local engineering company: it would have to take on massive new debts in order to fund the investment, which, if it failed, would lead to the financial collapse of the business. The investment is unrelated to the existing activities and the firm has no unique skill for reducing the risk. The investment is therefore speculation, a straight gamble.

 ## CASE STUDY – RISK AVERSION IN ELECTRIC CARS

Amidst growing concerns about global climate change and the depletion of oil reserves, car manufacturers are being forced to give up the predictable cycle of new product releases and instead start looking for an alternative to the internal combustion engine. There have always been wild ideas about jet engines and flying cars, but the real options for the future are frighteningly few. Indeed, the electric car seems to be the only feasible alternative. In theory, electric drive offers zero emissions, though in practice this depends on how the electric power is produced. It is counterproductive if the electricity is generated from a 'dirty' energy source, such as coal. Furthermore, electric cars suffer from their own problems, such as a short driving range and a high purchase cost. Nevertheless, all car manufacturers feel the pressure to have some sort of presence in the technology, ready for the day when the oil wells run dry.

Two such firms are Japan's Nissan and Mitsubishi Motors. In some ways, Mitsubishi looks to be the more courageous risk taker. After 40 years of research it revealed the i-MiEV in 2009, one of the first of the modern crop of electric vehicles and offering a decent range of around 160km from its lithium-ion battery pack. Nissan was much later to the technology, experimenting with electric drive in 1997 with a version of its Alta sedan. It then dramatically raised its commitment with the Leaf, an entirely new model, released to the public in 2009. Reported to be the result of a $3 billion investment, the car needs to sell in relatively high volumes if the investment is to be justified. So which company is the risk taker, and which is risk averse? Nissan has much higher ambitions in the market, and it has built new production facilities to meet the hoped-for demand, while Mitsubishi has developed the technology over many years and has used an existing small vehicle design as the host. The real answer probably lies in the prices for which the two cars are sold: in their home market they sell for almost identical prices, despite the i-MiEV being in a much lower market segment than the Leaf. Clearly, Nissan is taking a much higher risk with its pricing strategy...or is it?

Point of consideration: Apply the three risk-investment questions to these two company investments. Do you think they made the right decisions?

Source: Mitsubishi (2009)

MANAGEMENT SPOTLIGHT: ENTREPRENEUR AS EXTREME RISK TAKER

So if risk aversion is all about appetite, not character, then where does this leave the biggest risk taker of them all, the entrepreneur? We often think of entrepreneurs as being the superstars of the business world since they are able to run rings around the slow-witted industry giants, taking untried ideas and turning them into new market phenomena. So do they owe their success to their steely courage, their macho risk-taking attitudes?

We like to think that entrepreneurs can defy the norms of the industry and achieve something extraordinary but all they are really doing is applying the rules of business with exceptional clarity and energy. We can probably think of many examples of entrepreneurs, but one of the most famous is Richard Branson of the Virgin Group. While he is often portrayed as a business rebel, in fact he meticulously analyses the commercial environment for opportunities. Like many entrepreneurs, his advantage is not in backing entirely new ventures but in taking a new approach to an established style of business (Branson, 2011).

The entrepreneur's advantage, then, is to earn the high rates of growth that are expected of a high-risk investment but find a unique way of lowering the actual company-specific risk. In this way they can make a rational business case at a rate of return that would be difficult for competitors to accept.

Point of consideration: How can senior managers replicate the dynamic energy of the entrepreneur within the structure of their own corporations?

Source: Branson, 2011

RISK AND NORMAL PROFIT

We have so far looked at how risk is never a problem in itself as long as it is matched by the expected financial returns. It is only when the rate of return is too low for the risk that the investment becomes an irrational gamble. The competitive advantage is in finding some unique method for lowering the risk so that it comes into alignment with the expected rate of return in a way that rivals cannot replicate.

The expected rates of return are not fixed; they vary according to the structure of the industry, prevailing economic conditions and the strategies of the investors. Underlying the investment decision, though, is the concept of normal profit. It is not the same as the kind of profit shown in the company accounts, but rather it refers to economic profit, which includes opportunity costs. It occurs when total revenue equals total costs, that is, all possible costs that can be considered, so that economic profit then equals zero. It signifies that the company is using its resources at the most efficient (Shaikh, 2007).

If a company is demonstrating greater than normal profit then it is earning economic rent, which is a higher than expected revenue due to a market imperfection. A monopoly, for example, can use its total dominance of the market to impose higher prices, the economic rent leading to higher than normal profits.

Where higher than normal profits exist rival enterprises will enter the market in search of the same economic rents. In the case of monopolies it may take government intervention to prise the market open to these new entrants. With the heightened competitive pressures in the market prices are likely to fall, eliminating the economic rent. There will then be a tendency for profits to normalise.

If profits fall below normal then the full risks are no longer being accounted for. Firms will decide that their resources would be better employed elsewhere and they will leave the market. As the competitive pressures fall, prices in the market can rise until normal profits are attained. The rate of normal profit is difficult, if not impossible, to calculate in advance. In a stable market, though, it is the rate of profit that has been observed over the long term. This is very dependent on the industry and the entry/exit costs. For example, shipbuilding has very high fixed costs which inhibit players entering the market but also mean that existing companies will tolerate low financial returns as long as they are reasonably stable over the long-term.

TYPES OF RISK

Vague though the definition of risk may be, we have so far worked up enough of an understanding for us to see how businesses include the concept into their investment plans. For more detailed analysis we need to break business risk down into the different constituent parts. These are usually given in five main areas:

1. Political risk – the threat of government interference in business.
2. Economic risk – the chance that economic changes will impact on the business.
3. Foreign exchange risk – the likelihood of foreign exchange developments occurring.
4. Technological risk – the possibility of competitors or suppliers changing the nature of business through technological advances.
5. Market risk – the possibility that demand for the company's products will change.

The first three we can think of as systemic, that is, they are embedded in the structure of the country we are investigating. The last two are specific to the company and its competitive environment.

1. POLITICAL RISK

Government interference is as certain as death and taxes. Indeed, the government may even tax you in death so there is no escape there either!

Table 3.3 *Corporate income tax as share of total central government income*

Country	Corporate Tax Share of Total Income (%)
US	10.5
UK	12.5
Norway	20.0
India	38.6

Sources: IFS (2012), US Department of Commerce (2012), Royal Ministry of Finance (Norway, 2012), Ministry of Finance (India, 2012)

First of all there are the corporate taxes that contribute to government income, and Table 3.3 shows the extent to which governments differ in the corporate tax strategies. Naturally, the government strategy on corporate tax will be complemented by the strategy on personal tax.

The United States and the United Kingdom governments are able to make up their income from wealthy individuals through personal taxes, while Norway is able to gather taxes from its generous endowment of oil resources. India is forced to collect a large part of its tax revenue from corporations, given that a large proportion of the population is in a very low income group.

Government interference is much more involved than simply taking a share of corporate profits. When it comes to business governments are involved in four basic ways:

- Systemic
- Procedural
- Distributive
- Catastrophic.

Systemic risk is the kind of change that is present in most countries, whatever the political structure, and it refers to changes in government policy that affect all companies. This would include an increase in the national minimum wage or an adjustment to the rate of corporate tax. These changes should be reasonably predictable as they are usually publicised long in advance of being implemented or form part of an incoming government's declared intentions. However, it can also be highly controversial when central government attempts to rescue companies that are considered 'too big to fail', and therefore prop up a system that that is clearly in need of reform (Coffee, 2012, p. 1021).

Procedural risk is the likelihood that the government will become involved in the manner in which companies operate. In other words, they seek to change corporate procedures. Although these changes are less predictable since they tend to occur in response to some kind of crisis they are preceded by much public discussion. The banking industry is one recent example, with the Basel III proposals emerging at the height of the crisis in early 2010 but followed by a clear roadmap for implementation by 2019 (Slovik and Cournède, 2011).

In some way **distributive risk** is more dangerous for companies because it involves the appropriation of their taxes by government in order that it can be redistributed elsewhere in the economy (Holburn and Zelner, 2010). Since periods of higher than normal profits are a standard feature of the dynamic business environment, lasting only until the entry of new competition pushes prices back down, government intervention of this type is often partisan or self-serving. This can range from a windfall tax, a one-off tax on perceived high profits, or even complete nationalisation of the entire business.

MYTH BUSTER: VENEZUELA AND THE REDISTRIBUTION OF OIL WEALTH

The discovery of oil for any country is taken as a financial bonanza that will benefit rich and poor alike. Well, maybe not alike: in Saudi Arabia it is the ruling classes that are being showered with the benefits. In Venezuela, the wealth is being distributed to the poor; the government believes that this is to their enduring benefit.

Distributive risk is a particularly pernicious danger for international corporations. This is particularly the case in developing economies, where the wealth of foreign corporations is eyed with suspicion. It is often believed, rightly or wrongly, that they are exploiting the country's natural endowments for their own profit, with no benefits to the country.

When Hugo Chavez came to power as president of Venezuela in 1999 the oil industry was in a parlous state. The national oil company, PDVSA, was contributing decreasing amounts of tax to a government that was desperate for funds to inject into the economy. Over the next few years, the Chavez administration progressively nationalised the entire oil industry, including the assets of the US corporation Exxon. These had been valued by the company at US$10 billion but it received just US$255 million in compensation.

With total control of oil revenues the Venezuelan government was able to fund many social programmes. Criticised as bribes to the voting poor, and therefore creating a solid powerbase for President Chavez, the funds were also an effective method of improving the living standards of the most disadvantaged in society. The approach can also be contrasted with those countries where the oil wealth accrues to the elite classes. However, government interference in business can bring unintended consequences and the PDVSA is reported to be poorly managed and lacking in a commercial strategy. Furthermore, foreign firms have been deterred from investing in the country. Far from bringing long-term benefits to the nation and its poor, the government's redistribution policy may actually prolong the agony of poverty.

Point of consideration: Is it the government's job to decide whether corporate profits are too high? To what extent should they become involved in taxing profits?

Sources: BBC (2012), Oil and Gas Journal (2013)

The most unpredictable possibility, though, is that of **catastrophic risk**. This is the closest in concept to full uncertainty, and it relates to the sort of dramatic change that occurs when a political revolution sweeps aside an entire political system. Like other uncertain events, such as earthquakes, in retrospect they may seem inevitable but the exact timing of their occurrence is impossible to calculate. The political events that have shaken the Arab countries, the so-called Arab Spring starting with Tunisia in late-2010, appeared to take on a logical progression, yet the same type of political challenge was effectively suppressed in Iran. Similar protests in China twenty years before appeared to herald a political conflagration only to be extinguished within a few months.

2. ECONOMIC RISK

As economic actors, companies contribute to the economic landscape, but there is little that they can do to influence the associated risks that changes will impact on their business. Since governments are the only economic actors that can directly influence the economy it can be difficult to distinguish between economic and political risk factors. However, we are not trying to analyse the chain of events here, that would take us into the arena of economics, but we are interested in the direct impact on corporate operations.

Table 3.4 *Macroeconomic and microeconomic risk factors*

Macroeconomic	National output and income: GDP (gross domestic product), GNI (gross national income)
	Price stability: CPI (consumer price index), RPI (retail price index)
	Employment: unemployment, participation
	Savings, investments
	Balance of payments: trade, capital transfers
Microeconomic	Supply factors: costs, availability (global demand, seasonal effects)
	Demand factors: fashion, pricing

Political risk relates to actions taken by governments directly on corporations. Economic risk may have a political causality behind it but that is not our concern; instead, we are focusing on the way specific economic factors impact on corporations. These economic factors are systemic in the sense that they affect all companies at the same time, though not necessarily to the same degree.

We can divide economic risk factors into two broad perspectives: macroeconomic and microeconomic. Table 3.4 demonstrates the range of factors related to each viewpoint.

Macroeconomic risks are at the strategic level, but a company needs to retain enough flexibility in its plan to respond in the short term. Macroeconomic risks would be the focus of long-term strategic planning, where different economic scenarios can be costed and contingency plans put in place. For our purposes, macroeconomic risk is the most relevant since it can be matched by the appropriate allocation of resources and the required rate of return.

Microeconomic risk concerns factors that are more likely to be buffeted by the daily vicissitudes of business life, and therefore the appropriate response would be to adapt the current plan to the new conditions. These adaptations are usually short-term and tactical in nature.

Analysing the **macroeconomic environment** is highly complex given the broad range of factors involved. Fortunately, in most developed countries they are intentionally kept relatively stable. Since risk analysis is costly for companies, governments strive to create a stable and predictable environment within which to invest. For the sake of comparison, Table 3.5 shows how two economies have coped on some **key performance indicators (KPI)** over the 2007–2013 period, as recorded by the IMF (2014a). The countries are Germany and Ireland, partners in the EU and the Eurozone, but with the German economy in excess of sixteen times larger than Ireland's. The KPI chosen are:

- **Gross domestic product (GDP)** – a measure of the total output of the country
- **Unemployment (since 2009)**
- **Current account deficit (CAD)** as a proportion of GDP – shows the trading position of the country relative to the size of the economy.

Table 3.5 *Key Performance Indicators (KPI) for Germany and Ireland, 2007–2013*

Country	Factor	2007	2008	2009	2010	2011	2012	2013
Germany	GDP Growth	3.3	1.1	−5.1	4.0	3.3	0.7	0.4
	Unemployment rate			8.1	7.7	7.1	6.8	6.9
	CAD/GDP Balance	7.5	6.3	6.0	6.4	6.8	7.4	7.5
Ireland	GDP Growth	5.0	−2.2	−6.4	−1.1	2.2	0.2	0.1
	Unemployment Rate			12.0	13.9	14.6	14.7	13.1
	CAD/GDP Balance	−5.4	−5.8	−2.2	1.1	1.3	4.4	

Source: IMF Principal Global Indicators (2014a)

Although both countries operate in similar economic conditions (as members of the Eurozone) it is noticeable that the larger, more complex German economy suffers less variation than the Irish one during a period of economic and financial upheaval. Furthermore, the German economy underwent a dramatic reduction in output for only one year, returning rapidly to positive growth, while the Irish economy's recovery has proved to be painfully slow. This rough comparison demonstrates the need to analyse risk differently for countries according to the size and complexity of their economies. Most of all, developing economies need to be treated as a special case.

RISK ANALYSIS FOR DEVELOPING ECONOMIES

Developing economies around the world have made some impressive progress over the past few decades. In the vanguard are countries like China and India but in their wake we see high rates of growth in smaller countries like Vietnam and Ethiopia. However, this progress is frequently fragile and easily reversed. They are often dependent on trade in a narrow range of commodity items, the price of which can vary wildly from year to year. It is not only oil producers like Venezuela and Nigeria that are at the mercy of these price swings; agricultural economies like Kenya suffer when there is a bumper harvest amongst competitor countries that sends the world price crashing.

The vulnerability of developing economies means that organisations like the IMF often become involved. The organisation is criticised for having a prescriptive approach to rescuing economies; it seems to have a set of rules that it applies without consideration for specific circumstances. Be that as it may, the approach has a consistency that permits more reliable business planning for the desperately needed investors. Although the IMF does not publicise its economic rules, we can devise our own set in order to explore how the system works.

The first task is to select the most important KPI for developing economies. Since they have a less complex economic structure than developed economies, we can focus on a very narrow range of the most basic measures. We will therefore look at:

a) Growth of the economy in terms of GDP increase
b) Price inflation and its stability
c) Trading position in terms of the CAD/GDP balance.

The IMF uses measures like these to evaluate countries and decide on the extent of remedial action necessary. The organisation has been accused of being insensitive to the unique characteristics of each economy and using its restorative policies as a blunt tool (Stone, 2004). We will use these methods to evaluate developing economies in terms of their risk and, therefore, the matching required rate of return.

a) GDP Growth

Gross domestic product (GDP) measures the total value of everything that has been produced in the country, regardless of the nationality of the producer. The simplest measure is nominal GDP, which does not attempt to correct for the impact of inflation. Real GDP, though, corrects for the effects of price changes with use of a deflator and so reveals the true increase in the value of output. Our measure, using constant prices, is real GDP.

All countries seek a positive GDP growth as it shows the country as a whole is getting wealthier. However, the figure is an average, and it is possible that the advantages are mostly accruing to the rich in society or, if the population is rapidly expanding, the gains are being spread more thinly over a greater number of people. It is possible for GDP to increase while GDP per capita (i.e. per person) is falling. Other

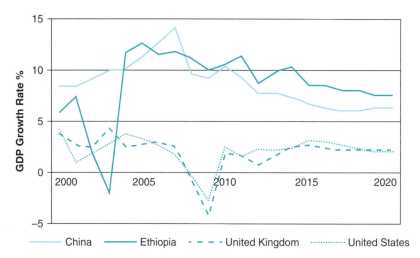

Figure 3.2 *GDP growth rate 2000–2020 constant prices (2015–2020 IMF forecast)*
Source: IMF, 2015

metrics have been put forward as being more valid for measuring the progress in the quality of human existence, one being GPI, or the Genuine Progress Indicator (Kubiszewski et al., 2013), but for the time being GDP is the most widely accepted method for evaluating the economy.

Figure 3.2 shows how GDP growth using constant prices (i.e. stripping out the effects of inflation), often known as real GDP, has fared for developed economies like the United States and UK. We can see how the results compare against China, as a leading emerging economy, and Ethiopia, a fast-recovering developing country.

The results show that developed countries, such as the United States and UK, can maintain growth of around 2.5% per annum over the long term, notwithstanding the odd economic accident. Emerging market economies like China can sustain much higher levels of growth, historically even beyond 10% per annum, as they bring untapped resources into use without risk of overheating the economy. More recently, China has been targeting growth of around 7% per annum. Developing economies like Ethiopia can sustain slightly higher rates of growth again, although progress tends to be much more volatile.

If growth is too fast then the economy will overheat and inflation will rise, necessitating an increase in interest rates to suppress borrowing and spending. A high rate of GDP growth can also boost imports at the expense of domestic industry. Although consumers experience this as a rise in their wealth it means that the economic development does not have deep roots in the growth of domestic industry.

If GDP growth is too low then the country's economic development will fall behind that of other countries. It will attract less investment, and this will only make matters worse as its industries become less competitive. If GDP growth is low or negative then the country is taken to be in **recession**. There is no precise definition of the term, and some commentators prefer to highlight employment figures as signifiers of a recession, but two quarters of negative GDP growth is the most widely accepted description (HM Treasury, 2010). In a recession the government can lower the cost of borrowing by reducing interest rates and the subsequent rise in demand will lift the country out of recession after about a year. A recession is a normal part of the business cycle and is usually partnered with a falling rate of inflation.

For emerging and developing economies there is a much higher obligation for economic growth: they need to grow faster than developed economies if they are ever going to have a hope of catching up. For them, the officially defined recession of negative growth for two quarters is not a normal part of the business cycle but represents an economic catastrophe. Since the IMF considers the world, including the developed economies, to be in recession when global growth falls to 3.0% (Abberger and Nierhaus, 2008), an argument could be made for stating that developing economies are in recession when they fall below 5.0% GDP growth.

For businesses, the state of the economy, as measured by GDP, is not itself a measure of the attractiveness of the country for investment. However, different GDP outcomes affect the risk of the investment and so the company must match that with the financial rate of return. In short, high risk is quite acceptable if the rate of return is also high. The purpose here, then, is to judge the level of risk related to GDP and then ensure the rate of return is appropriate. This is illustrated by Table 3.6:

Table 3.6 *GDP risk rates for developed, emerging and developing economies*

	Developed Economy		Emerging Economy		Developing Economy	
	GDP	**Risk/Return**	**GDP**	**Risk/Return**	**GDP**	**Risk/Return**
Recession	<0%, 2 quarters	High	<3.9%, annual	High	<4.9%, annual	High
Low Growth	0–1.9%	Medium	4.0–5.9%	Medium	5.0–6.9%	Medium
Sustainable	2.0–3.0%	Low	6.0–10.0%	Low	7.0–11.0%	Low
Overheating	3.1%+	High	10.1%+	High	11.1%+	High

b) Inflation

Inflation is often partnered with GDP growth rates and is frequently remedied using central bank interest rates, although that is not the only weapon in the government's arsenal. When GDP is high then prices will often rise due to high consumer demand and rising labour costs. As a gross measure of the economy, though, a booming GDP result may mask rising unemployment in a particular industry that is in decline, along with a widening equality gap. When the government attempts to constrain the overheating economy by raising interest rates this may cause undue pain on those in society who have missed out on the fruits of the boom. When GDP growth is low then the pressure in the economy is reduced markedly and it is likely that inflation will be low. Again, government attempts to kick-start the economy may result in some parts entering an unsustainable boom.

If a recession is a normal part of the business cycle then a **depression** represents a grave departure from it (Eslake, 2009). Again, there is no formal definition, but it is usually taken to mean two years of negative GDP growth accompanied by deep-seated problems in the financial sector. In this sense, a depression is due to the structure of the economy rather than vicissitudes of the business cycle. In some cases the economic stagnation is combined with rising inflation, known as **stagflation**, and high unemployment. The cause may be imported, such as a dramatic rise in the price of oil (Blinder and Rudd, 2013), and beyond the remit of the government. A reduction in interest rates would make prices rise even faster, so it is recognised as one of the most difficult of economic challenges for policy makers.

Although zero inflation might appear to be an attractive option it is precariously close to the kind of negative GDP growth that central banks struggle so hard to eradicate. Consequently, a small amount of inflation is generally thought of as a necessary evil, accompanied by a positive interest rate from the central bank. The European Central Bank (ECB) has an inflation target of around 2.0%, as does the US

Federal Reserve and the Bank of England also targets 2.0% but will accept 1% either side of that. The Bank of Japan has been struggling with deflation for years but is hoping to raise inflation to 2.0%. For the sake of argument this is the suggested inflation standard:

Table 3.7 *Global inflation rate risk*

Inflation Rate	Inflation Type	Risk
<0.0%	Deflation	High
0.0–0.9%	Low	Medium
1.0–3.0%	Price stability	Low
>3.1%	High	High

Despite the consensus around the 2.0% target in the developed countries there is some criticism that it is too restrictive for developing countries. This is particularly the case if they are dependent on commodity sales, whose global prices can be highly volatile. Nevertheless, there is a case for using inflation targeting as a method for bringing discipline to emerging economies (Gonçalves and Salles, 2008).

c) CAD/GDP Balance

The final KPI we can look at relates to the current account deficit (CAD) to the size of the economy (GDP) in the **CAD/GDP ratio**. As we have seen in the previous chapter, there is nothing inherently wrong with a deficit because it is funded by incoming capital, but it can be difficult for small, delicate economies to attract this capital to cover a sudden expansion of the deficit. An unsustainable deficit is one that causes a liquidity crisis and capital flight; the Chilean government therefore targeted a CAD/GDP ratio of 2.0–4.0% in the early 1990s (Morandé, 2000).

We can expect anything greater than 2.0% of GDP to be alarming. It is noticeable that India runs a persistent deficit, but it is usually around this figure. Figure 3.3 shows that the so-called **BRICS** (Brazil, Russia, India, China and South Africa) either have strong CAD/GDP surpluses or small deficits. India is notable. The CAD/GDP result we are looking for is therefore nothing in excess of –2.0%.

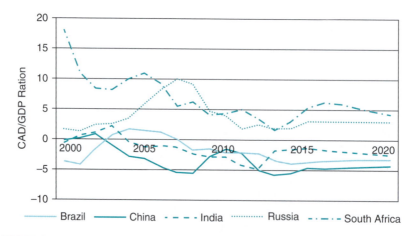

Figure 3.3 *BRICS CAD/GDP ratios 2000–2020*

If we put these three KPI requirements together we have a framework by which all developing and emerging countries can be evaluated in terms of associated risk. This is summarised in Table 3.8 and 3.9:

Table 3.8 *Guide limits for developing economy risk assessment*

Economic Measure	Low Risk	Medium	High Risk
GDP growth	7.0–11.0%	5.0–6.9%	<4.9% >11.0%
Inflation	1.0–3.0%	0.0–0.9%	<0.0% >3.0%
CAD/GDP	>−2.0%	−2.0	<−2.0%

Table 3.9 *Guide limits for emerging economy risk assessment*

Economic Measure	Low Risk	Medium	High Risk
GDP growth	6.0–10.0%	4.0–5.9%	<3.9% >11.0%
Inflation	1.0–3.0%	0.0–0.9%	<0.0% >3.0%
CAD/GDP	>−2.0%	−2.0	<−2.0% >10.1%

Institutions such as the IMF, World Bank and so on would use the results as the basis for recommending changes in the country. For an international business, such recommendations are unlikely to have any political influence and are not even necessary. In a high-risk environment it is only necessary to ensure that the financial returns are also high. So, there is nothing wrong with investing in a country suffering high economic turmoil as long as the risks are properly ascertained and the returns are secured. Even war zones are able to attract businesses but only those that are seeking very high rates of return.

RISK ANALYSIS FOR DEVELOPED ECONOMIES

The IMF is often criticised for evaluating all countries on the same criteria. It is as if they all arrived at their predicament by the same route and so will recover using the same set of remedies. We might argue that a country has been brought to economic collapse for many reasons, political, social or economic, and so the recovery strategy should be customised appropriately.

The IMF's defence would be that it is only prescribing economic solutions to economic problems, it is up to the country how it implements the recovery (Fernando and De Carvalho, 2000). This view is more difficult to support when it comes to developed economies, which are so much more complex. In theory at least, the countries of the Eurozone support each other so that the debt of one member country is a debt for all of them. In practice, the most indebted countries have been disappointed to discover the opposite.

If we apply the same quantitative criteria that we have formulated for developing nations to economies like the United States we would be obliged to come to a rather surprising conclusion, if, that is, we were unlucky enough to pick a bad year. Table 3.10 does this:

Table 3.10 *Quantitative Economic Risk Analysis for the United States, 2014*

Risk Factor	Result	Conclusion
GDP growth	–2.8%	High risk
Inflation	–0.32	Low risk
CAD/GDP	–2.6	High risk

Source: IMF, 2015

The conclusion from Table 3.10 would have to be that the United States is a high-risk investment because its economy is infected with a deep recession, there is deflation and the current account deficit is dangerously high. Indeed, the IMF figures suggest that the United States is at no point a wholly low-risk investment prospect because the CAD/GDP ratio is continually in excess of 2.0%. An investor would therefore require a high rate of return in order to cover the high risk. This suggests that many investors would be dissuaded from entering the US market, despite the fact that the country has the richest economy in the world!

For developed economies we therefore need a much more sophisticated approach to economic risk analysis. Generally, this involves gathering the views of experts in order to form a consensus. It is unlikely that any given company would have such resources at its disposal and so it would turn to a professional organisation, such as a firm of business analysts and consultants. The panel of experts would provide scores on different economic factors, each of these factors being assigned a particular weight according to their importance. For example, it might have been agreed that credit risk makes up 10% of the total economic risk. The panel members each provide their score and then they are averaged. They will repeat this for all economic factors to arrive at a total figure out of 100%.

The Economist Intelligence Unit (2014) rates countries on ten different risk criteria, including security, infrastructure and taxation. The ten criteria are rated on a score of 0–100, with 100 denoting very high risk. Around two thirds of the data used in the analysis is quantitative, gleaned from official data and 66 risk factors, but it is the skill of the analyst that makes sense of the risk factors. Even the lowest-risk countries are judged to have some risk attached.

 CASE STUDY: CALCULATING COUNTRY RISK

Euromoney is one of many organisations that will analyse countries for risk and sell the information to clients on a confidential basis. The analysts take a holistic approach, combining qualitative judgements with quantitative data. In recognition of the complexities and subtleties of individual economies, Euromoney gives the highest weighting (70%) to the qualitative judgements of its top country experts. There are three factors, each with their own weighting contributing to the overall total:

- Economic risk scores are as follows (30%) – bank stability, Gross National product (GNP) outlook, unemployment rate, government finances and currency stability.
- Political risk (30%) – corruption, government non-payments, government stability, information transparency, institutional risk, regulatory and policy environment.
- Structural risk (10%) – demographics, infrastructure and labour market.

For the quantitative measures of risk, Euromoney collects data from organisations such as the IMF and various credit ratings agencies. The three factors each carry the same weight of 10% towards the total.

- Access to bank finance/capital markets.
- Debt indicators – total debt stocks to GNP, debt service to exports, current account balance to GNP.
- Credit ratings.

The panel of experts work separately and score on a scale of zero to ten. The higher scores denote greater attractiveness (i.e. lower risk) to the investor, so a zero for corruption means the country is highly corrupt, while a ten for unemployment would signal that the numbers of people out of work was at a minimum. The scores are all combined without consultation between the experts in order to maintain the independence of their views.

According to Euromoney, at the beginning of 2013 Norway gained the highest score with 89.87%, meaning that it had been awarded the lowest risk rating across all factors. Countries like the Central African Republic, with little in the way of a functioning government, can have a score well below 10%. This does not mean that it is too risky for investors, but the returns would have to be very high and probably supported by government guarantees.

Point of consideration: Do your own analysis based on the methodologies of Euromoney and the Economist Intelligence Unit. How close can you get to the scores of their experts? Which do you think is the more useful method?

Source: Euromoney (2014)

3. FOREIGN EXCHANGE RISK

For international managers, foreign currency valuations are one of the most worrying aspects of doing business globally. Unexpected changes in currency valuations can render a profitable overseas investment suddenly uneconomic; they can raise the cost of imported components or the price of exported goods. Equally, the valuation changes can salvage an unprofitable overseas investment, reduce the cost of imported goods or conjure up a price advantage in export markets. It all depends on movements between the domestic currency and that of the target country. These movements are difficult to predict, even by experts, and impossible to control by international managers.

The **foreign currency exchange rate** is simply the value of one currency in terms of another. It is the nearest we can get to claiming that money itself has value, although even here it is not strictly true. As in any market, the value of a currency is a reflection of the availability of its supply and the level of demand. The relative valuations are influenced by macroeconomic factors such as interest rates and government spending.

Recent developments in foreign currency exchanges have given rise to a myriad of financial instruments. Some of these are obscure and have even been associated with some unscrupulous behaviour. In the main, though, there are four basic types of currency exchange:

- **Spot** – exchange rate values for an immediate transaction.
- **Forward contract** – an exchange rate for a transaction of any size at a particular time in the future.
- **Future contract** – an exchange rate for a standardised contract of transaction size and maturity, usually 3 months. As an off-the-shelf contract it is cheaper than a forward contract.

- **Swap** – currencies are exchanged for a period and then exchanged back. Comprises a spot rate for the first transaction and a forward contract for the second.

If the currency has a high value then imports are cheaper but exports are more expensive. In contrast, if the currency has a low value then imports are expensive but exports are cheaper. Sometimes a high value currency is said to be **strong**, while a low value one is **weak**, but these are emotive terms that have little real meaning. For example, an MNE in a country with a strong currency will find that it is able to import supplies at a relatively low price but then it will find that its own exports will be relatively expensive in host country markets. Such a currency only gives strength when importing, not when exporting.

The foreign currency exchange markets have grown to staggering proportions. According to the Bank for International Settlements (BIS), known as the central banker's bank, in April 2013 around US$5.3 trillion per day was being traded, up nearly a third on the same period in 2010. The vast majority of this is driven by financial institutions, such as banks and pension funds, rather than international trade. The most traded currency is the US dollar, being an element in 87% of all trades. Table 3.11 shows the top four currencies and their proportional presence in all currency trades, plus China as a representative of the dominant developing economies.

Table 3.11 *Proportion of foreign exchange market turnover by currency, April 2013*

National Currency	Proportion of Turnover (%)
US Dollar	87
Euro	33.4
Japanese Yen	23.0
British Sterling	11.8
Chinese Renminbi	2.2

Source: BIS (2013)

Few would be surprised by the dominance of the US currency, particularly when oil is priced in dollars, but it is curious to see that the British currency is still traded in huge volumes, while the Chinese renminbi is still only the ninth most traded currency in the world. Clearly, trade is only a small motivator for moving money internationally.

The location of these currency exchanges is also focused on the developed economies. Indeed, the trading is being conducted in just a handful of countries and in one rather surprising city most of all (see Table 3.12).

Table 3.12 *Location of currency exchange centres by volume, April 2013*

Currency Exchange Centre	Proportion of Global Trades (%)
UK	41
US	19
Singapore	5.7
Japan	5.6
Hong Kong SAR	4.1

Source: BIS (2013)

Not only does the UK hold the dominant position in the world for foreign currency trading but that activity is almost entirely contained within the limits of London. In April 2013 the average daily turnover was US$2.7 trillion. Estimates suggest that the foreign currency trading being conducted in London is 200 times greater than the total GDP for the country.

DETERMINING CURRENCY VALUES

It is because there are a number of macroeconomic factors influencing the valuation of a currency on the foreign exchange markets that the rates fluctuate so frequently. We can consolidate these factors into four main areas:

i) Purchasing Power Parity (PPP)

The law of one price suggests that in an era of globalisation it is not possible for the same good to have a different price according to location. If the good is selling for a lower price in one location then consumers will make their purchase there. In order to compete, the price in the second location must converge on that in the first.

Example: If a typical basket of goods in the UK costs £50 and the same in the United States costs $100 then this implies a PPP exchange rate of £1:US$2. If a good is priced in the United States at US$10 and for £10 in the UK then consumers will purchase the good in the United States until such time that the UK price is reduced. Alternatively, the exchange rate can change to reflect the price difference, the dollar rising in value and the pound falling until the rate of £1:US$1 is reached.

PPP shows how much can be bought if the money is generated locally. This has given rise to the (only slightly) humorous **Big Mac Index** (Economist, 2014). This uses the price of the McDonald's Big Mac around the world to impute the exchange rate and thereby illustrate the degree to which the currency is over or undervalued.

ii) Currency supply

As with any market, values depend on supply relative to demand. If a nation increases the amount of money in circulation then its value, relative to other currencies, will fall. There are a number of reasons why the supply of a currency might change:

- Rising income levels boost demand for goods, both domestically produced and imported. However, import volumes tend to rise fastest, as it is quicker to source the rising demand from global markets rather than from increasing domestic production. Increased import demand means a higher demand for foreign currencies, raising their values and depressing the value of the domestic currency.
- Inflation will depress the value of the domestic currency when prices are rising faster than overseas. In order to maintain the relative prices of goods the exchange rate is adjusted. See purchasing power parity (PPP) above.
- The international trade current account influences the relative demand for currencies. If a country persistently operates a current account deficit then it has a higher demand for foreign currencies than there is demand for its own. As a consequence, the domestic currency falls in value. This is partially offset by the demand for its currency in the capital account.

Under normal circumstances a country that is exporting (i.e. has a current account surplus) will have high demand for its currency from countries wishing to buy its products. This will push up the value of the currency and reduce the price competiveness of the goods. This is the **auction effect** of trade on currency values. Exporting countries thereby discover that they cannot compete on price alone but also must compete on product features and quality.

iii) Interest rates

As all investors know, money cannot be left idle; it must be earning interest. When money can be easily moved around the world then investors will seek out the highest rates of interest, even if only for a brief period. If a country raises its interest rates, perhaps to dampen domestic consumer spending, this will also attract inflows of money from overseas. Since these inflows need to be in the domestic currency, demand for it rises, thereby pushing up its relative value. The value will rise until such point that the additional interest payments to the overseas investor are negated by increasing expense of obtaining the currency. The rising value of the currency has the effect of reducing import prices and so stimulating consumer spending, which may be contrary to government intentions.

iv) Government foreign currency reserve policy

Governments are caught in a dilemma of wanting to reduce the value of the currency to render exports more price competitive, or raising the currency value to reduce the price of imports. Export-oriented governments will suppress the domestic currency value in order to stimulate exports as part of a strategy for economic development. However, this means that domestic consumers will be denied access to cheap imports, and companies will find that imported supplies are relatively expensive.

An export surplus should lead to a rise in the value of the currency, reducing the price-competitiveness in overseas markets. For countries with a national export strategy they have to continuously intervene in the foreign exchange markets to undermine the rising value of their currency. One effective way of doing this is through the capital account, to invest the incoming foreign funds back in their country of origin. They may also accumulate foreign currency reserves. In Table 3.13 are listed the top five holders of foreign currencies in the world. The United States and UK are then shown for reasons of comparison.

Table 3.13 Top five foreign currency reserves, plus US and UK, 2014

Country	Foreign Currency Reserves US$ billion
China	3,948.1
Japan	1,282.8
Switzerland	548.9
Russia	472.3
Taiwan	421.5
US	70.0
UK	42.8

Sources: Bank of Korea (2014), IMF (2014b)

Some of these foreign currency reserves seem vast, and they are, but they are not for spending. Rather like the ballast in a ship their purpose is to provide stability in the currency markets by providing ammunition to the government to intervene. Countries like the United States and UK have sufficient funds to do this in the short term and at a low scale. Where countries have very large reserves they dare not release them since that will then flood the market and reduce the value of that currency, thereby raising the value of their own currency and undermining their export strategy. Exporting countries with large foreign currency reserves are doomed to accumulating ever more currency; it is therefore a sign of poverty in government policy rather than national wealth.

Historically, governments have enjoyed varying success at controlling exchange rates. **Fixed exchange rates** are when the government sets an immutable price for its currency, although in practice it usually allows some mild variation. The government may also **peg** its currency to another, the US dollar being a common target. This can create a whole new set of problems when the overseas currencies are unstable and there is a constant battle to hold steady with them on the exchange markets. If the domestic currency then climbs high in value it opens up opportunities for illegal trading in the black market. The government may attempt to release pressure through a **crawling peg**, which means re-pegging the currency to a new level when the previous one becomes unsustainable.

Many developed economies have opted for **floating rates**. They can afford to do this if they have economies of enough sophistication that they are less likely to suffer wild swings in currency values. In effect, the currency valuation is diversified across many economic activities. The United States and UK have floating currency rates, while South Korea has stopped short of full liberalisation by holding routine **currency auctions**.

CURRENCY VALUE IMPACT ON BUSINESS

The risks to the international manager are at the microeconomic level because of the way currency values impact on relative international prices. It is not only the value of imported supplies against that of exported finished goods; any international transaction will be affected. This even includes the simple act of reporting the transaction in another currency, even when an exchange has not taken place.

Globalisation means that no business is entirely insulated from the effects of exchange rate fluctuations, although the degree of impact depends on the nature of the business. For an export business using domestic supplies, such as commodities, a low currency value hands it a price advantage in overseas markets. However, this would not be the case with exporters that are having to import those commodities for their production system. Service industries tend to import less, but they are still plugged into the global business processes as much as manufacturers.

The risk that international organisations are exposed to comes in two forms:

i) **Transaction risk** – contracts between buyers and suppliers are based on some agreed exchange rate. However, if the buyer assumes all the risk then the supplier will demand to be paid at the price set in the local currency. There is a chance that when payment is due the exchange rates will have moved against the buyer, a weakening in their own currency making the payment for them higher.

ii) **Translation risk** – cash sums do not have to cross borders or be exchanged to suffer from the effects of rate changes. An MNE must report its overseas financial dealings in its annual reports using its own currency. Where it is reporting profits from an overseas subsidiary, even if the local sums are constant year-by-year, the figures given in its report will rise and fall with the exchange rate. This can cost real sums of money: high taxes on inflated profits, or a falling share price on deflated profits.

FINANCIAL HEDGING

The company can protect itself from the worst effects of exchange rate risk by **financial hedging** (Makar and Huffman, 2011). This is a kind of insurance similar to the way that a casino or bookmaker will lay off a large bet. In such a situation the bookmaker taking the bet will place a similar but smaller bet with another bookmaker. If the gambler wins and the first bookmaker has to pay out then at least they can collect some funds from the second bookmaker. That way the loss is spread through the industry rather than one company taking the entire financial hit.

When a company hedges it will find some investment that diversifies the risk of its foreign currency transaction. As financial instruments have grown in sophistication the number of hedging options has multiplied. One method is to invest sums of money in the target currency. If interest rates in that country are raised, with the effect of increasing the currency value, it would normally mean that the company would have to find more of its own currency to fund the transaction. Fortunately, the sums are already there and the effect of translation will automatically raise the value in terms of the domestic currency.

Translation risk can also be reduced through **natural hedging**. We have seen how profits earned at an overseas subsidiary can fluctuate in terms of the domestic currency simply through the way that they are reported by the MNE. If the domestic currency rises in value then the subsidiary's revenues can be inflated, regardless of what was actually earned in the local currency. At the same time, costs at the overseas subsidiary, when translated into the domestic currency, will also rise. Since profit is basically the difference between revenues and costs this helps to dampen the wilder fluctuations due to currency translation. Exporters, with few local costs, have little natural hedging and will suffer the full effects of currency translation.

 ## MANAGEMENT SPOTLIGHT: ANTICIPATING EXCHANGE RATES

Forecasting exchange rates is a form of business alchemy that depends on the triumph of hope over experience. If it were truly possible to predict foreign currency exchange rates then international business would be no more risky than domestic business. Nevertheless, like forecasting the weather there is some purpose in the endeavour. There are three chief methods:

- **Judgemental** – a group of experienced experts pool their views of the economic forces that determine the currency values. The experts base their decisions on a 'feel' for the market. The approach appears subjective, but it is a very cost effective way of including many different variables, some of them qualitative. Has good long-term validity.
- **Technical** – based on trend analysis and chartism, or the observation of patterns in the data. Takes the view that there is some sort of momentum in the market, although this tends to be valid only for the short term.
- **Fundamental** – identification and processing of the most important variables. Involves detailed statistical analysis which is reliable but wholly dependent on the choice of variables for the validity of the forecast. Tends to take a long-term perspective.

The judgemental method is usually the most effective, but it can be tempting for international managers to suffer delusions in their own capabilities. If a panel of genuine experts cannot be employed then it is often better to use the technical or fundamental approaches as an objective standard. Lawrence et al. (2006) found that management judgement was indispensable but it needed the support of statistical techniques, known as 'bootstrapping'.

Point of consideration: A simple method for testing your own ability to forecast currency exchange movements is to record the changes for a five-year period up to some point in the recent past (e.g. one week, one month and three months). Then make your forecasts for the intervening period up to the present using judgement, technical and fundamental methods. Check your forecasts against the actual figures for an instant check.

Source: Lawrence et al., 2006

4. TECHNOLOGICAL RISK

It is often claimed that technological progress is gaining velocity at an exponential rate. **Moore's Law** is a version of this and it is based on the observation by George Moore (1965), co-founder of silicon chip manufacturer Intel, that computing capacity would double every few years. Such a rapid rate of development is seen as symbolic of the dynamism of the modern world. Technology can therefore be seen as a significant source of risk since firms can gain competitive advantage through technical innovations. While firms will include this risk assessment into their overall calculations in order to arrive at an agreeable rate of return on any investment, as always it is preferable if they can make a stab at predicting precisely what development will actually take place.

To the uninitiated, technological development appears to be made up of random forward leaps into the unknown. In fact, companies carefully manage their product launches in order to take their competitors by surprise and to maximise the impact on the market of the product launch. Behind the scenes there are research and development (R&D) departments that are feverishly working on forthcoming products that utilise the latest technology. If you were privy to the R&D strategy of a company you would realise that the immediate future has been mapped out with a degree of certainty. The apparent haphazard nature of technological development, in the short term, is therefore an illusion maintained by companies in order to keep competitors and consumers guessing.

PRODUCT LIFE CYCLE MODEL

Regular updates and replacements for existing products are probably the most predictable technological advances. This is embodied in the **product life cycle (PLC) model** that illustrates the rise and fall of a product in the market. We can see this in Figure 3.4. There is the initial introduction of the product, with low sales volumes and the high risk of failure offset by relatively high prices. If all goes well this is followed by a phase of rapid growth as general consumer demand catches on to the product's features. At maturity, sales volumes reach a plateau as consumer demand is satisfied and competitors have piled in to offer their alternative products. Finally, there is the inevitable decline as the product is superseded by new entrants that boast the latest technologies.

Although the decline phase can be managed through product redesigns, pricing structures and consolidation in production, there is as much risk attached as during the introduction phase. Many products enjoy a relatively gentle decline, perhaps because consumers are tied into the old technology, while others suffer a sudden death when there is a mass adoption of a new technology. There is some suggestion

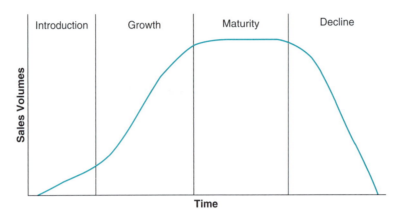

Figure 3.4 *Product Life Cycle*

that production can then be transferred to a developing economy, supplying the local market with a low cost, superseded product. However, globalisation means that developing economies gain access to the latest products almost at the same time as the rest of the world, any delay being due to the production limitations at the product's launch.

Manufacturers can enforce the predictability of the PLC model by routinely introducing new products. Cynics often call this '**planned obsolescence**', meaning that a company will launch a product that has not been fully developed so that they can then replace it at some point in the future with the completed version (Cooper, 2004). This would give the false impression of technical progress, although this in itself would be a highly risky strategy since it means withholding new technologies that rival firms may be ready to launch immediately. Car manufacturers, for example, will sometimes introduce a new model that is based on the preceding model and so avoid the enormous expense of developing new technologies. This can prove highly profitable if the consumers liked the old model anyway so only a styling refresh was needed, but it can also earn the company a bad reputation for seeming to pass off old products as new.

The PLC model is effective for anticipating linear progress of existing products, part of the regular updating that goes on in industries with a strong fashion element. In this way, the established structure of the supply chain is designed around the PLC and compels it to continue its prescribed cycles or risk having to restructure the supply chain (Aitken et al., 2003). However, the PLC model cannot anticipate the sudden emergence of **disruptive technologies**. These are technologies that are both technically and conceptually new. Their effect can be so dramatic that they change the very way we live. Yet even these are usually the result of years, even decades and centuries, of R&D to bring them to the market. We can characterise these advances in terms of paradigms.

PARADIGM PROGRESSION

Paradigms are often used in the sciences to show how most progress is not random but structured around new and disruptive ideas. Thomas Kuhn (1970) put forward the idea that scientific groups, or communities, gathered around new discoveries and created their own ways of working based on the founding principles of the discovery. Paradigms are a lot easier to understand in practice than in theory and Table 3.14 contrasts three paradigms in the medical sciences.

Table 3.14 *Medical paradigms*

Medical Paradigm	Central Principle	Future Developments
Virology	Pre-treatment of virus diseases through vaccination	Improved anticipation of future viruses in order to prepare the most appropriate vaccine. Complete extinction of viruses.
Bacteriology	Post-treatment of bacteria diseases through antibiotics	Careful administration of antibiotic treatment programmes to prevent 'super bugs'
Surgery	Invasive physical intervention	Smaller, less invasive techniques

Although the three approaches are all contained within the medical sciences their fundamental principles and procedures render them so utterly different that there is no common ground between them. Virus diseases are treated prophylactically, that is the body is forearmed by vaccines that allow the body to be prepared to fight the disease before it has appeared. Antibiotics, like penicillin, are not effective against viruses and surgery is simply out of the question. Similarly, neither viruses nor antibiotics are effective in treating, say, broken bones, although they might be helpful in dealing with any of the related complications.

Although there is very little common ground between different paradigms, it is possible to make basic predictions on how they might progress. Indeed, Kuhn would claim that the future problem-solving activities are part of the founding principle. So we know that the future of virology is to improve the accuracy of anticipating new viruses so that the correct vaccines can be produced in time for people to become immune to the virus. Ultimately, viral diseases could be entirely eradicated.

For bacteriologists it is the opposite problem because it is the bacteria that are developing the immunity. Some bacteria have become drug resistant, which makes them almost impossible to treat. The medical counter-attack has been to carefully control the use of antibiotics so that this bacterial immunity does not spread.

In the final medical paradigm, surgery has been on the same development path for centuries. Starting as little more than butchery, the principles of invasive surgery have remained constant even as the techniques have been, thankfully, refined. The natural and predictable progression for the paradigm is for the trauma of surgery to be minimised by reducing the scale of physical interference. So-called key-hole surgery, operating through tiny holes, is now commonplace.

For each of these three medical paradigms the future progression or purpose of the scientific discipline was obvious. Kuhn calls this the problem-solving period for the paradigm, building on the original discovery or theory and taking it to its logical conclusion. This period of problem solving can be very rapid, hence the application of Moore's Law to a new field in electronics. It is only when a new discovery is made that goes entirely against all preceding paradigms that science lurches forward into a wholly new paradigm. In medical science this might be in the form of the nanotechnology advances that could put microscopic robots into patients to deal directly with problem areas. This new paradigm, should it occur, will owe nothing to the previous paradigms of virology, bacteriology and surgery, although they will probably continue to co-exist for a period.

BUSINESS AND PARADIGMATIC PROGRESS

The concept of paradigms is less commonly applied in business but when we do it opens up a whole new view of the future. As we have seen, a paradigm is clearest when it is based on a highly defined technology or approach. A good example of this would be the iron and steel industry, which has progressed in

Table 3.15 *Paradigms in iron*

Technological Paradigm	Central Principle	Development Potential	Limitations
Wrought Iron	Iron ore smelted in a bloomer and hot iron is then beaten with a hammer to remove impurities	Scale up using large mechanical hammer	Iron is very soft, stop-go production process
Cast Iron	Blast furnace	High rates of production	Costly to create steel
Steel	Bessemer process using air to remove impurities	High rates of production of cheap steel	Difficult to adjust the production flow to meet demand

dramatic forward leaps throughout its history. Table 3.15 gives an idea of the fundamental technology and the implications for further problem-solving as all the potential benefits are exploited. We must always be aware, though, that each paradigm is exclusive; it does not lead into the next paradigm. The steady progress in the industry throughout the ages is therefore partly an illusion: it only occurs during the puzzle-solving within the paradigm, while the jump to the next paradigm is based on dramatic chance discoveries.

Other industries have similar defining technologies, materials and production processes. These prescribe the potential for future expansion while also putting a limit on it. Historically, shipbuilding underwent massive changes in the move from wooden hulls to iron and then steel. Metal ships could be made much larger but the ultimate development of the production process, involving huge dry docks and large amounts of steel, is inflexible and requires constant rates of production for it to be economically justified.

Where almost all countries could sustain an industry in the days of wooden ships this was not the case with iron and steel ships. As a result, countries either have very extensive commercial shipbuilding capabilities that are economically sustainable, or else their industries are dependent on government support to keep them out of bankruptcy. An independent, small-scale shipbuilding industry is simply economically unstable.

We are possibly experiencing a shift to a new production paradigm, that of **build-to-order (BTO)**, a process by which products are only manufactured and assembled when the customer's order is placed (Gunasekaran and Ngai, 2005). This has huge implications for managers because the entire supply chain must be capable of supporting such a lean strategy. Since the production hardware itself is unchanged by the strategy there are problems of idle production capacity when the orders dry up. The company may then be tempted to abandon BTO and instead build for stock which can then be sold when the market picks up again or else discounted to a lower price to clear the excess inventory. This suggests that BTO may not be a paradigm at all but just a lean approach to operating a production system while there are sufficient customer orders for full capacity utilisation.

It is because paradigms have known both potential for development and limitations on what is possible that we can make reasonable forecasts on the future technological developments. For example, once the jet engine had become a practical reality aircraft manufacturers could rapidly design a new breed of transcontinental airliner to transport large numbers of passengers at affordable prices. Yet supersonic travel is beyond the economic limits of standard jet engine technology, so the only airliner to travel faster than the speed of sound, Concorde, was operated by just two airlines and only then thanks to massive government subsidies.

CASE STUDY: APPLE – DOOMED TO TECHNOLOGICAL RISK?

Consumer electronics are the most exciting area of the retail market, and head of the pack is Apple. The company has an enviable reputation for anticipating where demand will be heading next and so is able to release the hottest new products. However, two theories are useful in predicting the new product releases by Apple. The first is the product life cycle (PLC) model, and it is clear that the company slavishly follows a routine of releasing new versions of old products, such as the iPhone. If it did not do this then consumers would either hold onto their existing iPhones or they would choose newer products by rival companies. Even if the rival products offered no real advantage over aging iPhones, in a fashion-obsessed market the newness alone will attract buyers. The PLC model forces Apple to release new products before the sales decline sets in.

Paradigm theories also help to explain the launch of new Apple products such as the iPad. Claimed by some to be a revolutionary product, others might argue that the iPad fits well within the existing mobile phone paradigm. In this paradigm, the miniaturisation of electronic processors and batteries was inevitable – that is how the phones get to be mobile – but the limiting factor then became the screen. Since the iPhone screen is already as small as it usefully can be the next development would be to make the screen bigger. On this basis the iPad is almost entirely predictable. The iPad is therefore part of the puzzle solving that goes on within the paradigm.

But could the iPad ever replace the desktop computer? If this were to occur it would represent a paradigm revolution in how we use computers and even how we work. Yet there is little evidence that people are struggling to use their laptops in a more mobile way; indeed they seem happy with them just the way they are. Market satisfaction with laptops signifies that the iPad will probably never spark the computer revolution that was originally heralded. For that to happen there would have to be a new technology, unforeseen in its capabilities and unpredictable in its impact. It is the technological risk of such a revolutionary new paradigm that would be the gravest threat to Apple. In the meantime, it is the iPhone that continues as the mainstay of the company's business.

Points of consideration: Looking ahead, how could Apple replace the iPad with an entirely new product? How would that product change the way we live and work? To what extent will that product replace the iPad or any other Apple products?

Source: Apple company reports (2014)

5. MARKET RISK

Market risk is also faced by domestic corporations but it multiplies for international corporations as they deal with higher numbers of markets. Market risk is that a shift in prices will adversely affect a business strategy. For an MNE market, risk includes foreign exchange risk and inflation. Generally, the risk is asymmetrical: an unexpected rise in price will dampen demand and reduce revenues below a level where the project would be viable.

Inflation, when it is out of control, can be a dangerous condition for a company. It affects the way that supplies and work-in-progress can be costed as part of the final product. It can also play havoc with the way that the product is competitively positioned in the market, the pressure to raise prices having to be referenced against price rises implemented by rivals. Deflation is rare but potentially more dangerous since it is usually symptomatic of a deep recession and falling demand (Bernanke, 2002). An overseas company would have to engage in price cutting to remain competitive in the market, thereby eroding profitability.

For international managers, investing in fast-growing, developing economies has a particular inflation dilemma in the form of the Balassa–Samuelson effect. Originally put forward by economists Bela Balassa (1964) and Paul Samuelson (1964), it describes a situation where an industry with strong international links will suffer high rates of wage inflation if it is growing at a rapid rate. This wage inflation will spread to other industries and raise the general rate of inflation. This then has knock-on effects for the exchange rate, which will rise (Égerta et al., 2003).

Although the Balassa–Samuelson effect signals an increase in exchange rate risk it also indicates higher spending power in the country as wage levels rise. This would suggest that new local market opportunities will emerge at a faster rate than in mature, developed economies. International managers might therefore decide to take a strategic view of the market, being prepared to take an unprofitable position in the belief that the situation will improve and the company would be at an advantage if it already has a presence.

To an extent market price risk can be ameliorated by forward contracts on commodity prices. This may not eradicate the influence of inflation, which will still be included in the contract, but it does avoid the worst effects of the uncertainty caused by inflation. It is then possible for managers to make business plans with greater confidence.

 ## CASE STUDY – THE DUTCH DISEASE AND THE WRONG KIND OF SUCCESS

The phrase Dutch Disease was coined by The Economist magazine to describe the malevolent effect on a country's economy when a vast new natural resource is discovered. In the original scenario the Netherlands discovered that it was endowed with huge reserves of oil. This should have brought an economic bonanza but instead the overseas demand for the oil raised the value of the currency. This rendered its other exported goods more expensive in overseas markets. It seemed as if the discovery of oil had turned out to be a poisoned chalice, destroying the economy it had been expected to help.

Other countries have suffered similar effects, such as the UK. When the pound became a petro-currency on the back of North Sea oil the exchange rate made exported goods uncompetitively expensive in the overseas markets. Given enough time the manufacturing industries might have moved into higher value-added products, where there is less price sensitivity, following the example of German industry. However, British industry could not adapt fast enough and many long-established companies, such as shipbuilding and car production, went into terminal decline.

The Dutch Disease is not restricted to developed economies, it also affects developing economies. Papua New Guinea is endowed with natural gas, which is exported as LNG (liquefied natural gas). Although the revenues from this trade have been invaluable in raising the national economy the exchange rate has had a devastating effect on old export industries, such as fishing. It did not have to be a commodity doing the damage either; inflows of foreign aid can have a similar effect.

The remedy to the disease is for the country to use the revenues earned through the current account to purchase overseas assets through the national capital account. It is also recommended that the revenues are used to subsidise the industries that have been worst affected.

Point of consideration: Vietnam is a rapidly expanding developing economy with a growing presence in manufacturing and technology. Oil was discovered a few years ago, threatening development with the Dutch Disease. How would you advise the country on avoiding its effects?

Source: Van Wijnbergen (1984)

RAISING EMPLOYABILITY: MANAGERIAL APPETITE FOR RISK

For too long, the notion of risk has been synonymous with toughness. The riskier the project the more it was expected to be led by a physically imposing man, the alpha male of his generation. Female leaders were held down by the **glass ceiling**, an invisible barrier that prevented them rising any further up the corporate hierarchy. Those that succeeded in smashing through were said to be more masculine than their male colleagues. Other groups were also kept down by the same prejudice, one that formed irrational and negative attitudes to the leadership qualities of certain races, colours and creeds.

The calculations used in risk analysis take the process away from the temptations of subjective judgement and into the hands of anyone capable of working the figures. This means we can at long last divest ourselves of the notion that powerful corporations can only be led by powerful men. Just as one would expect a surgeon to act on their diagnosis with whatever radical surgery was called for, without any reference to their own personal characteristics, so one can now expect managers to make their decisions based on the facts of their analysis. This enlightened attitude to business management widens employability to those that have the conviction to act on what their analysis tells them.

So how are we doing so far? A report by Grant Thornton (2014), with figures for the proportion of senior management positions being taken by women, finds that the leading country is Russia with 46% and the worst is Japan with just 3%. The United States has hardly anything to boast about with just 17% of senior positions going to women. Many developing nations are remarkable in their progressive attitudes, with Thailand, Philippines and Botswana all showing 39%.

When it comes to ethnicity it is more difficult to draw clear conclusions since much of it depends on the demographics of the country. For example, in 2012 in the United States, African Americans made up 12% of the total workforce but only 0.8% of the CEOs who were leading Fortune 500 companies (Center for American Progress, 2012). In South Africa in 2013 just 12% of top management posts went to blacks and 73% to whites; the black proportion of the total population is 79.2% and whites 8.9% (Guardian, 2013).

There are many other minority groups in society that are not finding places at the top table of management. There are campaigns continuing to correct the balance but progress is slow. Remember, this is not simply about social justice but making full use of the resources available, always the hallmark of a well-run business.

THE STORY SO FAR: LEARNING TO EMBRACE RISK

Business is nothing without risk: those that put their resources into an enterprise expose themselves to the loss of what they have invested. The reward for taking a chance is in the returns they receive, so it is vital that the risks and returns of a project are properly evaluated and matched. State-owned industries and government agencies are not burdened with risk in quite the same way and so do not need to pay such close attention to receiving the appropriate rates of return; they are notoriously inefficient with their resources as a result. Non-governmental organisations (NGOs) often take their returns in non-financial, subjective forms; a charity formed for a specific purpose that is wound up when all the money has been spent represents success in a way that would be alien to a business.

We have seen that risk comes in many forms: political, financial, technological and so on. For each of them there are no excuses for avoiding a proper evaluation of the risk and thus identification of the required rate of return. Risk aversion therefore has no meaning: investments are the result of objective decision-making processes. This also means that there is no place for the stereotyping of managers: corporate expansion no more requires a tough-talking, macho alpha male CEO than a contraction involving mass redundancies needs to be led by a gentle, caring woman. Equally, there is no advantage or disadvantage according to race, colour or creed.

There are still those that might be disadvantaged by the strictly objective approach to the calculation of risk: namely, developing economies. The IMF is often accused of being unsympathetic to the unique predicaments in which these countries find themselves. The organisation has been criticised for using a rigid set of rules that damn these economies to punitive correction measures in order to meet guidelines that the wealthier IMF member countries would themselves fail. Fortunately, entrepreneurs are not so hidebound by rules and can find opportunities in developing economies to everyone's benefit.

 WEB SUPPORT

1. Top tips for effective risk taking – this article from The Treasurer website puts a little too much emphasis on the macho side of risk taking but also reminds us of that old chestnut about golf: 'the more I practise, the luckier I get'.

    www.treasurers.org/how-be-effective-risk-taker

2. Perhaps sometimes you have only one option that is to gamble. Business Insider reports that FedEx was saved when founder Frederick Smith gambled the company's last US$5000 in Las Vegas ... and won. Was he really gambling, though, if he had no choice? And did he stack the odds in his favour because of certain gambling skills?

    www.businessinsider.com/fedex-saved-from-bankruptcy-with-blackjack-winnings-2014-7?IR=T

3. A short video from Murray Group on 11 Most Common Risk Management Mistakes Made by Small Business Owners. Concise, with plenty of food for thought, if you ignore the promotional aspect.

    www.youtube.com/watch?v=rHTojOrJDRk

Project Topics

1. Some nationalities are known to be risk averse, such as the Japanese. Consider, then, how Japanese companies like Sony and Toyota are able to be such pioneers in their fields.
2. Imagine you are an advisor to a large pharmaceutical firm. The senior managers want to diversify the firm into the expanding business of coffee shops. How would you advise them to minimise the risks?

3. 3D printers are a new technology that allows people to manufacture small, plastic items from a machine in their own home. Consider the product life cycle for this machine and how each stage should be managed in terms of production volume, marketing costs and product R&D. What kind of machine do you think would supersede it?

CASE STUDY – SUPERMARKETS RETURNING TO NORMAL

Few industries can be more stable than household retail. The average weekly shopping basket of groceries, routine food items, cleaning products and so on must be one of life's great constants. Of course, as exciting new products are released then brand loyalties will shift but the level of demand for each product type must be fairly unchanging. Despite this, supermarket chains have been showing impressive rates of growth for many years.

In the United States, Sam Walton started out with a simple Five and Dime store, selling household goods at the lowest possible prices, making up for slim profit margins with high volume sales. It was a simple business model that came to characterise supermarkets worldwide. The goods can be bought at any number of retail outlets, so price is the only differentiating factor. On the strength of the business model Walton's store became Walmart and the largest retailer in the world. The business is continuing to grow, although mostly through the opening of new stores: average comparable sales growth for 2012–2014 has been around 1.0% per annum. Operating income as a percentage of sales has been around 5.0% to 8.0% for the period 2009–2014.

In the UK the supermarket that enjoys equivalent dominance is Tesco. Starting earlier than Walmart, its great growth spurt came in the 1990s as it successfully broadened its appeal with more high-value products. By 2007 Tesco had nearly a third share of the market. Since then discount supermarket chains have appeared, tempting away price-sensitive consumers during an economic recession. In the 2013/14 financial year Tesco supermarket revenues grew by only 0.9% and underlying profit before tax was down 6.9%. The operating profit margin has fallen from 6.5% in 2012 to 4.1% in 2014.

Tesco is not alone in its suffering; other long-established UK supermarket chains are also slipping off their previous growth trends. There are some desperate management plans being implemented to return to the old expansionary ways, but it may all be in vain. Quite simply, the supermarket retail sector has been enjoying the benefits of above-normal profits for too long. As they opened vast new out-of-town stores and squeezed local independents out of business, the supermarket giants seemed to create local monopolies. However, the new discount supermarkets are based in high street locations and are much more convenient. Along with their low prices the attractions for consumers are irresistible.

During the years of high growth the supermarket giants seem to have lost touch with the simplicity of their business models: selling the goods people want at the best prices. If we remember that most goods sold in supermarkets are widely available elsewhere then price is the only defining factor for consumers. This being the case, the supermarket giants will need to relearn price competitiveness even if it means the end of fast-growing profits. What we are seeing then is not a rout of the supermarket giants by the discount entrants but just a return to normal profits.

Point of consideration: Should supermarkets add new services in the search for value-added business, or consolidate their businesses around an old-fashioned low-price, high-volume strategy?

Sources: Company reports, Tesco (2014) and Walmart (2014)

? MULTIPLE CHOICE QUESTIONS

1. Which of the following is considered an uncertainty?
   a. Volcanic activity within Japan.
   b. A Tsunami on the French Riviera in the next 10 years.
   c. England winning the football World Cup.

2. How is risk different from uncertainty?
   a. Risk can be calculated and included in the expected financial rate of return.
   b. Uncertainty is riskier than risk.
   c. Risk should be welcomed in business; uncertainty should be avoided.

3. For what kind of industry is it advisable to be risk averse?
   a. Healthcare – medics should not gamble with their patients' lives.
   b. Farming – the seasons are a certainty, there is no risk.
   c. No industry – risk is to be managed, not avoided.

4. How would you characterise a manager who is suited to taking risks?
   a. Objective, methodical and decisive.
   b. Courageous, dominant and tough.
   c. Cautious, sceptical and meek.

5. You are considering opening a chain of fashion boutiques in Nigeria but you are worried that the economy could be wrecked by rebel insurrection. What kind of risk concerns you?
   a. Political – the risk is that the rebels will take power in the next election.
   b. Economic – the rebellion is depressing the economy.
   c. Catastrophic – if the rebels take power it will dramatically change the entire political landscape.

6. Why are developing nation economies inherently high risk?
   a. They have a narrow economic base.
   b. They are too poor to remedy economic recessions.
   c. They are politically weak.

7. Which exchange rate policy best minimises exchange rate risk?
   a. Floating – it allows greater flexibility in economic control.
   b. Crawling peg – the currency value changes are entirely predictable.
   c. Fixed – there are no changes in currency values so there is no risk.

8. Sales of vinyl records have been falling for many years and are now close to zero. What does the product life cycle (PLC) model suggest manufacturers should do?
   a. Leave the industry.
   b. Reduce costs and compete on price.
   c. Invest in new product features.

9. Do smart watches represent a new technology paradigm?
   a. No, they do the same job as mechanical watches, i.e. tell the time.
   b. Yes, they deliver masses of information in an entirely new way.
   c. No, they are basically small smart phones.

10. If Kenya were to discover large and valuable reserves of oil some people would consider it to be the 'wrong' kind of success. Why?
  a. Coffee farmers would not be able to compete and would lose their jobs.
  b. The value of the currency would rise against other currencies, making all exports uncompetitive on price.
  c. The sudden influx of money would benefit only the elite of society, leading to high income inequality.

Answers
1b, 2a, 3c, 4a, 5c, 6a, 7c, 8a, 9c, 10b

REFERENCES

Abberger K and Nierhaus W (2008) 'How to define a recession?' *CESifo Forum (Vol. 4, pp. 74-76), Ifo Institute for Economic Research at the University of Munich*

Aitken J, Childerhouse P and Towill D (2003) 'The impact of product life cycle on supply chain strategy' *International Journal of Production Economics,* 85(2), pp. 127–140

Apple (2014) Financial Information from www.investor.apple.com/financials.cfm accessed 1 July 2014

Balassa B (1964) 'The purchasing-power parity doctrine: a reappraisal' *Journal of Political Economy,* 72(6) (1964), pp. 584–596

Bank of Korea (2014) Official Foreign Reserves (May 2014) from www.bok.or.kr/contents/total/eng/board View.action?boardBean.brdid=13893&boardBean.rnum=23&menuNaviId=634&boardBean.menuid= 634&boardBean.cPage=3&boardBean.categorycd=0&boardBean.sdt=&boardBean.edt=&boardBean. searchColumn=&boardBean.searchValue= accessed 2 June 2014

BBC (2012) Venezuela to pay Exxon $255m in oil dispute from www.bbc.co.uk/news/business-16381730 accessed 1 July 2014 Bernanke B S (2002) *Deflation: Making sure 'it' doesn't happen here.* Remarks before the National Economists Club, Washington, DC, 21 from www.federalreserve.gov/boarddocs/ speeches/2002/20021121/default.htm accessed 29 August 2015

BIS (2013) Triennual Central Bank Survey, Foreign exchange turnover in April 2013: preliminary global results from www.bis.org/publ/rpfx13fx.pdf accessed 2 July 2014

Blinder A S and Rudd J B (2013) 'The supply-shock explanation of the Great Stagflation revisited' in Bordo M D and Orphanides A (Eds.) *The Great Inflation: The rebirth of modern central banking.* Chicago: University of Chicago Press

Branson R (2011) *Losing my virginity.* London: Random House

Center for American Progress (2012) *The State of Diversity in Today's Workforce* by Burns C, Barton K and Kerby S 12 July 2012 from www.americanprogress.org/issues/labor/report/2012/07/12/11938/the-state-of-diversity-in-todays-workforce/ accessed 1 February 2015

Coffee Jr J C (2012) 'Political economy of Dodd-Frank: why financial reform tends to be frustrated and systemic risk perpetuated' *Cornell Law Review,* 97(5), p. 1019

Cooper T (2004) 'Inadequate life? Evidence of consumer attitudes to product obsolescence' *Journal of Consumer Policy,* 27(4), pp. 421–449

Economist Intelligence Unit (2014) World risk: Alert - Guide to Risk Briefing methodology from www.views-wire.eiu.com/index.asp?layout=RKArticleVW3&article_id=183328603&country_id=1510000351&refm=rkCtry&page_title=Latest%2520alerts accessed 1 July 2014

Economist (2014) The Big Mac index from www.economist.com/content/big-mac-index accessed 2 June 2014

Égerta B, Drinec I, Lommatzschd K and Raultc C (2003) 'The Balassa–Samuelson effect in Central and Eastern Europe: myth or reality?' *Journal of Comparative Economics*, 31(3), September 2003, pp. 552–572

Eslake S (2009) 'The difference between a recession and a depression' *Economic Papers: A Journal of Applied Economics and Policy,* 28(2), pp. 75–81

Euromoney (2014) Country Risk Analysis Methodology from www.euromoney.com/Article/2773899/Euromoney-Country-Risk-Methodology.html accessed 1 July 2014

Fernando J and De Carvalho C (2000) 'The IMF as crisis manager: an assessment of the strategy in Asia and of its criticisms' *Journal of Post Keynesian Economics,* pp. 235–266

Gonçalves C E S and Salles J M (2008) 'Inflation targeting in emerging economies: what do the data say?' *Journal of Development Economics*, 85(1), pp. 312–318

Grant Thornton (2014) International Business Report Q4 2014 from www.dataviztool.internationalbusinessreport.com/ibr.html#map/women-in-senior-management/quarterly accessed 1 February 2015

Guardian (2013) 'South African racial transformation starting but painfully slowly' by Davis R 13 September 2013 from www.theguardian.com/world/2013/sep/13/south-africa-race-transformation accessed 1 February 2015

Gunasekaran A and Ngai E W (2005) 'Build-to-order supply chain management: a literature review and framework for development' *Journal of Operations Management*, 23(5), pp. 423–451

H M Treasury (2010) Glossary of Treasury terms from www.webarchive.nationalarchives.gov.uk/20130129110402/www.www.hm-treasury.gov.uk/junebudget_glossary.htm accessed 25 August 2015

Holburn G L and Zelner B A (2010) 'Political capabilities, policy risk, and international investment strategy: evidence from the global electric power generation industry' *Strategic Management Journal,* 31(12), pp. 1290–1315

IMF (2014a) Principal Global Indicators from www.principalglobalindicators.org/default.aspx accessed 1 July 2014

IMF (2014b) Data Template on International Reserves and Foreign Currency Liquidity from www.imf.org/external/np/sta/ir/IRProcessWeb/colist.aspx accessed 2 July 2014

IMF (2015) World Economic Database from www.imf.org/external/pubs/ft/weo/2015/01/weodata/index.aspx accessed 25 August 2015

Institute for Fiscal Studies (IFS)(2012) A Survey of the UK Tax System from www.ifs.org.uk/bns/bn09.pdf accessed 1 July 2014

Knight F H (2012) *Risk, uncertainty and profit*. Mineola, NY: Dover Publications

Kubiszewski I, Costanza R, Franco C, Lawn P, Talberth J, Jackson T and Aylmer C (2013) 'Beyond GDP: Measuring and achieving global genuine progress' *Ecological Economics,* 93, pp. 57–68

Kuhn, Thomas S (1970)(2nd edn.) *The structure of scientific revolutions*. Chicago: Chicago University Press

Lawrence M, Goodwin P, O'Connor M and Önkal D (2006) 'Judgmental forecasting: a review of progress over the last 25 years' *International Journal of Forecasting*, 22(3), pp. 493–518

Makar S D and Huffman S P (2011) 'Foreign currency risk management practices in US multinationals' *Journal of Applied Business Research (JABR)*, 13(2), pp. 73–86

Ministry of Finance, India (2012) Receipt Budget 2011-2012 from www.indiabudget.nic.in/budget2011-2012/ub2011-12/rec/tr.pdf accessed 1 July 2014

Mitsubishi (2009) Mitsubishi Motors to bring new-generation EV i-MiEV to market from www.mitsubishi-motors.com/publish/pressrelease_en/products/2009/news/detail1940.html accessed 1 July 2014

Moore G E (1965) 'Cramming more components onto integrated circuits' *Electronics,* 38(8), April 19, 1965

Morandé F (2000) *A Decade of Inflation Targeting in Chile: Main Developments and Lessons*. Manuscrito, Banco Central de Chile from www.bcentral.cl/eng/policies/presentations/executives/pdf/2000/morandejulio132002.pdf accessed 26 August 2015

Norway (2012) Royal Ministry of Finance National Budget 2012 from www.statsbudsjettet.no/upload/Statsbudsjett_2012/dokumenter/pdf/nb_summary.pdf accessed 1 July 2014

Oil and Gas Journal (2013) Badly Damaged PDVSA Should Be Replaced, Founding Board Member Says from www.ogj.com/articles/print/volume-111/issue-3b/general-interest/badly-damaged-pdvsa-should-be-replaced.html accessed 1 July 2014

Samuelson P A (1964) 'Theoretical notes on trade problems' *Review of Economics and Statistics,* 46(2) (1964), pp. 145–154

Schencking J C (2008) 'The Great Kanto Earthquake and the culture of catastrophe and reconstruction in 1920s Japan' *The Journal of Japanese Studies,* 34(2), Summer 2008, pp. 295–331

Shaikh A (2007) 'A Proposed synthesis of classical and Keynesian growth' *The New School for Social Research,* Working Paper, (5)

Slovik, P. and Cournède B. (2011) 'Macroeconomic Impact of Basel III' *OECD Economics Department Working Papers*, No. 844, OECD Publishing from www.dx.doi.org/10.1787/5kghwnhkkjs8-en accessed 13 November 2014

Stone R W (2004) 'The political economy of IMF lending in Africa' *American Political Science Review,* 98(04), pp. 577–591

Tesco (2014) Annual report downloads www.tescoplc.com/index.asp?pageid=548 accessed 27 June 2014

US Department of Commerce (2012) Federal Gov't Finances & Employment: Federal Budget--Receipts, Outlays, and Debt from www.census.gov/compendia/statab/cats/federal_govt_finances_employment/federal_budget--receipts_outlays_and_debt.html accessed 1 July 2014

Van Wijnbergen S (1984) 'The `Dutch Disease': a disease after all?' *The Economic Journal,* 94(373) (Mar., 1984), pp. 41–55

Walmart (2014) Annual reports www.stock.walmart.com/annual-reports accessed 27 June 2014

Yahoo! Finance (2014) Finance www.finance.yahoo.com/ accessed 27 June 2014

4 International Market Analysis

Chapter Objectives

At the start of a company's globalisation strategy it must identify where it and its products or services fit in the target market. This chapter will discuss the different aspects of this positioning process:

- Defining the international market in terms of characteristics relevant to the intended consumers.
- Theories for evaluating the attractiveness of the market.
- Segmentation of the market and its subdivision into niches.
- Identifying gaps in the market.

DEFINING THE INTERNATIONAL MARKET

The term 'market' is an amorphous word describing a nebulous concept. Though frequently referred to in the business media as if it were an institution that exists in a physical form, in truth it is fundamentally nothing but a negotiation between a buyer and a seller for the purposes of a mutually beneficial exchange. If one of these two parties does not exist or is unwilling to close the deal then the market does not exist. Even if the deal does proceed but one of the parties is acting under duress, still the market does not exist. The concept of the market is based on a willingness to exchange, usually money for goods according to the agreed price. A more formal definition of a market might be a 'decentralised non-organised interaction between buyer and seller' (Roberts, 2005). At least this is the essence of the economic relationship, but forces of centralisation and organisation do exist to shape the market.

In theory at least (Stiglitz, 1987), an efficient market is one where both parties have access to the same information and neither is able to exert undue influence in extracting an advantageous price. This would imply limitless numbers of buyers and sellers with no barriers to entry or exit. It is also assumed that both parties are looking to maximise their profits. Sadly, at various times in our economic history this concept of the perfect market has been found to be illusory and players in the market have abused their positions for personal gain.

For example, trading in stocks and shares is usually conducted at a stock exchange. Not only are the exchanges made in some central location, like the New York Stock Exchange (NYSE), they are also bound by a series of regulations to protect both the buyer and the seller. NYSE derives its rules from a framework set down by the Securities and Exchange Committee (SEC), a US government agency. These rules are intended to prevent fraudulent or manipulative practices and allow the NYSE to discipline the transgressor (NYSE, 2014). Although the existence of the rules is an admission that a perfect market in stocks does not exist, they create the conditions for equitable trading in stocks within a clear boundary. The result should be a reasonable approximation of a perfect market within the confines of the rules.

International markets are not simply domestic markets multiplied; the entire relationship between seller and buyer has to be reassessed. Some overseas markets may differ from the domestic market in degrees of novelty, others may be entirely unrelated. Of course, both markets need to be analysed, but where the nature of the domestic market must be accepted and dealt with, overseas markets have a unique element of choice: the company can decide how, when and with what products it will enter each new foreign market. An international market entry strategy is therefore more detailed than a domestic market entry and based on meticulous market analysis.

 ## CASE STUDY: THE PERFECT MARKET IN HOLIDAYS

In some ways the market for holidays, or vacations, is one of the most open in the world. Consumers are not usually tied into a particular destination and the switching costs, before any deposit has been paid, are zero. Generally, the same information is available to all consumers and even the burgeoning discount websites are accessible to anyone with an internet connection.

Accommodation prices range from camping at the lowest end to high-class hotel suites at the top end. There is plenty of scope for small-time entrepreneurs to enter the market by offering bed and breakfast accommodation with very little additional cost to them; they can also exit the industry at very little cost. Taken as a whole, then, the tourism market is close to a perfect market.

The problems tend to occur within the particular segments of the market. Hospitality, which tends to serve business clients with the complete management of events, is dominated by specialist companies and hotel chains. The costs of entering or exiting this segment are very high but companies are also able to charge high prices to their clients.

In the tourism segments the access to information may be the same for all consumers but it also tends to be limited and therefore open to abuse by providers. There are many horror stories of hotels not being complete when guests arrive to start their holidays, by which time the costs for them to switch to another holiday are very high. Consumers do have some protection thanks to government regulation but this is often of little comfort in a foreign country.

Over the longer term, consumers can find themselves tied into deals such as time-share, where payment of an annual fee grants them access to accommodation. Again, there are switching costs when the consumers want to vacation elsewhere or they are unable to gain access when they want it.

Seasonality is also a restriction on the openness of the tourism market. Like it or not, skiing takes place during the winter and beach holidays during the summer. Consumers have some opportunity to defy the seasons by choosing to holiday in another part of the world, perhaps even opting for a different hemisphere, but providers in a given location need to make money while they can. This leads to high prices during the peak season. Out of season prices will be lower but so will the attractiveness of the location.

Overall, in a market this open few consumers have advantageous positions that they can exploit, with the result that there are few real bargains to be had. Of course, last-minute bookings can be remarkably cheap but then the consumer must accept whatever location and accommodation is available. At the other end of the scale, booking a honeymoon suite in a luxury hotel in Venice during the height of the tourist season is going to result in a substantial bill but also the holiday of a lifetime. For tourism, the old adage holds as true as ever: you pays your money and you takes your choice!

Point of consideration: The luxury end of the tourism market is constrained by a near oligopoly of major international hotel chains. If these large corporations were to extend their operations into the budget end of the market (backpacker hostels, campsites, etc.) to what extent would consumers be advantaged and disadvantaged by the strategic move?

Sources: Jang S (2004), Dolnicara S (2002), Papatheodorou A (2006)

INTERNATIONAL MARKET OPPORTUNITIES

That an overseas market exists is not sufficient; it needs to offer good enough opportunities for it to be profitable. When the company was originally founded the local market will have been familiar territory. At this initial stage the evaluation of the market might have been more visceral than verified, a gut feeling that impassions a fervent ambition in the entrepreneur. While blind faith should never be the basis of a business strategy, when it comes to one's own market familiarity engenders a certain unconscious understanding of the opportunities. Living and working within the target market means that the entrepreneur has a sense of what profits might be made.

This is not the case with new markets. With no innate understanding of the unfamiliar market, the managers must analyse the opportunities for profit from first principles. Fortunately, this is being done from a position of domestic strength: if the new market offers poor profitability then the company can abandon its attempt and look elsewhere. The process of market analysis then begins all over again. One of the most well-known methods of analysis is Michael Porter's Five Forces.

THE FIVE FORCES

Michael Porter takes the view that there are a number of different factors, or forces, that shape the opportunities in a new market. Even if other companies have already staked a claim it does not mean that a new company cannot take them on and win. Porter argued that it is the intensity of the competition that impacts on profitability. It is not the competition itself that is the worry, but whether that competition is powerful enough to prevent newcomers to the market from earning a sufficient financial return.

In Porter's characterisation of the market there are five forces, four impinging from outside and one internal (Porter, 2008). The most important of the forces is that of the **bargaining power of buyers**. Depending on where the company is situated in the supply chain, buyers can be client companies looking for component supplies or they could be the final consumers. Whoever the buyers are they have the power to influence the selling price of the product and therefore the profitability of the business. This incorporates the concept of value: if the consumers place a low value on the product then they will resist high prices. It may also be easy for the buyers to switch to alternative products, particularly if they are not tied into the product for technical reasons. In a similar way, resource dependency theory suggests that where there is a high dependence on a resource the buyer loses power to the supplier. Buyers can gain power by co-operating (Crook and Combs, 2007).

At the other end of the supply chain are the company's own **suppliers**. In an extreme case there may be only one supplier, in which case they would hold monopoly powers and could command the price they charge the company. Even if there are a number of suppliers they may still have enough of an oligopoly to strongly influence prices. It is a common feature of most industries that a company will have close ties with its supplier, and this makes it very difficult for the company to switch to an alternative supplier. Fortunately, the company is itself a buyer and has the same potential to wield power as we would normally expect of a buyer. The power of each is in balance when the company and supplier are in a close, symbiotic relationship and hold equal power; for either one to exert power over the other would destabilise the relationship and damage both parties. This implies that even when a buyer holds power over the supplier it should not be exercised (Benton and Maloni, 2005).

When a company has identified a market with low power amongst buyers and suppliers then this should be a highly profitable position. Like vultures to carrion, though, this will quickly attract further competition, depending on the existence of entry barriers. The threat alone of **new entrants** may be enough to suppress profitability. The profitable opportunity may be short-lived and so the company would have to put a new strategy in place for the long term. It may conclude that long-term profitability is not possible: the company may then consider a skimming strategy, one where maximum pricing and profits are extracted from the market in the short term, followed by an exit once the new entrants make this impossible. Alternatively, the company may conclude that without a long-term strategy there is no reason to become involved in the market in the first place.

The final external force is that of **substitutes**. These might seem similar to new entrants but they are subtly distinctive. Substitutes can take the place of the company's products in the market, yet they do not share the same characteristics. For example, tea is a substitute for coffee. Although a coffee company will be locked in competition with other coffee companies, consumers may decide that they just prefer to drink something different altogether. The market is broadly unchanged, but substitutes come in from new competitors in other industries and it is this that makes them dangerous. Although consumers may perceive little difference between the coffee and tea beverages, the industrial processes and supply chains are utterly distinct. Consumers might decide that herbal teas are refreshing in a way that coffee does not seem to be and the coffee industry would find it almost impossible to respond. Whatever the reason for the change in consumer shift towards a substitute it is very difficult to predict and so company managers are at a severe disadvantage in formulating their business strategies. Where the opportunity had looked profitable, the sudden appearance of substitutes can erode the financial returns.

CASE STUDY – BULOVA WATCHES IN JAPAN

Bulova is an American brand of watch which was credited with inventing the first electronic watch, the Accutron of 1960, based around a vibrating tuning fork driven by a small electrical current. Curiously, the watch did not tick but hummed! Although the company rose to prominence in its home market by associating itself with Charles Lindbergh, the first person to fly solo across the Atlantic, and later with the US space programme, manufacturing was always conducted in Switzerland.

Like the native Swiss watch brands, Bulova was gravely impacted by the rise of Japanese manufacturers and by 2007 had come under the ownership of Citizen, Japan. Small numbers of Bulova watches are still designed in the United States and manufactured in Switzerland.

With the centre of gravity for the watch industry moving from Switzerland to Japan it might be interesting to consider how the Bulova management could use Porter's Five Forces Model to evaluate the Japanese market for its products. It hardly needs mentioning that the Japanese watch market as a whole is considerable but the purpose of the model is to clarify the profitability of any sales opportunities.

Table 4.1 *Market forces and profitability*

Force	Strength of Force	Profit Potential
Buyer	High – consumers can easily switch to other brands	Poor
Supplier	Low – Citizen is the parent company so Bulova is part of the world's largest watch company	Good
New Entrants	Low – watch manufacturing requires high volume production for economies of scale. Bulova can access these through Citizen.	Good
Substitutes	High – many consumers choose not to wear a watch at all but get the time from a mobile phone or computer	Poor
Rivalry	High – not only is there intense competition amongst the Japanese brands but the Swiss brands continue to highly sought after	Poor

The conclusion from using the Five Forces Model is that the Japanese market for Bulova is rather hostile. However, the potential for profit at each turn has not been quantified here so it is not a simple matter of the two 'goods' outweighing the three 'poors'. It is interesting to note that Bulova has indeed benefited from its relationship with Citizen to maintain a small market presence in Japan and it sells into a small niche where consumers have an appreciation for a highly differentiated style of watch.

Point of consideration: Seiko has a line of premium watches of its own, the handmade Grand Seiko range, that rivals Rolex and Omega in quality. If you were a Seiko manager, using Porter's Five Forces Model how would you assess the profitability of entering the Swiss market with the Grand Seiko brand? Would the mainstream Seiko brand be more profitable in that market?

Source: Bulova company website, 2014

ADDITIONAL COMPLEMENTORS AND FORCES

A number of attempts have been made to add a sixth force to the Five Forces Model and so broaden the analysis by managers. Nalebuff and Brandenburger (1996) introduced the game theory approach as a way of explaining the role of **complementors** in motivating strategic alliances that are somewhere between competition and co-operation. These complementors are goods from rivals that complement those of the manager's own company.

Andrew Grove, ex-CEO of Intel, elevated the role of the government to that of a force (Burgelman and Grove, 2007). In the original, Michael Porter saw the government as a factor, acting on all industry participants equally. If viewed as a force then governments can directly influence the profitability of an industry for a company. This is often seen when a state-owned monopoly is introduced to new competition due to deregulation of the market, the government targeting its erstwhile champion for the beneficial rigours of competitive business.

Grove sees a role for complementors who may not be directly involved in the industry under review, but they play an important supportive role. E-commerce firms, such as online retailers, are highly dependent on the development of the internet and technological advances in the hardware. Interestingly, the online behemoth Amazon includes links to its smaller online retailers. On payment of a fee, and meeting certain standards set by Amazon, these retailers can trade under the Amazon umbrella. This broadens the coverage for both Amazon and the smaller firms.

Despite these critical attacks on the Five Forces Model it remains a useful tool for managers. It is intuitive in conception and application, directing managers away from tempting yet unprofitable market segments and focusing them on the vital concerns of optimising the financial rates of return. The model continues to enjoy strong validity, but only as long as managers are aware of the dynamic environment in which it is applied.

 ## MANAGEMENT SPOTLIGHT: FACTORS NOT FORCES

Michael Porter's Five Forces Model has found favour with managers since it has them focus on profitability rather than vacant gaps in the market or sales volumes. After all, it is the ultimate profit of the company for which managers must answer. Nevertheless, Coyne and Subramaniam (1996) accused Porter's model of making three unsupportable assumptions:

1. The main players in the industry (buyers, sellers, substitutes and rivals) are unrelated – in reality companies commonly work with each other, either as favoured partners or as co-dependents.
2. Erecting barriers to entry by new rivals creates a structural and financially rewarding advantage – this suggests that the advantages are static when evidence shows many firms are competitive through dynamic qualities of technical development ability to forecast future market changes.
3. Uncertainty is low and the profitability of a strategy can be predicted – this may be true of some industries, but those where managers most need a model like the Five Forces are also ones where uncertainty is high.

This does not mean that the Five Forces Model has no value for managers and under certain conditions may yield useful results, such as Grigore (2014) found when evaluating a market for books. Yet critics of the Five Forces Model argue that it only accounts for the pressures on profitability that exist in the market itself and that it does not account for the non-market pressures. The non-market pressures can originate from stakeholders, media, government and so on (Baron, 1995). For example, the defence industry is one that is heavily impacted by government policy to the extent that the contractors are almost an extension of the government. Indeed, the defence industry market is almost entirely controlled by governments, from supply and demand to specification and price.

The necessity to invest in R&D can also impact on profitability, such as in the pharmaceutical industry, where profits revolve around the release of successful new drugs and the length of time they are held under patent. While the patent is current it acts as a considerable barrier to entry for incoming competitors, yet this all changes when the product comes off patent and generic rival drugs can become readily available. Since Porter's model does not account for this time element, the shift from patent to no patent, two separate analyses would have to be conducted.

Michael Porter includes these non-market environmental influences as factors rather than forces. Whereas forces act individually to shape the attractiveness of the market, factors shift the entire set of forces. We can see this when government implements legislation restricting exhaust emissions from cars. The technical challenges affect the entire industry and so do not alter the relative powers of suppliers, new entrants, substitutes or rivals. The new requirements oblige all the industry players to make the same upgrades and the rise in cost is then passed on to the buyers, who are the final consumers. At the margin this may deter some consumers from buying a new car since they cannot afford the price rise, and the consequent fall in sales volumes will reduce the profits of the car manufacturers.

While this view preserves the integrity of the model it also ignores the disruptive effect that some changes can have. Porter seems to be assuming that there is a high degree of predictability in industry, but this is often not the case. In technology-based industries the profitability of individual firms is at the mercy of new product development and how well it is accepted by the market. When demand is not as strong as expected, or a company releases a popular new technology that was not anticipated, then the situation described by the Five Forces Model can be quickly disrupted. The source of the new technology may not even be a direct rival; it could be a new entrant or a substitute.

Point of consideration: If you were looking to launch a new technology, like a smart watch, in China, how effective would the Five Forces Model be in evaluating the market?

Sources: Coyne and Subramaniam, 1996; Grigore, 2014; Baron 1995

MARKET DIVISIONS

If **perfect markets** did exist then they would be infinitely fluid and dynamic. Any opportunity could be explored and exploited, there being no costs associated with entering or exiting the market. Companies could devise an almost infinite variety of product features. These products would appeal to primary buying motives, i.e. those motives derived from the basic human needs for food, warmth, etc. This creates a featureless and homogeneous market.

In opposition to the theoretical, homogeneous market is the real market made up of manufacturers who are limited by the capabilities of the production systems and the need to differentiate themselves from the competition. W R Smith (1956) observed that this diversity of supply to the market could be attributed to five reasons:

- Variety in production systems
- Access to different resources
- Product design innovations
- Variable quality control
- Different estimates of consumer demand.

It is due to this diversity of supply that producers divide up the market and target their products at groups of consumers. Companies need to cluster around these market divisions and serve proven demand by competing with similar products. These divisions in the market are the **market segments**.

The market can then be segmented in terms of distinctive, and related, consumer demand (Dickson and Ginter, 1987). Given the existence of economies of scale, as well as other entry and exit barriers, companies will tend to be conservative in how they structure the market. Rather than developing endless varieties of products they will instead focus on those with a proven track record, even if originating from a competitor. Through innovation and product differentiation they may test the outer reaches of the market segment, but generally these tend to involve product variations to appeal to selective buying motives, based on such characteristics as product colour and size.

The limits of a market segment are often defined by the economies of scale in production. If each of the manufacturers or service providers in that segment are able to benefit from economies of scale

Table 4.2 *Market segments and niches*

Market Division	Production Costs	Product Characteristics	Sales Volumes	Price	Product Example
Segment	Low cost – mass production, economies of scale	Generic, undifferentiated	High	Market price	Readymade suit
Niche	High cost – craft production, low scale	Differentiated, customised	Low	Premium	Tailored suit

then none of them has a cost advantage, thereby removing the opportunity for long-term competition based on price. Innovation will then focus on the product specifications as companies look for differentiation advantages, but these will be relatively minor as long as the company wishes to remain in the segment.

Sometimes the segment is too small to offer the sales opportunities to mainstream producers, in which case the segment is known as a **market niche**. The definition of niche is not clear-cut, but generally they are segments that do not offer the potential for sales volumes that would attain economies of scale in the long term. Without the likelihood of price competition based on low-cost production, niches are often populated by highly differentiated products marketed at premium prices. This acts as a barrier to entry for new rivals, but equally it is difficult for niche brands to break out into the mainstream market when additional sales volumes are needed. Table 4.2 summarises the main differences between segments and niches.

The low volume of sales in niches means that there are very few products competing within the niche, and on occasion the niche may be identified with a single product or brand. Savile Row is a centre for tailoring in London that has become most famous for handmade suits. The street is in an historic part of the capital, and there is no potential for the construction of large factories, placing a severe constraint on the output of bespoke suits. However, this also protects the makers of genuine Savile Row suits from new entrants since they could not bring with them any particular cost advantage in production. As a result, the number of tailors in Savile Row has remained stable for many years.

SEGMENTING THE MARKET

Since the market is simply a relationship between a buyer and a seller the precise form of the market depends upon the nature of the deals being negotiated. The market for gold, for example, can take many forms, from industrial use to financial investment and the crafting of jewellery, to name just three. When analysing the demand for gold, therefore, there will be many different factors involved such as industrial demand, the state of the financial markets and fashion, respectively. Fortunately, managers can call on the, still improving, power of computers to conduct multivariate and cluster analysis (Kuo et al., 2002).

Multivariate analysis will bring some coherence to the vast array of ways for characterising a market and its segments. In any purchasing decision there are a broad number of factors influencing the purchase decision but multivariate analysis should reveal the most important. For the housing industry, price inflation and income growth are often the most important factors for defining the market, although social factors such as average family size will have some relevance as well. In this section we will look briefly at the relationship of price and perception of value as one way of segmenting a market.

Value and price are two concepts that are easy to confuse but distinguishing them is a vital part of any manager's strategy. Value is a measure of how much a service or product matters to a consumer. Value can be ultimately expressed in monetary terms but the judgement is deeply personal, as embodied in the phrase 'everyone has their price'. A lump of gold might be highly valued by one person but considered entirely without value by another. Even this judgement cannot be directly translated into a price since this depends on the wealth of the consumer. In a free-market situation the price of a lump of gold is decided by the highest bidder but if they are very rich the expenditure will represent a small part of their fortune; despite the high price, the buyer is actually placing little value on the metal.

Even the richest people have their spending limits, and this means they will not, rationally speaking, pay more for an object than the value it has for them. This is because there is an **opportunity cost**; they could have spent the money on something else of the same price but perceived higher value. Let's say that the current price of gold is US$1300 per ounce. This is telling us that those who can afford to buy are currently pricing it at this level. If demand in the market pushes the price up we do not know if this is because buyers value gold more, perhaps because other investment opportunities are less attractive, or because they simply have more money to spend. Forecasting future price movements is therefore a complex process of economic analysis as all relevant factors have to be evaluated.

 MYTH BUSTER – THE VALUE AND PRICE OF MONEY

The difference between value and price is most starkly shown by something that you would think we can all agree on: money. If someone were to offer you a US$1 note how much would you be prepared to pay for it? If you were in the United States at the time you might be tempted to say that it was worth one dollar, but at that price it is not worth your bothering to buy it as you are getting back only what you paid. So where value equals price there is no reason to do the deal. Perhaps then you would like to buy the dollar for 50¢. It is a highly attractive price, of course, but you would soon be outbid by other interested buyers. Indeed, you could expect the price to quickly rise to 99¢, after which there is no point in doing the deal. So although everyone agrees that a dollar is worth a dollar, the market price of a US$1 note would have to be 99¢ and no more.

There are occasions where the dollar might be worth the same or more than its face value. Dollar coins featuring Susan B Anthony became commonly known as the Susan B, or Susie. It was only available for a short period of time because it was easily confused with the quarter (25¢) coin. The rarity of the Susan B then made it more valuable than its nominal, or face, value of one dollar. The same principle applies to precious metals like gold; the value can be increased by adding a new feature, such as forming the metal into something rare or unique. Gold is often traded in the form of coins, such as South African Krugerrands.

This distinction between value and price underpins many of the strategic decisions made concerning new products. Companies will improve the specification of a product by adding new features. They may therefore claim that they are adding value to the product, but that is only true to the extent that consumers will pay for it. The mistake is in adding a high-cost feature that has low value for the consumer. The consumer will only pay a price that is just less than the value they place on the feature. If the price is more than the value they place on the feature they will refuse to buy it, and if the price is the same as the value then it is not worth the trouble.

When digital watches first appeared in the 1970s the technology offered the possibility of adding features such as tiny calculators. In practice, people put very low value on having calculators strapped to the ends of the arms and were certainly not prepared to pay for them. Clearly, people put the value on a watch that tells the time reliably and stylishly, so that is all they are prepared to pay for. Design a watch with more style, then the value rises and the customer will hand over more money.

Point of consideration: Gold has few practical uses but as a soft, shiny metal it is highly suited to the crafting of ornamental objects. Under what circumstances do you think the price of gold would fall to that of, say, lead, another soft but more commonly available metal?

Source: Harper (2014), South African Mint Company (2014)

BEYOND THE SEGMENT

We have already covered the problems companies have in attempting to cover the entire market. Due to factors like economies of scale, inflexible production systems and difficulties in adapting products, companies tend to focus their resources on identified market segments. The segments can be characterised in a number of different ways, but cluster analysis will reduce these to the most influential for the segment, such as geography, demographics and so on.

THE DEMAND PROBLEM

The problem with segments is that they become self-defining. The market for the pop music segment tends to be characterised by a young demographic with low disposable income. As a consequence the music tends to be focused on achieving high-volume sales by appealing to mainstream tastes within the segment. In support of this strategy the music is set at a low price by selling individual tracks as internet downloads.

Sales volumes then become synonymous with **demand**, but in fact demand is a subtly different concept. There may actually be unsatisfied demand for different types of music outside the mainstream, or amongst consumers in another demographic. However, with little information on the potential of this mysterious, unrealised demand, producers prefer to stay within the confines of their segment. In an established market segment consumers buy what they are being offered but their true demand may go unacknowledged. There have been times when the pop music segment is shaken by the sudden popularity of an atypical piece of music that appeals to an alien demographic. However, these events are seen as anomalies and the music scene promptly regresses to the mean.

 CASE STUDY: AFRICAN POP FOR THE WESTERN MAINSTREAM

By any measure, Youssou N'Dour is a major figure in the world of pop music. In Africa his name is instantly recognisable, famous for developing a style of music known as *mbalax*. He has won numerous accolades around the world: in 2007 Time proclaimed him as one of the top 100 most influential people in the world, alongside Martin Scorsese, the Pope and Osama Bin Laden. He has been appointed to the position of government minister of his home country of Senegal and acts as a goodwill ambassador for the Food and Agricultural Organisation of the United Nations.

It is something of a surprise, then, that Youssou N'Dour is barely known at all in the American and European pop music markets. It is not as if his friends in the business have not extended him a helping hand. He has sung duets with some of the most recognisable names in Western contemporary music: Peter Gabriel, Paul Simon, Bruce Springsteen and many others. Yet the mainstream pop music fans have remained resolutely ignorant of his much-lauded talents. The highest chart rating he has achieved so far has been to number 3 in the UK pop chart with the song 7 Seconds, performed with Neneh Cherry; it reached number 98 in the US Billboard Hot 100. Most other songs have not even cracked the top 20 in any country.

It is difficult to know whether the demand for Youssou N'Dour's music is simply not present or if the buying public has been indoctrinated by mainstream pop music and is unable to grasp what they are missing. The fact that he has enjoyed some music sales and a lot of critical acclaim suggests that there is potential for growth, a latent demand if you will, and that with a bit of persistence the mainstream will make a space for his African style. The difficulty is in identifying the character of his market segment when that segment does not yet exist.

Point of consideration: For African music to find popular success in western markets is it necessary to sell to existing fans outside the market or to educate those already in the market on its delights?

Sources: Time, 2007; Observer, 2012

IDENTIFYING THE GAP

With companies focusing their efforts on identifiable market segments and niches there then arises the possibility of analysing the gaps between the segments for new business opportunities. This is a risky strategy because it means entering a part of the market about which nothing is proven, whatever the market research might be attempting to anticipate. As a consequence, established players in the market tend to encroach on these gaps progressively from the safety of their segment positions, while only new entrants are likely to aim for the vacancies directly.

The market, the segments and the vacant gaps can be measured in many ways, including consumer income, demographics, geography and so on. In Figure 4.1 we see a simple model for identifying gaps in the market for travel in Europe. The two dimensions in this case are value, as perceived by the consumer, and price.

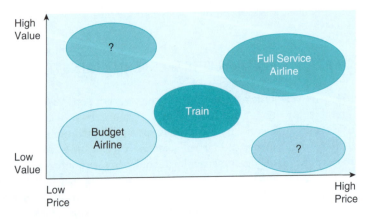

Figure 4.1 *Positioning by value and price*

Figure 4.1 illustrates the values and prices for three different methods for travelling across Europe. The reason why all consumers do not choose the budget 'no frills' airline is because it has a low value attached to it (Lawtona and Solomkob, 2005). Nevertheless, it is popular because the price of air tickets is very low. This motivates budget airlines to drive costs ever lower as a way of increasing their profits without raising prices.

The full-service airline is highly valued but of course the price reflects this. To capture revenues from the wealthiest of passengers these airlines will offer first-class seating, sometimes under their own brand name (e.g. Virgin Atlantic's Upper Class). First-class offers the usual refinements of more spacious seating, better food and personal service, all of which carry additional costs that need to be paid for. At the same time, first-class passengers will receive priority boarding, which costs the airline nothing extra but allows them to charge the customers more for the perceived value.

In the middle we have the train service, to which consumers attach a medium value and so pay medium-level prices. Although not as fast as a jet aircraft, because rail travel connects city centres, for many passengers an express train can rival air travel for time over the total journey. Trains also offer a more pleasurable passenger experience than budget airlines.

For each of these services, the consumer will only pay up to what they consider to be the value. For those that put a low value on the travel, maybe because they have no time pressures, the natural choice would be the budget airline. For those who put a very high value on the travel, perhaps because they have an urgent meeting to attend or prize comfort over price, then they will choose the full-service airline. In each of these segments it is important to note that value and price are strongly positively correlated; they rise and fall in step with each other. In this model the result is that the segments are aligned along a diagonal line. This has important implications for identifying economically feasible gaps.

IDENTIFYING MARKET GAPS

We can see from Figure 4.1 that the market, one that is described by the two dimensions given, can be laid out pictorially. For managers, this acts as a device to reveal where the gaps in the market might be. The gaps appear in two places:

1. **Between the existing segments** – on the diagonal line connecting the three existing segments there are visible gaps between budget airline and train, just as between train and full-service airline.
2. **Outside the existing segments** – in the high value–low price and low value–high price sectors of the model there are no identifiable current market segments.

Analysing these gap opportunities in more detail:

1. The gaps between the existing segments are unexplored combinations of value and price. They are still governed by the same correlation as in the other segments but there is yet to be any product offered there. Companies will readily explore these gaps because they are simply incremental steps from their existing segments so they can be tested as tactical moves within their overall corporate strategies.
   In our current illustration the budget airline could offer a higher class of service for a higher price. We can already see some of that in the additional services these airlines offer, such as in-flight food and priority boarding, both of which are available to travellers willing to pay the extra. The full-service airline might want to consider the opposite action of charging for items that were previously included in the ticket price, such as for headphones, in order to be able to offer special low prices. Finally, the train operator in the middle of the market can head into the gap below with cheaper

seats (e.g. third class) or into the gap above (e.g. *gourmet* dining). In each case, the company is not departing radically from its existing business model.

2. In Figure 4.1, there are two segments that are clearly not on the diagonal line connecting the three existing segments. These seem to indicate two possibilities: high value–low price and low value–high price. However, we need to be very cautious since they do not adhere to the same value-price correlation for the existing segments.

The **low value–high price** situation is where the consumer is being asked to pay a high price for something on which they place little value. We have all observed how our fellow consumers can apparently overpay for something, but this is not what is being described here. Let us say that the most expensive way to travel from Paris to Berlin is by taxi. This is a distance of over 1000km and would take at least 10 hours of constant driving, more when the poor taxi driver wants to take a well-earned break. It would also cost several thousand euros. Clearly for most international travellers such a journey would be too long and uncomfortable so would have very low value for them. Though attractive for a taxi firm, it would be quite irrational for consumers to choose such a method of travel and so the apparent gap in the market is just an illusion created by the value-price model.

This is not to say that long-distance taxi rides or car journeys are never taken, but they would be chosen by those few people that place a high value on them, or else they have found a way to reduce the price down to the value. Either approach would then bring the value of the journey and its price back into alignment. This shifts such independent modes of travel back onto the diagonal with the existing segments. These travellers might be people who suffer from a phobia of public transport, and even if they complain about the taxi fare it is still rational for them to pay for the service due to the relatively high value they place on the mode of travel compared to the alternatives. There are also people who would take the journey in their own cars: they put a relatively low value on the mode of travel but if they travel as a group they can bring down the price to each of them. Finally, there are hitchhikers, who would undoubtedly prefer to fly, so they too put a low value on road travel, but they can do it for free so it is a perfectly rational low value–low price option for them.

The value-price model also seems to indicate a gap in the market for high value–low price travel. This is such an enticing idea, where customers get to travel in the way they most desire but at a bargain price, that one wonders why no business has tried it. However, although the mode of travel would be rational for the consumer it would be entirely irrational for the business. In effect, the business is giving its service away since the consumer would readily pay more for the service, up to a price that almost equalled the value they placed on it. It is likely that only a government would have the funds and lack of business acumen to propose such a nonsensical strategy.

According to World Bank (2014) data, in Saudi Arabia car fuel in 2013 was priced at around 16¢, which is less than a fifth the price in the United States and less than a tenth that in the UK. This is probably the lowest price for gasoline anywhere in the world, even though most consumers could pay more. So what is the purpose of selling a product that has a high value to consumers but charging a low price? The answer is a political one, as the regime is one that is considered by many to be rigid and undemocratic, but it is able to survive by sharing the wealth derived from its huge oil industry. As long as the Saudi populace is able to enjoy access to cheap resources, such as gasoline, then it will not seek to upset the political *status quo*.

In other countries it is not the car fuel that is subsidised but the infrastructure, so that most roads can be used for free at the point of use. Although the roads are paid for through taxation, those who use them most frequently are receiving more than they paid for. This means they are receiving a high-value service for a relatively low price. The actual value of the road access to the driver can be derived in the locations where there is a separate toll, such as major bridges and tunnels. In some countries tolls are charged for a parallel road system offering a congestion-free motorway that the driver pays to access. Although the value-price model would indicate a gap in the market for high value–low price travel in the form of free motorway access, the business opportunity is to provide access to a motorway only on payment of a toll. The price of that toll is the one that best reflects the value placed on the service by the most economically viable number of customers.

INTERNATIONAL AND EMERGING MARKET SEGMENTATION

Value and price are just two factors that can be used in sub-dividing a heterogeneous market into its homogeneous segments. These segments, as we know, are made up of consumers united in the reasons for demanding a particular product. This is not to say that the consumers in a defined segment are all the same, they are still individuals, but with regards to that type of product they share a similar set of characteristics. Depending on the product, they might share a similar age, income, race, gender or leisure interest. This list is certainly not exhaustive and there will be many other characteristics that could be relevant. It is only by investigating the data, perhaps through cluster analysis, that the most important factors will be uncovered.

If we look at the housing market, for example, researchers have found that there are a number of ways of segmenting it (Goodman and Thibodeaub, 2003):

- House type – detached, semi-detached, terrace
- Structural characteristic – age, historic interest
- Neighbourhood – schools, crime rate, ethnicity.

For international companies, though, the temptation is to segment their markets at a much higher level of aggregation, preferring to characterise a market in terms of some putative national qualities. This often involves theories of cultural analysis, and if these are inaccurate they can lead to lost opportunities. European car manufacturers have long avoided shipping their small cars to the United States since a market obsessed with automotive leviathans was assumed to be hostile to anything on a more sensible scale. In fact, a number of small cars have sold well there, from the VW Beetle to the Mazda MX5 sports car.

Another mistake international managers make is to segment an overseas market in the same way as their own domestic market. Hofstede et al. (1999) suggest that the world market should be segmented holistically. The Mazda MX5 is a good example of this, as it was designed to appeal to the sports car segment in every market, unlike the Suzuki Cappuccino, which was a micro-sports car for the Japanese market alone. As a method of analysis the authors also recommend the **means–end approach**, an in-depth evaluation of the personal values that motivate the consumer's choice. Although there is good empirical support for its validity, it is a very resource-intensive method that is only suitable for a large-scale market entry.

When it comes to emerging economies the market may not be ready for segmentation because the market itself may barely exist. This means a form of **market making**, where the seller is almost constructing the consumer, shaping their demand in terms of the intended offer (Araujo, 2007). This activity generally exists only at the margins of the established markets of the developed world, such as in the financial markets or when a wholly new product is released into consumer markets. In developing economies the entire market may have to be built from the foundations up.

As a consequence, making a market in an emerging economy is a highly involved process. The Finnish mobile phone manufacturer Nokia has been on the back foot in Western markets recently, but in Africa it established its dominance from the beginning. Despite the entry of fierce competition from Apple and

Samsung in smartphone products, which have been hugely successful elsewhere in the world, Nokia continues to hold onto more than 50% of the African market (Telecoms.com, 2014). By establishing its position in the market early Nokia was able to take a defining position, one by which all rivals are then judged.

The opportunity to make the market in an emerging economy brings with it the potential for local dominance, even a monopoly. A number of companies have enjoyed these powers over the years, such as VW in Brazil, Shell in Nigeria and De Beers in Botswana, through its Debswana joint venture with the government. Emerging economies will tolerate such dominance in key industries, Botswana being a notable beneficiary of diamond industry revenues. However, it can also suppress the growth of indigenous industries. It may be hard to imagine now, but before World War II Ford and GM had the Japanese market to themselves: it was only the extreme political backlash that expelled them from the country and permitted Toyota et al. to flourish.

RAISING EMPLOYABILITY: THE VALUE OF EXPERIENCE

The evaluation of market opportunities is one of the core elements of a manager's job description. It demands a blend of academic ability and experience, the proportions of each dependent on the nature of the opportunity. Academic skills, though, are taught in class, while experience is a function of length of service and learning from real life. In business, academic skills and experience can compensate for each other: longer service for a lower ability to learn, or faster learning can compensate for a shorter length of service. What is certain is that the years in a senior position do not by themselves allow the manager to claim that valuable attribute they call 'business acumen'.

Used wisely, experience brings depth to the critical analysis. When companies are considering entering new overseas markets the local conditions are far too complex for theoretical analysis alone, and so time must be spent learning by experience (Johanson and Vahlne, 2003). To an extent, previous experience can be used but the need to treat the new market as novel and risky should not be underestimated. Experience is therefore dynamic, systematically destroying and creating knowledge over time.

According to Kolb's Experiential Learning Theory (ELT), for professionals learning is a continuous cycle of a real event, reflection, conceptualisation, experimentation and then back to real events again (Kolb and Kolb, 2012). Naturally, experience grows with time served, which means that there is always a role for the old lions in the corporate pride. However, it would be wrong to assume that experiences cannot be compressed into a shorter time frame. Careful career planning can accelerate the learning process with ambitious managers lining up a sequence of different jobs, overseas appointments and periodic returns to academia.

On the other hand, companies may delude themselves on the time value of experience, leading to a time-serving mentality where seniority comes to those that hang on in a job for the longest. Japanese corporations are not alone in their notoriety for promoting managers based on age rather than the quality of experience. At the extreme this can lead to *amakudari*, or 'descent from heaven', a revolving door of senior managers retiring from business only to enter the civil service as regulators of the very industry they have just left. This creates a cosy relationship between corporations and the government which has been blamed for nurturing a culture of complacency, possibly with occasional catastrophic results (Aldrich, 2011).

Those managers who have yet to enjoy the fruits of experience must rely on their inherent aptitude for critical analysis. These are the young hot shots, fresh from academic study and hungry for rapid advancement. This can become a source of friction in the corporation, as those managers with experience feel the threat of the upstarts. Both groups represent valuable human resources, but their contrasting talents demand careful handling.

Many international companies will structure the early years of the young management acolytes to take them around a variety of positions at home and overseas. This puts their critical faculties to work whilst exposing them to new experiences. The experiential learning can be accelerated by having these young pups of the organisation learn business tricks from the old dogs, those managers who have accumulated a vast store of experience. Through mentoring this experience can be passed on, and there are many institutions, both public and private, that will facilitate this process. One such is the US-based Management Mentors (2015), a consultancy that will help a corporation to establish its own network of mentors. Another organisation, Venture Capital for Africa (VC4A, 2015), holds a freely accessible contact list of experienced executives to provide advice on investments in the continent.

Analogous to the market positioning of products, managers balance experience and academic learning to position themselves in their careers. Just as products must evolve in the market, so must managers evolve and develop in their careers. If not, then they risk exceeding their sell-by-dates and end up collecting dust on the corporate shelf.

THE STORY SO FAR: MOVING INTO POSITION

Market analysis is where the sense of competition in business starts to make itself known. Any established producer, of goods or services, will jealously guard their position in the market from existing rivals and new entrants. The trouble is that the market is not a physical entity, so any position in it is essentially theoretical; it depends entirely on how the market is defined. Since the market can be defined in a multitude of ways, from demographics to fashion, a rival can analyse the market in a novel way that reveals a new opportunity.

However, it is risky to venture into unexplored parts of the market, so companies tend to cluster around nodes of recognised consumer demand, known as market segments. That way they can safeguard their established processes and strategies, focusing their competitive efforts on evolving their products and services. Only rarely does a completely novel innovation occupy a new segment. Most stable of all is the niche, a mini-segment usually occupied by low-scale, highly differentiated premium brands.

Globalisation has opened up a range of new market opportunities. In particular, emerging markets require market position analysis from first principles but the result can be the chance for the interested company to be a market maker. Such a firm can hold a dominant position over the whole market before later competitors can segment the market to suit themselves. Whatever the market, correct positioning can bring the company the highest rewards, but the complexity of the challenge will test the most skilled of managers.

 ## WEB SUPPORT

1. It always helps if you can express exactly what your positioning intentions are. A blog by Doug Stayman at eCornell sets out a format for a positioning statement, plus some useful links.

   www.blog.ecornell.com/how-to-write-market-positioning-statements/

2. Another blog, this time from Sherice Jacob at Kissmetrics.com, on how incorrect positioning decisions can lead to disaster.

   www.blog.kissmetrics.com/branding-failures/

3. Smarta.com have an interesting guide on their website for those worried that they might lack the experience for starting a business. It is particularly reassuring to learn that experience can be found anywhere in your life, not just while working in business.

   www.smarta.com/advice/starting-up/starting-your-own-business/how-important-is-business-experience/

Project Topics

1. Select a country and then segment its wine market according to different factors, e.g. demographics, income and culture. How does the method of segmentation reveal different opportunities in the market?
2. For decades, inventors and entrepreneurs have been striving to fill the gap in the market between cars and airplanes: the flying car. How attractive do you think this vacant market segment is?
3. Conduct an analysis of the tobacco industry in a country of your choice using the Five Forces Model. How would you include the role of the government in your analysis?

 ## CASE STUDY: BLACKBERRY SEEKS SALVATION IN EMERGING MARKETS

How the mighty have fallen. When the Canadian company Research in Motion (RIM) launched its BlackBerry smartphone it was not the first into the market; predictably, the Japanese had been early adopters, but the BlackBerry found its success in the vast North American market.

With a background in pagers and mobile email devices, RMI was able to install on the BlackBerry the kind of functions that are crucial to the manager on the move. Launched in 2003, the new smartphone had a miniature QWERTY keyboard, just like the laptop in the office, and secure access to corporate email systems. Not only did this mean that no manager need feel out of contact but also since email itself was in its infancy the kudos attached to having it on one's phone was considerable. By 2006 the BlackBerry had attracted 5 million subscribers, although in truth it was not dominating the market as a whole, only the business user segment. This meant that the product was surrounded by substitutes and potential new entrants in the wider industry.

In 2007 a battleship appeared on the smartphone horizon: Apple launched the iPhone. RIM held firm to their faith in the separate keyboard, while the iPhone boasted a touchscreen interface. For a while, RIM were vindicated, enjoying a 19.5% global smartphone market share in 2008 to the iPhone's 10.5% share. A year later growth of the BlackBerry had slowed, with a 20.7% peak global market share but the iPhone was advancing strongly and now the Android operating system had entered the market. This new system prised the market open to a multitude of new entrants, while RIM was beset by controversial failures in its service and lacklustre product innovation.

The company attempted to revive its fortunes in 2012 with a new CEO and mass layoffs of staff. To revitalise the brand the company even tried changing its name from RIM to BlackBerry, but by the end of 2014 the global market share was down to 0.5%. Taking the worldwide market as a whole the demise of BlackBerry seemed inevitable.

Yet it could be argued that there is no such thing as a worldwide market, despite the advance of globalisation. There are still highly varied, individual markets around the world, and while BlackBerry might have been pushed out of the developed economies, there is still potential in the developing nations. One such is Nigeria.

Although Nigeria has a great deal of oil wealth it still suffers from many of the income inequality and public infrastructure problems of other developing economies. To circumvent the poor telecommunications provision there is high demand for mobile phones. Furthermore, consumers require their phones to offer secure access to the internet in a country where connectivity is far below developed economy standards. A dedicated BlackBerry smartphone, with a slightly lower specification to reduce the price, found ready acceptance in the Nigerian market. It even enjoys the aspirational status it once had in the developed markets.

There is, of course, no escape from the iPhone's relentless invasion of all markets around the world, but BlackBerry has a firm foothold in other developing markets, such as Ghana and Kenya. By analysing them as markets in their own right, rather than as extensions of a uniform global market, BlackBerry has a chance to stake out a new presence for itself.

Point of consideration: Some emerging economies are highly receptive to the capabilities offered by smartphones, such as online retail, business-to-business (B2B) transactions and internet banking. How can BlackBerry serve these markets better than its rivals, heading off the threats from new entrants and substitutes?

Sources: Guardian, 2012; InvestorPlace, 2013

 MULTIPLE CHOICE QUESTIONS

1. The following is **not** an example of a market:
    a. Transfer pricing, where divisions within a corporation charge each other for goods and services.
    b. A local youth group offering to do odd jobs in the local neighbourhood in return for charitable donations.
    c. Defence contractors tendering for government contracts by submitting sealed bids.

2. Perfect markets do not exist because:
    a. Consumers are irrational and imperfect.
    b. Technological advances lead to new products.
    c. It is not possible for everyone to know everything at the same time.

3. When do consumers enjoy the power in the market?
    a. When they are relatively high in number.
    b. When they are relatively few in number.
    c. When they equal the number of sellers.

4. How can suppliers increase their power in the market?
    a. Grouping together to form syndicates.
    b. Introducing new product lines.
    c. Lowering prices of existing product lines.

5. What would be a substitute for an online social network like Facebook?
    a. Another social network, such as Twitter.
    b. Better use of time, such as healthy exercise.
    c. A return to writing real letters.

6. Which is a feature of a real market?
   a. A temporary competitive advantage for new products.
   b. Zero exit and entry barriers.
   c. Constant returns to scale, i.e. no economies of scale.

7. Why do market segments exist?
   a. Products are designed to fulfil specific purposes.
   b. They don't; they are a marketing expedient.
   c. Products compete with each other based on common features.

8. How are niches different to segments?
   a. The products in niches are very small.
   b. Niches often contain a few, very similar products.
   c. Product prices in niches are much higher than for segments.

9. What is the value of a World Cup final ticket officially priced at US$250?
   a. More than US$250 if it is going to sell.
   b. Equal to US$250 because that is the law.
   c. Less than US$250 because the ticket issuer can charge a high price.

10. Few brands are positioned in the low value-high price segment of their respective markets because:
   a. Only the rich can afford the high price.
   b. The sales volumes would not be economically viable.
   c. It would be irrational for any consumer to buy.

Answers
1a, 2c, 3b, 4a, 5c, 6a, 7b, 8b, 9a, 10c

REFERENCES

Aldrich D P (2011) 'Future fission: why Japan won't abandon nuclear power' *Global Asia*, 6(2), pp. 62–67

Araujo L (2007) 'Markets, market-making and marketing' *Marketing Theory*, 7, pp. 211–226

Baron D P (1995) 'Integrated strategy: market and nonmarket components' *California Management Review;* Winter 1995, 37(2), pp. 47–65

Benton W C and Maloni M (2005) 'The influence of power driven buyer/seller relationships on supply chain satisfaction' *Journal of Operations Management*, 23(1), pp. 1–22

Burgelman R and Grove A (2007) 'Let chaos reign, then rein in chaos—repeatedly: managing strategic dynamics for corporate longevity' *Strategic Management Journal.* Oct 2007, 28(10), pp. 965–979

Bulova (2014) Bulova from www.bulova.com/en_us accessed 2 August 2014

Coyne K P and Subramaniam S (1996) 'Bringing discipline to strategy' *McKinsey Quarterly.* 4, pp. 14–25

Crook T R and Combs J G (2007) 'Sources and consequences of bargaining power in supply chains' *Journal of Operations Management*, 25(2), pp. 546–555

Dolnicara S (2002) 'A review of data-driven market segmentation' *Tourism in Journal of Travel & Tourism Marketing*, 12(1), 2002, pp. 1–22

Dickson P R and Ginter J L (1987) 'Market segmentation, product differentiation, and marketing strategy' *Journal of Marketing,* 51(2) (Apr., 1987), pp. 1–10

Goodman A C and Thibodeaub T G (2003) 'Housing market segmentation and hedonic prediction accuracy' *Journal of Housing Economics* 12(3), September 2003, pp. 181–201

Grigore A-M (2014) 'Book publishing business in Romania – an analysis from the perspective of Porter's Five Force Model' *Review of International Comparative Management* 15(1), March 2014, pp. 31–47

Guardian (2013) 'Nigeria's BlackBerry addiction offers hope for Research in Motion' *Guardian* 15 November 2012 by Monica Mark from www.theguardian.com/technology/2012/nov/14/blackberry-nigeria-status-symbol accessed 5 February 2013

Harper D (ed.) (2014) *2015 North American coins & prices, 24th edition: A Guide to U.S., Canadian and Mexican Coins.* Fairfield, OH: Krause Publications

Hofstede F T, Steenkamp J-B E M and Wedel M (1999) 'International market segmentation based on consumer-product relations' *Journal of Marketing Research (JMR),* Feb 1999, 36(1), pp. 1–17

InvestorPlace (2013) 'Brief History of Research In Motion' from *InvestorPlace* Jan 29 2013 by Brad Moon from www.investorplace.com/2013/01/a-brief-history-of-research-in-motion/#.VNM9VqPyFi4 accessed 5 February 2015

Jang S (2004) 'Mitigating tourism seasonality: a quantitative approach' *Annals of Tourism Research,* 31(4), October 2004, pp. 819–836

Johanson J and Vahlne J E (2003) 'Business relationship learning and commitment in the internationalization process' *Journal of International Entrepreneurship,* 1(1), pp. 83–101

Kolb A Y and Kolb D A (2012) 'Experiential learning theory' in *Encyclopedia of the sciences of learning* (pp. 1215–1219). New York: Springer US

Kuo R J, Ho L M and Hu C M (2002) 'Integration of self-organizing feature map and K-means algorithm for market segmentation' *Computers and Operations Research,* 29(11), September 2002, pp. 1475–1493

Lawtona T C and Solomkob S (2005) 'When being the lowest cost is not enough: building a successful low-fare airline business model in Asia' *Journal of Air Transport Management,* 11(6), November 2005, pp. 355–362

Management Mentors (2015) homepage from www.management-mentors.com/ accessed 9 June 2015

Nalebuff B J and Brandenburger A M (1996) *Co-opetition.* London: HarperCollins Business

NYSE (2014) Rules from www.nyserules.nyse.com/nysetools/PlatformViewer.asp?SelectedNode=chp_1_2&manual=/nyse/rules/nyse-rules/ accessed 28 July 2014

Observer (2012) 'Youssou N'Dour: the singer who changed his tune' *The Observer,* 8 January 2012 by David Smith from www.theguardian.com/theobserver/2012/jan/08/observer-profile-youssou-ndour accessed 11 February 2015

Papatheodorou A (2006) 'Liberalisation and deregulation for tourism: implications for competition' in Buhalis D and Costa C (eds.) (2006) *Tourism management dynamics.* Oxford: Elsevier Butterworth-Heinemann

Porter M E (2008) 'The five competitive forces that shape strategy' *Harvard Business Review,* January 2008, pp. 25–41

Roberts R (2005) 'The reality of markets' from Library of Economics and Liberty featured article 5 September 2005 www.econlib.org/library/Columns/y2005/Robertsmarkets.html accessed 25 July 2014

Smith W R (1956) 'Product differentiation and market segmentation as alternative marketing strategies' *Journal of Marketing,* 21(1), (Jul., 1956), pp. 3–8

South African Mint Company (2014) Krugerrand Series from www.samint.co.za/%202012%20Coins/Krugerrand%20Series.aspx accessed 30 July 2014

Stiglitz J E (1987) 'Competition and the number of firms in a market: are duopolies more competitive than atomistic markets' *Journal of Political Economy*, Oct 1987, 95(5), pp. 1041–1061

Telecoms.com (2014) 'Africa gets smart: continent prepares for device revolution' *Telecoms.com* 09 January 2014 by Sahota D from www.telecoms.com/opinion/africa-gets-smart-continent-prepares-for-device-revolution/ accessed 12 February 2015

Time (2007) 'Youssou N'Dour' *Time* May 03, 2007 By Peter Gabriel from www.content.time.com/time/specials/2007/time100/article/0,28804,1595326_1595332_1615978,00.html accessed 11 February 2015

VC4A (2015) Venture Capital for Africa: Mentor Matching from www.vc4africa.biz/mentors accessed 9 June 2015

World Bank (2014) Pump price for gasoline (US$ per liter) from www.data.worldbank.org/indicator/EP.PMP.SGAS.CD accessed 31 July 2014

5 International Market Entry

Chapter Objectives

On the face of it the decision to enter a new market might seem to be a simple matter of evaluating the expected volume of demand and meeting that through production, product design and marketing. For international markets, though, companies can decide on their level of commitment according to the risks they perceive and the overall corporate strategy. In this chapter, we will be looking at:

- Whether to venture abroad at all or stay secure within the established domestic market.
- What new skills and knowledge are demanded by the new market.
- Assessing how to enter the market: blanketing the new market with the full range of products and services or, more tentatively, with a sample of the company's offerings.

DOMESTIC, GOING-ON INTERNATIONAL

This is the point at which the company transforms itself from being a purely domestic enterprise to one that operates in the international environment. The effect this has on the company may not be immediately obvious to outside observers but it can induce subtle changes on the company at every level. It is almost as if the company is being founded all over again. At its first foundation it was a purely domestic company and it had to find its way in a complex commercial world. Each corporate function needed to be configured for optimum effectiveness and all the functions needed to work together as a team. Ultimately, the company needed to have demonstrated its ability to deliver maximum value to the customer at minimum cost to itself.

A company that is launching itself into the international arena is likely to have proved itself in the domestic market. It may not be the domestic market leader but it should be one of the leading players. Occasionally, smaller firms are obliged to break out of a mature domestic market and seek growth amongst the international opportunities but these cases are rare. Rather, it is the larger firms that explore the new markets because the additional risks to them are proportionately lower relative to their existing home market strength than for small firms. If the overseas opportunities do not work out, then larger firms can continue to rely on their domestic market.

For these domestic market leaders, there are a number of reasons why the managers may feel it is time to look beyond the domestic scene:

1. The growth imperative
2. Efficiency imperative
3. Knowledge imperative

4. Globalisation of customers
5. Globalisation of competitors.

We will now look at each of these in more detail.

1. THE GROWTH IMPERATIVE

An increase in the size of a company seems an obvious sign of its success. If a company is expanding then its profits must be increasing and the owners getting richer. This seems simple enough to understand, and indeed most stakeholders would be suitably impressed by a company that is getting bigger. It is not only shareholders who require growth; debt also creates a pressure for the company to expand because the repayments are usually a fixed cost, so any additional revenues beyond that cost accrue to the company alone. There are also economic reasons for growth: if the economy is growing, which it should be, then in aggregate industry should be growing as well (Binswanger, 2009).

A wise manager, however, should not be swayed by growth alone. Just look at this for a moment. Let us say that if a company expands its output by 20% we would expect bottom-line profits to increase as well. If profits increased by 20% in step with output then we might argue, all other things being equal, that the company is right back where it started; the profit per unit produced has not changed. If profits do not go up faster than the growth of the company then it was hardly worth the bother. Furthermore, if profits grow at a slower rate than the rate of expansion then the company is actually worse off than before since the profit per unit produced has gone down. Even if profits grow faster than the rate of expansion the growth strategy is still not vindicated since risk will also have increased. If the risk is increasing then it must be offset by an increase in the rate of return.

Increases in production volume might be implied by the **product life cycle (PLC)**. When a product has been recently introduced volumes and profits will be low and marketing costs will be high, relatively speaking. With potential demand in the market still unsatisfied production will need to rise (Golder and Tellis, 2004). As it does so the marketing costs will become smaller in relation to sales revenues. Effectively, the company is growing in order to achieve its potential in the market, including those markets that are overseas. However, the PLC model only directs this growth to cover one product; there are no guarantees that this production capacity will be required for the next product.

Although we have dismissed the need to expand simply to impress the various stakeholders we should not underestimate the need to provide opportunities for dynamic managers. A company selling a mature product into a mature market can appear to be a pretty unexciting prospect for an ambitious manager. To attract and retain top talent the company may find it is obliged to explore international business opportunities. The risk of operating overseas must then be compensated for by improved performance in the mature markets: a kind of market conquest that only the best managers will be able to achieve. It is under these circumstances that a company can find itself embarking on an expansionist strategy when caution should have prevailed.

2. EFFICIENCY IMPERATIVE

So growth is not, by itself, a sign of success since the additional risk to the company of expanding out of its current market position must be compensated for by increased returns. However, if the growth in output is achieved by using up spare capacity in the company's existing production facilities then the risks are sharply reduced. Although the additional sales, either at home or abroad, do introduce their own market risks at least in production no new fixed costs have been incurred. The attractiveness of exports, then, is that the international sales help to utilise existing domestic production capacity.

For smaller firms, simply filling idle capacity may not be enough. They could be in the predicament of being too small to enjoy the kinds of **economies of scale** that are being accessed by larger competitors. With a persistent cost disadvantage the smaller firm must either accept long-term decline or grow to a point where economies of scale are within its grasp. Fortunately, the economies of scale may be accessible to the firm externally via the supply chain, so small firms may be sustainable as long as their suppliers grow to the extent of economies of scale (Henderson, 2003).

For both service and manufacturing companies a climb to economies of scale means investment in new, higher capacity facilities. This can be particularly costly in manufacturing where an existing plant has to be replaced with a larger one. This involves careful planning since the two plants will have to operate alongside each other as production at one is ramped up while the other goes into a managed decline. If the small firm is at a substantial scale disadvantage where it does not have the time to construct the larger plants that can offer optimum output levels then it may have to seek some kind of strategic alliance.

 ## CASE STUDY – BMW'S MINI AMBITIONS

The original Mini was a British small car introduced in 1959. Its diminutive proportions were cleverly packaged to create a surprising amount of interior space, enough for four adults even. It was also highly entertaining to drive, and all this came at a very reasonable price. Indeed, the price was possibly too generous to the customer because the company, the British Motor Corporation (BMC), made very little profit with it. At such a low price it was imperative that production was kept high in order to benefit from the economies of scale. Output exceeded 300,000 units in the early 1970s but that was still not enough for the company to justify further investment. The model changed only in detail over the years, and sales declined year-on-year until the British icon faded away in 2000.

In its latter years the Mini had come under the ownership of BMW. With access to far greater investment funds than BMC or its successors, BMW was able to devise a new Mini that completely refashioned the model. The new car was dubbed the MINI One, and with styling that paid homage to the original but with a much larger body and an emphasis on sportiness the model was priced for profit. BMW invested around £230 million in production capacity at its Oxford plant specific to the new car. The company expected the model to enjoy niche market success with around 100,000 units per annum. Not only was the company pleasantly surprised by the demand, it was positively embarrassed.

The new MINI One became an instant hit on global car markets. Production exceeded the planned output from the start, and although the plant had been designed to cope with higher demand if necessary it soon became clear that further growth in capacity would be needed. Another £100 million was spent expanding the plant without hindering continuing production. It was almost as if a new plant was being built around the old one even as production carried on unabated. Since 2000 a total of £1.75 billion has been invested in its production sites in the UK, most of it for the MINI.

On the face of it, growth of this magnitude seems the very epitome of success. Yet it has also been a very expensive experience for BMW. Constantly having to expand facilities beyond their intended output volumes has meant having to effectively rebuild the Oxford plant. Not only that, assembly has also had to be contracted out to two other firms. If the Oxford plant had been designed for 300,000 units per annum from the beginning then the company would be enjoying the full benefits of economies of scale. As it is, the profitability of the model has been dragged down by the failure to properly forecast demand.

Point of consideration: In terms of sales the MINI has been highly successful but do you think the growth in production volume is also a kind of failure? How could BMW have planned more wisely?

Sources: Automotive Intelligence (2000), BBC (2005), BMW (2014)

3. KNOWLEDGE IMPERATIVE

Innovation can occur anywhere in the world, and globalisation has made those advances highly accessible. It is becoming increasingly common to find that companies will locate a product development facility overseas as a way of exposing itself to new ideas. This may not be the core **research and development (R&D)** facility but an offshoot: a low risk dip of the corporate toe in foreign waters. It can involve tie-ups with university research departments and consulting agencies with a view to exploring the outer limits of current knowledge rather than the development of specific products. Mergers and acquisitions (M&A) with established operations is another approach and one that has been found to be effective in the pharmaceutical industry (Bollen et al., 2005).

The search for **knowledge** is not restricted to research of new products; it can also include the exploration of markets that are subtly different to the home market. The experience gained can then inform marketing strategies elsewhere. The company might choose a very competitive market in order to test its strategies in the extreme heat of the toughest environment. Alternatively, it may choose a very small market, almost as an experiment in marketing its products, before rolling out the product range in a much larger market.

To a certain extent, companies will establish overseas manufacturing with the purpose of discovering what production advantages may exist there. However, such facilities require a high level of commitment. They can be several years in the planning, not only for the plant itself but also for the network of suppliers. There are also questions over the size of the plant. As an exploratory move one would expect the company to experiment with low-level rates of production that are relatively inefficient but less costly to shut down when the experiment is over. However, if the experiment is a success then the company must commit even more financial sums rebuilding the facility as a full-size plant that can benefit from the economies of scale. For this reason such approaches often involve joint ventures or less costly forms of production.

 ## CASE STUDY – HONDA MOTORCYCLES LEAD THE WAY

In the 1970s, Japanese car manufacturers seemed to be enjoying an unassailable advance into the markets of the world. It is not even as if they were doing anything particularly magical: the cars were reasonably well designed, affordable, reliable and pretty much met the needs of the customers. Oddly, though, put all these qualities together and Japanese cars were in the vanguard of the industry. American cars were heavy on fuel, British cars were famously unreliable, German cars were expensive and rather austere. French and Italian cars had design flair but, like their British cousins, were often an uncertain ownership prospect. Japanese cars simply did everything that was required of them and as a consequence sales rose inexorably year after year.

Japanese managers were worried, though. It was not as if there was a great secret to their success and they wondered why their overseas rivals were not quickly adapting the same approaches to car design and production. Most of all, the Japanese executives wondered if their advantage was an inherent part of their culture. While they were manufacturing and exporting from Japan this was a positive advantage, but it meant that production overseas would be highly risky. If British workers could not make their own cars properly, how could they be trusted to work for Japanese companies with any greater attention to detail?

The Japanese response was to trial small-scale production and analyse the experience. Honda was lucky in this respect. As a latecomer to the car industry it had already built up a substantial presence in the motorcycle industry. The financial commitment for production plants is much lower than in the car industry, so the company was able to test production conditions in different countries. In Thailand, motorcycle production began in 1965 and was not joined by car assembly until 2000. In Europe, Italy was the test bed, motorcycle production starting in 1971 and car assembly in the UK in 1985.

Other Japanese manufacturers have been equally tentative in their own ways of internationalising. Toyota established a joint venture with GM at NUUMI plant in California in 1984. Mitsubishi has tended to license production to local companies. Without exception, the Japanese companies found that their production methods were readily transferable.

Consideration point: Imagine you are the CEO for a European beer brewing company and you wanted to expand your production to Africa in order to start sales in the region. In what country would you test out your strategy, how would you do it and what results would you expect?

Source: Honda, 2014

4. GLOBALISATION OF CUSTOMERS

Corporate managers may like to think that they are the masters of their own destinies but often they are pulled into markets due to consumer demand or the actions of their competitors. This is particularly prevalent in logistics, where global customers demand that one company handle the distribution of goods (Lemoine and Dagnæs, 2003). This has led to the rise of firms such as FedEx and Maersk.

When global markets offer similar sales opportunities to companies offering competing products then there is an obligation on them to enter those markets before their competitors do. If they fail to do this then not only will their competitors enter instead but the company's own home market will also come under attack from those competitors. Where once a company might have enjoyed a home advantage, perhaps through culture, language or local regulations, many markets now are effectively open to all competitors. For some products the world has become the home market.

CASE STUDY: ADAPTING TO LOCAL MARKETS

There are some products that lend themselves to global markets. There is essentially no difference between products sold in the home market and those sold overseas. Digital cameras are a good example of such items. You only have to observe tourists from around the world taking pictures to see that each nationality seems to have its own approach. The Japanese, to take one example, love to have a group of people clustering in front of the camera giving their ubiquitous peace sign and giving the international 'cheese' expression. For such photographers, innovations like face recognition software can be useful.

Yet this is not to say that one type of camera software would be unwelcome in other cultures. Face recognition may be useless for photographing scenery but even landscape photographers take pictures of people sometimes. Indeed, generally speaking the process of taking photographs is pretty much the same all over the world.

Japan has been a centre of camera design and production for several decades. The cameras themselves have long been internationalised, the dials showing western style numbers or internationally recognised symbols. Only the manual would need to be printed in a language appropriate to the market. Digital cameras, though, contain most of the user instructions internally, accessed via the screen on the back of the camera. By offering these instructions in a number of different languages the manufacturer no longer needs to publish a variety of different manuals. The same digital camera can be shipped to all markets; it is the customer who decides how it should be configured.

Other products are even more easily globalised, such as watches. Although there is more variation in time measurement than might be realised (China uses animal symbols, Ethiopia has its own calendar) the world has settled on a recognised 12/24 hour day using western numbers. Even high-class watchmakers like Omega can ship essentially the same product around the world, only going so far as to include a multi-language manual.

Globalisation of products has its limits, however. Food is a notable example, from the physical challenges of storing it during long freight journeys to the fact that it may not even be properly understood in its target market. Does anyone know how to prepare sea sponge?

Point of consideration: For your own country, try to think of a product that seems resistant to international sales. Now imagine you are a manager for a company that produces it: how would you market it overseas?

5. GLOBALISATION OF COMPETITORS

Eager to fill the globalising markets are the producers. Again, managers might like to think that it is they who decide which markets to enter, yet when the main competitors are rushing in then it would take a brave manager to resist the **peer pressure**. The most proactive of managers would want to enter the market first in order to enjoy **first-mover advantages**. This can mean setting the price and product expectations amongst customers in a way that best suit the specification of the company's own product. It can also mean that the company can grab the largest market share, leaving the remainder to the later arrivals.

The first mover may not have it all its own way. The second mover can observe any mistakes and enter the market with a revised strategy. In a sense, the first mover has done all the market research and it is the second mover that can act on it. Indeed, the first mover's only real advantage may be in the technology to which it has a legal claim, and even that advantage will soon attract rival developments. If the following companies can expand the market with their own products then the opportunities for profitability will not be diminished (Reid, 2000). Many companies, though, may be in such a hurry to enter the same market as a competitor that they fail to properly evaluate the opportunities. That peer pressure amongst managers to take their companies into new markets for fear of losing opportunities to rivals can sometimes be too hard to resist.

CASE STUDY – FORD AND GM RUSH INTO SWEDEN

Sweden is not a large country, with a population of just under 10 million people in 2013, providing homes for less than 300,000 cars that year. In better economic times, sales were higher but still not enough to sustain even one mass-market automotive company. Yet Sweden is also a wealthy country and has managed to sustain two car manufacturers, Saab and Volvo, plus their heavy truck operations, for many decades. The key to their survival has been their exports, which have allowed them to raise production levels somewhere near economic viability. However, from the 1980s full exposure to global competitors meant their independence was threatened.

Volvo was the first to succumb, Ford acquiring the car manufacturing side in 1999. For the next few years Ford progressively exerted its influence over its Swedish offshoot and new Volvos were heavily based on Ford's global vehicle architecture. Saab Automobile fell next, GM completing its ownership in 2000 when it purchased the 50% of the company it did not already own. Again, a progressive globalisation of Saab models began.

Despite the business logic of integrating the Swedish operations with those in the rest of the world, neither Ford nor GM was able to make much money out of their Swedish adventures. With a downturn in the economic cycle the two US corporations were more concerned with holding together their core operations. GM let go first, selling Saab to the exclusive Dutch sports car company Spyker in early 2010. Ford followed later in the year, moving Volvo on to Geely of China.

There is little evidence that the secret to success in the Swedish automobile industry has been recovered in the past few years. Spyker struggled on with Saab until the end of 2011 but with GM refusing to co-operate over intellectual property rights (IPR) Saab collapsed into bankruptcy. The company is now owned by the Chinese consortium NEVS, which is intending to manufacture electric vehicles, although little has emerged from the factory gates. Volvo has appeared to fare much better, but perhaps only because Geely has access to greater funding resources. It still suffers from low production output by global standards.

Point of consideration: Looking at Ford and GM's entry into the Swedish automobile industry, what do you think they were trying to achieve? Examine the reasons for their failure and suggest how NEVS and Geely might succeed where the US giants failed.

Source: Granstrand and Holgersson, 2013

LEARNING AND INTERNATIONAL MARKETS

We have seen the kinds of pressures on companies to enter foreign markets and the occasions when managers do not seem to be entirely in control. We now need to look at how managers can wrest control back so that they are once more directing the commercial advance of the company they command rather than reacting to external developments.

There are three kinds of capabilities that companies need to develop in order to successfully grapple with the international opportunities:

1. Learning about foreign markets
2. Learning about the management of foreign workforces
3. Learning how to develop foreign business units.

We will now look at each of these in turn.

1. LEARNING ABOUT FOREIGN MARKETS

A first step for a manager would be to engage in desk research, which means to gather data from all available sources without leaving the comfort of the office. In recent years this has been considerably aided by the availability of online data, much of it freely available. Nevertheless, it can be a challenge to interpret the data, and there is no real substitute for local knowledge. Even when the MNE is exposed to learning opportunities in overseas markets the transfer of that knowledge is dependent on the ability of the organisational structure to pass it on (Lord and Ranft, 2000). This has serious implications for international managers, who will then have to put the systems in place to ensure that local knowledge is disseminated throughout the organisation.

Many companies choose to engage international **consulting agencies** that have a worldwide perspective. They can advise, not just on the target country, but also any alternatives. There may be a bias towards making the investment so the client company will need to be cautious, but at least there should be much less of a specific country bias.

A company looking to invest overseas might also use the services of the broader **financial industry**. The financial industry is one that is suited to globalisation, and as a result banks are able to offer similar worldwide assistance as the consultancies. They often enjoy access to detailed local knowledge through their network of branches and experience based on a wide variety of clients. As before there will be a pro-investment bias in the advice given; after all, the bank hopes to make money on lending for the scheme, so managers would still need to exercise their own judgement.

Third-party agencies can be entirely sidestepped if the investing company forms a partnership with a local enterprise. A partnership offers a relatively low-risk and independent route to learning about a new location. The first step is usually for the company, or principal, to appoint a **local agent** to handle sales and marketing, sometimes in the form of a franchise. Using the agent's local knowledge, entry into the new market can be rapid. However, like all partnerships, it reduces the freedom for manoeuvre by the principal and it can become tied to the agent's own agenda. There have been cases where the local agent has wanted to take the company's products into market segments that are in contradiction to the company's global strategy. Given that the principal intends only to have a short- or medium-term relationship with the agent it is advisable to take a minority ownership of the agent (Puga and Trefler, 2010).

MYTH BUSTER: VW THE SHY MULTINATIONAL

It might be supposed that the industrial colossus we know today as VW would charge into any new market at full speed, offering all its available products and covering the entire country. Not quite so. In its early years after World War II it faced entrenched local competition. When the German car manufacturer VW first began to sell its quirky little cars in the UK it did so through a local importer. In 1957 this passed to the Thomas Tilling company, owner of the Stratstone group of dealerships, which had VW as one of its brands. At the time there were around 16,000 VWs on British roads, almost all of them the iconic Beetle.

In 1975 the import agency, now known as Volkswagen (GB) Ltd, had passed to the Lonhro Group. By now the Beetle was far too antiquated for sales in developed economies and the state-of-the-art Golf had replaced it, soon to be joined by the smaller Polo. Also gaining in popularity were the Audi range premium cars, a brand that VW had inherited in 1965.

Although Lonhro were instrumental in pushing VW and Audi to the forefront of the British car market, by 1992 VW was ready to take full control of the import agency. As the parent company has expanded its product portfolio the British unit now looks after Bugatti, Bentley, Seat, Skoda and Lamborghini in addition to the established VW and Audi brands. No longer a minority player in the market, VW brands now cover every segment.

The company has been similarly shy about entering other markets. It was happy to meet demand in Brazil with exports, a strategy that over the long term would have secured a small share of the local market and maintained production at the German factories. Instead, it was forced to invest in Brazilian assembly plants by a government looking for import substitution. Compelled to make the most of the obligation, VW then became the dominant brand of car in the country.

Point of consideration: At each stage in VW's British market growth, how do you think the role of the importer changed? Why did VW ultimately feel it had to take direct control?

Source: VW, 2014

2. LEARNING ABOUT FOREIGN WORKFORCES

Just as globalisation has dispelled some of the myths about a need to adapt products to each and every market, so we have come to learn more about differences in workforces. Notwithstanding the more obvious cultural variations around the world, when it comes to work most human beings apply themselves in similar ways. This does not mean that local idiosyncrasies should not be taken into account, but it does mean that with managerial flexibility they can be accommodated.

With workforces, local agencies are much less help; indeed they are themselves foreign workforces. There is no substitute for experience, but it is the high risk attached to commitment that puts off many corporations setting up operations overseas. A local partnership is often the key, and Japanese firms in particular have specialised in teaming up with local firms as a kind of bridgehead into the new location.

In some cases the local population may be resistant to incoming corporations who have chosen the location for their **foreign direct investment (FDI)**. Conflict can occur between the corporation and its new workforce to the extent that subsequent investment will be diverted to less troublesome regions. Governments are instrumental in these cases for smoothing the introduction of the international corporations (Menon and Sanyal, 2007). It is also worth pointing out that the increasing rates of labour migration mean that domestic corporations too will have to deal with international workforces on their own doorsteps in the home market.

3. LEARNING HOW TO DEVELOP FOREIGN BUSINESS UNITS

One might think that having established itself in the new location the company can breathe a sigh of relief. Sadly, as in all aspects of business, no company has this luxury. Whatever operations have been set up in the new location, from a basic sales outlet to a fully equipped new plant, the company will need to continue its learning about the many challenges and rewards of being there.

For managers this often means integrating the operations of the subsidiary into the overall global strategy. A great advantage for corporations is that globalisation goes a step beyond internationalisation by permitting an integration of the worldwide operation. The foreign location should not be seen as there simply to exploit local opportunities but additionally to contribute to the overall competitive advantage. Each location can then become a centre of excellence for particular core competencies.

 MANAGEMENT SPOTLIGHT: THE CORPORATE DNA

Senior managers encourage the idea that their corporations have characteristics as unique as those that define human beings as individuals. It is almost as if there is something inherent in the genetic makeup of the company, its DNA if you will, that sets it apart from other corporations. They point to the culture of the organisation and the way that people at all levels work together for the advancement of the company. While it is true that each company seem to have its own personality there is no evidence that it is better than its rivals. In a highly competitive industry each company may have its own style, but they are all converging on similar positions.

Precisely what constitutes **corporate DNA** is difficult to define, and if it were easy then companies would probably attempt to replicate each other. Nevertheless, sociologists have noted that any group of people will pool their individual personalities to arrive at a kind of group culture. In corporate society it is often derived from the most senior managers, the company founder most of all. GE under Jack Welch had a reputation for an aggressively meritocratic management style (Abetti, 2006), while rival aero engine manufacturer Rolls-Royce was always engineering-led, a characteristic perhaps derived from its founder, Henry Royce.

The challenge for international growth is not so much to achieve a better company character but to maintain consistency across the global spread of divisions. A failure to do this can mean that the different divisions end up speaking different languages, metaphorically as well as literally. The company needs to maintain the same style of approach in order for synergies to emerge between the different divisions. If a company has developed a management style involving consensus and corroboration, for one division to play the maverick with a more individualistic approach means that the division is effectively a standalone operation. It then loses some of the advantages of being part of a wider team.

In order to bring the international divisions into line with the corporate DNA the senior management need to effectively transmit their core beliefs and philosophy. This sometimes includes a mission statement, although this seems less fashionable than it was. This seems to have been replaced by more of a statement of attitude. For example, Google promises to avoid evil acts amongst other pledges. Taken as a corporate philosophy it helps to bind together the disparate parts of the business.

Point of consideration: Corporate DNA is the foundation of the company's culture. Critically analyse the ways in which the DNA can be established in a start-up or newly acquired business unit.
Source: Abetti, 2006

MANAGEMENT DECISIONS FOR MARKET ENTRY

A key difference between establishing a presence in an overseas market and that in the original home market is that the foreign excursion is being launched from an existing set of competencies. At its inception the company had to endure the birth pains of creating all the necessary functions of a company in a very short space of time. From production and marketing to accounting and human resources, all aspects of the firm need to be set up almost simultaneously. Once established, though, the firm can select the most suitable core competency to spearhead its assault on the overseas market.

There are five main areas of competency that an internationalising company can dip into, covering the following areas:

1. Choice of product
2. Choice of market
3. Choice of mode of entry
4. Directed and organic strategies for growth.

Taking each of these in turn we will see how the management team can use the corporate arsenal of competencies to its fullest effect.

1. CHOICE OF PRODUCT

Most firms start from some sort of domestic base with a portfolio of products that are already established in the home market. The entire portfolio does not have to be employed all at the same time, although this might be an option, and the company is free to enter the market with the product that suits the internationalisation strategy. The management team will have a number of questions they will be asking themselves:

- Should the firm globalize the entire portfolio, or use a subset?
  Usually a **product portfolio** reduces overall risk for the company because the fluctuations in demand and the effects of the **product life cycle** can be spread across different products. The risk attached to each product is unchanged, but if each product risk is balanced by another then the overall risk across the product range remains acceptably consistent and predictable. This may not be the case when entering a market with the entire product portfolio since they will all have product life cycles coinciding in that location. Effectively, they are all being launched as new products. Furthermore, if there are any problems with market positioning for one product then the effect is likely to exist across the range, amplifying the difficulties.
  A more likely local tactic is to enter with one product, perhaps the core or best known one, and use it to test the waters. If the product is not accepted then it can be withdrawn and revised for later re-entry without causing serious damage to the overall corporate strategy. An example of this was Toyota's entry into the US market in 1958 with the Crown. In contrast to the company's current enviable reputation, the Crown of that year soon revealed a set of surprising defects that rendered the model completely unsuited to the market. The model was improved and relaunched two years later to great effect, heralding the rise of Toyota as a major force in the industry (Toyota, 2014).

- To what extent does the product need adapting to local demand?
  Market demand varies from country to country, whether due to local tastes or regulations. It is often tempting to conclude that products need to be adapted to satisfy those local peculiarities. In fact, this is a wasteful and dangerous decision. Since the dawn of the industrial revolution the great advance of mass production and modern business methods has been to produce standardized products and for the company to convince disparate markets to accept them. Product adaptation adds cost, and as always in business this can only be justified if it adds value to the product the customer is willing to pay for. The maxim is quite simple: product adaptation should be kept to an absolute minimum.

- Does the product comply with local regulations?

  It is much more difficult to avoid product adaptation when it comes to regulations. For electrical products it is vital to match the local power supply: 240V in countries like Singapore and 110V in the United States, to take just two examples. Other products, though, may be granted exceptions if they are imported in small enough numbers.

  Many countries have vehicle type approval regulations that only apply to cars and trucks when they are imported in high enough volumes. Alternatively, governments may force adaptations on manufactures in the knowledge that it is adding cost, and therefore increasing the local selling price of the product, despite it providing no additional value to the customer. This kind of non-tariff barrier to free trade is one that the World Bank has been warning about for many years (Stephenson, 1997).

- What are the local competitor products?

  If the company is launching its products from a position of domestic strength then there will be a strong chance that it will be competitive in other markets as well. The nature of this competition might be quite different from that which was experienced at home and push the incoming product into an unfamiliar market segment. If the company is confident of future high-volume sales then it may try to compete on price, otherwise it may differentiate the product in pursuit of a low-volume, high-profit strategy.

  A market that might be considered one of the most competitive in the world would be sales of whisky in Scotland, the home of world famous Scotch whisky. Japan is also a production centre for whisky, though not on anything like the same sort of scale. One might expect that there would be little purpose in Japanese companies marketing their products to Scottish whisky drinkers but this is not the case. Connoisseurs of whisky enjoy broadening their palates by exploring rare brands. Japanese whiskies, thanks in part to careful study of the Scottish originals, have earned a high reputation for quality around the world. Although it is unlikely that companies like Suntory could ever compete in Scotland at the lower end of the market there is a steady and profitable demand for the company's finer offerings (Forbes, 2013).

2. CHOICE OF MARKET

In its original domestic market the company will have been pushing for a financially viable market share and, ultimately, economies of scale. If it can achieve economies of scale then no other company using the same production system will be able to beat it on cost, although it can achieve parity.

When the company internationalises it is able to be much more selective in all its operations, including the choice of market. This requires meticulous market research and the managers can evaluate the new market from two strategic perspectives:

- **Market potential**
- **Learning opportunities**

The market potential is no longer about the simple matter of expanding sales to a financially viable size but the way the market might fit with the company's overall strategic aims. The new market may have high strategic importance for a number of reasons. It may be a market that offers high demand for that product or is showing high rates of growth. Many western car manufacturers were falling over each other to enter the Chinese market in the 1990s when they first realised that the nascent demand had the potential for very high sales volumes in the future (Thun, 2008). Indeed, they have largely pushed the local competitors to the margins of the market so successful has their market entry been.

The market being entered is not necessarily the main point of interest, so a lack of potential may not be the flaw it might appear. The main strategic thrust might be for another market with similar characteristics but with much greater sales potential. The initial market is seen as a test case, or a learning opportunity, before taking the much greater risk of entering the larger market. Hong Kong is often used in this way by companies seeking a bridgehead into the Chinese market. The Chinese government is well aware of this, and even though Hong Kong returned to Chinese control in 1997 the central government has pledged to respect Hong Kong's political and economic structure. Many non-Chinese companies are reassured by this and have made the enclave the base for their investments in mainland China. There is also traffic in the opposite direction as Chinese companies use Hong Kong as the starting point for their foreign adventures (Zhang, 2005).

The company might also be attracted to a market because of the characteristics of the consumers. If these potential customers are sophisticated buyers then the learning experiences for the company can be tough but rewarding. The US market is one of the hottest retail markets in the world and most companies with international ambitions will have some sort of presence there. Even if it amounts to little more than a toe-hold in the market, the exposure to such fierce competition can help the company to become more competitive in other markets. In 2013, GM sold just 18 Buicks in the Japanese car market, a risible number by any view, but it is also a valuable source of practical market experience for the company (JAIA, 2014).

The strategic purpose of the market entry will then dictate the scale and pace of the entry process. This can range from an experimental dabbling to a progressive ramping up of market presence to a full-blown mass invasion. Alternatively, the company might decide to simply ignore the market altogether, although in the face of competitive pressure this can require as much courage from the management team as entering the market.

Ungson and Wong (2008) proposed a framework of four possible entry processes according to two dimensions. These dimensions rate the strategic importance of the market on one axis and the ability of the company to exploit that market on the other axis. Strategic importance is not just about the potential sales volumes; it can also include the importance of that market as a bridgehead to another market, the learning opportunities and other factors relevant to the internationalisation strategy. Then, whatever the importance of the market, the ability of the company to exploit it needs to be taken into account. Again this is a more complex issue that is about more than just the size of the company but also how effectively it can bring to bear its resources in the new location.

The framework suggests that there are four separate methods for entering a market:

- **Rapid entry** – the market is strategically important and the company can allocate the resources to make the most of the opportunities. There is no reason for the company to hang back, so it engages in a full-frontal invasion of the market before its rivals can respond with their own strategies. The company will control marketing activities directly and have a full distribution system in place.

   Globalisation of markets has now reached such an advanced form that there are few of strategic importance that have escaped the notice of the world's most capable corporations. Historically, though, corporations that have come to dominate their industries, such as Shell in oil and De Beers in diamonds, have been known to carry that power into new markets when they have appeared. Shell, for example, has a huge presence within Nigeria's oil industry (Shell, 2014).

- **Phased-in entry** – the market is an important part of the company's strategy, but it lacks the resources for rapid entry. Second-rank firms, those that cannot compete with the global giants, may have to enter even important markets in measured steps. The venture is relatively high risk for them due to their smaller size, so each progression needs to be secured before the next step can be taken.

   In the early 1980s it was clear that the Indian car market offered some tempting long-term growth opportunities. Local competition was manufacturing outdated designs under licence and often in low-technology plants. At that time Suzuki was a relatively minor Japanese car manufacturer and its first step into India was to license production of its small car, the Alto. With no serious rivals the car became a hit, and the company has since released a number of other models to complete a full range of products. Suzuki is now the controlling partner in the Indian operation (Nayak, 2005).

- **Opportunistic entry** – global corporations have the resources to enter almost any market they choose, particularly when they have already explored the most strategically important markets. Those remaining will have less importance, but a successful entry will still provide a welcome marginal increase in sales and revenue. A low-risk experiment is worth a small gamble.

  The British wine industry likes to claim a heritage going back to the Roman days, but the truth is that it is new, largely experimental and trades on consumer curiosity. This curiosity is strong enough for British wines to capture small-volume sales even in the wine-growing regions, particularly when the harvest in the UK has been relatively good (Daily Telegraph, 2014). There is little likelihood of serious market penetration.

- **Ignore for now** – despite the apparent pace of market globalisation there are still some that are not yet worth the risk of entering, particularly for companies that are less capable of exploiting what opportunities do exist.

  In the United States, micro-breweries, companies that brew traditional ales in small volumes, have collectively taken a significant share of the domestic beverage market. As part of an opportunistic strategy they have also opened sales channels in European countries. Samuel Adams is perhaps the most well-known but with most sales in the United States and just 20 overseas markets there are clearly many markets where it has yet to make its mark (Boston Beer, 2015). This is not to say they never will look at exports to these markets but have decided for the time being to cautiously avoid them.

3. CHOICE OF MODE OF ENTRY

When a company is born it must appear with all its vital functions in place. The product must be fully developed, the means of production prepared and the marketing strategy laid out. It is the necessity to co-ordinate these different functions all at the same time that makes the early years of a company so vulnerable. A slip up in any one area can bring the entire company crashing down.

To a certain extent the company's exposure to risk can be mitigated by outsourcing some of the functions. For manufactured goods the components can be bought in and for services the support operations have some scope for outsourcing. Nevertheless, the most important functions of the new company are integral to its strategy and form the heart of its operations. It is these that define the purpose of the new company being born in the first place.

Most companies do not internationalise until they have established themselves in the home location. When they do enter a new location they are not being born again and they do not have to reveal themselves in some fully functioning or vertically integrated form. Instead, they can select the functions that will spearhead the company's emergence in the new market.

Some commentators have put forward the idea of companies entering new markets in a series of stages. One of the more well known of these is the **Uppsala internationalisation process model** (Johanson and Vahlne, 1977, 2009). This is a stage model, arguing that due to the risk of entering new markets the ones that are closest to the home market, geographically or culturally, will be entered first. The authors argue that it is the markets that are close in the psychic sense that will be targeted first. This is known as **psychic proximity**.

The commitment to the market will be commensurate with the knowledge that the company has about that market. Of course, more knowledge will become available as local experience is gained, but the company can only act within the knowledge it has: this is known as **bounded rationality**. As the bounded rationality expands with new knowledge then the company can increase its commitment. Although this undermines the reliability of any legal contracts (Korobkin, 2003) going beyond the limits of the bounded rationality would take the company into an unknown territory where the risks are unknown and uncertainty rules.

As a result, a company will tend to enter a new location in four progressive steps:

1. Opportunistic exports
2. Export strategy using local agents
3. Control of the local operations
4. Local production facility.

If this seems to be a logical sequence then you are overestimating the chaotic world of business! The model might apply to a company that has never ventured outside its own national boundary before but even then much depends on company and location-specific factors. We have already seen how the nature of the product and the market will have a strong influence on the market entry decision. For firms that have an innovative product with indications of high potential demand in overseas markets the tentative stages of the Uppsala model are an open invitation to rival companies to leap ahead.

It is quite possible for firms to jump the stages of the Uppsala model, and some strategies, such as licensing and franchising, are difficult to place within the framework at all. The Uppsala researchers updated the stage theory in their later work (Johanson and Vahlne, 2009) to look at business relationships in terms of networks, accumulating knowledge as the relationship deepens. This seems to indicate that while it is reasonable for companies to progressively intensify their commitment to a market this does not mean that they all need to start and finish at the same place. It is more likely that managers will evaluate the market opportunities, cross reference these with the corporate competencies and then select the opening market entry mode from a palette of possibilities, like an artist choosing a colour for a painting. Figure 5.1 shows how a range of entry modes can suit local conditions and fit with the corporate strategy.

Mode of Entry	Local Conditions	Advantages	Disadvantages
Exporting	Low production efficiency, Generic demand, Low trade barriers, Uncertain local conditions	Swift market entry, Low risk, Scale benefits at home plant	Transport costs, Poor local learning, Lack of responsiveness
Licensing	High trade barriers, Cultural and political obstacles, Low technology product	Swift production entry, Use of existing structures	Risk of internal competition, Loss of control, Limited contract period
Alliances	High trade barriers, Cultural and political obstacles, Unique local conditions	Learning from competitor, Low investment costs	Risk of internal competition, Corporate culture conflicts
Foreign Direct Investment	High trade barriers, Poor local competition, High sales potential, Greenfield or acquisition feasible	First mover, IPR protected, High control in greenfield investment, Existing infrastructure in acquisition	High investment cost, Acquisition may meet cultural conflicts, Greenfield requires infrastructure

Figure 5.1 *Palette of entry modes*

Like the Uppsala model there is a sense of progression to the modes of entry, from exporting to foreign direct investment since each of them has a higher commitment to the new location. However, this is not how a manager would use the array of options. Instead, they would make a selection dependent on the factors specific to the firm and the entry conditions. Briefly looking at each one:

- **Exporting** – often seen as the lowest risk entry strategy since it may not involve much investment in new facilities. If the additional production volume for export is found in idle production capacity in the domestic location then it can even reduce unit costs. Exports are best suited to open markets that do not require much local adaptation or flexible responses to changing market conditions because the purpose here is to make full use of existing production capabilities.

  Exporting also implies rather lacklustre local competition. However, if the local rivals improve, or other foreign companies enter the market, then the exporter can find it difficult to respond quickly to the new conditions. The exporter will also be missing out on the benefits of learning about the specifics of the local market, although the importance of this depends on the market and the product.

- **Licensing** – as a low-commitment step into local manufacturing, licensing is an effective way of gaining a presence while avoiding the kinds of tariff and non-tariff barriers that can confront exporters to the country. If it is a way of evading trade barriers then it may not be the first choice of the company, exporting might have been preferable in theory but impossible in practice, thereby compelling the licence route to market entry. For companies where the advantage lies with intangibles, such as brand or service, then the hardware investment can be safely left to the licensee without necessarily putting the product at risk.

  Since the production capability already belongs to the licensee the mode of entry is often much quicker than setting up a wholly owned facility from scratch. However, the licensee may have their own agenda, ranging from a desire to fill a hole in their own product strategy to wanting to learn about the product technology for their own advantage. The foreign firm may be restricted in how it can develop its local presence beyond the confines of the licence agreement, and may even find that it is nurturing a potential future rival. As a safeguard, licensed production is often for low-technology or generic products.

- **Alliances** – similar to licensed production, alliances, which come in a number of different forms, are a way of gaining a local production presence without making the high-risk commitment of a wholly owned facility. Again, it can be a way of avoiding trade barriers but, if so, then the company is engaging in the alliance as a second best option. Perhaps it would have preferred the scale advantages of using existing production capacity at home for exporting but host country factors prevented it.

  An alliance is much more of a partnership of equals than licensed production. The two parties can learn from each other and new developments should bring mutual benefits. For this reason there is less likelihood of one partner extracting an unfair advantage to the disadvantage of the other. However, an alliance can still be constraining and both companies can find it difficult to terminate the partnership when their strategic needs change.

- **Foreign direct investment (FDI)** – the highest form of overseas commitment since it involves owning and managing an overseas facility. Even if the company might have preferred to take a more progressive line with its entry, as advocated by the Uppsala model, various factors may have obliged the company to jump to a fully functioning local presence. Trade barriers and other obstacles may make exporting unattractive, while the restrictions of licensed production and alliances may also be undesirable. It is quite common to find that firms need to invest in a country in order to gain political support for their presence there. Furthermore, economies of scale may have a crucial importance, particularly if the local competition is strong.

At least with this level of commitment the investing company is the master of its own destiny. It should be able to protect its own intellectual property and any other unique advantages it may hold. It can also act on its own strategies for the locality without having to compromise with a local partner or agent. Of course, this means that the company is entirely exposed to the risk of the investment. In the most extreme cases the political support may be inverted and the company's assets expropriated by the host country government.

The range of options shown in Figure 5.1 is a more realistic framework for managers than the Uppsala model because it acknowledges that corporate strategies are as varied as their competitive positions in the market. There is no single, prescribed route into a market and it is more important that the one chosen is aligned with the corporate strategy. We will now look at those different strategies.

4. ORGANIC AND DIRECTED INTERNATIONAL GROWTH

Growth is not simply about expanding the size of the company. Indeed, it is possible for a company to expand beyond the ability of its own resources. For example, the management team may not be qualified to run the enlarged company, or the expansion in facilities may take the company into diseconomies of scale. The growth we are talking about here is not a basic increase in corporate size but the extension of the company's structure into new locations. It is even possible that a subsequent restructuring could result in the company shrinking in terms of output or personnel employed if the international structure gives rise to greater efficiencies.

Wolcott and Lippitz (2007) distinguish between two types of growth, one being the kind of organic growth where the company expands by following a sequence of market opportunities, the other being growth directed by management with an **entrepreneurial** attitude. In essence, then, there are two types of corporate growth:

- Organic growth
- Directed growth.

Organic growth is less risky because it means following the demands of the company's own consumers. Existing product lines are renewed and production adjusted to meet the changing fortunes in the market place, the costs of any expansion being met using existing resources. This works very well when a company has a unique product in a fertile market. The product itself may not be especially innovative but, like Coca Cola for example, if it has a strong enough presence in the market then it can even enter new markets and capitalise on instant recognition.

A company like this is relatively self-contained, and growth does not mean that the company undergoes a character transformation with unfamiliar products or production. It also means that the company is dependent on its existing product line and so can be caught out when the market shifts to newer products. Wolcott and Lippitz (2007) point out that Sony had all the credentials for devising a miniaturised music player, given its track record with the Walkman range, but instead it was Apple that produced the innovative iPod.

Directed growth is pushed forward by management vision and is often ambitious and innovative. It may take the company beyond the mature markets or established product lines with which it has enjoyed stable fortunes. The management will be looking for growth by seeking out alliances, mergers and acquisitions. Any kind of alliance, including joint ventures, is a way of jumping on a fast-moving bandwagon. It means that the company can reach further along the economies of scale curve and, if the partner is a local one, immediately tap into local knowledge. The problem is that it can also act as a straitjacket, constraining further growth and development since any change must be agreed with the partner.

Wolcott and Lippitz (2007) take a slightly narrower view of directed growth by arguing for a corporate entrepreneurial attitude. The form this takes will be company-specific based on two dimensions:

- Decision-making authority – focused on a small group or diffused throughout the organisation.
- Funding authority – finances originating from a central source or by authority devolved to the local business unit.

Although the entrepreneurial spirit can drive a domestically based company into new and profitable markets, the problems are magnified for international companies. Yeung (2002) cautions that in overseas locations companies operate according to their own business systems as dictated by local ownership patterns, organisational structures, institutional authorities and employment conditions. The transnational entrepreneur is therefore one who can engage with and control the different national business systems confronting the MNE.

We can think of the transnational entrepreneur as being a development of the traditional homegrown variety. How then can an entrepreneur move from having a constrained, domestic purview to the global arena? Yeung puts forward three ways:

- Engaging with global managers and financiers
- Conducting international research
- Learning from educational institutions.

These approaches are of interest to MNEs as they attempt to nurture the same entrepreneurial attitudes in the management culture, turning managers into so-called **intrapreneurs**. The intended result is that managers leverage the internal resources of the company to direct growth towards new opportunities. If this is achieved then it will have combined the predictability of organic growth with the dynamism of international entrepreneurship. Perhaps Sony would have then invented the iPod.

 CASE STUDY – THE GOOGLE CORPORATE PHILOSOPHY

Google has around 70 offices located in 40 countries around the world. As a member of the knowledge industry it is very dependent on its people and so needs a clear philosophy to maintain the corporate DNA. The company states ten items which it claims to 'know to be true', to which brief explanations have been added:

1. Focus on the user and all else will follow.
    The company sets out to be customer-oriented.

2. It's best to do one thing really, really well.
    The company pledges to concentrate on its core competency as an internet search engine, although it has diversified into many other software and hardware products.

3. Fast is better than slow.
    Speed is a major source of competitive advantage.

4. Democracy on the web works.
    The company uses its customers as a resource and as the basis for its searches.

5. You don't need to be at your desk to need an answer.
    The company will actively pursue mobile technologies that can operate with its software.

6. You can make money without doing evil.
    In business this is a worthy but nebulous concept. Although the company has been often criticised for its dominant presence online, it does have stated principles in relation to advertisements:
    *   *They should be relevant and informative*
    *   *Text advertisements are less distracting to readers and more effective in attracting genuine interest*
    *   *Google will not be influenced by advertisers when conducting searches*

7. There's always more information out there.
    Google strives to improve its service. Similar to the Japanese concept of kaizen (continuous improvement).

8. The need for information crosses all borders.
    Google is global, not American.

9. You can be serious without a suit.
    The company projects a relaxed image.

10. Great just isn't good enough.
    See Item 7 above.

Point of consideration: To what extent can this philosophy be applied to other companies? Look at doing this for two case study companies, one similar in its operations to Google (e.g. Yahoo!) and the other quite different (e.g. a house builder).

Source: Google, 2014

RAISING EMPLOYABILITY: MARKET ENTRY THREAT TO EMERGING ECONOMY MANAGERS

Market entry strategies carry with them connotations of commercial imperialism: the invasion of vulnerable emerging economies by powerful developed economy MNEs. This perpetuates the advantages of those MNEs and further strengthens their management structures. The other side to this is that managers of companies in emerging markets are denied the opportunity to develop their own skills and raise their employability because of a national deficit in industrial experience.

University education is often seen as a way of leapfrogging the drawn-out process of learning by experience and instead raising the skills of the young so that they can more quickly take leading management positions in domestic companies. China, in one of its customary five-year plans, is investing US$250 billion a year in university-level education, with over 2400 colleges now established (New York Times, 2013). In some ways, though, this swaps the industrial experience deficit for an educational skills deficit, highlighting the shortage of suitably qualified teachers.

This can be addressed by having students educated overseas in the universities of those very countries that pose such a threat. Throughout Europe and North America business schools are continuing to expand thanks to the mass influx of students from emerging economies, most notably India and China. Often, though, they do not have visa permission to work locally and so lose out on gaining the practical knowledge that is such a vital element in employability. An alternative national strategy is to have the foreign university build branch campuses in the domestic market. Even North Korea is getting in on the act with its first foreign-funded university, the Pyongyang University of Science and Technology (YPF, 2015). Most of its faculty are from the United States, despite the deep political problems between the two countries.

Although the centrally funded schemes are headline news, and the vast numbers of students involved are certainly impressive, there is a lack of depth to management training in the industries of developing economies. The Indian giant Tata is a rare example of a corporation with an advanced programme for improving local skills, having a management training centre in Pune, near Mumbai. The centre works with the Harvard Business School and has its own journal for publishing research (TMTC, 2015). However, in a country as immense as India, to make a real impact on the national pool of management talent, such centres need to be the rule, not the exception.

Until developing economies can build up their business skills, whether through the creation of academic courses or the accumulation of relevant experience, they will continue to be dependent on wealthy countries for both these attributes. As with the mutual benefits of international trade, by raising business standards across all nations, in the long term all nations will benefit. Politically, though, wealthy countries are extremely parsimonious in handing out the work permits, even to business students who are expected to pay generously for the privilege of studying in the country in the first place. Countries like Canada and Australia, proud examples of immigrant success, have highly restrictive immigration rules based on points. Furthermore, the fact that these policies mean they cherry pick the best candidates only serves to further deny developing economies their brightest and best talents.

THE STORY SO FAR: DIP IN A TOE OR JUMP IN AT THE DEEP END?

Globalisation has prised open access to many new markets. Some of these have been long in existence and temptingly attractive, but hidden behind trade barriers; other new markets are economically less attractive but offer development potential. In either case it is not only the market possibilities that need evaluating but also the company's own ability to exploit those opportunities. Taking these into account, the next step for the management is to decide how it should enter the new market. It is fortunate in this regard since it has the domestic market as a foundation: the new market permits a range of strategies, from a tentative exploration with a limited product range to a full-blown invasion and a substantial local presence. For developing economies this is part of a reciprocal relationship, companies in both countries entering each other's markets. Developing economies are not so fortunate and the looming presence of foreign MNEs can threaten their own nascent industries. For them, the economic benefits can seem a very long way off.

WEB SUPPORT

1. Like French Champagne and Cuban cigars, there are some things best left to the countries that specialise in them. The finest whisky, of course, comes from Scotland. Well, perhaps also the United States. Then there are Canada, Ireland and Japan. And now Taiwan. Take a tour around the Kavalan website and devise an appropriate market entry strategy for a country of your choice.

   www.kavalanwhisky.com/en/

2. SsangYong Motor is South Korea's least known car manufacturer. It specialises in a range of low price SUVs and one luxury limousine. Severely lacking in economies of scale it has carved out a fairly stable, if small, niche for itself at the bottom of the global market for off-roaders. What to do with that luxury car, though? Check out the details and formulate a market entry plan somewhere in the world.

   www.smotor.com/en/index.html

3. Yahoo! was once one of the world's dominant internet search engines. Then Google upset the plans. Where did it all go so wrong for Yahoo! and so right for Google? Compare the two home pages and consider how Google managed to enter the market and wipe out the competition with such ease.

   www.us.yahoo.com/?p=us

   www.mygooglehomepage.com/United-States/

Project Topics

1. The benefits of international growth are often taken to be self-evident. Find a company that you believe has expanded too rapidly and analyse the mistakes that have been made.
2. The Japanese company Suntory has been making whiskey for nearly a century but has never produced it in Scotland, home of Scotch whisky. Had it done so what kind of knowledge would it have gained and how would the Japanese whiskey industry be different now?
3. The German supermarket chains Aldi and Lidl have gradually found success in a number of European countries. Using the framework for market entry (phased-in, rapid entry, opportunistic entry and ignore for now), how would you advise the companies to start operations in North America?

 CASE STUDY: INVITING MARKET ENTRY INTO EMERGING ECONOMIES

It is a harsh truth but emerging economies have little to offer the profit-hungry multinational enterprise (MNE). The rights of the investor are often poorly protected, the infrastructure is patchy, suppliers lacking and consumer spending is low. There may be few, if any, competitors in the field but then the market is barely definable at all. The incoming MNE will, in all likelihood, be perfectly capable of exploiting any opportunities; it is just that without specific demand data, current or predicted, the strategic importance of the market cannot be known.

The host country needs to prepare the ground for the nervous MNE by stimulating the latent demand. In Ethiopia the government has done this by allowing the establishment of a beer-brewing industry. Although beer is not consumed in Ethiopia at anything like the rate it is in Europe, other countries in the region, such as Kenya, show that there is no cultural obstacle to increasing its take-up.

In the ancient walled city of Harar, in the extreme east of the country, amongst the coffee roasters and the performing hyenas, the Ethiopian government built a brewery in 1984. Thanks to Czech hardware and knowhow, the brewery was able to produce a very creditable range of European-style beers. However, it has always been a challenge to obtain reliable supplies of malt barley and hops, as well as water, so they often have to be imported in order to maintain stable production.

In 2011 the government sold the Harar operation to the Heineken company for the sum of US$78 million. Another brewery, Bedele, in the west, was sold to Heineken at the same time for US$85 million. Together, the two breweries held 18% of the Ethiopian beer market. Yet Heineken was not interested in just taking a financial stake in the existing operations, it was clear that the company's senior managers had been satisfied that there was still plenty of untapped demand in the market. In 2013 they also pledged US$156 million for a large-scale brewery close to the capital, Addis Ababa. To support this expansion, assurances have been made for reliable supplies of malt barley.

With the UK firm Diageo also moving into the country with its purchase of the second biggest brand in the market, Meta, there seems to be a sudden tidal wave of interest where before there was only indifference. Yet by these companies pushing into a domestic brewing industry that could then stimulate market demand, the Ethiopian government was able to demonstrate the strategic importance of the market to the global industry's MNEs.

Point of consideration: To what extent has the Ethiopian brewing industry contributed to the country's economic growth? Would the government have been better stimulating a high-technology industry instead? You might want to make comparisons with similar stories from other developing economies.

Source: Financial Times, 2013

? MULTIPLE CHOICE QUESTIONS

1. Economies of scale mean that:
    a. Only the very largest companies will prosper.
    b. There is a theoretical size of plant that offers minimum production cost.
    c. A plant must produce at the rate of 120% of capacity in order to be competitive.

2. The best place for a corporation to find innovation is:
    a. Anywhere.
    b. In the R&D department.
    c. Where the staff are incentivised to innovate.

3. Globalisation means that customers are becoming the same around the world.
    a. False – demand is unique to each market.
    b. True – markets around the world are converging.
    c. Neither – humans have their basic needs and wants, but there will always be some local variation.

4. Why is first-mover advantage so important?
   a. The first mover in a market can charge a high price.
   b. The first mover defines the market segment.
   c. The first mover owns the intellectual property rights.

5. Do second movers ever catch up?
   a. No – they only react to the first mover's innovations.
   b. Yes – the first mover's products become old first, while the second mover has newer products.
   c. Sometimes – if the first mover makes mistakes the second mover can snatch the advantage.

6. What is the disadvantage of using local agents?
   a. They have no in depth understanding of the company or its products.
   b. They are working to their own advantage, not the company's.
   c. They have a short-term strategy.

7. Can local workforces be trusted to work as effectively as the home workforce?
   a. No – they lack the experience and the dedication.
   b. Yes – they are eager to work hard for lower pay.
   c. Certainly – it is a matter of training and good management.

8. How much should a product be adapted to the local market demand?
   a. As much as necessary.
   b. Not at all – global markets are converging.
   c. Absolute minimum – it is costly and should be avoided.

9. The only market worth entering is one that is strategically important.
   a. True – the market entry strategy should be aligned with the corporate strategy.
   b. False – markets can be explored opportunistically.
   c. Perhaps – if the company has high economies of scale then only strategically important markets matter.

10. Could you sell sand to the Arabs?
    a. Yes, because different grades of sand have specific uses, e.g. construction.
    b. No, they seem to have enough already.
    c. No, Arabian sand is the highest quality and can be used in all domestic applications.

Answers
1b, 2a, 3c, 4b, 5c, 6b, 7c, 8c, 9b, 10a

REFERENCES

Abetti P A (2006) 'Case study: Jack Welch's creative revolutionary transformation of General Electric and the Thermidorean reaction (1981–2004)' *Creativity and Innovation Management* 15(1), pp. 74–84, March 2006

Automotive Intelligence (2000) BMW Manufacturing Oxford Plant from www.autointell.com/european_companies/BMW/mini/oxford-plant/BMW-plant-oxford.htm accessed 4 August 2014

BBC (2005) BMW cash to fuel Mini production from www.news.bbc.co.uk/1/hi/business/4246215.stm accessed 4 August 2014

Binswanger M (2009) 'Is there a growth imperative in capitalist economies? A circular flow perspective' *Journal of Post Keynesian Economics* 31(4), pp. 707–727

BMW (2014) BMW Group to build new MINI Hatch also at VDL Nedcar from www.press.bmwgroup.com/global/pressDetail.html?title=bmw-group-to-build-new-mini-hatch-also-at-vdl-nedcar&outputChannelId=6&id=T0166729EN&left_menu_item=node__5247 accessed 4 August 2014

Bollen L, Vergauwen P and Schnieders S (2005) 'Linking intellectual capital and intellectual property to company performance' *Management Decision* 43(9), pp. 1161–1185

Boston Beer (2015) Investor relations: SEC filings from www.bostonbeer.com/phoenix.zhtml?c=69432&p=irol-sec accessed 1 September 2015

Daily Telegraph (2014) 'British vineyards could enjoy a better harvest than their French rivals' *Daily Telegraph* 11 July 2014 from www.telegraph.co.uk/foodanddrink/wine/10962844/British-vineyards-could-enjoy-a-better-harvest-than-their-French-rivals.html accessed 9 August 2014

Financial Times (2013) 'Heineken to build Ethiopia's biggest brewery' *Financial Times* 7 Mar 2013 by Irene Madongo from www.blogs.ft.com/beyond-brics/2013/03/07/heineken-to-build-ethiopias-biggest-beer-factory/ accessed 20 February 2015

Forbes (2013) 'Fine whiskey from Japan – the next big thing' by Larry Olmsted from www.forbes.com/sites/larryolmsted/2013/02/20/single-malt-whiskey-from-japan-the-next-big-thing/ accessed 9 August 2014

Golder P N and Tellis G J (2004) 'Growing, growing, gone: cascades, diffusion, and turning points in the product life cycle' in *Marketing Science* 23(2), pp. 207–218

Google (2014) Ten things that we know to be true from www.google.co.uk/about/company/philosophy/ accessed 10 August 2014

Granstrand O and Holgersson M J (2013) 'Managing the intellectual property disassembly problem' *California Management Review* 55(4)

Henderson J V (2003) 'Marshall's scale economies' *Journal of Urban Economics* 53(1), pp. 1–28

JAIA (Japan Automobile Importers Association) (2014) from www.jaia-jp.org/english/j/stat/nc/ accessed 9 August 2014

Johanson J and Vahlne J (1977) 'The internationalisation process of the firm; a model of knowledge development and increasing foreign market commitments' *Journal of International Business Studies* 8, pp. 23–32

Johanson J and Vahlne J (2009) 'The internationalisation process of the firm revisited; from liability of foreignness to liability of outsidership' *Journal of International Business Studies* 40, pp. 1411–1431

Korobkin R (2003) 'Bounded rationality, standard form contracts, and unconscionability' *The University of Chicago Law Review* pp. 1203–1295

Lemoine W and Dagnæs L (2003) 'Globalisation strategies and business organisation of a network of logistics service providers' *International Journal of Physical Distribution & Logistics Management* 33(3), pp. 209–228

Lord M D and Ranft A L (2000) 'Organizational learning about new international markets: exploring the internal transfer of local market knowledge' *Journal of International Business Studies* pp. 573–589

Menon N and Sanyal P (2007) 'Labor conflict and foreign investments: an analysis of FDI in India' *Review of Development Economics* 11(4), pp. 629–644

Nayak A K (2005) 'FDI model in emerging economies: case of Suzuki Motor Corporation in India' *Journal of American Academy of Business* 6(1), pp. 238–245

New York Times (2013) 'Next Made-in-China Boom: College Graduates' *New York Times* 16 January 2013 from www.nytimes.com/2013/01/17/business/chinas-ambitious-goal-for-boom-in-college-graduates.html?pagewanted=all&_r=1& accessed 22 February 2015

Puga D and Trefler D (2010) 'Wake up and smell the ginseng: international trade and the rise of incremental innovation in low-wage countries' *Journal of Development Economics* 91(1), pp. 64–76

Reid G C (2000) 'Free trade, business strategy and globalisation' *Global Business and Economics Review,* 2(1), pp. 26–38

Shell (2014) Briefing notes from www.shell.com.ng/aboutshell/media-centre/annual-reports-and-publications.html accessed 9 August 2014

Stephenson S M (1997) 'Standards and conformity assessment as nontariff barriers to trade' World Bank Policy Research Working paper, (1826) from www-wds.worldbank.org/external/default/WDSContentServer/WDSP/IB/2000/02/24/000009265_3971110141409/additional/102502322_20041117162503.pdf accessed 1 September 2015

Thun E (2008) *Changing lanes in China: Foreign direct investment, local governments and auto sector development.* Cambridge: Cambridge University Press

TMTC (2015) Tata Management Training Centre homepage from www.tmtctata.com/ accessed 22 February 2015

Toyota (2014) Toyota USA Automobile Museum – Cars from www.toyotausamuseum.com/pdf/cars.pdf accessed 9 August 2014

Ungson G R and Wong Y Y (2008) *Global strategic management.* Armonk, NY: ME Sharpe

VW (2014) The Volkswagen Timeline from www.volkswagen.co.uk/timeline/index accessed 5 August 2014

Wolcott R C and Lippitz M J (2007) 'The four models of corporate entrepreneurship' *MIT Sloan Management Review* 49(1), pp. 75–82

Yeung H W C (2002) 'Entrepreneurship in international business: an institutional perspective' *Asia Pacific Journal of Management* 19(1), pp. 29–61

YPF (2015) YUST PUST Foundation homepage from www.yustpust.org/ypf.php accessed 22 February 2015

Zhang K H (2005) 'Why does so much FDI from Hong Kong and Taiwan go to Mainland China?' *China Economic Review* 16(3), 2005, pp. 293–307

6 International Marketing

Chapter Objectives

Marketing is a method of communicating with existing and prospective customers with the ultimate purpose of making a sale. It is a highly flexible concept, industrial products being marketed in a distinct way from consumer financial services. The role of the manager is to ensure that the marketing is kept in alignment with the overall business strategy to maximise the benefits, or value, to the customer. In this chapter, we will look at the topic from a wide range of angles:

- How consumers value a product- or service-based on the features that promise the benefits they require.
- Aligning the overall company strategy with the existing product range.
- Making decisions on the commitment of resources to international markets.
- Devising the marketing mix.

PRODUCT FEATURES AND VALUE

A common mistake by managers is to confuse product features with benefits. Features are product specifications but there is no guarantee that the customer will value them. Product features only have value when they bring a benefit to the customer that they are prepared to pay for. For this reason, when marketing a product it is not sufficient to point out its features in the vague hope that potential customers can imagine how the feature relates to them (Khalifa, 2004). The proactive marketing approach is to communicate to the customer the benefits so that the customer can perceive whether it has value for them.

Table 6.1 demonstrates the difference between features and benefits for a standard domestic washing machine. The customer then makes a value judgement on the benefit: prepared to pay extra if positive, less if negative and no change in price if it is of neutral value. The manufacturer is only interested in product features of positive value.

Note that the specification of the hypothetical washing machine needs to be spelt out for the customer in order to clarify the potential benefits, but the final decision on value, and whether they will pay for it, lies with the customer. Energy efficiency and colour choice would be valued positively, so any company that offered these features would be able to charge a higher price. However, Wi-Fi connectivity is certainly a modern feature, offering the capability of remote control, but if it is not a benefit customers care for then the company cannot earn money on the feature. Even worse is the apparently wise feature of having the machine refuse to operate if it is only partly loaded: there is a benefit to the customer in that the machine will only operate when it is efficient to do so but this

Table 6.1 *Product features and benefits – domestic washing machine*

Product Feature	Benefit to the Customer	Value to the Customer
Energy efficient	1. Good for the environment 2. Saves money	Positive – will pay extra
Range of available colours	Can match personal colour scheme	Positive – will pay extra
Wi-Fi connection	Machine can be operated remotely by smartphone	Neutral – will not pay extra
Automatic shutdown for partial loads	Machine will only operate at its most efficient loads	Negative – will pay less

would not impress customers who demand convenience from their appliances. A domestic appliance that only operates when it decides it should do so would definitely need a large price discount in order for it to sell!

DOMESTIC AND INTERNATIONAL MARKETING

Marketing for the domestic market implies a comprehensive array of corporate activities to ensure that product development results in features that represent value for the customer. There should also be a reverse flow of information: what the customer values is communicated to the company and translated into product features. Marketing is therefore an activity that pervades all areas of the business, from product design to customer service. Since the home market is often the most important to the company it is vital that the product is designed to maximise the value to the domestic customer. This may entail a substantial redesign of the product if it is underperforming in that prime market.

International marketing is fundamentally no different to that in the domestic market. It is still communicating product benefits to customers in alignment with the corporate strategy, only it is being done in multiple domestic markets. As a result, international marketing is confronted by the diversity of markets each of which has its own peculiarities. We can highlight some of the international marketing mistakes that have been made, Craig and Douglas (2005) quoting the case of Microsoft in India neglecting to show the disputed region of Jammu-Kashmir as Indian territory on its maps in Windows 95, thereby attracting political ire and banishment from the market. Yet we could argue that this was due to poor marketing research within India; in other words this was not international marketing but simply inadequate local marketing research.

International marketing is different to domestic marketing because it has to reconcile the diversity of national markets with the unified corporate strategy. To treat every market as unique is to adopt a multi-domestic strategy, which is not international marketing but domestic marketing multiplied. What makes international marketing distinct is that it is attempting to find enough commonality across multiple markets that products can be sold with only the minimum adjustments being made to the product. Returning to the example above, Microsoft learnt its lesson by ensuring the next version of Windows had the disputed territory depicted under Indian control.

The Microsoft example shows us that the company was able to return to the market at a later date with a different product, and one that was minimally different from versions sold in other markets.

We can conclude that international marketing is distinguishable from domestic marketing in two core aspects:

1. The international corporate strategy is selective: the corporation is free to choose the market, the product it sells and the mode of entry.
2. The product will only be adapted to the local market if the case for doing so is absolutely compelling.

It is this second point that international managers are often guilty of overlooking. Entry into new, foreign markets is a high-risk venture, so companies will only embark on it from a position of established strength. The managers can reduce the risk of the overseas adventure if they adhere as closely as possible to the established strengths. Any diversion from these strengths takes on higher risks and incurs additional costs. This gives rise to a simple management axiom:

All adaptations incur additional costs and should be minimised at all times

The challenge for international corporations is to deliver value to customers in each market while minimising any adaptations and therefore keeping costs under firm control. Japanese firms, for example, have resolved these issues by designing global products, i.e. products that are acceptable in all intended markets (Calantone et al., 2006).

STRATEGIC ADVANTAGE AND TARGET

Michael Porter can always be relied on to give managers a generic model for corporate strategy. In this situation the model directs managers towards distinguishing between focused or broad strategies based on the competitive advantage of the company. The result is something like a 2×2 matrix (Porter, 2008). There are two dimensions, one of which is the strategic, or competitive, advantage of the company; the other is the scope of the target market:

1. Competitive Advantage.
   - Products with unique features valued by the customer
   - Generic products differentiated on cost.
2. Competitive Scope
   - Broad – mass market, multiple segments
   - Narrow – market segment or niche.

For any given pair of target and advantage, the model delivers a recommended strategy:

- **Unique product for a mass market** – perhaps the most coveted position for any company to be in since it implies a product without competitors, at least for the moment, with very high market acceptance. The matrix calls this a **differentiation** strategy and it is often seen with fashion items or new technologies. Such novel items are in high demand and for a limited period have the market to themselves.
- **Low-cost product for a mass market** – this position exemplifies modern industry: cheap goods for the masses. Such goods are often generic in nature, or have become so as more competitors have emerged, and depend on high sales to ensure efficient rates of production. In the matrix this is the **cost leadership** strategy.

- **Unique product for a narrow market** – here the company has a product without much competition, but not much of a market either. It therefore needs a **focus** strategy that concentrates on dominating a single market segment.
- **Low-cost product for a narrow market** – the closest thing to a business nightmare; not only is the product generic, so customers can only be induced to buy it on its low price, but the market for it is not very large either. Again, the matrix recommends a **focus** strategy. Products may find themselves in this position during the decline stage of the life cycle when the competitor products are still in the market but the market itself is disappearing.

The model appears useful as a management tool because it combines company-specific conditions with market-specific opportunities. On closer consideration, though, it becomes much less attractive. First of all, it is noticeable that the 2x2 matrix only gives rise to three strategies, not four. It seems extraordinary that targeting a narrow market opportunity with a unique product or a low-cost one entails employing broadly the same focus strategy. Clearly, two such distinct conditions should have only one strategy each.

More importantly, the model fails to recognise the relationship between cost and differentiation, and Charles Hill (1988) has been especially critical of the model in this regard. He points out that production systems are often common to an industry, so cost minimisation is not an area that a company can excel at in contrast to rivals. Although Porter conceded that a company could be low-cost and differentiated, he saw this state as a poor compromise and a temporary condition.

As Hill (1988) agrees, differentiation and low-cost are mutually exclusive so can, and should, co-exist. Differentiation is about delivering value to the customer in a way no other product can quite manage. Cost, on the other hand, is about the company minimising the costs of delivering that value. As argued throughout this book, the purpose of all businesses is to deliver value to the customer while simultaneously minimising the cost of that delivery. Value indicates the downstream price that can be charged to the customer; cost indicates the upstream price to the producer that must be covered. The difference between value and cost is where the profit lies.

If we return to Porter's matrix we can see that for each entry an alternative perspective can be included. For example, the historic Ford Model T was unique when it was released in the early twentieth century but it was also intended for the mass market. Famously, the uniqueness of the Model T was its affordability, and yet it was also Henry Ford's obsession with minimising production costs, enabling successive price cuts, that kept the car at the forefront of the car market for as long as it did. Inevitably, Henry Ford became a very rich man.

A similar argument can be made for products that are said to compete on their low cost. This is a highly undesirable position for a company to be in because low production costs are often a feature of the industry the company is in and can be replicated by competitors. Though this might also be said of unique product features, that eventually they will be copied, some aspects of product differentiation, such as branding, are within the ownership of the company. For this reason manufacturers of the most generic products will still attempt some sort of differentiation. Even amongst the most generic of product categories, such as foodstuffs, there will be attempts at branding and other forms of differentiation. Indeed, it is part of the manager's axiom: *they have minimised the cost to the company, now they must maximise the value to the customer.*

The axiom can be applied to international markets as much as national but the strategy is no longer tied to the comprehensive requirements of domestic operations. Whereas the domestic location is home to all the corporate functions, from R&D to customer support, the international markets can be cherry-picked for their choicest financial returns.

There are dangers, though, that selling a narrow range of products according to the local market demand characteristics may also lead to the company losing out on **economies of scope**. This is ironic for MNEs because they are often large companies with broad product ranges that have been enjoying these very efficiency benefits. Should the company find that a particular local market is genuinely unreceptive to the full product range it can then be compelled to rapidly expand into further markets in the search for economies of scope across all markets.

INTERNATIONAL MARKET COMMITMENT MODEL

Since the new market is almost certainly an addition to the company's access to other markets it can be flexible in its commitment. This is in contrast to the home market where commitment is total, from dedicated product design to retail and distribution. When it comes to the overseas markets the company can dip a strategic toe in the local water with a low commitment entry, such as exporting a broadly unchanged product, to the other extreme of including the new market in a vast global, strategic plan. For clarity we can distinguish between four levels of rising local market commitment, although in practice they merge into one continuum.

- **Production focus** – simply a matter of finding demand anywhere in the world to support output. Low specific market commitment, little marketing effort.
- **Sales focus** – additional demand sought to fill spare production capacity. Specific markets identified, some marketing effort.
- **Tactical market focus** – opportunities in market segments and niches identified. Market research looking for a small but stable market presence.
- **Global market strategy** – integrated view of production capacity, long-term market opportunities and product specification.

1. PRODUCTION FOCUS

At the most basic, companies seek out international sales opportunities simply because they have a production system that requires support from additional demand to achieve economic efficiency. This is likely to be for a generic product or service that needs little or no adaption to local market conditions. While there is a need to locate new customers, their location is irrelevant and there may be no particular home market. Indeed, any international aspects are entirely incidental.

The kind of products this would suit are commodities and raw materials with high economies of scale from inflexible production systems. Mining products would generally fit this category but also agricultural goods from large-scale farming regions. Since the products are generic there is little reason or opportunity to adapt the product to specific markets. Marketing activity will be focused on individual sales as they appear and not on any market development. Commodity producers will often form co-operatives, notably in agriculture, since there is little to distinguish their products. The co-operative boosts the market power of the producers and allows them to make long-term production plans.

This is not to say that differentiation of the commodity is not possible, but Pennington and Ball (2009) state that this is only possible if there is some variation in the quality of the commodity and the customers are in a position to choose which version they want to purchase. When these conditions are met, product differentiation and branding becomes possible. The researchers put forward Idaho potatoes as an example of a commodity that is genuinely appreciated only by connoisseurs of the tuber but has now gained enough brand visibility to justify a dedicated marketing effort.

CASE STUDY – SHIPBUILDING IN FINLAND

Finland is one of half a dozen or more countries that open onto the Baltic Sea. It has no particular economic advantages over its neighbours; indeed it is very much overshadowed by Germany, Sweden and Russia. Yet it has established an indigenous shipbuilding industry with a global sales presence.

As a littoral state Finland has always had a local maritime industry but it was its unfortunate position next to Russia, or the USSR as it was then, that pushed the country to rapidly industrialise. Despite a brave defence of its independence during World War II, once the hostilities were over Finland was obliged to make reparations to Soviet Russia. Since these demands included large numbers of ships, Finland was forced to invest vast sums in expanding its maritime industrial sector. Not only new shipyards but also an entire supply industry had to be brought up to standard.

So it was that the Finnish shipbuilding industry found itself, quite without prior strategic intention, to be one of the most competitive in the world. While the European shipbuilding companies were interdependent the Finish maritime cluster was almost completely self-sufficient, around 90% of vessel content being of domestic origin. Although Finnish industrialisation meant there was a rising local demand for ships, this was never enough to sustain the domestic shipbuilding industry after Soviet demands had been satisfied. Shipbuilders had to look for sales around the globe.

The current shipbuilding cluster in Finland is as competitive as ever. Capable of constructing almost any sea-going vessel, from offshore platforms to ice-breakers and passenger ships, it is only in the warship sector that Finland has little presence. The largest cruise liners in the world, the gigantic Oasis class, were built to a gross tonnage of 225,000 for the US-based Royal Caribbean International. Of the 200 companies that comprise the Finnish maritime industry cluster around 80% conduct their business internationally. A number of foreign companies have also been attracted to the cluster, such as Rolls-Royce.

Point of consideration: The shipbuilding cluster in Finland is heavily dependent on international sales for its products in order to be economically efficient. To what extent, if any, do these ships have to be adapted from the demands of the domestic market to those of the international market?

Source: Meridium, 2010

2. SALES FOCUS

A company may already have a strong home market or other overseas outlets but they are not enough to sustain the most economic levels of production. Additional sales are therefore sought in new locations. It is now important to identify those markets through research, and this may involve some need to adapt the product to the local conditions. The presence in the market may be exploratory or even temporary.

The sales focus approach is suitable for companies that are looking to grow but do not have the resources to make a concerted assault on a new market. Instead they are looking to gain a reasonable market presence for as long as they can. For example, wine producers can find that if they have a larger than usual output one year, perhaps due to a bumper harvest, they are obliged to expand their market cover. Market research may be limited to working with a local wholesaler and product adaptation limited to changing the labels on the wine bottles to the local language. Next year's production may not require the additional sales, but wine customers are famously fickle, so the lack of long-term sales in the market may be expected as a matter of course.

An interesting example of a product that benefited from a substantial sales focus was the French wine, Beaujolais Nouveau. Considered by wine buffs to be a wine of simple and rather uninteresting character, the fact that it does not respond well to the aging process was turned into a virtue by Georges Duboeuf in the 1980s with an impressive marketing campaign. This created a sense of excitement at the annual release date of the year's consignment with races to see who could sell the first bottle in the designated market. This proved very effective at lifting production volumes beyond what would normally be expected of what is fundamentally an unremarkable beverage. As the palates of global wine drinkers have become more educated the demand for Beaujolais Nouveau has waned, although it remains popular in Japan (Cogan-Marie and Charters, 2014).

CASE STUDY – INDIAN WINE TO THE WORLD

Few products are more international than wine. Even if French wines are still lauded as the preeminent art form there are few countries in the world that do not have their home-grown versions. From the soggy hills of southern England to the perfect vine growing climate of Chile, hardly a corner of the world is without an enterprising vineyard. Few places are more challenging, though, than India.

The sub-continent should be prime grape-growing country, and indeed it has a long history of wine making. There is evidence that it existed more than two thousand years ago, and the Mughal Emperors are known to have introduced the Shiraz variety. The Portuguese brought their expertise with them to their colony in Goa, introducing a new type of wine they called vin d'ail, from which we get the word vindaloo. Even the British had a go at winemaking, not normally a prospect viewed with enthusiasm by wine connoisseurs. However, local demand was never significant.

In recent years the promise of the climate has encouraged some entrepreneurs to invest in new vineyards. There have been some setbacks, but there are now 50,000 hectares under vine cultivation, and, though only 1% of that is destined for wine production, the market for Indian wine has been expanding at over 30% in some years. There are thought to be about 60 wineries in the country.

Perhaps most startling, around 15% of Indian wines are exported. For those who have become blasé about European wine these rare Asian alternatives are a little bit of excitement for a curious palate. Even the French are buying them.

Point of consideration: Despite a climate that lends itself to viniculture the wine industry in India is still minute by global standards. How would you propose marketing Indian wines in foreign markets in order to raise production volumes?

Source: Indian Grape Processing Board, 2014

3. TACTICAL MARKET FOCUS

If the company believes that it has the resources to hold a long-term presence in the market, but is unwilling or unable to make a high commitment from the start, then it will take a more short-term tactical approach. This means actively seeking out market demand that is specific to the company's product, including identification of market segments and niches. However, this medium level of commitment means that the company will not allocate substantial resources to product adaptation, only what is deemed necessary to hold a small market share. The approach is tactical in the sense that the company is flexible in its hold on the market, prepared to leave and try another market if the short-term gains do not emerge.

This is a useful approach when companies are not convinced that they can or need to engage in a full assault on the new market. Small specialist firms, such as manufacturers of high-end consumer products may take this route if they see little competition within their market niche. Larger firms may also use this approach as exploration of an unfamiliar market with a limited product range, keeping the high-commitment general market strategy in reserve. Both these players will conduct minimal product adaption to the local market but will display sensitivity to demand characteristics. However, this tentative approach may also be symptomatic of managers who take a short-term view of the market because they lack the necessary analytical skills or perhaps because their own career planning objectives are short-term (Lages and Lages, 2004).

This is not to say that short-term perspectives have no value; on the contrary, we can expect these tactical ventures to have significant organisational learning opportunities. Research by Lages et al. (2008), though, revealed that export performance in one year did not lead to significant strategic changes in the next year. The reasons for this are not clear, but it may be that firms with a short-term tactical focus are not interested in making long-term strategic adaptations. If this is the case then the tactical market focus is not an interim step towards a more intense market commitment but is an end in itself.

 ## CASE STUDY – RICOH FORGETS ITS CAMERAS

Ricoh is a Japanese corporation founded in 1936 to exploit technical innovations in sensitised paper for use in specialised printing machines. Within two years it had also shifted into cameras but it did not lose sight of the business support market and in 1955 released its first office copier. The company continued to advance the concept of office automation and is now one of the largest manufacturers of business machines in the world.

As the company has grown, it has structured itself around two major divisions. One is the Imaging and Solutions division, comprising the copier business. The other is the Industrial Products division, which includes hardware such as semiconductors and electrical components. The famous camera brand is not in either division; instead, it has been shunted into a third division known, rather disparagingly, as Other.

For European consumers this seems odd when the brand is associated as much with the cameras as it is with office equipment. In the United States, though, the camera range is very much the poor relation. There are just a few retail outlets offering the Ricoh cameras, and sales volumes are almost insignificant. It would appear that camera sales are not part of Ricoh's corporate strategy in the United States. So why do they bother?

The main reasons are probably tactical. With a large organisation already in place to support the office equipment side of the business it would not have taken much of an investment to also support a few camera sales. With strong brand recognition in the country a reasonable number of cameras would have been sold for relatively little specific marketing effort. Furthermore, withdrawal from the camera market would have incurred few costs, leaving the rest of the organisation to continue with the far larger office equipment side. With low entry and exit costs the camera side of the business was simply taking a tactical approach to earning revenue where it could.

As a footnote to this, Ricoh in 2011 acquired the famous Pentax camera company. This has greatly increased the exposure of the company to the camera market in the United States and it is likely that Ricoh-branded camera sales will be pulled up by joint distribution with Pentax.

Point of consideration: Why do you think Ricoh did not take a more strategic view of its cameras in the United States? If the company had implemented a camera strategy in the market what form would you expect it to have taken?

Source: Ricoh, 2014

4. GLOBAL MARKETING STRATEGY

The highest level of market commitment, the global marketing strategy, integrates production, product specification and marketing into one world view. The production system is configured to operate at the highest possible efficiency when capacity is fully utilised, but this means the product must have the potential to be sold in global markets. This takes extensive marketing research and any market presence must be defended with tenacity. This may mean accepting financial losses in some markets for periods of time. In order to accommodate the peculiarities of each market the product must be flexible enough to readily accept adaptation without radical redesign. The company may also have to develop the market through targeted promotion if the product is unfamiliar to it.

According to Zou and Cavusgil (2002), the global marketing strategy encompasses three main strands:

- Standardisation – commonality of the global marketing mix (i.e. product, price, promotion, distribution, etc.) to benefit from economies of scale, scope and synergies.
- Co-ordination – the extent to which marketing is centralised.
- Integration – ensuring that marketing in different locations is dependent on each other.

The authors warn that these three aspects of global marketing are only the basics and need supporting through continuous analysis of the company's global performance.

Most MNEs will follow the global market strategy. An obvious example would be the worldwide sale of films on DVD. The DVD technology allows manufacturers to offer the same product in different world markets because they can be offered with various language options. Some DVD films allow the viewer to select the language of the subtitles, particularly useful for the hard of hearing. There are also differences in the broadcast format yet the underlying technology is standardised across all DVDs and the marketing of the film itself is broadly common to all markets.

🔍 MANAGEMENT SPOTLIGHT: DECISIONS ON MARKET COMMITMENT

The market commitment model put forward earlier is an attractive management tool. It is simple to use and the requirements at each stage can be mapped onto the particular characteristics of the company. The model also encourages managers to question their strategic view of the foreign sales intentions. Is it just to fill temporarily vacant production capacity or is the company taking a long-term view of the new markets? Are they prepared to commit substantial resources developing the market or are they snatching a sales opportunity that happens to have come their way? The model forces managers to clarify their long-term and short-term plans.

As in other stage models the market commitment model is dynamic; as conditions change managers know they must move up or down stages. This means that even if the market commitment is short-term there is still the capacity in the model for consideration of the long-term strategy. However, much of this depends on the quality of the information that is put into the model. Like SWOT (Valentin, 2001) and PESTLE there is too much opportunity to input prior judgements, with the consequence that the output of the model is in fact predetermined. Suppose that a manager had erroneously decided that the company had sufficient resources for a full product range entry of a new market. The model would compound the error by directing the manager to a global market strategy. It is therefore important that the information that is put into the model has itself been subjected to an analytical process.

Another observation of the model is that it gives the illusion of companies being able to progress from one stage to the next in a linear fashion. If only the business world were so neatly arranged. In fact, companies can dodge around from one stage to the next, jump stages and even mix them together. For example, an MNE with a wide range of products might market one in a standardised form in many markets according to a global marketing strategy, whilst simultaneously selling another product in a highly adapted form in a few select but lucrative market niches. We have also seen that the short-term tactical market focus, which tends to eschew a strategic perspective, can be an end in itself and so be an obstacle to progression (Lages and Lages, 2004).

Despite the weaknesses in the model it is still a useful planning tool. It can help to structure the analysis and provide a core strategic message which can then be customised to the company's own particular strategic requirements. Once the strategy is in place the more detailed planning of the marketing mix can begin.

Point of consideration: For a company of your choice make a case for each one of the four market commitment stages. What does this tell you about how you should use the model?

Sources: Valentin, 2001; Lages and Lages, 2004

THE FOUR PS

Perhaps the most famous management planning model in marketing is the Four Ps, proposed by Jerome E McCarthy (1960) and further popularised by Philip Kotler (2006). Like similar management models such as SWOT and PESTLE it has high utility in the profession due to its intuitive application and memorability. It might even be said that only a marketing practitioner could have concocted the famous mnemonic.

The Four Ps is a framework to direct marketing managers to consider the most important aspects of bringing products closer to the customer. It aims to be a comprehensive checklist to ensure that all the marketing angles have been covered. The four main areas of marketing are, according to the model:

- Product
- Price
- Promotion
- Place.

In formulating the marketing mix, managers should consider each of these areas in a sequence of decision-making.

1. Product

As we have seen in Table 6.1 at the beginning of this chapter, a product is not a bundle of specifications but an object of benefit and value to the customer. Value is what the customer is prepared to pay for, and in basic terms the amount they pay should always exceed the costs to the company of delivering that value, i.e. the product cost.

One purpose of marketing is to identify the value in the product. In the international arena different markets have different values and this may mean a degree of product adaptation specific to the market is necessary. Of course, at all times management need to take care that the product adaptation intended to enhance value does not also incur marginal costs that then exceed the marginal value.

Uncovering the value of a product is a highly complex process since it is dependent on customer perceptions. These perceptions in turn are derived from many cultural sources, the following two being just the tip of the iceberg:

- **Custom** – e.g. US cars having large cup-holders thanks to the American propensity for taking fast food while driving.
- **Religion** – e.g. under certain religious rules foodstuffs may need special preparation or be banned outright.

There are a multitude of other factors that will influence customer perceptions. Economic conditions in the market will also impinge on the product and how it is valued. If the product is being lined up for a developing economy then it may be necessary to lower the specification of the product by deleting those features that have no value, i.e. they may be desired but there is not enough wealth to pay for the features.

An added complication of international marketing is that there may be technical and legal reasons why a product must be adapted. Electronic products often have to be redesigned to accept a different electrical voltage, for instance. Another area of rising concern is the ecological environment, so the product may have to meet requirements on waste and emissions, perhaps by promising recycling potential. Sometimes countries can use legislation as a non-tariff barrier to trade, demanding new product specifications in the name of health and safety when the real purpose is to burden the company with enough additional costs to render sales uneconomic.

When international markets are very different from each other the cycles of **new product development (NPD)** can fall out of synchronisation, as a fast-moving market demands a new product, while a slow-moving market does not. Factors that can accelerate demand for shorter product life cycles are R&D-intensive industries, such as electronics or fashion, highly competitive markets and relatively wealthy consumers who can afford higher value-added products.

Since marketing can quantify the connection between product specification and value it is vital that it serves to link product R&D with market demand. By communicating effectively with the customer marketing can identify where value is being added in the production process as a whole. This should result in products that are specifically designed to meet consumer perceptions of value, produced with the quality that consumers expect and in volume that is appropriate for the level of demand. Problems occur when attempting to integrate the various market demand characteristics.

Füller et al. (2006) argue that online technologies mean that virtual groups of product innovators can work in a spirit of community-based innovation. This somewhat addresses the concerns of Zou and Cavusgil (2002) relating to the standardisation, co-ordination and integration of global marketing.

2. Price

The marketing principle concerning price is that the customer must feel they have made a net gain because the perceived value exceeds the price paid. It is immaterial whether non-customers think the value is not reflected in the price since they will not be buying it: the only matter of importance is that enough customers do consider that, for them, the value is indeed greater than the price.

 MYTH BUSTER – DO CONSUMERS SHOP FOR VALUE OR PRICE?

Although a product or service value is made up of the features that customers value, it is not the same thing as the price they are willing to pay. Moreover, value needs to exceed price if the customer is to buy. This is the consumer surplus, the difference between the price paid and the highest price that the customer would have paid, which represents the value of the item. The consumer surplus represents the gain that the consumer has made in their purchase (Bapna et al., 2008). If the price and the value coincide then there is no consumer surplus and no rationale for making the purchase.

We can see this most clearly if we consider something that has indisputable and quantifiable value, such as cash. Let's say that you are in Europe and have a five euro note that for some personal reason, like the serial number is your unlucky number, you decide to sell. How much is it worth? Surely a five euro note is worth five euros because it will buy five euros of goods just like any other five euro note.

Unfortunately, you will be disappointed. Your intended customer will see no point in spending five euros on something that has the value of five euros. Having made the effort to do the deal, they will find themselves right back where they started. There is absolutely no incentive for them to buy your note, unless of course you drop the price below its value. If you were to hold an auction you should find that the highest price you could earn for an ordinary five euro note is €4.99, since above that the buyer is making no net gain.

There are occasions when cash money, notes and specie do have a price that is the same or higher than their face value but that is because the buyer is deriving some additional value. For example, people will buy gift vouchers for higher than face value because they hold the additional value of being gifts, an emotional impact that cash money does not quite have. The same is also true of rare notes and coins, or money that is made out of metals that have greater value than that denoted on the money itself.

Point of consideration: As an experiment, put an item of small but clear nominal value on sale in an auction. The item could be a gift voucher or cash; anything as long as it has an apparently incontrovertible face value. Then wait to see what price it sells for …

Source: Bapna R, Jank W and Shmueli G (2008)

Most companies face a **price elasticity of demand** for their products, usually experienced as falling volumes of sales, as the price, relative to consumer wealth and market competition, rises. Trying to find a price that maximises revenue is challenging for any company, even more so if the production system is inflexible. If demand is underestimated then waiting lists will result, which means stable rates of full capacity production but also the opportunity cost of lost sales. Alternatively, overestimated demand means surplus output accumulating in warehouses and either production stoppages or price discounting to get rid of the stuff, both costly options.

Market research on pricing will provide some indication of price elasticity, although most companies will simply price against the competition. This might be as a starting point, facilitating estimates of demand in order to plan production output. If the production system is inflexible then the price point will be set to ensure full capacity output.

In the international arena there are, as always, further complications. First of all there can be a set of local price limitations. The authorities sometimes impose maximum or minimum prices, often in regard to products that have health implications like alcohol and tobacco. Indeed, price is seen to be the most effective lever on public behaviour for such products (Tauras, 2006). The authorities will also impose tax and duty on products that effectively raise the price of the product into a market segment beyond the company's original plan.

In extreme cases the company may attempt to sell its product at an artificially low price, and when this is below the cost of production it is known as **dumping**. An apparently irrational strategy, the company is effectively buying market share by driving its competitors out of the market. Once it has bought a dominant position it can restore its prices to a more realistic level, or even higher. In the short run the consumer gains from the very low price, which is why they flock to the product in large numbers, but in the long run consumers suffer less choice in the market and higher prices. Only companies with large financial resources, or backing from their home government, can afford to engage in dumping and it is clearly an abuse of market power. Under WTO rules the host country has the right to impose **countervailing duties** to raise the price of the product in the local market to where they consider it should be (WTO, 2012). The countervailing duties may even be imposed on a product from that country not directly involved in the dispute, often giving rise to international diplomatic tensions.

Despite the price restrictions companies still have a reasonable range of prices that can be chosen according to the corporate strategy. There are two basic strategies (Palmer, 2000) that a company might choose for an overseas market:

- **Skimming** – setting a high price for short-term profit. A price strategy for a company that is uncertain how long its product will be in the market, perhaps because the product is new and there is a limited window of opportunity before the competition mount a counter-attack. A company that does not have the resources to defend its market position in the long-term must make all its financial gains while it can. Stronger companies will rapidly release a new product before it has to reduce prices to meet the competition.
- **Penetration** – the acceptable low price strategy, unlike dumping. The company has the resources and the long-term strategic view to position the product at a low price and so buy market share. The revenue shortfall can be made up by the progressively higher volume of sales until prices can be raised at a later date.

There are numerous other pricing strategies that focus on targeting some kind of rate of financial return (Cannon and Morgan, 1990). For example, the cost-plus strategy takes the costs of production and bringing the product to market, adding some predetermined profit. Usually defined as a percentage of cost, there is the danger that any sudden changes due to inflation, transport costs, etc., can lead to a rise in the 'plus' and consequent dramatic rise in price to the consumer. The rise in price will then negatively impact on consumer demand.

International sales bring additional risks. Currency exchange rates can be volatile, meaning that either prices, and consequently demand, or profits will be affected. If the company has a **fixed price** strategy then it is profits that come under pressure, but if a **variable price** strategy is in place then sales volumes will rise and fall according to price elasticity. New tariffs might also be imposed if the local government fears the foreign threat, or there might be a **voluntary export restraint (VER)** agreement that limits sales volumes to an agreed market share. Limiting sales can push the company into something like a skimming strategy, with higher prices to maximise the profits from the constrained sales volumes.

The risks associated with one market do not end there. If two markets in close proximity have different pricing strategies then there is an opportunity for arbitrage. Properly known as **parallel imports**, but more widely as **grey imports**, products being sold at a cheaper price in one market can be imported into the higher price market without the permission of the producer (Richardson, 2002). The price difference represents a largely risk-free profit for the trader. In the interests of liberalising trade many countries, like New Zealand, have legalised parallel imports and the EU allows it within its borders.

Although the producer is still making a sale it is outside their established sales network so not under their control. This causes friction with the established retail outlets, which are losing sales to the cheaper grey imports. It also raises concerns about product reputation since grey imports are not supported by the producer's usual warranties. The product specification may also be incorrect for that market, affecting its functionality. Some products that are commonly passed into the used market after a few years, such as cars, may be difficult to sell if they are non-standard for that market.

3. Promotion

This is the most visible aspect of marketing, as it involves advertising and other means of stimulating the interest of potential customers. There are two types of strategic driving force behind it (Urban, 2005):

- **Push strategy** – used for low fixed-cost/high variable-cost products. This means a production system that is not expensive in itself, the major part of the costs being in the materials directly used in the manufacture of the product. A sales campaign can lead to a sudden, perhaps temporary, increase in sales. Also, generic products that are differentiated only by price, or when the company has a market penetration strategy that requires a rapid increase in market share.

  A push strategy is often a high pressure campaign, perhaps only in a selected location, that particularly lends itself to one-to-one personal selling tactics, where the salesperson is paid a commission on each sale. It is also suited to service industry sales campaigns, where temporary staff can be hired for the occasion.
- **Pull strategy** – used for high fixed-cost/low variable-cost products. This implies a costly production system that requires long-term, relatively stable demand in order to maximise efficiency. Also products that are identified with a particular lifestyle and strategies suited to long-term cost-plus pricing strategies. The promotion focuses on creating demand by stimulating consumer curiosity in the product. Usually co-ordinated centrally as part of a national or international campaign.

When deciding between a push or a pull promotion there are a number of factors that need to be taken into consideration. Sophisticated consumers are more likely to be convinced by a pull strategy in the mass media that creates an image of how the product fits with their lifestyle and values. This is also the case where the production has high economies of scale such that it is preferable to establish stable demand for the long-term by insinuating the product's brand values into the lives of the consumers. Of course, this means nothing if the media outlets for the promotion are not available: promotion in developing economies is often of the push type because of lack of access by consumers to television, magazines and other mass media.

Table 6.2 illustrates the push and pull approaches with a range of products and their characteristics. The product type is either generic and undifferentiated, or differentiated and specific to particular consumer lifestyles. For the sake of simplicity the product is assumed to compete on price or brand values.

The push strategy tends to promote a conscious desire in consumers to obtain the product. It gives rise to increases in sales that may last only as long as the promotional campaign, but at least weaknesses in the promotion can be rapidly resolved. In contrast, the pull strategy is intended to imbed the product in the consumer's unconsciousness and so lead to high loyalty with long-term sales. The problem with the pull strategy is that it takes some time for its effectiveness to be understood, by which time it may be too late to resolve any weaknesses in the approach. The two strategies are not mutually exclusive, and a push strategy that merges into a subsequent pull strategy is an effective method for launching a new product.

A major component of a pull strategy is the **brand image**. Consumers identify themselves with the brand, and for the most high-profile brands it can validate them as people. This can lead to tribal loyalties, as consumers identify with the brand not just as individuals but also as groups. This can often be perplexing to outside observers, such as the fanatical loyalty some computer users have for particular types of software.

The push and pull strategies are not necessarily mutually exclusive and they can be used for the same product to stimulate demand in different ways. They are analogous to **transactional** and **relationship marketing** (Zineldin and Philipson, 2007). Transactional marketing focuses on making the deal in the short-term, as seen in push campaigns, and so tends to emphasise price or the immediate benefits of the product to the customer. Relationship marketing is more like a pull promotion, creating demand by emphasising the long-term connection between the seller and the buyer. However, any sales campaign may have elements of both marketing styles. A cut-price introductory offer, for example, is a classic short-term transactional approach, but the long-term intention is for the customer to return for repeat purchases.

International branding decisions are complicated by the selective nature in which foreign markets may be entered. If the company is entering the market with just one product then the brand will be closely identified with that single item. However, if the company is making an all-out assault on the mass market with a range of products then the corporate brand becomes more important. This can create problems if the local branding strategy is at variance with the branding strategy in other markets.

Table 6.2 *Push and pull promotions*

Product	Product Type	Competitive Features	Promotion
Double glazing	Generic	Price	Push
Malt whisky	Lifestyle	Brand values	Pull
Blended whisky	Generic	Price	Push
Fashionable clothes	Lifestyle	Brand specific design	Pull
Household cleaning goods	Generic	Price	Push

4. Place

A less conspicuous aspect of marketing is that of place, a concept that runs the full spectrum of back-room planning of **distribution** to **point-of-sale** placement in front of the customer. As the product makes its journey from the production site to the customer a range of different specialisms come into play. Distribution involves not just the **logistics** of moving products around but also assessment of the types of distribution networks appropriate to the product, the culture and the retail outlets.

When entering a new, foreign market it is often advisable to find a local partner to handle the distribution. They can offer a **turnkey** service that includes import administration, stock handling, storage and other logistical matters. Equally important is to plug into the local retail network, and in developed countries this often means selling the product to national retail chains that have their own distribution systems. It would be nice to think that it is therefore possible to leave the task of bringing the product to the customer to the local partner, but this invites the **moral hazard** of the partner acting in their own interests (Corbett et al., 2005). In particular, the partner may give prominence to a rival brand if it brings higher financial returns. In extreme cases the overseas company may be obliged to take charge of its own distribution and retail network.

To an extent, a company can take a dynamic view of its product distribution network. It may nominate a local partner only for the initial entry into the market, replacing this with its own distribution system once it has gained sufficient experience of local market conditions. Another approach would be an exploration first of a regional market before expanding to national coverage. These two strategies could be merged, exploring the regional market with a local distributor before going national with a wholly owned distribution system. Larger MNEs, in the interests of economies of scale and other efficiencies, also have the option of connecting the new market with an existing global distribution network.

Some products are highly sensitive to the organisation of distribution – foodstuffs and fashion being the most obvious examples – where they have to be brought to the point-of-sale within a specified time limit. This means that speed of delivery, not just the geographical reach of the distribution system, is paramount. When there is a broad range of products, as in a cost leadership strategy, there is a need for a system that can handle multiple products. This may entail sophisticated stock handling and advanced warehouses, perhaps even wholly owned if there is no local partner equipped for the challenge.

Cultural issues come into play when customers are used to purchasing similar goods in a way peculiar to that region. In Africa, Avon found that its distribution system based on personal selling suited a culture that promoted cosmetics by personal recommendation (Scott et al., 2012). Related to this is the retail system in the country, which can range from out-of-town shopping centres to village mom-and-pop stores. In India, for example, there are a large number of small, local retail outlets that can make a mass-market entry of a cost-differentiated product very challenging. It can even act as a non-tariff barrier to trade.

If the distribution network has administrative challenges then the point-of-sale is a science in its own right. Many studies have been made of the effects of background music on behaviour and how customer flows through large stores determine where departments should be placed. Then product-specific concerns include matters of shelf placement and point-of-sale promotions. It can be a struggle for managers to ensure that the company's products are positioned within the store to their full advantage when the store itself may prefer to promote a rival item.

MANAGEMENT AND THE FOUR PS MODEL

The Four Ps model is an easy to remember mnemonic and a handy checklist of marketing items. It is the kind of plan that lends itself to back-of-the-envelope scribbling by managers who prefer to make their decisions on the fly. As a strategic tool, though, it lacks sufficient rigour to guide managers towards a definitive marketing plan. Each item covers a huge range of different considerations, each one vulnerable to the subjective rationale of the manager. Although it is known as the marketing mix it actually implies input across the functions of the firm, creating co-ordination and control problems (Goi, 2009).

Although the Four Ps is a useful marketing primer it does not direct detailed analysis. If we take the first P, product, as an example, we can immediately see that the model reminds us to include these considerations in the marketing strategy but provides no further clue on what or how they should be evaluated. Our principle may be that product adaptation should be minimised, but the model does not direct the manager to conclude what degree of adaptation is permissible.

When we look at the other Ps there is a similar lack of guidance. Price is determined by many different factors, such as pricing strategies like skimming and dumping, according to the overall long-term strategy for the market. The decision-making process may even prove irrelevant when it is the pricing strategy of a dominant rival that sets the prices in the market. The P of promotion does have some strategic clarity, dealing as it does with the narrow issue of communicating the product benefits to the customer, but there is a degree of overlap with the multifaceted P of place.

The Four Ps model is of little use to specialists working in each field, so a logistics expert would hardly use the P of place as the starting point for analysing a distribution network. The value of the model is mainly to senior managers who want a checklist to ensure that the marketing strategy for a new, foreign market is coherent and complete. Yet there is still a grave limitation on the model: it is most effective with the considerations that are internal to the firm, particularly when it comes to manufactured products. However, as Goi (2009) points out, the model does not include the role of the customer and this is most pertinent when it comes to the service sector.

THE FOUR PS AND THE SERVICE SECTOR

In processes that involve the production of physical products, such as manufactured and agricultural goods, the flow in the transformation process lends itself to many business models. This is certainly so with the Four Ps when a product is manufactured according to the prior lessons of market research, adapted to its intended market, priced, promoted and then placed where the customer can buy it. The Four Ps may be guilty of being an *aide-memoire* devised by marketing executives for marketing executives, like a snappy slogan with little substance, but it does serve as a senior management checklist when preparing a marketing strategy.

Unfortunately, the non-linear structure of the service sector industries means that the Four Ps struggle to be applied. With some services, such as banking, money is both the input and the final product. With other service industries, like dining out or going to concerts, the customer has far cheaper alternatives waiting for them at home, yet they can still be enticed away. The point is that the service sector is not about just the physical product, assuming there even is one. To state the obvious, the service sector is about service.

This is not to say that the Four Ps are a complete failure, but they are inadequate and fail to direct managers to the core marketing elements of the service sector. Kotler himself was concerned that the model did not take sufficient account of buyers (Kotler, 2006). To illustrate the inadequacies, Table 6.3 is a Four Ps exercise for a product we know well, coffee. Not an ordinary coffee, we can make that at home, but a so-called gourmet coffee, such as latte or cappuccino, from a specialist coffee shop.

Although the marketing strategy in Table 6.3 is a credible one it has also been written retrospectively. We probably already have a particular brand of coffee in mind when writing it so there is no real analysis. Instead, we are using the Four Ps to describe a business with which we are familiar. The model is simply not prescriptive enough; the quality of the strategic response given by the model is only as good as the information put into it.

Table 6.3 *The 4 Ps of coffee*

4 Ps Factor	Application to Coffee	Marketing Strategy
Product	Product brand identity Cultural taste preference	Coffee branded by source, Fair Trade Sweet flavour according to national market
Price	High price for a quality product Local competitors	Skimming Priced nationally
Promotion	Lifestyle product	Pull promotion
Place	Instant access to fresh product	Shops located in high streets, tourist and refreshment areas

In Japan coffee is available in hot cans from **vending machines** more than from coffee shops, which are still relatively rare in the country. If we revisit Table 6.3 with the Japanese vending machine information the model would present the same strategic responses, only the P of place would now be a vending machine. It hardly needs mentioning that the retail experience of a vending machine is quite different to that of a retail outlet like a coffee shop.

The crucial aspects of the service industry are related to social behaviour. In a coffee shop customers are looking for personal service, an artisan approach to making the coffee and a suitable ambience in the shop. It is therefore important that the member of staff speaks to the customer in a friendly way, the making of the coffee is displayed as a performance in its own right and the shop offers a relaxing place where the coffee can be enjoyed. Fortunately, the Four Ps model can be extended to include more Ps, as below:

5. People

People are a central part of any service industry company, comprising all those in customer-facing roles who are integral to the purchase experience. Staff will often need training in the type of service that should be offered, ranging from casual friendliness to cool professionalism, as appropriate to customer expectations. There may also be differences between national markets.

In the service sector staffing can become the costliest part of bringing the product to the customer. Restaurants would be a good example of this, as the staff need to behave towards the customer in a manner appropriate to the experience the customer is seeking. Fast food restaurants tend to be casual, personable and child friendly, while staff in high-class restaurants would be expected to be almost invisible, even faintly haughty if the occasion demanded it. Generally, improved service by staff will increase value to the customers, but managers need to balance this with the staff training costs of delivering that value.

6. Process

In some services the customer is buying into the process. Many high-class products are custom-made to order. The final result may not, in reality, have any tangible advantage over mass-produced products, which have the added advantage of a lower price. Yet customers will pay premium prices if they perceive added value in the process, and the company will promote this aspect. The product may not be expensive in absolute terms but will be relative to its mass market versions. We can see this in branded malt whiskies, which are somewhat more expensive than unbranded blended whiskies. The malt whiskies will proudly display the number of years they have taken to mature, ten or fifteen years being common, when such slowness would be considered desperately unacceptable in most other products.

There is an increasing opportunity for managers to enhance value because of the process. Fair Trade products are gaining market share because consumers place a high value on the production method and, of course, high value can be translated into a higher price paid. Supermarkets are getting in on the act by having product packaging, such as for meat, declare the farm where it was sourced.

7. Physical evidence

In the service industry much of what the customer is buying into is an intangible experience. Even in the process, where the customer gains value from the way the product is prepared, the equipment that is used in the process is a tool; it is not the process itself. Equally, the attention being given by the people, or staff, is not something physical that can be packaged and sold separately. When a gentleman is being measured for a handmade suit it is important that he receives personal attention from the tailor and that the clothing really will be put together by a craftsman, not by machine. Yet these two aspects do not capture the full value of the experience. The customer also needs the physical side of the experience.

The physical evidence of service is more subtle and intuitive than the Ps of people and process. A bank needs to show that the employees have a professional attitude. The physical evidence is that the staff wear business clothing and the money transactions are conducted behind protective glass. Furthermore, the bank needs to exude an ambience of financial success and stability. As a consequence, banks are often housed in solid-looking buildings with modern, stylish interiors. The challenge for managers then is to devise some marketing approach that has the physical evidence the customers expect but still differentiates it from the competition. Some banks have been experimenting with an office style with desks but no protective glass.

ALTERNATIVES TO THE SEVEN PS

Adding the three additional Ps to the famous Four Ps model encourages a more holistic approach to international marketing for managers. It introduces vital elements that are important features of any marketing strategy, not just the service sector. For managers in manufacturing industries, for whom the Four Ps might have been sufficient, the additional Ps can guide them to uncover new value by encouraging them to analyse the customer relationship.

An empirical study by Akroush (2011), though, has found that the additional three Ps can be conflated into just one general P for people. The argument is that the customer's perception of service integrates all three. If we accept that the Four Ps model has value then the inclusion of the P for people gives us a possible **Five Ps** model.

Kotler's awareness that the Four Ps, and by extension the Seven Ps, was focused only on the internal operations of the firm led to the proposal of the customer-centric **Four Cs** (Kotler et al., 2013). A switch in perspective then takes us from product to customer solution, price to customer cost, place to convenience and promotion to communication. The Four Cs approach recognises that the customer is looking for value, which we can think of as a product solution at the right price, accessible for purchasing and with the benefits effectively communicated. We could continue this equivalence exercise into the additional three Ps of people, process and physical evidence.

Kotler states that the Four Ps marketing strategy should be built on an understanding of the Four Cs but this is probably missing the duality of the situation: if the Four Cs represent the customer's search for value then the Four Ps represent the firm's ability to deliver that value to the customer. This being the case then the Four Ps and Four Cs should be combined; perhaps we could call the resultant model the **Eight PCs**. It is the implicit resolution of the capability Ps and the demand Cs in such a model that requires the customer management skills of marketing specialists.

RAISING EMPLOYABILITY: CAREER OPPORTUNITIES FOR MARKETING SPECIALISTS

Managers are often generalists; their job is to recognise the expertise in others and to create the right conditions for them to flourish in their assigned roles. Senior managers often come from a variety of business backgrounds, but it is their acumen for leadership that allows them to take on the wider strategic responsibilities of running the company. In the process of attaining these dizzy heights of success many of them may have returned to academic studies at various points in their lives or broadened their experience through positions at other companies.

There is still some disagreement whether academic qualifications or experience count: Rachel Key, Business Development Director of Thales Training & Consultancy (ILM, 2013), takes the view that formal qualifications should be identified and achieved on the job. Nevertheless, it is important for managers to have a grasp of theoretical concepts. Models such as the Four Ps and Porter's product strategies can provide a simple framework with which to interpret the market challenges of new, international markets. The models are easy to remember and implement, promising a coherent overview of the marketing strategy. However, the models are no replacement for the kind of specialist theoretical knowledge that comes from academic learning.

Marketing is certainly an area of business that demands dedicated training and experience. From an academic point of view there are countless university degrees designed to build a firm foundation in the discipline. On top of that, experience is vital for gaining that 'gut feeling' for a market that comes from dealing with customers face-to-face. Experience in sales brings invaluable insights into the animal spirits that inhabit that jungle we call the market.

For those planning their career development in marketing up to the highest levels of management a newspaper careers service held an online forum with industry experts and distilled out the main points (Guardian, 2009):

1. Marketing qualifications are only the first step – consider mixing studies with part-time work or internships in marketing.
2. Marketing requires well-rounded individuals, so ensure that the CV or résumé demonstrates a broad range of activities.
3. Marketing takes drive, resilience and innovation.
4. Marketing pervades many areas of a company's activities – seek out these opportunities and use them as a platform for gaining experience.
5. Basic experience is vital – starting from the bottom puts the career ladder on a solid footing.
6. Technological advances are having a significant impact on marketing, so keep up with the latest developments.

It is this mix between theory, experience and personal drive that makes marketing one of the most dynamic business disciplines. It is also the reason why so many top managers owe their success to a start in marketing.

THE STORY SO FAR: PUTTING THE PRODUCT IN FRONT OF THE CUSTOMER

Marketing is more than a specialised function within a business; it cuts across almost all the activities of a company. It is vital that the market intentions of the product are in alignment with the overall corporate strategy, in particular whether the organisation is chasing a broad market with a price-sensitive product or defined segments with a highly differentiated product. Ultimately, though, the company must attempt to resolve both issues as cost and differentiation are not mutually exclusive. For new, international markets the company can at least be selective in where and what it chooses to sell, and to whom. This requires extensive evaluation. Market research informs product design, marketing campaigns bring the product to the attention of the customer and logistics ensure the customer can actually obtain what they want. The Four Ps model provides a useful checklist, but service industries in particular need the full range of market sensitivities provided by the Seven Ps and other such models. To cope with these challenges marketing managers need to develop a range of skills from lofty intellect of market theory to the low animal cunning of the salesperson. No wonder that marketing is perhaps the most dynamic activity in business.

 WEB SUPPORT

1. The difference between features and benefits. A 2011 blog from Ardath Albee of Marketing Interactions on the crucial point about adding product features willy-nilly or providing benefits that the customer will actually value (and pay for). Worth exploring other posts as well.

   www.marketinginteractions.typepad.com/marketing_interactions/2011/12/the-difference-between-benefits-and-features.html

2. The four faces of mass customization. A combination of mass production with customised products, and this article from the Harvard Business Review is comprehensive. Remember, though, the first priority is always to keep production going at full capacity and minimise the costs of product adaptations.

   www.hbr.org/1997/01/the-four-faces-of-mass-customization

3. Philip Kotler: Marketing. The man himself giving an hour-long lecture at the Chicago Humanities Festival in 2012. Quite a treat.

   www.youtube.com/watch?v=sR-qL7QdVZQ

Project Topics

1. Product features are not the same as customer benefits. For a newly launched product, discuss how some new features may not offer benefits and the impact this will have on the value of the product for the customer. Should the company have developed an alternative product design?
2. What has greater influence on sales volumes, product price or perceived product value?
3. When a bank is advertising its mortgage products, to what extent is it a transactional marketing strategy and to what extent is it a relationship marketing strategy?
4. Using the Four Ps model, how would you devise a marketing strategy for organic vegetables? If you think the Four Ps model is insufficient, how many more Ps do you think there should be?
5. If the Four Cs model is the customer-centric equivalent of the Four Ps, how would you convert the Seven Ps into Seven Cs?

CASE STUDY: ARE EMERGING MARKETS ALL ABOUT PRICE?

To state that consumers in emerging markets lack only spending power would be fatuous; of course they lack spending power, that is what poverty means. Yet the mistake made by so many corporations is to believe that poverty is about money alone. Based on this assumption, when marketing a product or service in an emerging market, only the low-cost marketing strategy makes any sense.

The low-cost strategy suggests that companies simply need to offer versions of their existing products that have been stripped of features in order to lower the price in emerging markets. Yet poverty is not a condition that affects only the purchasing power of the consumer; it pervades their entire lifestyle. As a consequence, it is not sufficient to compete solely on price; the product specification is also crucial. As in any other market, low cost and differentiation win the heart of the fair consumer.

Research by Eyring et al. (2011) came to the same realisation after looking at a number of different emerging markets. In India the researchers found that the need was not for standard refrigerators that stored perishable food supplies and ice-cold drinks but machines that could preserve leftovers from meals for a couple of days and keep drinks refreshingly cool. In response, the domestic manufacturer, Godrej, designed an entirely new refrigerator that was a compact, top loader that did without the usual complexities of a compressor and instead used more basic, reliable cooling techniques. At US$69 it was affordable, easily portable and met the needs of the consumers in that market.

The authors of the research suggested a new and systematic approach to markets. Their model comprises four elements:

- Customer value proposition (CVP) – consumer demand, affordability
- Key resources – commitment needed for the project
- Key processes – core skills required for the project
- Profit formula – costs and revenue expectations.

In developed markets the researchers claim that product differentiation takes precedence, so the analysis is conducted from the CVP and continues down. In emerging markets, where price is paramount, then the analysis starts at the bottom with the profit formula and works up to CVP. However, it could be argued that their research supports the idea that all markets require both simultaneous cost minimisation and value maximisation. It is not that poverty leads consumers to give price the highest priority; it is that often they are forced to accept what is available at the price they can afford. As Godrej found, even the least wealthy have their own specific product requirements; the successful product is the one that delivers what the customer wants at the price they can afford. For all markets, price and differentiation are simultaneous.

Point of consideration: One of the most over-used compliments to an expert salesperson is that they could 'sell refrigerators to Eskimos'. The idea is, of course, that no one living in a land of permanent snow and ice needs an appliance for keeping things cool. In fact this is wrong and there is demand for such devices, just not of the type we are used to seeing in the rest of the world. How would you go about analysing the need for such an appliance and what type of product would you propose?

Source: Eyring, Johnson and Nair, 2011

? MULTIPLE CHOICE QUESTIONS

1. Do customers value product features?
    a. No, they only value product benefits.
    b. They might, if they see the benefit.
    c. Yes, customers are always looking for product developments.

2. Customers will always pay more for product benefits
    a. True, the benefits are the reason why they want the product.
    b. False, some benefits have no value.
    c. Maybe, if the price of the benefit does not exceed the value.

3. To what extent should products be adapted to local market conditions?
    a. Minimally, as adaption means cost.
    b. As much as necessary to gain market acceptance.
    c. Not at all; markets are converging so the same product is sold worldwide.

4. According to Michael Porter, what is one way that products gain a competitive advantage?
    a. Differentiation – uniqueness meaning there are no rivals.
    b. Low price – the lowest price winds the highest volume of sales.
    c. Generic product features – appealing to the average consumer.

5. What is the most intense form of commitment to overseas marketing?
    a. Production focus.
    b. Sales focus.
    c. Global market strategy.

6. Which is better, product differentiation or minimum cost production?
    a. Production differentiation – it means there are no rival products.
    b. Minimum cost of production – it means there are no rival producers.
    c. Both – the two are mutually exclusive and should be targeted.

7. Senior managers should use the Four Ps model because:
    a. It is a quick and easy checklist.
    b. It forms the basis of a comprehensive market analysis.
    c. It results in a definitive strategy.

8. What price strategy would suit the sales of Korean whisky in Scotland?
    a. Skimming – low sales at a high price due to entrenched local competition.
    b. Penetration – high sales at a low price in order to beat the local competition.
    c. Cost plus – the cost of production plus an additional percentage to cover overheads.

9. How does 'dumping' impact on consumers?
    a. Low prices to the benefit of consumers.
    b. Long term higher prices and less product choice.
    c. A requirement on consumers to pay countervailing taxes.

10. What kind of product is suited to a push strategy?
    a. New houses in a large development area.
    b. High fashion clothing.
    c. Umbrellas on a rainy day.

Answers
1b, 2c, 3a, 4a, 5c, 6c, 7a, 8a, 9b, 10c

REFERENCES

Akroush M N (2011) 'The 7Ps classification of the services marketing mix revisited: an empirical assessment of their generalisability, applicability and effect on performance evidence from Jordan's services organisations' *Jordan Journal of Business Administration* 7(1), pp. 116–146

Bapna R, Jank W and Shmueli G (2008) 'Consumer surplus in online auctions' *Information Systems Research* 19(4), pp. 400–416

Calantone R J, Kim D, Schmidt J B and Cavusgil S T (2006) 'The influence of internal and external firm factors on international product adaptation strategy and export performance: a three-country comparison' *Journal of Business Research* 59(2), pp. 176–185

Cannon H M and Morgan F W (1990) 'A strategic pricing framework' *Journal of Consumer Marketing* 793, pp. 57–68

Cogan-Marie L and Charters S (2014) 'Can wine tourism remedy poor wine marketing? The case of Beaujolais from Academy of Wine Business Research', 8th International Conference, June 2014 www.academyofwinebusiness.com/wp-content/uploads/2014/07/CS03_Charters_Steve.pdf accessed 4 September 2015

Corbett C J, DeCroix G A and Ha A Y (2005) 'Optimal shared-savings contracts in supply chains: linear contracts and double moral hazard' *European Journal of Operational Research,* 163(3), pp. 653–667

Craig C S and Douglas S P (2005) *International Marketing Research*. Chichester: John Wiley & Sons

Eyring M J, Johnson M W and Nair H (2011) 'New business models in emerging markets' *Engineering Management Review, IEEE* 42(2), pp. 19–26

Füller J, Bartl M, Ernst H and Mühlbacher H (2006) 'Community based innovation: how to integrate members of virtual communities into new product development' *Electronic Commerce Research* 6(1), pp. 57–73

Goi C L (2009) 'A review of marketing mix: 4Ps or more?' *International Journal of Marketing Studies* 1(1), pp. 2–15

Guardian (2009) 'How to make it in marketing' *The Guardian* Friday 4 September 2009 by Eustice K A from www.careers.theguardian.com/best-of-the-forums-marketing-careers accessed 26 February 2015

Hill C W (1988) 'Differentiation versus low cost or differentiation and low cost: a contingency framework' *Academy of Management Review* 13(3), pp. 401–412

ILM (2013) Should senior managers have a university degree? 24 April 2013 from www.i-l-m.com/Insight/Edge/2013/May/should-senior-managers-have-a-university-degree accessed 11 June 2015

Indian Grape Processing Board (2014) Wines of India from www.igpb.in/indian-wine-sector/wines-of-india.html accessed 21 November 2014

Khalifa A S (2004) 'Customer value: a review of recent literature and an integrative configuration' *Management Decision* 42(5), pp. 645–666

Kotler P (2006) 'Alphabet soup' *Marketing Management* March/April 2006, p. 51

Kotler P, Armstrong G, Harris L C and Piercy N (2013) *Principles of marketing* (6th European edition). Harlow: Pearson Education

Lages L F and Lages C R (2004) 'The STEP scale: a measure of short-term export performance improvement' *Journal of International Marketing* 12(1), pp. 36–56

Lages L F, Jap S D and Griffith D A (2008) 'The role of past performance in export ventures: a short-term reactive approach' *Journal of International Business Studies* 39(2), pp. 304–325

McCarthy J E (1960) *Basic marketing: A managerial approach*. Homewood, IL: Richard D. Irwin

Meridium (2010) The Finnish marine industry: directory from www.meridiem.fi/uploads/images/Gallery/Fiiliskuvat/Final_MARINE%20DIRECTORY%202013%2005%2007_ml.pdf accessed 21 November 2014

Palmer A (2000) *Principles of marketing*. Oxford: Oxford University Press

Pennington J R and Ball A D (2009) 'Customer branding of commodity products: the customer-developed brand' *in Journal of Brand Management Jun2009*, 16(7), pp. 455–467

Porter M (2008) *Competitive advantage: Creating and sustaining superior performance*. New York: Simon and Schuster

Richardson M (2002) 'An elementary proposition concerning parallel imports' *Journal of International Economics* 56(1), pp. 233–245

Ricoh (2014) Company profile from www.ricoh.com/about/company/ accessed 22 November 2014

Scott L, Dolan C, Johnstone-Louis M, Sugden K and Wu M (2012) 'Enterprise and inequality: A study of Avon in South Africa' *Entrepreneurship Theory and Practice* 36(3), pp. 543–568

Tauras J A (2006) 'Smoke-free air laws, cigarette prices, and adult cigarette demand' *Economic Inquiry* 44(2), pp. 333–342

Urban G L (2005) 'Customer advocacy: a new era in marketing?' *Journal of Public Policy & Marketing* 24(1), pp. 155–159

Valentin E K (2001) 'SWOT analysis from a resource-based view' *Journal of Marketing Theory and Practice* 9(2) (Spring, 2001), pp. 54–69

WTO (2012) 'Anti-dumping regional regimes and the multilateral trading system: do regional anti-dumping regimes make a difference?' by Jean-Daniel Rey in *World Trade Organization Staff Working Paper* ERSD-2012-22, 31 October 2012

Zineldin M and Philipson S (2007) 'Kotler and Borden are not dead: myth of relationship marketing and truth of the 4Ps' *Journal of Consumer Marketing* 24(4), pp. 229–241

Zou S and Cavusgil S T (2002) 'The GMS: a broad conceptualization of global marketing strategy and its effect on firm performance' *Journal of Marketing* 66(4), pp. 40–56

Part III Global Locations

International business is a risky activity replete with traps for the unwary at every turn. The markets might be entirely unknown, from the peculiar preferences of the consumers to the mechanisms of delivery. No wonder these traps can become graves for the unwise speculator. Fortunately, internationalising companies do not have to jump in at the deep end and can progressively explore the new global locations that lie open before them.

Exporting is probably the simplest first step into overseas markets. According to stage theories of overseas expansion, such as the Uppsala internationalisation process model, exports are the first tentative step towards exploration of unfamiliar markets and locations. For some companies, it may be true that the managers are more comfortable dealing with psychically close locations first, i.e. those that are most familiar to them, if not actually geographically the closest.

As the lowest risk international strategy, exporting has its attractions. It often makes better use of existing production facilities and requires little product adaptation. Such leveraging of existing company assets serves to reduce unit costs and thereby raise profitability. It would be wrong, though, to believe that there are no risks attached. For example, the hands-off attitude to exporting can mean that the product is too much under the control of a local agent, who may have their own market strategy, one at odds with the company's. Such is the principal–agent problem.

Even getting the product to the market can be a challenging process. Administrative complexities inevitably increase costs, and it is unlikely that the product can be deposited in the market without any changes at all. At the very least, the packaging would have to reflect local language and culture. Freight costs can also be substantial. The company may even suffer an embarrassment of success when increased sales mean additional production facilities need to be built, negating all those cost advantages of filling the vacant production capacity it already had.

Success with exporting may oblige the company to look at putting roots down in the overseas market. Foreign direct investment (FDI) enables the company to retain management control in a way that licensing and franchise agreements do not. This can be important if the vital competitive advantage lies with the product, the process or the way the company fits together. Whichever it is will decide if the company should go for a joint venture with a local partner, or take the wholly owned route with a new built greenfield site or the takeover of an established local enterprise.

FDI does not only benefit the investing company but also the local industry. For poorer countries, it is often touted as an engine for economic development and, although this has probably been overplayed, the employment alone is more than welcome. That said, the impact of FDI is not related to the condition of the local economy; rich countries also benefit from the incoming investment. In fact, the wealth of their markets means that they attract far more FDI than do the poorer countries.

Globalisation, though, is not solely concerned with companies extending themselves into overseas locations through exporting and FDI. International markets are now so transformed that companies can exploit globalisation without themselves being globalised. They do this through the international supply chain, management of which presents perhaps the most modern of management challenges.

Admittedly, there is nothing modern in the extraction of maximum value from the company's various activities, although Michael Porter's Value Chain Model is a useful management tool. The advance that globalisation has brought is to include the value chains of suppliers and buyers around the world in the management analysis. This has meant that companies can exploit the core competencies, not only of their own companies, but of all the companies with which they interact. It is because of this that no company, no matter how small, can claim to be untouched by globalisation.

7 Managing Exporting and Importing

Chapter Objectives

The least committed form of internationalisation is for a company to engage in exporting and importing. There may be perfectly good reasons for this: for example, mining companies are tied to their location, so exporting is the only route to overseas markets. Equally, there are companies that must import their supplies since they are just not available in the home markets. Then there are those companies for whom exporting is the first tentative step into the great overseas markets. In this chapter, we will look at the strategies and mechanisms of importing and exporting:

- Opportunities and risks of exporting.
- Management decision-making process.
- Different types of exporting and importing.
- Financing exports and imports.
- Emergence of e-commerce.

STEPPING ONTO THE WORLD STAGE

Firms that are exploring international markets have the luxury of being able to choose which markets to enter and how to do it. This is because they are almost always working from an established base in their home market. The only exception to this are the **'born global'** firms, usually operating online so the minute they are launched they are accessible to customers around the world.

Although online enterprises claim to be in the vanguard of a global business revolution, for the time being the traditional approach still dominates. This means companies, for a variety of reasons, look to extend their established home market activities into new, foreign markets. From their domestic redoubts they can choose how, when and where to enter. They can also be selective about the product with which they enter.

Some theoretical models, such as the **Uppsala internationalisation process model**, argue that companies will enter unfamiliar markets in predetermined series of steps. Critics, such as Ruzzier et al. (2006), counter that this is unnecessarily restrictive, particularly in the modern evolution of globalisation with its dynamic pace of business. In reality, managers will devise a strategy for internationalisation based on their analysis of the company's capabilities and market opportunities. While this is not a process for the faint hearted, neither is it a time for taking unnecessary risks: there is quite enough risk already in just entering foreign markets, and any more would be plain reckless.

A manager's job is to minimise risk for any investment. Even when the investment is high risk by nature, the actual risk should never be higher than it has to be. One relatively low-risk method for entering a new market is to export a product from an established production site in the domestic base.

The manager's task is to evaluate whether this lower risk strategy is appropriate to the capabilities of the company and the market opportunity.

RECORDING EXPORTING AND IMPORTING ACTIVITIES

Exporting and importing are the activities that comprise international trade. They are simply mirror images of each other: an export by one country is an import by another, and vice versa. Any kind of goods and services that can be traded count as exports and imports, the flows being measured in the **current account** of the nation's **balance of payments** (IMF, 2009). They do not include financial investments, transfers or grants. Exports of services do not, by definition, involve flows of physical goods but should not be confused with financial transfers. Many developed economies depend heavily on the export of their expertise in service industries. For example, over a third of UK exports are made up of services (ONS, 2014).

Although **trade in services** has become increasingly important with the rise of mass communication, which has enabled the rapid improvements in knowledge transfer, it is still **trade in goods** that demands the greater investment commitment. There is a much higher requirement for physical infrastructure in product freight and handling. For some countries, trade in goods can be quite volatile, particularly when it comes to seasonal products.

Trade in goods is measured in two distinct ways with respect to whether the reference is to exports or imports, as defined by the International Chamber of Commerce (ICC, 2010). Exports are measured as **FOB**, or free on board. We can think of this as the cost of the products as they are loaded onto ships and aircraft waiting to be dispatched to overseas markets. When the countries are joined by a land border then it is the value of the goods as they sit on the truck or train waiting to be carried over the border. FOB is the cost of the product and the handling charges up to the point where they will leave the country, but free of any further charges related to international freight. The value of the product is the same as it would be if it were about to be delivered to a warehouse for storage, retail outlet or customer in the domestic market. It is then possible to make comparisons between the value of goods produced for export and those produced for the domestic market.

At the other end of the trade the product is being imported. At the port of arrival the value of the product is measured as **CIF**, or cost insurance freight. This is the cost of the product plus charges for the freight and insurance during the period of carriage. In the host country the cost of the import as it is unloaded at the port can then be directly compared to the cost of a domestically produced product as it leaves the factory gate. CIF can be thought of as export FOB with the addition of international transport costs. Figure 7.1 illustrates the concepts of CIF and FOB as they might relate to the movement of goods across the English Channel.

Although exports and imports should match in value it is the cost difference between the FOB and CIF measurements that mean imports are recorded at a higher value than exports. Further anomalies in trade figures are due to variations in the way countries measure their trade and even the fact that at any one time a large number of goods are still in transit, recorded by one country as an export but yet to be recorded by the other as an import. This is most noticeable for trade in very large, high value products like aircraft and ships.

CHARACTERISTICS OF EXPORTERS

The stereotypical exporter would be a large corporation that has come to dominate its home market and is now looking for new markets overseas. Many people might also imagine it to be led by an ambitious management team that are known to be aggressive risk takers. Professional managers, however, know

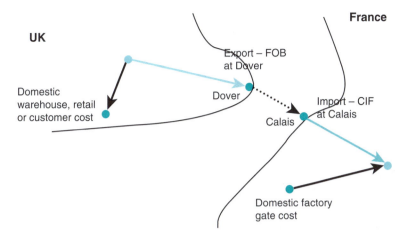

Figure 7.1 *Recording exports and imports*

that an export strategy is rooted in an objective evaluation of the company and its market opportunities. As business itself has globalised, so all companies will need to consider exporting as part of their strategic planning. Indeed, small companies can have an advantage in some industries because they can respond more quickly to changes in their export markets (Verwaal and Donkers, 2002).

There is some truth in the common view that exporters tend to have already gained a leading position in their domestic, home markets. Inevitably, this means that they are often relatively large enterprises compared to their home and host country rivals. There are exceptions to this rule and smaller firms may use exporting as a route to growth, building up their production capacity to attain a more efficient size.

The management team may also appear to be comparatively risk tolerant, but this should not be taken as a sign of an aggressive style but more to do with managers who are prepared to act on their convictions. If, after objective evaluation, they find that exporting is the logical step, then they are obliged to take the appropriate action. To uninformed observers the new internationalisation strategy may appear dramatic, but in fact it is the result of a cold decision-making process.

At a national level exporters can play a crucial role in the economy. For developing economies, it means that the companies can find markets for their goods that may barely exist at home, providing them with sufficient revenues to justify reinvestment the business and raise it to international standards of competitiveness. For developed economies, exporters play a role in the balance of payments, offsetting the value of imports. Indeed, the top 1% of exporters in the world are the 'international superstars', making up 53% of the value of the goods and services being traded around the globe. Some individual companies, like Nokia in Finland and Intel in Costa Rica, can contribute 20% of total national exports (World Bank, 2012).

OPPORTUNITY AND RISK OF EXPORTING

As an example of corporate growth the expansion opportunities of exporting might look self-evident. Yet it is not growth itself that managers need to pursue but opportunities for improved rates of return. If export sales offer low rates of profit or require expensive investments in new production facilities then the expansion in units produced can actually result in a lowering of financial returns per unit. In this type of situation the total revenues grow but not as fast as the production volumes, so the company is actually less profitable. The first task for a manager, then, is to analyse the opportunities and their value to the company.

- **Exploiting existing production capacity.** The drive to export may come from the company's need to fill idle production capacity in the short term (Malmberg et al., 2000). This may involve diversification of sales, finding markets where demand is in an opposing cycle to domestic demand, with the effect that the sum of the two cycles results in a constant rate of production. The pressure to do this depends on the nature of the production system, and it is most pernicious in the case of high fixed cost, capital intensive operations. In such cases the marginal cost of exporting can be low since it mostly comprises comparatively minor variable costs.

  In the longer term the company may be looking at accessing the economies of scale in the industry, particularly if rivals have already reached this level. The company will then be looking for sufficient additional sales to justify a larger plant that can offer the required scale.
- **Low risk route to overseas expansion.** Identifying the sales opportunities in new markets is only part of the story; managers must also minimise the risks of supplying that demand. Building a new plant in the target market represents a heavy commitment and therefore a high risk. If the rates of return in the market do not justify the financial outlay of a new local facility then exporting from an existing home facility could be the better option. Buch et al. (2009) also found that exporting can, in some respects, offer lower risk than domestic expansion because it offers diversification across multiple markets.
- **Increases in revenue.** As economists would argue, the marginal increase in revenue must at least equal the marginal increase in cost. In other words, the additional effort made in winning export orders must be compensated for by an equivalent increase in income. Better still, the marginal revenue should exceed the marginal cost of exporting. If not, then the company could find that it is making less profit than its rivals.
- **Learning effects.** Stage model theories of internationalisation are founded on the notion of psychic proximity: companies choose the most similar market to enter first and do so from an existing domestic production base. They are then able to use exports as a way of learning about the foreign market environment before progressing to subsequent commitment stages such as production. The commercial reality is that the mode of entry is dictated by the nature of the market opportunities and the company's own ability to exploit them. Nevertheless, companies in developing nations can find that exports give them insights into foreign technologies that can then be incorporated into new product development (Das et al., 2007).

Having assessed the opportunities the manager then needs to set these against the risks which can be firm-specific, country-specific or external to both (Alvarez, 2004). Clearly, if the increased risk of entering unfamiliar markets is not justified by the financial rate of return then the export strategy is not recommended. Managers therefore need to take the following issues into consideration:

- **Loss of control and responsiveness.** A major disadvantage with exporting is that the company is generally a step or two removed from the new market. There are barriers to communication such as language differences or the intermediary position of a local agent. For geographically distant markets there is the simple matter of items being in transit for extended periods over a lengthy supply line. This has particular importance for goods with a short shelf life, such as perishable goods or items of fashion. Responses to market changes can be handicapped by time lags that local competitors will not suffer from and can exploit to their advantage.

- **Lack of local knowledge.** Unlike when it first took to the stage in its home market a company may be entering the foreign market completely blind. SMEs (small medium enterprises) are most vulnerable since they have a smaller management team who are less likely to have experience of those markets. Larger firms have extensive management teams that can offer a more diverse range of overseas experience. Indeed, larger firms may be more capable of attracting an international range of managers in the first place.
- **Intimidated by 'foreignness'.** This goes beyond a lack of knowledge and brings into question the psychology of the management team, especially at SMEs. If they have no experience of operating overseas then the managers may perceive obstacles to exporting that in reality are not as great as they suppose. Stage model theories suggest that the company can first explore psychically close markets, those that are geographically and culturally familiar. However, the sense of apprehension may prevent even that small step.
- **Freight and tariff costs.** Exports are most effective when freight and tariff costs are low relative to the value of the product. When freight costs are high, perhaps because the product is bulky and of low value like cement, or because the target country is attempting to repel imports by high tariff and non-tariff barriers, then local production would be the preferred option. This means, though, that the local market would then have to be large enough to justify entering with such a high-commitment, high-risk strategy. A common compromise solution is to export the good in a partly disassembled, kit form which is then assembled locally.
- **High costs in the target market.** Even where high freight costs and barriers to entry point to local production, if production costs in the market are relatively high then exporting can still be the better option.

 ## CASE STUDY – EXPORTING CHICKEN FROM AN EMERGING MARKET

Brazil may be considered a developing economy but it has become a major player in international trade. According to the United Nations, in 2013 Brazil imports were valued at US$239.6 billion while exports amounted to US$242.2 billion. Most of the trade was in the traditional form of commodities from Brazil for manufacturing into finished products in other countries and then importing back to Brazil. As a result, Brazil has grown to become one of the world's biggest exporters of iron ore and oil.

As a developing economy Brazil has also been dependent on its agricultural industry, exporting soy beans and sugar. Symbolic of its growing economic stature, though, has been its rise to prominence as an exporter of chicken meat. In 2011 the country produced 13.1 million tons, making it the third biggest producer in the world behind the United States and China. Of this, 30.2% went for export and was worth US$8.2 billion to the Brazilian economy. The biggest overseas market was the Middle East, followed by the continents of Asia and Africa. The most important single market was Saudi Arabia.

As the Brazilian industry has expanded it has enabled particular regions of the country to specialise. This has increased the learning effects and allowed companies to access economies of scale. The industry has also broadened its scope, increasing output of related products like turkey, duck and egg products. Increasingly, these products are processed, helping Brazil to industrialise. It is interesting to note that the poultry industry is conducting genetic research, which has positive knock-on effects for the nation's scientific community.

Point of consideration: Brazil's neighbour Argentina has long been a major exporter of beef. In a similar way to Brazil's poultry industry, how can Argentina use the beef industry as an export 'superstar', helping the national economy as a whole?

Sources: United Nations, 2014; Brazilian Poultry Association, 2012

EXPORT DECISION-MAKING PROCESS

Although the stage model theories of how companies build up their export commitment have little empirical or practical support this does not mean that managers simply throw themselves into an exporting strategy with little planning. On the contrary, the planning process should go through a systematic series of evaluations to ensure that the export opportunities are financially justifiable and that the company has the capability to exploit them to its benefit. Naturally, there is little point in chasing export sales that are unprofitable and cause the company to lose its hard-won competitive position.

Figure 7.2 sets out the kind of sequence of decisions that managers need to go through when evaluating how and when to implement a new export strategy. It is an iterative process in the sense that it should be practised each time the company finds a new export market. Note that it explicitly includes a role for external expertise in the decisions in order to avoid the kind of problems described by Elbanna (2006), amongst others, with reference to internal resources, company politics and management competence.

With exporting, the company is looking to boost the volume of output using the existing resources as much as possible. It is because of this that the strategy is often perceived as low risk, though if the opportunity cost of exporting is the failure to embrace an even greater opportunity for manufacturing overseas then the reduced risk is an illusion.

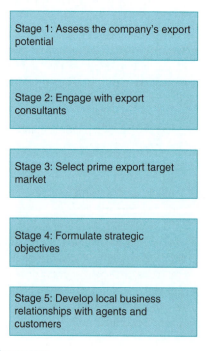

Figure 7.2 *Export decision-making process*

In the early stages the company managers need to identify and quantify the capacity available for exports. This is not just about filling idle production capacity but also unused capabilities throughout the organisation. These capabilities include product development, particularly when it comes to adapting products to local markets. Other capabilities comprise marketing, administrative functions and management time. If any substantial investments have to be made in order to make exports possible then the management team need to acknowledge that they are moving beyond the limits of a basic export strategy and are encroaching on a separate investment strategy.

The risk in exporting comes from the lack of familiarity with the new market. The company may be fortunate in having internal managerial resources, principally personnel who have direct experience of the market, but often the company will be dependent on bringing in consultants from outside the company. Government assistance can be invaluable because governments are generally very supportive of exporting. For example, the Canadian government has a Trade Commission with representatives around the world and its own *Step-by-Step Guide to Exporting* with a handy checklist for managers (Canadian Trade Commissioner Service, 2014):

- Assess your company's export readiness
- Build an export plan
- Research and select your target market
- Create an export marketing plan
- Determine the best methods of delivering your product or service to your target market
- Develop a sound financial plan
- Understand the key legal aspects of international trade.

The home government will often help in identifying target markets, but host government assistance in the target market is often less constructive because imports are seen as competition for the domestic companies. The Canadian Trade Commission, for example, has no equivalent guide for imports but instead invites foreign direct investment (FDI) which would substitute local production for imports.

In any case, imports tend to experience a pull effect from the market, so in a free-market economy the government would not be in the business of promoting particular products when the consumers can decide for themselves. Naturally, market research becomes vital when formulating the strategic objectives but they continue to play a part, as they always should, as the company develops its strategies and tactics in response to events.

As an alternative, local agents can act for the company in the new market. They will have the market knowledge to be able to anticipate levels of demand and how to implement a distribution system to bring the product to the market. However, these local agents may reduce risk for the company but they also introduce a new element of risk. This is the classic **principal–agent problem** where the principal, here the exporting company, is at the mercy of its agent. If the strategies of the principal and the agent are not aligned and the agent acts for its own advantage then, *ipso facto*, the company will find its own strategy is not being properly implemented.

EXPORT OPTIONS

The traditional form of exporting involves shipping products to a foreign market and then selling them through the normal distribution and retail networks. Conceptually at least, there is little difference between that and the home market except that the foreign market is so much more unfamiliar. It is due to this lack of familiarity that exporters often use local agents until they have built up enough experience to go it alone. Depending on the company's familiarity with the market, what we call the psychic distance, and the strategic objectives there is a choice of two styles of exporting (Hessels and Terjesen, 2007):

- Direct export
- Indirect export.

To this we can now add a third export option:

- E-commerce.

DIRECT EXPORT

Direct export selling is what we might call the traditional form of exporting. The company is effectively treating the export market as an extension of the domestic market. As always in business the company strives to minimise the amount of adaptation to local market conditions so that it can avoid incurring additional costs. At the extreme, if the product is so thoroughly customised to the local market that it almost constitutes a new product then the whole rationale behind the export strategy is called into question. Under these circumstances it might even be worth the company considering local production, even in a limited form.

On the one hand the exporting company enjoys the economic benefits of leveraging its existing resources, perhaps also smoothing out the fluctuations in its production flows where the new market offers a diversification in demand. On the other hand there is also the significant matter of heightened risk due to the lack of knowledge about the new market. In practice, the company is likely to employ the services of some kind of local agent, although of course this itself introduces additional risks and costs. Even direct exporting involves the use of an intermediary of some sort.

The type of intermediary that the company might choose depends on the level of knowledge that it has on its chosen market. The company's knowledge can range from understanding all aspects except the final point-of-sale retail activity to complete ignorance of the entire export and distribution process. Categorising these levels of knowledge into three we have the following approaches that the exporter can make:

- **Sales to foreign retailers** – when the exporter has a high degree of confidence in its ability to manage much of the export process then it may sell directly to the local retailers only at the last stage. This means that the exporting company must take responsibility for all import administration, distribution and marketing. This would be particularly appealing when the product's brand reputation precedes it so that it already enjoys good recognition in the local market.

  This does not help with the challenge of distributing the product to the retailers. Under certain circumstances the local postal service can be used but this is only suitable when the product is relatively small and sold in low volume. There could also be significant difficulties in the customer-facing tasks at the point-of-sale if the product is not already well known.
- **Sales to local agents** – local sales agents are used where the problem is only how to bring about the final transaction with the customer. The exporting company may need help with communicating with the customers due to language problems. The local sales agents will act in place of the company's own sales force, speaking with customers, processing orders and dealing with inquiries.

  The problem with this approach is that the company risks losing control of the vital customer relationship: the local agents might attempt to sell too aggressively, or have interest only in short-term sales gains. It is therefore important that the company's management prepares the contractual details with great care to ensure that the local sales agents behave as the company's own internal sales team would do.

- **Sales to distributors** – creating a distribution network from scratch can be very challenging. It requires a close study of demand patterns throughout the new market and the logistics needed to serve that demand. Without that knowledge the exporting firm can hand the tricky job over to a local distributor. Since the distributor would already be established in the market and would be diversified across a variety of products the distributor should be able to offer a flexible package. For example, the first target could be sales in major cities before moving on to peripheral areas. If the distributor has the complete network in place then the transition should be a smooth one.

  The kinds of problems that might occur include selecting a local distributor that cannot offer full market coverage and so is relatively inflexible when it comes to developing the local strategy. The exporting company can then find itself trapped in a distribution network that is incapable of reaching all its potential customers. There may also be problems with the distributor's own ability to handle the exporter's products, leading to product damage and high warranty claims from customers.

INDIRECT EXPORT

As we have seen, the direct exporter can run into difficulties tackling the idiosyncrasies of the local market. It therefore finds it has to rely on the services of various intermediaries and agents, all of which introduce additional costs and new risks. The direct exporter is closely involved in the local market but their efforts are augmented by the knowledge and skills of local enterprises.

For many analysts (e.g. McCann, 2013) any export activity involving intermediaries is considered indirect. Since all exporting involves some sort of local intermediary let's clarify the definition of indirect exporting: indirect exporting avoids the problems of the company dealing with the local market by simply avoiding any contact with it at all. Instead the entire process is handled by intermediaries, from specialist export–import agencies to government-to-government contacts. These bodies are not augmenting the local operations of the company, they are taking full responsibility, which implies that the company is therefore denied the opportunity to gain international experience (Yasar, 2015).

- **Export management companies (EMC)** do not handle the product themselves but will arrange for companies to do so. EMCs are adept at the administrative side of international trade and will ensure that the complexities of paperwork and bureaucracy do not become an impediment to doing business in the target market (Market Network Exchange, 2014). Sadly, this means that marketing activities tend to take a backseat and the exporting company needs to engage other agencies. All this will eat into the exporter's profits and reduce its ability to control its own affairs, meaning that it may miss out on new opportunities emerging in the market.
- **Export trading companies (ETC)** take a more hands-on approach than EMCs. They are responsible for shipping, storing and distributing the product in the target market. They may also take a more active role in marketing the product. This is a turnkey operation with all the advantages for the exporter of having a strategy put in place with impressive rapidity. Naturally, there are costs to pay, from the fees to the ETC to the danger of new opportunities going undetected. As with the EMC the nature of the relationship means that the exporter is not learning about the local market for itself and so will find it difficult to establish its own capabilities in the future.
- **Government-to-government (G2G)**. When an industry is of crucial national importance then governments will express an interest. Often this is seen in arms deals where there are significant

political and security implications. For political reasons, governments do not want to be identified with supplies of arms to countries with poor human rights records. Equally, it can be highly embarrassing to be in a conflict with a country where it is facing its own weapons systems, though militarily this may not be a disadvantage. Indeed, there may be intelligence and logistical advantages to being the enemy's weapon supplier.

When governments take control of the exports of a company the partnership can be highly constructive. As the government's anointed supplier the company will find all domestic competitors are eliminated and the target government will most likely have entered into an exclusive deal to eliminate international competition as well. The volume of sales and price would be guaranteed, removing much of the risk of the deal. Governments tend to be very reliable customers, so there is often the possibility of repeat sales for many years to come.

G2G exports can also be highly restrictive. Some markets will be completely closed to the company because the home government would not sanction the exports. The government may also interfere in the internal affairs of the company, directing investment programmes and product specifications. Even in free-market economies this can mean that the company has a quasi-nationalised structure which often implies a lack of commercial discipline.

E-COMMERCE

Over the past few decades, the rise of the internet and online retailing has opened up many new international business opportunities. Fans of internet trading foresee a world without borders where free trade truly can be free. This kind of electronic or e-commerce is seen as categorically separate from direct and indirect forms of exporting because it operates without reference to national borders. With e-commerce the world is seen as one single market and many of the intermediaries of trade, such as sales agents, are eliminated. It opens up the channels of communication between all buyers and all sellers so that even narrow segments of the vast global market can be financially rewarding (Grandon and Pearson, 2004).

In such a utopian commercial world a consumer in China could order an item from a company based in South Africa, communicating with the company via its website. Neither party in the transaction has any concern for the other's location: the consumer has seen a product that they want at the right price and they place their order just as they would if the company was based in their own country. Although an export–import process takes place this is only in the physical movement of the good, all other processes are virtually automatic and have no respect for location.

The payment could be conducted by credit card or through one of the online payment organisations. The foreign exchange transaction would be handled by the financial organisation, the transaction costs being passed to one or other of the transacting parties. The product would be sent through an existing distribution network, such as the postal system, so there would be no need to create a new network. For both parties, then, e-commerce transactions hardly differ between domestic and international sales.

That, at least, is the theory. In practice, many of the challenges seen in direct exporting still exist in e-commerce. For the exporting company there may be fewer of the risks of operating in the foreign market but then it is also much less engaged. Since it will not necessarily be actively targeting the foreign markets where it is selling its products the company will be much more passive in its international strategy. It could even be argued that it has no international strategy at all. The company will not have conducted local market research, it will not be adapting its product to local market conditions or regulations and it will have no ability to learn from trading in the country. Essentially, the company is completely passive.

For the consumer the risks of dealing with an online company domiciled in a foreign country actually increase. First of all, perhaps most obviously, there can be language problems in navigating the company's website. Beyond this, though, Yao-Hua Tan (2000) argues that questions of trust come to the fore. There will also be question marks over the product's specification and whether the consumer will even be able to use it; electrical items, for example, may run on a different voltage. At least in a shop the consumer can inspect the physical item. Then, of course, the e-commerce consumer may be anxious about sending money overseas, or divulging their credit card details, to companies that are beyond the jurisdiction of their home country. Online payment organisations can alleviate some of this worry, but not all.

As a consequence e-commerce is not quite the retail revolution that was predicted. Online companies have to develop different versions of their website and include prices in the local currency. It is now a common feature of more popular websites to have the option to see it in various languages and currencies. The companies also need to offer products in specifications appropriate to the local market. The company may even find that it has to establish a new operation in the target market, serving local customers from its local website and distributing products in close proximity. When this happens e-commerce is less about exports and internationalisation, more about localisation.

In the business-to-business (**B2B**) sector the online revolution has been more subtle in its effects. **Information technology (IT)** means that the entire supply chain can be electronically connected, allowing the instant order and despatch of items. However, this can only be achieved within the limitations of the physical delivery system and it does nothing to create demand for the product in the market. Indeed, the system seems to work well during periods of stability when its efficiency means that products are delivered to the market in a timely fashion. Unfortunately, B2B e-commerce delivers fewer advantages during periods of instability or uncertainty when the obstacles exist in the marketplace itself. It is during these volatile periods that the IT system underlying the supply chain management needs to offer maximum flexibility (Iyer et al., 2009).

 ## CASE STUDY – RFID IN THE SUPPLY CHAIN

Radio frequency identification, or RFID, has become an indispensable part of stock and supply management. Although the term refers to a range of different technologies, they all have the common purpose of reading an identification label, such as a bar code, and transmitting the information in the code by radio to a computerised data handling system.

The RFID units can be used in a wide number of different applications to monitor the movement of stock. They can be found in situations as diverse as manufacturing plants and ports. They are most conspicuous as hand-held devices used in retail. Shop workers shine the laser scanner at a bar code and it then provides a readout of how much of the product is held in stock; the worker then has the ability to update the stock quantity. By feeding the information back into the central data system more stock can be automatically ordered.

The US retail chain Walmart was in the vanguard of this supply chain revolution. Beginning in 2003, it required its suppliers to identify all deliveries using the RFID tags. This had the twin benefits of establishing an RFID standard and reducing the cost of the tags thanks to economies of scale. The tags contain a 96-bit EPC (electronic product code), enough to identify every product ever made. Raising the visibility of items in stock means efficiencies can be made in reduced buffer stocks and less labour input, while increasing sales through greater product availability.

There is concern that RFID capability is too detailed. In some cases the tags have triggered video surveillance so that consumer behaviour with the product can be observed. The technology has also been used to monitor employees as an anti-theft measure. There are even suggestions that human beings could be implanted with a tag acting as a key to unlock personal information.

Point of consideration: If human beings were tagged at birth, what advantages would that bring to society? How would it threaten the freedom of individuals?

Source: Lockton V and Rosenberg R S (2005)

MANAGING IMPORTS

It is the demand for imports that powers international trade. Many countries have configured their economies around the importing of goods and services to the degree that they have become entirely dependent on them. Sometimes this is because they are completely incapable of providing the items themselves, as is often the case with fuels and other raw materials. It might also be that the country is using the functions of free trade to specialise in their comparative advantage and trade the surplus for imports of those items in which it has a comparative disadvantage. It is the mutual benefits that spring from the exchange of imports and exports that underpin the push towards global free trade.

Where importing differs from exporting is in the nature of the strategy. Exporting requires an explicit strategy that targets a market with a select product or service. The strategy needs to be implemented in a manner that recognises the challenges specific to that market. This takes meticulous planning from the management.

Importing, however, is often much less explicit, and the final customer may not even be aware that the item they have purchased is an import. They benefit from the wider choice of products that comes with access to global producers as well as the possibility of lower prices. Overseas producers may be in a low-cost location, perhaps due to lower labour costs, or they may have the advantages of specialisation and economies of scale. The consumer will be unaware of any increased risk due to the overseas origin of the product because the risk will be carried by the retailer or supplier in accordance with domestic consumer laws.

For corporate managers it is not quite so simple because importing usually involves the procurement of supplies for inclusion in a complex production process. Since these supplies come from overseas markets this means that there are a number of risks involved:

- **Exchange rate risk** – that the price paid is different to the one agreed. Fortunately for the company it is often the supplier that carries this risk.
- **Supply risk** – whether the product is delivered at the agreed time. Production systems are increasingly run according to lean principles, so delivery times have become crucial.
- **Product specification** – the item being supplied must meet local market and legal requirements.
- **Product support** – the ability to continue providing service, maintenance and other support over the life of the product.

Since much of the import risk can be transferred to the supplier the strategy of buying overseas becomes implicit rather than explicit. A company will simply define the product specification and then evaluate tenders from suppliers without regard to their actual location. The creation of a **global supply chain** offers a wider choice of production specifications and prices, with some benefits from the diversification of supply. However, the importing of supplies only affects the operations of the company where they offer incremental improvements. For example, a firm may import capital equipment to replace the local workforce; it is not the importing that changes the operations but the equipment. The fact that the equipment has been imported is incidental to any changes that may be made to the production system. This is one reason why importing is not a strategy in its own right, like that of exporting, although it may be part of a strategy to build a global supply chain.

A global supply chain is not location specific. The company is at liberty to secure supplies from where it finds the specification and price that it needs. Indeed, it is quite possible that the supplier could be domestic. For smaller firms the search and co-ordination costs of a global supply chain may outweigh the benefits, so it will tend to source locally. Yet the globalisation of supply means that even then they may be unwittingly purchasing items that comprise imported components.

Firms that are running a global sourcing strategy will tend to be large since these firms are more likely to be controlling their own supply chains. The strategy is non-discriminatory in the sense that specific countries will not be targeted, although it may well be that a close relationship may develop with one supplier in a particular location. Again, it is the supplier that is identified, not the location.

GOVERNMENT RESISTANCE TO IMPORTS

It is this pervasive globalisation that confounds political campaigns to buy domestically produced goods and services. These campaigns claim to support domestic industry in spite of the known benefits of international trade. The government in its role as a major consumer may have a 'buy domestic' policy but sourcing a product that has been produced solely with domestic inputs can be almost impossible. Even if the physical components are sourced domestically, the technical knowhow could be foreign.

Governments are on more rational ground when they require domestic purchases for security reasons. Weapons for national defence are the most obvious example but there may also be policies for agriculture in order to guarantee food supplies during time of conflict. Most developed countries, which have comparative advantages in manufacturing, will also subsidise the agricultural sector in order to maintain production even when it is not economically efficient to do so. In addition to this, concerns about disease can also give rise to anti-import regulations, Adamson and Cook (2007) making reference to the very real threat of 'exotic' species to a geographically isolated country like Australia.

FINANCING IMPORTS AND EXPORTS

As we have seen, there is heightened risk, particularly on the financial side, for companies that join international trade. For the importer there are concerns that what they have paid for will actually be delivered, and for exporters that what they have delivered will be paid for. These conflicting anxieties over exploitation by either party in the deal create a need for an intermediary who can secure both payment and product.

This is a role that banks commonly take on. It can be a complicated process with the bank holding title (i.e. ownership) to the product even if it does not have the product in its physical possession (Levi, 2005). The transfer of goods and payment goes through a number of steps:

1. The importer makes an agreement with the bank for the bank to pay for the good on its behalf.
2. The bank agrees with the exporter to pay for the good.

3. The exporter transfers the title to the good to the bank and the bank effectively takes ownership, if not physical possession.
4. The bank pays for the good.
5. The bank transfers the title to the good to the importer and thus physical delivery to the importer can take place.
6. The importer pays the bank.

The fees for the transaction are a significant addition to the total costs of the deal and need to be set against the risks of doing business directly between exporter and importer. If the risks are small in relation to the value of the deal, or the costs of transacting through an intermediary are high, then a direct approach might be preferable.

A compromise solution might be to use an **escrow account**. In this a third party holds an account in which the funds for payment are deposited. The escrow account holder has control over the release of the funds but does not take title of ownership over the good. The funds are released for payment once the contractual terms of the transaction have been fulfilled. At the extreme this may mean that the funds are not released until the good has been physically delivered to the purchaser. In this way the seller is guaranteed to receive payment once delivery has taken place and the buyer knows that the payment will not be final if delivery has not taken place. The US agency, International Trade Administration, does warn, however, that this can create cash flow problems for the buyer since their money is tied up ahead of receiving the goods (ITA, 2013).

Escrow accounts have become especially popular with small firms that are trading online. They guarantee payment for them while providing reassurance to the customer. However, these transactions do not involve contractual obligations for the payment to coincide with delivery. Instead, online escrow payments act as a quality assurance mechanism. For the buyer this means they feel reassured that the seller is legitimate and, most importantly, is not gaining direct access to their personal bank account. Since increased numbers of customers will be attracted by this additional level of security it is the seller who pays the fee. Online businesses that do not offer payment secured through escrow would struggle to sell their wares.

CASE STUDY – PAYPAL

A major problem with online retail is that customers worry that their payment will go to an unscrupulous dealer who has no intention of shipping the item, and even that they will suffer the nightmare of giving away their personal bank details for subsequent criminal exploitation.

To an extent credit cards help to alleviate such anxieties because they can act as intermediaries. They guarantee payment to the seller and require settlement from the purchaser by a certain date in the future. In some countries the credit card provider is jointly responsible with the seller for the delivery of a product in good condition. The reassurances are useful in attracting customers so the transaction fee is paid by the seller.

PayPal was launched in 1999 as a spin-off from Confinity, a more basic form of online payment system, but it was in 2000 when X.com took control that PayPal began to realise its potential. It then really got into its stride after it was purchased by eBay in 2002. The online payment system was the perfect partner to the myriad of small businesses and private sellers who were trading on the eBay platform. Unlike credit cards PayPal makes it very easy for money to flow backwards and forwards between sellers and buyers while maintaining enough separation between them for security. Not only payments but also refunds could be swiftly completed. Over longer periods interest can be earned on outstanding balances. It is the sellers who pay for the service, the cost being dependent on the status of the seller and the value of the deal.

Customers soon became familiar with PayPal and realised that it could be used for more than just purchases on eBay. By 2008 PayPal transactions outside eBay exceeded those within it for the first time. In 2013 the company handled over US$212 billion. Unassailable though PayPal may seem there are rivals waiting in the wings. For example, with the wider use of smart phones for internet access consumers find it useful to transfer payments via their phone charges. Banks are also using the same platform to fight back, permitting payments through smart phones.

Point of consideration: Evaluate the advantages to eBay consumers of having PayPal as an integral part of the company. Suggest what the disadvantages might be, not only to eBay consumers but also other online shoppers.

Source: PayPal, 2014

Governments are another source of intermediary funding. It is common for them to provide loans to support export activities, particularly for industries that are considered to be of core economic importance or where there are vast sums of money involved. Both Airbus and Boeing, fierce rivals in the civil aviation industry, are highly dependent on government financial support when launching new products or chasing export orders. There is much less need for importers to seek similar government support since they are not as vulnerable to being exploited.

 MANAGEMENT SPOTLIGHT: THE BUREAUCRACY OF TRADE

It seems inevitable that trading across national borders will lead to businesses becoming entangled in international red tape. These are the bureaucratic obstacle courses that add to the management burden and increase the costs of exporting and importing. It is for this reason that larger companies have specialist administration teams handling the processes but bureaucracy also acts as a serious disincentive for smaller firms who fear they cannot spare the managerial time. We will look at just a few of these various bureaucratic considerations (Tradegoods.com, 2014):

1. **Export licence** – some products, particularly those that are high value or security sensitive, require a special licence before they can be allowed to leave the country. Government departments are notoriously slow in granting these licences, which is then an impediment to the company's competitive position. Foreign rivals have an opportunity to sneak in and take the opportunity.
2. **Import licence** – although the theoretical benefits of free trade are generally accepted there is still reluctance from many governments to allow imports to pour into the country unchecked. Some governments require that an import licence be obtained. Import licences are often used for agricultural goods on health and safety grounds and they act as a non-tariff barrier.
3. **Letter of credit** – issued by the buyer's bank to the seller as proof of ability to pay. The payment will be made when the agreed terms have been met.
4. **Bill of lading** – a document issued by the carrier of the good to the exporter. It is more than a receipt, it is a legal document stating that the good has been received and is ready for transportation.

5. **Bill of exchange** – the document setting out the price to be paid by the importer and the date of payment. A **sight bill of exchange** must be paid when the importer has seen it, a **usance bill of exchange** must be paid within a time limit.

Kneller and Pisu (2011) noted that these kinds of procedures acted as one of the major barriers to trade. Firms are intimidated by the bureaucratic challenges and report the highest number of problems in the early years of tackling them. However, experienced firms report far fewer problems, so there is clearly a strong learning effect as companies absorb the administrative demands into their normal routines.

Point of consideration: Experience is vital for creating a smooth process for export administration. How can nascent exporters access this experience as they start out?

Sources: Kneller and Pisu, 2011; Tradegoods.com, 2014

COUNTER TRADE

Companies can find exporting and importing a bureaucratically exhausting process. As we have seen, at each stage in the process the parties involved need to assess potential markets, modes of entry and the risks of achieving the expected financial rates of return. Naturally, companies will strive at every turn to reduce the risk and simplify the process. An approach comprising a number of different variations is for companies to counter trade with each other in lieu of cash payment. The approach has the additional advantage of finding political support since governments like to be seen to be balancing imports with exports.

While counter trade looks like a neat solution there are a number of obstacles to its use. One disadvantage is that the companies may have no direct use for the imported goods they are receiving so must take on the task of marketing them in their home market. Another problem is that counter trade is in opposition to the principles of the global supply chain. In theory, countries may export raw materials, or components, to be manufactured in another country and then imported as finished products. So iron ore may be exported and then manufactured steel goods, like domestic appliances, are imported as a return flow of trade. At the company level, though, the flow of material is in only one direction: when a mining company sends iron ore down the global supply chain it does not expect to receive thousands of washing machines coming in the other direction. As Yoffie (1984) points out, counter trade can be 'messy' and the financial results elusive, although it also creates strong bonds between the contracting parties.

The traditional method, and probably the original form of international trade, is to **barter** (Barter News Weekly, 2014). Companies can avoid the problems of bill payments and exchange rate risk by simply swapping their exported goods for imported goods from the same company. This completely avoids any problems with bill payments or currency values. It does mean, though, that the two types of good must be ready for exchange at the same time, and this is not always practicable. Agricultural goods generally have a limited shelf-life and their value is often seasonal. When bartered for manufactured goods the quantities required to make the deal can fluctuate throughout the year.

The essential problem with bartering is that it does not allow for value to be stored for any period of time. The exchange of goods needs to be simultaneous, even if the moment may be to the disadvantage of one party. The invention of money permitted the separation of the exchange of goods across time because it acts as a store of value. **Counter purchase** plays a similar role to money because it introduces a promise to hold the value of the deal while the exchange is conducted in two distinct phases. One set of goods is dispatched in the first phase, followed by the exchanged goods in the subsequent second phase. During the intervening period the value of the deal is held according to the contract and it means that each party can rely on the value of the goods they are trading.

In a global supply chain it is highly unlikely that each trading party will have a need for equivalent quantities of goods from each other. In an **offset** agreement the seller promises to purchase only a proportion of the value of the deal with the buyer. It is a conventional export sale but some of the revenue will be spent with the importer. While it only reduces, but does not entirely avoid, some of the problems of marketing goods received in lieu of cash payment the approach does at least attract political approval. A variation on the offset is a compensation or buyback agreement, an agreement by the seller to purchase some of the buyer's production output.

A compromise between traded goods and cash payment is **switch trading**. Here, the two companies contract with a third party, a trading house, who purchases the rights to the counter trade and sells them on to a buyer that has a direct need for the goods. This means that the two trading companies can convert the value of their counter trade into cash.

MANAGEMENT IMPLICATIONS FOR COUNTER TRADE

The complexities of counter trade are sure to keep any senior manager very busy. The kind of 'horse trading' that goes on is more reminiscent of dealing in used cars than international business. Small firms would therefore find the intricacies of counter trade too intimidating to engage in, so it is generally the larger firms that will engage in it. For this they will have a specialist team, most likely based in a central location or group headquarters.

Another reason why counter trade tends to be practised mainly by larger firms is that they usually involve large-scale transactions. The trade will often involve quantities of raw materials or manufactured goods that then need to be placed on the appropriate market for onward sale. Due to the nationally strategic nature of these large deals governments are often involved; indeed they may be encouraging counter trade as a way of promoting the country's overall trading position. The government's role may relieve the company of some of the administrative burden but it can also prolong and delay payments.

Small-scale transactions are more likely to be settled in cash terms, or by credit. For small firms this will be the most attractive option since they are unlikely to have the necessary managerial skills to deal with counter trade. Nevertheless, the increasing use of e-commerce for **business-to-business (B2B)** transactions does open up the potential for counter trade between smaller companies.

For large or small firms the greatest challenge of counter trade is the extent to which it distracts managers from their other tasks. What we are talking about here is a method of payment. It is not usually a central component of the company's strategy but a way of facilitating the strategy. Like all payment methods counter trade should be seen as a tactic rather than a strategy. The trouble is that as a tactic it can become so convoluted that it obscures the real purpose of the strategy.

 ## CASE STUDY – BAE AND THE AL YAMAMAH COUNTER TRADE

Al Yamamah is a defence industry contract between the UK defence contractor BAE and the government of Saudi Arabia. Although the UK had been a defence industry supplier to Saudi Arabia for many years, it was when the United States reduced its defence exports to the kingdom due to the powerful pro-Israel lobby in government that the UK came to the fore. The first agreement, a Memorandum of Understanding (MoU), was signed in 1985 and involved the supply of Tornado fighter/bombers, training aircraft, missile defence systems and full spares support. The second agreement, Al Yamamah II, was signed in 1988 and contracted for further Tornado deliveries.

The total value of the deal has never been fully disclosed but it is thought to be one of the most lucrative export deals the UK has ever contracted for. Some estimates have put the value of the two Al Yamamah phases at £43 billion. BAE has taken such a major role in the supply of arms to Saudi Arabia that the kingdom has become the company's second home market. BAE can almost be thought of as the Saudi defence industry. In 2005, BAE agreed with Saudi Arabia to continue the relationship with the supply of Typhoon fighter jets.

The unusual feature of the Al Yamamah agreements is the way in which the defence supplies are paid for. Saudi Arabia, perhaps not surprisingly, is paying in oil. This has been up to 600,000 barrels per day but rather than it going to BAE it went to the UK government which then sold it on to oil companies. A crucial reason for this was so that BAE would not be subject to volatile oil prices, which over the period have fluctuated from less than US$20 to over US$120. These variations in revenue would be a disaster for a company that needs predictable flows of cash in order to operate its business day to day. Naturally the UK government was willing to be involved since the deal was of huge importance to the UK economy as a whole, with knock-on benefits throughout the supplier network.

Point of consideration: In what way could similar government-to-government (G2G) contracts be used to encourage trade between developed and developing countries?

Source: Guardian, 2010

RAISING EMPLOYABILITY: EXPORT MANAGERS SPECIALISE IN EVERYTHING

Career opportunities for managers in exporting, when they come up, bring with them one of the widest job descriptions imaginable. After all, exporting is essentially an activity that covers all company activities. For a manager to specialise in exporting is for them to specialise in all company activities. A glance through some of the recent management vacancies demonstrates the range of skills required.

Prostaff Holdings Group (2015) is a South African recruitment agency serving a range of industries, from mining to medicine. A vacancy for an export development manager included some of the following items in the job description for the post:

- Managing all international business by region
- Managing key accounts
- Achieving sales targets
- Evaluation of markets
- Maintaining good relations with clients
- Upholding profit margins
- Improving market intelligence.

So broad is this job description it is almost as if the export manager is being asked to establish a whole new multinational corporation on their own. Not surprisingly, applications were being sought from managers who could demonstrate excellent achievements across the business spectrum. These included:

- Business qualifications
- Export experience
- Sales experience
- Excellent communication skills
- Financial acumen
- Language skills
- Experience of bulk shipping.

One might wonder if Prostaff had not realised that it was really looking for a team of managers rather than a single person, but then other agencies around the world carry similar advertisements. The career path to such a height is therefore a complex one that takes careful planning. Most likely starting with sales, it is important to gain experience with companies already engaged in international sales across a variety of markets. Companies do not, in general, have export departments as such, but international sales departments are the most closely involved in exports. Certainly, most export management job descriptions contain a strong element of sales.

The Prostaff vacancy, in common with other similar advertisements, also indicates that experience in logistics is important. International distribution tends to be the preserve of specialist freight companies but this is quite a separate activity from sales. The career planner would therefore need to consider strategic moves between sales and logistics to build up the required experience. This is a risky practice but essential for broadening the skills base.

In parallel with the accumulation of targeted experience is the necessity to sharpen general management skills in finance, business analysis and communication. As so often for the ambitious manager, regular returns to academia should be part of the career plan. Interestingly, though, when the full array of export management skills have been put in place, they have good transfer potential as well: having proved themselves in exports the manager will be well placed for promotion to CEO.

 ## WEB SUPPORT

1. Trading Economics. An excellent repository of a range economic data for a multitude of countries. Easy to navigate, although the data itself is sourced from elsewhere so its quality cannot always be guaranteed.

   www.tradingeconomics.com/

2. Import Documentation. A video from Tata Autocomp Systems that bravely tries to clarify the arcane bureaucratic procedures for importing. It is enough to put anyone off international trade for life.

   www.youtube.com/watch?v=zISENL1Vyqw

3. Export Import Bank of the United States (EXIM). See how the world's most powerful economy promotes trade. Predictably, and despite the name, there is almost nothing in support of imports.

   www.exim.gov/about

THE STORY SO FAR: TESTING THE INTERNATIONAL WATERS

Exporting, along with its twin activity, importing, is the staple of international trade. It is seen as a badge of honour for a sophisticated, advanced economy with giant corporations acting as industrial superstars for their home nations. Exporting is seen as an activity practised by large companies, but they do not have the field to themselves. Small companies, acting with the assistance of specialist intermediaries and their own governments, can also exploit openings in overseas markets. For companies of all sizes there are a variety of reasons for entering the international arena, from filling idle production capacity to simply exploiting a good idea before anyone else does, but the risks of going overseas are considerable. The demand in the new markets is Exporting helps to minimise the risks and may be the foundation stone of a truly global corporation. Before that, there are numerous bureaucratic and financial obstacles to overcome. The rewards, though, are considerable and the support mechanisms highly sophisticated. So pervasive has exporting become that companies now need reasons not to engage in it.

Project Topics

1. If you were the owner of a boutique coffee shop in a developed country of your choice, what risks would you face when importing coffee beans directly from the developing country farmer?
2. How has e-commerce changed the operations of utility suppliers like water and power companies?
3. What would be the advantages and disadvantages in switching from money payments for imports to paying with countertrade?

CASE STUDY – SUPPORT LOCAL, BUY INTERNATIONAL

Almost all countries have had moments in their history where politicians have campaigned with a 'buy local' slogan. Their urging to support domestic industry appeals to the deep-rooted patriotism of the voters and seems to offer an easy path to economic regeneration. Since it means that consumers are obliged to accept products of a price and specification they would normally reject any buy local campaign is in fact a tax on consumers to subsidise uncompetitive industries. It can also lead to retaliatory actions by trading partners, thereby negating any hoped-for gains.

The Buy British campaign of 1931 was a government-instigated scheme to overcome the balance of payments problems the country was experiencing in the early 1930s. The international economic turmoil led to Britain leaving the stability of the gold standard in September 1931. The country was one of the few to remain loyal to the concept of free trade, so the raising of import tariffs was not an option. Fortunately, Britain was at the centre of its own domestic–international trade bloc: the British Empire.

The Empire Marketing Board was given the job of cajoling the public into making patriotic purchases. However, it was not a simple Buy British campaign but a 'Buy British From The Empire At Home And Overseas' campaign. The implication was that first priority should go to domestic firms, but if not them then at least those from within the empire. There were anecdotal reports of consumers switching to South African wine, Australian butter, New Zealand meat and so on.

The effects of the campaign, though, were short-lived. More budget-conscious consumers started to drift back to buying products on price rather than origin. The government, meanwhile, abandoned its adherence to free trade principles and decided to embrace the more predictable outcomes of tariffs. However, the main economic stimulus came from a most unwelcome quarter: the build up to World War II.

The war had a catastrophic effect on the British economy. Economic resources were hurriedly reallocated to war work and at the peak over 70% of national GDP was dependent on public funds (UK Public Spending, 2015). Ultimately emerging victorious but broke, what remained of the British Empire after the war was progressively dismantled. Many of the newly industrialised colonies began their own 'buy local' campaigns as part of strategies to industrialise using domestic resources. It seemed that the newly empowered politicians were basing their development policies on national pride rather than economic sense.

Global trade did not exhibit its now customary strong rate of growth until the 1980s as countries around the world lowered their entry barriers under the aegis of first GATT, and then WTO, agreements. Founded on comparative advantages, global economies, both developed and developed, began to enjoy unprecedented periods of economic expansion.

Recently, however, the global financial economic meltdown that began in 2008 has led many governments to wonder if international trade leaves their countries dangerously exposed to the economic vicissitudes of their trading partners. Politicians have begun to hint that they would like to see a rebalancing in the global economy, meaning that their countries should repatriate the very manufacturing and service industries that they ceded in favour of their trading partners just a few decades ago. This return to buying locally rather than globally will undermine the principles of international trade and wind back the economic clock. The outcome is predictable.

Point of consideration: Updating the buy local policy to the twenty-first century, how would a 'Buy European' campaign help to boost the economic growth of the Eurozone?

Source: Constantine, 1987; UK Public Spending, 2015

? MULTIPLE CHOICE QUESTIONS

1. The acronym FOB refers to:
   a. First overseas business – first mover into a new market.
   b. Free on board – the cost of goods at the moment they are loaded.
   c. Final outbound barter – the countertrade that concludes the trade deal.

2. What is one reason why companies export?
   a. To use spare production capacity.
   b. To sell old products.
   c. To sell products that do not meet domestic standards.

3. Which of the following is considered an export risk?
   a. Lack of local market knowledge.
   b. A local economic recession.
   c. Poor product design.

4. Exporting requires very little planning:
   a. True – it replicates sales processes in the home market.
   b. False – every single aspect of the process is unfamiliar.
   c. Partly true – sales processes are different but local agents are looking to help.

5. A state-owned coal industry sends its products overseas to similarly state-owned enterprises; the orders are processed through a website. What kind of export activity is this?
   a. Direct – it is irrelevant who owns the businesses or how the sales are administered.
   b. Indirect – it involves state-owned enterprises so it must be a government-to-government (G2G) deal.
   c. E-commerce – the deal only occurred because of the online sales process.

6. What kind of export activity would you suggest to a manufacturer of highly advanced medical equipment to a developing nation?
   a. Direct – it is little different to domestic sales, only needs some local agency representation.
   b. Indirect – the deal is full of risk and it is likely to require government grants for funding.
   c. E-commerce – high technology equipment is considered e-commerce.

7. What advantages are there to a country importing rather than producing locally?
   a. The country can specialise in its comparative advantage.
   b. The importing industry boosts domestic employment.
   c. Importing promotes political trust and reduces international conflicts.

8. Why do governments resist imports?
   a. They have no control over the producer.
   b. They earn no tax revenue.
   c. Voters perceive imports as a threat to employment.

9. What is an escrow account?
   a. It is a money account controlled by an independent intermediary.
   b. It is an aviary food store.
   c. It is the part of the balance of payments that reports on international debt.

10. What business skills does an export manager require most of all?
    a. Experience of international trade.
    b. Technical skills in international accounting and finance.
    c. All of them, and more.

Answers
1b, 2a, 3a, 4c, 5a, 6b, 7a, 8c, 9a, 10c

REFERENCES

Adamson D and Cook D (2007) 'Re-examining economic options for import risk assessments' 51st Annual Conference of the Australian Agricultural and Resource Economics Society (AARES), February 2007, Queenstown, New Zealand, pp. 13–16

Alvarez R (2004) 'Sources of export success in small-and medium-sized enterprises: the impact of public programs' *International Business Review* 13(3), pp. 383–400

Barter News Weekly (2014) The low down on the barter industry from www.barternewsweekly.com/the-low-down-on-the-barter-industry/ accessed 14 November 2014

Brazilian Poultry Association (2012) Annual Report 2012 from www.brazilianchicken.com.br/files/publicacoes/d220421fe22b294a31a584138b5fda95.pdf accessed 10 August 2014

Buch C M, Döpke J and Strotmann H (2009) 'Does export openness increase firm-level output volatility?' *The World Economy* 32(4), pp. 531–551

Canadian Trade Commissioner Service (2014) *Step-by-Step Guide to Exporting* from www.tradecommissioner.gc.ca/eng/guide-exporting.jsp accessed 10 August 2014

Constantine S (1987) 'The Buy British Campaign of 1931' *European Journal of Marketing* 21(4), pp. 44–59

Das S, Roberts M J and Tybout J R (2007) 'Market entry costs, producer heterogeneity, and export dynamics' *Econometrica* 75(3) (May, 2007), pp. 837–873

Elbanna S (2006) 'Strategic decision making: process perspectives' *International Journal of Management Reviews* 8(1), pp. 1–20

Grandon E E and Pearson J M (2004) 'Electronic commerce adoption: an empirical study of small and medium US businesses' *Information & Management* 42(1), pp. 197–216

Guardian (2010) 'BAE and the Saudis: How secret cash payments oiled £43bn arms deal' by Leigh D and Evans R in *The Guardian*, Friday 5 February 2010 from www.theguardian.com/world/2010/feb/05/bae-saudi-yamamah-deal-background accessed 14 November 2014

Hessels J and Terjesen S (2007) 'SME choice of direct and indirect export modes: resource dependency and institutional theory perspectives' *Scientific Analysis of Entrepreneurship and SMES* 5–9

ICC (2010) Incoterms 2010 from www.store.iccwbo.org/incoterms-2010 accessed 5 September 2015

IMF (2009) *Balance of Payments and International Investment Position Manual* (6th Edition) from www.imf.org/external/pubs/ft/bop/2007/bopman6.htm accessed 5 September 2015

ITA (2013) *Trade Finance Guide*, US Department of Commerce, International Trade Administration from www.export.gov/static/TradeFinanceGuide_All_Latest_eg_main_043219.pdf accessed 6 September 2015

Iyer K N, Germain R and Claycomb C (2009) 'B2B e-commerce supply chain integration and performance: a contingency fit perspective on the role of environment' *Information & Management* 46(6), pp. 313–322

Kneller R and Pisu M (2011) 'Barriers to exporting: what are they and who do they matter to?' *The World Economy* 34(6), pp. 893–930

Levi M D (2005) *International finance*. Abingdon, Oxon: Routledge

Lockton V and Rosenberg R S (2005) 'RFID: the next serious threat to privacy' *Ethics and Information Technology* 7(4), pp. 221–231

Malmberg A, Malmberg B and Lundequist P (2000) 'Agglomeration and firm performance: economies of scale, localisation, and urbanisation among Swedish export firms' *Environment and Planning A* 32(2), pp. 305–322

Market Network Exchange (2014) Homepage from www.mnxconnect.com/4formsmodernbarter/ accessed 14 November 2014

McCann F (2013) 'Indirect exporters' *Journal of Industry, Competition and Trade* 13(4), pp. 519–535

ONS (Office for National Statistics)(2014) UK Trade from www.ons.gov.uk/ons/index.html accessed 10 August 2014

PayPal (2014) History from www.paypal-media.com/history accessed 12 August 2014

Prostaff Holdings (2015) International Exports / Business Development Manager (Africa, Europe, North America / South America) job vacancy advertisement from Prostaff Holdings (Pty) Ltd www.linkedin.com/jobs2/view/12420285 accessed 28 February 2015

Ruzzier M, Hisrich R D and Antoncic B (2006) 'SME internationalization research: past, present, and future' *Journal of Small Business and Enterprise Development* 13(4), pp. 476–497

Tradegoods.com (2014) Trade forms from www.tradegoods.com/helper/06lc/lc_112.html accessed 14 November 2014

UK Public Spending (2015) A century of public spending from www.ukpublicspending.co.uk/past_spending accessed 11 June 2015

United Nations (2014) UN Comtrade Data from www.comtrade.un.org/ accessed 10 August 2014

Verwaal E and Donkers B (2002) 'Firm size and export intensity: solving an empirical puzzle' *Journal of International Business Studies* 33(3), pp. 603–613

World Bank (2012) 'Export superstars' World Bank Development Team Policy Research Working Paper from www.openknowledge.worldbank.org/bitstream/handle/10986/12069/wps6222.pdf?sequence=1 accessed 10 August 2014

Yao-Hua Tan W T (2000) 'Toward a generic model of trust for electronic commerce' *International Journal of Electronic Commerce* 5(2), pp. 61–74

Yasar M (2015) 'Direct and Indirect Exporting and Productivity: Evidence from Firm-Level Data' *Managerial and Decision Economics* 36(2), pp. 109–120

Yoffie D B (1984) 'Profiting from countertrade' *Harvard Business Review* May/Jun 84, 62(3), pp. 8–16

8 Foreign Direct Investment

Chapter Objectives

Foreign direct investment (FDI) is one of the major driving forces of globalisation. It is a high commitment investment, tying the company into the location for the long-term and obliging management to take a controlling interest in the venture. In this chapter, we will consider:

- The rise of FDI as a major new force in global business.
- The strategic push for FDI.
- Management decision-making processes that lead to FDI.
- Impact of FDI on developed and developing economies.

THE RISE OF FDI

As markets around the world open up to traded goods and services, corporations are increasingly finding that they need to move their operations closer to the centres of action. From manufacturing to financial services, firms are extending their domestic operations to international locations by investing locally. The local operation demonstrates a high level of commitment by the investing firm in the **host country**. The new operation is part of a long-term strategy that transforms the very nature of the firm into that of a **multinational enterprise (MNE)**.

It is not only the nature of the firm that is changed by FDI. The host country will be looking to improve its economic progress, thanks to the incoming investment. Its own internal industries may provide a degree of organic growth, that is growth based on the fundamental improvement across the economy as a whole, but FDI offers the chance of a direct injection of new capital and technology. In this way, FDI is often looked to for accelerating economic growth.

We most often hear about FDI as a mechanism for boosting developing economies. This can come at a cost, the main casualty being the organic, locally based growth. Unable to compete with the incoming MNE, the local firms may be forced out of the industry. Furthermore, the MNE's own strategic purpose will be to grow its own business, any wider benefits to the local economy being mostly coincidental.

The MNE's home country will be in a contrasting position to the host country. As Vahter and Masso (2006) acknowledge, the general belief is that the MNE is effectively exporting jobs, capital and technical expertise to the new location. The home country is therefore losing those very economic assets that previously contributed to its economic strength. Anxieties over the bleeding of these assets to other countries can lead to political resistance in the home country. The advantages are less conspicuous, but the MNE benefits through its access to new markets and new factors of production. In short, it can sell better products at lower prices to more customers and in the process becomes a more competitive firm. This is the very soul of international trade and is the reason why FDI continues to grow at impressive rates.

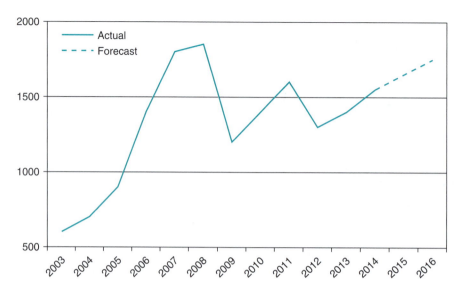

Figure 8.1 *FDI inflows, global and by group of economies, 1995–2013, and projections, 2014–2016 (US$ billions)*

Source: UNCTAD, 2014

The United Nations Conference on Trade and Development (UNCTAD) publishes an annual global report on FDI flows. Figure 8.1 shows how these sums have rocketed in recent years (UNCTAD, 2014).

There was a palpable euphoria for FDI from 2004 to 2007, faltering in 2008 and then collapsing in 2009. This was, of course, the global economic slowdown related to the banking crisis that caused so much financial damage. Yet even in the midst of the economic chaos, the upward progress of FDI reasserted itself, albeit at a slightly more cautious rate. Even the relapse in 2012 was viewed by UNCTAD as a temporary setback.

Clearly, there is a momentum behind FDI that has defied the retarding effect of one of the biggest economic slowdowns in modern history. One might have expected the various overseas investments to have been hit hardest by the worldwide recession, with MNEs withdrawing from their foreign adventures to focus on their main home markets. Yet this would be to mistake the importance of FDI to MNEs. Their investments in foreign locations are part of a long-term international strategy; they are not exploratory ventures to assess market potential. As MNEs they view the world as a single entity and they will pursue the opportunities wherever they occur. Just because there is a global recession does not mean that opportunities will only appear in the home market. On the contrary, they may increase their investment overseas due to the paucity of opportunities at home.

We would anticipate that most MNEs will originate from the largest and wealthiest market in the world, one where they have been able to hone their competitive skills and then transfer them to other locations. In Figure 8.2 we can indeed see that US companies are by far the biggest overseas investors.

In fact, as a nation of foreign direct investors, the United States is nearly three times more active than the next country in line, Japan. Both these countries are home to highly competitive corporations that have come to dominate overseas markets with their exports, so it is no surprise that they are also investing in operations around the world. It is perhaps a little more remarkable to see China in third place given that we tend to think of the country as being a recipient of FDI, not an investor.

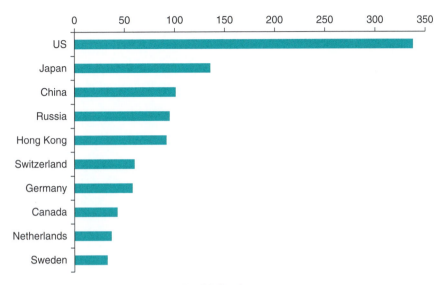

Figure 8.2 *Top 10 investor economies, 2013 (US$ billion)*
Source: UNCTAD, 2014

In Figure 8.3, we can see where the FDI flows are going. We might hazard a guess that China would be in the highest position because much of its dramatic economic expansion is based on inviting western corporations to invest in the country. In fact, Figure 8.3 gives us a rather surprising result: the United States is by far the biggest FDI target in the world.

This time China is in the second highest place, while Japan is notable by its absence from the list. Indeed, Japan is the exception. In general, countries that invest in FDI receive FDI in comparable

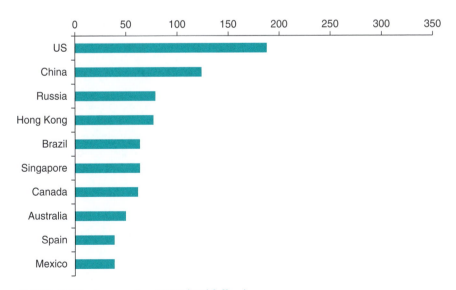

Figure 8.3 *Top 10 host economies, 2013 (US$ billion)*
Source: UNCTAD, 2014

quantities in return. This is because FDI is a two-way street: those countries with vibrant economies that have MNEs investing overseas are themselves attractive to MNEs from other countries. Furthermore, far from being a tool for supporting developing economies, FDI is attracted to developed economies and the fastest growing developing economies. It is clear that FDI is rooted in conventional strategic decision-making, where the business opportunity is the key factor, rather than about economic development.

DEFINITION OF FDI

Overseas investments are certainly not a new phenomenon and some historic European empires promoted the growth of their business enterprises into the new colonies. For example, the Hudson's Bay Company in Canada was founded in 1670 in London as a mechanism for co-ordinating certain business activities in the British North American colonies, principally Canada. Its activities became so widespread that in some places it acted as the local government (O'Leary et al., 2002). The company still exists but in the more prosaic form of a retailer.

Conventional businesses do not operate with the broad powers of the old Hudson's Bay Company. The simplest view of a company is to characterise it as a profit-seeking enterprise, delivering value to the customer at a minimum cost to itself. For analysts, the difficulties arise when trying to comprehend the essential processes by which this is achieved.

PORTFOLIO BEGINNINGS

For many years, it was believed that companies engaged in FDI in order to **diversify** their financial risks. They would invest overseas to broaden their portfolios, seeking out the highest rates of interest on their money. Pioneering work by Stephen Hymer (1976 posthumous publication of 1960 PhD thesis) found that this was not the case and that companies were actually seeking out foreign opportunities that they were uniquely capable of exploiting. These advantages might range from host country advantages in low labour costs to the availability of factors of production, such as raw materials. Alternatively, the advantages might lie within the company itself, such as the new technologies that it has developed. Whatever the source of the advantage, the company is uniquely positioned to exploit it. Instead of trying to spread risk across a portfolio of investments the company is extending its current operations into the foreign locations.

An essential element of Hymer's theory is that a company needs to maintain operational control over the foreign facility. FDI is a tool of the company's international strategy and so it needs to ensure that its investment is being implemented according to plan. This demands a long-term commitment, and although it is difficult to define exactly what this means in practice it certainly implies that the company would have to make substantial changes to its strategy. Indeed, reversing out of an FDI signals a clear failure of strategy in contrast to the selling of a portfolio investment, which could signal either success (profit taking) or failure (loss cutting).

According to the OECD (2008) definition, the lowest threshold of ownership that can be considered FDI is 10%. In other words, the investing corporation needs to have at least 10% of the voting rights in the target enterprise. It is at this level that there is the minimum managerial influence for the project to be considered as FDI. For higher ownership levels, such as 50% or more for a subsidiary and 100% for a wholly owned branch operation, the FDI commitment is even higher. Despite the clarity of the OECD definition of FDI, which is generally accepted, the funding structure of equity and debt can be highly complex.

PARENTAL CONTROL

FDI tends to be the mark of an elite, highly competitive company. Helpman et al. (2003) found that the least competitive companies could not even survive in their domestic territories and so exited the industry. The more capable firms would export, but only the industry leaders would invest in facilities overseas. This is not to say that there were no advantages for them in exporting but, having established their dominance at home, their high rates of productivity would also have meant few idle resources that could be put at the disposal of export activities. The company would therefore be obliged to transplant some of its activities to exploit the resources available overseas, maintaining control in order to protect the competitive advantages that had made it successful at home.

The investing company may have a number of different activities that it wishes to have under its operational influence in the overseas location. These activities can include the supply chain, the production system, the product itself and the distribution network. Each of these may require its own set of management priorities:

- **Supply chain** – secure access to supplies that the open market cannot match. The market may be risky due to unreliable rates of supply or unpredictable changes in price. FDI in the supply chain involves backwards integration.
- **Production system** – companies often gain much of their competitive advantage through the production system because they can control cost and quality. The necessity for managerial control is a major reason for FDI. Not, though, for all companies, as production can often be outsourced if the production system is generic or the production partner is under close control (e.g. licence agreement). For these companies, FDI is not required.
- **Product** – not only is the product usually the main source of competitive advantage but it may also comprise intellectual property rights (IPR) and R&D costs that the company needs to keep within its control. The management would risk losing that control if the product was licensed to another company, so FDI is the chosen route into overseas markets.
- **Distribution network** – a competitive advantage in logistics can sometimes be the hidden core capability. Some online retailers are best known for the products they sell when in fact their true talent is in the logistics of getting the product to the customer. It is in this that the management need to hold control through FDI.

In addition, the cultural drivers of FDI should not be underestimated; research by Filatotchev et al. (2007) found that amongst **newly industrialised nations (NIEs)** there was a strong tendency amongst family-owned firms to look for FDI opportunities in locations that had some cultural links. This manifested quite clearly in Taiwanese firms that invested in mainland China, and we should not discount the emotive element in this, but it may also go some way to explaining the cross flow of FDI between the United States and other English-speaking countries.

Even if a common culture can help support the FDI decision it does not supply the strategic rationale for making the investment. FDI needs to be rooted in the strategic direction of the firm, one that links the need for control with the opportunities presenting themselves in new locations.

STRATEGIC NECESSITY FOR FDI

FDI represents the highest commitment by a company to the opportunities of doing business beyond the home market. The move into the foreign market carries all the same risks as when the company was originally founded except that this time it is conducting its business in an unfamiliar environment.

Fortunately, having built up a presence in its home market, the foreign adventure can be attempted from a position of strength. The company can enter the new location at a time of its choosing and with only those resources that are appropriate to the new operation. It is due to this flexibility that FDI can come in many different forms.

Management of the **product life cycle (PLC)** was once seen as a major driver of FDI (Vernon, 1966). The product life cycle is usually depicted in four stages: introduction, growth, maturity and decline. A product is most vulnerable in the early periods, the introduction followed by growth stages. It is during these first two stages that the company experiences the initial market reaction to the product's launch, implementing any necessary product changes and observing the first responses from competitors. Since close operational control is necessary it is preferable to keep the lines of communication short, and that means producing in the home market for the home market.

According to this theory, once the technology has become standardised throughout the industry, there is a greater focus on reducing production costs, in particular by seeking out low labour cost sites (Buckley and Casson, 1981). The theory introduces a dynamic element to FDI by arguing that it is the passage of time that encourages a company to invest overseas.

The PLC view, though, has been rendered out of date by globalisation: most markets are porous to new products and the trade may be conducted in unconventional ways. If demand for a new piece of technology is high enough then consumers will find a way of obtaining it, whatever market they may reside in. It is no longer possible for companies to delay the launch of a product in a new market until its sales are declining in the old market. These days new product launches around the world are no more than a few months apart, subject to production constraints. FDI is not about exploiting these opportunities but how and why management control should be retained.

STRATEGIC ADVANTAGES

As Hymer originally argued, the FDI decision is a narrow one that focuses on the need for management influence over local operations. To compensate for the heightened risk of operating overseas the company must enjoy particular benefits from maintaining that control. Theories of FDI tend to categorise these advantages into three main areas:

1. Ownership – what should be invested
2. Location – where the investment should take place
3. Internalisation – how the investment should be organised.

The **ownership advantage theory** argues that firms gain their competitive edge due to some resource or asset exclusive to them. If posed as a question it would ask: what should be invested overseas? An early proponent of this view was Caves (1971), who pointed out the importance of product differentiation and, as a consequence, the necessity to claim ownership of the essence of this uniqueness. If this unique resource or asset were to be transferred to another company then it would not enjoy the same kind of success; the advantage is company specific.

The ownership advantages can range from physical technology to intangibles like the brand image and the corporate culture. It might even be embodied in one person, such as a particularly charismatic leader. The ownership advantages are often difficult to define or quantify but are soon destroyed when another company takes responsibility. This can mean that corporate takeovers often have to be handled with delicacy for fear of losing the most important asset during the change in ownership. Buckley et al. (2007) found that Chinese firms are acutely aware of the need to maintain their unique network structures, known as *guanxi* and valued as relational assets, ownership of them being protected by FDI.

Theories about **location advantages** are often more easily quantified and so are more readily comprehended. The question is simple: where should the investment be made? This includes the classic search for low labour costs which was alluded to earlier in reference to the product life cycle. However, cost reduction is an activity that all organisations are engaged in at all times as a cornerstone of their operations; it is not a temporary campaign. As Bellak et al. (2008) found in their research of FDI in Central Europe, labour productivity is a much better predictor of FDI because it is labour cost per output that matters, not labour cost alone. After all, countries like Germany have high labour costs but this is compensated for by high rates of output.

The location choice is not limited to labour-related costs either: there are many other locational advantages that a company may be seeking, such as access to suppliers, raw materials, infrastructure and other factor inputs specific to the location. In China, a country that has long been viewed as the epitome of cheap labour, Du et al. (2007) concluded that the assurance of legal frameworks and protection of intellectual property were just as important when choosing the location to invest.

Internalisation advantages are a little more difficult to define since they depend on the synergies that exist between the different units of a company. This is not like ownership, though it is easy to confuse the two kinds of advantage. Whereas ownership is about the resources and capabilities that give the firm its competitive power, internalisation concerns the way these assets are organised to release further advantages or to avoid costs. Alan Rugman was an early investigator of internalisation, and he argued that it was a firm-specific advantage based on using its unique knowledge base to make efficiency gains (Rugman, 2010). These knowledge advantages cover branding and management capability, thereby showing strong parallels with transaction cost analysis (TCA) theories of the firm.

OLI THEORY

Although it is generally agreed that FDI can involve the assertion of ownership, location or internalisation advantages much of the debate surrounds the relative importance of each one. Some theories of FDI combine two of them but the unique aspect of the OLI (ownership, location and internalisation) theory is that it combines all three. It is often also known as the OLI or Eclectic Paradigm (Dunning, 2001).

The OLI theory does not add much to the theories of ownership, location and internationalisation on which it is based. The unique part about it is that it insists that all three must be present at all times in order for the investment to be defined as FDI. This approach embraces the complexity of FDI, acknowledging that a firm's intention to operate overseas will comprise a variety of different factors. However, Rugman (2010) has been critical of the OLI theory for being too eclectic. For example, he points out that the Ownership advantages include local factor endowments when these should be categorised separately as country factors. Furthermore, there is confusion with the Location advantages when, for example, a company is attracted by natural resources (Location advantage) but then acquires it (Ownership advantage).

The OLI theory is in danger of describing the FDI process without giving appropriate emphasis to the most important factors. It may be true that a company engaging in FDI benefits from all three OLI factors, but it may also be true that just one was critical to the FDI decision. We have already seen that for each type of advantage (ownership, location and internalisation) there are empirical examples of companies that have specifically targeted one over the others. We could argue, then, that an MNE may place a high strategic importance on one advantage, rendering it non-negotiable in any FDI analysis, while freeing itself to be flexible on the other two.

CASE STUDY – THE OLI OF THE PHARMACEUTICAL INDUSTRY

Pfizer is now one of the largest pharmaceutical companies in the world: a true MNE. It is also one of the oldest, starting out in 1849 in Williamsburg, New York, as the creation of two German immigrants: cousins Charles Pfizer and Charles Erhart. Combining skills in pharmacology and confectionery, the fledgling company found success producing drugs that were both effective and palatable.

Over the succeeding decades the company released products with medical and food benefits. For soft drinks it became a huge producer of citric acid, while the manufacturing of penicillin contributed significantly to the allied victory in World War II.

After the war Pfizer began to expand rapidly overseas with FDI. Far from being a simple extension of the manufacturing facilities at home the overseas units were encouraged to build strong connections with the local governments and communities. Pfizer invested in R&D throughout three continents in order to access new innovations. Major production and R&D centres now include those in the UK, Germany and Japan.

Pfizer has shown itself to be an excellent example of the OLI theory in action. Spanning the world with different operations, ownership of them allows them to share research advances while safeguarding IPRs (intellectual property rights). It is also exploiting locational advantages such as the microbiology soil screening research centre in Nagano, Japan. Finally, internalisation advantages are crucial in the pharmaceutical industry, where the profits from sales of existing drugs are used to fund the research of the next generation of medicines.

Point of consideration: It is possible that the MNEs in the pharmaceutical industry particularly stand out as examples of the OLI theory due to the specific nature of the industry. Analyse why this might be the case and compare Pfizer with Levi Strauss, the US jeans manufacturer that has closed all domestic US factories and now sources its products from overseas contractors.

Source: Pfizer, 2014

FDI MANAGEMENT DECISIONS

There are three basic types of FDI operation. These involve a management decision whether to create a brand new operation from scratch, buy an existing one or share with a local partner.

1. GREENFIELD

Starting from scratch has a number of advantages for an MNE that is putting a high priority on extending its control into every detail. It is called greenfield to indicate that a fresh site is being used that is empty of pre-existing facilities relevant to the FDI operation, although it may not actually have been a genuine green field before the start of production. It is the form of FDI that is most politically acceptable since it implies a new and net increase in investment in the country. It is the form of investment that is often most welcome in developing economies.

Greenfield FDI tends to be most often associated with manufacturing due to the nature of the production system. Though modern production systems often employ unskilled labour the manufacturing activity will still be a highly sensitive area for the MNE; the best way to keep the inner secrets of a new product confidential is to make sure that it is manufactured in a facility controlled by the MNE. At the same time the investing firm may gain knowledge about the new market; Branstetter (2004) found that when Japanese firms set up product development facilities in the United States it enabled them to uncover how Americans conducted such research.

This ground-up style of FDI is also the riskiest in terms of its operation. The workers will have to be recruited and trained well in advance of the opening of the facility. Where there are cultural and linguistic challenges this can be highly challenging, often involving the transfer of host country supervisors over to the home plant for early training so that they can pass on best practices on their return to the new facility when it opens. From the start of production there will have to be a steady ramp up of output as the new workforce gain experience. All of this assumes that there is sufficient demand to utilise the planned level of output, possibly including conquest sales being made at the expense of less competitive local firms.

2. BROWNFIELD

Where the investing MNE acquires a pre-existing operation, it is known as brownfield FDI. It is much quicker to implement since the facility is already operating and there may be no interruption in its output. The workforce can carry on as before with no significant additional training. Equally, there may be no pressing need to change the supply or distribution side. It is in the character of brownfield FDI that the investing MNE will inherit all the advantages, and disadvantages, that were part of the operation before the change in ownership.

The risks to the MNE are that it has taken control of an operation that is unfamiliar to it. This is not to suggest that there will necessarily be friction between the new management and the existing workers, but there will certainly be enough potential for it that needs careful handling. The company may find that the training needs, compared to greenfield FDI, have simply been pushed back to a later time and not avoided at all. Whereas the greenfield operation requires prior training for the workforce, the brownfield operation requires training to take place after acquisition. The extent of training required in brownfield is dependent on how tolerant the MNE management is of the inherited work practices.

Brownfield FDI tends to attract the strongest **political resistance**. It implies a shift in ownership control beyond the country's borders. There will be fewer economic advantages compared to greenfield FDI, as it displaces the previous owner and may not signify a net increase in national FDI inflows. Since it is dependent on existing capabilities, at least in part, there may be a national perception that little new knowledge or technology is being introduced, or even that existing knowledge is being spirited away to the MNE's home location. There are also fears that financial resources will drain out of the host country, as noted by Kim (2009) when comparing cross-border mergers and acquisitions (**M&A**) with greenfield FDI in South Korea. A way to placate these concerns is often to simply maintain the outward appearance of the local firm, preserving brand names for products or the local management structure. The investing company may also promise to invest in local training or R&D activities, areas that are most desirable for developing economies.

Such political agreements can prove vital when the company attempts to address the paradox at the heart of brownfield FDI: the new management will have to work the facility in a different way to the previous management if it is to be more successful. If the new management cannot make a better job of it, then the FDI investment has introduced no new advantages. For this reason brownfield FDI can end up being just as disruptive as greenfield.

3. JOINT VENTURE FDI

Sometimes seen as a compromise between greenfield and brownfield, a joint venture FDI has the potential to combine the best elements of both. Teaming up a local company with an incoming investing MNE can still result in a greenfield operation being built but this time with the help of the experienced local management team. Raff et al. (2009) found that joint ventures suited all parties where greenfield FDI was perceived as a local threat and the investing firm was not looking for a merger.

A joint venture can avoid the heritage problems of a brownfield site and the uncertainty of a greenfield project. It also tends to enjoy political support since it implies a net increase in national FDI inflow and appears to guarantee a transfer of knowledge to the local partner. Joint ventures are often seen as the FDI route to economic salvation for developing countries.

This political support can be taken to the extreme of requiring investing MNEs to engage in FDI only with a local partner, forbidding both greenfield and brownfield FDI. Certainly, joint ventures do have their own strategic advantages, and partner firms will frequently engage in them to their mutual advantage, but it is probably hoping for too much that the political requirement for a joint venture will coincide with the MNE's strategic preference. The investing MNE will become cautious in sharing any knowledge or experience in the face of a conspicuous desire by the government to acquire those skills for national needs. It will be obvious to the investing MNE that in its partner it is creating a future rival. Where greenfield and brownfield FDI might result in the natural dissemination of skills through the economy, the more forced pace of knowledge transfer in a government-induced joint venture can actually constrain the benefits.

 ## CASE STUDY – FDI FOR EMERGING ECONOMIES

China's rise as an economic superpower has been apparently meteoric, even to the point where many assume the country will overtake the United States as the global economic power of the twenty-first century. This growth, though, was not, in the main, generated internally.

The government has carefully picked out the types of FDI it wants to see in China as a mechanism for building the national economy. In particular, it has welcomed foreign companies that are willing to help in a number of vital areas: these include infrastructure, energy usage, the development of new technologies, raising national competitive advantages in existing industries and lifting rates of exports. Joint ventures have been the preferred tool for achieving these benefits, and according to Guoqiang Long (2005, p. 317) in 2003 43% of FDI came in this form, with 37% being wholly owned by the MNE. Eighty per cent of FDI was for greenfield sites.

The investing MNEs have conducted a significant amount of R&D within China. This is not only because it curries favour with the government; there is substantial technical skill in the country to draw on. In any case, the products being manufactured need perpetual redesigning to keep them current in the local market. It therefore makes business sense to have a local R&D capability.

China is fortunate in that it has a domestic market large enough to avoid the crowding out effect of FDI, in which a dominant MNE is able to squeeze local rivals out of the industry. To exploit this in-built advantage the government needs to permit a freely competitive market where local enterprises can enter the industry by their own volition. However, the Chinese government tends to restrict the domestic market with the consequence that there is little compulsion to evolve goods into custom designs for Chinese consumers. For this reason goods manufactured by MNEs tend to be derivatives of global products designed, in the majority, elsewhere in the world. This has the effect of taking the heat off technology development in China. Unless that changes, product innovation will continue to be forged in the white hot competition of the developed countries.

Point of consideration: Consider FDI as a tool of economic development for a smaller emerging economy, such as Vietnam. Should the government restrict the competitive powers of the investing MNE to protect local firms from being crowded out?

Source: Long, 2005

 MANAGEMENT SPOTLIGHT: FDI DECISION-MAKING PROCESS

The OLI theory of FDI may be of particular academic interest when analysing the mechanisms, but it is of little use to professional managers when making a decision on whether to engage in FDI or not, and if so what type. According to Raff et al. (2009), companies select their FDI strategy according to firm-specific factors. In Figure 8.4 we see how that might look if the management team comes to a decision by a process of elimination.

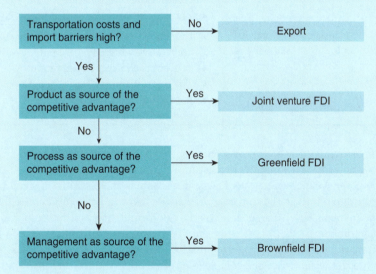

Figure 8.4 *FDI management decision-making process*

The flow design of Figure 8.4 aids the management decision-making process by using a series of steps to guide the team to a single decision. At each stage a decision is required for FDI based on the nature of the specific advantage:

- Product
- Process
- Management.

This is analogous to the OLI theory related to ownership (product), location (process) and internalisation (management). However, in an important break with the theory the OLI factors have been separated into distinct decisions. For the purposes of illustration, in Table 8.1 we can include some examples of how the final decisions are arrived at:

Table 8.1 *Decisions for FDI strategies*

FDI Strategy	Competitive Advantage	Example	MNE Decision-Making Process
Export		Premium Swiss watch	• Compared to the high value of the product, transportation costs will be low and import barriers low
Joint Venture	Product	Cars for Chinese market	• Transport costs to China are significant, import barriers very high • The production process can be shared but the IPR ownership must be retained
Greenfield	Process	Online retailer	• International transport costs from a central hub are very high • The products are not specific to the company, only commodities to be sold • The efficiency of the distribution system is crucial
Brownfield	Management	Cement Production	• For a bulky, low-value product the transport costs are relatively high • Cement is a fairly generic product • The distribution system is generic • It takes a talented management team to extract cost savings and synergies

The advantage for managers of a process like that shown in Figure 8.4 and Table 8.1 is that it is simple and repeatable. It also culminates in a definitive answer, which is of great practical importance to managers. Even when a strategy goes awry, if it is simple and definitive it should be reasonably straightforward to unpick it and find out where it went wrong. Academic approaches, such as the OLI theory, are not nearly so amenable to strategy formulation and reformulation, at least for industry practitioners.

As so often with prescribed business approaches, though, the FDI decision-making process fails to incorporate all the subtleties and complexities of FDI that the academic approaches are able to do. If we look back at the examples shown in Table 8.1 we could argue that the actual reasoning behind the FDI strategy was different to that given in the table. For example, the business case for exporting expensive watches from the manufacturing base in Switzerland rather than producing overseas is rational, but the main reason is that the country of origin is an integral part of the product's brand image.

We can make similar points about the other examples given. Again, the business case for manufacturing cars in China as a joint venture with a local firm is a sound one, but the main reason for doing so is the requirement by the Chinese government. In the rest of the world, car manufacturers consider a joint venture to bring additional risk due to the constraints of sharing production capacity, the clashes between the two styles of management and the underlying fear that the local partner is being groomed to become a future rival. Similar criticisms can be levelled at the remaining two examples given in Table 8.1, basically that there are firm- and location-specific reasons for engaging in a particular style of FDI. Although the decision-making process model is effective at laying out the relevant factors, it does not indicate the most crucial ones.

Point of consideration: For a company of your choice, allocate an FDI strategy at random and then work backwards to see if you can justify it.

Source: Raff et al., 2009

DECISION-MAKING MATRIX

There is no escaping the complexity of the FDI decision-making process. Rather than a linear decision flow process a matrix structure might better guide management decision-making. Indeed, Raff et al. (2009) argued that an FDI decision can be arrived because it is already known that certain strategic factors are not open to negotiation.

Returning to the OLI model for its comprehensive coverage of the issues we can consider the importance of maintaining control over each factor. This can be combined with the areas of control shown in Figure 8.4: the product, the process or the management. There are three possible outcomes that we are looking for, depending on the level of control that we need:

- Joint Venture where low control of the shared enterprise is acceptable
- Brownfield for a compromise level of control where there is high strategic control but low operation control is acceptable
- Greenfield for high strategic and operational control.

For each type of FDI there are areas where the MNE is prepared to negotiate but also areas where its control is sacrosanct and utterly non-negotiable. Where the company can find no grounds for negotiation at all then the most likely result is that it will stay secure within its home market and export to overseas markets. The FDI outcomes are shown in Figure 8.5.

The purpose of Figure 8.5 is to assume that one of the three OLI factors (be it ownership, location or internalisation) is non-negotiable. This is the crucial factor, the one that the flow decision-making model fails to emphasise. It is then a matter of deciding to what extent control can be relinquished in the other two factors in order to decide the overall level of control.

If the source of the company's competitive advantage is its product then ownership is not negotiable; it must be retained at all costs. It then becomes a matter of deciding the level of control required in terms of location and internalisation. This can be seen in Figure 8.6.

In the case of the product we can take it for granted that total control of the IPR will be retained but the management may be much more flexible on the need to internalise the operation with its benefits from various synergies. There is also a low priority on where the operation should be located.

For foreign car manufacturers entering China it is important for them to hold onto the specific product technology. The production system, though, is broadly similar to those in the rest of the world, the priority being to benefit from economies of scale. There is therefore less importance placed on internalisation of the production site since there is less urgency for the MNE's management to have direct control over operations. The foreign car firms are also much less choosy about precisely where

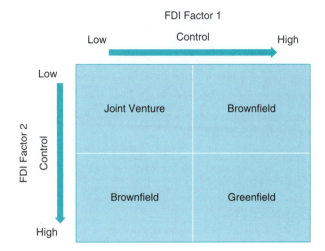

Figure 8.5 *Basic FDI decision-making matrix*

the operation should be located in China as long as there is an effective infrastructure in place. The matrix then indicates that a joint venture would be acceptable. Licensed production is the non-FDI equivalent strategy where ownership of the design is, again, non-negotiable but control over location and internalisation is entirely relinquished.

It is a similar routine for an FDI decision where the production process is the source of the competitive advantage. Here, as shown in Figure 8.7, location becomes key because of the availability of the necessary factor inputs. For example, if low labour costs are being sought then it would never be acceptable to invest in a high labour cost location. This means that any negotiation would surround internalisation and ownership issues. Competitive advantage in process often implies, but does not compel, a high priority for internalisation as well, so the resultant FDI is often greenfield.

Be aware that when national or regional governments are trying to attract an FDI manufacturing plant they may do so on the basis that they can guarantee certain labour costs and other factor inputs

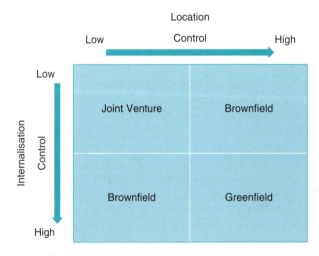

Figure 8.6 *Product FDI controlling for ownership*

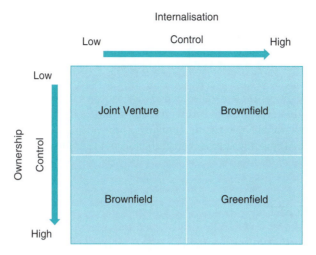

Figure 8.7 *Process FDI controlling for location*

in a given location because this is the principal requirement of the investing firm. It may appear that the negotiations surround those costs, but in fact the company is quite fixed in its demands: it is up to the other party to ensure that these requirements are met in order to attract the investment in the first place. For the company, the location characteristics it is seeking are non-negotiable.

When the investing firm's main advantage is in its management then internalisation of operations is the non-negotiable side of the FDI proposal. Figure 8.8 therefore shows the decision-making process surrounding issues of ownership and location.

As we saw with the example of the cement product given in Table 8.1, if the competitive advantage is in the management skills then there is much less need to have control over ownership of product IPR or the precise location. A greenfield site might be considered, but this indicates excessive control over location and ownership rights. Nevertheless, a management competitive advantage still implies a high level of control over all aspects of the business so a joint venture is also unlikely, though it is not entirely off the table. A brownfield site is therefore going to be the most common outcome where management control through internalisation is non-negotiable.

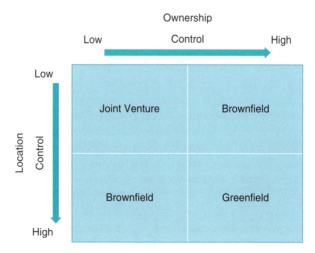

Figure 8.8 *Managerial FDI controlling for internalisation*

The matrix approach captures some of the subtleties of the FDI decision-making process in that it allows fine-tuning of control levels. This means that it also incorporates consideration of the importance or weight of each factor in a way that the OLI theory fails to do. This means it is more dynamic, and therefore more relevant to real management decision-making than the flow diagram in Figure 8.4.

There is some possibility of more detailed negotiation within each of the three FDI categories, for example by indicating that even a joint venture may still require a heightened level of control but not quite to the level of a brownfield investment. Similarly, a brownfield investment might need enhanced powers for the new management when the matrix analysis put the FDI decision close to, but just short of, a greenfield project.

FREE TRADE AND FDI

FDI and the emergence of MNEs is having a huge impact on the way that business is conducted around the world. This affects all stakeholders, from producers to employees and customers, along with everyone else in between. It is even said to be affecting the ecological environment. We have seen that theories of free trade argue that, in the long run, we all benefit from being able to do business with each other without hindrance. In practice it is not quite that simple, at least in the short term.

FDI is not free trade, although it is part of the same trend towards opening the world to the free movement of goods, labour and capital. If free trade is about the movement of goods then FDI is about the free movement of capital and, to a much smaller degree, labour. Where discussions on free trade and FDI meet is in the restructuring effect they have on national economies. Just as free trade promotes specialisation in some comparative or competitive advantage at the national level so FDI promotes similar effects at the corporate level. It is the growth of MNEs and their related industrial structures that lead to international trade based on Michael Porter's view of competitive advantage.

A major difference between free trade and FDI is that trade is an international phenomenon, whereas FDI tends to involve a bilateral restructuring of operations between two countries or regions. So when a company decides to replace its exporting strategy with local manufacturing the impact is on the home country and the host country rather than the international economic environment.

HOME COUNTRY IMPACT

Outflows of FDI are not usually conspicuous, so overseas investments by domestic corporations tend not to attract much attention. This is particularly the case when domestic operations are not directly affected. The act of investing overseas almost certainly means the omission of an investment at home of course and so results in a net loss of investment for the country. Fortunately for the MNE, this attracts little comment by the media or politicians on the basis that they cannot object to what never happened. Federico and Minerva (2008) found that, over the short-term at least, outward FDI had no impact on home country employment. The explanation for this could be that FDI is usually practised by companies that are already successful at home, so the overseas investment is taken as a positive sign of domestic strength, not weakness.

Outflows of FDI are perceived in a more negative light when the loss to the home country is demonstrable. This is particularly so when large manufacturing plants or specific functions are closed down in favour of the overseas investment. This can increase local unemployment rates and lead to a 'brain drain', a loss of specific skills. If the plant was dominant in the region then it could undermine the viability of the industry cluster that had grown up around it. This can have tragic consequences for single industry towns that depended on one plant to support the entire local economy, directly and indirectly. Not only the suppliers to the company are affected; the sudden drop in average earnings for the area can affect local businesses from large supermarkets to high street shops.

The negative aspects of FDI outflows are countered by the positives. The dreaded 'brain drain' may turn out to be the start of a knowledge exchange that actually benefits knowledge accumulation for both sides, as noted in the working paper by Athreye and Kapur (2009). Less conspicuous to the general public are the benefits that relate mainly to the internal operations of the company. By exploiting advantages built up in the home market the company can further bolster its international competitive standing with successful FDI. It can reduce its costs and raise revenues by locating operations overseas. Having a physical presence in those markets means that it can be more responsive to changes in demand there and so further strengthen its competitive position. In the long run this means the MNE is more sustainable, which secures employment in its home location.

Management need to understand how the balance of advantages and disadvantages of outward FDI will play out in their home country. This involves a delicate public relations (PR) campaign to reassure the country that the investments are part of the ongoing success of the company and will underpin its long-term sustainability.

HOST COUNTRY IMPACT

1. Developed nations

Inflows of FDI are what cause all the public excitement. It means a fresh injection of funds as resources are transferred and there will be promises of a reduction in local unemployment. A rise in local income should have a positive effect on the entire economy of the area. At the national level the balance of payments should improve as imports are substituted by local production and any exports will improve matters further. Incoming FDI is also expected to offer knowledge spill overs, the effect of new skills being disseminated into the wider economy; research by Kokko (1994) found that the technological benefits of FDI were greater for those countries equipped to exploit them. The new investments are often highly conspicuous and warmly welcomed by the country.

In developed economies the inflows of FDI are often part of a broader flow of global investment funds. As was shown in Figures 8.2 and 8.3, the United States is the pre-eminent investor and receiver of FDI funding. Below it in the rankings are numerous other developed economies, demonstrating how these countries are investing in each other; for every outflow for politicians to draw a veil over there is an inflow to celebrate. For these countries the benefits in FDI are complementary and targeted at specific industries or even companies.

- **Employment** – declining industries are a natural part of any dynamic economy as it constantly shifts its economic structure to meet new opportunities. Even as some areas thrive with a new industry, another area can sink into a localised depression. FDI can help to alleviate the problems in these economic blackspots.
- **Balance of payments** – with their sophisticated, multifaceted economies developed countries do not generally suffer the volatile balance of payments problems of developing countries. Nevertheless, developed countries can fall into periods of chronic economic decline where they suffer outflows of capital. FDI can reverse that flow and restore levels of domestic investment. This can rebalance the current account by substituting for imports of goods and services.

- **Technological spill overs** – developed economies already have a high level of general technological skills. The FDI inflow may augment specific areas of weakness or it may employ existing skills but within the structure of a successful foreign MNE. Joint ventures can spread the risk of the most far reaching, but risky, of new technology investments.

FDI between developed economies tends to be an exchange of investments between equals. It is analogous to international trade in that it permits the two parties to specialise in their comparative advantages without entirely losing capabilities in any one area. Most developed economies support domestic capabilities in traditional heavy industries, new technologies, services and agriculture. For them, FDI is not transformative but supportive.

2. Developing nations

The reason why FDI is so often associated with developing economies is because of its transformative potential. Even if until recently they have attracted only a minority of total global FDI inflows (UNCTAD, 2014), the impact on the developing economy host can be substantial. Usually the FDI inflows are seen as positive but they can also distort the local conditions and produce a seismic shift in the national economy.

- **Employment** – the most immediate impact of FDI inflows is to employ more labour. Developing countries may not have high official unemployment rates, but this is because the labour is simply under-employed. Lacking the support of welfare payments, many people will subsist on temporary or seasonal work which is poorly paid and irregular. FDI projects will offer regular work and reasonable levels of pay.

  The benefits, though, may be relative. If the investing company is seeking low labour costs then it will not be willing to pay the same rates as it does in its home location, but at least they will be good compared to the going rate in the local area. Furthermore, the working conditions may be lower than the home country. These issues create moral dilemmas that can cause public relations disasters but there are also indirect effects. The arrival of an MNE able to pay higher wages has knock-on effects for local firms that are unable to do the same, and so they lose their workers to the MNE. FDI then squeezes out the local nascent industry.
- **Balance of payments** – developing countries are often in the position of exporting large quantities of low-value unfinished products and commodities in order to import lower quantities of high-value finished goods and services. This puts them at the mercy of a limited range of export price changes which can be volatile. Local production of high value goods by an MNE can substitute for the imports and may also be exported.

  As with employment there can be unwelcome effects, particular with the currency exchange rates. Developing countries often have low currency values which have the benefit of limiting imports and stimulating exports. Large-scale production by an MNE can boost the value of the currency, which then makes the country's other exports less competitive on price. The arrival of the MNE can therefore suppress organic growth in related local industries.
- **Technological spill over** – this is perhaps the most eagerly anticipated benefit of FDI for developing economies. In theory, the incoming MNE trains local workers to have new, high-value skills. Subsequently, the high-value skills are disseminated throughout the economy as workers leave to start up new companies and new workers are taken on to replace them. There is a similar knock-on effect amongst local suppliers. New technologies may develop around the MNE that are applicable to other local industries, raising their competitiveness and opening opportunities for trade.

However, these spill overs may not be the economic panacea they first appear to be. MNEs will jealously guard their IPR, as it is the source of their competitive advantage. This means that the core capabilities in R&D and innovation will be conducted in the home country. In any case, Noorbakhsh et al. (2001) discovered that without the necessary skill base developing nations are barely capable of being receptive of any new technologies. Even where high-value skills are promoted the workers are reluctant to leave the secure employment of the MNE and take risks on setting up their own business.

For developing economies FDI is seen as a short cut to prosperity. On the whole it does bring immediate and significant benefits, but often at the cost of distorting the local economy and suppressing the growth of local rivals to the MNE. Some important contributions to this argument were put by Jagdish Bhagwati (1958) and act as cautionary notes to headlong economic expansion. The spread of new technology can also be held back by the MNE that owns it. Fundamentally, business is built on knowledge, not the hardware that results from it. The problem with FDI is that it puts the hardware first and hopes the knowledge will follow.

GOVERNMENT POLICY AND FDI

1. Home country

Home governments are generally relaxed about outward FDI. It is usually perceived as a matter for individual corporations, their success in the domestic market excusing their overseas investments. Their expansion into foreign markets is seen as bolstering their competitive position and, politically, as a feather in the cap for the country.

This tends not to be the case when the overseas investments are preceded by redundancies and closures at home. This is seen as a net loss to the country and a sign of declining competitive advantage. To prevent outward FDI the government may instead offer export incentives, such as loans, in order to encourage production in the home location. In certain circumstances the government may cite security concerns in allowing valuable technologies to be used outside the country's borders.

2. Host country

As we have seen, governments give a warm welcome to incoming FDI. Indeed, so keen are they that it can spill over into a war of words between different governments as they slug it out for the MNE's money. It may not even be international; regions within a country may vie with each other for the incoming investment. These internecine wrestling matches do nothing for the country's overall FDI and may even damage it, as the wealthier regions offer generous incentives to the MNE and the poorest regions lose out on the investment they so sorely needed.

The reason for the government incentives is to attract MNEs to locations where they would not normally go. If we look again at the OLI theory, the MNE has sole responsibility for the ownership and internalisation factors, so the government can only influence the location factors. The incentives can include the construction of new infrastructure, loans on easy terms and tax breaks. The MNE then needs to calculate whether the short-term or one-off incentives are enough to compensate for the long-term burdens of high labour costs or distribution and co-ordination problems.

In certain circumstances governments will try to encourage a new industrial cluster by creating enterprise zones. These are areas designated for attracting specified industries offering specialised infrastructures and financial inducements.

MYTH BUSTER: SPECIAL ECONOMIC ZONES LEAD NATIONAL GROWTH?

It is no easy task to galvanise an entire national economy into action with FDI. Even MNEs can be intimidated by the enormity of the task: the lack of infrastructure, the low skills of the workforce, the undeveloped nature of the market and so on. An alternative approach is to focus energies on a Special Economic Zone (SEZ), laying down a location-specific infrastructure and offering packages of incentives to any interested MNE.

SEZs come in many forms. For example, the UK and United States have used Enterprise Zones to revitalise depressed industrial areas by offering incentives to new industries. Other countries, like Singapore, have created free trade areas where businesses can conduct their operations without having to worry about local tariffs; useful, if the MNE is engaged in importing and exporting.

India has tried a number of different types of enterprise zone, the most famous of which is probably Chennai in the south of the country. Huge investment has gone into upgrading its communications, thereby facilitating the IT industry, and, as a port city, it has been very attractive to foreign automotive firms who use the location as an export hub.

Although SEZs tend to become headline acts for the economic resurgence of countries like India, there are some disadvantages attached to them. There is no escaping the fact that they are the beneficiaries of market distortions, enjoying low tax rates and generous government funding which rivals outside the zones are denied. This can also serve to limit the dissemination of FDI benefits since MNEs will prefer to stay within the zones rather than expanding operations through the rest of the country. Indeed, the very existence of SEZs suggests that, fundamentally, the country is not a good target for investment.

Point of consideration: For a country of your choice suggest how an SEZ might accelerate the benefits of FDI. Explain how you would plan to dismantle the SEZ after a set period of time in order to ensure the benefits of FDI can then flow to the rest of the country.

Source: Muthu, 2012

The high costs of inviting FDI inflows is part of the reason why developing nations struggle to attract sufficient MNEs. They lack the funds themselves to offer new infrastructure or easy loans, and although they can offer tax breaks this also means that the government is denied the badly needed income. Often MNEs are offered coastal sites so there is less need for infrastructure networks and the company can easily import suppliers and export finished goods. The MNE gains an export hub, while the country gains relatively well paid jobs.

RAISING EMPLOYABILITY: FDI SPILL OVERS FOR MANAGEMENT EMPLOYMENT

FDI does not only have an impact on the employment of workers; it also brings changes to management practices and employability. Doeringer and Terkla (2003) looked at how the spread of Japanese corporations into new markets also brought with it the kinds of management practices that had made them the envy of the business world. Specifically, the researchers looked at the way Japanese FDI was influencing the management styles in their US-based FDI operations.

In general, Japanese corporations were found to invest heavily in social capital, that is, the development of a workplace culture. This was found in the nurturing of team-based work and a sense of common purpose between the workers and the managers. High performance management practices brought in flexible working, quality circles and intensive training, all to the benefit of productivity.

It has been found that these Japanese management practices have been readily diffused throughout US companies. While technology spill overs from MNEs can be held back by IPR and a reluctance to disclose competitive advantages, this need not be the case for management practices. They can be readily replicated or be transferred with managers as they move from job to job, their employability enhanced by the accumulation of their new skills. In a developed economy like that of the United States the transfer of practices is facilitated by companies being at similar levels of technical development. In developing countries the gulf between MNEs and indigenous companies is both technical and managerial.

The worry is that MNEs will leave behind their management standards when they enter developing economies because they are there to exploit only their technical advantages. However, Prakash and Potoski (2007) found that corporations that had the ISO 14001 accreditation, which sets management standards, actively promoted these same standards in their FDI operations in developing economies. Part of the reason for this was political: by maintaining global standards there was less pressure on MNEs to make changes in their management practices in their home locations.

As MNEs raise the standard of management in their facilities around the world it also raises standards in the supporting supply industries and beyond. These management spill overs into developing economy companies bring their managers up to globally desired skill levels, greatly improving their employability in turn. This could even suggest that developing economy governments should accept that future organic growth will be thanks to the emergence of an indigenous management pool that knows how to manage, rather than growth based on direct technology transfers from MNEs.

 WEB SUPPORT

1. United Nations Conference on Trade and Development (UNCTAD). We have mentioned the World Investment Report on a few occasions but UNCTAD is also a source of many other high quality reports and statistics.

   www.unctad.org/en/Pages/Home.aspx

2. fDi Intelligence. A news service from the Financial Times with very brief reports for those who want to keep up with the latest FDI developments. Sister site fDi Markets.com has full reports but they need paying for.

   www.fdiintelligence.com/Trend-Tracker

3. Theodore Moran: Foreign Direct Investment and Development. Video lecture from the Peterson Institute, 1 June 2011. Moran summarises his book in a presentation but other speakers also respond.

   www.piie.com/events/event_detail.cfm?EventID=184

4. How Beneficial Is Foreign Direct Investment for Developing Countries? An IMF report by Prakash Loungani and Assaf Razin in June 2001 for the *Finance & Development* magazine (Vol.38, No.2). Short, concise and very thought provoking.

   www.imf.org/external/pubs/ft/fandd/2001/06/loungani.htm

THE STORY SO FAR: FDI ACTS LOCALLY TO BENEFIT GLOBALLY

FDI marks the point in the evolution of an MNE when it stakes its place as a permanent player in an overseas market. While exports can ebb and flow, or financial investments can be cashed in, FDI means establishing a physical presence in the local market with a long-term commitment and a minimum of managerial control. How long a commitment should be for it to count as long term is difficult to say, but it generally involves the deployment of resources that would be highly costly to withdraw.

The commitment can come in the form of greenfield, brownfield or joint venture agreements, depending on where and how much control the MNE needs to retain. The decision is the responsibility of the MNE, but the economic benefits can induce a bidding war amongst governments wanting to attract increased investments. For developing countries, FDI is often seen as a short cut to economic salvation, but the advances may not be as deep rooted as they hope. For every dollar of FDI they attract developing nations receive more, and the majority of MNEs are still domiciled in developed economy nations.

Research Projects

1. Is inward FDI (IFDI) really the fast route to economic prosperity or would countries be better advised to nurture their own native industries?
2. Once a country has reached economic maturity would it be advisable to deter any future IFDI and instead develop its own capabilities?
3. For a developing economy of your choice, imagine you are a consultant advising the government on FDI. Explain why you believe the country is ready to start outward FDI (OFDI) and the benefits this will bring to the country as a whole. What reservations might you have about OFDI that the government should be cautious about?
4. Special enterprise zones (SEZs) have been used in many different situations as a way of stimulating economic growth. Why not simply declare the whole country an SEZ and so maximise the benefits?

 CASE STUDY – EMERGING ECONOMY OUTWARD INVESTMENT

We are very used to the idea that inward FDI (IFDI) can boost the economy of a developing nation. The injection of new capital, knowledge and wages has knock-on effects throughout the country. It can create other, more negative, issues such as the squeezing out of native enterprises. In the long run, though, the country should experience a substantial up-lift in its fortunes to the extent that it too can join the ranks of the international investors: outward FDI (OFDI).

The leading developing economies are now showing signs of such economic maturity, with emerging market enterprises (EMEs) engaging in substantial overseas commitments. Researchers

Luo et al. (2010) note that home country governments continue to play an important strategic role, just as much as they did when inviting the earlier wave of IFDI. For OFDI, the government needs to implement trade agreements, provide financial incentives, protect against risk and act as an agent for the EMEs.

China in particular has come to the fore, with investments throughout the developed and developing worlds. Where IFDI has brought in certain new technologies at the discretion of the investing MNE, OFDI means that Chinese EMEs can go searching for the technology they want. Not only technologies but other inputs, such as commodities, helping to accelerate the country's mercantilist strategy of importing raw materials in order to export finished goods. OFDI has financial benefits as well, bringing in new revenue streams for the EME and taxes for the government.

In other developing economies EMEs are becoming fully-fledged MNEs, capable of competing with those originating from developed economies. In India, Tata Group has built up a dominant position as a provider of IT services and Tata Consulting Services now operates in 44 countries. The group also owns the Corus steel production company, the second largest in Europe, and the UK premium car manufacturer Jaguar Land Rover. Out of Mexico comes Cemex, provider of building materials such as cement. The company now operates in 50 countries, often by acquiring brownfield sites.

Despite all this headline-grabbing success, and perhaps a hint of national pride after centuries of imperial repression, OFDI is not by itself symbolic of national economic success. There are two arguments we can make here. The first is that OFDI is a sign of weakness in the home market. Instead of investing locally, either by expansion of its existing operations or by moving into other business activities, through OFDI the EME is conceding that the only growth opportunities are overseas. In the case of Tata Motors the company has not only struggled to find traction in its own market, it has also failed to penetrate neighbouring developing markets. As a consequence it has taken the rather desperate action of acquiring a Western manufacturer and funding its recovery in the wealthy markets of the developed world. Apart from the financial returns the UK acquisition has done little to help Tata at home.

The second argument against OFDI is that it denies investment in the home nation. Whereas East Asian conglomerates like Hyundai and Mitsubishi have vertically, and horizontally, integrated a huge number of different operations to promote widespread industrial development, Mexico's Cemex has ploughed much of its money into other countries. Granted, many of these countries have developing economy status but it does mean that Mexico loses the opportunity to have Cemex as the foundation of a national industrialisation strategy. This is not to say that developing nations should not take pride in their international champions, they are certainly very positive symbols, but true economic development is broad based and touches all citizens. Until that occurs, these champions of the developing world will remain exceptions to the rule.

Point of consideration: Supported by case study examples, consider whether OFDI by EMEs is a sign of domestic economic strength or an indication of a lack of opportunities at home.

Source: Luo et al., 2010; Tata Group, 2014; Cemex, 2014

❓ MULTIPLE CHOICE QUESTIONS

1. How is FDI different to any other kind of international commerce?
   a. It is purely financial in nature.
   b. It involves taking a minority shareholding.
   c. It includes managerial control.

2. What is the definition of a company that engages in FDI?
   a. A globalised corporation.
   b. A multinational enterprise (MNE).
   c. A conglomerate.

3. Which type of country benefits most from FDI?
   a. Developed economies as they are by far the biggest recipients.
   b. Developing economies because they need it the most.
   c. Countries suffering an economic recession.

4. What is the role of the product life cycle (PLC) in FDI?
   a. As products age it is more cost effective to manufacture them in low labour cost locations.
   b. Due to globalisation of markets the PLC no longer has a role in FDI.
   c. The newest products demand the highest investment.

5. Branding brings what kind of OLI advantage?
   a. Ownership – it differentiates the product in the market.
   b. Location – the power of the brand depends on the location of the market.
   c. Internalisation – the company needs to retain the brand within its organisation because it would be more costly to transact in the market for brands.

6. Greenfield is the most committed form of FDI.
   a. True – it requires investment in capital and labour.
   b. False – there is no requirement for costly reorganisation of existing facilities.
   c. It depends – it is costly in the short-term but there may be benefits in the long-term.

7. Why is joint venture the most common form of FDI in China?
   a. Because of the geographic distances.
   b. It is a government requirement.
   c. Because it is a high risk for FDI.

8. As the owner of a Hollywood film company, how would you engage in FDI in Bollywood?
   a. Brownfield – buy an existing company and brand but introduce Hollywood style film making.
   b. Greenfield – start with a brand new site and avoid the legacy issues of managing an Indian operation.
   c. Joint venture – share facilities, combining the best of both operations.

9. If you were investigating FDI for the American brewer Budweiser, what would **not** be up for negotiation?
   a. Ownership – the brand is what makes the beer special.
   b. Location – it is where the beer is brewed that differentiates the product.
   c. Internalisation – all beers taste the same, it is the efficient production system that has made Budweiser so much more profitable.

10. What is the most immediate benefit of FDI for developing economies?
   a. Technological spill over.
   b. Balance of payments
   c. Employment.

Answers

1c, 2b, 3a, 4b, 5a, 6c, 7b, 8a, 9a, 10c

REFERENCES

Athreye S and Kapur S (2009) 'The internationalization of Chinese and Indian firms—trends, motivations and strategy'. Working paper from Birkbeck Working Papers in Economics and Finance 0904, January 2009 from www.eprints.bbk.ac.uk/7558/1/7558.pdf accessed 28 September 2015

Bellak C, Leibrecht M and Riedl A (2008) 'Labour costs and FDI flows into Central and Eastern European Countries: a survey of the literature and empirical evidence' *Structural Change and Economic Dynamics* 19(1), pp. 17–37

Bhagwati J (1958) 'Immiserizing growth: a geometrical note' *The Review of Economic Studies* 25(3) (Jun., 1958), pp. 201–205

Branstetter L (2006) 'Is foreign direct investment a channel of knowledge spillovers? Evidence from Japan's FDI in the United States' *Journal of International Economics* 68(2), pp. 325–344

Buckley P J and Casson M (1981) 'The optimal timing of a foreign direct investment' *The Economic Journal* 91, pp. 75–87

Buckley P J, Clegg L J, Cross A R, Liu X, Voss H and Zheng P (2007) 'The determinants of Chinese outward foreign direct investment' *Journal of International Business Studies* 38(4), pp. 499–518

Caves R E (1971) 'International corporations: the industrial economics of foreign investment' *Economica* 38(149), pp. 1–27

Cemex (2014) Corporate website from www.cemex.com/ accessed 22 August 2014

Doeringer P B and Terkla D G (2003) *Foreign Direct Investment, Management Practices, and Social Capital: New Evidence on the Host Country Effects of Japanese Multinationals*. Boston, MA: Boston University, Institute for Economic Development

Du J, Lu Y and Tao Z (2008) 'Economic institutions and FDI location choice: evidence from US multinationals in China' *Journal of Comparative Economics* 36(3), pp. 412–429

Dunning J H (2001) 'The eclectic (OLI) paradigm of international production: past, present and future' *International Journal of the Economics of Business* 8(2), pp. 173–190

Federico S and Minerva G A (2008) 'Outward FDI and local employment growth in Italy' *Review of World Economics* 144(2), pp. 295–324

Filatotchev I, Strange R, Piesse J and Lien Y C (2007) 'FDI by firms from newly industrialised economies in emerging markets: corporate governance, entry mode and location' *Journal of International Business Studies* 38(4), pp. 556–572

Helpman E, Melitz M J and Yeaple S R (2003) 'Export versus FDI (No. w9439)'. National Bureau of Economic Research from www.time.dufe.edu.cn/spti/article/helpman/helpman008.pdf accessed 7 September 2015

Hymer S (1976) *The international operations of national firms: A study of direct foreign investment* (Vol. 14, pp. 139–155). Cambridge, MA: MIT Press

Kim Y H (2009) 'Cross-border M&A vs. greenfield FDI: economic integration and its welfare impact' *Journal of Policy Modeling* 31(1), pp. 87–101

Kokko A (1994) 'Technology, market characteristics, and spillovers' *Journal of Development Economics* 43(2), pp. 279–293

Long G (2005) 'China's policies on FDI: Review and evaluation' in Moran T H, Graham E M and Blomstrom M (eds.) (2005) *Does foreign direct investment promote development*. Washington DC: Institute for International Economics and Centre for Global Development

Luo Y, Xue Q and Han B (2010) 'How emerging market governments promote outward FDI: experience from China' *Journal of World Business* 45(1), pp. 68–79

Muthu D S (2012) 'Special economic zones and exports' in Soundarapandian M (ed.) (2012) *Development of Special Economic Zones in India: Volume Two*. New Delhi: Concept Publishing

Noorbakhsh F, Paloni A and Youssef A (2001) 'Human capital and FDI inflows to developing countries: new empirical evidence' *World Development* 29(9), pp. 1593–1610

OECD (2008) *OECD Benchmark Definition of Foreign Direct Investment - 4th Edition* from www.oecd.org/daf/inv/investmentstatisticsandanalysis/40193734.pdf accessed 13 August 2014

O'Leary M, Orlikowski W and Yates J (2002) 'Distributed work over the centuries: trust and control in the Hudson's Bay Company, 1670-1826' in Hinds P J and Kiesler S (eds.)(2002) *Distributed work*. Cambridge, MA: MIT Press

Pfizer (2014) History from www.pfizer.com/about/history/history accessed 15 August 2014

Prakash A and Potoski, M (2007) 'Investing up: FDI and the cross-country diffusion of ISO 14001 management systems' *International Studies Quarterly* 51(3), pp. 723–744

Raff H, Ryan M and Stähler F (2009) 'The choice of market entry mode: greenfield investment, M&A and joint venture' *International Review of Economics & Finance* 18(1), pp. 3–10

Rugman A M (2010) 'Reconciling internalization theory and the eclectic paradigm' *Multinational Business Review* 18(2) pp. 1–12

Tata Group (2014) Corporate website from www.tata.com/default accessed 22 August 2014

UNCTAD (2014) *World Investment Report 2014* from www.unctad.org/en/PublicationsLibrary/wir2014_en.pdf accessed 13 August 2014

Vahter P and Masso J (2006) Home versus host country effects of FDI: Searching for new evidence of productivity spillovers. William Davidson Institute Working Paper No.820, March 2006 from www.deepblue.lib.umich.edu/bitstream/handle/2027.42/57200/wp82?sequence=1 accessed 6 September 2015

Vernon R (1966) 'International investment and international trade in the product cycle' *The Quarterly Journal of Economics* 80(2) (May, 1966), pp. 190–207

9 International Value and Supply Chains

Chapter Objectives

Globalisation is not only an opportunity for aggressive MNEs to invade overseas markets, it also allows companies of all types to access supplies from those global markets. To do this, a company must understand its own internal processes before it can go looking for external inputs. We will cover the following points in this chapter:

- The company's internal value adding and support activities.
- How the value adding activities of many companies makes a supply chain.
- Lean production and just-in-time delivery systems.
- Internalising supplies through vertical integration.
- Group network style supply structures, *keiretsu* and *chaebol*.
- New technology impact on supplies.

ADDING VALUE

Business, being almost as old as the history of human civilisation, seems doomed to rediscovering the most fundamental principles of commerce on a regular cycle. It is as if each new generation of managers believes that the modern methods of business were born with them. In fact the basic purpose of business has not changed over the centuries. There is no harm in restating it:

> **The purpose of business is to deliver maximum value to the customer at the minimum cost of production.**

Ironically, in this value delivery process managers are usually the most highly paid, yet they are seldom directly involved in the value creation. They may like to believe that their role is pre-eminent, that they are acting as leaders or visionaries for the company, but in fact their purpose is as simple as that of the business itself: the job of managers is to ensure that the system of value creation and cost reduction is working at its most effective. Exactly how this is done may be industry, company or product specific, but the underlying principles have not changed since the dawn of commerce.

Since time immemorial the job of the manager has been to identify what the customer values and then deliver it at the minimum cost to the company. It is in the difference between value and cost where the company makes its money. Of course, as always the devil is in the detail. The value in a business can occur anywhere in the production process, from the initial procurement of supplies to the distribution and later servicing of the finished products. At each stage costs will be incurred and so the company is engaged in a perpetual battle to keep them to a minimum.

It is due to the complexity of this process that management roles are often divided into specialisms. Identifying product value is usually the task of marketing or product development functions while cost reduction might come under production, procurement or logistics functions. For each function there is a manager to oversee it. No matter how effective each manager is there is a danger that they will focus only on their own responsibilities with no one to take a wider, holistic view of the company. This view should cover not only how well the company operates as an internal system but also how it interacts with its external business environment. For the internal system, we have the value chain; for the external environment, we have the supply chain.

VALUE CHAIN

All companies, even the smallest, are made up of a complex series of activities operating under a unified management. This is what makes them companies in the first place. Each of these activities undoubtedly incurs costs but they may also be a source of value to customers. Value is not simply embodied in a product feature but is something that the customers are attracted to and are prepared to pay for having. If the customer is not willing to pay for the product feature then the sad truth is that they do not value it.

Managers need to identify the sources of value in order to maximise them and quantify the costs of delivery in order to minimise them. Michael Porter (2008) characterises this as a value chain, each activity adding value for the customer but also incurring cost. The business activities can be categorised into one of two types: primary, directly related to the final product, and supporting, which includes those vital but indirect administrative functions. Both types can have implications for value delivery and cost, Porter's definition of margin being what is left after the costs have been subtracted from the value. It is because of the way the firm's entire value chain operates interactively that it needs to be analysed as a complete system, not activity by activity.

1. Value and cost – primary activities

The primary activities of the firm follow the transformation process of creating the finished product from the basic inputs, either components or raw materials (Porter, 2001). We can divide this into five distinct activities, although these might not accord with management functionary titles:

- **Inbound logistics** – this covers access to supplies, such as raw materials and components, as used in the production process. This would not, for example, include office supplies. From the customer's point of view value can be added when supplies of a higher specification or quality are obtained. However, this is pointless if the cost of obtaining them exceeds the additional value that customers are prepared to pay for having them. **Just-in-time (JIT)** deliveries can be crucial in minimising costs.
- **Operations** – this is the transformation process where the inputs are fabricated into the finished products, usually measured as output. In a manufacturing operation this includes such activities as processing of raw materials to assembly of components. Customers value the implications for quality that this function has on the product, but the company needs to reconcile this with the need for economic forms of production that deliver a product at an affordable price for the customer. Economies of scale are often key here.
- **Outbound logistics** – far less complex than inbound logistics, it involves the delivery of the product in a timely and convenient way that the customer will value. Generally this means fast delivery and to the customer's location, be it their home or their own business. To facilitate the function for the customer's

needs it may be necessary to carry stock in a warehouse but this then raises costs. Doctrines of **lean management** and JIT deliveries have become highly influential in controlling costs.

- **Marketing and sales** – as a customer-facing function this is a vital area where intangible value can be maximised. This includes customer relationship management (CRM) and the anticipation of customer needs. Advertising campaigns come under this umbrella since it communicates to the customer how the product might be valued by them but these campaigns can be very expensive and only viable if they deliver sales to justify their costs.

- **Service** – it is often said that we live in a throwaway society where things are never repaired, only replaced. This may be true of products that have fulfilled their intended purpose but legislation and customer expectations of quality mean that companies need to be prepared to deal with items that are returned for repair, exchange or refund. This often represents the last opportunity for the company to maintain a positive customer relationship and retain their loyalty. Product recalls can be notoriously difficult to manage from both a public relations and a servicing perspective.

Although it is clear that each activity offers varying degrees of opportunity to enhance value to the customer, but always at a cost that needs controlling, firms gain their competitive advantage by innovating in their own unique ways. Table 9.1 puts forward some examples of approaches suited to different businesses and shows how the most important primary activity offers value to the customer but also increases costs:

Table 9.1 *Value and cost in dominant primary activities*

Business	Dominant Primary Activity	Value Added	Benefit to the Customer	Cost to the Business
Fashion retail	Inbound logistics	Anticipation of coming fashions	Access to new fashions as they emerge	Specialised staff to search for coming fashions
Handmade furniture	Operations	Customer involved in design	Control over final product	Slows the design process; designer needs sales training
Digital cameras	Marketing & sales	Periodic camera firmware updates post-purchase	Updates bring it to similar standard of new cameras	Disincentive for buying new camera
Online retail	Outbound logistics	Next day delivery	Convenience	Requires high speed delivery system
Car retail	Routine maintenance	Collection and delivery service	Convenience	Employment of additional driver

It would be a mistake to believe that the main area for looking to add value is in the area for which the business is best known. The purpose of the Value Chain Model is to identify where the greatest difference between value and cost lies since that is the main source of the company's financial return. Where the company enjoys a high level of expertise with the value/cost equation then it is said to have competency, which is a company-specific advantage, although not one that is necessarily permanent (Teece et al., 1997).

This point of highest value/least cost is the **core competency** of the company and is not always what is expected. Indeed, the company may find that it is adding most value for the least cost in an area that is otherwise taken for granted. For example, high class shops sell expensive products with which they are synonymous in the eyes of the customer, but the shop has little responsibility for the product; their job is only to sell it. The shop's core competency is in selling the high class experience, which is expensive to provide but the customer is happy to pay for through higher prices. The shop can therefore sell a variety of products as long as they suit the shopping experience and can contribute to the high costs of offering that experience.

Although a firm's core competency is usually in one of the primary activities, a wise manager understands that competitive advantage can be extracted almost anywhere in the company. Even in the support activities it is still possible to provide value to the customer for a low cost to the company.

2. Value and cost – support activities

Strictly speaking, the support activities are functions that do not affect the customer directly but assist the primary activities in providing value to the customer. The various activities may not relate to specific nominal company functions but their roles will be embodied within them; just because there is no department known as Procurement does not mean that procurement as an activity does not occur. Support activities are also not tied to any one primary activity but can be spread across all of them (Porter, 2001). The advantages found in the support activities often rely on the way the company is organised, additional capabilities and advantages being released through inter-departmental synergies.

- **Infrastructure** – this is made up of the basic administrative tasks that tend to toil away out of the limelight but are essential nonetheless. Included in this are the accounting, finance and legal departments. They come to the notice of customers when settling bills or during a dispute.
- **Human resource management (HRM)** – this function has no direct contact with customers, but through the ability to recruit and train the most suitable staff it can have a huge impact on customer relations. For this reason HRM is increasingly seen as playing a strategic role in the development of the company.
- **Technological development** – this refers to the use made by the company itself of different technologies. This covers **IT**, management information systems and **customer relationship management (CRM)**. It is the least distinct of the supporting activities since it tends to work in the background of other functions, only coming to wider attention when it fails. Nevertheless, technical advances are bestowing an increasingly vital importance on new technologies.
- **Procurement** – the ability to source supplies of the highest specification for the lowest price is one of the great gains offered by globalised markets. Companies can exploit this by have a procurement strategy that actively seeks out supplies from around the world, broadening the specifications available and obtaining them for more competitive prices. Depending on the component supplies that are found this can improve the value of the final product to the customer while lowering the cost of delivering that value for the company. This is the very essence of good business.

The support activities are often portrayed as routine, even bureaucratic, with little or no value to the customer. Treated as a necessary evil, the temptation for managers is to minimise the costs of support activities by starving them of investment, ignoring the indirect effect this might have on the value to the customer.

It is not only the final customer that is affected by the support activities. It can sometimes be useful to characterise the functions of the firm as entities in their own right who are trading with each other through **transfer pricing** (Colbert and Spicer, 1995). In that sense each function of the firm is a customer of the other. It is then just as important for the technology support activity to deliver value at a low cost to the marketing function as it is for it to enhance any final customer experience. Table 9.2 considers how support activities can deliver value both internally and externally for some of the same businesses that were shown in Table 9.1.

Table 9.2 *Value and cost in support activities*

Business	Support Activity	Value to the Company	Value to the Customer	Cost to the Company
Fashion clothes	Procurement	Securing supplies before rising demand bids up prices and reduces supply	Access to reliable supplies of latest fashions	Large team of experienced buyers
Handmade furniture	Human resource management	Flexible and innovative labour	Access to expert advice	Highly experienced workers difficult to source
Online retail	Infrastructure	Efficient integration of functions	Fast delivery	Current infrastructure may inhibit future innovation
Car retail	Customer relationship management (CRM)	Effective communication of new car sales and maintenance deadlines	Automatic reminders for maintenance	Investment in latest technology

MANAGEMENT SPOTLIGHT: STRATEGIC ADVANTAGE OF THE VALUE CHAIN MODEL

Porter's (2008) value chain model is a useful prompt to managers that value can be found anywhere in the organisation. It can also help to redefine the core competency and thereby signal where future investments should be focused. The model is directive; it points managers towards the corporate activities that need evaluating. In this sense it is a practical management tool.

The problem with the model is that it does not specify how value itself can be identified and measured. This is not to reject use of the model altogether: value is specific to the customer, you might say it is in the eye of the beholder, and no generic model can instruct managers on how and where to find new value. The model does not exactly help itself by having generic categories like 'operations' that can include any number of activities.

Service companies in particular can struggle to apply the Value Chain Model. Inbound and outbound logistics are difficult to identify, as is the services activity. If the company is itself a provider of support services then its internal support activities can become confused with its primary activities. An accountancy firm has its own internal accounting department, for example.

Instead, managers need to adapt the Value Chain Model to their own circumstances. Service industries are often quite a test for any business model, as they often lack the distinct processes of manufacturing industries. The challenge in trying to depict, say, banking activities is that there is no linear flow: the money the banks deal in is both sourced from and lent to customers. This is in contrast to manufacturing, where commodity inputs are delivered at the start of the production process and emerge utterly transformed at the end of the process, ready for the final customer.

For all sectors of the economy implicit in the idea of supply chain management is the practice of **lean production**. Although this is essentially about minimising inputs by eliminating waste the complexities of producing goods and services means that there are a wide range of areas demanding management attention, from defining the role of stakeholders to collaboration with partners. In the shadow of Toyota's success with such an approach, and now the growing importance of IT, it is difficult to argue with the proposition that inter-firm competition is dead, replaced by competition between supply chains (Cox, 1999).

How a firm positions itself within the supply chain, though, is not about co-operation *per se* but self-preservation. Andrew Cox (1999) argues that firms do not simply identify value and then appropriate it by internalising the activity; it is more that a firm needs to have ownership over those resources specific to its needs, those upon which the value creation activity of the firm depends. This is analogous to transaction cost analysis but with the emphasis on value, not cost. Strategic use of the supply chain can create a unique advantage for the firm: what Cox calls entrepreneurial supply chain thinking.

Although Toyota is often given as an example of a company that has mastered its supply chain and made it work to its strategic advantage, there is little evidence that it is unique in doing this. For example, in the United States GM took a strategic view of its supply chain by internalising its body supplier, Fisher, in 1926 (Casadesus-Masanell and Spulber, 2000). It is perhaps more pertinent to say that it is not that Toyota has gained strategic advantage through supply chain management but that other firms have failed to keep up.

Point of consideration: Dell builds computers to special order direct from customers. To what extent has it been successful in maximising the benefits of its value chain?

Sources: Casadesus-Masanell and Spulber, 2000; Cox, 1999; Porter, 2008

THE SUPPLY CHAIN

The Value Chain Model is the internal analysis of value and cost for one company, focusing in particular on its core competency with the highest margin. This, though, is a narrow view of a wider business world. For many products passing through a multi-corporation production system on their way to the final customer, one company is simply a link in a much longer sequence of events: the supply chain.

Although the supply chain implies a single route for a product, at the planning stage there are potentially an infinite number of different routes that the product could go down. If we imagine a domestic appliance manufacturer, perhaps of washing machines, each component starts in the form of raw materials and journeys through successive companies until it reaches the appliance manufacturer's final assembly plant. From there the finished product is passed on through the distribution network to the end customer. This constitutes a single supply chain but when the manufacturer was devising its production strategy it could have chosen any number of possible suppliers. The final production flow selected was far from inevitable.

In practice the free flow of the supply chain can be managed to the extent that it coagulates around preferred suppliers (Chen and Paulraj, 2004). The best supply chain can be thought of as linking together the core competencies of all the companies that make up the complete production flow. Each company is minimising its own costs and maximising the value of its product to the next company in the chain. The intention, at least, is that the final product will be the sum of all those maxima and minima, offering the highest value to the customer at the lowest cost and, by implication, lowest price.

MYTH BUSTER – NO COMPANY IS AN ISLAND

We know that the company's internal value chain indicates where most value is being added in a firm's numerous activities and invites cost analysis in order to reveal the profit margin. The intention of this management process is clear when the firm's inputs are made up of raw materials and the output is finished products direct to the customer. The purpose of this analysis is to identify the company's unique strengths and then defend them against the competition.

If we accept this approach on its own then we will find ourselves concluding that each company, the successful ones at any rate, enjoy some kind of lofty separation from the hoi-polloi of the rest of the industry. Yet few businesses are quite so insular and most are dependent on upstream component suppliers and downstream buyers and retailers. In this way, almost all firms are merely players in a multi-firm supply chain, most likely one that stretches across the globe.

Within the supply chain each firm is taking value from its input supplier but doing its best to minimise the cost to itself. After these supplies have passed through the firm's processes the firm will then hope to maximise the price that it can charge to its downstream buyers. These buyers are the firms and retailers it supplies, or the final customer. In this way the firm hopes to become the lead enterprise, maximising its share of the total value of the finished product at the expense of both its suppliers and buyers. It is the search for minimum cost inputs from anywhere on the globe that has pushed the supply chain into international markets.

The Californian technology company Apple has proved itself particularly adept at monopolising value within its own supply chain. It buys many of its components from manufacturers in low labour cost areas and much of the assembly work is done in China. Apple is able to maintain its position as lead firm in the global supply chain by ensuring that the inputs can be readily substituted so that it has the power to switch suppliers if it can find a better deal elsewhere. Downstream it holds power over its buyers by closely controlling its retail outlets. As a result, Apple remains one of the most profitable companies in the world even while it is operating in one of the most ferociously competitive markets.

Point of consideration: How can Apple's suppliers expand their share of the final product's value and so earn higher margins on their own activities?

Source: Linden et al., 2007

ASSESSING THE SUPPLY CHAIN

The supply chain plays to the strengths of the free market. Having a large number of potential suppliers, a company is able to select the preferred candidate on the basis of their product specification, delivery capability and price. When market access is globalised the supply chain is broadened and some of the emphasis is changed, but the basic character of the business relationship remains unchanged.

- **Product specification** – the greater the number of suppliers, the wider the choice of products on offer. Even for generic products the possibility for future innovation can be very attractive. Sourcing products internationally means an even greater number of suppliers to choose from but it also increases the risk that the product delivered may not match that which was specified. It is also more difficult to monitor product quality.

- **Delivery** – a company needs to be sure that it can rely on agreed delivery schedules. This is the riskiest part of the relationship with the supplier. The company is utterly dependent on its supplier to hold up its side of the bargain otherwise its own output will suffer. For a safety margin the company can hold buffer stocks to cover shortfalls in deliveries, but these stocks represent waste in the form of working capital tied up, so it is good management practice to minimise stocks. At the most extreme a supplier can withhold deliveries to extract improved terms from the company, a situation known as a hold-up (Casadesus-Masanell and Spulber, 2000). An international supply chain is at even higher risk, exacerbated by the logistical challenges of moving goods over an extended distance that can introduce random delays.
- **Price** – the chance to drive down costs of supplies is the prime advantage of sourcing from a broad number of suppliers. This can create a mercenary attitude amongst buyers as they focus on driving down supply costs with the result that suppliers may cut corners on product quality or take unethical action with the workforce. Global markets, with their access to low labour rates, have offered dramatically lower supply costs but there are concerns about employee welfare.

MANAGING THE SUPPLY CHAIN

In a perfectly **free market** where companies are at liberty to compete with each other, the outputs and inputs of each company value chain are transparent. This means that it is the **market mechanisms** that decide how the supply chain should be configured; all the individual companies have to do is select the most suitably specified product for the lowest price. If each company plays its part then the entire supply chain will deliver maximum value at minimum cost to the final customer.

Sadly, free markets do not exist in this perfect state. Complete information is not available, and the quality of the information that can be obtained is highly dependent on the source. Supplies may not meet the promised specification or price. Some supplies are also widely available, which means that the buyer has the power to influence the price, while other supplies may be restrictive, and it is the seller that has the pricing power.

It is tempting for managers to concentrate on just one aspect of global supply sourcing, usually price. More recently, enlightened managers have come to realise that the supply chain is a source of competitive advantage when it is actively managed. Instead of each company in the chain attempting to monopolise the added value in the short term at the expense of other actors, companies develop sustainable shares in a spirit of co-operation (Li et al., 2006).

In this way, far from leaving the supply chain to the mysterious self-regulating powers of the market, companies are increasingly finding that they need to become involved in the relationships between companies. By working with suppliers and buyers, product innovation can be encouraged and deliveries brought into closer alignment with production schedules. As a consequence the supply chain becomes less a range of short-term choices, where the company switches from supplier to supplier at will, and becomes more a unified system operating at its optimum over the long term. For some companies this can extend to active participation in the internal affairs of the supplier companies in the supply chain, training their workers, improving quality control and guiding product innovation. In creating dedicated co-operative relationships the entire supply chain can be improved to compete more effectively with alternative supply chains.

LEAN PRODUCTION

One of the greatest business reinventions of the last few decades has been the concept of lean production. This managerial philosophy seeks to reduce waste at every stage in the production process. While the approach has garnered a lot of attention amongst new generations of business professionals there is very little that is new in its operation. On the basis that cost is the enemy of profit, all successful businesses since the dawn of commerce have been obsessive about minimising cost.

Taken to its utmost lean production should be more correctly termed **fragile production**, a term originally put forward by John Krafcik (1988). This approach argues that smooth rates of production, resulting in reliable rates of output over the long term, are not necessarily indicative of a well-run system. It may well be the case that the constant rate of production is being held to that of the slowest element; a bottleneck in other words. This means that the other elements of the production system are operating well below their individual capacities. The fragile production approach seeks to expose the bottleneck by pushing the rate of production higher until it essentially breaks down. Given that the bottleneck is the weak point its failure attracts improvements, and when production is restored output can rise. The principle of fragile production is that this is not the end of the process: output is pushed ever higher, exposing each weak point in turn.

Of course, the principle of fragile production is only applicable when rising demand supports increasing output. It might also be argued that when demand is rising then it is that, not management philosophy, that pushes output higher and reveals where improvements need to be made. Furthermore, to the casual observer there is very little apparent difference between the lean approach and that of a **mass production** system operating at full speed. There is some suggestion that both these industrial paradigms will be replaced by that of **mass customisation**, a system where a large facility can produce short production runs of more specialised products by use of flexible manufacturing (Mourtzis and Doukas, 2014). Again, there is little evidence that this is more than just an adaptation of established mass production methods.

If theories of lean and fragile production are teaching old knowledge to a new generation of managers, they are at least articulating principles that were previously held as tacit knowledge, the kind that comes through years of experience. Modern managers often learn their skills in an academic environment and so do not have the luxury of being able to hone their knowledge in the traditional way.

JUST-IN-TIME DELIVERY

Applying the principles of lean production to the supply chain we arrive at the concept of just-in-time (JIT) delivery systems. This attempts to bridge the gap between separate companies, a space over which no manager has direct responsibility, and ensure that the companies are working together in the most efficient manner possible. The fundamental purpose is to eliminate waste between the companies just as lean production seeks to eliminate waste within companies.

The most effective way to do this is to have the supplier's output rate synchronised to that of its client's assembly process. Component supplies are only delivered at the moment they are needed: just-in-time in other words. Taken to its logical conclusion the supplier's operation should be located in close proximity, or even inside the client's own plant. Such a close relationship necessitates careful co-ordination by both company management teams to ensure that what is being delivered is exactly what was required at exactly the required time. Absolute precision may be vital for both production systems to be run at their optimum.

Not only does JIT require considerable managerial resources but it also carries significant risk for the company that relies on it. As a consequence, it is integral with strong supply chain management and quality control (Kannan and Tan, 2005). Should the supplier fail, for whatever reason, the impact on the company's own production is immediate. It is because of the danger of this that in practice JIT means deliveries are not made directly from the supplier's own production but from the buffer stocks held in their warehouse. The quantity held in stock depends on the nature of the component.

One of the reasons why the lean philosophy has taken hold is that improving IT resources mean that it is much easier to monitor supplies, stock and production with accuracy. When the supplies are timed to be delivered straight into production, eliminating stock entirely, then such absolute synchronisation demands the processing power that only advanced IT can deliver. JIT then becomes a strategic decision because it involves investment in the appropriate IT resources. Nevertheless, the underlying principle remains the same: waste elimination is a management obligation, not a computer function.

LEAN PRODUCTION IN THE SERVICE SECTOR

The principles of lean production are most readily applied to manufacturing, where there is a linear production flow and observable quantities of stock and wasted resources. The service sector deals with many intangibles, such as customer service, and there may be no physical product at all. Nevertheless, Piercy and Rich (2009) found that the principles of lean management were still applicable to good effect in service sector activities like call centres.

One of the difficulties is in identifying where waste may actually be occurring in service operations. The fast food industry is the showcase for lean production in service but most of what is lean is in the physical side of the production. The preparation of burgers, for example, is clearly a manufacturing process on a small scale. The pure service side concerns the relationship with the customer. To save time, menus are often represented by pictures of the food rather than text explanations and orders are taken at a counter rather than having to wait for table service. The service, if not the food, is lean.

While this is efficient up to the moment of delivery, the customer will want to relax to eat their meal and they will not appreciate being hurried. This does not mean that the principles of lean production should be abandoned, as the company will not want to have to provide more dining space than is necessary. Yet the customer needs to feel that they have sufficient time to eat even if not necessarily wanting to linger. It is far from easy convincing customers that they want to eat at their own pace but still quickly. Fast food outlets will encourage customers on their way with skilful use of the right kind of restaurant ambience.

The problem for the service sector is that customer values and company costs converge and coincide. It is different for the manufacturing sector, where the value for the customer is in the product while the costs are in the production system. In the service sector the value for the customer is contained within the production by the company. Banks, for example, do not just provide the process of securing customers' money and offering loans, they also need to provide tangible evidence of their dependability by the use of quality furnishings. The customer wants to feel that they are receiving quality attention and they find evidence for it in what is apparently a wasteful, unproductive set of attributes. Health care providers are also introducing lean philosophies (Boyer and Verma, 2010), but this can give rise to suspicions amongst clients that the treatments themselves are being minimised or eliminated altogether.

INTEGRATING THE SUPPLY CHAIN

The make or buy decision

All companies have suppliers in some shape or form, delivering anything from office supplies to major sub-components for final assembly. At one extreme may be a company that is little more than a corporate shell, all the production activities being taken on by suppliers. At the other extreme may be companies that take on all the major tasks themselves, the functions organised in a vertically integrated corporate structure. The extent of vertical integration comes down to the make-or-buy decision, whether to produce component parts in-house or to outsource to suppliers. As Ronald Coase (1988), the famous business professor observed, this goes to the very heart of why a firm exists at all.

There are a number of risks in procuring supplies in the open market. Managers do not have full knowledge of all aspects of the market, instead they have a 'bounded rationality' that places limits on their ability to make the most suitable decisions. Not only is the free market something of an economic utopia, often talked about but never quite reached, there are also various risks attached to procuring the desired product specification, delivery and price from external sources. If the risks are too high then the company may simply decide that in-house production is the better part of supply and so will opt to vertically integrate the different processes within its corporate boundary.

The main consideration of managers when confronted by the make-or-buy decision is to evaluate the **transaction costs** of any supply relationship. This was an approach first put forward by O E Williamson (1973), and it is characterised as the friction that exists between suppliers and buyers. Transaction cost is not, therefore, simply about the price of the supplies, although that does come into it, but the broader implications of two companies simultaneously working together and looking after their own interests. When these two approaches are in opposition there will be friction between the two parties and, like the physical friction between objects, this implies losses.

O E Williamson particularly focuses on the **hold-up**, the power that the supplier has to hold up its client by altering the terms of the association to its own advantage and in contradiction to the original agreement. Let's see how such **opportunism** might emerge in the three main areas of the supplier–buyer relationship:

- **Product** – the supplier may not be able to deliver on the product specification as promised. It may have exaggerated its ability to do so in order to win the order, or it may decide to cut corners and reduce the product quality in order to lower its own costs. When the product technology is new and still rapidly developing, the supplier may offer later innovations on the product to other companies.
- **Delivery** – despite the best of intentions the supplier may not be able to meet promised delivery schedules. This could be due to unforeseen problems in its production system or because of logistical challenges over an extended distance. The supplier may have difficulties with its own supply chain or the buyer want to buy more than the supplier is able to deliver. In the worst case, the supplier may have switched allegiance to a more lucrative deal, putting a higher priority on delivering to the alternative buyer.
- **Price** – this is where the most scurrilous hold-ups can occur, with the supplier simply raising its price in defiance of the agreement. The buyer would suffer very high switching costs in attempting to locate a new supplier so may be obliged to absorb the higher price.

Transaction cost analysis (TCA) takes into account the different frictional risks across time. This means taking a long-term strategic view of the relationship the buyer has with its suppliers and the open market. Of particular importance are switching costs which are dependent on the specific nature of the assets being employed. This **asset specificity** can take many forms, covering the specialist machinery used in production to the human specialists involved in design or knowledge creation.

Some analysts, such as Benjamin Klein (2006), have argued that the only asset specificity of any critical importance is that of the humans involved. There is, of course, the danger that designers can be enticed away to a rival by the promise of higher salaries, or even that they will steal ideas and sell them to the highest bidder. In fact, humans are decisive in all aspects of the supplier–buyer relationship, and it is they who ultimately decide on the outcome of the transaction costs.

1. VERTICAL INTEGRATION

When transaction costs of the open market are calculated to be too high then the company will opt to make rather than buy. This involves internalising the functions of the suppliers into the vertical structure of the firm, more specifically known as **backward vertical integration** (Monteverde and Teece, 1982). The company instantly loses all the advantages of buying in the open market: options over product specification, future development and price are restricted. Indeed, the company has created its own internal market, one that is highly controlled.

The single most important advantage for the company is that its exposure to opportunism is sharply reduced, bringing down the frictional losses of the transaction costs. Product specification is now guaranteed or at least can be closely monitored and controlled. Delivery schedules will be highly predictable and the price will be fixed. At the heart of this corporate structure are the individual employment contracts. Employees are much less likely to engage in opportunism to their own advantage because the company they are supplying, their employer, owns their labour. This is not to say that vertical integration can prevent illegal activity, but it does mean that any innovations or advantages automatically belong to the firm.

In an unstable, fast developing or uncertain business environment, vertical integration offers a ready solution. There are a number of different areas where this style of corporate structure offers security of supplies:

- **Technology innovations** – where the technology is fast developing, or its precise form is still uncertain, then ownership of the **intellectual property rights (IPR)** means that the company can control and benefit from any new developments.
- **Guaranteed supplies** – components and raw materials may be in short supply. In the absence of a fully open market the company is at the mercy of its suppliers. Owning the source of the supply will ensure there are no interruptions.
- **Fixed prices** – this is the most seductive of reasons for vertically integrating. Through its ownership of supply the company can fix the price at a level that suits it, thus maintaining its profitability. However, by denying its newly internalised division the right to raise prices in accordance with the rest of the market it is missing out on the potential high revenues to that division. The company may be gaining as a customer, but it is losing as an investor. This kind of vertical integration is often a way of shifting profits internally through transfer pricing, subsidising one part of the corporation with another.

Forward vertical integration

So far we have only looked at the vertical integration of companies with their suppliers. This kind of integration is called backward because it extends the company boundary back up the supply chain to the source of the production inputs. Most firms, though, are not at the end of the supply chain and are not supplying the final customer directly. Rather, they have their own client companies, including distributors and retailers. To internalise companies further down the supply chain is to engage in forward vertical integration (Acemoglu et al., 2010).

Although the reasons for doing this are slightly different to backward integration the transaction cost considerations still apply. In the case of downstream functions the worries are no longer about the product specification but how the product is used, the route to the customer and the price that will be received, not paid.

- **Product use** – the supplier trusts that its product will be used in the intended manner. If it is not then its reputation may suffer and it will find it difficult to find new buyers. There is also the danger of opportunism on the part of the buyer, either passing the product on to a rival supplier to be studied or even for a copy to be manufactured in-house. It can be notoriously difficult to protect product IPR in certain overseas markets.

- **Marketing and distribution** – when a product is passed on to a wholesaler or retailer, the supplier is at the mercy of the buyers own marketing and distribution strategy. If the buyer's marketing strategy is not in alignment with the supplier's then demand and production output may fall short of original plans. The buyer may also market the product for short-term profit, a market skimming tactic, which has the effect of spoiling long-term growth prospects.
- **Revenue** – the buyer may be guilty of creating a hold-up, refusing or delaying payment for their own advantage. This can be a particular problem for international deals.

Forward vertical integration allows the company to control sales and distribution to ensure that they are kept in alignment with strategic expectations. This means that the product is correctly positioned in the market, it is fully available to customers and revenues are secured. As with backward integration this provides particular advantages during periods of great uncertainty, such as when launching a new and technically novel product, or entering a new market. At the same time, it means missing out on the specialist skills of an established independent company.

Vertical integration in the service industries

The supply chain in the service industries is not as well defined as it is in manufacturing because there is much less sense of a raw material being progressively transformed into a finished product, yet there are still decisions to be made over the organisation of inputs and outputs. Robinson and Casalino (1996) looked at the US healthcare industry and found that vertical integration led to unwieldy bureaucracies of salaried managers as the heavy reliance on human assets exceeded saturation point. It is because the service industries are dependent on human assets and have less distinct processes than manufacturing that the degree of vertical integration tends to be company-specific, and may even be project-specific.

If we look at the television broadcasting industry we can consider the final product to be the programme that is transmitted to viewers. To feed this output there need to be inputs and it is here that the supply chain can become confusing. For a drama programme, the initial input comes from the writer and the director. If they are employees of the television company then there is backwards vertical integration and their work, through the employment contract, is automatically owned by the company. If the writer or director has a brilliant idea for a new programme there is no fear about a rival company benefiting since the idea is owned by the employer. However, artistic creativity is difficult to predict so the company will still take some new proposals from outside the company, for which it will have to pay the market rate. When negotiating with external enterprises the company will want to secure **exclusive rights** to the programme idea in order to prevent it being passed to a rival. Programme makers will often use material from a writer who is long dead and avoid any copyright issues, but then there will be no exclusive rights either.

Larger television companies will have the scale to internalise most of the functions of programme making. The studios will be in constant use and the crews will move from programme to programme as one ends and another begins. Smaller firms will **outsource** or partner with other programme makers; some broadcasters make no programmes at all and specialise in rebroadcasting programmes that were hits for larger television companies years before.

Although there is no pattern for vertical integration in service industries the principles of TCA still apply. The transaction costs need to be taken into consideration when dealing with the make-or-buy decision. For television programme making the open market offers broad access to new and creative ideas but it also means that those ideas can be passed to another, higher bidder. When the programme material can never be internalised, such as for news or sports, then the company will attempt to implement an **exclusive contract**. Not only will this be preceded by some frantic negotiations but these will be repeated when the contract comes up for routine renewal.

International vertical integration in service industries brings its own peculiar challenges. Their customer-facing role means that service companies are confronted by the idiosyncrasies of each local market far more than are manufacturers. Consequently they will deal with local culture, legislation and demand factors. The result can be a strategic tension as the organisation strives to achieve global coverage and scale without alienating the local customers.

Service industries also face a degree of **political resistance** due to their high public profile. When international fast food chains open outlets, it often causes local resentment as it can be taken as a threat to existing, local firms. This can be contrasted with incoming manufacturers who are generally welcomed.

2. HORIZONTAL INTEGRATION

We have so far looked at vertical integration, which is effectively an internalised chunk of the overall supply chain, and it is characterised as being linear in form. The inputs and outputs remain as they were, passing from one transformative process to the next, whether they are vertically integrated within the company or sourced on the market. However, integration is not limited to this kind of backward and forward internalisation; it can be horizontal as well. Strictly speaking horizontal integration extends the firm's boundary outside the linear supply chain and into alternative sources of supply. It may even take the company into an unrelated process.

Horizontal integration is less suited to using TCA as a management evaluation process because there are fewer transactions taking place. Even if a firm has both internalised and outsourced functions, such as when firms engage consultants to augment their existing capabilities, the fact that the bulk of the work is being done internally means that the company is still reasonably well protected from opportunism by external players.

When the structure of the organisation is changed by horizontal integration, then it is related to risk diversification rather than internalisation. In diversification a well-chosen additional process will be as unrelated as possible, with business and product life cycles that are the opposite, or counter-cyclic, to the company's existing processes. The result is a conglomerate, an integration only at the group level but not at the operational level.

CONGLOMERATES FOR DEVELOPING ECONOMIES – LESSONS FROM ASIA

Vertical integration is a way of making up for some market failure within the supply chain. In developed economies this failure can come in the form of opportunism and other factors highlighted in the TCA approach. In developing economies the external market may hardly exist at all, the suppliers have simply not entered the industry yet, so the company is obliged to create its own supply chain almost from scratch.

These kinds of groups have come to prominence in South Korea and Japan, where they are known as **chaebol** and **keiretsu** respectively. The Japanese keiretsu grew out of the pre-war **zaibatsu** family-owned industrial groups. The South Korean chaebol are similar to the zaibatsu but more recent, and continue to dominate the South Korean economy. When the country targeted economic growth from the 1960s onwards, the South Korean government needed to establish new industries. It did this by building on the existing economic structure, identifying prominent firms and providing them with loans from overseas institutions. The close co-operation between the government and selected companies stimulated rapid growth of core industries.

The chaebol have features of both vertical and horizontal integration. Centred on core industries, such as chemicals or steel production, they will have other business units downstream that will take some of the production but not all. For the wider economy to benefit, companies outside the chaebol will also be customers for particular processes. This promotes national economic development and overcomes one of the main problems of vertical integration, which is the matching of efficient production rates for the different processes. It is unlikely that two distinct processes will have economies of scale that coincide, so when they are vertically integrated within a single production system one might be economically efficient while the other is not. The chaebol structure allows one process to expand to its most efficient scale and sell its surplus production to an external customer. One of the most famous chaebols is Hyundai, a group with interests in steel production, car and truck manufacturing as well as many other industries.

In the longer term industrial groups that dominate can have the same effect as monopolies and they inhibit competition. This restricts choice in the market and maintains high prices. This can be particularly disastrous for developing economies where other producers depend on the industrial group for their own inputs, such as component supplies and technical development. This has not happened in South Korea because the role of the chaebols in economic development was only a part of the government's broader industrial strategy. The government retained control of the strategy, and the chaebols have been kept in check.

 ## CASE STUDY – ZAIBATSU TO KEIRETSU

The Japanese zaibatsu were industrial groups centred around some of the more powerful ruling families in Japan. Their roots were in the Meiji Restoration, a revolution in 1868 that restored power to the Japanese Emperor from the Tokugawa Shogunate. With integrated companies as their foundation, they expanded through cross equity holdings that permitted a relatively small number of family members to exercise control of a vast number of companies. It was not necessary to vertically integrate the members of the group and many were legally separate entities.

The dominant zaibatsu were Mitsubishi, Mitsui and Sumitomo, but there were a number of others. By 1937 the ten largest zaibatsu controlled 37% of the corporate equity in Japan. Their economic power meant that they were closely identified with the martial government during World War II. After the Japanese surrender in 1945, General MacArthur decided to destroy the power of the zaibatsu by forcing them to break up.

The three main zaibatsu evaded this enforced restructuring by forming themselves around an even more complex form of equity cross holdings and informal exchanges of senior executives. Thus the illegal zaibatsu became the legal keiretsu, and the three were soon joined by other similar large corporate groups.

There are basically three types of keiretsu:

- Vertical keiretsu – manufacturers and their suppliers
- Horizontal keiretsu – groups of companies centred on a bank
- Distribution keiretsu – retail networks attached to manufacturers.

It is the existence of the keiretsu that often gives rise to misunderstandings of how Japanese companies operate. For example, they may appear to benefit from enviably close co-operative business relationships but, behind the scenes, they are enforced by equity holdings and management links. The keiretsu structure also makes it very difficult for non-Japanese companies to break into the market because retailers are often tied to their related manufacturers.

Point of consideration: Mitsubishi is so extensive it is said that if you work for the company you never need handle a product made by a rival company: Mitsubishi manufactures everything from cars to TV sets to pencils. How do you think this structure has helped the car division to survive during business downturns? What are the disadvantages of the keiretsu structure during an economic slump?

Source: Lincoln and Simotani, 2009

Disappointingly, this is not a model for economic development that has been taken up in other parts of the developing world. There may be three reasons for this: lack of industry to build on, no economically dominant families and an absence of the most suitable political support.

Many developing economies, such as those in Africa, are heavily dependent on agricultural production, which does not lend itself to industrial development. Usually, the related processes, such as turning milk into butter or wheat into bread, are low value, offer little opportunity for product differentiation and have low impact on the wider economy. We can contrast this with steel production, which can support a wide diversity of high-value industries and thus enjoy high impact on the wider economy.

A rare example of a chaebol in Africa could be the De Beers diamond group. It dominates many aspects of the industry, from mining extraction to diamond cutting and retail. However, it suffers from the same problems as agriculture: its greatest local impact is in the low-value task of employing unskilled labour in mining. Much of the high-value work is conducted overseas in diamond centres like Antwerp and, in any case, there are few related industries for it to stimulate in the local areas.

TECHNOLOGY IN THE SUPPLY CHAIN

In the business-to-business (**B2B**) sector the online revolution has been more subtle in its effects. **IT** means that the entire supply chain can be electronically connected, allowing the instant order and despatch of items. However, this can only be achieved within the limitations of the physical delivery system, and it does nothing to create demand for the product in the market. Indeed, the system seems to work well during periods of stability, when its efficiency means that products are delivered to the market in a timely fashion. However, B2B e-commerce delivers fewer advantages during periods of instability or uncertainty, when the obstacles exist in the marketplace itself. It is during these volatile periods that the IT system underlying the supply chain management needs to offer maximum flexibility (Iyer et al., 2009).

A development that is generating a great deal of excitement is that known, rather prosaically, as the '**internet of things**'. This is an IT network that does without people almost entirely, physical objects communicating with each other using their own digital language. Although the possibilities are discussed in the media with feverish excitement there is still little agreement on how it will come to fruition. For certain, though, it will be made up of smart objects that have some understanding of their environment which they can then communicate to human users or to other objects. For example, safety clothing can have sensors woven into it which can detect toxic chemicals so that the wearer may be alerted (Kortuem et al., 2010).

A study by Gubbi et al. (2013) attempts to peer even further into the future, setting out a common operating picture (COP), where smart objects communicate with each other over wireless networks. This will move the internet with which we are currently familiar, one made up of pages of information, to the web2 social networking and then to web3, where it is computers that are doing the communicating. This will be a true internet of things, where production machines can order their own component supplies and vehicles can book themselves in for repair. This has given rise to nightmares about machines taking over the world, as if computers will be talking about us behind our backs, but will probably be no more dangerous than self-stocking supermarket shelves.

 ## CASE STUDY – RFID IN THE SUPPLY CHAIN

Radio frequency identification, or RFID, has become an indispensable part of stock and supply management. Although the term refers to a range of different technologies they all have the common purpose of reading an identification label, such as a bar code, and transmitting the information in the code by radio to a computerised data handling system.

The RFID units can be used in a wide number of different applications to monitor the movement of stock. They can be found in situations as diverse as manufacturing plants and ports. They are most conspicuous to consumers as hand-held devices used in retail. Shop workers shine the laser scanner at a bar code and it then provides a readout of how much of the product is held in stock; the worker then has the ability to update the stock quantity. By feeding the information back into the central data system more stock can be automatically ordered.

The US retail chain Walmart was in the vanguard of this supply chain revolution. Beginning in 2003, it required its suppliers to identify all deliveries using the RFID tags. This had the twin benefits of establishing an RFID standard and reducing the cost of the tags thanks to economies of scale. The tags contain a 96-bit EPC (electronic product code), enough to identify every product ever made. Raising the visibility of items in stock means efficiencies can be made in reduced buffer stocks and less labour input, while increasing sales through greater product availability.

There is a concern that RFID capability is too detailed. In some cases the tags have triggered video surveillance so that consumer behaviour with the product can be observed before purchase. The technology has also been used to monitor employees as an anti-theft measure. There are even suggestions that human beings could be implanted with a tag acting as a key to unlock personal information.

Point of consideration: If human beings were tagged at birth, what advantages would that bring to society? How would it threaten the freedom of individuals?

Source: Lockton V and Rosenberg R S (2005)

RAISING EMPLOYABILITY: NEW SUPPLY CHAIN MANAGERS REQUIRED

There is an argument that there is nothing new in business, just new managers. Even in this modern world of instant communications and global trade, the basic principle of business, to maximise value and minimise cost, remains the same. Yet globalisation has brought a subtle change in the way businesses are managed: for the first time it is possible to have influence on the entire process from beginning to end, not just within the boundary of the company itself.

It is this new challenge of managing the supply chain that requires a new breed of manager. They need to be able to combine skills in logistics, procurement, information processing and relationship management. Such managers need to be part of a shift in corporate culture towards that of the learning organisation. Supply chain management (SCM) goes beyond logistics because it takes the manager outside the confines of the company and into the entire supply chain.

Research by Mangan and Christopher (2005) concluded that these new managers needed a so-called T-shaped skills profile, providing depth of knowledge in one key area of the business coupled with a broad scope of knowledge across all other areas. This will necessitate the ability to foster relations both within the company itself and throughout the supply chain.

SCM is not just an opportunity to enhance the competitive positions of the company itself, it can also bring wider social benefits. Hervani et al. (2005) argue that it is only to be expected that the pressure on corporations to improve their environmental performance is being extended to the whole of the supply chain, but this creates a problem in allocating responsibilities for implementing the required changes. This has come to prominence in recent years, where retailers have been held partly responsible, at least by consumers, for tragic events at distant suppliers who have not been respecting duty-of-care standards.

It is this new-found ability to intervene in the global web of suppliers and buyers that makes SCM a new force in global management. The role of the international manager, then, is to unearth the unique competitive advantage the company might be able to enjoy because of, not despite, all the other players in the industry. Indeed, SCM may be the very definition of globalisation in business.

(www) WEB SUPPORT

1. What is value chain analysis? Web article from Business News Daily (26 January 2015). A clear explanation along with links to some handy templates guiding you through the analysis. Lacks a critical perspective, however.

   www.businessnewsdaily.com/5678-value-chain-analysis.html

2. Supply Management. A website that ambitiously attempts to cover all aspects of supply chain management, including careers. UK based but with a global overview.

   www.supplymanagement.com/news

3. When and when not to vertically integrate. An article by John Stuckey and David White for McKinsey and Company, the global management consultancy. Although a little dated (August 1993) the principles are still valid.

   www.mckinsey.com/insights/strategy/when_and_when_not_to_vertically_integrate

THE STORY SO FAR: MANAGING VALUE AND COST IN A GLOBAL BUSINESS

As businesses strive to provide value to the customer while minimising the cost to themselves, they must constantly review their operations. Only managers have the broad enough perspective to seek out further sources of value in all aspects of the business, whether in primary or support activities. This is particularly challenging for service companies, where the demarcation between different activities may not be distinct. Extending this out to the supply chain, managers need to come to a make-or-buy decision: whether to produce inputs internally or to source them on the open market. For companies in developing economies, the opportunities for vertical integration are much less, but the conglomerates of Japan and South Korea may provide a clue as to how control of the supply chain can be a tool of economic development. As pressures rise on all companies throughout the world to minimise their costs while behaving in socially responsible ways, supply chain management is proving to be the bedrock of globalisation.

Project Topics

1. Identifying the core competency in a firm's value chain is easier than it looks. As examples, you might say for Toyota it is car design, for Rolex it is product quality and for Ali Baba it is product price. However, competitors often do these activities just as well if not better. Conduct a value chain analysis to see what alternative core competencies you can reveal.
2. Sub-contracting and outsourcing are two alternative methods for sourcing inputs from the market. Compare them and suggest case study companies that show how the methods offer advantages and disadvantages.
3. IT has the potential to bring great changes to global supply chains. However, are all these changes for the good?
4. The keiretsu corporate group structure has been instrumental in accelerating economic growth in South Korea. How could such a system work in other developing economies, and what challenges would you anticipate in its introduction?

 ## CASE STUDY – GIVE AWAY THE PRODUCT, CHARGE BY THE USAGE

Customers may express the value they place on a product by how much they are willing to spend, but frustratingly for the manufacturer the customer is not so skilled on estimating that value in the first place. That is why the firm has to advertise the product and try to communicate its benefits. In some industries the manufacturers have given up attempting to charge for the full value of the product; instead they make their money on the service items. They do this in the knowledge that the consumer will undervalue the product until they begin to use it. If they can sell the product and the service as a single bundle then they can price the bundle in accordance with the total value.

Computer printers for home use are a good example of this. Lack of prior experience leads first-time printer buyers to believe that a printer will have only occasional use. This is, after all, a paperless age when there should be little need to print anything from the computer. Since the buyer puts a low value on the printer, the manufacturer can only charge a price that equates with that value, a price that may barely cover the cost of production.

No matter, because once the buyer has got the printer home they will soon find they are frequently printing off photographs, dinner recipes, maps and all manner of internet discoveries. To keep up with their new-found delight in printing anything and everything the customer will find they have to make frequent purchases of printer ink cartridges. It is in the relatively low-technology ink cartridges that the manufacturer makes back its money. The customer may not value the printer, but they certainly do value the ink and they have to pay accordingly. The overall profit comes from bundling the printer and the ink by ensuring the cartridges are specific to the printer.

Experienced buyers have a much better idea of the value of a printer. They may even have learned to evade the high cost of ink cartridges from the manufacturer by purchasing from an alternative source. It is likely, though, that they are more discerning in the kind of printer they want and for this reason premium printers sell for a premium price.

This kind of product bundling can also be seen in subscription and membership charging, where the company will be hoping that the customer has overvalued the purchase. For example, they may believe that they would buy every issue of a particular monthly magazine, so an annual subscription that offers twelve magazines for the price of ten sounds like a bargain. In reality they may have only bought half that number once they had had a chance to flick through the pages in the newsstand copy. The publisher comes out the clear winner.

Point of consideration: Imagine you have just opened a new hotel in the industrial German city of Düsseldorf. There is a lot of competition from better known hotel chains for business travellers, and the city of Düsseldorf attracts few tourists. How would you offer a bundle that combines a stay at your hotel with another service in order to attract both business travellers and tourists?

Source: Bar-Gill, 2006

? MULTIPLE CHOICE QUESTIONS

1. What is the most basic purpose of a business?
   a. To maximise the value to the customer at the minimum price.
   b. To deliver maximum value to the customer at minimum cost to the company.
   c. To minimise the price to the customer at the maximum cost to the company.

2. Which of the following is a primary activity in the value chain?
   a. Dealing with warranty claims on faulty products.
   b. Obtaining the cheapest component supplies.
   c. Ensuring the staff are trained to work efficiently in production.

3. What is the core competency of a dairy farm?
   a. The production of milk.
   b. Managing the cows to ensure maximum yields.
   c. Impossible to say – the core competency could occur in any of the farm's activities.

4. Is there any value in support activities?
   a. Yes – even support activities can add value from the consumer's perspective.
   b. No – support activities are administrative processes that should be minimised.
   c. Impossible to say – it depends on how the company operates.

5. Who manages the supply chain?
   a. The supply chain consultancy.
   b. National governments.
   c. All participating companies and their managers.

6. What is one advantage of vertical integration?
   a. It minimises transaction costs.
   b. It provides access to the cheapest supplies.
   c. It provides access to the latest technologies.

7. What is one reason for horizontal integration?
   a. It diversifies risk across a broad range of products.
   b. It increases group profitability.
   c. It increases the chances of synergy between the business units.

8. Is it possible to have lean production in the healthcare industry?
   a. No – efficiency has no place in patient care.
   b. Yes – cost minimisation means that more money can be spent on patient care.
   c. In part – administrative costs should be minimised, but patient care should have no budget restrictions.

9. What does mass customisation seek to do?
   a. It provides individual products for the mass market.
   b. It brings craftsmanship back to production.
   c. It allows some limited customisation of products within the mass production system.

10. What is the 'glue' that holds a keiretsu together?
    a. The Japanese cultural inclination towards mutual trust and co-operation.
    b. Ownership crossholdings administered by the group's own bank.
    c. Business networks centred on the founding family.

Answers
1b, 2a, 3c, 4a, 5c, 6a, 7a, 8b, 9c, 10b

REFERENCES

Acemoglu D, Griffith R, Aghion P and Zilibotti F (2010) 'Vertical integration and technology: theory and evidence' *Journal of the European Economic Association* 8(5), pp. 989–1033

Bar-Gill O (2006) 'Bundling and consumer misperception' *The University of Chicago Law Review* 73(20), pp. 33–61

Boyer K and Verma R (2010) *Operations and supply chain management for the twenty-first century*. Mason, OH: South-Western, Cengage Learning

Casadesus-Masanell R and Spulber D F (2000) 'The fable of Fisher Body' *The Journal of Law and Economics* 43(1), pp. 67–104

Chen I J and Paulraj A (2004) 'Towards a theory of supply chain management: the constructs and measurements' *Journal of Operations Management* 22(2), pp. 119–150

Coase R H (1988) 'The nature of the firm: influence' *Journal of Law, Economics, & Organization* 4(1) (Spring, 1988), pp. 33–47

Colbert G J and Spicer B H (1995) 'A multi-case investigation of a theory of the transfer pricing process' *Accounting, Organizations and Society* 20(6), pp. 423–456

Cox A (1999) 'Power, value and supply chain management' *Supply Chain Management: An International Journal* 4(4), pp. 167–175

Gubbi J, Buyya R, Marusic S and Palaniswami M (2013) 'Internet of Things (IoT): a vision, architectural elements, and future directions' *Future Generation Computer Systems* 29(7), pp. 1645–1660

Hervani A A, Helms M M and Sarkis J (2005) 'Performance measurement for green supply chain management' *Benchmarking: An International Journal* 12(4), pp. 330–353

Kannan V R and Tan K C (2005) 'Just in time, total quality management, and supply chain management: understanding their linkages and impact on business performance' *Omega* 33(2), pp. 153–162

Klein B (2006) The Economic Lessons of Fisher Body - General Motors (October 13, 2006) from www.ssrn.com/abstract=937510 accessed 7 September 2014

Kortuem G, Kawsar F, Fitton D and Sundramoorthy V (2010) 'Smart objects as building blocks for the internet of things' *Internet Computing, IEEE* 14(1), pp. 44–51

Krafcik J F (1988) 'Triumph of the lean production system' *Sloan Management Review* 30(1), pp. 41–51

Li S, Ragu-Nathan B, Ragu-Nathan T S and Rao S S (2006) 'The impact of supply chain management practices on competitive advantage and organizational performance' *Omega* 34(2), pp. 107–124

Lincoln J R and Simotani M (2009) 'Whither the Keiretsu, Japan's Business Networks? How Were They Structured? What Did They Do? Why Are They Gone?' available from Institute for Research on Labor and Employment, UC Berkeley from www.escholarship.org/uc/item/00m7d34g accessed 17 September 2014

Linden G, Kraemer K L and Dedrick J (2009) 'Who captures value in a global innovation network?: the case of Apple's iPod' *Communications of the ACM* 52(3), pp. 140–144

Lockton V and Rosenberg R S (2005) 'RFID: the next serious threat to privacy' *Ethics and Information Technology* 7(4), pp. 221–231

Mangan J and Christopher M (2005) 'Management development and the supply chain manager of the future' *The International Journal of Logistics Management* 16(2), pp. 178–191

Monteverde K and Teece D J (1982) 'Supplier switching costs and vertical integration in the automobile industry' *The Bell Journal of Economics* pp. 206–213

Mourtsis D and Doukas M (2014) 'The evolution of manufacturing systems: from craftsmanship to the era of customisation' in Semančo P and Modrák V (2014) (eds.) *Handbook of research on design and management of lean production systems.* Hershey, PA: IGI Global

Piercy N and Rich N (2009) 'Lean transformation in the pure service environment: the case of the call service centre' *International Journal of Operations & Production Management* 29(1), pp. 54–76

Porter M E (2001) 'The value chain and competitive advantage' in Barnes D (ed.) (2001) *Understanding business: Processes.* London: Routledge

——— (2008) *Competitive advantage: Creating and sustaining superior performance.* New York: Simon and Schuster

Robinson J C and Casalino L P (1996) 'Vertical integration and organizational networks in health care' *Health Affairs* 15(1), pp. 7–22

Teece D J, Pisano G and Shuen A (1997) 'Dynamic capabilities and strategic management' *Strategic Management Journal* 18(7), pp. 509–533

Williamson O E (1973) 'Markets and hierarchies: some elementary considerations' *The American Economic Review* pp. 316–325

Part IV Global Strategies, Alliances and Structures

Business globalisation will not get very far without global strategies to push it forward. As companies prepare to meet the international opportunities and transform themselves into MNEs the managers need to make long-term plans to reallocate resources to where they are most needed. This is quite distinct from the tactical considerations that would have occupied managers in their day-to-day decisions for the domestic market.

One of the more basic strategies, put forward by Michael Porter, suggests that managers need to decide whether to take their companies into a cost leadership or a differentiation strategy. Maybe at one time this was reasonable advice for domestic companies but to compete globally companies need to embrace both challenges simultaneously: minimising costs of production while ensuring the product is unique in its value to the consumer.

The generic international strategies come in four types: international, multidomestic, global and transnational. Each strategy needs to be aligned with the company's core competences, the nature of the product and the demand characteristics of the market. They might also be thought of as progressive steps, starting with exporting as part of the international strategy and ending with global integration as part of the transnational strategy. However, there is nothing to say that the steps should be taken in that order or that there is even a concluding step.

Whatever strategic steps are taken, it is always a time-consuming and risky affair globalising a business. A shortcut can be to form an alliance with another firm. At first glance such co-operative agreements seem attractive as they purport to share out the risk. The problem from a business point of view is that this necessarily means sharing the returns on the investment. Given the business maxim that risk and rate of return should match, reducing both by the same amount has no net effect. Instead, the key point is that uncertainty, the unquantifiable threat to the investment, is what is being shared.

The uncertainty element in the investment can manifest itself in one of a number of ways. These can cover production in a new location, research of a new technology or the development of a new product variant. It may even be the case that regulations exclude the company from a designated region. For each of these there is a suitable type of alliance: joint venture, equity alliance, non-equity alliance and multi-regional strategic alliance. All of them, though, are inherently short-term since they only last for as long as the uncertainty exists. One new type of alliance, the vertical joint venture, may have staying power but only by virtue of the interdependencies that tie the partners together in perpetuity.

Underpinning the international strategy must be an organisational structure that supports it. If there is a single, ideal structure for an MNE it will probably never be seen since structures are not something that can be reconfigured just to suit the latest strategy. Instead, firms arrive at their organisational structures through their unique paths of development. Most, but not all, start with the classic unitary U-Form, one centred on the owner and founder who heads the nascent enterprise as the CEO.

The close involvement of the CEO in all aspects of the business may be effective up until when the company is so large it requires a specialist team of managers to run it. This is the multi-divisional M-Form with a headquarters staffed by professional managers. As the company continues to expand and extend itself into overseas markets, the M-Form will evolve into ever more sophisticated structures, one probably unique to the company. Nevertheless, the structure that the company proclaims in its literature may be more flexible than realised. In emergencies, even the most complex of M-Form companies can revert to the short communication lines of the U-Form, if only temporarily.

The corporate structure that is not amenable to sudden developments is the matrix form. When a company is dealing with a multitude of different processes and technologies then it is paramount that all sides of the business should be communicating with each other at the same time. This provides internal flexibility but it can also lead to costly confusion as power of authority gets lost in the structure and poor decision-making takes hold. It is not uncommon for the first project under the matrix structure to suffer appalling delays and cost over-runs. The matrix structure is not one that a company falls into by accident, therefore, but one that is imposed by a management team with a clear strategic conviction. As always in business, the overall corporate strategy is paramount.

10 International Business Strategies

Chapter Objectives

The strategy decision is one that cements the role of manager as captain of the corporate ship. It requires the systematic commitment of resources to achieve long-term goals set for the organisation. In this chapter, we will be looking at how strategies for international businesses are put together:

- Distinguishing strategy from tactics.
- Generic strategies for general business.
- Generic strategies for international business.
- Factors affecting the strategy decision.

OBLIGATIONS FOR STRATEGY

Success in business would be assured if there were prescriptive strategies that managers could pluck off the shelf and apply to their own situations. As we are constantly reminded, even for a simple domestic company this is a near-impossible task given the infinite variety of market conditions, economic factors and firm-specific issues. The question of growth is not as clear cut as a popular maxim might suggest, i.e. expansion is good; contraction is bad. Given the irresistible force of the economic cycle, there will be periods when managers will need to plan for stability or shrinkage of the business, or even terminal decline.

When this is extended to the international arena the strategic options are only complicated further due to the wider number of business permutations. At birth the company probably had to deal with one new product and only the local domestic market. Much of the business strategy would have been implied by the nature of the product and the market. For example, the requirement to recover the costs of development and manufacturing would bear heavily on the pricing decision. In international markets the pressure to do this is not quite so prescribed, with opportunities to place the product in a different price segment and increase revenues to offset the risk of operating overseas.

International operations enjoy much greater room for manoeuvre, so managers find they can evaluate a range of overseas markets and perhaps a choice of the products already launched in the home market. In order to select the best course of action from the several available the senior managers need to conduct a detailed strategic analysis. The resultant strategy is the plan, or business model, that provides the framework for the company. Within that framework, there will still be flexibility in order to react to changes on the ground. These local responses are tactical and are the responsibility of managers further down the hierarchy. We should first distinguish between tactics and strategies.

STRATEGY AND TACTICS

'Strategy' is perhaps one of the most overused business terms. It suggests a bold approach to business, a grasp of the big picture. Whenever a manager unveils a new plan it is invariably heralded as a strategy with far-reaching implications. In practice, it is more often a tactical response to the immediate changes in the business environment. Strategy can be seen as providing the overall direction for the corporation, while tactics involve the real-world adjustments that have to be made in a dynamic business environment (Casadesus-Masanell and Ricart, 2010).

The business strategy involves a model or framework that allocates resources and structures the corporation in order to set it on an intended course. A new strategy can only come after meticulous analysis of the business environment and the corporation's own capabilities. For the new strategy to be implemented it is necessary to re-allocate resources to bring greater emphasis to some capabilities over others. For example, the move by Lenovo into the mobile communication business has required a huge commitment of resources, RMB5 billion (US$800 million) over the 2012 to 2017 time period (Lenovo, 2012).

With the strategy in place and the resources allocated, adjustments will need to be made as tactical responses to changes in the business environment. This may involve changing production output to meet demand, switching output to alternative products or making continuous developmental changes to the product. Tactical responses are not necessarily minor, they may involve major changes to the design of a new product, but there is often greater scope for middle and junior managers to exercise their judgment. At a high managerial level Lenovo purchased patents for mobile technology from NEC in 2014 (Lenovo, 2014), but at a lower level the company will run local sales campaigns. Both these tactics fit within Lenovo's overall mobile communications strategy.

Where some of the confusion between strategy and tactics occurs is when the strategy is implemented at the departmental level. The same principles apply, though: strategy involves the allocation of resources according to a long-term plan while tactics are the actions taken in support of the plan as conditions change. So if a company decides to add online advertising aimed at younger consumers to its established media channels, such as TV or newspapers, then it represents a new marketing strategy. Within that strategy there may be the tactical decision to conduct a limited run of sales promotions as a way of introducing the brand to younger consumers.

The relationship between tactics and strategy can be reversed when a tactical exploration of a market or technique is translated into a full strategic plan that restructures the company. Trial marketing of new products is a commonly used method for low-risk sampling of real demand in order to make short-term forecasts for the full market (Fader et al., 2003). On the operations side, firms may develop new techniques that are merely incremental improvements, which are then expanded to reconfigure the entire organisation. For example, we have seen how IT has gone from a bulky computer crunching sales data to a network of such fundamental importance to the management that it begins to raise questions of corporate governance (Peterson, 2004).

 MYTH BUSTER – BMW AND THE BUBBLE ECONOMY CAR

BMW is now one of the most famous luxury car brands in the world, a status it has enjoyed throughout much of its existence. Less well known is that the company owes its corporate life to the manufacture of some very small, and frankly cheap, cars.

The company traces its origins in 1916 to a manufacturer of aircraft engines. Indeed, the company's emblem is meant to evoke a rotating propeller. Within a year the company had merged with a small manufacturer of engines, Bayerische Motoren Werke GmbH, from which we get the BMW brand name.

The company changed its strategy in 1923 when the BMW division began to produce complete motorcycles, and the strategy changed again in 1928 when BMW entered the car industry. It did this through the expedient of acquiring Dixi, a car manufacturer in Eisenach. These were no sports cars, however, but licence-built versions of the diminutive British Austin Seven. The launch of the BMW car brand could not have had a more humble start.

Continuing as a supplier to the aircraft industry, the company's aero engines were in high demand during World War II. In order to raise output the company was obliged to implement the disreputable tactic of employing forced labour. BMW today bitterly regrets this dark stain on its history.

After World War II BMW lost much of its manufacturing capacity due to appropriation of its resources by the allied powers. Once again the company found itself fighting for its existence. The company recovered its capabilities by initially manufacturing kitchen utensils. Perhaps more amusing when compared with BMW's current range the company also resorted to the licensed production of the Italian Iso Isetta microcar. Due to their minuscule size, motorbike engine and single front door in a canopy-style body, it was almost inevitable that they would be known as bubble cars.

BMW's occasional descents into ignominious low-technology manufacturing were never real strategies. The company's tactical diversions were simply desperate, short-term attempts to keep the company running while it reintroduced its strategy for building quality cars and motorcycles. After courting bankruptcy in the 1950s, the company released the New Class range in 1961 and set itself on the course to global prominence.

Points of consideration: If BMW had designed its own bubble car, would you consider that to have been a strategy or a tactic? The New Class range was a major financial commitment that marked the birth of the modern range of cars – was that investment a new strategy or a tactic within the old strategy?

Source: BMW, 2014; Robson, 2005

MICHAEL PORTER'S GENERIC STRATEGIES

Michael Porter (1998) has looked at the ability of businesses to exploit opportunities in the market. To do this a manager must define the source of the company's competitive advantage and then evaluate the scope the company has for holding a position in the market. This position relative to rival firms will ultimately decide if the firm is going to earn normal profits for the industry, or be able to defy the odds and earn a more favourable rate of return by sustaining its competitive advantage.

Porter argues that there are three fundamental competitive strategies for a firm, which are derived from the two approaches open to it: a cost or differentiation approach to the product, and a broad or narrow approach to the market segments.

In Porter's model, a company has two possible advantages: either its cost structure, which then affects its ability to compete on price, or the differentiation, the uniqueness, of its product. Either of these should lead the management to decide if the product is defined by its cost or the uniqueness of its features. If cost is the advantage then the product can compete by undercutting rivals on price. The company earns a higher than normal profit by selling high volumes of the product. Alternatively, if the product features are what set it apart then it will not have any direct rivals. In this scenario, the company earns its higher rates of return by setting a higher price.

When we turn to the competitive scope in the market, Porter finds that the company can aim for one of two types of position: a broad one where it dominates the market, or a narrow one where it can concentrate its energies in a smaller part of the market, like a segment or even a niche. The broad scope means that it is taking on its competitors across the entire industry, while the narrow scope means that it is limiting the potential competition.

If we combine the competitive advantage of the company with the competitive scope available to it in the market, Porter argues that there are three possible generic strategies:

- **Cost leadership** – the company has advantages in the costs of production across a broad range of products. Since it can compete on price in all market segments it has a cost leadership position for the industry as a whole.
- **Differentiation** – although the company does not have a cost advantage, perhaps because it lacks the size required for economies of scale, all its products have unique features that consumers value. Its strategy is therefore one based on product differentiation.
- **Focus** – when the potential market segments are few the company is obliged to take a targeted approach. This may be discretionary; an international company entering a new market may decide to do so in only one or two segments, at least in the beginning. Within these limited segments the company may compete on product price or differentiation. However, what earns the company the higher returns is the fact that it is focusing on a part of the market it can call its own, the price/differentiation decision being a secondary issue.

Porter has also added a fourth strategy, the pitiful **stuck in the middle** approach. This is where companies end up when they are unable to make any of the other strategies stick. It has no unassailable cost advantage, nor products with uniquely appealing features. Somehow the company has lost its perspective on the market, not knowing whether it should be competing across all segments or maintaining a tight focus on just one or two.

Companies can end up in such a predicament if the original strategy is allowed to drift. This can happen when companies neglect to pursue low-cost production or fail to invest in product development. If such a company finds it is earning above-normal profits then it will be due to the unusually favourable conditions within the industry. MNEs can find themselves in this position when entering weak markets in developing economies. However, the advantageous positioning will last only until another MNE, or local rival, enters the market with a more defined generic strategy.

GENERIC STRATEGIES AS A BUSINESS TOOL

The attraction of this model is that it has clarity. We know that it cannot represent every nuance or subtlety in the commercial world but to be useful it should provide a basic sense of strategic direction. We therefore need to test the model to find if it can be reliably used as a business planner without sending the company in an erroneous direction. First, consider the source of the competitive advantage: examples abound of companies that sell low-priced items as opposed to those companies that charge a higher price for a unique product. Indeed, it is difficult to think of a market that is not divisible in this way. We can see this clearly in a grocery store that sells branded goods on their perceived features alongside similar products sold under the store's own brand but at a lower price.

Up to this point the choice between cost or differentiation strategies appears clear-cut. In reality we find that the distinction is not quite so neat and that differentiated products do still have price concerns while low-price products can be differentiated from rivals. This is not a problem as long as the main thrust of the strategy is in the right direction. Our lingering concern is whether the model has underestimated the importance of these exceptions and could send the company on the wrong strategy.

Another view is that being stuck in the middle, as Porter puts it, is not actually a hopelessly compromised position but a hybrid strategy that gains strength from taking a comprehensive approach to business. Instead of being a 'jack of all trades and master of none' the hybrid strategy means that a company is competing to the fullest extent in all its functions. Research by Pertusa-Ortega et al. (2009) found that the hybrid approach opened up greater combinations of cost and differentiation considerations, resulting in a unique and profitable corporate strategy.

COST VERSUS DIFFERENTIATION

On the question of cost we must first emphasise that this is not the same as price. Cost is economically definable in monetary terms and is derived from the production factors. The concept of low cost is related to the ability of a company to produce the same good or service at a lower cost to itself than its competitors. What *price* the company actually charges the customer is another matter entirely.

Relative **price** level (high, medium, low) as a concept is much more difficult to pin-down as it is derived from consumer perceptions of value and need. The price that consumers are willing to pay is also affected by personal circumstances, fashion, product availability and a multitude of other factors. Prices are often set in the market according to the principles of supply and demand, varying quite independently of the cost that the producer must cover. If the price is set high, the consumer may perceive the quality of the product to be high as well, even as the value-for-money declines (Dodds et al., 1991).

A related phenomenon is **psychological pricing**, where the price ends in the digit 9 to make it appear, in the minds of the consumers, to be considerably lower than the price just one unit higher ending in a zero (e.g. $14.99 appears much lower than $15.00). Although this pricing tactic is common its effectiveness is unproven (El Sehity et al., 2005). This is despite the fact that many businesses now trade on this concept, naming their businesses after their strategies of selling everything for 99 cents, 99 yen and so on according to the local currency.

At the other end of the price spectrum, for most people a car represents one of their biggest expenditures in their lives. The most affordable are generally made at the highest rates of production by the largest manufacturers, yet the buyers would hardly term them cheap. These same manufacturers make more expensive cars using essentially the same production techniques, the difference in price being explained by the greater use of resources, the lower rate of sales and the greater propensity to spend amongst the target consumers.

In both cases one economic principle is inviolate: production must achieve the lowest possible cost. If it does not and a rival company launches a similar product at the same price but with a more cost-efficient production system then the rival will earn greater profits. These profits can be reinvested in the business to perpetuate the economic advantage. Although Porter's model might suggest there is a choice between cost and differentiation in fact cost is always of crucial importance. Even products that have no apparent rival still face threats from substitute products; an expensive watch may be rejected in favour of jewellery if the watch is not perceived to offer sufficient value for the price.

On the matter of differentiation there is also the possibility that Porter's model could lead a manager astray. There are plenty of examples of products that might be called generic but still respond to **branding** strategies in attempts to differentiate them. Low-cost airlines are conspicuous in this regard, promoting their brand livery to the point where they are as famous as the national flag carrier airlines. Again, the model would have suggested to managers that the branding of their low-cost airline is a secondary issue, worthy of little attention, when experience shows that differentiation is important in all areas of the market.

Michael Porter (2008) gives the example of a budget airline that lost its way due to a drift from low cost towards differentiation. The airline was Laker, the 1970s predecessor of the modern budget airline. The company began to offer additional services when it should have focused purely on cost, and therefore price. This was not, though, the reason why the company failed; the company collapsed due to the intense competition from state-owned flag-carrier airlines (Francis et al., 2007). The offer of additional services to customers was part of the normal value adding exploration that all companies practise.

SCOPE, BROAD AND NARROW

If the Generic Strategies model puts a false separation between cost leadership and product differentiation, at least when it comes to scope there is a little more to hope for in the model. The breadth of the market that a company can compete over is dependent on the availability of internal resources and the nature of the product. While the metrics are not absolute, the company's scope is still broadly quantifiable and limited. As an example, let us consider a firm like Schaefer Shelving that makes industrial shelving for warehouses in the United States. It could, to an extent, sell to private users looking to equip their workshop at home, but the sheer scale of warehouses, and the requirement for industrial strength construction, means that this will always be the main market for the firm (Schaefer Shelving, 2015). It is therefore the product characteristics that limit the scope that is available to the firm.

Even where the scope is broad it is still closely tied to the qualities of the firm and its product. Cosmetic manufacturers are fortunate to be involved in products that can be sold to all age groups and even skin tone. The products, by their nature, are readily adapted and so a broad range of fundamentally similar products can be sold.

This itself may be limited by its own internal resources. A specialist furniture manufacturer, even though it had the workforce skills to make any pieces the customer desired, would find that it was wasting its resources attempting to compete with mass-market furniture brands. The model would advise some sort of focus and in this way it is providing sound advice.

MANAGEMENT SPOTLIGHT: RESOLVING COST AND DIFFERENTIATION

The Generic Strategies model from Michael Porter (1998) we have explored so far has some use to domestic managers in terms of guiding them on the scope dimension of the market. They should be able to analyse the capabilities of the firm, the product features and the opportunities in their market to decide whether to choose a focused strategy or a leadership one. There is some possibility of competing across a broad number of market segments but with a single representative product in each segment. However, a skilful compromise like this is not truly broad and is rather a multiple-focused segment strategy within a broad market strategy. In clarifying the distinction between broad and narrow scopes the Generic Strategies model is still serving a purpose.

This is not the case with the competitive advantage dimension. As far back as the 1980s, Charles Hill (1988) was warning about the dangers of perceiving cost and differentiation as mutually exclusive. It would be unwise for a firm to pursue a cost strategy alone when a rival could replicate the same cost base while providing significant product differentiation. Equally, a firm with a highly differentiated product could be making a fatal error if it neglected the cost issues. Even where the product is unique, and enjoying an effective monopoly in its segment, it is still vying for the consumer's money within their limited budget. If the company charges monopoly pricing but does not control its cost base then it will not earn the financial returns that it could. Furthermore, when the promise of high returns attracts a new entrant with lower costs, that entrant company will be able to offer the consumer a more competitive price and still earn higher financial returns.

As a business tool the model is therefore one that should be used with caution. It can indicate areas for investigation but it cannot prescribe a particular strategic outcome. For the domestic market it provides a framework for discussion without providing any conclusions.

International managers are in a slightly different position because they can explore new markets in a number of different ways. Despite having a broad range of products to draw on they may decide to focus on just one or two market segments. The company may be a cost leader in its domestic market but then the managers decide to market the product as highly differentiated and at a higher price point.

Porter's Generic Strategies model can serve some purpose as a point of departure for discussion but when it comes to exploring foreign markets it fails in another way: it is not dynamic. The model does not allow for companies to start with one strategy and then transfer to another as the situation develops. This is a critical deficiency since MNEs often have the luxury of being able to test the new market while explicitly planning for a future strategy changeover.

It is this fluid attitude to strategies for international business that distinguishes them from domestic strategies. In the next section, we will look at generic strategies for companies operating in the international arena.

Point of consideration: Chanel manufactures perfumes that can be said to be differentiated products with little regard to cost. Re-evaluate this contention, suggesting how even high-class perfumes need to be produced with attention to both cost and differentiation.

Source: Hill, 1988; Porter, 1998

CASE STUDY – HARD-DISCOUNT RETAILERS OFFER NARROW SAMPLES OF BROAD RANGES

Aldi and Lidl are two budget supermarket chains, or hard-discount stores, based in Germany. They have gained fame for their relentless pursuit of cost reduction, with the result that they offer the lowest prices in household goods in the market. In fact, they appear so obsessed with this strategy alone that they appear to have neglected to make any attempt to differentiate themselves from each other. The product lines are severely limited in number and little attempt is made to decorate the stores. As a result they are almost indistinguishable from each other, or from how supermarkets were when they first appeared over fifty years ago.

In terms of Michael Porter's Generic Strategies model the two German brands slot firmly into the low cost, narrow scope category. When they expanded into the UK market for the first time, they did so with around 800 products against 40,000 offered by the supermarket incumbents. This has led some analysts to label the stores 'limited assortment discounters'. The brands are usually in-house and entirely unfamiliar to British shoppers. With this business model they are occupying the same market segment as the Japanese ¥100 shops and the American 99 cent or dollar stores. At the budget level the brand itself has little value to the consumer; all that matters is the price of the goods.

Aldi and Lidl, along with other rising stars in the hard-discount firmament, have hit on a business model where the most popular product types are available, so competing fairly broadly, but there is limited choice within each type. We can say that the stores are offering narrow samples from a broad range of possible products. The two companies are able to stretch their product ranges by selling specific products for limited time periods. This paradox between broad and narrow focus only exists when interpreted through Michael Porter's model. In the real world of retail it is an entirely rational strategy, where consumers expect to find the goods they want, at the right quality and the lowest price. Concentrating on a sample of goods and selling only from existing stock is an approach that market traders know well.

The ruthless logic of the hard-discount model can be applied to any market but it does not mean that established supermarket chains have no defence. A number of attempts have been made to respond at the margins, such as offering own-brand budget products or entering joint ventures with hard-discount chains. Ultimately, though, the hard-discount brand model may be hoist by its own petard. As they grow more numerous they will have to differentiate themselves from one another, and customers will become more demanding as they expect low price along with a broad product choice, including their favourite brands. This takes the discounters into the territory occupied by the established supermarkets, which have economies of scale on their side and who only need to re-learn the importance of price competition. The once stagnant world of the supermarket could become dynamic once more!

Point of consideration: Think about an established supermarket chain and look at how it has drifted from its original business model. Devise a business model that will allow it to respond to the rise of the hard-discount retailers.

Source: Steenkamp and Kumar, 2009; Daily Telegraph, 2014

GENERIC INTERNATIONAL STRATEGIES

Despite the increasing globalisation of business, which implies that the world is becoming a single, unified playground for companies to explore at will, there are still enough differences to force managers to implement distinct strategies for overseas. There are a number of different reasons for treating the international arena as different from the domestic, as the company feels two contrasting pressures:

- **Marketing need** to respond to local market conditions – if the market is very dynamic then it may be necessary to become closely involved for greater responsiveness.
- **Economic need** to create the most efficient international structure – some operations offer greater efficiency if they work together across the world.

It is these pressures to be responsive or not to the local market, and to have a structure that is highly integrated or not, that give rise to the four generic international strategies shown in Figure 10.1.

The four strategy model shows how MNE can approach the development of their businesses overseas in different ways. Three of these approaches are familiar to international managers but Bartlett and Ghoshal (2002) put forward a fourth, transformational approach. The concept has been further developed over the years and is known as the transnational strategy (Bartlett et al., 2008).

Each of the four strategies is international in form but is derived from a different corporate attitude to the international operations. The differences can sometimes appear subtle so in order to clarify the link between the attitude and strategy some handy mnemonics have been added to the following list:

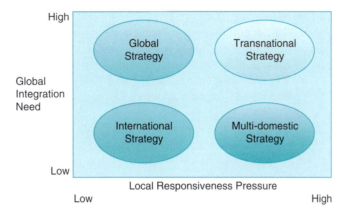

Figure 10.1 *Four generic international strategies*

Source: Bartlett and Ghoshal (2002)

1. International Strategy

Mnemonic: Missionary Strategy. Like a missionary spreading the good word, the corporation extends operations into overseas markets in order to convert them to its products and services. There is little appetite for local learning, only teaching. The objective is to offer an alternative to local rivals and hold a profitable market share.

Strategic requirement: low integration/low responsiveness. The corporation has little need of integrating overseas functions with its domestic operations and puts a low priority on responding to local market developments.

Strategic considerations: when a company first internationalises it does this usually from the familiarity of the domestic market. Quite likely it has a position of strength in that market. At this first tentative international adventure the managers will not want to unnecessarily disturb a domestic strategy that is clearly working, so they will opt for as few changes as possible. What the managers are looking for is an international strategy that supports the domestic operations, so changes to the product, production and marketing will be kept to a minimum.

For some products, there may be no advantage to having operations spread across the world and there may even be disadvantages:

- There is unused capacity in existing domestic operations which new overseas sales can utilise.
- The new, local market is small and would not support dedicated local operations.
- The product has special features, or is highly technical, and operations are not easily transferred. There may be risk that the technology could be appropriated by overseas competitors.

The local market itself may not warrant particular attention if the product is one that can be sold in all markets with significant change:

- There is very little local competition.
- The product is highly generic and follows a common global standard.

Strategy implementation: the international strategy is most often seen as one that emphasises exporting from existing facilities, or at most only low value-added activities are transferred to the new location. High-end audio manufacturers, such as Revox of Switzerland, maintain operations integrated in their domestic locations because they need to closely monitor their operations and there are no substantial economic benefits to extending operations overseas. Demand for these premium products is international, so a high proportion of output is exported to a multitude of markets, albeit in small volumes to each.

The weakness with the strategy is that it suffers from poor local responsiveness. If a rival, either another MNE or a new local enterprise, can justify a commitment to operations in the region then they can gain a significant advantage in their ability to meet the peculiarities of local demand.

2. Multidomestic Strategy

Mnemonic: Charitable Strategy. Just as a charity seeks to help its beneficiaries achieve independence, the corporation wants to help each local business unit develop in its own way. It does this by providing mainly financial assistance from the centre.

Strategic requirement: low integration/high responsiveness. Although the corporation has little necessity for its global diaspora of business units to be integrated with each other, there is a high priority for each business unit to be able to respond to local developments.

Strategic considerations: if the pressure for a new overseas operation needs to work with operations in other international locations is low, and it is focused on serving local demand, then the new operation can operate largely independently of the rest of the world. There are a number of conditions where this strategy is suitable:

- The local market is dynamic and consumer demand is unique to that area.
- The local market is large enough to support economically efficient operations.

Bartlett and Ghoshal refer to this globally fragmented strategy as *multinational*, but this invites confusion with the term *multinational enterprise* (MNE). For this reason, the alternative term *multidomestic* is preferred here.

Strategy implementation: from a marketing point of view the Multidomestic Strategy is a powerful option since it strengthens the ability to exploit new local opportunities. It was a common strategy for US car manufacturers who were always comfortable with their European business units being run quite independently of the American side of the business. Although this seems sensible on the marketing side given that the European car preference was quite different to the American one the strategy also served to encourage a divergence between the two sides of the business. Without integration there was little opportunity for synergies when the product ranges have nothing in common. There were occasions when world demand for a particular type of car was met by separate product designs for each market.

When the Japanese car manufacturers emerged in the 1970s, they took a contrasting approach. They demonstrated that it was possible to sell broadly the same products in all global markets. They consequently benefited from the economic efficiencies in both production and product development costs. It is an important principle in business that products should be standardised in all markets whenever possible, and it is a principle that is flouted by the Multidomestic Strategy. In general, the global automotive industry follows the Japanese custom of maximum standardisation but with certain local inputs in product design variations and components (Sturgeon et al., 2008). In this way a Multidomestic Strategy can nest within a Global Strategy.

3. Global Strategy

Mnemonic: Chess Strategy. Like a game of chess, the business units are now pieces that specialise in tasks but are controlled, sometimes sacrificed, by the headquarters in the service of a greater strategy. The corporation develops a set of rules and regulations in its home base that it wishes to impose on its business units in the rest of the world. Similar to the Missionary Strategy but now with aggressive control from the centre as all business units are co-ordinated. The objective is to out-compete local rivals and other MNEs in all locations.

Strategic requirement: high integration/low responsiveness. The priority shifts to the internal efficiency of the corporation. The world is treated as a single region, both as market and production location.

Strategic considerations: modern international business has progressed to a state where the global strategy prevails. In this strategy, operations are scattered around the world but they work closely together on standardised products. The global strategy treats the world as one location, replicating the domestic strategy but on a worldwide scale. Just as the domestic strategy sets out central control over domestic production, engineering and marketing operations, so the global strategy has a headquarters function (HQ) co-ordinating facilities in different parts of the world.

Strategic implementation: The advantages of this approach are that economies of scale can be achieved in all operations since they are potentially serving the entire world. At the same time, each operation is specialised in its activity, so continuous improvements can be made thanks to learning effects. In some product categories standardisation is forced on a company due to a need for compatibility, which allows the company's products to operate with those made by other companies, with laptops and printers being one example (Besen and Farrell, 1994). Any local advantages, such as low labour costs or local skills, are additional benefits. The aircraft industry caught onto this strategy some years ago and it is now common for parts of airplanes to be sourced from specialist operations around the world.

Weighing against the advantages are a number of disadvantages. There is poor local responsiveness since the operations are focused on the unified world market, not local demand. Fortunately, most mainstream products, particularly high technology, need little adaptation for different markets. Digital cameras, for example, are usually programmed with a number of language settings, so the consumer can choose the one appropriate to them for the display screen. Another disadvantage is that of co-ordination cost in keeping the global elements of the business working together. This often results in corporations that have an elite class of managers stationed in headquarters, or around the world, whose task it is to keep the scattered operations in alignment.

4. Transnational Strategy

Mnemonic: Parental Strategy. On the face of it the most charming strategy, one that has parallels with the way parents raise their children to play and grow together. The corporation seeks to have all the various parts of its business 'family' working and developing in harmony.

Strategic requirement: high integration/high responsiveness. The corporation attempts to retain the global efficiencies of operating internationally while also being responsive to local markets. Instead of dictating strategy from the centre the management devise one that evolves through feedback from the periphery.

Strategy conditions: this can be thought of as the ultimate international strategy. It is one that combines the advantages of the Global Strategy, with its highly efficient specialised operations, with the Multidomestic Strategy and its high local responsiveness. Although there are still considerable managerial co-ordination costs most control is delegated to the local business unit. Unlike the Multidomestic Strategy the products are basically standardised but with plenty of margin for local adaptation. Local economies of scale can be exploited, while any learning effects can be disseminated throughout the international group.

Strategy implementation: the Transnational Strategy represents such a perfect confluence of apparently contradictory elements that it is no wonder true examples are difficult to find. Financial services are one of the few industries that lend themselves to the approach. The principles of finance are fairly common throughout the world, but it is important to adapt the actual financial services to the local market. HSBC, originally a Hong Kong-based bank, boasts that it is the 'world's local bank' (Koller, 2007). In fact, there is nothing unique about that declared market position since all international banks are made up of strong national branches reporting back to a central headquarters. The headquarters itself can be located anywhere in the world, HSBC having relocated from Hong Kong to London in 1991 without having any negative effect on the worldwide banking operations; the move was for cost rather than strategic reasons.

MANAGEMENT DECISIONS AND THE GENERIC INTERNATIONAL STRATEGIES

The Generic International Strategies model is dynamic to the degree that the first exploration of the overseas environment can be conducted within the International Strategy framework. As the corporation grows in experience and confidence the strategy can progress to the Multidomestic and Global strategies. The fully mature MNE can reach for the Transnational Strategy. Although this progression has a strong rationale it does not account for the requirements of different industries. For some, flexibility in the market is an option due to the nature of the product, while in other industries the product is inflexible and so the focus is on minimising the cost of production.

A further obstacle to the use of the model as an aid to dynamic decision-making is that the Multidomestic Strategy could prove to be something of a dead end. The approach is predicated on granting semi-autonomous powers to the overseas business units with weak control from the centre. To move from that to the Global Strategy would mean reversing the structure and imposing tight control from the centre. Even a shift to the Transnational Strategy would mean retaining the core competencies of the business units while creating a new international managerial structure over the top of them.

In practice, it is likely that the Generic International Strategies model presents a two-step decision-making process at best: first, the tentative International Strategy to explore the overseas opportunities, then a full-blooded attack in the form of one of the three remaining strategies. Table 10.1 illustrates the range of decisions for each strategy outcome according to the industry.

In Table 10.1 the ability to respond to local market conditions is represented by the adaptability of the product and the flexibility of the production system. If both of these are high then it is possible to supply all markets with customised products from one production location. This is because the product can be easily adapted to the demands of markets around the world, and the production system is flexible enough to make those adaptations.

Before coming to this conclusion, though, it is necessary to evaluate the need to integrate global functions, here represented by the economies of scale in production and co-ordination by the management. If the economies of scale are high then the production sites will be large but minimal in number, implying a reluctance to proliferate production across globally disparate locations unless local market demand

Table 10.1 *Generic international strategies and industry*

Industry	Product Adaptability	Production Flexibility	Economies of Scale	International Coordination	Strategy
Steel Production	Low	Low	High	High	International
News media	Low	High	Low	Low	Multidomestic
Film industry	Low	Low	High	High	Global
Pharmaceutical	High	High	High	High	Transnational

is high enough to support large-scale production. Equally, when there is a high need for co-ordination then there will be a similar reluctance to allow unfettered international expansion until the appropriate control mechanisms are in place.

Returning to Table 10.1 we can look at each industry in more detail, as follows:

- **Steel production** – a commodity product that is manufactured in broadly standard form with very little flexibility in production. The economies of scale are high and it is important that the corporation has close control over output so that efficiency is maximised. International markets are usually served through exports in order to maintain stable output at the production location. This suits the International Strategy but Multidomestic is feasible where the local market is large enough.
- **News media** – television news are specific to their local market in terms of their language and content; there is little possibility of adapting news in one country for another. At the same time, the programmes can be produced using small, highly responsive production teams. There is little need for global co-ordination, although news teams may borrow each other's material as necessary. Generally Multidomestic, although there are a few examples of the International Strategy (e.g. BBC World Service, Al Jazeera).
- **Film industry** – like television programmes movies tend to be specific to their market, but the production is much less flexible and the economies of scale tend to be high. For these reasons movie making tends to be concentrated in particular locations with a small number of companies (e.g. Hollywood) but the movies themselves are made with broad appeal in mind to maximise global sales. Depending on the film, the production location can be almost anywhere but co-ordination from the centre will still be strong. International movie makers generally have a Global Strategy, although some domestic market producers enjoy the occasional international hit.
- **Pharmaceutical industry** – vast sums are spent on R&D to continually develop drugs or replace them with entirely new ones. The R&D centres are often in close proximity to knowledge-intense clusters, such as universities, and as a consequence are spread around the world. The need to co-ordinate the various research programmes and keep them working with each other points to a Transnational Strategy. The production system is flexible but has high economies of scale and so by itself it suggests a Global Strategy. However, given the importance of co-ordinating production with R&D the Transnational Strategy remains the preferred option.

These four examples suggest that the four Generic International Strategies are more prescriptive than the originators intended. Furthermore, the Transnational Strategy may not be the ultimate evolution of the MNE but simply a strategy that suits a particular requirement for market responsiveness and corporate integration. If this is so then we would expect there to be little movement from one strategy to the other, even if the International Strategy represents a common first step.

CASE STUDY – HOLLYWOOD FEELS THE HEAT FROM BOLLYWOOD

There is no doubt that the global movie industry is dominated by Hollywood, California. In its home city of Los Angeles it is known simply as The Industry. The city's industry cluster report (2010) showed that the movie and TV industry employed over 112,000 people, and the highest earning films bring in over US$1 billion from worldwide sales. Often accused of playing to the lowest common denominator in the market, they nevertheless are able to build on the advantage of a large domestic audience whose language and culture is recognised throughout the world.

Although many movies are indeed produced in Hollywood they are also made on location anywhere in the world. Furthermore, movies made in other English-speaking areas are able to ride the Hollywood bandwagon and sell in the same markets. One of the best examples of this is the British-based James Bond franchise. Hollywood, though, remains the home of the largest movie making firms in the world. In terms of the Generic International Strategies Model, the Hollywood industry is truly a global one.

The Indian movie industry has similarly clustered in a single location, in this case the city of Bombay from which the industry derives its name, Bollywood. Like its American cousin it serves a huge domestic market, by population nearly four times larger than that of the United States. It is also a very diverse market, the movies having to appeal to a wide variety of languages and cultures. At the same time there is widespread poverty throughout the country. As a result Bollywood movies have to be made on far lower budgets than the American blockbusters, and they tend to follow a formulaic approach in order to appeal to the widest sections of Indian society.

Bollywood has enjoyed some success in overseas markets. The global Indian diaspora have taken their movie preferences with them, so Bollywood films are being shown in cinemas where there are sufficient emigrants. The movies are also finding favour throughout Asia and even into Saudi Arabia. The Bollywood industry is now valued at around US$3.5 billion and is larger than Hollywood, employing 2.5 million people and selling over 4 billion tickets annually to Hollywood's 3 billion.

Despite the impressive metrics, Bollywood operates according to an International Strategy. Though, like all movies, location filming takes production out of the city's studios there is no question that the city remains firmly in the director's chair. It is rare for movies of this style to be made anywhere else, so there is no sense of knowledge and experience feeding back to Bollywood, or of Bollywood companies co-ordinating worldwide empires of movie making.

The contrast in Hollywood and Bollywood strategies does not mean that Bollywood is somehow less developed, or that one day it will advance to the Global Strategy commanded by Hollywood. The Bollywood industry structure is different to that of Hollywood, focusing on a particular social stratum within a broad but identifiable ethnic group. It is difficult to see how an Indian Canadian movie company, for example, could produce a film for Canada and find popularity in Asia as well. The two markets are just too different.

It is likely, then, that Hollywood will continue to succeed with its Global Strategy for worldwide sales while Bollywood uses the International Strategy to serve the popular end of the Asian, mainly Indian, market. There is equal success in both of these strategies.

Point of consideration: At one time Italy gained international fame for its 'Spaghetti Westerns', competing against Hollywood westerns in global markets, including the United States. Indeed, this was how Clint Eastwood launched his career. Determine which Generic International Strategy this was and suggest reasons why it did not last.

Sources: Los Angeles County Economic Development Corporation, 2010; Punathambekar and Kavoori, 2008

RAISING EMPLOYABILITY: GLOBAL EMPLOYMENT FOR MANAGERS

It is not only corporations that are stepping onto the international stage with a sense of trepidation; the managers too are walking gingerly into the unknown. Whatever logical argument might pop out of the analysis leading to the decision to globalise the corporation, the strategic move needs managers to lead it. This can create something of a paradox: companies need internationally experienced managers to globalise them, and managers need globalised companies to give them the international experience.

Of course, the situation is not quite as critical as stated: there have been companies operating internationally since before the time of Marco Polo, extending themselves to the limits of their known worlds. In the modern age, some of the more basic international strategies, such as exporting standard products from a single home location, can rely on the stock of international management experience inherited from previous eras. The problem with globalisation is that it is more than internationalisation *in extremis*; it means taking a holistic perspective of the business as it operates across the world. Where internationalisation means transacting with enterprises overseas, globalisation means actively working with them. Few managers have this experience.

Corporations can foster this new breed of global managers by seconding them to overseas divisions as the organisation progressively explores international markets. However, as Daily et al. (2000) discovered, managers face a dilemma when offered such opportunities. They are concerned that in being posted far from the home headquarters they risk being side-lined from the most important corporate developments. This harms their ambitions to climb to the top of the corporation, yet, interestingly, it enhances their employability with other corporations. The lesson here is that managers who want to lead international corporations must first join the elite group of managers who are prepared to hawk their skills around the corporations of the world rather than pinning their hopes to just one. The best international managers are those that have a career strategy, not a job strategy.

For the small and medium-sized enterprise (SME) there is often a lack of resources in entering international markets at all, so the managers are denied the opportunity to build up their experience. Furthermore, SMEs are often young companies with managers who lack even domestic experience, never mind the international kind. Yet this gloomy perspective may not be true of the companies that are part of the new wave of industries. Reuber and Fischer (1997) looked at the Canadian software industry, one that is by nature born-global with few international entry barriers to deal with, and found that firm size alone was not an impediment to international growth. Instead, these SMEs were able to extend operations overseas through a combination of overseas partnerships driven by a commercial compulsion to secure sales beyond the domestic market. A note of caution, though: the relative ease of globalisation may be specific to the industry.

As always it seems that the developing economies do not have it so easy. With industries heavily dependent on commodities, businesses tend to lean towards exports with little necessity to adapt to individual overseas markets. If we take coffee, one of the most traded commodities, as an example, the multitude of flavours that have been concocted for the beverage have their origin in the markets of the developed economies; the coffee farmers do little more than supply the beans. With few opportunities to engage with the international markets, managers in emerging economies are denied the opportunity to gain the relevant experience, perpetuating the domestic bias of their companies.

A possible route out of this predicament would be to encourage knowledge transfer by offering employment to managers from developed economies on a short-term basis. The managers gain the international experience they need for their career plans, while the developing economy enterprises gain the overseas management skills. Sadly, the only way to attract ambitious managers from wealthy nations is to offer them sufficient financial rewards, the very resource that developing nations lack.

WEB SUPPORT

1. Understanding Goals, Strategy, Objectives And Tactics In The Age Of Social. An article from Forbes by Mikal E Belicove, published in 27th September 2013. Suggests a neat mnemonic, G'SOT, for remembering the difference between goals, strategies, objectives and tactics. Worth exploring the various links too.

   www.forbes.com/sites/mikalbelicove/2013/09/27/understanding-goals-strategies-objectives-and-tactics-in-the-age-of-social/

2. Strategy: Low Cost or Differentiation. A post by M Dana Baldwin, senior consultant, on the Simplified Strategic Planning Blog. It clarifies the difference between the concepts, thankfully also conceding that they can be mixed in one blended strategy.

   www.cssp.com/strategicplanning/blog/strategy-low-cost-or-differentiation/

3. Hollywood copy from Bollywood. A video from Bollywood Life listing five Hollywood movies that are said to get their plots from original Bollywood movies. Even if you are not convinced, think about how developed economies can increasingly learn from developing economies in the future.

   www.youtube.com/watch?v=d4D0orWHnb0

THE STORY SO FAR: GENERIC STRATEGIES FOR INTERNATIONAL MANAGERS

In this chapter we have looked at two sets of generic strategies: Michael Porter's strategies for the domestic market followed by the generic international strategies of Bartlett and Ghoshal. The two models are linked by the compulsion companies have to extend their operations beyond their own national borders. The problem is that both models struggle to contain all the possibilities open to companies. In attempting to systemise the strategic options the models inevitably fail to grasp the infinite variety of corporate success. If it were possible to guarantee success by choosing one of three or four possible strategies then risk and strategy could be eliminated from the business landscape!

So why give these two approaches any room in a manager's analysis? Because the models provide frameworks to what would otherwise be a chaotic and subjective decision making process. If the most suitable strategy is not one that is included in either of the models, the reasons for the exception can still be systematically inspected via the models. Like a camera lens, the two models bring the most important factors into sharp focus for us to then make our own decision.

Project Topics

1. Suppose you are the manager of a company manufacturing suitcases, a mature product that has changed little over the past few years. Your company has come to dominate the market in your country. A large foreign competitor enters your domestic market with a product priced much lower than yours and their market share rapidly expands.
   a. Should your response be tactical or strategic? Try to analyse the merits and demerits for each strategy.
   b. With reference to Michael Porter's Generic Strategies Model, what kind of strategy would be most suitable for your company? Does your company's predicament suggest improvements that could be made to the Generic Strategies Model?

2. Fifty years ago the global watch and clock market was dominated by Swiss brands, many representing small companies. The Japanese manufacturers entered the market with cheap and accurate electronic watches, quickly taking a large market share.
    a. What does this upset in the market tell you about the apparent choice between product differentiation and cost?
    b. How did the Swiss industry respond to the Japanese expansion?
3. Ethiopia is reputed to be the birthplace of coffee, and even today the growers have a good name for a high-quality product. However, it is the Brazilian coffee growers that supply most of the world with its coffee needs.
    a. In terms of the Generic International Strategies model compare and contrast the approaches made by companies in the two countries.
    b. What kind of strategy would you recommend to a coffee grower in Ethiopia in order to expand internationally?

 CASE STUDY: DIFFERENTIATION AND COST IN AIRASIA

Budget airlines, or low cost carriers as they are officially known, started to appear in the 1980s to exploit a trend towards deregulation in the airline industry. This allowed for much greater competition on air routes and a downward pressure on prices. The new airlines fit Michael Porter's Generic Competitive Strategies model quite well, starting out as cost-focus businesses with a narrow scope in the beginning and a strong emphasis on lowering costs. It is this ruthless programme of cost minimisation that marks out the budget airlines as unique and quite unlike the regional flights offered by major airlines over similar routes.

The existing regional airlines were run as offshoots of the main company. For these short-haul routes all customer reservations, baggage handling, aircraft maintenance and so on were run using the same systems as for the long-haul routes. In terms of the generic strategy mode this represented a confusion of strategies. Budget airlines brought much greater clarity to the strategy by relentlessly pursuing lower costs at every turn. In general they moved their business models to customers doing their own online reservations; dynamic pricing meant prices changed according to demand and there were strict limits on baggage allowances. On the operations side the aircraft cabins were low maintenance, easy to clean and inflight services were only available at additional cost. Flights were routed to lower cost destinations that were sometimes, famously, inconveniently far from the passengers' ultimate destination.

The new airlines made efficiency gains if they could maintain high rates of occupancy with load factors typically over 80%. It was this need to fill the aircraft as much as possible that made budget airlines high risk and many of the ventures failed. The major airlines tried to compete by launching their own budget subsidiaries but since they had to be structured around the same low cost strategy they had to be almost entirely separate from the main business; as investments they were just as risky as independent budget airlines. The British Airways budget subsidiary, Go, lasted just four years until it was absorbed by EasyJet in 2002.

One of the latest newcomers is AirAsia, a long-haul budget airline based in Malaysia with routes throughout Asia and Oceania, including Australia and China. It started with a low-cost focus strategy based around the established core competencies of budget airlines:

- High capacity utilisation with high load factors and aircraft embarking on their return flight within 25 minutes of arrival at the airport terminal.

- No frills approach that does without a dedicated airport lounge, no customer loyalty programmes and in-flight service only available for an additional fee.
- Point-to-point network that avoids the expense of stopovers at intermediary airports.
- Standardisation of the aircraft fleet to streamline flight crew training and minimise operational costs.

As the airline has expanded into long-haul routes, though, its strategy is not so readily explained by Porter's generic competitive strategy model. Although the scope of AirAsia's network means that it has assumed cost leadership it has also differentiated itself in the market by promoting its brand values. Rather than simply competing on price it promotes itself to the youth market by sponsoring sports and entertainment events. It also denotes funds to charities, such as disaster relief. By building up the brand identity the company is hoping to compete on more than just price and so encourage good rates of customer retention. If the managers had followed the theoretical model more closely, the company would be constantly defending itself against rivals offering cheap deals and introductory offers.

All budget airlines follow a similar pattern, competing first on price alone but then strengthening their brand image so that they become the first point of contact for customers looking for a flight. The same principle can be applied to other markets since low-costs, and therefore competitive prices, can usually be replicated by rivals in a short space of time. The additional power of the brand provides the differentiation that cannot so easily be copied.

Points of consideration: Budget airlines are continuing to take business from the larger, full-service airlines. Using Michael Porter's Generic Strategies model, to what extent are the budget airlines low-cost leaders? Can these budget airlines be said to be undifferentiated?

Source: AirAsia, 2014

? MULTIPLE CHOICE QUESTIONS

1. Is growth always good for a business?
   a. Yes, it increases revenues.
   b. Yes, it diversifies the product ranges.
   c. No, it is risky and requires skilled management.

2. Managers are only concerned with strategy, not tactics.
   a. True – strategy is about the overall command of the corporate direction, which is a management remit.
   b. False – corporate strategy may set the overall objectives but tactics involve the day-to-day management decisions.
   c. It depends – sometimes tactics become the corporate strategy.

3. Which of the following is an example of tactics?
   a. Designing a range of cosmetics for older consumers.
   b. Advertising on afternoon TV to reach older consumers.
   c. Merging with a company that manufacturers cosmetics for older consumers.

4. Cost leadership means cheap products and high-volume sales.
   a. False – expensive products can also be sold at high volumes.
   b. False – it is not about cheapness to the consumer but low cost to the producer.
   c. True – high-volume sales are needed to increase the revenues from the low-price products.

5. Which group of products are suited to a differentiation strategy?
    a. Fountain pens, custom watches, sports cars.
    b. Pencils, low price quartz watches, family cars.
    c. All products can be differentiated in some way.

6. Which company would be suited to an international strategy?
    a. Wine producer.
    b. Silk textile manufacturer.
    c. Business hotel chain.

7. Which company would be suited to a multidomestic strategy?
    a. Fast food chain.
    b. Aluminium producer.
    c. Tourist hotel chain.

8. Which company would be suited to a global strategy?
    a. Pharmaceutical company.
    b. Hollywood film company.
    c. Bollywood film company.

9. Which organisation would be suited to a transnational strategy?
    a. Red Cross charity.
    b. Car manufacturing company.
    c. Shipbuilding company.

10. Why do so few companies implement a transnational strategy?
    a. The company needs to be very large.
    b. The strategy carries high risk.
    c. It involves complex co-ordination and control.

Answers
1c, 2b, 3b, 4b, 5c, 6a, 7c, 8b, 9a, 10c

REFERENCES

AirAsia (2014) Annual Report 2013 from www.airasia.com/docs/common-docs/investor-relations/annual-report-2013.pdf accessed 16 July 2014

Bartlett C A and Ghosal S (2002) *Managing across borders: The transnational solution* (2nd edn.). Boston, MA: Harvard Business School Press

Bartlett C A, Ghosal S and Beamish P (2008) *Transnational management: Text, cases, and readings in cross-border management* (5th edn.). London: McGraw-Hill

Besen S M and Farrell J (1994) 'Choosing how to compete: Strategies and tactics in standardization' *The Journal of Economic Perspectives* pp. 117–131

BMW (2014) Milestones from group website www.bmwgroup.com/e/0_0_www_bmwgroup_com/unternehmen/historie/meilensteine/meilensteine.html accessed 13 July 2014

Casadesus-Masanell R and Ricart J E (2010) 'From strategy to business models and onto tactics' *Long Range Planning* April 2010, 4392/3), pp. 195–215

Daily C M, Certo S T and Dalton D R (2000) 'International experience in the executive suite: the path to prosperity?' *Strategic Management Journal* 200, 21(4), pp. 515–523

Dodds W B, Monroe K B and Grewal D (1991) 'Effects of price, brand, and store information on buyers' product evaluations' *Journal of Marketing Research,* pp. 307–319

El Sehity T, Hoelzl E and Kirchler E (2005) 'Price developments after a nominal shock: Benford's Law and psychological pricing after the euro introduction' *International Journal of Research in Marketing* 22(4), pp. 471–480

Fader P S, Hardie B G and Zeithammer R (2003) 'Forecasting new product trial in a controlled test market environment' *Journal of Forecasting* 22(5), pp. 391–410

Francis G, Dennis N, Ison S and Humphreys I (2007) 'The transferability of the low-cost model to long-haul airline operations' *Tourism Management* 28(2), pp. 391–398

Hill C W (1988) 'Differentiation versus low cost or differentiation and low cost: a contingency framework' *Academy of Management Review* 13(3), pp. 401–412

Koller V (2007) '"The world's local bank": glocalisation as a strategy in corporate branding discourse' *Social Semiotics* 17(1), pp. 111–131

Lenovo (2012) 'Lenovo establishes industrial base in Wuhan' from *Lenovo News Rel*eases 7 May 2012 www.news.lenovo.com/article_display.cfm?article_id=1587 accessed 13 July 2014

———(2014) 'Lenovo to buy mobile patents from NEC Corporation' from *Lenovo News Releases* 4 April 2014 www.news.lenovo.com/article_display.cfm?article_id=1784 accessed 13 July 2014

Los Angeles County Economic Development Corporation (2010) Industry Clusters in Los Angeles County from www.laedc.org/documents/industryclusters_online.pdf accessed 23 July 2014

Pertusa-Ortega E M, Molina-Azorín J F and Claver-Cortés E (2009) 'Competitive strategies and firm performance: a comparative analysis of pure, hybrid and "stuck-in-the-middle" strategies' in Spanish firms' *British Journal of Management* 20(4), pp. 508–523

Peterson R R (2004) 'Integration strategies and tactics for information technology governance' Van Grembergen W (ed.) (2004) *Strategies for information technology governance*. London: Idea Group

Porter M E (1998) *Competitive advantage*. New York: The Free Press

———(2008) *Competitive strategy: Techniques for analyzing industries and competitors*. New York: Simon and Schuster

Punathambekar A and Kavoori P A (2008) *Global Bollywood publisher*. New York: NYU Press

Reuber A R and Fischer E (1997) 'The influence of the management team's international experience on the internationalization behaviors of SMEs' *Journal of International Business Studies* 00472506, 1997 4th Quarter, 28(4)

Robson G (2005) *BMW: Driven to succeed*. Yeovil: Haynes Publishing

Schaefer Shelving (2015) About us webpage from www.schaefershelving.com/t-about.aspx accessed 5 March 2015

Steenkamp J-B E M and Kumar N (2009) 'Don't be undersold!' *Harvard Business Review* Dec 2009, 87(12), pp. 90–95

Sturgeon T J, Memedovic O, Van Biesebroeck J and Gereffi G (2008) 'Globalisation of the automotive industry: main features and trends' *International Journal of Technological Learning, Innovation and Development* 2(1–2), pp. 7–24

11 Global Strategic Alliances

Chapter Objectives

Not all companies are capable of making the leap to full global operations; instead they need to take the intermediate step of forming a partnership with another firm. This has the effect of diversifying the risk but with it goes some of the authority to control the investment, as well as a part of the profits. We will be looking at the purpose of entering a partnership and the forms that an alliance may take:

- The sharing of risk and the division of profits.
- Types of global strategic alliance.
- Managing the alliance.
- Ending the partnership.

PARTNERS IN RISK

A major part of any manager's job is to reduce risk to the company. This is not to say that risk *per se* is to be shunned, despite the reputation of some managers to be either **risk takers** or **risk averse**. In fact, risk is an inherent part of business and the extremes of risk aversion and risk addiction are both short routes to business destruction. To avoid risk when competitors are taking it means to be pushed to the rear of the industry, but to embrace risk without due care and attention is little short of a game of Russian roulette with company resources.

According to Amit and Wernerfelt (1990), risk reduction for its own sake has just three purposes: minimisation of management risk (e.g. bankruptcy, loss of earnings), preservation of cash flows in an uncertain environment and reduction in transaction costs due to risk management. If we accept that these are common to all operators within an industry then a manager has two purposes with regards to risk for the company:

1. First, ensure that the financial return matches the risk. High risk is perfectly acceptable if the rate of return is also high. Assuming that other managers in the industry make the same objective assessment the company's competitive position should be at least equal to the competition and earn it normal profits.
2. Second, ensure that the company specific risk is minimised. This is one source of the company's competitive advantage over its rivals.

If a manager can lower the risk to the company while continuing to enjoy the same rates of return as the rest of the industry, then the result will be higher than normal profits. If the risk reduction is company specific, then the higher than normal profits may be secure for the long term.

Apart from the initial period during the founding of the company perhaps the riskiest time is when it launches itself in overseas markets. While it already has an established position in its home market, perhaps even a dominant one, in the new market it is just like starting over. The product it is offering will be new to that market, and it could well be up against competing products from existing players in the market. There are also marketing and distribution challenges, exacerbated by the complexities of international logistics. The option of local manufacturing brings with it another set of problems.

SHARE THE RISKS; SHARE THE PROFITS

A neat way of reducing much of the risk of international operations is to team up with another company in a **global strategic alliance**. As the old adage might have it, a risk shared is a risk halved. We do need to add a small caveat to this: dividing the risk between the partners will also mean a division of the profits.

It is because the financial rewards of any partnership have to be shared that alliances are not a panacea to be used in all instances of risk reduction. Rather, the alliance approach is just one risk reduction strategy in the manager's toolbox. There are a myriad of other techniques, from exports to the wholesale acquisition of a local company. The role of the alliance is to create a strategic compromise, an intermediate stop in order to avoid shouldering all the risk. The cost of this is in relinquishing some of the rewards.

Conventionally, a company would make its investment based on its calculations of risk and reward. On the assumption that an alliance reduces both of them equally, the end result should be that the company is no better off than if it had plunged in with a solo commitment to the project. The missing element is **uncertainty**, the incalculable face of risk. Research by Inkpen and Currall (2004) considered this to be a crucial reason for firms seeking joint ventures.

The impossibility with uncertainty is that there is no sure way of finding a matching rate of return. To invest in an uncertainty is to gamble, and this is not what professional managers do. The priority then is to eliminate uncertainties or convert them into calculable risks. The purpose of the alliance, then, is to sharply reduce the uncertainty by dividing it with a partner. The fact that this means dividing the spoils is immaterial: the risk, and the commitment, is also lower.

WEIGHING UP STRATEGIC ALLIANCES

The uncertainties that strategic alliances seek to reduce or eliminate can occur in any area of a company's operations. Looking at a selection of these in turn:

- **Research and development (R&D)** – when a technology is in its early stages, its potential is at its most uncertain. Not only is it difficult to know when the technology will be ready for the market, it may never make it to the market at all. Sharing the R&D with another organisation will inevitably divide the returns but also reduce the incalculable uncertainties. Sampson (2007) found that the firms that benefited most from R&D alliances were those that were already capable of doing *some* of the work and had the potential to learn the rest from a partner.
- **Production** – economies of scale for the industry are usually understood, but it is difficult to know whether demand in a new market will justify a full-scale production operation. A risk assessment of the new market should provide a reasonably reliable range of output expectations, but economies of

scale are related to a precise output figure. Sharing a production plant reduces the danger that the company will be lumbered with a full-scale plant running at a costly low-capacity utilisation. Japanese companies have been particularly adept at this kind of alliance as a method for expanding production sites around Asia (Hatch and Yamamura, 1996).

- **Marketing** – market research will assess the risks associated with entering a new market, but uncertainty rises in line with the novelty of the product. An entirely new product will be almost entirely beset with uncertainty since the marketing team has no existing customer behaviour on which to base its research. A local partner will have specialist knowledge that can convert some of that uncertainty into definable risk. Teng and Das (2008) cite the alliance between Coca-Cola and Danone to market the US firm's Minute Maid drink in France, but warn that a subsequent merging of brands in the minds of the consumers can be difficult to unpick when the alliance is terminated and the partners go their own way.

Due to the reduction of uncertainty, strategic alliances find their greatest use in exploring new opportunities that are beyond the company's customary mode of operations. Such co-operation is often seen in developing untried technologies, entering entirely unfamiliar markets or setting up production in unfamiliar locations. Aside from the business case for an alliance, the company may also be obliged to enter into an alliance due to local political pressure. This has the additional benefit of eliminating a potential competitor since the local rival is tied into a contractual relationship.

FRICTION IN THE PARTNERSHIP

Unfortunately, there are a number of risks attached to strategic alliances (Anderson et al., 2006). To an extent, we can dismiss the reduced financial return since the risk is also reduced through sharing. However, there is an increased risk that one partner will learn about the other's unique competitive advantage and exploit it. Indeed, where there is a legal obligation for the alliance the political agenda is for this very transfer of knowledge to take place.

Alliances appear very appealing on the surface since they suggest a more convivial approach to business in place of the traditional reputation for ruthless competition. Some business commentators believe that by working together companies can reduce wasteful duplication of effort and resources. For example, the **C3 Behaviour** model advocates the nurturing of co-operation, co-ordination and collaboration (Humphries and Wilding, 2004). There is little doubt that where C3 is observed the business relationship is found to be highly efficient, avoiding much of the economic friction that transaction cost analysis (TCA) warns against. Yet it also seems that C3 is the result, not the cause, of the close working team. Indeed, in the early stages the business relationship needs to be based on enforceable contracts or the investment of **reputational capital** before the successive iterations of business dealings give rise to a sense of trust between the parties.

The point about a collaborative team spirit is that this utopian business state is alien to most commercial enterprises, perhaps even unnatural when you consider that most businesses are forged in mutual competition. Bringing two rivals together to work in harmony so that they can compete against the rest of their peers is a paradox that is not easy to resolve. The relationship itself is very challenging at the start as it means overcoming a sense of mistrust built up over years of rivalry. The early days of the alliance are therefore secured by complex, costly negotiations and contracts in order to reassure both parties.

Even when the companies have formed the agreement, the practice of working together is fraught with difficulties. There may be the mysteries of culture clashes as the two partners have contrasting approaches in their businesses, and these can only be worked out with experience. Then there are technical obstacles thrown up by such things as different IT systems and even, as when working with US firms, differences over measurements.

All this means that management resources become stretched, as the minutiae of the alliance need fastidious care in a way that each partner would normally have taken for granted. Alliances may save costs in many areas but not usually in management resources. Finally, the alliance can prove restrictive, preventing individual partners from developing the shared project according to their own vision. Only once the relationship has proved itself can the spirit of collaboration emerge along with its promise of a frictionless, costless partnership.

MYTH BUSTER – NASA AND THE SCIENCE OF MEASUREMENT

Science is logical, rational and objective. At its base is a set of universal rules that apply to all of us. Fundamental to this is one unified system of measurement. At least, you might think so. There are three countries left in the world still regularly using the medieval British measurement system of feet and inches: Burma, Liberia and the United States. With the rest of the world, including the UK, having turned over to the metric system, it was only a matter of time before something got lost in translation. That something was a US$125 million space probe.

In 1999, two major contractors had finished work on a probe that was intended for landing on the surface of Mars. The two collaborators were Jet Propulsion Laboratory (JPL) and Lockheed Martin, both American but each using a different system of measurement. JPL were using the metric system while Lockheed Martin had stuck to the traditional British measurements. The crucial mistake was made when JPL were working on the navigation system for the craft, believing they were inputting metric-seconds when in fact they were inputting pound-seconds.

The launch of the craft went without a hitch but then it steadily drifted away from its intended course over a journey of 461 million miles (or 741.91 million kilometres, if we are not to compound their error). By the time the space craft had reached the planet it was plunged too deep into the Martian atmosphere and was destroyed.

NASA was unsure which company to blame. Each of them had acted in good faith but neither had put in sufficient additional monitoring mechanisms to check what the other was doing. It is true that Lockheed Martin should have been using the metric system, but the JPL should have been aware that they were not. Ultimately, the fault lay in that vacuum between the two companies.

Point of consideration: What simple strategy could have been used to minimise the costs of the partnership while preventing these kinds of mistakes? Why do you think this strategy was not used?

Source: Los Angeles Times, 1999

Ultimately, strategic alliances are intended to overcome specific challenges facing the partners. The best alliances deliver mutual and equal benefits to both partners. Once the problem has been overcome the agreement can be dissolved and the two partners go their separate ways. The worst alliances end in recriminations over the waste of management resources, appropriation of IPR and restrictions on future development.

DOMESTIC AND INTERNATIONAL ALLIANCES

There are many forms of co-operation, of which the strategic alliance is just one. For instance, co-operation is commonly observed in the form of companies working closely with their suppliers without the need to create a formal alliance. Indeed, such a close working relationship is so common that it attracts little notice outside the two companies involved. These co-operative arrangements can be long-lived, as the companies have complementary, not competitive, roles. At this level, though, they are using the working relationship to reduce many of the transaction costs that exist between companies and so improve the efficiency of the overall process. Since the supplier and buyer are working together on defined projects, they do not necessarily share the same strategic vision, so there is less danger of friction between them.

Strategic alliances bring together two or more partners, so that in partnership they can achieve their strategic purposes. The partners may not have the same vision in the long term but short-term pooling of resources will help them to progress. This can lead to tension in the later stages of the partnership as one begins to explore an independent path before the other partner is ready to do the same.

The opportunities and the risks of engaging in alliances have expanded as business itself has globalised. At the domestic level, strategic alliances are often observed when companies are exploring a new technology that is replete with novel uncertainty. There may also be a political agenda, obliging the companies to work together in order to force the pace of development for a national benefit, or to preserve the capabilities of an industry made up of independent companies that are judged too small to be sustainable.

Globalisation of markets and industries has broadened the opportunities for strategic alliances. Domestic companies looking at overseas locations for the first time may lack the resources to explore every opportunity that comes their way, so they will divide their resources over a number of alliances. These companies are also taking on uncertainties about the new markets and overseas locations that an alliance can alleviate. Global strategic alliances have therefore come to prominence in recent years.

TYPES OF GLOBAL STRATEGIC ALLIANCE

As in all attempts to categorise business structures there are as many structure types as there are businesses. Every business has its own unique structure, and as a consequence each strategic alliance must have its own special character. Nevertheless, we can broadly categorise global strategic alliances into four main types:

1. Joint venture
2. Equity strategic alliance
3. Non-equity strategic alliance
4. Multi-regional strategic alliance.

None of these co-operative styles is exclusive to global strategic alliances. In other guises they may be domestic and non-strategic. To take just two examples, joint ventures regularly occur between domestic firms sharing production facilities and an equity alliance could be a tactical manoeuvre to protect one partner from a hostile takeover. The same reasons for an alliance exist at the international level but with the added complications of distance and unfamiliar conditions. Here, though, we will discuss the four main types of global alliances that have a strategic purpose.

1. Joint venture – the resource multiplier

'Joint venture' is a vague term applied to many different kinds of inter-company co-operation. In the popular media, it is often used to describe the purpose rather than the structure of the arrangement, conveying a sense of a commercial venture that is being conducted within a spirit of teamwork. For our purposes, though, a joint venture is a separate organisation that has been created by two separate companies in which they hold an equal share. Since the joint venture is a standalone operation it is a legal entity in its own right. The two partners agree with each other what resources they will put into the venture, whether those that they have in common or those that are complementary.

In general, though, joint ventures tend to involve a sharing of common resources. Each partner has the ability to own and run the operation by itself but either lacks the quantity of resources to do so or is not prepared to commit those resources. The purpose of the joint venture is to multiply the resources of each partner since the shared operation delivers greater benefits than could have been achieved in sum by two separate and smaller operations. A push for **economies of scale** is a common motivator for the joint venture: the economic efficiency of one large operation is better than that for two smaller ones, Boersma et al. (2003) giving the DSM-BASF merger as an example.

Joint ventures are commonly seen in production where there are no great secrets in the type of production but there are high economies of scale. There is little risk of one partner stealing the other's competitive advantage in this area, at least not in terms of technology, but if the plant is built to full size and is fully utilised then both partners get to share in the economies of scale. Since the benefits of economies of scale apply to every unit of production both partners gain all the same advantages as if they were filling the plant with their own production.

If a company does have a significant and specific competitive advantage in its production system then the risks of losing that knowledge to a partner outweigh the advantages from the production economies of scale, so the joint venture is not feasible. It is unlikely that Coca-Cola and Pepsi will ever share the same production facility given the closely guarded secrets of their soft drink recipes.

 CASE STUDY – EXPLORING GRAPHENE

Graphene is one of 500 new wonder materials, just one molecule thick and therefore effectively a two dimensional structure. This gives it special characteristics the possibilities of which are only slowly being explored. Graphene is a sheet of carbon, many times stronger than steel weight-for-weight, impermeable to even the smallest of molecules, and it is a superb conductor of electricity.

Although graphene has been known about for many years it was only in 2004 that Andre Geim and Konstantin Novoselov, researching at the University of Manchester, found a way to strip away microscopic layers using 'mechanical cleavage'. To do this they used the simple application of sticky tape, but at least this was an advance on the alternative: rubbing a pencil on a piece of paper.

The commercial potential for graphene is quite extraordinary. It makes possible instantly rechargeable batteries, flexible screens for smartphones that can be folded away, water filters and could replace silicon in microchips. A large number of enterprises have been established in order to bring some of these ideas to fruition.

Once such enterprise is Graphene Nanochem, which has an Advanced Materials division search-ing for industrial applications. Much of the work is still experimental, but in Malaysia the company has two manufacturing operations. In April 2014 a subsidiary of Graphene Nanochem, Platinum Nanochem, entered a 50:50 joint venture with Scomi Oiltools to establish a manufacturing plant in Malaysia producing chemicals used in drilling for oil.

There are similar joint ventures around the world trying to productionise the possibilities offered by graphene and bring products to the market. Despite the apparent confidence, this is still a very uncertain business. It is quite possible that graphene will instead become a niche product, one of the great might-have-beens in industry. It is therefore difficult to predict precisely what production volumes will be needed, hence the desire for joint ventures in manufacturing.

Point of consideration: Investigate one of the joint ventures that has been put together to com-mercialise graphene. If successful, how do you expect the joint venture to progress? What do you think would happen to the joint venture and the partners if that particular use for graphene was not successful?

Sources: Graphene Nanochem, 2014; Morning Star, 2014

This is not to say that the partner companies will not take a sly glance at each other's working practices in order to learn something of value to them. Joint ventures are a fertile opportunity for managers to observe each other and the joint labour force in order to improve their own practices.

A well-designed joint venture has both partners working together in a stable relationship over the long term disturbed by few external influences. It is not suited to dynamic conditions where demand, the product or the production system are likely to fundamentally change in the short term. The inherent stability means that joint ventures are relatively inflexible, holding back a partner that may want to expand and develop beyond the confines of the joint venture.

Horizontal and vertical joint ventures Joint ventures can be structured in two ways: horizontal or vertical. The horizontal joint venture is the most common and most closely identified with what we understand a joint venture to be. It is horizontal in that the partners, and competitors, share in the same process (Duncan, 1982). If this is in product assembly then the two partners will work together in production but will maintain their own upstream and downstream operations of product design and marketing, respectively.

The horizontal joint venture is intended to alleviate an acute and identifiable problem. In the case of a production joint venture there is an identified lack of scale. The horizontal joint venture brings the two partners together as common owners of a function that should have all the scale advantages of a wholly owned function of the same size. In particular, it allows two small companies to build a facility that can access the economies of scale for that type of technology. Outside the joint venture both companies maintain independent activities.

Figure 11.1 shows two such companies, A and B, who have decided to share in an assembly process. Individually they would have operated two assembly processes at less than optimal scale, but as a team they can have one full-size plant and both benefit from the economies of scale. They design their own products, which are variants of a common technology. The partners sell the products separately, the market intelligence then feeding back to the R&D function for more product design.

In a horizontal joint venture, there is some danger of one partner appropriating the technology and techniques of the other, so care needs to be taken in defining the limits of the teamwork. This style of

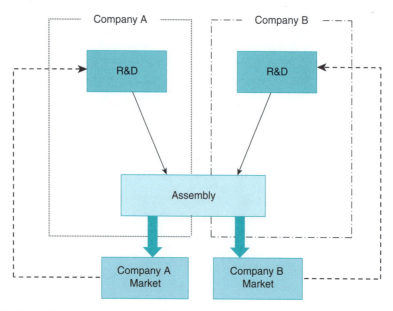

Figure 11.1 *Horizontal joint venture in assembly*

joint venture is also restrictive, and it is difficult for one partner to innovate or develop their part of the shared facility: any improvements must be passed on to the partner and expansion in output by just one partner is impossible. As horizontal joint ventures are a response to a specific, acute problem they last only as long as the problem exists. They have little scope for further development.

Vertical joint ventures are much rarer but they have greater long-term potential (Wynn-Williams, 2009). The partners are not sharing in a single function but the entire product creation system, from R&D to the market. They do this within the system by taking sole responsibility for the distinct functions in which they hold a comparative advantage. This is shown in Figure 11.2:

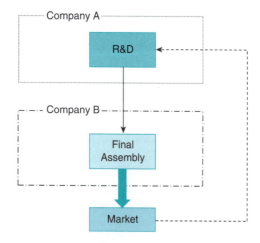

Figure 11.2 *Vertical joint venture*

The vertical joint venture replicates the vertical integration of a single company but divided across the partners. This is not, though, a matter of outsourcing nor is it a buyer–supplier relationship. Instead, the vertical joint venture retains the symbiotic relationship between functions of full vertical integration. It therefore benefits from the same minimisation of transaction costs.

There is no danger of appropriation of **intellectual property rights (IPR)** or opportunism since each partner has sole responsibility for their specialism. Just as a vertically integrated firm may innovate in production, with direct benefits for production efficiency and indirect benefits for the firm as a whole, any innovations or developments each vertical joint venture partner makes will stay within their specialism but benefit both partners. Vertical joint ventures therefore promise long-term stability since they can contain dynamic developments just as well as a vertically integrated firm structure.

The price for the long-term stability in vertical joint ventures is their extreme short-term instability. In a horizontal joint venture the two firms maintain their own vertically integrated structures and share in one of them. This does not affect their own vertical integration, and when the joint venture is dissolved they can return to their original structures. The vertical joint venture involves a radical restructuring for both partners. They must identify where they each have core competitive advantages and, if they are complementary, they will relinquish their competitive disadvantages to their partner and retain only their core competitive advantage.

So, in a simple two stage company with R&D and assembly, the partners must first agree that one has the advantage in R&D and the other in assembly. The R&D specialist must then relinquish all assembly tasks to the assembly specialist and vice versa. This results in the structure shown in Figure 11.2. Once achieved, this structure is stable, but the transformation is likely to be traumatic and highly risky. There will be opposition to the strategy from politicians and labour, who fear rising unemployment and the loss of a skill base.

Where a horizontal joint venture can be useful for exploring new market opportunities, a vertical joint venture is a last resort for a company that concedes it will never recover in the area where it has a competitive disadvantage. The best it can do is hope to maintain its remaining competitive advantage through a partnership. The vertical joint venture therefore needs special conditions:

- Two partners with complementary competitive advantages.
- Each partner concedes that its competitive disadvantage is fatal and cannot be remedied within the lifetime of the company.
- There is political and labour support for the radical restructuring, probably because they understand all other options have been exhausted.

For companies to give up vast amounts of their structures permanently in favour of a rival suggests that they would have to be in desperate straits. This would be because the company is in long-term and irreversible decline, or close to bankruptcy. Consequently, at least one partner could be in an unstable condition that requires swift action by the other partner.

Since the conditions for a vertical joint venture involve so much uncertainty they generally do not occur in that form. Some firms are able to close the function in which they are weak and outsource. Many specialist sports car manufacturers have been obliged to stop manufacturing their own engines due to the high cost of meeting the latest emissions regulations, and they simply buy engines from larger car companies. Other firms may find they have such an impressive competitive advantage in one area that they focus all their resources on it and sell off their other functions. IBM, once the most famous computer manufacturer in the world, is now a specialist in providing business solutions.

Where the semblance of a vertical joint venture structure is observable it is usually because one partner has actually collapsed into bankruptcy. The other partner then acquires the functions in which it is lacking, gaining local political and labour support for at least saving a part of the failed business. The vertical joint venture structure is replicated and secured through ownership: not strictly speaking a true joint venture but a close approximation. The two companies maintain their separate characters, and their core competitive advantages, but under the umbrella of common ownership rather than a joint venture agreement.

This style of relationship is being seen a lot recently with companies based in the developing economies, such as China, which have built up considerable production capability, often in partnership with a partner from the developed economies. However, having grown dependent on their partners for product design they have not quite managed to develop their own abilities to a sufficient degree. In acquiring the remains of collapsed corporations in the developed economies they can access the technical knowledge they lack. As noted by Balcet et al. (2012), the purchase of the Swedish car manufacturer Volvo by Geely of China in 2010 is an example of this.

2. Equity strategic alliance – a hold on the future

When the production process or the nature of the product is entirely new then companies face the highest level of uncertainty. The management can be in a quandary over it because they know that they need to be scanning the business horizon for potential new developments, but they do not yet have a clear enough view to make a commitment. What the management would like to do is to have a minimal commitment in the new approach but still high enough that the company has some claim on it. Owning a small equity in the project is often enough to fund the development, along with other partners, and secure sufficient ownership that the company can directly benefit should the project be successful but without excessive exposure to its possible failure.

Equity strategic alliances are often implemented for so-called **blue skies** projects, new research that has been dreamt up by scientists and has clear market potential but is still well short of being released to the public. It is the uncertainty over whether the technology will ever actually make it to the market that inhibits any one company from making a full commitment.

Blue skies research does not, itself, generally yield lucrative business opportunities; it is too abstract for that. It is usually the task of universities to conduct this kind of research, funded by government money and sometimes with corporate partners. The money-making opportunities come at the application stage, when the technology is transformed into a new kind of product by commercial corporations. The original research partners are not, therefore, too worried that their reduced ownership share of the blue skies research will earn a reduced financial return. Far more important is that they hold a claim over the fundamental technology, which they can then use as the basis for a product of their own design. This secures them a first-mover advantage in the market and means they can start one step ahead of their rivals, including those who were partners in the research.

An example of this kind of alliance was the compact disc (CD) developed by Sony of Japan and Philips of the Netherlands (Immink, 1998). The original blue skies research was conducted by Philips with a small team reminiscent of the kind of fundamental research usually done at universities. At a later stage, when the product could be readied for the market but its success was uncertain, Sony stepped in as a risk-sharing partner. Both companies were then able to use the basic technology of the CD in machines of their own design and manufacture, as well as licensing it to other firms.

3. Non-equity strategic alliance – sharing the workload

When the uncertainty is very low the company may have the confidence to look for a non-equity alliance secured by a contract. This will only be done when the company is reasonably sure about the transaction costs and feels that all aspects of the relationship can be accounted for in the contract without significant risk of opportunism by the partner. The relationship with the partner is like that with a supplier except that it is less a buyer–supplier relationship and more a partnership of equals.

A non-equity strategic alliance in production duplicates the company's production capability in a partner and has the effect of increasing production capacity. This is particularly useful for products that are variants of the original, made in low output volumes that would otherwise interfere with the main production system. A derivation of non-equity alliances is the contractual joint venture (CJV), often observed between Hong Kong and mainland Chinese firms in low-technology production (Wang and Nicholas, 2007).

Non-equity strategic alliances last for the lifetime of the contract. If the contract is renewed then it will most likely be for a new product. Since it is up to the partner to win a new contract, either from the existing client company or a new one, much of the uncertainty in the non-equity strategic alliance is carried by the partner. It has become a common feature of Italian car design houses to offer contract production so that they can provide a full turn-key operation on their styling proposals. In particular, they can demonstrate a high-style version of an existing car, such as making a convertible soft-top out of a standard closed car, and include the offer of manufacturing it. The original car manufacturer is then free from having to consider possible market demand or commit production capacity. However, the volatility in contract production, as one model reaches the end of its life-cycle long before the next contract is ready, means that some of these design houses have been under considerable financial strain as they struggle with the periods of idle production.

4. Multi-regional strategic alliance – marriage of convenience

A new breed of strategic alliance has been made possible by the rush to globalise by corporations even while political, legal and cultural frameworks try to hold them back. These are the strategic alliances that attempt to provide wider coverage by linking together corporations that are tied to their home regions. It is also used by corporations with a limited product range who are seeking to broaden it by re-branding products from another corporation.

The unusual feature of this kind of alliance is that the firms do not set up a separate operation in which they share equal interest; they hold no equity in each other and there is only a relatively simple agreement binding them together. Indeed, they are hardly working together at all since they are carving up the globe according to their own spheres of interest. Instead of sharing to compete as a team it is more a case of divide and conquer. The partner firms maintain their dominant positions in their home regions but can sell access to their partner's operations as if they were an extension of their own.

Companies will often engage in this kind of alliance because there is local opposition to entry by foreign organisations. A way round this is for a foreign company to market its products under the name of a local partner. For example, car companies have done this as a way of mitigating cultural suspicions of foreign imports, while the local partner agrees because it means an additional product for the model range. In South Korea during the 1990s, the mid-size Mercedes-Benz E-Class was assembled locally by SsangYong and sold under its brand as the Chairman luxury car (Haley, 2000). In Germany, the high-end camera manufacturer, Leica, sells Panasonic cameras under its own brand in order to offer more affordable models alongside its premium products.

The multi-regional alliance creates a virtual extension to each company. From the customer's point of view there may be little or no awareness of where the main company's operations end and the partner company's begin. This can create problems when the partner company cannot match the values and standards of the main company. For example, the Panasonic cameras marketed under the Leica brand are technically almost identical to the mass market Japanese versions but carry a significant price premium. Published reviews of the Leica versions point out that the higher price is not reflected in any technical advantage. Fortunately, these kinds of alliances find their success in the emotional power of the brand in overcoming rational objections.

CASE STUDY – INTERNATIONAL AIRLINE ALLIANCES

International airlines suffer from two basic problems. The first is that they provide a service that offers only marginal differentiation. They have little control over the design of the aircraft they use or their speed. The world's aircraft are generally held to the same safety standards and the airport experience is one for which airlines can only apologise. Even the inflight meals the airlines serve is often sourced from a single supplier. As a result, they strive to differentiate themselves in the marginal areas where they do have control, such as the décor of the aircraft cabin and the service skills of the cabin crew.

The other problem airlines have is that no matter how popular they may be in their markets, entrenched national market protectionism often precludes them from competing in other markets. This often means that they are restricted to offering flights only from hub airports in their own country to single destinations in other countries. Not only is this inefficient but it also makes travel planning difficult for passengers who have journeys that take them beyond the main city-to-city routes.

In response to these market restrictions, international airlines have formed themselves into multi-regional strategic alliances. Although they are ostensibly rivals the fact that they are prevented from competing in the same markets means there is little risk of one partner appropriating the competitive advantage of another. There is therefore little reason to tie up the partnership with equity cross holdings, complex contracts or joint ventures. They only need to agree to share their flight codes, enabling passengers to plan their complex journeys using both airlines. Indeed, the passenger may not even be aware that they will be carried by two different companies.

These multi-regional strategic alliances have grown from bilateral agreements to constellations of multilateral agreements, with all partners integrated into the codesharing, passenger check-in and marketing strategies. Amongst the bigger constellations have been Star Alliance (twenty-seven members, including United and Singapore Airlines) and One World (fifteen members, including British Airways and American Airlines). Although all members benefit from their increased global reach not all members benefit equally and much depends on airlines strengthening their bilateral ties. There is also a degree of passenger resentment to their finding that the airline they selected for the journey is not necessarily the one that will carry them the full distance.

Point of consideration: Healthcare around the world should have little to differentiate it, country to country. How do you think travellers would benefit from healthcare organisations forming multi-regional strategic alliances? What problems do you foresee?

Source: Lazzarini (2007)

THE GLOBAL STRATEGIC ALLIANCE

Partner selection

An alliance involves a company stepping outside its existing boundary, or inviting an erstwhile rival within it. This creates considerable risk, and it is therefore beholden on the managers to ensure the decision process is robust and systematic. A five-step process can aid decision-making:

1. Gap analysis
2. Partner assessment

3. Contract formulation
4. Operations
5. Termination.

We will now consider each one in more detail.

1. *Gap analysis* An alliance is intended to overcome a weakness or disadvantage within the company that it does not have the resources, or sufficient justification, to correct internally. The gap between the strategic target and the resources available to achieve it needs to be analysed before concluding that an alliance is necessary. This gap analysis involves the standard assessments of the company and its environment.

SWOT and PESTLE are simple analytical techniques but due to the lack of definition they are vulnerable to subjective inputs. For example, van Wijngaarden et al. (2012) found very little empirical support for the use of SWOT and even less clarity on how the analysis should be conducted. Despite the criticism, with care the two techniques often serve as quick and cheap techniques that can form the basis of more detailed, subsequent analysis. The next step might be value chain analysis to determine the core competitive advantage of the firm, what we might call its comparative advantage, to identify where not to share knowledge with a partner. As part of the same analysis the comparative disadvantage will be identified and it is the need to strengthen this that will form the focus of the alliance.

Transaction cost analysis (TCA) takes a very detailed look at the risks and costs of working with a partner. Jones and Hill (1988) used the approach to good effect when looking at how it influences corporate structures. TCA will take into account the dangers of opportunism, such as IPR theft, and hold-ups. This is particularly important when the alliance means the kind of close working relationship seen in horizontal joint ventures. The other alliance types, equity, non-equity and multi-regional, have less exposure to partner opportunism.

2. *Partner assessment* A similar gap analysis is used to assess potential partners. The information will necessarily be limited to that accessible in the public domain but the steps will be the same, progressing from a perfunctory SWOT or PESTLE and leading to a detailed transaction cost analysis. The conclusion of the process should identify the preferred partner.

Once the company has conducted its analysis of itself and the preferred partner it can make its first approach. This should trigger a similar set of internal and external analyses in the preferred partner, releasing additional information. The assessments by the two firms will be built on iterations of the analysis steps until both are satisfied that they have sufficient information.

An attractive partner is one that is able to fulfil a number of conditions to ensure that both companies are on a converging strategic path, at least with regards to the project in mind. Kale and Singh (2009) state that the qualities being sought are compatibility, complementarity and commitment, though both partners should also be ready to make sacrifices.

- **Compatibility** – the potential partner should share a similar corporate strategic vision so that they share the same intentions for the alliance. There should be few cultural differences and the corporate functions should be comparable. Technologies should be similar, particularly where they will be pooled in the alliance. Views on governance, ethics and corporate social responsibility should be in convergence.
- **Complementarity** – although the alliance is intended to remedy a lack of resources or commitment it is preferable if one partner is not significantly weaker than the other. They may be offering complementary capabilities, but one partner should not have power over the other. When this occurs it is not a true alliance. Some capabilities may be difficult to scrutinise, such as managerial talent.

- **Commitment** – it is the nature of alliances that the partners will be dependent on one another. The degree of commitment, though, is related to the structure of the alliance and the power to enforce it. In a non-equity alliance the commitment is set out in the contract, while an equity alliance implies commitment through ownership, although it is no more enforceable than any other shareholding. Vertical joint ventures are self-enforcing because of the co-dependency. Horizontal joint ventures and multi-regional joint ventures are less enforceable and can be the victim of poor commitment by the partners.

3. *Contract formulation* With the detailed information in place the two partners are in a position to set out the form of their new business relationship. The type of alliance has its own contractual requirements, each one seeking to create a degree of definition for the roles of the partners (Kale and Singh, 2009):

- **Joint venture** – horizontal joint ventures need to be carefully defined in terms of what is included in the shared organisation and what is not. Much of the complexity is alleviated by having the joint venture as a separate entity from the two partners. Nevertheless, the partners need to be on guard against opportunism. Vertical joint ventures achieve a similar result by separating the partners into their own specialist competencies.
- **Equity alliance** – like the joint venture the contract details are simplified by the ownership rights and the separation of the alliance from the partner organisations. Statutory law governing ownership underpins the contract and so allows the contract to focus only on the specific details of the project. The purpose of the equity alliance is to enable each partner to take any benefits as they arise, so opportunism is, in a sense, an intended outcome; if the partners do not take benefits from the alliance then it has no purpose. At the same time the partners need to be cautious about the technology they invest, as it will be accessible to the other partners.
- **Non-equity alliance** – separation is maintained between the partners, so there is no need to establish a new, third-party facility. The relationship is governed by a supplier–buyer style contract, if more detailed. There is some danger of opportunistic behaviour by the supplier partner but the main gains they will make will be their own learning, which will be passed on to the next client.
- **Multi-regional alliance** – the two partners do not share operations but rather customers. The contract is mainly concerned with ensuring consistency of customer service. There is little likelihood of opportunism by a partner and indeed if one does copy the other it can enhance the continuity of the customer experience. The business relationship is often a loose one open to the addition of new partners.

4. *Operations* Despite all the preparations in the preceding stages there are substantial challenges in the operational aspects of the joint venture. There can be significant clashes in managerial culture and communication that can delay a project even after allowing for the inevitable warm-up period. Indeed, some joint ventures have come to grief because the two partners have never really learned to work with each other. There may also be instances of opportunism, or suspicions of it, that fatally undermine the relationship. The two sides may defend their distinct identities so fiercely that they fail to share competencies as intended.

At the assessment stage the management need to consider how such friction between partners will be tackled. On a routine basis this can absorb significant managerial resources during the period when the working relationship is settling down. Over time much of the friction between the partners should be eased and the alliance operates according to plan.

5. *Termination* Most alliances are strategically static: they have a single purpose and the alliance lasts only as long as that purpose exists. Termination is therefore an event that can be planned (Reuer, 2000). In the case of an equity alliance it is a simple matter of selling out, whereas the non-equity alliance will have an end date included in the contract. The multi-regional alliance is often loosely structured and partners can enter or depart the partnership at their convenience.

The horizontal joint venture is the alliance type that can be the most difficult to close down. With time the two partners find their operations become enmeshed in one entity as they learn to work as a unified team. Horizontal joint ventures are often traumatic to conclude. The rule is not applicable to the vertical joint venture which is so structured to promote change, not contain or avoid it. Since the structure replicates that of a vertically integrated corporation the end of the vertical joint venture is analogous to corporate collapse. The partners will only survive if they have maintained a separate and external operation in parallel to the vertical joint venture.

 MANAGEMENT SPOTLIGHT: END OF THE AFFAIR

The death of an alliance is almost inevitable and requires managing as much as the living alliance. The original need for it will have been because two established businesses found they had a need to team up with a rival to overcome common or complementary weaknesses. In a competitive environment it is not a natural state of affairs and the conditions for the co-operative agreement will usually be unstable (Sadowski and Duysters, 2008). There are three possible reasons for the termination of an alliance:

1. **Failure**
   o The alliance proved more costly than going it alone, e.g. conflicting strategies in a horizontal joint venture.
   o The objectives were not achieved or were unachievable, e.g. unsuccessful blue skies research in an equity strategic alliance.
   o Management obstacles due to insurmountable cultural and practical differences, e.g. management friction between partners in horizontal joint venture.
   o One partner changed its strategic objectives or was unable to continue investing in the alliance, e.g. vertical joint ventures when one partner collapses.
2. **Success**
   o The purpose of the alliance was static and the objectives were met, e.g. equity strategic alliance completes blue skies research.
   o One partner acquires the other, e.g. multi-regional strategic alliance where the rules are changed to allow expansion by acquisition.
   o The contract period comes to an end, e.g. non-equity strategic alliance in production of a specific product.
3. **Irrelevance**
   o The objective is no longer necessary, e.g. equity strategic alliance in research.
   o In a dynamic market the partners no longer need to share activities, e.g. non-equity strategic alliance in production of a specific product.

It is because most alliances, domestic or international, have a shelf-life that managers need to have a contingency plan ready for the day when the partnership reaches the end of the road. Given that there are a number of possible outcomes, there is a similar range of termination strategies for managers to consider. Reuer (2000) puts forward four managed routes out of an international joint venture:

1. One partner buys the entire operation
2. One partner is replaced by a new investor
3. Both partners sell the entire operation to a new investor
4. Both partners break-up the joint venture.

Reuer's research found that termination of the relationship was an integral part of the alliance's life cycle and that if properly planned it could enhance value to the shareholders of the partner firms. Furthermore, the longevity of the partnership was no indicator of its success; only the achievement of strategic aims could do that. Indeed, a poorly planned termination could undo all the good achievements of the alliance. It is therefore vital to take a holistic view of the alliance across all stages of its life cycle.

Point of consideration: Throughout its long history Shell Oil has traded as a single company, but in fact from 1907 to 2004 it was made up of two companies, one British one Dutch, with individual ownership structures. This apparent alliance ended with a full merger. Does this merger signal a failure of the alliance and should it have been planned for years earlier?

Sources: Reuer, 2000; Sadowski and Duysters, 2008

MANAGING THE ALLIANCE

Alliances of all types can consume significant amounts of management resources. Not only does the operation itself require the usual management input but the relationship between the partners needs additional management effort in a way that an in-house, wholly owned operation does not. It would be trite to compare an alliance to a marriage, but like all relationships they require work in order to work.

There are three main areas where the two partners need to expend effort in order to have the alliance achieve its potential:

1. Decision-making
2. Building trust
3. Learning from partners.

Taking each one in turn we will consider their implications in detail.

1. Decision-making

This is the area where alliances can become bogged down in bureaucracy, delay and mounting costs. Even companies that are relatively compatible will be exposed to new risks purely because of the alliance, thereby requiring new control mechanisms (Gulati and Singh, 1998). Companies have a single chain of command, but in an alliance this is more than doubled as decisions made within the alliance then have to be passed through the hierarchy of decision-making at both partners. As much as possible, decision-making needs to be devolved to the managers within the alliance itself. The importance of doing this depends on the type of alliance.

The worst offenders are the equity alliance and horizontal joint venture since they mix the chains of command. Differences of opinion can be highly distractive from the intended purpose of the alliance. Fortunately, in the equity alliance the power of each partner to influence decision-making is predetermined by the size of their shareholding. In a horizontal joint venture disagreements can be avoided if the operation is set up correctly in the first place, but disagreements between equal partners can become entrenched and intractable.

The non-equity alliance and vertical joint venture have a single chain of command that significantly reduces the chances of interruptions to the normal decision-making process. The multi-regional alliance has very little in the way of a chain of command at all and each partner continues to make decisions on its own account. This does, though, exacerbate the problems of this kind of alliance in presenting a single, coherent business approach to the customer.

2. Building trust

Co-operation is at the heart of the alliance paradox: companies working together in harmony so that they can better compete. It would be charming to think that companies could one day do business with each other in a spirit of common purpose and teamwork, all for mutual benefit of all stakeholders. If only the spirit of competition were not striving to create disharmony and dissonance through opportunism, exploitation and innovation.

Nevertheless, trust does develop in the business world, Das and Teng (1998) finding that control mechanisms were a necessary basis for its emergence. There are a number of control levers in the hands of the management:

- **Legislation** – companies are required to honour contracts and ensure they are financially viable. Relevant to non-equity alliances.
- **Equity** – companies may own shares in each other in order to ensure transparency and accountability. This approach underpins equity alliances.
- **Co-dependency** – over time companies learn from experience to depend on each other. Vertical joint ventures are entirely structured around this principle. It is much more challenging for horizontal joint ventures and can take an extended period to nurture. In multi-regional alliances the co-dependency is the clear purpose of the relationship, but it is a much looser arrangement, based on customer service standards and **reputational capital**, the risk to one's own good name if the company misbehaves.

3. Learning from partners

The reason why firms enter into alliances so tentatively is the fear that a partner will exploit the close relationship to steal advantages. This is balanced, amusingly, by the opportunity to steal advantages oneself. A properly designed alliance introduces a sense of propriety by permitting a controlled relationship where ideas can be exchanged. It does this by bringing together equal partners who can learn as well as teach. As Inkpen and Currall (2004) point out, the route to this happy partnership is made up of a steady progression in trust and control.

The learning purpose of the alliance needs defining at the outset if it is to avoid the potential for opportunism. In an equity alliance the partners will have their own strategic intentions beyond the project and have the right as co-owners to benefit from any knowledge advances. In a horizontal joint venture the enmeshed relationship heightens the possibility of knowledge appropriation by one partner. It is critical to ensure balance so that each partner has the same learning opportunities and a fair exchange is affected. The learning in vertical joint ventures, non-strategic and multi-regional alliances will be internal, as the partners' own development is stimulated by the success of the alliance.

The promise of learning is what drives many of the alliances between companies in developed and developing economies. In China, for example, there is a political tendency to require 50:50 joint ventures in the belief that this will accelerate and enforce knowledge transfer to local industry benefit. In practice, the foreign firm only protects its core competitive advantages all the more, somewhat negating the government's desired outcome.

RAISING EMPLOYABILITY: LEARNING TO MANAGE ALLIANCES

As if managing a company is not challenging enough, involvement in an alliance means that a manager must learn to cope with the partner company as well. This requires a manager with a broad knowledge base and a talent for business relationships. As argued by Schreiner et al. (2009), the alliance manager must be skilled in co-ordination, communication and bonding.

It would appear, though, that most managers in alliances lack these skills given the high failure rate of the partnerships. Due to the unique nature of these partnerships few managers have the background to prepare them for working together with managers from other organisations. Draulans and Volberda (2003) discovered that companies found their ability to cope in alliances grew with experience, a minimum of six alliances being the critical number. The researchers concluded that it was important for companies to engage in alliances almost routinely in order to build up experience, bolstering this with training for managers if necessary. Interestingly, the skills related to alliance management are most relevant to middle, not senior, management since it is they who have to deal with the crucial operational aspects of the partnerships.

It is this experience effect that hands an advantage to larger, more sophisticated organisations. They are more like to have opportunities within their various operations for alliances, and so their middle rank managers accrue the relevant experience. Indeed, the rapid pace of technological development suggests that firms will increasingly engage in serial alliances (Kale and Singh, 2009). This might indicate a disadvantage that companies in developing economies have in forming alliances with companies from developed economies: simply that they are smaller and less sophisticated. However, relative to companies from other developing economies there are still numerous opportunities to find partners and form sustainable alliances.

To overcome the lack of internal management skills a number of external organisations can provide training or advice. Some of these, such as AllianceStrategy.com (2015), do this from an academic basis. Other providers help to smooth the mechanisms of alliances, helping the partners to overcome the problems of merging their business systems, an area that has proven to be the weakness of so many failed alliances. For example, Tata Consultancy Services (TCS) of India provided the IT platform for an airline alliance, enabling them to access a shared data centre (TCS, 2014).

Since the ability to handle an alliance partner is part of the skillset of a mid-ranking manager it would seem that it holds few benefits for advancement further up the organisation. Nevertheless, it will improve employability for those that are looking to transfer across to other organisations, particularly those that are only just embarking on their first alliances. Just as the alliance is a learning opportunity for the learning organisation, so it is for the aspiring manager.

WEB SUPPORT

1. Do Women Take as Many Risks as Men? An online article from the Harvard Business Review by Doug Sundheim and published 27 February 2013. Slightly provocative discussion and one we hope will eventually become irrelevant. For the sake of argument you could, of course, replace women with any other social group.

   www.hbr.org/2013/02/do-women-take-as-many-risks-as/

2. Develop Your Reputation Capital. An article by Roger M. Ingbretsen, available on the SelfGrowth. com website. We have looked at how important reputational capital is for the company but what about you? This article briefly discusses how you can maintain your own personal brand qualities.

   www.selfgrowth.com/articles/develop_your_reputation_capital.html

3. Best Practice Guideline D2: Joint venture arrangements. A set of joint venture guidelines from the Construction Industry Development Board in South Africa, published in March 2004. In a concise document provides the industry view of joint ventures, at least for the construction industry in South Africa. Think about how the guidelines could transfer to other industries.

   www.cidb.org.za/toolkit06/toolkitpages/module5/20supplementaryinformation/5s14%20 pgd2-jv%20edition%201.0.pdf

THE STORY SO FAR: UNITED THEY STAND

There are many routes to growth for a company, all of them risky. The attractions of new technologies, economies of scale, overseas sales and so on may be clear enough, but they can require substantial commitment of internal resources. A wrong step can have pernicious consequences, particularly for smaller companies. The formation of an alliance reduces risk for each partner but also the financial returns, which must be shared. A well-designed alliance goes further by reducing uncertainty, and this is where the partnership can enjoy a net gain.

There are as many ways of structuring an alliance as there are companies willing to engage in them, but for international players there are essentially four types: joint venture, equity, non-equity and multi-regional. Each has its own costs and benefits but all require special skills from the mid-ranking managers that are directly involved. United, the partners can make an intermediate step towards their growth plans, but such are the challenges that most alliances collapse in failure and division.

Project Topics

1. If companies could work together in a spirit of co-operation, co-ordination and collaboration then they could avoid the expense of using contracts. Select a corporation and discuss how it might benefit from such harmony with a supplier. What are the weaknesses of such a cosy relationship?
2. Fusion energy has the promise of delivery unlimited clean energy at a low price. However, it is still very much at the stage of blue skies, university-based research. How would you advise an energy supplier to collaborate in the research to its own future benefit?

3. The European Space Agency brings together European organisations to put satellites and scientific instruments into space. It can therefore be considered a kind of alliance. Under what circumstances would you envisage the agency coming to an end, and how would you, as an advisor to the agency, plan for such an eventuality?

 ## CASE STUDY – EAST AND WEST AT NUMMI

By the 1970s it was looking like the Japanese automotive industry was an unstoppable force, particularly in North America. The Big 3 in the United States were GM, Chrysler and Ford, vast corporations that had grown fat on the American love affair with huge cars and cheap fuel. The oil crises during the decade had caught them out badly, desperately trying to shift their product ranges to more fuel-efficient models while smaller, imported models began to gobble up market share.

Most shocking for the Big 3 was that the new Japanese cars were not just efficient with their fuel; the production method was also highly efficient. It seemed that the Japanese had found a new advantage in addition to the customary economies of scale. The Americans, with their large domestic market, had been able to construct gigantic factories that promised minimal production costs. The Japanese, though, had found another advantage: lean production.

At the forefront was Toyota, the largest Japanese producer and one that had developed the Toyota Production System (TPS). The company had made serious in-roads into the US market with its exports, and the Japanese factories were running at full speed, maximising output and efficiency without compromising quality. It seemed as if TPS was the perfect production machine and that the Big Three only had their dominant, but waning, domestic presence as a final defence. The Big 3 could deliver cars to customers much faster than Toyota because their plants were closer to the market.

Toyota management knew that they had to establish a manufacturing facility in North America but they were, by nature, cautious. American workforces had a reputation for industrial militancy and low quality standards. Toyota managers were worried that manufacturing in North America would result in lower productivity and poor product quality, effectively trashing the company's hard won reputation for excellence. The answer was to dip a toe into the United States by way of a joint venture.

GM had a plant in Freemont, California, that it had closed due to the appalling inefficiency and product quality. Yet there is nothing more inefficient than an idle plant, so the company was looking for a way to reopen it. Toyota saw their chance, and in 1983 the two companies formed a joint venture that took over the plant under the name New United Motor Manufacturing Inc. (NUMMI). For GM, NUMMI was an opportunity to unlock the secrets of lean production and TPS; for Toyota, it was a time to find out if the American worker could be tamed.

Toyota took the precaution of ensuring that it had operational control of the NUMMI plant, something that GM was keen to agree to given its own experience and desire to learn from the new industrial masters. Somewhat surprisingly, Toyota was able to turn the plant into one of the most productive even within its own empire, never mind the United States. Workers per vehicle amounted to 20.8 per vehicle, close to the 18.0 at Toyota's Takaoka plant and almost half what it had been for Freemont under GM. Both companies sat up and took notice.

For Toyota, it was the reassurance it needed to roll out an investment programme across North America. It understood then that with proper recruitment and training any workforce could learn the TPS way. For GM, the learning was more gradual: the advantages of lean production had been made obvious but the company found it much harder to embed the TPS philosophy in the corporate culture. Nevertheless, over time GM was able to rotate increasing numbers of its executives through the NUMMI facility to learn about TPS first hand. The experience fed directly into the creation of a new GM Opel plant in Eisenach, Germany, in 1992.

NUMMI was a classic joint venture: it was the solution to the specific problems of the two partners, allowing them to trade knowledge without putting at risk their core competencies. Sharing the plant meant that both received the full benefits of the economies of scale even while the risks for each were reduced. As long as the business conditions remained the same, the joint venture could have continued indefinitely.

Then in 2009 GM collapsed into bankruptcy and emerged as a new entity thanks to government funding. As part of its restructuring, GM relinquished its share in the NUMMI joint venture to Toyota. However, without the rationale for the joint venture Toyota had no reason to keep the plant operating and it too pulled out in early 2010. The facility has more recently switched to electric car production for Tesla but at drastically reduced rates of output.

Point of consideration: NUMMI was very effective in meeting the strategic needs of GM and Toyota, but the benefits seem to have been static. Once conditions changed, with the bankruptcy of GM, the NUMMI operation could not offer new benefits for the restructured GM or to Toyota. Do you agree with this view, and how do you think Toyota could start a new joint venture at the plant with Tesla?

Source: Inkpen, 2008

? MULTIPLE CHOICE QUESTIONS

1. Which is better in business, to be risk averse or a risk taker?
   a. Risk averse – the purpose of management is to minimise risk.
   b. Risk taker – the bigger the opportunity the bigger the risk.
   c. Neither – if the rate of return matches the risk then the opportunity should be acted upon.

2. Companies are better off in alliances because the risks are reduced?
   a. True – any risks are shared with the partner.
   b. False – it is the uncertainty, which has no matching rate of return, which is reduced.
   c. False – an alliance is always a sign of corporate weakness.

3. Smart watches are a new technology becoming popular in the market. In what way can an alliance reduce the uncertainty?
   a. Form an alliance in research and development due to the novelty of the technology.
   b. Outsource the technology development to a supplier in a fixed-price contract.
   c. Form an alliance in marketing, splitting the revenues with the partner.

4. Why is reputational capital important?
   a. It is part of the brand equity.
   b. It delivers costless competitive advantages.
   c. It is difficult to gain and easy to lose.

5. How can companies be more co-operative?
    a. Create strong interdependencies.
    b. Engage in trust building activities.
    c. They cannot – co-operation has no place in competitive markets.

6. What is the essential feature of a joint venture?
    a. The sharing of intellectual property rights.
    b. The 50:50 ownership split.
    c. The high risk of opportunism by one partner.

7. What is the main purpose of an equity strategic alliance?
    a. To ensure that any future rewards are shared.
    b. To diversify the financial portfolio.
    c. To trade the shares on the global stock markets.

8. How is a non-equity strategic alliance different to a supplier–buyer relationship?
    a. More money is involved in a non-equity strategic alliance.
    b. A non-equity strategic alliance is a step towards a full corporate merger.
    c. A non-equity strategic alliance involves more team work between the partners.

9. What sort of company is suited to a multi-regional strategic alliance?
    a. Medicinal drugs.
    b. Fast food brand franchises.
    c. Time-share apartments.

10. All alliances come to an end at some point.
    a. False – the best planned alliances have no end point.
    b. True – alliances are inherently limited.
    c. False – alliances are separate entities and last as long as any independent corporation.

Answers

1c, 2b, 3a, 4b, 5a, 6b, 7a, 8c, 9c, 10b

REFERENCES

AllianceStrategy.com (2015) Homepage from www.alliancestrategy.com/AboutUs/Overview.html accessed 7 March 2015

Amit R and Wernerfelt B (1990) 'Why do firms reduce business risk?' *Academy of Management Journal* 33(3), pp. 520–533

Anderson S W, Christ M H and Sedatole K L (2006) *Managing strategic alliance risk: Survey evidence of control practices in collaborative inter-organizational settings.* Altamonte Springs, Florida: The Institute of Internal Auditors Research Foundation

Balcet G, Wang H and Richet X (2012) 'Geely: a trajectory of catching up and asset-seeking multinational growth' *International Journal of Automotive Technology and Management* 12(4), pp. 360–375

Boersma M F, Buckley P J and Ghauri P N (2003) 'Trust in international joint venture relationships' *Journal of Business Research* 56(12), pp. 1031–1042

Das T K and Teng B S (1998) 'Between trust and control: developing confidence in partner cooperation in alliances' *Academy of Management Review* 23(3), pp. 491–512

Draulans J and Volberda H W (2003) 'Building alliance capability: management techniques for superior alliance performance' *Long Range Planning* 36(2), pp. 151–166

Duncan J L (1982) 'Impacts of new entry and horizontal joint ventures on industrial rates of return' *The Review of Economics and Statistics* pp. 339–342

Graphene Nanochem (2014) Corporate overview from www.graphenenanochem.com/about-us/corporate-overview accessed 21 September 2014

Gulati R and Singh H (1998) 'The architecture of cooperation: managing coordination costs and appropriation concerns in strategic alliances' *Administrative Science Quarterly* pp. 781–814

Haley U C (2000) 'Corporate governance and restructuring in East Asia: an overview' *Seoul Journal of Economics* 13(3), pp. 225–251

Hatch W and Yamamura K (1996) *Asia in Japan's embrace: Building a regional production alliance (No. 3)*. Cambridge: Cambridge University Press

Humphries A S and Wilding R (2004) 'Long term collaborative relationships: the impact of trust and C3 behaviour' *Journal of Marketing Management* 20(9–10), (November 2004), pp. 1107–1122

Immink K A (1998) 'The compact disc story' *Journal of the Audio Engineering Society* 46(5), pp. 458–465

Inkpen A C (2008) 'Knowledge transfer and international joint ventures: the case of NUMMI and General Motors' *Strategic Management Journal* 29(4), pp. 447–453

Inkpen A C and Currall S C (2004) 'The coevolution of trust, control, and learning in joint ventures' *Organization Science* 15(5), pp. 586–599

Jones G R and Hill C W (1988) 'Transaction cost analysis of strategy-structure choice' *Strategic Management Journal* 9(2), pp. 159–172

Kale P and Singh H (2009) 'Managing strategic alliances: what do we know now, and where do we go from here' *Academy of Management Perspectives* 23(3), pp. 45–62

Lazzarini S G (2007) 'The impact of membership in competing alliance constellations: evidence on the operational performance of global airlines' *Strategic Management Journal* 28(4) (Apr., 2007), pp. 345–367

Los Angeles Times (1999) 'Mars probe lost due to simple math error' *Los Angeles Times*, 1 October 1999 from www.articles.latimes.com/1999/oct/01/news/mn-17288 accessed 18 September 2014

Morning Star (2014) Graphene NanoChem's Malaysia venture signs PlatDrill sales agreement 11September 2014 from www.morningstar.co.uk/uk/news/AN_1410428042048893800/graphene-nanochems-malaysia-venture-signs-platdrill-sales-agreement-.aspx accessed 21 September 2014

Reuer J J (2000) 'Parent firm performance across international joint venture life-cycle stages' *Journal of International Business Studies* pp. 1–20

Sadowski B and Duysters G (2008) 'Strategic technology alliance termination: an empirical investigation' *Journal of Engineering and Technology Management* 25(4), pp. 305–320

Sampson R C (2007) R&D alliances and firm performance: the impact of technological diversity and alliance organization on innovation *Academy of Management Journal* 50(2), pp. 364–386

Schreiner M, Kale P and Corsten D (2009) What really is alliance management capability and how does it impact alliance outcomes and success? *Strategic Management Journal* 30(13), pp. 1395–1419

TCS (2014) A leading airline alliance consolidates data center operations to realize efficiencies and achieve 99.98% system availability from www.tcs.com/SiteCollectionDocuments/Case%20Studies/Airline-Alliance-data-center-operations-0114-2.pdf accessed 7 March 2015

Teng B S and Das T K (2008) 'Governance structure choice in strategic alliances: the roles of alliance objectives, alliance management experience, and international partners' *Management Decision* 46(5), pp. 725–742

van Wijngaarden J D, Scholten G R and van Wijk K P (2012) 'Strategic analysis for health care organizations: the suitability of the SWOT-analysis' *The International Journal of Health Planning and Management* 27(1), pp. 34–49

Wang Y and Nicholas S (2007) 'The formation and evolution of non-equity strategic alliances' China in *Asia Pacific Journal of Management* 24(2), pp. 131–150

Wynn-Williams M (2009) *Surfing the global tide: Automotive giants and how to survive them.* London: Palgrave Macmillan

12 Organisational Issues

Chapter Objectives

For a manager to manage effectively the enterprise must be organised around a structure. This structure must allow the co-ordination and control of the company according to the aims of the strategy put together by the manager. In this chapter, we will look at the issues related to organisational structure:

- The necessity to divide an enterprise into specialist functions.
- The chain of command.
- Distribution of power and control.
- Command and control for international strategies.
- The organisational structure.

CONTROLLING THE ENTERPRISE

If there is one thing that makes managers of all kinds uneasy it is this: no matter how lofty their position within the company, they do not actively produce anything. You might say this is the elephant in the room. Managers make tactical and strategic decisions, they direct operations and they are rewarded with status and remuneration. Ultimately, though, it is not obvious to outside observers that managers directly make money for the corporation. This chapter discusses the role that managers can play in providing the most logical and efficient structure for the organisation. Like airline pilots, who seem to spend 90% of their time enjoying the view and 10% of their time saving lives, if everything is set up correctly managers should not have anything to do!

In creating an appropriate organisational structure managers need to take many factors into consideration. These include issues surrounding **communication**, the **chain of command** and the **distribution of power**. At the same time the links within the organisation may have grown organically, even randomly, over time and the organisational structure needs to support, not obstruct, these links. Inevitably, the structure put in place will be customised to the particular needs of the company and may not adhere to the theoretical structures shown in textbooks. In large MNEs there may be multiple structures in place throughout the group, and the organisation may shift from one structural form to another in response to environmental changes. Managers need to remain flexible in the decisions on organisational structures if they are to meet new challenges as they appear.

CHAIN OF COMMAND

The organisational structure needs to optimise the flow of information to the management and the communication of orders in the return direction. The chain of command charts these simultaneous flows, although it is often more accurate to portray them as a complex web of connections rather than a chain. For the sake of simplicity, though, we tend to characterise the chain of command as **linear**, a basic flow up and down the management **hierarchy**. More complex organisational structures, such as those for MNEs, may have **non-linear** chains of command.

A linear chain of command is usually associated with a formal hierarchy, with information being passed up to the appropriate management level and the subsequent orders being passed back down. The classic example of this style of command would be the security services, where orders are disseminated, verified and modified by a communications system that carries them up and down the hierarchy (Builder et al., 1999), but it also exists to a lesser degree in the commercial world. It is suited to an organisation that requires strong leadership from the top or one where there is a clear allocation of roles. For example, a theatre or film company would be expected to have a linear chain of command.

The advantages of the linear style are that it allows for close adherence with a strategy or plan. Decision-making responsibilities are precisely defined so commands should be given in a timely fashion in response to new information. Naturally, it is these advantages that the security forces look for. However, there are disadvantages. The linear chain of command is only as strong as its weakest link; if one manager is incompetent then it has a negative impact on all commands downstream of them. Equally, if authority is not appropriately delegated then decision-making can be delayed, as the information and commands have to be communicated too far along the chain of command. If the commands are perceived as unjust then those affected may step outside the chain of command altogether to make their grievances known (Kassing, 2009).

Non-linear chains of command are often informal and difficult to chart. Information and commands may be traveling horizontally as well as vertically and they may by-pass the accepted centres of power. This is not the same as insubordination, when the chain of command breaks down, but is a healthy sign of vibrant communication. In a **matrix** form of organisational structure all the different parts of a company may be working on a single project together all at the same time. The marketing department may have suggestions for a design change that involves actions by the engineering, finance, human resource and production departments. Equally, some new financial restrictions may force changes on the product design and thus marketing as well. In complex projects the matrix approach can be more effective if the participants agree to work together on an informal basis and largely ignore the formal, hierarchical chain of command.

 ## MYTH BUSTER – WHISTLE-BLOWERS AS HEROES OF SOCIETY

Like referees in a game of football, whistle-blowers expose illegal activities, wrong doing and unacceptable behaviour in organisations. There is another thing they share with referees: they are about as popular.

In many cases whistle-blowers are seen as traitors to the organisation and consequently suffer reprisals. They may lose out on promotions or be dismissed altogether. If they work for the government they may even be incarcerated. Whistle-blowers face a tricky dilemma between doing their moral duty and damaging the organisation they serve.

Mordechai Vanunu was an Israeli engineer who was working for the government on their secret nuclear arms programme. Becoming embittered by the project, he left his job and embarked on a life of travel. In 1986, in violation of his non-disclosure agreement, he sold photographs of Israel's nuclear arms facility to the British newspaper, *The Sunday Times*. In an attempt to limit the damage to the national reputation, the Israeli secret service organisation, Mossad, enticed Vanunu to Italy where they drugged him and spirited him back to Israel. After a closed trial he was sentenced to 18 years in prison. By anti-nuclear protestors he was hailed as a hero, but many others have accused him of being reckless with the country's security.

More recently there has been less ambivalence towards whistle-blowers. For example, the scandal at US energy provider Enron first came to light through the revelations of an employee. Many governments have put in place legislation to protect whistle-blowers from retribution. However, the motivation for being a whistle-blower is not clear cut, with researchers Heyes and Kapur (2009) noting that the reasons may be based on morality, welfare or a desire to punish the organisation. This complicates the issue of how to deal with the information they divulge since it will be biased to the purposes of the whistle-blower. The broader benefits to society may be unintentional and may even be ultimately damaging.

Point of consideration: What are the implications of protecting all whistle-blowers under the law? In what ways could this legal privilege be abused by rival corporations?

Sources: Sunday Times, 2010; Heyes and Kapur, 2009

NETWORK COMMUNICATION

Other forms of non-linear command structures include the social networks that exist in all community groups, including commercial companies. The people within the company have a web of personal and professional connections that have evolved over time, often with the most experienced person being in a highly influential position, even if they do not hold a formal hierarchical position. In fact this network may work independently of the formal linear command structure and can be the source of a significant, if hidden, competitive advantage.

Social Network Analysis (SNA) uses statistical methods to reveal interactions in terms of nodes (usually the people who make up the network) and the ties that define their social relationships (Tubaro, 2012). The resultant visualisation of the network is depicted using arrows for the direction of the information communicated along the ties, as well as the thickness of the ties to denote the strength of the relationships. The study can reveal hidden structures within the corporation's formal hierarchy and indicate where the real power centres lie. It is not necessarily those that have the greatest number of ties that enjoy the greatest influence within the organisation, it may also lie with those that have strategic positions in the network. Some corporations are infamous for having CEOs that are only accessible through their personal assistants.

Non-linear command structures are highly flexible and encourage innovation. SNA techniques can help to develop social networks within the corporation that foster the most effective professional relationships. However, these structures can be very difficult to co-ordinate and control, leading to confusion and delay in large projects. When the corporation merges or is acquired by another firm, the informal network can be severely upset when a new linear, formal structure is imposed. There are also dangers of the most experienced personnel building their own power bases that subvert the formal structure. SNA should therefore be seen as an iterative process, being repeated at regular intervals to monitor the dynamic evolution of the corporation.

🔍 MANAGEMENT SPOTLIGHT: WHAT IS A FIRM?

It is believed that the oldest firm in the world was Kongo Gumi, a Japanese temple construction company founded in 578 and succumbing to economic misfortune in 2007 (Businessweek, 2007); still, a 1400 year corporate life-cycle is not a bad attempt. By contrast, the oldest theory of the firm is not even one century old: Ronald Coase wrote his treatise on the nature of the firm less than 80 years ago (Coase, 1937). This gives some idea of how far behind practice the theory is.

Although the deeper philosophical arguments over the precise nature of the firm are still raging, we can be clear that it is defined by its organisational structure. Without it the firm, company or corporation is an ad hoc gathering of activities unified only by ownership. The organisational structure brings coherence and efficiency to the activities contained within a legally defined boundary. The structure imposes sense on the company in a number of different factors:

- **Division of labour** – a company differs from sole traders, partnerships or co-operatives in that it brings together specialists, skilled and unskilled, to work together as an interdependent team. The company structure allocates the specialist roles, from marketing to final assembly. Within each function the workers are dedicated to one particular task, or set of related tasks, and this promotes efficiency and learning effects. There is also specialisation within the ranks of managers, most notably for MNEs where the overseas management teams may be allowed a degree of local autonomy.

- **Mechanism for co-ordination** – as the company is divided into its specialist areas the organisational structure must impose a system of co-ordination and control. This releases synergies between the corporate functions, the benefits they get from working together. If these benefits do not exist then the managers should look at transacting within the market instead.

- **Organisational boundaries** – companies have a choice between transacting with other companies in the open market, or vertical integration, where the buyer–supplier relationship is internalised and company divisions make transactions with each other. The limits of the company are marked by its boundary with the external market and this is defined by the organisational structure.

- **Control and responsiveness** – all companies need to balance the need to respond to local changes with that of controlling the overall operations. Strong managerial control from the centre is intended to direct strategy and ensure that different parts of the company are operating together at their optimum. It can also mean inflexibility when confronted by exogenous shocks. This dilemma is exacerbated by international operations where the need for both central control and local responsiveness is heightened.

- **Distribution of decision rights** – companies can circumvent some of the control and responsiveness dichotomy by delegating decision-making powers to lower management positions and beyond. This can include those workers on the factory floor or facing the customer, where they may be given sufficient authority to act on their own initiative relevant to their position. In other operations it may be necessary to retain decision-making powers with senior management if further delegation is not possible.

To these factors we can add the additional dimension of internationalisation. When a firm extends itself into international operations and turns itself into an MNE, it may well have to change its organisational structure accordingly, seeking to resolve the tension between local and international control mechanisms.

Point of consideration: For obvious reasons, crime syndicates are precluded from having legally defined corporate boundaries. What advantages and disadvantages do you think this might have for the organisation?

Sources: Businessweek, 2007; Coase, 1937

MANAGEMENT POWER

Vertical power distribution

In any command structure, whether linear or non-linear, the vertical links lead to the decision-makers, the power centres in the structure. In a linear command structure these links are strictly arranged up and down the hierarchy, but they also exist to an extent in non-linear command structures. In the non-linear structure these links may be very short. The power can be distributed in one of two ways:

1. *Centralised command structure* In the organisation's command structure power can be distributed in two ways: centralised and decentralised. A **centralised command structure** has decisions travelling as far up the command chain as possible, with all major decisions, and even relatively minor ones, being made centrally. This supports a tightly controlled strategy with strong co-ordination and highly consistent decisions. It also promotes efficiency because decisions are not duplicated. It does not have to be a rigid system and a centralised command structure can make swift decisions when conditions compel them. It is analogous to a military system, one which allows the senior strategists (i.e. the senior military officers) to leave the field as the mission commences, as the command system is robust enough to deal with exogenous developments (Builder et al., 1999).

Despite the clear advantages to centralised command structures they are out of favour with modern management styles, particularly when they are stretched internationally. The vertical links can become lengthy and this delays decision-making and may isolate distant managers from local developments. This can be a particular handicap for an MNE when the competition is based locally and has much shorter links in the chain of command. This can make the MNE look slow-witted by comparison.

The centralised structure tends to be formed around a core of professional managers, and this has specialisation advantages, but it also disempowers managers further down the chain of command. For an MNE, this can mean that local managers have little incentive to develop their knowledge, as they feel their views will be overruled by their superiors. A centralised structure can therefore smother innovation before it has started.

This is not to say that centralised command structures do not work at all. In industries where innovation at the local level tends to be relatively minor in relation to the grand global corporate strategy then it is more important to maintain strong co-ordination and control. For example, multinational oil companies are most concerned with co-ordinating global exploration and production, so they hold onto the power to control them; it is highly unlikely that a local unit would discover a new method for either of these activities, so there is little need for them to hold the power. In some industries innovation at the local level is positively discouraged, such as service industries where one level of service is delivered worldwide. Fast food MNEs are careful to minimise local variations unless absolutely necessary.

2. *Decentralised command structure* The decentralised command structure is gaining in popularity, particularly for international corporations. It liberates the senior management from making routine decisions and allows them to focus on the greater corporate strategy. Managers further down the hierarchy feel empowered by their additional responsibilities and this acts as an incentive to innovate. Such managers may find they have the power to act almost as if they were regional CEOs, responding to local developments with the authority to exploit new opportunities in a timely fashion. The shorter links in the chain of command should lead to greater flexibility and mean that the unit of the MNE can react as swiftly as the local competitors. There should also be greater accountability, with decisions being made in the same place where they are implemented.

Despite the attractiveness of decentralisation, especially for the managers involved, a certain amount of caution is wise. Local business units can became detached from the global corporate strategy as the unit develops according to its own agenda. This may mean that the corporation's core competitive advantages are not being fully exploited, or that the learning effects from one location cannot be transferred to another. Andersen (2004) found that decentralisation was a far too simplistic way of depicting the corporate decision-making structure: power may be devolved to the overseas business units, which themselves have a centralised structure. Alternatively, the corporate structure may be decentralised but underneath lie processes that integrate and co-ordinate strategies.

Andersen argues that the choice between centralised and decentralised structures does not have to be as stark as it appears. They exist on a continuum, managers able to choose how centralised or decentralised they need the company to be. Some of this can be down to the corporate culture and the management style, the resultant command structure reflecting the personalities as well as the business strategy. For MNEs, it is also possible to have a centralised command structure for the international group, directing strategy from a high level, while each regional business function has its own dedicated structure, from centralised to decentralised, as required.

Horizontal power distribution and specialisation

When the power to make decisions is distributed horizontally in the corporation it permits the company to structure itself around sub-units with specialised functions. A typical structure might involve R&D, production, marketing and accounting functions. Specialised functions avoid the duplication of the tasks elsewhere, so there are efficiency gains and the benefits of learning effects. For example, an accounts department can process the financial administration tasks for production, R&D and so on, thereby freeing those departments to concentrate on what they do best. With each function specialising in this way the process should release significant efficiencies and cost savings. However, it also puts in place a barrier between parts of the company, preventing them from transferring knowledge to each other.

Horizontal separation of the corporate structure is a considerable boon to value creation functions. These functions usually focus on R&D and marketing, but in fact customers can find value in many aspects of the company. Product service is often an opportunity for the company to interact with the customer long after the original sale took place. If the service department is given sufficient autonomy then it can develop its value-added activities in a manner that is specific to the way in which it works.

International corporations will find that a horizontal separation of decision-making is a useful way of carving up their world markets. This will often mean each regional centre having responsibility for its own activities, almost to the extent that it appears to operate as a semi-independent and self-contained organisation. This in turn may lead to the very same duplication of functions, such as production and R&D, which the horizontal separation was meant to have avoided.

The most extreme form of horizontal command structure is the **matrix**, where a single project has multiple corporate functions all attempting to have equal say. When this is working well there is a sense of partnership but it can also descend into confusion if there is no hierarchical power to arbitrate conflicting interests.

A conglomerate is an example of a horizontal command structure that has become so disparate there is no sense of interaction at all. In this case the conglomerate headquarters holds the strategic power for the group but the individual sub-units are left to their own devices. This has advantages of specialisation but surrenders the opportunity for synergies across the business units. Nevertheless, Suehiro (1993) points out that family businesses are structured horizontally, family members taking charge of different parts of the business while maintaining equal status with one another. The family connections in a *zaibatsu* conglomerate create a social network that overcomes the weaknesses of the structure, even promoting innovation and flexible responses.

FORMING THE MANAGEMENT STRUCTURE

We have seen so far that the command chain may be linear or non-linear in the way information and decisions flow, with links between power centres that are vertical or horizontal. This has much in common with the informal network of business relationships that is revealed through social network analysis (SNA). While the informal network is a vital part of management efficiency, the company still needs a formal structure within which to operate. The foundation of the management structure is decided by the structural variables, the business activities being monitored and the degree to which the management will needs to be imposed.

Structural variables

In selecting how decision-making in the company should be structured, managers need to take a number of variables into consideration. Among these are:

1. Historic structure One reason why there are such a plethora of organisation structural types is the enormous challenge of **restructuring** in order to better meet new developments in the industry or market. So risky is the restructuring that most firms prefer evolution to revolution. An experienced manager can recognise what elements of the existing structure have brought the company to its current level of success and so preserve them in the new structure. Done effectively, the company should end up with a management structure that is customised to its current situation and can cope with continued evolution.

2. Management culture It is easy to forget that corporations are not simply business machines working towards a strategic objective but communities of people with all their idiosyncrasies. Averaged across the corporation their personal characteristics take on the form of a culture, an identifiable set of customs and mores. The management are a sub-group of the corporation and have their own unique culture, one that tends to set the tone for the company as a whole (Bartlett and Ghoshal, 2000). This culture is often centred on the most senior figures. Some management teams are known to be aggressive and more suited to a linear and vertical command structure. Management teams in other firms, even in the same industry, may be more conciliatory and prefer a non-linear, horizontal command structure. These cultural styles are not always obvious to outside observers and can cause huge problems when two apparently similar companies merge their operations.

3. Business and product strategy These are perhaps the most important variables in the design of corporate structure. The structure needs to be supportive of the strategy, one which may call for close supervision from the centre or local autonomy and responsiveness. At a more detailed level, the same principles apply to the product strategy. If the product is to be marketed in a broadly unchanged form in all world markets then strong central control would be appropriate. However, if the product needs to be produced in a multitude of variants to suit local demand then a decentralised structure would be preferred.

4. Responsiveness to dynamic changes In markets that are in a high state of flux the organisation needs to have a structure that can cope with change. It may be necessary to give marketing or R&D a high degree of autonomy so that responses to changing conditions are readily available. The largest MNEs may even have enough dominance to be market leaders and induce those changes in the competition.

5. Future structural requirements Even when the structure has been carefully devised and implemented, exogenous changes in the industry can render it out of date. For industries that are slow moving this presents less of a problem since the company may be able to evolve quickly enough to keep pace. In other industries, such as electronics or e-commerce, rapid development of new technologies means that a radical restructuring may be forced upon the company. This has implications for the other variables since a restructuring obliges new approaches across the board.

Monitoring business activities

Although the chain of command describes the flow of information and decisions it does not show how management can ensure that actions are carried out. This is where the control system comes in: a collection of approaches for determining that a business plan is being acted upon. The monitoring of a business plan by management has three distinct phases:

1. Setting the standard It cannot be known if a project was a success or not unless the standard of achievement is set in advance. Managers often use a well-known mnemonic, **SMART**, in devising the intended outcome target:

- S – specific targets that are easily understood and unequivocal
- M – measurable outcomes
- A – achievable targets that motivate the participants
- R – relevant to the existing strategy and the participants
- T – time-bound to further incentivise participants to achieve the target by a reasonable deadline.

SMART defines what success means and how it can be achieved. It brings a sense of purpose to the project that motivates all those involved and allows management to monitor its progress with precision (Rubin, 2002).

2. Comparison with results When the project has reached some sort of completion point, such as delivery to the customer or the time set as the deadline, the management then need to compare the outcomes with the intentions. The success of the project may be measured against an array of metrics, from financial returns to customer satisfaction data, about which the management will need to make judgements. Whether the intended outcomes for the project have been met or not the management will then need to deliberate on the next stage.

3. *Response action* An inevitable feature of all projects is that as they reach a conclusion they have to be replaced by the next project. Management will use the experience of the completed project as the basis for the next. Where the project has been successful and the intended outcomes met then management needs to exploit the advantage and maintain the momentum in the market. If the outcomes were not met then it may be necessary to take remedial action and rerun the project with a new set of intended outcomes.

Imposing management intentions

Throughout the three phases of the management monitoring, there are a battery of different techniques available to managers for ensuring their will prevails. In some cases an authoritarian style is appropriate, but this is increasingly frowned upon in a modern business environment that calls for a sense of common purpose and co-operation throughout the company.

- **Bureaucratic control** – the classic form of management control by edict: managers issue orders that demand obedience, enforced by the threat of penalties. A more enlightened approach also provides for incentives, such as financial bonuses.
- **Personal contact** – a subtle and much less confrontational approach to imposing the will of management. Over time, managers can build a network of informal contacts reinforced by co-dependency. It is a very effective management tool but it is slow to create and quick to be destroyed. It also tends to grow organically and not necessarily in the manner the corporate strategy demands.
- **Cultural** – the values of the company become embedded and approaches to projects are part of the corporate furniture. The culture often originates from the founder and is absorbed by the rest of the workforce almost by osmosis. The more the corporate culture is centred on an individual, the more likely it is that the management structure can disintegrate when that individual is no longer around.

If it were possible for managers to settle on a particular style once and for all then their jobs would be very much easier. Sadly, autopilot is not a facility available to managers and they need to be flexible in a dynamic business environment. For this reason it will be necessary to mix the three approaches to the imposition of management intentions according to the conditions prevailing at the time.

Command and control for international strategies

Major challenges for the management structure arise when the company extends itself into overseas markets. This does not mean that the company needs to completely restructure; that would be highly risky, so evolution is still the order of the day. The structure will need to adapt in order to serve the new strategies. There are four generic international strategies given by Bartlett and Ghoshal (2002):

- **International** – standardised product for world markets, dominant home operation
- **Multidomestic** – custom products for local markets, local business unit autonomy
- **Global** – standardised product for world market, centralised control of worldwide design and product by interdependent business units
- **Transnational** – standardised and custom products, central co-ordination of semi-autonomous local business units, high levels of knowledge transfer between business units at all levels.

Each of these strategies requires its own type of command structure according to the contrasting needs for local autonomy or central control. A number of other **control factors** should also be taken into consideration:

- **Vertical links** – the strength of hierarchical links in the chain of command. Control may be held in the central headquarters or devolved to the local strategic business units. Co-ordination permits limited local autonomy but ensures business units are operating in accordance with the overall corporate strategy.
- **Horizontal specialisation** – how specialisation of corporate functions is structured. At its simplest the choice is between specialising in a standard product and finding markets for it, or specialising in the market and adapting the product.
- **Co-ordination necessities** – the importance within the strategy for co-ordination of the different worldwide business units. A conglomerate, made up of unrelated business units, has less need to co-ordinate them.
- **Integrating mechanisms** – the existence of management systems and structures for controlling a far-flung business empire. Often a heritage issue, the company was founded with a particular set of systems that have persisted as the company has grown.
- **Performance ambiguity** – management by specific targets issued from central control or the 'fuzzy logic' of general guidance for local autonomy. In dynamic markets, or those with unique local characteristics, greater ambiguity in the results can be tolerated.
- **Cultural control** – the degree to which the MNE is bound together by a common adherence to a corporate culture. Often originating from the founder, it evolves only slowly while the individual is present but may undergo a revolution when they leave.

In Table 12.1, we see how the characteristics of each control factor can be matched against a given international business strategy. A manager can use this to evaluate the extent to which the control factors support the strategy, and whether they need adjusting, or how the strategy might need adapting to fit the control factors.

Table 12.1 *Control factors for international business strategies*

Control Factor	International Business Strategy			
	International	**Multidomestic**	**Global**	**Transnational**
Vertical Links	Centralised control around core competency; limited local autonomy	Decentralised; localised management hierarchy	Centralised with local operational autonomy	Mixed – centralised global control with local multidomestic control
Horizontal Specialisation	Product	Market	Product	Product and/or market
Coordination	Moderate	Low	High	Very high
Integrating Mechanisms	Few	None	Many	Very many
Performance Ambiguity	Moderate	General guidance	Specific targets	Specific targets for global issues, general guidance locally
Cultural Control	Moderate	Low	High	Very high

Characterising strategy and control by corporation type

In Table 12.1, we see how basic forms of international business strategy call for a particular set of control factors, and, of course, vice versa. We can now characterise how a corporation would look for a given combination of strategy and control factors:

- **International strategy**
  The corporation has gained market leadership with a product that is enjoying acceptance in many overseas markets. The management need to retain total control over the product, its design and production. Any local autonomy will be limited to fairly peripheral tasks such as retail sales and the brand quality will be maintained at all times. Central management will need to co-ordinate the different local operations to ensure they are serving the designated markets and they are not competing with each other. Each business unit is effectively an extension of the main home operation, but there is little need to integrate the overseas business units with each other. Due to the strict central control being focused on the product some local variation is permitted in terms of marketing tactics and culture.

  Example corporation: Google

- **Multidomestic**
  The corporation is totally decentralised, devolving the majority of powers to the local business units. Indeed, these business units are then free to make their own decisions on fitting their specific local strategy with their control factors. Each business unit could end up with their own unique organisational structure. The holding corporation, meanwhile, works at a distance, assigning the business units to their regional markets and leaving them to make their own product decisions. As long as the business units stay in their regions there is little global co-ordination to deal with and there is no call for integration. Performance targets are in the form of aggregated requirements, such as return on investment or market growth, it being the local managers who set specific sales targets. There is almost no common culture holding the global corporation together.

  Example corporation: News Corporation

- **Global**
  A complex strategy that symbolises the stateless, truly multinational enterprise. The corporation retains strong control over its core competency, most likely the product, with just some minor adaptation if the local market demands it. The different business units are equally stateless, not simply serving their local markets but worldwide as well. This takes high levels of co-ordination and an internationally minded central management team. They will need to work on integrating the disparate business units so that they can serve the global market as a combined enterprise. This is only possible with the imposition of specific targets and a common corporate culture.

  Example corporation: Boeing

- **Transnational**
  A style of strategy that hopes to take into account all local variation and meld it into a single, unified corporate structure. To have local business units that can focus on their own markets autonomously, yet work with other business units if they develop a product with global applications, means knowing when to impose central control and when to defer to local expertise. Co-ordination needs to be detailed and the various business units integrated with each other at any level. The business units will have their own specific targets but the parent corporation will have another set of targets as well, both global and local. Corporate culture will be very important in holding together such a complex command and control structure.

  Example corporation: Unilever, Tata (tea, steel, etc.)

Checklist for international managers

Matching the international business strategy with the control factors involves a high number of variables that will lead to the entire evaluation process getting bogged down in scenario planning. A useful tool is an algorithm for decision-making, a systematic approach that brings consistency and a sense of logic. Peter Drucker was a famous management consultant who published widely, including seminal works such as *Concept of the Corporation* (Drucker, 1993) and *The Practice of Management* (Drucker, 1954). Drucker suggested a checklist for senior managers that act as guiding principles:

1. *Clarity* Like Occam's Razor, when confronted by two complex ideas of equal value the simpler of the two should be chosen. For an organisation, an unnecessarily complicated structure should be avoided since it will store up trouble for the future. Complexity in an organisation slows down decision-making, obscures accountability, wastes resources and reduces productivity. This is not to say that an MNE's organisational structure will not be complex, only that it should be no more complicated than is absolutely necessary.

2. *Economy* Control mechanisms should only be put in place where they are necessary. When control is allowed to spread unchecked it disenfranchises and demotivates the very people it was supposed to be managing to better effect. There are dangers of diseconomies of management as the bureaucracy begins to smother the activities within the company. An economical attitude to control means delegating authority to where it is most effective, even to the extent of empowering the frontline and shop floor workers where appropriate.

3. *Direction* The overall strategy for the MNE should provide a clear vision for the product and its benefits to the consumer. In targeting the customer in this way the process for delivering the product falls into line behind the vision. This is especially pertinent in industries with very high economies of scale where it is the demands of the process that seem to dictate the product strategy. Allowing the demands of the production process to take over creates a gap in the market between customer needs and product supply which can be exploited by rival companies.

4. *Understanding* As MNEs expand their operations it can be easy for individuals to feel lost in the vast corporate structure. Managers need to combat this by devising an organisation structure that recognises the role of the individual. The kinds of measures that are available include an HR strategy that is aligned with the corporate strategy.

5. *Decision-making* Even the most hierarchical and centralised of corporations delegates some power lower down the chain of command. Drucker's view was that the authority to make decisions should be delegated as low as possible. This should mean that power lies with those who can best judge what needs doing and can act upon it. Managers are often tempted to concentrate power in their own hands when their remote position can lead to slow or erroneous decisions. At the opposite extreme, power may be devolved to those who lack a wider perspective or cannot act on the decisions. Some worker empowerment programmes have been scaled back because the participants were making judgements about corporate strategy when they did not hold all the facts and could not act strategically even if they did.

6. *Stability* The organisation's structure needs to support the corporation and provide coherence in a dynamic business environment. Managers who tinker with the organisational structure sow confusion and distract the corporation from meeting the competitive challenges. At the same time, the structure should not be a rigid one that is incapable of evolving.

7. *Perpetuation and self-renewal* Strategic planning is based on a reasonable degree of certainty about the short- and medium-term business environment. In the long term the company needs to be structured so that innovations can take root. This may entail a radical restructuring of the organisation.

Drucker's checklist acts more as a cautionary tale rather than an algorithm that concludes in a specific course of action. This is not to undermine its utility for international managers and perhaps we can summarise in a single manager's axiom:

Management decisions should be definitive, economic, responsive and transparent.

SHAPING THE ORGANISATIONAL STRUCTURE

If the command structure needs to be formed with the corporate strategy, the organisational structure must also be shaped to serve the strategic purpose. The organisational structure defines the limits of the firm's boundary and sets out the divisions of the firm's operations. It is almost like a map or an architectural drawing of the firm, delineating its main features and showing how it works. Henry Mintzberg (1980), for example, put forward five structural forms:

- Simple – an organisation largely devoid of bureaucracy and hierarchy with an informal network of communication. Often displayed by companies in their formative years.
- Machine bureaucracy – rigid structure with a centralised structure and formalised procedures. Suited to firms engaged in mass production.
- Professional bureaucracy – the centralised structure is rendered unnecessary by a common standard of professionalism that binds the firm together. A legal firm, or accounting partnership, would be examples.
- Divisionalised form – the structure of the market obliges the firm to structure itself around divisions overseen by a central headquarters. It is effectively an umbrella structure, sheltering organisation structures appropriate to each market. Commonly observed in multinationals.
- Adhocracy – creative experts are allowed broad freedoms to practise while authority within the structure is passed to administrative staff. Frequently manifested in a matrix form. Can be seen in universities and research dominated organisations.

Given the manner in which firms evolve in response to their environmental changes we can expect there to be as many structures as there are firms. Despite this we can distil from the infinite variety some core structural forms that are instructive on the basic organisational forces moulding the corporation into shape. We will start with the two most basic structural types: the U-Form and the M-Form. Both of these were originally proposed by Alfred Chandler in the early 1960s (Chandler, 1990).

U-Form

Chandler's argument was that the U-Form is the ancestor of all succeeding organisation structures. Its full name is the unitary form and it shows the firm at the beginning of its life with the simplest of structures (Moschandreas, 1994). Preceding that is what we might call the post-natal corporate structure, one that has yet to take on any recognisable shape.

It is assumed that the firm was founded from scratch by a single person who started out working in all the operations of the nascent firm, or at least was responsible for those operations. At this post-natal stage the firm has no real structure but is an amorphous mass of activities all somehow embodied in the role of the founder. Since the founder is obliged to be a jack-of-all-trades, and not devote themselves to their own personal competitive talent, the firm is not operating at its most efficient. To compensate for this the founder may find themselves working extended hours, for instance doing the accounts long into the night.

Through dint of sheer hard work and brilliant innovation in specific areas the firm grows to an extent where the founder can no longer be personally engaged in every activity. This means forming an identifiable organisational structure. Specialist staff are recruited and the company creates distinct functions around them. Typically, these would include R&D, production, marketing and so on. The founder remains in position at the top of the firm as the **CEO**, where they continue to exploit their deep knowledge of the company and exert control of each function of the company. The firm's structure is depicted in Figure 12.1.

In the U-Form the command structure can be characterised as both vertical and linear: vertical in the sense of a hierarchy, linear in the sense of information being passed in order of seniority through the organisation.Information is processed by the specialist functions and passed to the CEO, who then hands down the decisions. The structure has a number of advantages, in accordance with Drucker's checklist, and is at least an advance over the preceding amorphous firm structure:

- The CEO is able to specialise in strategic decision making while remaining in touch with all operations of the firm.
- Each function is transparent to the CEO so strategic alignment is readily achievable.
- The chain of command is very short, so the company can be highly responsive.
- In emergency situations the CEO can quickly take charge of any function based on experience.

These advantages are fine for a small company but as it grows a number of problems with the U-Form come to light, most notably in connection with a CEO micro-managing an organisation that now demands an entire senior management team to steer it. For the growing company, the disadvantages of this basic structure are:

- The CEO only has time to focus on strategic decision-making but is distracted by the temptation to continue interfering in functional operations.
- Each function is itself becoming too large and unwieldy, particularly if the firm has grown to international scope.
- Managers have little opportunity to show initiative because the CEO continues to make all the major decisions.

With the operations of the firm now so expansive, and possibly internationalised, the next step is to restructure the firm around specialist divisions. This is the M-Form, or multidivisional form.

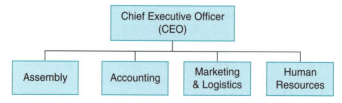

Figure 12.1 *U-Form organisational structure*

M-Form

The M-Form creates a series of semi-autonomous specialist divisions and moves the CEO, along with a senior management team, into a separate headquarters division. The headquarters division is made up of professional managers, the kind that have earned academic qualifications. They have skills in strategy formulation and implementation. It is not necessary for them to have risen through the firm like the founder. Of course, the founder could still be in place as the CEO but they are eminently replaceable by another CEO who is new to the company and may even be new to the industry.

The role of the **headquarters (HQ)** division is to set the strategic direction of the corporation and monitor progress from the data fed to it by the other divisions. These other divisions typically specialise around discrete business activities, be they a particular product range or regional market. The semi-autonomous nature of these divisions means that they can evolve within the limitations set down by the HQ. These limitations are defined by benchmarks and targets which, if met, mean the HQ need have little operational involvement in the divisions.

An M-Form corporation is one where the divisions are left to develop their assigned roles and report results, often in the form of sales volumes, financial returns but also any other metric that is deemed appropriate. These results are then analysed by the management team at the HQ. As a consequence, **divisional management** tend to have risen up the ranks within that division or have gained vocational experience in a related business, while the **HQ management** tend to be professionals with academic qualifications such as an MBA. Figure 12.2 shows the organisational structure of the M-Form corporation.

Returning to Drucker's Checklist we can see how the M-Form can serve the needs of the corporation when it has outgrown the U-Form structure:

- A U-Form corporation has a structure that is simple in form, but as the firm grows, particularly internationally, the different management command and reporting processes can become so complex that decision-making is impeded. The M-Form separates out strategic HQ management from operational divisional management and so restores clarity to the management of the organisation.
- The creation of an HQ division implies an expansion of management, but there should still be no more management staff than is necessary. Thus the most economical approach is maintained.
- A specialist HQ that is able to focus on strategy provides a clear direction for the company that might have become lost in an overburdened U-Form.
- The M-Form brings greater definition to the role of managers, such as whether their duties are operational, tactical or strategic.

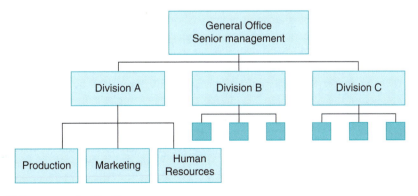

Figure 12.2 *M-Form organisational structure*

- Authority can be delegated to those that are best able to use it: operational and tactical control is with the divisional managers, strategic control with the HQ managers.
- The M-Form should be a stable structure due to the limitations that are put on the divisions by the HQ; the divisions are not free to make their own strategic decisions. However, it can be guilty of rigidity when divisions are in a position to exploit new strategic opportunities but are prevented from doing so by the HQ.
- The ability of the M-Form corporation as a whole to respond to the changing environment can become a challenge as it loses the role of the U-Form CEO, who enjoyed personal and professional influence over the various corporate functions.

Blending the M-Form with the U-Form

Many of the advantages offered by the M-Form are theoretical and might not be realised in a pure state. For example, a corporation may have some sort of HQ division but it will not be staffed only by professional managers who hold their positions purely on the basis of academic qualifications. There will be many others who have risen up the ranks of the divisions, their skills perhaps supplemented by additional qualifications as they advanced their way up the corporate ladder. This means that there is not quite the separation of strategic and operational management indicated by the model.

At the very top of the M-Form structure is the CEO, and the model suggests that this person will be the most remote from operational decision-making, devoting themselves almost entirely to strategic matters. In fact, a CEO needs to exercise much more flexibility and involve themselves as necessary. In an emergency this can mean taking direct operational control. When this happens it is almost as if the U-Form structure is reasserting itself, suspending divisional autonomy and allowing the CEO to take command of corporate functions.

In fact it could be argued that the M-Form is not a development of the U-Form intended for large, complex organisations but an unrelated structure serving a different purpose. If this is the case then the two forms could co-exist within a single corporation:

- The U-Form structure describes the chain of command, the flow of information from the corporate functions answered by the corresponding orders from the CEO and the senior management team. Any corporation facing a catastrophe needs fast response times so the senior management team may override existing communication procedures to deal directly with the situation. In this way the U-Form structure is used to temporarily re-establish the most effective chain of command.
- The M-Form describes a structure for a management information system (MIS), the emphasis being on the formulation, implementation and monitoring of the corporate strategy. In a vertically integrated company the M-Form manages the internal market in order to extract the full benefits of synergy and minimise the economic friction between the business units.

The U-Form and M-Form are simple to illustrate because they often describe the structure of the corporate processes rather than the physical structure. However, it is not always easy to identify exactly what structure the corporation has in each case. For example, if an international corporation has an HQ in the home country and semi-autonomous divisions around the world then it is clearly an M-Form, both in the way that management communicates and in the physical location of the divisions. But when an emergency situation obliges HQ managers to take direct operational control then the U-Form comes to the fore even though there has been no tangible restructuring. The picture is further complicated when the corporation has a custom structure to meet its own competitive and strategic requirements.

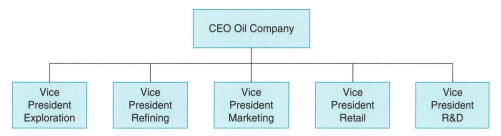

Figure 12.3 *Functional organisational structure*

Custom corporate structures

Between the basic U-Form and the more complex M-Form there are a number of hybrid structures. The first of these is the **functional organisational structure** and this is shown in Figure 12.3. This extends the departmental specialisation of the U-Form into semi-autonomous functions with a greater degree of their own decision-making power. The functional structure retains the tight chain of command of the U-Form as well as the specialisation of tasks without duplication. However, the semi-autonomous nature of the divisions means they can begin to act with growing independence of one another, raising co-ordination challenges.

This is a structure suited to oil companies, for example, where each function is highly specialised and there is much less need for them to be working together. The marketing division is hardly likely to request the exploration division to search for a newly fashionable type of oil, so there is little need for them to work together.

A more complex form of structure occurs when the corporation organises itself around specific products. This is a variant of the M-Form and it groups together value-creating activities into related divisions for a **product organisational structure**, as seen in Figure 12.4. This is often seen in high-tech corporations where the underlying technology is related but the products have distinct markets.

Samsung would be just such an example with various types of mobile phone and computer in its product range. Although the corporation as a whole has established itself as a technology leader, each division has a degree of freedom to develop its assigned products and markets within the corporate strategy. For each product this means good responsiveness to the demands of the market, but it also means a lack of knowledge transfer across the divisions along with other co-ordination difficulties. Like the M-Form it also tends to give rise to duplication of tasks, as each division has its own marketing, human resource management and so on.

As a domestically based firm begins to explore international opportunities it may start the process by creating an international division. This recognises that the challenges are distinct from those in the domestic market, and so the specialist function concentrates the learning effects of exploring the new

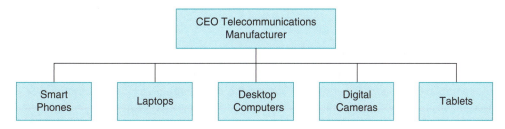

Figure 12.4 *Product organisational structure*

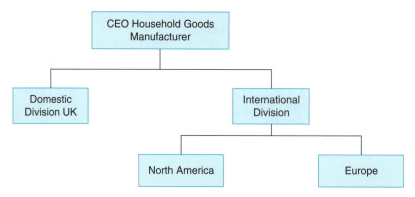

Figure 12.5 *International organisational structure*

markets. However, it is a simplistic view of the world since there is no global market, just a disparate array of internationally spread domestic markets. It tends to suit small firms manufacturing niche, premium products that will undergo minimum adaptation to world markets. The **international organisational structure** we see in Figure 12.5 brings with it the co-ordination and knowledge transfer problems of the M-Form to a company that may still be essentially U-Form in its main domestic operations.

A more advanced version of the international division form is the **area organisational structure**. This divides the international division into discrete areas, each division having its own decision-making powers. The product is still broadly the same for all markets but the marketing activities will be very different.

Manufacturers of foods and household goods are suited to this structure when they are selling those products in multiple markets. The area divisions then have equal status with the domestic division, and so there needs to be an M-Form style HQ to oversee the group. The divisions can be highly responsive to local market changes but it can mean that there is pressure to adapt the product to local demand and target different market sectors. There are also the M-Form problems of co-ordination, knowledge transfer between divisions and the duplication of functions.

Each corporate structure tends to be a custom fit according to the specific requirements of the organisation. Each structure is therefore founded on a key aspect or competitive advantage of the company. So if the company has a highly competitive product range that requires little product adaptation then it will structure itself around the products. However, it may also have production sites located around the world that need a degree of local autonomy in dealing with supply chain, human resource and other issues. This would imply an Area Structure. The two do not have to be mutually exclusive: the product is standardised to a global market under the control of a product team but is manufactured at the different locations under the control of the local area teams. It is possible for the two organisational structures to co-exist because they are related to different aspects of the organisation's activities. Sometimes, though, they are so interdependent that a whole new organisational structure is necessary: the matrix.

Matrix organisational structure

The matrix is less a structure and more a set of processes that brings the different functions and divisions of the corporation together into a network of contacts. It can exist within a formal organisational M-Form arrangement such as a Product or Function Structure but they all work together on a single project. This brings the various business units into alignment so that marketing, R&D and production, for instance, are able to respond to and include each other's requirements. Figure 12.6 shows a typical Matrix Structure.

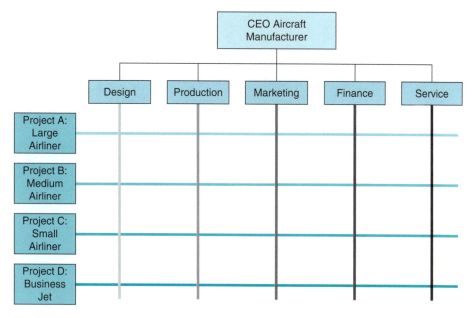

Figure 12.6 *Matrix structure*

This form of organisational structure is suited to highly complex projects, particularly those that include technical advances of uncertain potential. The aerospace industry uses this structure because new aircraft are supremely complicated machines gathering together the very latest technologies which must meet the needs of customers. A further difficulty is that aircraft designs are closely regulated by the authorities and are difficult to change once production has started; some of the most successful aircraft can remain in production for decades.

In a complex project it is vital that various divisions and functions within the corporation are able to work together. For example, a change in the product specification demanded by potential customers has immediate knock-on effects for product design, production and finance. The structure permits good communication and co-ordination with flexible responses to a dynamic situation. However, it can also lead to long delays as any new developments have to pass through the various divisions of the corporation.

The matrix structure may appear democratic but with no inherent management hierarchy any conflicts can become very difficult to resolve. These problems are not only structural but can also be blamed on the interpersonal friction between the participants (Sy and Côté, 2004). When a matrix project runs into trouble the delays can become intolerable. In such cases there needs to be a senior manager in the HQ division with the power to oversee the project.

Since the matrix structure exists in parallel to the overall organisational structure it can be implemented in any corporation at any level. It may be that a corporation that is structured around its product ranges can oblige the product teams to communicate with one another in order to encourage knowledge transfer. The matrix can even be used within a small U-Form company for the same reason.

On occasion a project may be unique to the extent that it demands a custom corporate structure as an alternative to a matrix. These suit complex, high-value products and systems (CoPS) such as warships, nuclear power stations and so on that have a very limited production run. The resultant **project based organisation (PBO)** will be highly suited to the specific demands of the project but do not adapt well to the more routine tasks of producing for broader markets (Hobday, 2000).

CASE STUDY – MATRIX AND THE BOEING DREAMLINER

The aircraft industry is the last of the great, romantic engineering enterprises. Once Victorian pioneers would risk everything crafting technical miracles like magnificent iron bridges, graceful ocean-going liners and steam locomotives that could pull with the power of a thousand heavy horses. In the place of these technology heroes it seems only the aircraft companies still stand.

There are just two aircraft companies of global stature left in the world: Boeing of the US and Airbus of Europe. Yet even companies of their grand scale must bet the farm with almost every new aircraft launch. They cannot afford even a single failure.

Boeing is perhaps best known for the 747 Jumbo but this design is now over 45 years old. These days public demand is shifting away from long-haul travel between massive hub airports, which are best served by large capacity aircraft, and towards short-haul journeys between local airports. Boeing's analysis has identified a need for smaller aircraft. At the same time Airbus was taking the opposite view with the 555 seat A380 superjumbo.

Boeing recognised that its new smaller aircraft would have to demonstrate a clear competitive advantage for all stakeholders. Not just the airlines but also the passengers would need to feel that they were benefiting from the most advanced airliner of the modern era. All major aspects of the design needed to bring added value. The larger windows, for example, provided an increased view for passengers and reduced the costs of artificial lighting but required technical advances in fuselage materials.

In order to achieve a quantum leap in aircraft design Boeing introduced advanced technologies, such as composite materials, and promised to raise fuel efficiency by 20%. With so many state-of-the-art technologies Boeing had to put in place a global supply chain comprising many of the world's leading aerospace companies. The company instigated a new style of supply chain with tiers of suppliers culminating in the senior Tier 1 companies who conducted major sub-assembly work. Up to 70% was outsourced in this way, from delegating parts of the fuselage and wings to Japan, the tail to Italy, the landing gear to the UK and so on.

That the Dreamliner project proved more a nightmare in practice should not be used to point the finger of blame at Boeing. The Dreamliner entered service in 2011 as the 787, three years later than originally planned, but the hugely complex matrix structure was a necessary step to taking the aircraft into the twenty-first century. Meanwhile Airbus was struggling with its own pan-European production system for the A380; that aircraft entered service in late-2007, a full two years behind schedule.

Point of consideration: Should Boeing have been more cautious in implementing the matrix structure for its Dreamliner project? Could the company have used another organisational structure at the same time in order to prevent the worst of the delays?

Source: Tang et al., 2009

RAISING EMPLOYABILITY: MANAGEMENT LEADERSHIP AND THE TEAM

There is a sense amongst managers that if they want to improve their employability and attain high positions in the corporate structure then they need to become leaders (Carroll and Levy, 2008). Management, it seems, is about learning the right technique for a known problem, while leadership is about creating new approaches to unexpected problems. We might say that management is about dealing with the present, while leadership carries the organisation into the future. Managers are therefore tactical, looking to the short term, while leaders have a long-term strategic purview. Leadership brings with it additional connotations of higher professional status and self-esteem.

Teaching leadership skills has, not surprisingly, become big business, as ambitious managers attempt to augment their qualifications with its perceived qualities. Some of this may have been due to the cult of the CEO, as embodied in such superstar leaders as Jack Welch of GE, who has a whole management institute named after him. In fact, despite his domineering reputation, Welch was well aware that leadership means also knowing when to step aside and let the team take over (Slater, 2003).

It is on this point that management fashion and practice diverge. Superficially, at least, managers like to characterise themselves as leaders in the military idiom, taking control in the vanguard of some courageous strategic advance. This, though, is not what is implied by the organisational structure which is intended to bring out the best in the entire corporation. As Welch himself would admit, the role of the leader is to put together the best team, give them a sense of direction and then leave them to do what they do best.

There would appear to be strong cultural perspectives on leadership. In China there is a special network of business relationships known as **guanxi**, a mutually supportive form of cross-corporate teamwork that would not respond well to an aggressive form of leadership from the top. Instead, guanxi pertains more to the concept of a leader as a servant, perhaps closer to the Western idea of the public servant (Han et al., 2010).

Chen and Tjosvold (2006) found that the kinds of participative teamwork promoted by guanxi were vital when managers from the United States work with companies in China. Yet it was not as if the American managers could not make the transition and in being able to do so prove that they could adapt to management leadership practices in other cultures too. International managers need to understand that there is no single set of metrics that define good leadership. Instead, the style of leadership that is required is determined by the nature of the team. After all, it is the team that does the actual work.

We can look to Japan for a more systematic approach to teamwork. It is expressed in concepts like **TQM**, total quality management, a holistic approach to business that originated in the country (Vouzas and Psychogios, 2007). TQM is, at its heart, a teamwork-based activity that uses all those involved as resources. With such an intensity of commitment it is necessary that the management training for TQM is rigorous, with strong support from senior management (Palo and Padhi, 2003).

This is perhaps no more true than for the kinds of groups upon which our lives depend, such as airline crews or medical teams. Gaba (2010) took the idea a step further by looking at how the concept of the 'crew' could be transferred to clinical teams and their ability to cope with the extremes of crisis resource management. With sufficient training such groups can deal with emergencies and head off catastrophes. Some of the training schemes that are available include Stanford's (2015) ACRM technique and TeamStepps, both intended for enhancing teamwork and communication in medical contexts but with lessons for business management.

The clinical team techniques emphasise the importance of taking a long-term and deep view of teamwork training, involving all personnel for the entirety of their careers. However, it should be noted that medical teams also need to be thoroughly drilled so that they can treat emergencies almost as routine, which is unlikely to be necessary in the business environment. Indeed, it could be argued that since innovation and dynamism are the hallmarks of a successful business, ultimately effective managers do not render dramas routine, they cause them to happen in the first place.

WEB SUPPORT

1. Chain of Command in Organizational Structure. A short article by Sophie Johnson of Demand Media for Houston Chronicles website. Succinct and accurate; there is also a link to where you can try out designing an organisational chart.

   www.smallbusiness.chron.com/chain-command-organizational-structure-59110.html

2. Social Network Analysis & Mapping - For Future Intelligence. Video presented by Juliet Fox, Partner at Future iQ Partners. The sound is not exactly hi-fi, but good enough, and the ultimate purpose is to advertise the company. Nevertheless, it provides a clear overview of what network analysis is for and how it can reveal paths to more effective organisational structures.

   www.youtube.com/watch?v=vgezXsE6-vg

3. The Most Misunderstood Business Concept In China. For those confused by the Chinese concept of *guanxi* try this article by Anthony Goh and Matthew Sullivan of US-Pacific Rim International for Business Insider, published 24 February 2011. It neatly demystifies *guanxi* but clings to the idea that it belongs only to China. Think about how *guanxi* manifests itself in your own business culture.

   www.businessinsider.com/the-most-misunderstood-business-concept-in-china-2011-2?IR=T

THE STORY SO FAR: MANAGEMENT AND STRUCTURE

Managers act by co-ordinating and controlling the enterprise, but they need a structure through which to do this. They have to devise routes by which to communicate, either receiving information or passing down orders. This chain of command runs through the enterprise in a multitude of different ways, horizontally and vertically, as well as through networks of contacts. Where the power is concentrated in this chain depends on the demands of the overall business strategy in place, and in some cases managers in far-flung locations may have a great deal of responsibility devolved to them. The structure of the company, whether U-Form, M-Form or one of many other types, should support the control and co-ordination approach that has been chosen but the structure should always be the servant of the manager.

Project Topics

1. When starting a new software company working on a small number of unrelated projects, how would one choose between the U-Form and M-Form organisational structures?
2. A hospital is made up of medical specialists of equal professional stature but often competing demands for resources. How should power be distributed within such an organisation, horizontally or vertically?
3. Shipbuilding brings together many advanced technical disciplines in an assembly process which has not, at the conceptual level, changed in character for many years. What necessity would you see to using a matrix structure in such an industry and what problems are likely to emerge?

CASE STUDY – BP AND THE MANAGEMENT OF DEEPWATER HORIZON

BP is one of the largest and most successful corporations in the world. With nearly 84,000 employees working in 80 countries it produces over 3 million barrels of oil per day, with another 18 billion barrels thought to be in reserve. Although oil is a commodity like coal or iron ore the industry is vertically integrated to an unusual degree. Oil companies will often be involved in much of the production and delivery processes, from oil well to service station. BP is typical in this regard.

The company divides itself up into five distinct categories:

- Exploration – surveys and test wells
- Development and extractions – drilling the main wells and releasing the oil
- Transportation and trading – selling and distributing oil
- Manufacturing – refining oil into fuels and other products
- Marketing – sales of oil products to industrial and retail customers
- R&D – research into alternative sources of energy.

The different categories are technically quite separate, perhaps only the drilling of test wells and the subsequent production wells sharing a common technology if not a common management approach. Indeed, the only shared feature of these activities is the oil running through them. Any of these activities could be readily outsourced, as is often the case.

It is hardly surprising, then, that BP is a prime candidate for the M-Form of organisational structure, most resembling one based around the functional structure in Figure 12.3. Each function will make the operational decisions pertinent to the corporate category for which they are responsible. As long as each function is operating as normal the M-Form structure allows them to flourish while keeping the BP headquarters adequately informed. Then on 20 April 2010 it all began to fall apart.

The Deepwater Horizon was a mobile drilling rig, owned by Transocean and leased to BP under the Marshall Islands flag of convenience. On that morning in April the rig had been drilling exploratory wells when it was overpowered by high-pressure methane gas, which ignited and engulfed the entire platform in a maelstrom of fire. Eleven workers simply disappeared, presumed dead, while another 94 were rescued by boat and helicopter. The stricken rig was unable to shut down the shattered oil well and raw crude gushed into the open sea at the rate of 62,000 barrels per day.

The damage to the environment was catastrophic and public venom was directed at BP. As an oil company it should have been prepared for such an eventuality, but as the weeks ticked by with little sign of progress the company looked increasingly incompetent. It was quite apparent that the classic M-Form structure, with its remote headquarters, could not cope with disaster on such a scale. The chief executive, Tony Hayward, was flown over from the UK to take direct operational control, thereby imposing a local U-Form-style structure.

While such a tactic might have overcome the problems of the M-Form it also introduced one of the main problems of the U-Form: everything hinges on the CEO. Whatever technical capabilities Mr Hayward may have had, handling the public relations disaster was not one of them. He was soon replaced by an American BP executive, Bob Dudley, but it was not until 15 July that the well was capped, bringing to an end 87 days of corporate panic.

Point of consideration: If BP had been structured globally as a U-Form corporation, might the Deepwater Horizon spill never have happened? What different kinds of disasters might have befallen such a corporation instead?

Sources: National Commission on the BP Deepwater Horizon Oil Spill and Offshore Drilling, 2011; BP, 2014

? MULTIPLE CHOICE QUESTIONS

1. A company is defined by:
   a. All the contracts that it holds, particularly employment contracts.
   b. The strength of the brand name.
   c. The ownership structure.

2. The corporate chain of command is a system for passing down orders.
   a. True – it is the management communication system.
   b. True – it is a one-way information flow, from top to bottom.
   c. False – information flows both up and down the hierarchy.

3. What does social network analysis (SNA) do when applied to an organisation?
   a. It maps the informal connections in an organisation.
   b. It shows how the managers are talking to each other.
   c. It reveals which online social networking services are most used.

4. What improvements can be suggested by SNA?
   a. To spend less time using online social networking services.
   b. How to make more efficient use of computers.
   c. Where to strengthen the connections.

5. What is the advantage of a centralised command structure?
   a. It protects the power of senior management to make decisions.
   b. It is simple and reliable.
   c. It promotes innovation at all levels.

6. What kind of firm is suited to a decentralised structure?
   a. A software company innovating in new products.
   b. A security firm operating a prison.
   c. A sole trader.

7. The best way to impose management will is through bureaucratic control.
   a. True – bureaucracy is reliable and systematic.
   b. False – bureaucracy is famously inefficient.
   c. False – there are other ways of managing.

8. As a firm internationalises does it need a new organisational structure?
   a. No – it needs to evolve the existing structure.
   b. Yes – the stretched lines of communication demand a new approach.
   c. Yes – the restructuring will drive the internationalisation.

9. Why did the M-Form of organisational structure emerge?
   a. It is the organisational structure for modern business.
   b. As firms grow they need more complex structures to distribute management responsibilities.
   c. On the basis of divide-and-rule it is easier for the CEO to control the company as a whole if lower management responsibilities are separated.

10. When would a firm use a U-Form of organisational structure?
    a. When the CEO is the source of product innovation.
    b. When a corporate emergency demands a direct command and control structure.
    c. When it is testing out international opportunities.

Answers
1a, 2c, 3a, 4c, 5b, 6a, 7c, 8a, 9b, 10b

REFERENCES

Andersen T J (2004) 'Integrating decentralized strategy making and strategic planning processes in dynamic environments' *Journal of Management Studies* 41(8), pp. 1271–1299

Bartlett C A and Ghoshal S (2000) *Transnational management* (Vol. 4). Boston, MA: McGraw Hill

——— (2002) *Managing across borders: The transnational solution* (2nd edn.). Boston, MA: Harvard Business School Press

BP (2014) Company information from www.bp.com/en/global/corporate/about-bp/company-information. html accessed 21 December 2014

Builder C H, Bankes S C and Nordin R (1999) *Command concepts*. Santa Monica, CA: Rand Corporation

Businessweek (2007) 'The end of a 1,400-year-old business' by James Olan Hutcheson in *Businessweek* 16 April 2007 from www.businessweek.com/stories/2007-04-16/the-end-of-a-1-400-year-old-business-businessweek-business-news-stock-market-and-financial-advice accessed 25 November 2014

Carroll B and Levy L (2008) 'Defaulting to management: leadership defined by what it is not' *Organization* 15(1), pp. 75–96

Chandler A D (1990) *Strategy and structure: Chapters in the history of the industrial enterprise* (Vol. 120). Cambridge, MA: MIT Press

Chen Y F and Tjosvold D (2006) 'Participative leadership by American and Chinese managers in China: the role of relationships' *Journal of Management Studies* 43(8), pp. 1727–1752

Coase R H (1937) 'The nature of the firm' *Economica* 4(16), pp. 386–405

Drucker P F (1954) *The practice of management*. New York, NY: Harper and Brothers

——— (1993) *Concept of the corporation*. Piscataway, NJ: Transaction Publishers

Gaba D M (2010) 'Crisis resource management and teamwork training in anaesthesia' *British Journal of Anaesthesia* 105(1), pp. 3–6

Han Y, Kakabadse N K and Kakabadse A (2010) 'Servant leadership in the People's Republic of China: a case study of the public sector' *Journal of Management Development* 29(3), pp. 265–281

Heyes A and Kapur S (2009) 'An economic model of whistle-blower policy' *Journal of Law, Economics, and Organization* 25(1), pp. 157–182

Hobday M (2000) 'The project-based organisation: an ideal form for managing complex products and systems?' *Research Policy* 29(7), pp. 871–893

Kassing J W (2009) 'Breaking the chain of command: making sense of employee circumvention' *Journal of Business Communication* July 2009, 46(3), pp. 311–334

Mintzberg H (1980) 'Structure in 5's: a synthesis of the research on organization design' *Management Science* 26(3), pp. 322–341

Moschandreas M (1994) *Business economics*. London: Routledge

National Commission on the BP Deepwater Horizon Oil Spill and Offshore Drilling (2011) 'Deep Water: The Gulf Oil Disaster and the Future of Offshore Drilling'. Report to the President, January 2011, available from www.gpo.gov/fdsys/pkg/GPO-OILCOMMISSION/pdf/GPO-OILCOMMISSION.pdf accessed 21 December 2014

Palo S and Padhi N (2003) 'Measuring effectiveness of TQM training: an Indian study' *International Journal of Training and Development* 7(3), pp. 203–216

Rubin R S (2002) 'Will the real SMART goals please stand up' *The Industrial-Organizational Psychologist* 39(4), pp. 26–27

Slater R (2003) *29 Leadership Secrets from Jack Welch*. New York: McGraw-Hill

Standford (2015) Anesthesia Crisis Resource Management from Standford Medicine from med.stanford.edu/VAsimulator/acrm/ accessed 10 October 2015

Suehiro A (1993) 'Family business reassessed: corporate structure and late-starting industrialization in Thailand' *The Developing Economies* 31(4), pp. 378–407

Sunday Times (2010) 'Israeli nuclear whistleblower freed from jail again' by Jamie McGinnes 8 August 2010 from www.thesundaytimes.co.uk/sto/news/world_news/Middle_East/article366995.ece accessed 8 March 2015

Sy T and Côté S (2004) 'Emotional intelligence: a key ability to succeed in the matrix organization' *Journal of Management Development* 23(5), pp. 437–455

Tang C S, Zimmerman J D and Nelson J I (2009) 'Managing new product development and supply chain risks: the Boeing 787 case' *Supply Chain Forum: An International Journal* 10(2), pp. 74–86. KEDGE Business School

Tubaro P (2012) Introduction to social network analysis from University of Greenwich seminar, 26 March 2012 from www.chairereseaux.wp.mines-telecom.fr/files/2012/06/SNA.pdf accessed 4 December 2014

Vouzas F and Psychogios A G (2007) 'Assessing managers' awareness of TQM' *The TQM Magazine* 19(1), pp. 62–75

Part V Global Regulations and Finance

The globalisation of business has taken centuries to achieve, mainly due to interference from national governments who fear the imagined consequences of open borders. Some anxiety is justified: free trade means having a market that is accessible to foreign competitors who may bring down domestic firms before they bring new employment. Even worse than this, many argue, would be to have completely open borders that allow influxes of migrant workers who cause greater unemployment and are a strain on public resources. No matter how supportive theories might be of dismantling trade barriers for the long-term national good, the short-term reality is that people are afraid of the personal consequences of economic restructuring.

It seems slightly ironic, then, that the way to bring nations together in a spirit of openness is to regulate trade still further. Or rather, the steps towards free trade need to be controlled in order that the global transition can be an orderly one. The target is for all countries to be granted the status of most favoured nation (MFN), which means that they all have equality in trade to the same degree as the closest trading partner. For example, Canada and the United States have always traded liberally with each other but now, as part of NAFTA, member country Mexico has obtained the same privileges.

NAFTA is the North American version of a free trade agreement (FTA), a trade bloc that enjoys internal liberalisation of trade. By clubbing together in an FTA nations enjoy internal free trade but still put up barriers against countries outside the agreement area. Certain restrictions continue even within the area, such as those against the movement of labour across borders. Successively closer agreements include customs unions, common markets and, finally, full economic and fiscal union of the countries within the trade bloc. This would replicate the economic structure within some federal countries, but so far it is not an agreement that has been made between countries.

Overseeing the progression towards free trade is the World Trade Organisation (WTO). While it does not legislate as such it is able to bring governments together so that they can reach some sort of settlement. Nevertheless, it will be many years before trade barriers around the world are fully dismantled.

The most detailed regulations cover money matters. Countries have developed their own approaches to the principles of financial accounting according to their own economic needs. In Japan, for instance, banks are the main source of business funding, so accounting reports are generally biased towards their information requirements. This system worked agreeably well before globalisation integrated companies across national boundaries. National accounting principles act as a barrier to global business because they prevent the ready comparison of results reported under different jurisdictions. Clearly, what is needed is the harmonisation of accounting principles across the world but the negotiations towards this are proving as tortuous as they are for free trade.

At least global finance is less constrained. It is the job of the company's chief financial officer (CFO) to evaluate investment opportunities around the world, and there is little argument on how to do this.

The customary tools include returns on investment, capital, equity and so on, plus weighted average cost of capital (WACC) and the all-important net present value (NPV). The calculations may be challenging but they are the closest business analysis gets to being scientific. The results are intended to be incontrovertible in theory if not always in practice. Yet despite the prescribed methods that should render finance the dullest of business activities, it is also the one where the most notorious of reputations can be made.

13 The International Regulatory Framework

Chapter Objectives

The advantages of free trade for the economies, and businesses, of the world have been reasonably well accepted for many decades. Yet there is a lingering sense that an overnight abandonment of all trade barriers would destabilise many economies and be utterly ruinous for the weakest. Progress towards free trade is therefore painfully slow and in this chapter we will investigate the mechanisms at work:

- Impediments to free trade.
- Intermediate steps towards global free trade.
- Institutions for protecting and promoting global free trade.

IMPEDIMENTS TO TRADE

It is an axiom of globalisation that **free trade** should result in a net gain for global businesses. These gains may take some time to appear, and in the process there will be winners and losers, but overall, once the dust has settled, all consumers and all business should benefit. The businesses will be able to gain from specialisation and from economies of scale, while consumers make welfare gains in terms of higher product specifications, wider choices and lower prices.

There is, though, an obstacle in the way of this commercial nirvana: the world is made up of countries, and their denizens don't like to give away the wealth they have accumulated throughout their history. As consumers they are quite happy to receive the benefits of free trade, but as workers, employers and patriotic citizens they do not like to see their industries impoverished by more competitive foreign rivals.

THE CHIMERA OF FREE TRADE

Absolute and perfect free trade, so attractive in theory, will probably remain an illusion. There are a number of impediments standing in its way:

- Lack of perfect markets – in practice, no market is perfect.
- Temporal misalignment – progress towards free trade takes time for countries to adjust, some faster than others.
- Socio-political resistance – citizens have a preference for familiar, indigenous products and practices so they distrust any shift to unfamiliar alternatives from outside. Politicians defy this preference at the peril of their careers.

- Cultural differences – different groups of people have their own ways of doing things and products brought in from outside may not be accepted.

It is these obstacles to free trade that create friction between potential trading partners and prevent them realising the full benefits.

IMPERFECT MARKETS

Perfect markets have only ever existed in theory, but it is a theory with a long heritage, the great Frank Knight (1923) being one of its most famous articulators. The perfect market, or perfect competition, has no more chance of being found in the real world than does an economic paradise but the concept offers a standard to aim for; some markets may have actually achieved something close. A perfect market is one where no participant has the power to set prices, more specifically:

- **There are an infinite number of buyers and sellers** – thus the law of supply and demand has no effect on prices. Very large markets with a high number of operators may offer a close approximation of a perfect market, e.g. car dealerships throughout the United States.
- **All factors of production are perfectly mobile** – all industry locations have equal access to the same resources at the same prices. Difficult to achieve given national rules on immigration but the EU for one is working towards this.
- **There are no exit or entry barriers to the market** – those already operating in the market cannot raise entry costs to exclude new entrants, with the result that competition is never impeded. Equally, zero exit barriers mean that companies can dip a toe into a new market with the assurance that the experiment will have cost them nothing should they decide to quit. An absence of such barriers is only possible where there is negligible need to invest in trained staff or special machinery. There is some sense of non-barrier markets amongst ticket touts (illegal vendors), who tend to proliferate at large sports events.
- **All participants in the market have complete access to the relevant information** – no one can use early intelligence of developments to their advantage and there is no insider trading. It is surely too much to ask that all people know everything all at the same time, but more-or-less equal access to media channels indicates that most people can learn about news events with no advantages in when or what they learn. However, commercially sensitive information often has to be carefully regulated to prevent anyone gaining an advantage by accessing it early.
- **There are no transaction costs** – it costs nothing to do the deal, implying that any information obtained is comprehensive and costless. This would mean that spending time meticulously research- ing a product or conducting due diligence would bring no additional benefits.
- **Products are homogeneous** – meaning that no product has an advantage due to its unique or inimitable character. However, this is the polar opposite of what companies work for, differentiating their product in the market. It is probably the case that French Champagne is really no better than any other sparkling white wine of the same grape, but the producers would beg to differ!
- **Property rights are perfectly well defined** – business deals are transparent and not open to mis- interpretation. All dealings are contract free and costless.
- **Companies seek to maximise their profits** – production output is set at the point where marginal cost equals marginal revenue. Surprisingly, some companies exist for reasons other than maximis- ing profits; e.g. government-owned housing can charge below market rates of rent in order to help the poor.

- **Constant returns to scale** – larger firms have no cost advantage over smaller rivals. This may not seem likely in a world of giant corporations, but many types of restaurants and shops exist in all manner of sizes, i.e. there is no particular advantage in a restaurant being larger than its rivals.

As you can see, the perfect market is more of a theoretical ideal than an actual state of business. The purpose of the concept is to have it as the ultimate standard so then we can make comparisons with the current condition of the market. The principle gives us an idea of how far short a market might be of the perfect state.

RESTRICTED TRADE AND CORPORATE MANAGEMENT

Globalisation has brought us many of the benefits associated with perfect markets, yet is taken so much for granted that we often forget how much we would lose if trade were to become restricted. Trade liberalisation has brought us access to markets, market knowledge and local suppliers (Meixell and Gargeya, 2005). The loss of international free trade, or the approximation to it that we currently enjoy, would return us to an era of economic history where businesses were faced with numerous obstacles to their operations. They would have far less choice of suppliers and fewer sales opportunities, probably because they would be restricted to their home markets.

Trapped in small closed markets there would be a lack of wider competition which would mean that businesses, and their managements, would lose their competitive edges. Economies of scale might be unobtainable and there would be fewer funds available for investment in plant and product R&D. These relatively small firms would dissipate their resources on wider product ranges, compounded by the inability to specialise, thereby further reducing efficiency in production and learning effects. For those firms that are able to dominate their local market all the problems associated with monopolies may rear their ugly heads.

A lucky few firms may find that the closed markets in which they are domiciled are very large and relatively wealthy, the United States being a shining example. With plenty of sales opportunities and economies of scale, firms can refine their competitive strengths and develop into formidable corporations. This holds them in good stead when they start to explore overseas markets where, despite the trade barriers, they often bring with them indomitable advantages that suppress local rivals.

POLITICAL RESISTANCE TO THE PERFECT MARKET

Political interference in business is at its most pernicious when it comes to the mechanisms of the market. Liberalisation of markets inevitably gives rise to degrees of uncertainty with which political institutions are uncomfortable (Fernandez and Rodrik, 1991). There are five main reasons why governments baulk at the idea of a completely unfettered, free market:

- Economic development
- Power to influence corporate strategic control
- Collection of taxes
- Consumer protection
- Power of the electorate.

Apart from a few notable exceptions, almost all governments favour economic development based on home-grown talent. Although they may tolerate inflows of **foreign direct investment (FDI)** the government will often apply pressure, both explicit and implicit, on the incoming MNE to maximise the knock-on benefits for the wider economy. When this threatens property rights it can gravely undermine the desire to invest by an MNE, very much to the cost of countries like Zimbabwe (Busse and Hefeker, 2007). In extreme circumstances the government may even expropriate the local assets of the MNE through **nationalisation**. In circumstances where the firm is a domestic one then the government may nationalise it to promote it as an industrial champion, one that will serve as a foundation for the economy. Strategic industries like mining and steel production often fall prey to this kind of nationalisation. In Japan the government has historically attempted to create national champions by obliging small firms to merge and create large corporations.

A major concern of governments is that corporations, particularly the foreign owned, will have strategies that serve their business desires rather than the national economic needs. Political influence can be exercised by restricting the ability to make staff redundant or permitting new investment only where the government considers it would be best placed. Planning laws can be used in this way, most noticeably in many countries where the government wishes to control the location of large retail centres, offices or factories.

Taxation is another area where governments can restrict the free market. Although use of tariffs to slow down import volumes is waning with the advance of globalisation it is increasingly accepted that there are still industries which should be subjected to punitive rates of tax. The tobacco industry is a favourite target in developed economies, and there is also the occasional imposition of windfall taxes when profits in an industry are perceived as excessive. Equally, governments may proffer favourable tax rates to those industries that they want to encourage, particularly in the cases of an **infant industry** that is not yet developed enough to withstand world-class competition (Chang, 2003).

Perhaps one should not be quite so beastly to the politicians; they are not always interfering in the free market simply for the pleasure of wielding power. Consumers need legislation to protect them from **unfair trading** practices or poor quality standards. In addition, many products need to meet basic standards of **health and safety**. We might broaden this to include the protection of suppliers from intimidation by more powerful client corporations. Ultimately, of course, all governments are at the mercy of their citizens, although it may take the threat of revolution to make them remember it. Consequently, the domestic market will only be as perfect as the people want it to be.

STRUCTURAL IMPEDIMENTS TO THE PERFECT MARKET

Some markets are held back from perfection for structural reasons; to take one example, it is obvious that shipbuilding, by its very nature, exhibits increasing returns to scale and there are high barriers to entry or exit. It takes huge capital investment to enter the industry, and when the commercial rationale disappears there are equally huge challenges when attempting to exit, including redundancies and local economic devastation. Even though this means the shipbuilding market is far from perfect a manager can still use awareness of theoretical perfect market conditions in order to identify where improvements could be made, perhaps in the face of their own misgivings. Table 13.1 shows how each condition is currently manifested in shipbuilding and how the improvements might come.

The purpose of the exercise in Table 13.1 is not to show what will happen but to forewarn managers of the consequences of what might happen should industry deregulation and privatisation lead towards a more open market, if not a true perfect market. As part of this evaluation it would be useful to apply probabilities to each outcome in order to develop future scenarios and contingency plans.

Table 13.1 *Working towards a perfect market in shipbuilding*

Perfect Market Condition	Current Shipbuilding Market	Potential for Change
Infinite buyers and sellers	Small numbers of large fleet buyers and large shipbuilders.	Deregulation breaks up large fleets; privatisation of shipyards.
Mobile factors of production	Raw materials and components are traded globally. Labour less mobile.	Relaxation of labour laws brings greater labour flexibility.
Entry and exit barriers	High capital costs create high barriers.	New composite materials may require less capital investment and broadening of the supplier base.
Access to information	Generally transparent industry.	Information technology advances bring greater accessibility to global suppliers.
Transaction costs	Susceptible to sudden high costs due to economic volatility.	New financial services can smooth out the fluctuations.
Product homogeneity	Highly homogeneous product.	Modularisation of ship design allows shipyards to specialise.
Property rights	Long-established industry with few problems over property rights.	New entrants may emerge in countries with less rigorous property rights.
Profit maximisation	Often seen as a national champion attracting government subsidies with profits secondary.	Governments may be obliged to reduce subsidies.
Constant returns to scale	Increasing returns to scale except for specialist ships and luxury yachts.	New flexible manufacturing methods may lower the economies of scale.

MONOPOLIES

At the other extreme from the perfect market is the monopoly, an organisation that enjoys complete dominance of its market. This is either because it is the only supplier in the market, or it has such a high market share that no other operator can offer significant competition (OECD, 1993). Unlike the perfect market the monopoly is not a theoretical construct but a realistic market possibility.

Monopoly powers allow the company to select prices in the market without fear of competitive responses. It can also make decisions on product specification, which usually means that expensive, risky new product development is scaled back. The management will avoid any action that threatens the monopoly's incumbent power in the market. It is a comfortable position that rewards an unimaginative and risk-averse leadership style, and Table 13.2 lists some of the temptations for allowing a monopoly to emerge.

Monopolies decide on the price and specification of the product but this does not mean that they can charge any price they like. Although they are faced with a fairly inelastic demand curve, meaning that price rises will not result in much of a fall in demand, consumers still have limited budgets and the monopoly can only charge up to the consumer's willingness to spend. For example, if a national airline company raises its prices, the lack of substitutes means that at least some of its customers will simply decline to travel at all.

Beyond a certain point the monopoly pricing becomes self-defeating. Just like a company operating in a competitive market, a monopoly seeks to maximise its profits by ensuring that marginal

Table 13.2 *Monopoly conditions*

Monopoly Condition	Example
No substitute goods	Creative artists if they are sufficiently differentiated to the point of uniqueness, e.g. famous rock bands can charge monopoly prices for their live performances
Legal barriers preclude new entrants	a) Government – protecting a national champion for economic development or national security, e.g. defence manufacturers b) Patents – allow companies to charge monopoly prices for a limited period to fund product development, e.g. pharmaceuticals
Technological barriers	Company specific technical advances or product specific features, e.g. secret recipe for Coca-Cola
Economies of scale	If the economies of scale match the market capacity then there is room for just one supplier, e.g. NASA's Space Shuttle
Learning effects	Company continually develops its product ahead of the competition, e.g. social media like Twitter, Facebook
High capital costs	High investment requirement can inhibit new entrants e.g. aircraft industry
Incumbent pricing power	The sole or dominant supplier sets prices to its own advantage, e.g. dropping prices below economic cost for short periods (dumping) to expel weaker rivals
Incumbent power over suppliers	Monopoly manufacturer sets prices from suppliers, e.g. multinationals operating in low labour cost developing economies
Consumer loyalty	The company creates a highly differentiated brand image, e.g. French cognac versus generic brandy
Network economies	The company can hold monopoly powers by creating an industry standard, e.g. Microsoft Windows software

revenue equals marginal cost. There is little reason for it to inflate prices to a point where so many consumers flee the market that manufacturing output falls to the extent that production cost per unit actually rises.

In some cases, the prices charged by the monopoly can be lower than if there were competitors in the market forcing the pace. For example, if the company can access the benefits of economies of scale then the minimum production costs allow for relatively lower prices for the consumer, though the company can still be exercising monopoly pricing power at the same time.

Product specification may also improve if a company is given temporary monopoly powers in order to guarantee a return on its product development investment. Pharmaceutical firms are allowed a patent on their new drugs for around 15–20 years. During this period the firms can charge monopoly prices in order to maintain funding in new research. They may attempt to extend the patent by developing new variants of the drug, but they often face pressure to reduce prices, particularly in developing markets where high prices are often perceived as unethical.

Legal monopolies exist in other areas of creativity, such as intellectual property rights. In effect, an inventor or artist holds monopoly power over their creative output. This is usually balanced by the fact that most creative output is untried, so the pricing power in the market is unknown. Nevertheless, successful artists with an established track record for pricing can earn staggeringly large sums of money for their creations.

Governments may also create monopolies for their own purposes since it allows them to influence the management of the company. This is particularly important in matters of public utilities and national security, so it is very common to find that defence firms are state-owned, or very closely monitored by the government. It also allows the government to have close control over technical research projects, but in order to pay for this it allows the company to charge inflated prices for its products.

Generally, though, the great danger with monopolies is that they evolve in corporations that are more concerned with serving the needs of the management rather than the customers. With the inevitable drift towards high prices and low investment in new products the company can revel in high earnings. These are known as 'higher than **normal profits**', meaning that if competitors were to enter the market the rivalry would lead to a decrease in prices and then profit levels would be expected to decline. This result is not guaranteed since monopolies, having long evaded the pressures to be efficient, often settle into a surprisingly unprofitable condition. The introduction of competition into the market can, conversely, raise the profit levels for all the participants by promoting efficiency savings. Furthermore, not only does the customer gain by the lower prices but competition will also stimulate product development.

MONOPSONY

A monopsony is a condition where a single, dominating buyer now has the power, rather than the supplier's dominance we saw in a monopoly. The monopsony buyer can dictate, within certain limits, prices and product specification. They are also in a position to effectively decide on production volume, even if this is not their intent. A monopsony is often referred to as a buyer's monopoly.

Monopsony conditions emerge in cases where there is one large customer that comprises almost the entire market. Supermarket firms are often accused of acting like monopsonies with the fear that they will squeeze their suppliers for ever-deeper price cuts (Towill, 2005). This can result in the suppliers, such as farmers, lacking funds to invest in the future of their business and having to live on low personal incomes. Weakened by the power of the monopsony buyer the supplier may find they cannot then resist new, stronger entrants to their industry. Alternatively, the supplier may simply go out of business when the prices forced on them fall below their costs of production.

Governments will legislate against monopsonies by confining them to areas within which only competitors can open additional operations. The area is often measured by **isochrones**, lines of equal distance radiating out from the outlet. In the United States, new car dealerships are not allowed to have showrooms within a set distance of another dealership selling the same brand of car. To do so is considered encroachment of a relevant market area (Lafontaine and Morton, 2010). Some manufacturers have responded by increasing their outlets within their areas using the expedient of creating multiple brands. For example, upscale Hondas carry the Acura brand, though elsewhere in the world they are known by the Honda name.

Suppliers may also organise themselves at the local level, coming together in the form of co-operatives. This is commonly seen in agriculture, where farmers will join together to establish a central processing organisation, such as a storage facility, product distributer or marketing organisation. Japan Agriculture (JA) was established after World War II in order to improve food production after the ravages of conflict (Kazuhito, 2013). It was given wide-ranging powers covering the distribution of agricultural products as well as financial services. Its support of protective trade policies have minimised foreign imports of food, but this has also inhibited consolidation and investment in Japanese farming. As a consequence, Japanese consumers pay high prices and have less choice.

CASE STUDY: JAPAN AGRICULTURE

At the end of World War II the Japanese economy was shattered and there was a desperate need to get farms producing food for the near-starving population. An organisation already existed for controlling agricultural funding, and so the government adapted this into Japan Agriculture (JA), a co-ordinating body for farmers. Usually, an agricultural co-operative is founded by farmers for the sake of the farmers; it represents their interests and allows them to gain market power by acting as a single unit. JA, though, seems to have been acting according to its own agenda.

JA was instrumental in lobbying for high tariffs on imported food, most famously rice, which carries a 777.7% penalty compared with the locally grown varieties. Even during periods of harvest failures there is intense resistance to sales of imported rice, backed up by a cultural obsession with the high quality of the domestic crop. Shielded from cheap imports from Thailand and the United States, the more inefficient Japanese farmers have little incentive to leave the industry and sell their land to their more efficient neighbours. Farms have remained small with barely enough work for part-time farmers; their average age is 70 years old. In the shops, Japanese consumers are having to pay high prices for their staple food, but they are also denied the freedom to choose foreign varieties which are cheaper and, amazingly, just as tasty.

As farmers retire or simply die there is often no one in the family prepared to take on the work and so the fields are left vacant, further exacerbating the inefficiency of Japanese agriculture. One might expect JA itself to begin to shrink in step with farming but instead it has managed to increase its membership by offering various financial services. The organisation's bank is one of the top three in the country. JA currently has almost 10 million members and a headquarters workforce of around 240,000 people.

The main threat to JA's existence is the possible entry by Japan into the Trans-Pacific Partnership (TPP), a free trade agreement comprising some of the countries surrounding the Pacific, including the United States and Australia. Membership would allow cheap foreign rice into the country, to the benefit of local consumers. Japanese farmers would be forced to adjust and the least capable would be compelled to leave the industry. However, in the longer term, the more efficient farmers would be able to purchase land and expand their operations to further increase their efficiency. Ultimately, once the short-term pain has been overcome, both farmers and consumers should benefit from free trade.

Point of consideration: As a management consultant, how would you advise the Japanese rice farmers to consolidate? How could you convince some of them that they would be better leaving farming?

Sources: The Economist, 2013; Kazuhito, 2013

Just as monopolies are sometimes advantageous, so monopsonies are on occasion encouraged. This is usually at the national level, where the government is seeking to guarantee specific products at a predetermined price. In countries like Canada, with a publicly funded medical care system, the availability and cost of drugs can be closely controlled. If the government were attempting to co-ordinate a multitude of suppliers then the costs of oversight would be high. To combat this, the government will often instigate consolidation in the industry. In other countries, where the government is autocratic, both the supplier and buyer are under the same political influence. A good example of this is the defence industry, where it can result in a state-owned industry monopoly facing the government's own monopsony.

🔍 MANAGEMENT SPOTLIGHT: CAREER DEAD-END IN A MONOPOLY

Although businesses thrive in a stable economy they are stimulated by the dynamic competitive forces of rival companies and the demands of consumers. Monopolies and monopsonies act like a dead weight on the market, stifling competition and creating stagnant business conditions. They slow down the market and dampen the forces of change. Managers are then restricted in their strategic decisions, as they are obliged to accommodate the requirements to maintain the dominant market presence. In the case of state-controlled organisations the rationale of the company's existence may be public service rather than commercial profit, as Gordon (1991) found with the US telecommunications company, AT&T.

In these conditions it is difficult for managers to justify levels of investment that are comparable with rivals in more open markets. There is less incentive to develop new products and the manufacturing system may fall steadily behind the global standards. At the same time, the company will be expected to meet demand in its own market with a wide variety of products so that it becomes a jack-of-all-trades. An open market would allow it to specialise in a narrow range of goods, as foreign rivals would be able to make up the total variety of goods facing the consumer.

A restricted or closed market can also suffocate a business in other ways. There will be less choice of suppliers, which means that component price and specification may be less than the best that is available. Meanwhile, competitors in other countries may have access to the higher quality suppliers and will consequently benefit.

For managers working within a monopoly, their lives might appear easy, as they often enjoy security of employment. This balances a lack of financial incentives since the organisation does not place a high priority on measures of efficiency or financial returns. However, a lack of pressure to develop new technologies or to pursue efficiencies means that opportunities for professional advancement become rare.

There is a tendency in monopolies for the management structure to become **bureaucratic**, apparently creating work for itself rather than for the good of the consumer. This can prove demotivating for the most talented managers and they leave for other, more dynamic companies. When eventually the market is forced open, the once mighty monopolies are often amongst the first to collapse due to their uncompetitive products, bloated cost structures and bureaucratic management teams.

Point of consideration: AT&T suffered something of a corporate culture shock when it was released from the security of being a regulated monopoly to exposure to market competition. How could the managers have been incentivised to prepare the company for the change?

Source: Gordon, 1991

INSTITUTIONS FOR FREE TRADE

It is an irony that free trade, which is defined by an absence of market interference, needs to be protected by powerful institutions in order for it to flourish. The rationale behind this is that the economic logic of free trade will result in benefits for producers and consumers such that the system becomes self-sustaining. Since this often entails dismantling existing economic structures, eliminating vested interests and surviving an adjustment period, it can be a painful and forbidding process implementing the principles of free trade. Not all countries are up to the challenge.

To make the changeover period more palatable for the country, the economic advance is usually done in stages. At each progression, there are organisations at all levels whose purpose is to promote and protect the principles of free trade. The trading parties seek to grant each other **most favoured nation (MFN)** status, which means that they will enjoy the maximum trade benefits that any country could be given (Horn and Mavroidis, 2001). The organisations supporting free trade exist at the national, international and supranational levels. The early stages of moving to free trade usually comprise bilateral free trade agreements covering a limited number of traded goods, progressing in later stages to customs unions and ultimately full economic union joining the countries together into a single unit. Transcending these arrangements are the supranational institutions that oversee international economic issues.

Some of the more famous free trade areas will already be familiar, but in fact most of the countries of the world are covered by agreements of some sort. Figure 13.3 provides a selection of them.

From Table 13.3 it can be seen that whatever the resistance to free trade, almost all countries are members of at least one and Europe seems to have more than any. Despite their impressive credentials,

Table 13.3 *Global trade agreements*

Type	Characteristics	Agreement
FTA – Free Trade Agreement	• Zero tariffs between partner countries • No common external tariff • Rules of origin	NAFTA – North American FTA AFTA – ASEAN Free Trade Area CEFTA – Central European FTA CISFTA – Commonwealth of Independent States FTA COMESA – Common Market for Eastern and Southern Africa GAFTA – Greater Arab FTA SAFTA – South Asia FTA GCC – Gulf Cooperation Council SICA – Central American Integration System TPP – Trans-Pacific Partnership
CU – Customs Union	As FTA but also: • Common external tariff • No national trade policy	Mercosur – Southern Common Market CAN – Andean Community EAC – East African Community CUBKR – Customs Union of Belarus, Kazakhstan, and Russia EUCU – European Union Customs Union SACU – South African Customs Union
CM – Common Market	As FTA but also: • Internal free movement of labour and capital • Factor markets are unified • Common product regulation	EEA – European Economic Area EFTA – European Free Trade Association CES – Common Economic Space
Customs and Monetary Union	As CU but also: • Currency union	CEMAC – Economic and Monetary Community of Central Africa UEMOA – West African Economic and Monetary Union
EU – Economic Union	Combines CU and CM	CSME – Caribbean Single Market and Economy EU – European Union
Economic and Monetary Union	Combines EU with monetary union	EU – European Union (Eurozone); lacks fiscal union

none of them are any more powerful than the national governments that delegate to them limited sovereign powers. There are also a number of international organisations arrayed against them, lobbying to protect their clients wishes.

 MYTH BUSTER: IS THE EU THE HIGHEST FORM OF ECONOMIC INTEGRATION?

Curiously, there is a form of economic integration even more closely bound than the EU; it is called the United States. Strictly speaking, it is a federation of states with sovereign power allocated between federal and state authorities. Each has their own distinct area of jurisdiction and there should not be occasions where one is contradicting the other, although disagreements do occur.

The original thirteen British North American Colonies each had their own form of self-government but under the overall rule of the government in London. It was a disagreement with the central authority over taxes that united the colonies into the Revolutionary War, or War of American Independence. Even when British power had been ejected, the country remained a rather weak political confederacy until the federal government was formed in 1789.

Currency union did not occur until the federal government was safely in place, Philadelphia keeping its pound (not linked to the British currency) up to 1793. The challenges of implementing a national currency were remarkably similar to those experienced in Europe in more recent times with the creation of the Euro.

Although each state retains the right to raise taxes for their spending plans the US government has the power to levy federal taxes for national spending programmes as well. It is the fiscal union provided by the federal government, along with the monetary union of the US dollar, that distinguishes the US economy from the Eurozone, which has a monetary union but no fiscal union. In a sense, all countries that control their own taxes and currency are operating a type of economic and monetary union within their borders.

Point of consideration: Assess the implications of California leaving the monetary and fiscal union of the United States and becoming a member of the NAFTA trade area. What lessons are there for a European country leaving the Eurozone but remaining within the EU?

Sources: Sala-i-Martin X and Sachs J, 1991; Grubb, 2004

INTERNATIONAL FREE TRADE AGREEMENTS

At their most basic, **free trade agreements (FTA)** are made bilaterally between two governments looking to deregulate trade, though they may be limited in scope at the beginning. They do not extend to a common policy on external tariffs, which means that it is possible for importers to avoid the high tariffs in one country by shipping the goods through the low-tariff partner country, and then into the intended country with no further tariffs being paid. This can become very complicated when the imported goods are components used in the final assembly of another good. To combat this, the FTA partners will agree on rules of origin, specifying how much of a good should be locally manufactured in order to enjoy the FTA tariff arrangement.

The negotiations between the trading parties are often protracted as the two sides seek to balance their gains and losses with each other. This takes a lot of sensitive handling since any agreement needs the approval of politicians who may be reluctant to appear to be supporting a foreign industry over a domestic one. The power to regulate trade usually remains with the participating government, the only central organisation being essentially administrative. The final result, though, can be impressive, with substantial increases in trade between the countries (Baier and Bergstrand, 2007).

CASE STUDY: SOUTH KOREA AND THE UNITED STATES CREEP TOWARDS KORUS

KORUS FTA, the free trade agreement between the Republic of Korea and the United States, has been through some tortuous negotiations. The process started in early 2006 and concluded just over a year later. However, international negotiations are usually conducted between teams of delegates who are given authority only to move the process along; they do not have the right to put the agreement into effect. For this it is necessary for the treaty to be ratified by the two respective governments. It is the introduction of politics into the process that is so often the cause of hold-ups. The treaty negotiators may understand the rational argument for free trade but the politicians need to be seen to be defending the rights and livelihoods of their citizens.

The respective presidents Bush and Moo-hyun did indeed sign the agreement, but in the United States there were major problems over the threat posed by the South Korean car industry. On the other side, South Korean anxieties were related to their agricultural sector, which was seen as weak in comparison to that of the United States. This typifies the kind of conflict that occurs in trade negotiations: neither side wants to be seen to abandon a national industry. In fact it is this very abandonment, in return for concessions elsewhere, that allows the two countries to benefit from free trade.

After a string of further negotiations and assurances, the KORUS FTA went into effect in March 2013. It has been agreed that within five years 95% of bilateral trade will be free of tariffs and all remaining tariffs eliminated after ten years. Recognising that tariffs are not the only barriers to trade, the South Korean government has promised new legislation that will allow US financial firms to offer their services in the Asian republic. The United States believes the FTA will boost manufacturing jobs by 70,000 and rebalance the trade deficit in goods by US$3.3 billion. South Korea has already reported an increase of 10.4% in its exports to the United States directly attributable to the FTA.

Point of consideration: How could the KORUS negotiations have been made to progress faster? What would have been the political costs of such a move?

Sources: Office of the US Trade Representative, 2014a; US Korea Connect, 2014

If bilateral FTAs are challenging enough to negotiate, the difficulties increase exponentially for multilateral negotiations. The **North American Free Trade Agreement (NAFTA)** is a trilateral treaty between Canada, Mexico and the United States (USTR, 2014b). The idea for it was first tabled in 1986 and it was not signed until 1992 with still another two years before it came into force. The FTA was very controversial, particularly in Canada, where the majority of voters were opposed but the FTA-supporting party won because its backing was more unified. There were also deep fears in the southern states of the United States that manufacturing jobs would bleed south to Mexico where labour rates were lower, though they also hoped for a reduction in Mexican immigration. In the event, NAFTA brought economic benefits even if many of the details did not play out as planned (New York Times, 2007).

For businesses within a new FTA there is likely to be an initial period of adjustment. If they had a domestic scope to their operations before then they will find themselves thrust unceremoniously into international competition within the FTA. Some least competitive companies may lose their independence or go out of business altogether, but the more competitive ones will expand their sales in the new markets and benefit from increasing returns to scale.

In preparation for a country entering an FTA, business managers will need to engage in intensive evaluation of the company's competencies as well as a detailed scan of the new, broader competitive environment. This will involve all aspects of business management, including value and supply chain analysis, risk assessments and so on.

FTA IN MATURITY

An FTA allows the partner countries to benefit from trade in the usual way, once they have gone through the adjustment period. However, there is the fear that third-party countries will use the partner country with the lowest import tariffs as a low-cost route into the free trade area. The country of origin rules designed to combat this are costly to monitor and over time lose their relevance as companies from third-party countries establish operations in different parts of the free trade area. For example, VW of Germany has two car manufacturing plants inside NAFTA, one under its own brand name in the United States and the other under the Audi brand in Mexico.

Although a free trade area allows countries to specialise it also brings enough mutual benefits that the national economies can converge. The pattern of their trade then resembles the international trade that occurs between fully developed countries, with all partner countries exchanging both labour- and capital-intensive goods. Once this point has been reached there is no longer a need for partner countries to have their own tariff structures protecting selected national industries. The period of the FTA has raised all the partner countries to a level where they can compete internationally. The weight of the economic argument pushes the FTA countries to upgrade their agreement to that of a customs union.

CUSTOMS UNION

In a **customs union (CU)** the partner countries agree to an FTA between themselves, with the addition of a shared tariff structure with external parties. This abolishes the need for rules of origin and relieves the cost of policing the imports. It means that all the hard work is done with the implementation of the FTA, the CU emerging as a natural evolutionary step. Nevertheless, progress may be slow.

Mercosur, or Southern Common Market, began in 1991 as an FTA for South America with Brazil as the dominant partner (Klonsky et al., 2012; BBC, 2012). The purpose has always been to progress towards complete economic and political union but progress is slow, so far attaining only customs union status. The common external tariff has been set high, at around 35%, and this is holding back the development of trade with other countries. There are also internal political tensions, with Paraguay suspended in 2012 and the entry of Venezuela threatening to destabilise the trade bloc. A common currency, the gaucho, is planned but momentum towards it has slowed.

For business managers there is more time to prepare for a CU than during entry to an FTA. It is likely that the CU will have been preceded by an FTA, and so managers could suitably restructure the corporate operations to be more international in their scope. The CU should not introduce significant additional threats after the FTA but rather bring greater transparency to the way the free trade area works.

COMMON MARKET

A common market seeks to intensify the internal business relationships of the partner countries. In addition to reducing the trade tariffs it also attempts to level the playing field for business by allowing free movement of **labour** and **capital**. No company within the common market should be at a disadvantage over **factors of production** because all companies will enjoy the same access. The result should be an efficient allocation of factors of production and therefore cheaper prices.

The relatively high level of integration necessary for a common market means that there needs to be a powerful political force behind it. Canada is a federation of ten provinces and three territories. Unusually, a law guaranteeing free movement of people, goods, services and investment (Agreement on Internal Trade) was very late coming: it did not come into force until 1995. So not only is Canada a sovereign nation; it is also a common market (Government of Canada, 2014).

By this stage in the progression towards comprehensive free trade, most managers and their businesses will be accustomed to competing in an international arena, if one that encompasses a limited number of countries. A common market is another step towards replicating global free trade, only with the restricted geography of the region affected. Companies can sell products throughout the regional market with minimal modification, although as always they are faced by the competition from partner countries enjoying the same benefits. For all parties, the ability to access factors of production throughout the region means they have a much wider choice of employees and funding.

CUSTOMS AND MONETARY UNION

A step on from the customs union is one that includes a monetary union, which means creating a **common currency**. To achieve this each of the partner countries must give up control of its own currency and join with the other countries in the union. This can have a huge political and economic impact. Governments can no longer use interest rates as a tool for expanding or contracting their own economies. They also lose control of their currency exchange rates, so they will not be able to influence the prices of imports and exports as part of their economic strategies.

At company level the impact of the closer trading relationship is much less marked. Although managers will no longer have to deal with exchange rate risks their threat is often overestimated. Sweden and the UK are two EU members that have not joined the Eurozone monetary union but have not directly suffered as a result. This is because the international financial markets have evolved services that can help companies to cope with the uncertainty of exchange rates, such as the use of hedges. Monetary union as an addition to a CU does not, by itself, impact greatly on the work of company managers.

ECONOMIC UNION

When a common market is combined with a customs union to regulate the trade bloc's external trading relations then we have an economic union. For the internal market, it means that companies can compete with each other on equal terms, facing the same product regulations and having access to the same factors of production.

Company managers will find that it no longer makes any sense to focus on the domestic market since it no longer exists in any real legal sense. Their own government may be the sovereign power, but many laws concerning commerce will be made centrally by the supranational administration for the union. This is not to say that all obstacles to business have been removed since there may still be some social or locational issues. For particularly sensitive items, such as food and finance, people often prefer to buy from domestic firms. Established domestic firms also retain a home advantage in their close relationship with the local market, which can be difficult for firms from other partner countries to overcome. Nevertheless, the opportunities are there throughout the region for firms prepared to take the plunge.

ECONOMIC AND MONETARY UNION

Generally, this is the level of trade agreement which almost eradicates the definition of the country altogether. As with economic union, almost all the most important regulations concerning business are now conducted centrally, and so companies can compete with each other on equal terms, no matter where they might be located within the region. Furthermore, monetary union means that the most important decisions concerning interest rates and international exchange rates are beyond the control of the national governments.

The last vestige of national government control concerns fiscal policy, which is government spending funded by taxation and debt. Normally, fiscal policy works in parallel with monetary policy, but in a monetary union the two can come into direct conflict. This is precisely the problem that has beset the Eurozone since the start of the global financial crisis. Within the **Eurozone**, monetary policy is conducted by the **European Central Bank** (ECB, 2014), while fiscal policies remain under the control of national governments. This can create a situation where one country can exploit a period of low interest rates, for example, to accumulate large public debts. When it finds it is unable to service the debts, perhaps when interest rates begin to rise or the economy falls into recession, then there is a danger that it will default on the loans.

Companies are not directly affected by the tension between monetary and fiscal policy, but the indirect impact of economic changes can be pernicious. If governments are struggling to pay their debts then they may have to raise the rate of corporation tax, which can dramatically increase costs to businesses. For companies, this demands the kind of crisis management that would be needed during any other economic drama and can oblige it to restructure substantially. This may even require the firm to close down domestic operations and move them to other locations, both inside and outside the union.

SUPRANATIONAL ORGANISATIONS

As we have seen, within many of the trade blocs there are organisations that take on the duties normally retained by national, sovereign governments. The decision-making processes that are devolved in this way vary in their power. In FTAs these supranational organisations are little more than administrators, publishing information and facilitating negotiations. The real activity of negotiating and implementing the deregulation of trade is conducted by the partner countries. As the trading bloc becomes more defined the central administration gains power. Once full economic and monetary union is achieved then the two major areas left where national governments exercise political power is over domestic laws and foreign relations. The only step after this would be for the states to merge into unified countries.

Just as the ultimate purpose of these trading blocs is to achieve complete global free trade, so there will need to be supranational bodies in place to administer and govern. Some of these institutions already exist, such as the United Nations, but the three of interest to the business world are the International Monetary Fund (IMF), World Bank and the WTO. The three organisations have their roots in the 1944 **Bretton Woods** conference. They do not generally work directly with companies but they can have significant influence in reshaping the business environment.

International Monetary Fund (IMF)

The purpose of the IMF is to promote stability in the trading relations between countries (IMF, 2014). This entails the surveillance of monetary policies and exchange rates, intervening when these reach unmanageable levels, as during a balance of payments crisis. It can assist countries by loaning them foreign exchange currencies but these usually come with conditions attached: in order to root out underlying problems the IMF often imposes stringent restrictions on government spending and obligations for increases in taxation.

It is a criticism of the IMF that these remedial actions can seem punitive, forcing the government to cut back on economic development programmes and shifting a greater financial burden onto already distressed taxpayers. In the IMF's defence, it is usually being consulted at a time when the country in question has exhausted all other avenues and is in a desperate predicament requiring emergency action. The country does not have to accept the IMF's plan and, in any case, it could be argued that the IMF is only instructing the government to cut back where it should not have been spending in the first place. Governments often find it politically expedient to blame the IMF for the severity of the remedial strategy even while implementing it. In many cases the IMF reforms are lost in the political machinations of the country (Stone, 2004).

Business managers have little influence over IMF actions. Before the IMF intervenes in the economy the company will be attempting to ride out the financial storm, so the managers will be in survival mode. All their attention will be focused on running the business day-to-day with scant regard for the uncertainties of the long-term economy. The arrival of the IMF does not mark the end of the instability because this may lead to massive restructuring of the economy. Not only retail sales but also business supply contracts and government spending can be severely reduced. However, the future will come into much sharper focus, as government policies will be clarified by the IMF's requirements. Managers can then start to make long-term plans based on their scans of the business environment.

World Bank

The World Bank's aim is to help developing countries put in place the foundation stones of economic progress by providing loans for infrastructure, sanitation, healthcare, education and the promotion of social equity. The **World Bank Group** should not be confused with the bank itself; the group is an umbrella organisation comprising The World Bank, the International Finance Corporation (IFC), the International Centre for Settlement of Investment Disputes (ICSID) and the Multilateral Investment Guarantee Agency (MIGA).

The World Bank is actually made up of two organisations (World Bank, 2014):

- **International Bank for Reconstruction and Development (IBRD)** – loans to middle-income developing countries.
- **International Development Association (IDA)** – loans to the poorest developing countries.

The two organisations work closely with each other and are essentially two sides of the same institution. They recognise that developing countries are caught in a poverty trap: the lack of valuable assets means that commercial loans are available only at very high rates of interest, which further suppresses their economic development and prevents them from creating the valuable assets to be eligible for loans. The World Bank attempts to break this vicious cycle by offering loans at lower interest rates that then permit sustainable development. Once lifted out of the poverty trap the country can attract commercial loans at under sustainable conditions.

Thanks to its robust financial foundation, IBRD has the highest credit rating available and as a consequence can obtain investment funds at the best rates. This enables it to make loans to the governments of middle-income developing countries at the same rates as would be available to developed countries. It also offers a range of financial products such as currency swaps and guarantees to private projects.

The IDA makes loans to the world's least developed nations, sometimes known as fragile countries. These countries find it impossible to repay commercial loans even on the best terms, so the IDA's loans are concessional or **soft loans**, often carrying zero interest. There is a clear mismatch between the high risk of the borrower and the low rate of interest, so the IDA requires frequent injections of cash from its wealthier members to cover the losses. These top-ups invite criticism of the IDA by the wealthy funding countries who consider that much of the money is wasted by corrupt governments. However, it is inevitable that the poorest countries will also have the least developed institutions, so a higher degree of fund wastage probably has to be accepted as part of the development process (Weiss, 2007).

World Bank funding can directly benefit companies connected to national **infrastructure** investments, such as the construction industry. It also provides an indirect boost to companies throughout the economy, permitting managers to engage in long-term planning thanks to the reliability of the infrastructure and the sustainability of economic growth. Even though the World Bank funding is intended for government projects, the private finding commitment can also be guaranteed, further aiding in the formulation of company strategies.

Another member of the World Bank Group, the **International Finance Corporation (IFC)**, can assist directly with companies. It shares the vision of the World Bank Group for the reduction of poverty and it does this by offering financial services to the private sector (IFC, 2015a). The IFC can be thought of as a commercial financial organisation with a strong ethical lending policy. Managers looking to obtain a loan must demonstrate that the project will alleviate poverty based on a rational business case. In return they will receive specialised advice and funding at market rates. A loan from the IFC is a stamp of approval that the borrower has reached a level of financial sustainability. Indeed, the borrower could seek funding from any other commercial lender on broadly similar terms.

WTO

The WTO (WTO, 2014) went through the most prolonged birth of the Bretton Woods institutions, not surprising since it directly targeted global free trade. Even though countries, and politicians, may accept the advantages of free trade they are still reluctant to take responsibility for selling it to their own citizens. Allowing countries to specialise in economic activities where they are strong inevitably implies they must relinquish activities where they are weak. This involves an adjustment period with industry closures and rising unemployment and no apparent guarantee that the remaining industries will pick up the economic slack at the same speed.

While the other Bretton Woods institutions got off to a flying start, international agreement on trade was much more protracted. Attempts were made in 1946 to establish the **International Trade Organisation (ITO)**, but when this failed in 1950 the only other alternative was the **General Agreement on Tariffs and Trade (GATT)**, which had been signed in 1947. Although it began as a multilateral agreement, it subsequently took on the duties of an institution for free trade. Through a tortuous series of further rounds of negotiation, eight altogether, the final Uruguay Round concluded in 1994. It represented a convergence on the closest agreement to global free trade so far seen, and GATT became a full-fledged institution in the form of the WTO in 1995.

Like all the supranational organisations that came out of the Bretton Woods Conference, the WTO oversees government-level relationships. Its purpose is to encourage the liberalisation of trade while allowing for protection of consumers and vulnerable industries. All member countries of the WTO accord each other most favoured nation (MFN) status so that they extend the same trading rights to all countries equally.

As an institution the WTO has no power of its own but instead works as a forum for negotiation, bringing aggrieved parties together in a government-to-government discussion. The negotiation cannot be dragged out to the advantage of one party, agreement must be reached within a year, and the conclusion should be binding and transparent.

While the WTO cannot enforce a judgement on the parties, it can sanction the corrective action of one government against another. For example, if one country is accused of **dumping** its goods in the market of another (i.e. selling them for below cost prices in order to eliminate local competition) then the opposing country can apply countervailing duties that raise the market price of the imported goods. It is through this mechanism that the price of the imported good is lifted to a point where it might be considered fair, though this is also an opportunity for the importing country to take its revenge by raising the price to an uncompetitive level.

The role of the WTO is abstracted from the world of business in that it promotes the principles of free trade within which companies can compete on an equal footing; the WTO does not directly interact with companies. This might indicate that there are no managerial implications at the company level, but the WTO does allow for some protection of vulnerable industries. During the progression towards free trade industries adjust at different rates. Not only does this depend on the nature of the industry itself but also the extent of the advantage enjoyed by corporations in developed economies. WTO allows for limited protection of **infant industries**, those that have recently started and have yet to evolve to a standard where they can compete globally.

Infant industries are vulnerable to competition from established multinationals due to market imperfections and high economies of scale. WTO-sanctioned protection gives companies an adjustment period during which the managers should plan for the ultimate reduction in the tariffs and loss of their protected status. They need to use this time to thoroughly evaluate the competitive landscape and prepare the company for full exposure to international competition.

RAISING EMPLOYABILITY: IMPROVING MANAGEMENT IN DEVELOPING ECONOMIES

In developing economies it is not only companies that are caught in a poverty trap; managers too are in a skills and experience trap. In order to lead their companies to a sustainable future they need to gain the same kinds of skills and experience that benefit managers in the developed economies. Sadly, because the companies that could offer these opportunities to learn barely exist in their countries the managers are unable to gain the experience that could create such companies. Held back by this vicious circle of low experience and poor opportunities managers in developing economies are condemned to a being permanently disadvantaged.

Even emerging economies that have taken a lead in rapid development lack many of the basic managerial skills. A report from ACCA found that China has around 130,000 qualified accountants across the public and private sectors, far short of the 300,000 that would normally be expected. The same report stated that across Africa there were difficulties in attracting and retaining qualified staff (ACCA, 2010).

One of the IFC's roles is to invest in management skills in developing economies and so equip managers with the skills to compete with the rest of the world. The IFC supports a number of innovative student funding programmes, including crowdfunding and social impact bonds (IFC, 2015b). In Chile, for example, the IFC supports Duoc UC, a commercial organisation that extends loans to students who cannot afford conventional bank loans. The maximum loan is US$4500 per year and the payback period is related to the length of study. It has found particular appeal amongst working adults looking to enhance their employability by taking night classes.

Local training schemes will encourage the organic growth of management skills, but the transfer of knowledge can be accelerated by sending experienced managers from developed economies. The UK does this through its Voluntary Service Overseas (VSO) programme, seeking managers with at least four years' experience and a relevant qualification (VSO, 2015). Not only does this transfer management skills to the developing nation but the volunteer gains valuable experience at the same time. This is a rare and heartening example of how co-operation between developing and developed economies can enhance the employability of managers on both sides.

 WEB SUPPORT

1. Perfect Competition. Presented by Dr. Mary J. McGlasson, this is Episode 26 of a series of online lessons. It starts with a restatement of perfect markets and then takes you step-by-step through the whole price/competition story. The video assumes knowledge of the other episodes but they might be worth checking out as well.

    www.youtube.com/watch?v=61GCogalzVc

2. There's No Such Thing as an Unregulated Market. An article by Howard Baetjer Jr, economics lecturer at Towson University, published on The Freeman website on 14 January 2015. You might think that only governments regulate but the market itself regulates as well, weighing on price as well as quality. Indeed, the article argues that governments interfere with that natural regulation to everyone's detriment.

    www.fee.org/freeman/detail/theres-no-such-thing-as-an-unregulated-market

3. Free Trade Agreements. The European Commission lists the EU's free trade agreements, both already in effect and those that are a work in progress. Includes background data on each FTA so a useful research tool, if lacking in critical perspectives.

    www.ec.europa.eu/enterprise/policies/international/facilitating-trade/free-trade/index_en.htm

THE STORY SO FAR: REGULATING THE FREEDOM TO TRADE

The benefits of free trade have been articulated for decades, but there is still a degree of trepidation in those countries wanting to take the plunge. It requires the economy to undergo a painful restructuring as long established, even historic, industries are allowed to decline if they are uncompetitive on the global stage. In their place will grow new industries in which the country is competitive, but it is difficult to know how or when these industries will appear. Understandably, the people of those countries fear for their personal futures and their politicians have little stomach for accelerating the liberalisation of trade. Instead, countries take a step-by-step approach, forming progressively closer trade blocs. At the international level there are institutions charged with bringing coherence to trade relationships or stimulating trade with financial support. A great deal of this support is targeted at developing economies with a view to bringing them into the global trade network and, in the best traditions of international trade, benefiting all sides.

Project Topics

1. China became a member of the WTO at the end of 2001. What advantages has membership brought to the economy, and why do you think it did not join the organisation earlier?
2. Without the help of supranational organisations like World Bank and WTO how could developing countries progress economically under conditions of free trade?
3. Why are the Eurozone countries reluctant to complete their economic union with common fiscal policies? If fiscal union were to take place, what new problems would emerge?

CASE STUDY – FTA AND DEVELOPING ECONOMIES

The inclusion of Mexico within NAFTA was the source of both hope and fear. Hope that membership would pull the Mexican economy up towards the lofty heights of the United States and Canada, fear that the new industries in Mexico would steal jobs from the southern states of the United States. However, the liberalisation of trade does not always turn out as expected, and while the FTA has clearly boosted the Mexican economy, it was not in the way that was originally thought.

Prior to NAFTA coming into force Mexico had attempted to promote economic development through government-controlled industrialisation, supporting those specific industries involved in import substitution and imposing restrictions on foreign firms. Manufacturers enjoyed financial subsidies and high domestic prices for their products. Although broadly successful, industrialisation did occur and imports were substituted, nevertheless exports were limited and in later years it proved too difficult to substitute for high technology imports. A financial crisis for the government in the early 1980s meant that it could no longer afford to be so generous.

The government changed tack and decided to widen the scope of economic development through trade liberalisation. In 1990 it began negotiating to join NAFTA and finally achieved its aim in 1994. In the ensuing years Mexico was able to build on the pre-NAFTA momentum and continue its economic development through increasing exports. Where once oil exports had dominated, growing industrialisation meant that manufactured products came to the fore. Foreign firms were allowed free rein to invest and the country was able to catch up in technology.

The experience of Mexico seems to suggest that an FTA between a developed country and a developing one can accelerate economic development in the poorer partner. Perhaps the nearest examples are the countries of Eastern Europe that are entering the EU. However, before joining their trade blocs, they and Mexico had already put in place industrialisation strategies, albeit ones that were running out of steam.

Many of the poorest nations in the world are not even at this stage and do not, in any case, have a close neighbour that is economically developed. For many of the nations of Africa, with their almost total absence of industrialisation, an FTA with a rich country may simply condemn them to the position of an economic colony. Trade liberalisation may indeed raise living standards, but at the price of ceding control of their economic destiny. It is these countries that are caught in a poverty trap, and it is for this reason that they need, and deserve, special attention. The question then is how a solution can be articulated within the structure of an FTA.

Point of consideration: If Kenya were to enter an FTA with the US, how would you expect the trade liberalisation to impact on Kenya's coffee industry? What other FTA partnership could more effectively accelerate economic development in the African country?

Source: Moreno-Brid et al., 2005

? MULTIPLE CHOICE QUESTIONS

1. There is no such thing as a perfect market in the real world because:
   a. Consumers are irrational and will purchase items on a whim.
   b. It is a theoretical construct, although the principles underlie all markets.
   c. New products upset the established equilibrium in the market.

2. Monopolies are always bad.
   a. True – they can raise prices at their own convenience.
   b. True – they put a freeze on new product development as there are no competitors.
   c. False – as national champions they can support wider economic development.

3. When is regulation a positive influence on markets?
   a. When health and safety laws protect consumers.
   b. When it holds prices to a fair level.
   c. When it ensures there is no waste from over-production.

4. Is a successful firm one that can earn above-normal profits?
   a. Yes – the purpose of a business is to earn higher profits than the competition.
   b. No – the advantage is brief and lasts only until the competition responds.
   c. Yes – the higher profits will attract new investment.

5. When is a monopsony good for consumers?
   a. When the lone buyer is an institution that brings stability to production and prices.
   b. When the buyer forces prices below the cost of production.
   c. When the monopsony is working with a monopoly.

6. Under the rules of global free trade, which country has most favoured nation status (MFN)?
   a. The United States.
   b. Wealthy trading countries, i.e. members of the OECD.
   c. All trading countries should be accorded MFN status.

7. What feature is NAFTA missing that prevents it from being a customs union?
   a. Zero tariffs between the member countries.
   b. Rules on country of origin.
   c. A common set of external tariffs.

8. Where can we observe complete economic and monetary union in practice?
    a. The United States.
    b. ASEAN.
    c. The Eurozone.

9. How does the World Bank promote global free trade?
    a. It regulates on how international business should be conducted.
    b. It invests in poorer countries to improve their terms of trade.
    c. It promotes economic development so that countries can afford to import more goods.

10. Why does the WTO allow certain cases of protectionism?
    a. Wealthier countries dominate the organisation and set trade rules to their own advantage.
    b. The organisation lacks its own regulatory powers to prevent protectionism.
    c. Infant industries in developing economies need protection until they can compete globally on equal terms.

Answers
1b, 2c, 3a, 4b, 5a, 6c, 7c, 8a, 9b, 10c

REFERENCES

Association of Chartered Certified Accountants (ACCA)(2010) Improving public sector financial management in developing countries and emerging economies from www.accaglobal.com/content/dam/acca/global/PDF-technical/public-sector/tech-afb-ipsfm.pdf accessed 12 March 2015

Baier S L and Bergstrand J H (2007) 'Do free trade agreements actually increase members' international trade?' *Journal of International Economics* 71(1), pp. 72–95

BBC (2012) Profile: Mercosur - Common Market of the South 15 February 2012 from www.news.bbc.co.uk/1/hi/world/americas/5195834.stm accessed 14 November 2014

Busse M and Hefeker C (2007) 'Political risk, institutions and foreign direct investment' *European Journal of Political Economy* 23(2), pp. 397–415

Chang H J (2003) 'Kicking away the ladder: infant industry promotion in historical perspective' *Oxford Development Studies* 31(1), pp. 21–32

European Central Bank (ECB)(2014) Homepage from www.ecb.europa.eu/home/html/index.en.html accessed 14 November 2014

The Economist (2013) 'With fewer, bigger plots and fewer part-time farmers, agriculture could compete' *The Economist*, 13 April 2013 from www.economist.com/news/asia/21576154-fewer-bigger-plots-and-fewer-part-time-farmers-agriculture-could-compete-field-work accessed 5 October 2014

Fernandez R and Rodrik D (1991) 'Resistance to reform: status quo bias in the presence of individual-specific uncertainty' *The American Economic Review* pp. 1146–1155

Gordon G G (1991) 'Industry determinants of organizational culture' *Academy of Management Review* 16(2), pp. 396–415

Government of Canada (2014) Agreement on Internal Trade from www.ic.gc.ca/eic/site/081.nsf/eng/home accessed 14 November 2014

Grubb F (2004) 'The circulating medium of exchange in colonial Pennsylvania, 1729–1775: new estimates of monetary composition, performance, and economic growth' *Explorations in Economic History* 41(4), pp. 329–360

Horn H and Mavroidis P C (2001) 'Economic and legal aspects of the Most-Favored-Nation clause' *European Journal of Political Economy* 17(2), pp. 233–279

International Finance Corporation (IFC)(2015a) Homepage from www.ifc.org/wps/wcm/connect/corp_ext_content/ifc_external_corporate_site/home accessed 15 March 2015

_____(2015b) Student finance: learning from global best practice and financial innovation from www.ifc.org/wps/wcm/connect/7fd7c8804783059296b2f7299ede9589/Student+Finance+Brochure_FINAL_web.pdf?MOD=AJPERES accessed 12 March 2015

International Monetary Fund (IMF)(2014) Homepage from www.imf.org/external/index.htm accessed 14 November 2014

Kazuhito Y (2013) 'Understanding the Japan Agricultural Cooperatives' in Nippon.com 30 July 2007 from www.nippon.com/en/currents/d00082/ accessed 5 October 2014

Klonsky J, Hanson S and Lee B (2012) 'Mercosur: South America's fractious trade bloc' Council on Foreign Relations from www.cfr.org/trade/mercosur-south-americas-fractious-trade-bloc/p12762#p9 accessed 5 October 2014

Knight F H (1923) 'The ethics of competition' *The Quarterly Journal of Economics* pp. 579–624

Lafontaine F and Morton F S (2010) 'Markets: state franchise laws, dealer terminations, and the auto crisis' *The Journal of Economic Perspectives* pp. 233–250

Meixell M J and Gargeya V B (2005) 'Global supply chain design: a literature review and critique' *Transportation Research Part E: Logistics and Transportation Review* 41(6), pp. 531–550

Moreno-Brid J C, Santamaria J and Rivas Valdivia J C (2005) 'Industrialization and economic growth in Mexico after NAFTA: the road travelled' *Development and Change* 36(6), pp. 1095–1119

New York Times (2007) 'NAFTA should have stopped illegal immigration, right?' by Uchitelle L in *New York Times*, 18 February 2007 from www.nytimes.com/2007/02/18/weekinreview/18uchitelle.html accessed 11 March 2015

OECD (1993) 'Glossary of Industrial Organisation Economics and Competition Law.' Khemani R S and D. M. Shapiro D M (eds.), commissioned by the Directorate for Financial, Fiscal and Enterprise Affairs, OECD, 1993 from www.stats.oecd.org/glossary/detail.asp?ID=3262 accessed 18 October 2015

Sala-i-Martin X and Sachs J (1991) 'Fiscal federalism and optimum currency areas: evidence for Europe from the United States' Working Paper No. w3855) from National Bureau of Economic Research from www.core.ac.uk/download/pdf/6586898.pdf accessed 10 March 2015

Stone R W (2004) 'The political economy of IMF lending in Africa' *American Political Science Review* 98(04), pp. 577–591

Towill D R (2005) 'A perspective on UK supermarket pressures on the supply chain' *European Management Journal* 23(4), pp. 426–438

US Korea Connect (2014) Home page from www.uskoreaconnect.org/ accessed 5 October 2014

US Trade Representative (USTR)(2014a) U.S. - Korea Free Trade Agreement: New Opportunities for U.S. Exporters Under the U.S.-Korea Trade Agreement from www.ustr.gov/trade-agreements/free-trade-agreements/korus-fta accessed 5 October 2014

_____ (2014b) North American Free Trade Agreement (NAFTA) from www.ustr.gov/trade-agreements/free-trade-agreements/north-american-free-trade-agreement-nafta accessed 14 November 2014

Voluntary Service Overseas (2015) Volunteering opportunities overseas for business managers from www.vso.org.uk/volunteer/opportunities/management-business-and-it/business-managers accessed 12 March 2015

Weiss M A (2007) 'The World Bank's International Development Association (IDA)' from Congressional Information Service, Library of Congress from www.fpc.state.gov/documents/organization/84308.pdf accessed 12 March 2015

World Bank (2014) Homepage from www.worldbank.org/ accessed 14 November 2014

World Trade Organisation (WTO)(2014) Homepage from www.wto.org/ accessed 14 November 2014

14 International Accounting

Chapter Objectives

A crucial aspect of international business is to keep track of progress in strategies and operations. Fundamentally, this means knowing where the money is coming from and where it is going; accounting is the final arbiter on whether the money flows are going well. In this chapter, we will look at the accounting issues for international business and evaluate possible alternatives:

- Profit as the purpose of business.
- Accounting for stakeholders.
- Disclosure and deceit.
- International accounting issues.
- International taxation.

PROFIT AND THE ART OF MAKING MONEY

Accounting is a system for monitoring the performance of a corporation using objective metrics, usually with a financial basis. As far as possible the data that is produced should be incontrovertible. In other words, the figures should be valid (measure what they are supposed to) and reliable (produce results in the same way each time). The ultimate purpose, according to the Federal Accounting Standards Advisory Board in the United States, is to produce a fair and representative record of the state of the corporation expressed in financial terms which are consistent with generally accepted principles (FASAB, 2014).

Given that all firms, whatever their size or industry, must ultimately make a profit to the satisfaction of the owners one might think that the reporting of that profit should be a simple enough process. Indeed, at its most basic the profit is simply the difference between the revenue being earned and the costs of running the business. This simple equation ought to be the definitive method of indicating whether the firm is making money. As always in business, though, it is not quite that simple.

Whether a business is profitable (i.e. making money) depends on the type of business operation being undertaken at the time, the time frame being considered and the interests of the stakeholders. If we look at each of these in turn, we can see how a sustainable and healthy company might report variable profits:

- **Business activity** – at its core, a company needs to make money in its business operations. Thus the cost of production must be met by the revenue of sales. However, output will fluctuate as part of the business cycle. Other activities might never make money by their nature, such as administrative support functions, product development and marketing.
- **Time frame** – during the start-up period the company might be sucking in funds from investors and not be reporting any positive cash flows. Once the operations have normalised, at least this area

should be cash positive, although the burden of debt could drag down final profits for an extended period. With maturity, the company should be earning more than it is costing, but this may change if large new investment opportunities require further financial inputs.

- **Stakeholder interest** – the focus will be on the particular area of the business in which the stakeholders have an interest. Employees, for example, will want to know that the company is operationally profitable and can afford to pay them; it matters much less to them that a management strategy for investment is raising debt costs. Taking another perspective, the government will want to encourage investments so will tax only those funds that remain after the operational and strategic needs of the company have been met. Finally, the shareholders will be focusing on the funds left over after all other commitments have been satisfied and thus are available for distribution in the form of dividends. Shareholders may tolerate never receiving a dividend if instead the funds are directed towards growing the business and thereby increasing its overall value.

Somewhere between cost and revenue stakeholders make their own concept of profit. However, if we are to reconcile the different views of 'making money' out of the cost revenue process we should first settle on a more systematic definition of profit.

THE POINT OF PROFIT

Profit can be measured wherever the company is making money. The most encompassing concept is that of **normal profit**, which does not restrict itself to financial reporting but takes in issues such as opportunity costs (Simshauser and Ariyaratnam, 2014). Normal profit is the financial benefit required by those with a financial interest in the firm in order to justify their commitment. Since the owners of the firm may have their own reasons for continuing their commitment, for example they may simply enjoy being associated with the organisation, the quantification of normal profit can vary from case to case.

At the industry level, normal profit is that which is required for companies to remain in the industry. The actual level of profit may be low, but if the returns are stable and the costs of exit are high then companies will be happy to maintain their position. If profit levels fall below normal then companies will exit the industry and if profit levels rise above normal new entrants will be attracted. Normal profit therefore denotes stability in the industry.

In order to provide a systemised view, accounting practices take a narrower view of profit expressed purely in financial terms, but this still results in a range of definitions according to the information being demanded. The accepted approach is to sample the financial condition of the company at points along the cost–revenue process:

1. **Gross profit** – cost of the goods or services subtracted from the sales revenues. This measures the ability of the management to make efficient use of labour and other direct production inputs in the core activity of the company. A positive figure indicates that the company's day-to-day operations are being properly managed. This is reassuring for investors and employees if the company is suffering financial pain elsewhere in its finances.
2. **EBITDA** (earnings before interest, taxes, depreciation and amortisation) – often taken as a proxy for cash flow, though not quite the same, it is intended to show how the normal operations of the company can cover the costs of financing. It is vulnerable to manipulation by management so needs to be used with caution.
3. **Operating profit** – also known as **EBIT** (earnings before interest and tax). The measure provides a wider perspective on the firm since it incorporates considerations such as operating expenses and

depreciation costs. The focus is still on the company's core operations but a positive result suggests that the company is sustainable in the long-term. This is good news for investors when the firm is heavily indebted.

4. **Net profit before tax** – also known as EBT (earnings before taxes). Allows investors to strip out the effects of different tax regimes and compare similar firms in different locations.
5. **Net profit/income** – popularly known as the bottom line. These are the final funds available for distribution to shareholders since all other financial commitments have been met. Sometimes taken as the final measure of a successful management strategy, although it may to prove to be a short-term view.

Each of the above metrics represents company profitability from a particular perspective, and so should not be accepted as a measure of management success by itself. Stakeholders then need to make their decisions based on their own expectations. This may lead to further analysis, perhaps including some of the following calculations:

- **Return on investment (ROI)** – intended to reveal the financial return on an investment for the purposes of comparing efficiencies with other opportunities. However, the lack of rigour in the technique means that its objectivity can be questionable, particularly for long-term investments.
- **Return on equity (ROE)** – used by shareholders to show how well their investment is being used by the management to create growth. Care needs to be taken that new share issues are included in the calculations.
- **Return on assets (ROA)** – a measure of how effectively the management are using the company's assets.

Whichever measure of profitability or performance is used, and there are many more, it is important to remember that the metric can only deliver the information that it is designed to give. No result is capable of definitively stating that the company is a good financial bet or not; it all depends on what information the stakeholder is seeking.

When one considers the diversity of stakeholders it comes as no surprise that company accounts need to serve a wide variety of information needs. For expediency, we will divide these stakeholders into those that are internal to the company, and those that are external.

ACCOUNTING FOR STAKEHOLDERS

The company accounts should serve the interests of different sets of stakeholders. The internal users tend to be:

1. Internal services – management information systems (MIS)
   - Information for investment and credit decision
   - Assessment of cash flows
   - Available resources and their commitments
2. External functions
   - Communicate the financial position to stakeholders
   - Report income to the government
   - Evaluation of performance against stated targets.

Not only must the reported accounts service the diverse needs of the different stakeholders, internal and external, but they must also balance the requirement to disclose information with the commercial necessity to withhold sensitive data. This is the data that rivals and other interested parties could use to their own advantage. It is this tension between the many different requirements and users of accounting reports that has resulted in a surprising degree of variability in what is intended to be an objective approach to reporting a company's health. The basic requirements are common to all accounting report objectives:

- Clarity – the data being reported is valid and understandable
- Transparency – all the relevant data is reported
- Comparability – financial data alone is not of interest, it needs some kind of standard by which it can be judged.

The need for these requirements to be met is only intensified when operating internationally.

1. Internal services

The main users of internal accounting are managers through their **management information system (MIS)** and **enterprise resource planning (ERP)**. These systems increasingly rely on IT hardware so they can be customised to the corporation's strategic needs and organisational structure. Similarly, the internal accounting methods are configured around the information that is required and who requires it. There is therefore no standardised approach to internal accounting services.

Since the accounting data is for internal use it can be an active component in strategic planning and implementation. At this stage, managers tend to be most interested in cash flow projections for different scenarios so that they can then make **net present value (NPV)** calculations (Ross, 1995). This information is often highly confidential since it may indicate to competitors likely strategies by the corporation, or alternatively it may unduly alarm investors when it includes contingencies for emergency planning. The data is available to managers of many different departments and it therefore comprises a wide variety of inputs, including:

- Daily sales – by product, client, region
- Cash flow – by department, retail outlet
- Work in progress
- Inventory
- Procurement.

Other sensitive information is covered by internal surveys of available resources and commitments. These can range from training needs for supporting a new strategy, to the physical resources that the company has on hand. Oil companies will regularly assess their accessible reserves, and although they will publish some of the results, internally the managers will engage in more conjectural activities, where they evaluate a range of possibilities. Needless to say, this is not information they would like to see passed to competitors.

There is a temptation with internal accounts for managers to mine them for endless quantities of information. This can lead to paralysis in decision-making as the volume of data obscures its quality. It also raises costs and means that companies find that they are expanding their accounting divisions at the expense of other departments. At the same time, as an administrative support function accounting is rarely seen as a source of competitive advantage in its own right, so there is an opposing pressure to reduce the burden of its cost.

One solution to this dilemma is to **outsource** accounting activities to specialist firms, often in low-cost overseas locations. As a cost reduction strategy it is one open to all firms, even the smallest

(Everaert et al., 2010). The problem here is that it puts at risk the sensitive nature of internal accounting. At least with in-house accounting the company has almost complete control over the information by integrating it into the MIS and ERP systems. It also means that the accounting function can develop in alignment with the corporation's strategic direction. For these reasons a company will retain some accounting ability in-house. Outsourcing tends to be most useful in collating the more routine data, the responsibility for interrogating the results remaining with the corporation's management team.

As a company grows it evolves internal accounting systems that are unique to its own operations. When it begins to expand internationally, the systems can become unwieldy with regions, products, cash flow and managers multiplying accordingly. This often necessitates an organisational restructuring, but the problems can be exacerbated after a merger or acquisition that imports a new structure into the organisation. This compels an urgent consolidation and simplification in the MIS that can bring disaster if it is not completed in sufficient time.

2. External functions

While internal accounting services can be custom designed for the corporation, this is not the case when providing accounting data for external stakeholders. There are a variety of information needs, some conflicting, according to the nature of the stakeholder.

- **Investors** – use standardised formulas to calculate financial returns that can be compared directly with other investment opportunities.
- **Bank** – need asset values and cash flows in order to evaluate creditworthiness.
- **Government** – require profit and loss for taxation.
- **Trade union** – interested in profit, management incentives and employee salaries for wage negotiation.
- **Analysts** – use a variety of metrics (cash flow, financial returns, profits before tax, investment, debt etc.) for interpreting the strength of the company and making comparisons.
- **Competitors** – experiment with a variety of metrics for estimating the strategic path of the company.

The contradictory demands of the various stakeholders can create a paradox for the company. It may be attempting to impress investors and banks with its apparent financial strength while at the same time playing down its financial resources in order to minimise demands for higher wages or taxes. As a result, national regulations oblige companies to report their accounting data according to standard formats that are equally accessible to all stakeholders. Usually this means two main reports, each providing information from different perspectives:

1. **Profit and loss (P&L)/Income Statement** – measures the financial performance of the company by relating the costs of running the business to the income over a period of time. The concept is simple, but due to the complexity of financial structures deciding how profitable a company is can be challenging. A start-up in a capital intensive industry, for example, could show years of losses when the cost of debt is included, so operational profit (revenue minus cost of sales) becomes the primary metric.

   Eventually, though, any company must show a profit after it has met all its fiduciary commitments, such as tax and interest payments. The surplus represents the change in wealth for the owners of the firm. Since the legal requirement is for the P&L account to be calculated at certain points in the year it provides a statement of the financial progress of the company in the periods between reports. This includes changes in the value of assets, such as by depreciation.

2. **Balance Sheet** – measures the value of a company by relating the assets to the liabilities, including the owner's equity, at a specific point in time. By definition these items must balance, so if the assets or liabilities change it should be reflected in the owner's equity. If the liabilities increase at the expense of assets, the owner's equity will fall. Conversely, if the assets rise and liabilities fall then the owner's equity will rise.

   Generally, the owners would like to see the value of the company rising, but they may decide to draw down cash from the firm, a common method in lieu of salary for partners of a firm. It may also be part of a planned withdrawal from the industry.

Even for the largest corporations these two reports are succinct, often just a few pages. Such a brief summary is usually too short to be of much practical use, so numerous notes are added. In Toyota's annual report the financial section was over eighty pages long, yet the consolidated balance sheet, income and cash flow statements took up just five of those pages such was the volume of notes and management guidance (Toyota, 2014).

The accounting notes are an opportunity for the managers to explain their actions during the year that have concluded in the financial results, but it is also time-consuming and costly to compile the report. Nevertheless, managers would still need to reconcile the conflicting requirements of the report for the different stakeholders. Given the standardised format of accounting procedures this can lead to some creative attempts to circumvent the regulations.

DISCLOSURE AND OFF-BALANCE SHEET REPORTING

It is just as well that corporations are obliged by law to release their basic financial results because there are many reasons why they should want to be selective in what they release. On the plus side the managers will want to impress the owners with good news about the way their investment has been handled. They may focus on one specific measure of profitability, such as EBITDA (earnings before interest tax depreciation and amortisation), which strips out the burdens of debt and the non-cash expense of the falling value of aging assets. It presents a picture of the effectiveness of the management in the day-to-day operations of the company, but it also takes attention away from high levels of debt or the long-term cost of renewing capital investments.

If the experienced investor can study the financial reports to make their own decisions, the management will still want certain figures to be kept out of the report altogether. Research and development (R&D) costs, warranty claims on faulty products and variations in regional profitability are rarely broken down in any detail since they represent valuable information for rival companies.

Certain information can be withheld temporarily, such as during mergers and acquisitions. In these situations a **non-disclosure agreement (NDA)** is made between the provider and recipient of the sensitive information (Wang, 2012). The provider is usually, but not always, the originator of the information. The NDA should have limits on the information it covers, how it may be used, the time period covered and the people that will be permitted to view the sensitive information.

Confidentiality agreements become even more pertinent during a process of **due diligence**, when one firm requires access to the most important data that the provider holds in order to obtain final proof of the target company's financial state (Meister and Alsup, 2014). Sometimes this proof is at such variance to the published data that the deal is hurriedly called off.

Some financial data does not need to be declared at all, quite legally and reasonably. Capital items that are leased cannot be claimed as assets, and so the company is not able to use them to boost the value of its stock. Company pension funds are not assets either, although the net liability (i.e. the amount the company would have to spend to top-up the fund) should be declared.

Where off-balance sheet reporting becomes murky is where the company is exposed to an investment but the shareholders are left unaware. For example, options are a commitment to buy, or sell, at a prearranged price. These commitments can often risk large sums of money, but they do not appear in the financial reports. If the managers of the company are less than transparent then the liability may not appear even in the notes.

CASE STUDY – FERRANTI AND INTERNATIONAL SIGNAL AND CONTROL

International Signal and Control (ISC) was a US electronics company specialising in electronic sensors for military applications. Some of these involved obscure dealings with national security. The company expanded, acquiring a number of other operations in the United States and overseas, including the Marquardt Aircraft Company, a supplier to the Space Shuttle programme.

In 1987, ISC was itself acquired by Ferranti, a British company with a worldwide reputation for high technology products in the computing and defence industries. It paid US$670 million for ISC and was soon enjoying increased profits. Sadly, by 1989, it became clear that the vast majority of ISC's income was from illegal contracts, the revenue being effectively laundered by the legal operations. Once the illegal income was uncovered and extinguished, Ferranti found it was left with a deeply unprofitable acquisition and losses of US$500 million.

Unable to sustain such heavy losses Ferranti collapsed and was snapped up for a bargain price by the British high technology engineering conglomerate, GEC. The founder of ISC, James Guerin, received a 15-year prison sentence for fraud. GEC itself embarked on its own disastrous investment spending spree in the late 1990s as it attempted to turn itself into an international giant of the telecommunications industry. Its failure and subsequent break-up finally snuffed out Ferranti and marked the tragic end of what had been a dominant industry player.

Point of consideration: Do you think this business disaster was due to poor management, the inadequacy of accounting procedures or was it just a tragic one-off?

Source: Wilson, 2013

The most extreme form of off-balance sheet activity is **money laundering**, where the income is from illegal activities and it needs to be 'cleansed' before it can be enjoyed. The purpose here is to find some way of declaring the income as if it were legitimate. There are three distinct phases to the process (ABCSolutions, 2015):

1. Placement – the dirty money leaves the hands of the criminal and enters the legitimate financial system. There are a multitude of methods, including the purchase of travellers' cheques or simply smuggling the money into another country. This part of the laundering carries the highest risk, sometimes diversified by using an army of 'smurfs', criminal associates who conduct the placements.
2. Layering or structuring – the money is put through a long series of transactions, many of them international, to put as much distance between it and the original illicit source as possible.
3. Integration – the money is routed back to the criminal, apparently from a legitimate source. It can now be spent as the criminal sees fit.

For example, an organised crime group might have a small business, such as a local cinema, that in reality has few customers but the syndicate declares as income revenues that originate from its illegal activities. In a show of ultimate respectability, it will even pay tax on the 'profits'. Unsuspecting tax officials will accept that the funds come from the cinema, not the business of crime.

🗨 MYTH BUSTER: PUBLIC TAX EVADER NO.1

Take evasion is wrong, but it is rarely seen as dangerous. Alphonse Gabriel Capone, better known to history as Al Capone, was born in Brooklyn but rose to fame as a gangster in Chicago in the 1920s. This was not, though, the crime for which he was incarcerated.

Rising up through the gang hierarchies by good fortune rather than low cunning he was able to profit from the city's close proximity to Canada. While the Prohibition era in the United States prevented the production and sale of alcoholic drinks, it was relatively easy to smuggle supplies across the border a few miles to the north. Illegal though this was, to the thirsty citizens of Chicago the illicit trade brought welcome relief from the trials of healthy living.

Publicly hailed as a Robin Hood-style hero, Al Capone lived up to his acclaim wearing sharp suits and entertaining in a lavish style. With little public appetite for Capone to be convicted he seemed almost untouchable. His mistake was in arranging to wipe out a rival gang in the brutal St Valentine's Massacre in 1929. Capone's men gained entry into the North Side gang's illegal warehouse by posing as police on a raid. The North Side gang put up no resistance, probably assuming that the police were simply putting on a public show and could be quietly paid off. Instead they were lined up against the wall and gunned to the floor.

Public sentiment turned against Capone, but it proved difficult to pin charges against him under the prohibition laws. Instead, the authorities levelled a series of ad hoc charges against him, from carrying a gun to vagrancy. The breakthrough came when it was decided to charge Capone on tax evasion. In fact the crucial evidence against Capone of his untaxed earnings was provided by his own lawyer.

The tax evasion trial was little more than a proxy for the more serious charges relating to Capone's gangster activities. As such he received an 11-year jail sentence, excessive for tax evasion but mild for the trail of murders in Capone's past. Yet even as he was sent down he was already a fading force in Chicago, and in his absence organised crime continued to flourish as before.

Point of consideration: Does it make sense for illegal organisations to be legally required to file their accounts? Should their accounts follow the standard format?

Source: Hoffman, 2010

INTERNATIONAL STANDARDS OF ACCOUNTING

Just as corporate accounting reports serve a multitude of stakeholders, so they are shaped by the needs of the country in which they are being formulated. In the United States, the capital structure is often slanted towards investors who are interested in their share of the profit, and so have their investment focus on the corporation's income statement. The American approach to accounting has its roots in the Stock Market Crash of 1929, leading to the formulation of five accounting principles by the American Institute of Accountants to clarify the kinds of income that could be declared (Zeff, 2005). The purpose was to get as close as possible to a true and fair representation of the company's financial condition. The problem is that truth and fairness are ephemeral concepts.

For many years, the American accounting system has excluded the revaluation of assets in order to prevent companies inflating the value of those assets, leaving the income statement as the primary instrument of assessment by investors. This protected investors in manufacturing industries, where many of the physical assets would generally lose value over time, but in asset-rich industries, such as oil and gas, the inability to reflect changing market prices would lead to a serious misalignment between reported and actual values (Zeff, 2005).

The British system shares with the American approach an attempt to report a true and fair view to the investor. In both systems there is room for interpretation by professional accountants. In contrast, German accounting is more in sympathy with the continental view that accounting serves the needs of creditors and as such works within a strict legal framework (Heidhues and Patel, 2008). This precludes the kind of professional judgements that American accountants can make. The German method suits a corporate capital structure where banks are dominant but is less suited to investors who make their deals on the stock exchange.

Japan has tended to follow the American accounting system, partly due to the country's close relationship with the United States after World War II (JICPA, 2013). At the same time, traditional Japanese conglomerates, known as *keiretsu*, often have banks at their centre as the most influential shareholders. As a result, Japanese corporations can sometimes withstand the wild fluctuations in share prices that result from the release of dismal financial reports. Nevertheless, if the keiretsu had been free to develop their own accounting styles they would probably have concocted something that suited their corporate structures rather than the American system.

Other nations have their own accounting approaches containing nuances that suit the evolution of their commercial practices. In each case they represent a compromise between business confidentiality and public reporting. Inevitably, this means that the system cannot meet the needs of all the stakeholders, but the strains are most obvious when companies extend their operations overseas and look for international sources of capital. This has led to a drive towards harmonisation of accounting practices.

INTERNATIONAL MANAGERS SEEKING INTERNATIONAL CAPITAL

As corporations have internationalised there has been an increasing need to fund their expansion using international sources of capital. This means that capital has to be able to flow freely across international markets. Unless this occurs corporations will overburden their current sources of finance and contribute to a local increase in interest rates. At the same time, this movement of capital across national borders brings with it a whole new set of risks. International managers are therefore faced with a complex series of financial decisions concerning which capital sources to access and how this might influence the capital structure of the company.

The broadening in the stakeholder base puts additional stress on the established accounting system used by the corporation. On the one hand, in order to service the growing need for international capital, corporations have to report financial results to investors around the world in a standardised format. On the other hand, international managers will find that their reports are demanded two distinct sets of investors: primarily by shareholders in one country and primarily by creditors in another. A company like Sony, headquartered in Japan, may have just six pages of financial data to release as part of its fiduciary duty to its financial backer, but the full report runs to over ten times that number (Sony, 2013).

ACCOUNTING HARMONISATION AND CONVERGENCE

International corporations find that their stakeholders are spread across a multitude of regions, but there are still a basic set of requirements for clarity, transparency and comparability. Added to this is the need for simplicity since the added complexities of international finance are likely to have a multiplying effect on the volume of inputs in the accounting reports. The consequent drive to develop common accounting practices as two forces behind it: that of changes in the rules and regulations of accounting that require corporate compliance, and then spontaneous adoption of common standards in order to reassure international investors (Canibano and Mora, 2000).

The purpose of **harmonisation** is to ensure that accounting practices do not, in themselves, become a barrier to international growth. Under harmonisation the different national systems continue in parallel with each other but are in broad alignment on common standards. The use of common standards means that overseas investors and banks can make informed judgments on the relative attractions of different investments. This is analogous to the advantages of globalisation, where all participants can benefit by promoting shared sets of principles. It is not only those large corporations that can scan global financial markets to find the lowest rates of interest; it is also possible for specialist lenders to find additional projects outside the home market in which to invest.

The movement to harmonise accounting standards has been a long time coming. The United States began exploring the idea in the years following World War II, yet progress remains painfully slow. Most countries adopt a conservative attitude to their approach, preferring not to meddle in a system that has served them well for many years. Accounting is not generally perceived as a tool for advancing business operations, more as a system of checks and balances to ensure that businesses are kept in order. There is often resistance to the idea of innovation in accounting, let alone that of changing established practices in favour of those used in competitor economies.

A more radical approach is **convergence**, where different systems come together into one. This would eliminate all national differences, as there would simply be one approach to accounting all over the world. For some countries this could imply massive configuration of accounting methods and periods of confusion as companies change their accounting procedures and restate previous accounts. This might be overkill, a costly solution when all that is necessary is that financial reports are broadly comparable.

CLOSING THE GAP WITH GAAP

In the United States the **Securities and Exchange Commission (SEC)** has delegated power to the **Financial Accounting Standards Board (FASB)** to drive forward the international harmonisation process (FASB, 2014). The aim is to bring US **Generally Accepted Accounting Principles (GAAP)** to the same level as the **International Financial Reporting Standards (IFRS)** as formulated by the **International Accounting Standards Board (IASB)**.

The problems with harmonising GAAP and IFRS begin almost before there is time to argue over the details. They are each based on distinct philosophies that affect their perspective on corporate accounting. Despite its title, GAAP is less interested in principles than it is on rules. It comprises sets of guidelines that are intended to deal with any likely scenario. IFRS, on the other hand, is intended to define the objectives of business reporting and then interpret them for specific industries (AICPA, 2014). There is less margin for confusion with GAAP since the guidelines can be more easily followed.

If US companies were to adopt the IFRS rules there are concerns that corporations would in some way lose out to foreign competitors. For example, under GAAP rules companies can value their inventory in a manner they believe is suitable, such as **FIFO** (first in first out) and **LIFO** (last in first out). For firms that have large inventories, particularly those dealing in raw materials, a change in the way the inventory is valued can dramatically alter the value of the company as a whole (PWC, 2012).

It could be argued that under a common accounting system the main strengths of accounting, that it is consistent and transparent, come to the fore. Once the harmonisation with IFRS has been completed then all the firms within an industrial sector can be globally compared. The disadvantage for GAAP firms is that they must bear the adjustment cost which their rivals, already using IFRS, will not have to. There may also be a personal element to this: senior managers in the United States often receive incentives based on the value and declared profit of the firm, and these results could be temporarily upset by the move to another accounting approach.

Although the SEC itself has reservations about the adoption of IFRS it seems that a process of evolution is bringing GAAP and IFRS into convergence anyway. US firms are finding that they need to have a clear understanding of how IFRS works when they are engaged in **mergers and acquisitions (M&A)** across the globe. Not only that, the US economy is by far the largest recipient of foreign investment, and in order to continue to attract funds it needs to present financial results that are comparable with the rest of the world. Finally, US subsidiary companies based overseas are themselves required to file accounts in the IFRS format. In return, if IFRS can accommodate some GAAP concerns, then the conservative world of accounting might actually reach a global consensus.

TRANSLATING FOREIGN MONEY

A major challenge for modern accounting approaches is that they need to record international transactions like never before. The funds being moved across international borders come in a number of different forms:

- Dividend remittances
- Royalties and fees
- Loan repayments
- Transfer prices.

Although these payments are not unique to the international business arena they are much more complicated than the issues confronting domestic businesses. The two factors that affect the movement of money across borders are taxation and exchange rates. To confuse matters further, their impact can be real, affecting the quantities of money, or they may be reported, meaning only that they vary when prepared for publication in the company accounts. This reporting variation is known as **translation risk**.

TRANSLATION RISK

The effect of translation risk is essentially an illusion in the sense that its effect is only seen in the official report. Although a company might be quite happily operating overseas using the local, or **functional currency**, at some point it will need to file a financial report in some sort of common, or **presentation currency**. Naturally, there is an IFRS instruction, IAS 21, on how to report foreign exchange (IFRS

Foundation, 2012). At the point when the financial report is due, functional currencies should be translated into the presentation currency of the organisation as follows:

1. Monetary items, such as revenues and debt repayments, should be accounted for using the exchange rate in effect at the close of business on the day the accounts are being prepared.
2. Historical, non-monetary items should be accounted for according to the exchange rate in effect at the time of the original transaction.
3. Non-monetary assets measured by fair value, such as the assets of an acquired operation, should be accounted using the exchange rate in effect when the fair value was decided.

While IAS attempts to bring some consistency to the reporting of overseas transactions there is still plenty of room for exchange rate fluctuations to distort the impression of the company's financial health. This distortion can be either positive or negative, but the perceptions of financial impact often need careful investor relations handling. In 2012, IBM reported a 2.3% fall in total revenues attributable purely to the rate of exchange being used to prepare the annual report. If the rate from the 2011 report were used then revenues presented would have been flat (IBM 2012). Over the two years IBM's operations had been continuing unchanged, it was only the numbers as reported that had moved.

When money is not being physically moved across borders then no actual currency exchange takes place. In these circumstances it might appear that currency translation affects only the numbers being reported. Sadly, there is the reality of taxation to deal with. In IBM's case the apparent fall in reported revenue would have reduced the amount of corporation tax being paid, all other things being equal. However, in another year currency translation effects might take steady local revenues, even falling revenues, in the functional currency and give them an upward boost when they are converted into the presentation currency for the sake of the financial report. This can lead to the payment of higher taxation on the higher reported profits, despite there being no justification for this at the local, functional currency level. This can have a devastating effect on companies that are hit with the double whammy of stagnant revenues and rising taxes.

NATURAL CURRENCY HEDGE

Companies can use currency translation effects when investing overseas to balance the reported costs and revenues with the use of a natural hedge. A natural hedge is a financial mechanism that counters the effects of exchange rate fluctuation as an inherent part of its process (Brooks and Chong, 2001). You can think of it like aircraft stability in flight: when an aircraft slows down it loses aerodynamic lift and starts to enter a dive which then increases the aircraft's speed, creates more lift and allows it to regain some altitude. By harnessing this natural effect the aircraft is able to avoid a deadly spiral to the ground.

A natural currency hedge works by ensuring that currency translation gains are balanced by translation losses elsewhere. Aside from the reported revenues we have looked at, other accounting items affected by currency translation include the value of assets and debts. If the functional currency loses value against the presentation currency then the value of assets, such as manufacturing plants, can appear to lose value. If the plant was sold at that point and the funds repatriated then the loss would be a genuine one. However, if the plant is part of a long-term commitment then the reported changes in value with the exchange rate can be a distraction that creates a false impression of how the company is faring in the overseas location.

Fortunately, the loss in value of the assets is partly balanced by the parallel fall in value of the debts. This means that the company can report lower interest payments in its presentation currency even while the functional currency payments remain the same. This is where the natural hedging occurs because if the variations are reversed so that the changing currency translation rates give rise to an apparent rise in revenues, which could increase the corporate tax burden, an equally apparent rise in costs will suppress the reported profit. Over the long term, reported revenues and costs work against each other to smooth out the financial results affected by currency translation. This serves as a major reason why companies move production to their most important overseas markets.

INTERNATIONAL TAXATION REGIMES

There is no doubt that accounting standards are an attempt to bring order, fairness and transparency to the byzantine world of money flows. Accounting regulations enable interested parties to evaluate the company on the basis of a unified set of financial results. A lot of assumptions have to be made in the process but with the trend towards greater harmonisation in accounting standards there is at least a reasonable amount of consistency. Taxation, however, is not like this.

Tax is, of course, how governments earn their money. Without taxation all public services would have to be funded as a private good. It would be wrong to say that there would be no roads, schools, welfare or national defence but it would certainly be difficult to achieve a national consensus. Instead, there are likely to be good services in areas that can afford them and bad services in those that cannot. This can be economically inefficient: for the country to operate at its most efficient there need to be well-maintained roads everywhere, not just in the wealthy areas.

In practice what exactly constitutes a public good varies from country to country. In some political regimes all property belongs to the state, while in others the state has minimal influence beyond national defence, infrastructure and basic welfare. Adherents of one system look on the alternatives with a sense of incredulity.

As a consequence, the taxes raised around the world vary from country to country. For international companies this means that their profits are taxed at different rates depending on the country where they are earned. Their carefully compiled accounting reports showing a consolidated set of results for their global operations are in fact based on any number of different tax regimes. Indeed, countries will use their tax policies strategically by setting them at a level that incentivises international companies to invest locally.

In Table 14.1, we can compare the different taxation strategies for a selection of countries.

Table 14.1 *National taxation strategies*

Country	Corporate Tax Rate, %	Personal Income Tax Rate, %	Indirect Tax Rate (VAT, GST etc.), %
China	25	45	17
Hong Kong	16.5	15	0
Ireland	12.5	48	23
Saudi Arabia	20	0	0
Sweden	22	56.6	25
United Kingdom	23	45	20
United States	40	39.6	0 (state taxes apply)

Source: KPMG, 2014

Globally we know that it is easier for corporations to move location than to transfer labour. Even in areas where labour mobility is permitted, such as large countries like India and economic regions like the EU, there are still many cultural and psychological barriers to movement. Although this means that it is easier to tax the workforce rather than the company there is an opposing force in the shape of public resistance to the payment of tax. Governments need to negotiate a tricky balance between encouraging commercial investment with the offer of low corporate taxes and maintaining public support among individual taxpayers who also want to minimise their payments.

Table 14.1 shows a number of countries that are clearly incentivising corporations. China, Ireland, Sweden and the UK are all placing the greater taxation burden on the workforce rather than the corporation. Indeed, both Ireland and Sweden show a difference between the two taxation rates of around 35 percentage points. According to KPMG (2014), Sweden has the second highest personal tax rate in the world and there are a number of other Scandinavian countries that are very close. This is due to a cultural tendency in the region towards generously funded welfare systems.

In Ireland's case it has a history as a relatively poor country that has grown its economy on the back of incoming foreign corporations, including the likes of Google and eBay. It is the twin attractions of an educated workforce and low corporate taxes that have led to an inrush of like-minded multi-nationals, many of them making Ireland the centre of their European operations. Of course on the other side of the taxation balance it means that a larger proportion of the burden must fall on the workers but the assumption is that it is the corporate tax strategy that brings the high-paying jobs into the country in the first place.

The United States and Hong Kong, however, like to treat individuals and companies alike. Both these countries are known for their entrepreneurial spirit and the taxation strategy will be a contributory factor. The government is effectively signalling that it does not distinguish between businesses and individuals. This means that individuals are emboldened to take on the risk of forming their own companies rather than sheltering under the employment umbrella of a large corporation. The intended result is a more dynamic national economy. The alternative view is that of governments like Ireland, where the corporate dynamism is being imported from outside.

In Table 14.1 there is one country that places the entire tax burden on the corporations, not the people. This is Saudi Arabia, holding the world's second largest oil reserves. When it comes to natural resources the corporations have no choice but to come to the country. There can be no threat of them leaving for elsewhere unless oil goes out of fashion. This is unlikely to happen anytime soon, so the government has taken the opportunity to keep the people happy by shielding them from the need to pay income tax. Zero rates are also observed in other Arab nations.

MANAGEMENT SPOTLIGHT: TAX EFFICIENCY

Tax is a major cost consideration for managers, and countries will compete with each other to offer the most attractive rates to MNEs. This has elements of a zero-sum game and the EU, for one, is working to prevent the most harmful practices (Ambrosanio and Caroppo, 2005). Some countries will play on this by turning themselves into **tax havens** or **tax shelters**, ultra-low tax locations for registered head offices. These head offices may have minimal staff, or no staff at all, but since the location is the official place of domicile for the company it is able to report its financial results with a reduced tax burden. More recently there has been a trend towards acquiring companies in low-tax locations in order to report financial results from there and avoid high taxes in the home country. There is mounting legislation around the world to put a stop to these practices.

A common method for minimising the tax bill is to use **transfer pricing**. This is a perfectly standard way of managing the internal finances of a firm by having the departments buy and sell services and goods within the company boundary. This creates an artificial market in which the departments trade with each other, so for example the R&D department might 'sell' its services to the production department. Although the pricing is decided by the management, not the market, treating each department as if it were a standalone operation means that it is easier to monitor efficiencies and to set incentives. It also creates a greater sense of discipline by giving departmental managers responsibility for their budgets.

On an international scale transfer pricing has become an effective method for moving revenues around the world and escaping the clutches of the tax authorities (Gravelle, 2015). For example, a company might have a plant in Country A supplying components to a plant in Country B. If Country B has a low corporate tax rate then the company would want to report its greatest profits there. It can do this by setting a low transfer price for supplies from Country A so that the plant in Country B is able to report lower costs. Assuming the price it then sells its own products for remains the same the transfer pricing strategy widens the gap between costs and revenues. In Country B the company is able to report high profits in a low-tax regime and in Country A low profits in a high-tax regime. It is a neat corporate trick but in recent years companies have suffered public defamation for appearing to avoid their share of local taxes.

The ability to play off one tax regime against another presents a tricky moral dilemma for managers. Presumably governments implement particular tax strategies in order to attract foreign firms, usually with the intention of making up the revenues by taxing the income of the employees. To then criticise multinational corporations for exploiting this opportunity smacks of political duplicity. In any case, one might argue that the payment of taxes should never by a moral issue since that would be an invitation to taxpayers to withhold taxes when they disagree with the government's spending policies. Such a stance would undermine the very purpose of government to spend on behalf of society as a whole. It might be concluded that the only way to have companies pay their dues is to change the tax regime accordingly and accept that this might deter them from investing in the country.

Point of consideration: When developed countries set their corporate tax rates low to attract MNEs at the expense of developing countries, does that count as unfair competition?

Sources: Ambrosanio and Caroppo, 2005; Gravelle, 2015

VAT VERSUS GST

As individual taxes are often unpopular, governments need an additional, less conspicuous, form of taxation. Consumption taxes are levied on consumers when they buy products and services. Such taxes include **VAT (value added tax)** and **GST (general sales tax/goods and services tax)**. They are considered to be economically efficient but sometimes difficult to collect, dependent as they are on meticulous record keeping by the companies who are responsible for ultimately paying the tax.

A significant advantage over corporate taxation is that consumption tax avoids the cascading problem where individual firms in the supply chain are taxed, which then creates an artificial incentive for vertical integration of the supply chain into a single firm. Nevertheless, there is greater resistance to the use of consumption tax as an alternative to income tax. It is regarded as both a **progressive** form of taxation in the sense that wealthier people, who spend more, pay higher taxes, and also as **regressive** because poorer people pay the same rate of tax as the wealthy (James, 2011).

GST (general sales tax) is a retail sales tax levied on the consumer at the point of purchase. In many countries it is also known as a goods and services tax. This has the effect of placing the entire tax burden on the retail outlet. Those outlets that are selling higher value products will pay the highest rates of tax which then has a distorting effect on the market and encourages tax evasion by retailers. It may appear progressive but it also means that less wealthy buyers, perhaps a student saving up to buy high-grade computer equipment, would find they are obliged to pay a higher tax rate on the upgrade.

VAT is more sophisticated in that it taxes only the value added by each company in the supply chain. This means that although the company must charge its customer a rate of tax levied on the selling price it can also subtract the tax it paid on the price of the components, raw materials and other inputs. The effect of this is that the VAT is then only due on the additional value that the company has brought to those inputs in putting the final product together. If you follow the supply chain all the way to the end only the final customer is paying the full amount of VAT since they are not adding any more value. VAT broadens the tax base and means that exports do not escape without being taxed (US Treasury, 1984).

The VAT system works best when it is applied as a unified rate across all products. This is economically efficient and cost effective to implement. However, there is often resistance amongst consumers who see VAT on basics such as food and clothing as a tax on the poor. European governments in particular shy away from a comprehensive imposition of VAT by excluding items like clothing and uncooked food. Yet not only does this shift the tax burden onto other items, making them even more unaffordable to the poor, but they also bring greater tax relief to the wealthy who buy food and clothes just like anyone else but at a higher price point.

TAXES FOR SOCIETY AND TRADE

Consumption taxes are also used on occasion for social and redistributive reasons. We can see this most readily with alcohol and cigarettes, which in many countries attract punitive taxes. Not only is this intended to discourage their use but it is also seen as a way of extracting payment from those who may suffer health effects later on and need care by the state. In other words, smokers and drinkers create an externality in the form of a financial obligation on the state to look after them which can be internalised by forcing them to pay more for their predilections through **redistributive taxes**.

Consumption tax revenues can be increased by the addition of **duties**, which are taxes on specific products and often of fixed amounts that need adjusting for inflation at regular intervals. When applied to traded goods they can be used to shape the trading patterns of that country, for example by shifting favour to domestic goods by applying the greater duties on imported goods.

In developing countries it is difficult enough to raise tax revenues when those citizens that can afford to pay are also the ones most capable of devising ways to avoid it. VAT is therefore seen as a practical method to ensure that everyone contributes something, and for this reason the IMF encourages the adoption of VAT. The **OECD (2010)** notes that developing countries favour the so-called New Zealand approach, which applies a single rate of VAT across a broad base of products. This is intended to result in an overall lower rate for all.

The United States has long struggled with the concept of VAT. Although there is no national sales tax individual states and cities have always been able to levy their own taxes as they see fit. Seattle, in the Pacific Northwest, has a sales tax of 9.5% comprising 6.5% for Washington State, 2.6% for Seattle itself and the remaining 0.4% for the Regional Transit Authority (Washington State, 2014). Other states in the union will have their own approaches, some even more complicated.

RAISING EMPLOYABILITY: ACCOUNTING FOR PROFESSIONALS AND AMATEURS

Accounting is a discipline reserved for professionals; it is not meant to be a business activity to be dabbled in half-heartedly. Decisions of strategy and tactics are dependent on accessing financial information that is valid, reliable and transparent. Internally, this means that managers need data they can rely on in their day-to-day operations. Externally, there is a legal requirement to publish financial results according to a set of standards and principles.

Most countries demand that accountants hold official certification. In the United States this process is supervised jointly by AICPA and FASB with some input from the Public Company Accounting Oversight Board (PCAOB). AICPA administers the Uniform Certified Public Accountant exam for the entire country, although to be licensed to practise as an accountant each state has its own additional requirements for education (i.e. a degree) and experience. Certified accountants from certain other countries, such as Canada and Ireland, need only take the International Qualifications Examination (IQEX) to be qualified in the United States, though it is still only the State Board of Accountancy that can issue the licence to practise (AICPA, 2014).

In the EU while each country has its own rules and regulations for certifying accountants it is the European Commission that has set the overall accounting rules. The declared purpose of these rules is to improve the management of companies, attract investors and increase access to bank loans (European Commission, 2015). In recognition of the heavy burden that such rules can have on the managers of small and medium size enterprises (SMEs) there are a different set of standards.

All these rules and regulations are designed to place the important task of financial reporting in the hands of qualified experts. Managers who wish to gain this expertise must complete the accredited training programmes. The danger with this is that it can create an echelon of elite financial experts who are isolated from the rest of the management team. What is needed is oversight by managers who have enough accounting knowledge to hold a degree of insight into the discipline.

For this reason there are many financial qualifications for managers that stop short of certifying them as accountants. The ACCA (Association of Chartered Certified Accountants) is a global body working to raise accounting standards (ACCA, 2015). Apart from the many courses for those wishing to become fully fledged certified accountants it is also possible to attend courses to gain a basic knowledge of the discipline. Another global organisation, the Chartered Institute of Management Accountants (CIMA, 2015), offers courses and certificates specifically intended for managers looking to gain a working knowledge of accounting.

It is by the use of such intermediate qualifications that the gap between the professional accountants and general managers can be bridged. This is vital since the very purpose of accounting, to open the financial state of the company to fair and transparent inspection, is in danger of being obscured by the arcane nature of the profession. More than ever managers need to be educated in accounting practices in order to maintain oversight and leadership of the business.

www WEB SUPPORT

1. Profit. A neat tutorial from Economics Online, including some colourful graphics, on the fundamentals of profit. Brief but you can always amuse yourself exploring the rest of the website.

   www.economicsonline.co.uk/Business_economics/Profits.html

2. Economic profit vs. accounting profit. Video tutorial from the Khan Academy, a MOOC provider. It does not go into great detail but it helps to clear up any confusion between the two notions of profit.

   www.khanacademy.org/economics-finance-domain/microeconomics/firm-economic-profit/economic-profit-tutorial/v/economic-profit-vs-accounting-profit

3. Business Stakeholders: Internal and External. Although the explanation is a little too sparse to be of anything but passing interest, the rest of the Boundless.com website might be worth revisiting from time to time. It looks like this MOOC provider has high ambitions.

   www.boundless.com/accounting/textbooks/boundless-accounting-textbook/introduction-to-accounting-1/overview-of-key-elements-of-the-business-19/business-stakeholders-internal-and-external-117-6595/

THE STORY SO FAR: ACCOUNTING AS THE BUSINESS DISCIPLINE

If business is about making money then it is crucial to track the money flows in order to have a clear understanding of the health of the business. The concept of profit, the indisputable measure of a company's success, is one that is defined by accounting techniques. Yet even this simple idea is open to interpretation. There are many different measures of profitability, and stakeholders have their own ideas of what financial information is important to them. There is also a tension between what the stakeholders may wish to know and what the company is prepared to let them know. Rules of accounting ensure that there is some semblance of a standard approach that permits financial performance to be assessed and compared, but so far these agreed accounting principles have proved resistant to globalisation. As multinationals wrestle with the demands of moving money across borders and balancing the costs of taxation policies around the world, the pressure to harmonise international principles of accounting is becoming irresistible.

Project Topics

1. To what extent do accounts provide a fair and representative view of the financial condition of all companies? How might certain companies be under-valued or over-valued?
2. What objections might a multinational corporation based in Germany have to adopting the American GAAP system of accounting?
3. When multinational corporations use transfer pricing as a way to exploit international tax differences are their actions morally indefensible?

CASE STUDY – MANUFACTURING CARS IN AUSTRALIA

Australia is the sixth largest country in the world by land area but with a population of just 23 million people, around a tenth the size of the United States. The market would generally be too small to justify manufacturing goods locally with any benefits from mass production efficiencies. With so many goods being manufactured in high volume these days the advantages of economies of scale are lost when production is located in a small market. Fortunately, for the Australian car industry the local market is also very isolated.

Historically, the rough road conditions in Australia tended to favour the kind of large, mechanically unsophisticated cars made in the United States. However, the high freight costs from North America to Australia favoured local assembly. Ford, through its Canadian subsidiary, was the first to begin assembly in the 1920s. Vehicle bodies were produced locally by Holden, a long established Australian coachbuilder, until Ford set up its own body plant. Holden was then acquired by GM, Ford's great North American rival. Holden then manufactured complete GM cars for the local market under its own brand.

The Australian car industry reached maturity in the early 1970s. Ford's Falcon became sufficiently localised that it could be considered indigenous. GM's Holden had its own range of vehicles culminating in the famous Commodore line. Other brands included British Leyland, with its P76 large car, and Mitsubishi, with the Magna. Toyota arrived in 1963 with a simple assembly operation and building up from there. However, in recent years the country has struggled to justify the need for local production.

A surge in total new car sales for the entire Australian market to nearly 390,000 units in 2008 would have been reasonable output for one manufacturer but with four companies to feed it meant that economies of scale were out of reach. As tariffs were reduced and the value of the Australian dollar rose on booming commodity exports there was little justification for local assembly. Toyota was importing nearly 190,000 cars at the same time as it attempted to boost local output to barely more than 100,000 units even with the addition of overseas exports.

Australian production had depended on having an industry that can produce vehicles for the local road conditions while international freight costs and import tariffs were high enough to offset the costs of small-scale local production. Once the plants could be accounted for as sunk costs there was little saving to be made in closing them down unless, of course, additional investments in new facilities were due.

Eventually, new investments became inevitable as machinery needed replacement and new products were released. In recent years Ford and GM have wanted to pension off their unique Australian models and consolidate around a truly global range of products. Toyota did have the more internationalised product range but was struggling to make the plant part of its global network. Consequently, all three manufacturers were facing serious financial commitments to stay in the country.

In the end the accountants just could not make the financial argument stack up. Imports were cheaper and promised a wider choice of products than a small local industry could ever hope to offer. In short order the remaining three car companies announced they were pulling out of the local industry, and 2017 marks the death of the Australian car industry.

Point of consideration: Thailand is even closer to the major car production centres of Japan and China yet its automotive industry continues to attract investment. Why is Thailand such an attractive location when Australia is not?

Sources: Automotive News, 2014; Federal Chamber of Automotive Industries, 2014

? MULTIPLE CHOICE QUESTIONS

1. If a company is not in profit then it should be closed.
   a. Yes, if there is no profit then the company is insolvent.
   b. No, there is a time element; any company can have periods of losses.
   c. No, if the company is a family firm it does not need to make profits.

2. When a company is heavily in debt and making losses, which profit measure shows that its long-term prospects are still good?
   a. Operating profit.
   b. Net profit.
   c. Net profit before tax.

3. In the long run, which measure of profit is a shareholder interested in?
   a. Operating profit.
   b. Net profit.
   c. Net profit before tax.

4. What are the three main objectives of accounting?
   a. Honesty, brevity and reliability.
   b. Obfuscation, obscuration and incorrigibility.
   c. Clarity, transparency and comparability.

5. Why do companies have internal accounting systems?
   a. Monitoring targets set by management.
   b. To keep sensitive information confidential.
   c. To give advance warning of bad news.

6. Which of the following are stakeholders of a company?
   a. Management, workers and administrative staff.
   b. Consumers, suppliers and the local community.
   c. They all are, but to differing degrees.

7. What does it mean if a balance sheet does not balance?
   a. The debts exceed the value of the assets.
   b. The company is technically insolvent.
   c. It has been compiled incorrectly.

8. What is the purpose of a non-disclosure agreement (NDA)?
   a. It allows a company to withhold information.
   b. It restricts sensitive information to the signatories of the agreement.
   c. It protects the intellectual property rights.

9. Is money laundering a victimless crime?
   a. Yes, although crimes might have been committed in obtaining the money.
   b. No, it denies an honest living for hard-working criminals.
   c. No, it denies tax revenue for the government and income for honest businesses.

10. Can translation risk be considered a genuine risk?
    a. Yes, because it impacts on the tax liability.
    b. No, the changes in value exist only on paper.
    c. Yes, it impacts on the value of the money being transferred.

Answers
1b, 2a, 3b, 4c, 5a, 6c, 7c, 8b, 9c, 10a

REFERENCES

ABCSolutions (2015) 'Money laundering: a three stage process' from www.moneylaundering.ca/public/law/3_stages_ML.php accessed 12 March 2015

ACCA (2015) Homepage from www.accaglobal.com/uk/en.html accessed 25 March 2015

Ambrosanio M F and Caroppo M S (2005) 'Eliminating harmful tax practices in tax havens: defensive measures by major EU countries and tax haven reforms' *Canadian Tax Journal* 53(3), pp. 685–719

American Institute of Certified Public Accountants (AICPA)(2014) Homepage from www.ifrs.com/index.html accessed 2 November 2014

Automotive News (2014) 'Why Australia's auto industry is going the way of the dodo' *Automotive News* 15 February 2014 from www.autonews.com/article/20140215/OEM01/140219896/why-australias-auto-industry-is-going-the-way-of-the-dodo accessed 1 November 2014

Brooks C and Chong J (2001) 'The cross-currency hedging performance of implied versus statistical forecasting models' *Journal of Futures Markets* 21(11), pp. 1043–1069

Canibano L and Mora A (2000) 'Evaluating the statistical significance of de facto accounting harmonization: a study of European global players' *European Accounting Review* 9(3), pp. 349–369

CIMA (2015) Homepage from www.cimaglobal.com/ accessed 26 March 2015

European Commission (2015) Accounting – financial reporting from www.ec.europa.eu/finance/accounting/index_en.htm accessed 25 March 2015

Everaert P, Sarens G and Rommel J (2010) 'Using transaction cost economics to explain outsourcing of accounting' *Small Business Economics* 35(1), pp. 93–112

FASAB (2014) *FASAB handbook of federal accounting standards and other pronouncements, as amended.* Federal Accounting Standards Advisory Board 30 June 2014 from www.fasab.gov/pdffiles/2014_fasab_handbook.pdf accessed 19 October 2015

FASB (2014) Homepage from www.fasb.org/home accessed 2 November 2014

Federal Chamber of Automotive Industries (FCAI)(2014) Vehicle sales from www.fcai.com.au/sales accessed 1 November 2014

Gravelle J G (2015) *Tax Havens: International Tax Avoidance and Evasion.* Congressional Research Service, 15 January 2015 from www.fas.org/sgp/crs/misc/R40623.pdf accessed 19 October 2015

Heidhues E and Patel C (2008) Convergence of accounting standards in Germany: biases and challenges in *Working Paper Macquarie University ResearchOnline* from www.lby100.com/ly/200806/p020080627326687493812.pdf accessed 2 November 2014

Hoffman D E (2010) *Scarface Al and the crime crusaders: Chicago's private war against Capone.* Carbondale, IL: SIU Press

IBM (2012) 2012 IBM Annual Report from www.ibm.com/annualreport/2012/bin/assets/2012_ibm_annual.pdf accessed 2 November 2014

IFRS Foundation (2012) IAS 21: The Effects of Changes in Foreign Exchange Rates from www.ifrs.org/Documents/IAS21.pdf accessed 2 November 2014

James K (2011) 'Exploring the origins and global rise of VAT' in Phillips C (ed.) *The VAT reader: what a federal consumption tax would mean for America.* Arlington USA: Tax Analysts

JICPA (2013) History and Background: Development of CPA Profession from www.hp.jicpa.or.jp/english/accounting/history/development.html accessed 2 November 2014

KPMG (2014) Tax Rates Table from www.kpmg.com/GLOBAL/EN/SERVICES/TAX/TAX-TOOLS-AND-RESOURCES/Pages/corporate-tax-rates-table.aspx accessed 2 November 2014

Meister M L and Alsup D M (2014) 'Confidentiality agreements and due diligence' from Modrall Sperling Lawyers www.modrall.com/files/4701_ConfidentialityAgreementsandDueDiligence.pdf accessed 2 November 2014

OECD (2010) 'An International Perspective on VAT' by Charlet A and Owens J in *Tax Notes International*, 20 September 2010, p. 943 from www.oecd.org/ctp/consumption/46073502.pdf accessed 1 November 2014

PWC (2012) IFRS and US GAAP: similarities and differences from www.pwc.com/en_US/us/issues/ifrs-reporting/publications/assets/ifrs-and-us-gaap-similarities-and-differences-2012.pdf accessed 2 November 2014

Ross S A (1995) 'Uses, abuses, and alternatives to the net-present-value rule' *Financial management* pp. 96–102

Simshauser P and Ariyaratnam J (2014) 'What is normal profit for power generation?' *Journal of Financial Economic Policy* 6(2), pp. 152–178

Sony (2013) *Annual Report 2013* from www.sony.net/SonyInfo/IR/financial/ar/2013/shr/pdf/AnnualReport_E.pdf accessed 19 March 2015

Toyota (2014) *Annual Report year ended March 31, 2014* from www.toyota-global.com/investors/ir_library/annual/pdf/2014/ar14_e.pdf accessed 19 October 2015

US Treasury (1984) *Tax Reform for Fairness, Simplicity, and Economic Growth: The Treasury Department Report to the President, November 1984-11/01/1984* from www.treasury.gov/resource-center/tax-policy/Pages/tax-reform-index.aspx accessed 1 November 2014

Wang E H (2012) *Reviewing the M&A Non-Disclosure Agreement* from www.dlapiper.com/reviewing-the-ma-nondisclosure-agreement-08-02-2012/ accessed 2 November 2014

Washington State Department of Revenue (2014) *Section II - State and Local Retail Sales Tax* from www.dor.wa.gov/content/fileandpaytaxes/fileoramendmyreturn/retailing/retailingact_statesalestax.aspx accessed 2 November 2014

Wilson J F (2013) *Ferranti. A history Volume 3: Management, mergers and fraud 1987–1993.* Manchester: Manchester University Press

Zeff, S.A. 2005. *Evolution of US Generally Accepted Accounting Principles (GAAP).* Rice University, USA. [Online] Available from www.iasplus.com/resource/0407zeffusGAAP.pdf accessed: 7 October 2013

15 International Finance

Chapter Objectives

Finance is the fuel of business. Without it managers could not make long-term investment plans and businesses would survive on a hand-to-mouth existence of cash revenues paying for the immediate costs of doing business. In this chapter, we will see how financial tools can be used to turn money into a strategic asset:

- The role of the chief financial officer (CFO).
- Matching risk and rates of return across time.
- Sources of funding.
- Evaluating rates of return.

RISK MANAGERS

When a business is born it is often of a scale so small that it is little more than an extension of the personal finances of the founder. They may have used their savings to form the initial injection of capital and then run the business on its revenues. Such a firm is driven forward on the passion of the founder who remains the sole owner and operator of their commercial offspring. Any new equipment would have been funded from those revenues so that debt would not have been an issue. With the founder as the owner equity decisions would not have been a problem either.

This homely vision of the sole trader devoted to their commercial creation and beholden to no one is a romantic one and it is even less likely as the company grows. In modern business it is not enough to take financial surpluses built up from past transactions and invest them in the present in order to benefit future profits. This kind of revenue-to-investment approach means any new opportunity is constrained by the amount of cash on hand. Avoiding risk also means missing opportunities and sole traders often suffer poor rates of growth (Foreman-Peck et al., 2006).

We know that on a personal level a risk-averse approach may suit daily spending since it avoids the unwitting accumulation of unaffordable debts. Even so, the most important financial decisions involve a strategic approach to spending. Our old friend Shakespeare may have declared 'neither a borrower nor a lender be' but for us this means that big ticket items like a house purchase could take a lifetime of savings. It makes no financial sense to pay out on housing rent whilst saving any cash that is left over for a house purchase, only moving into the house at the end of one's life. A mortgage means that the house can be owned from the start, with the payments spread out into the future. Interest has to be paid, of course, but the inflationary effects on rent and house prices are avoided.

We should not take the analogy of house buying too far when applying it to a business. A business is not a home, neither is it a money saving device. A business is about making money and it is to facilitate this that companies borrow funds for investment purposes. Financial management is about identifying the most suitable investment projects and sourcing the funds. As a consequence, the CFO's position has risen to one of unprecedented importance within the corporation (Zorn, 2004).

CFO

The CFO is charged with responsibility for the strategic and tactical financial planning for the company. The CFO oversees the three main financial management tasks:

- Evaluating investment opportunities
- Evaluating funding sources
- Managing current financial resources to best effect.

The CFO is therefore responsible for a wide number of different tasks. On a daily operational basis, these tasks include the accounting functions of the firm, from the statutory reports to the financial data disseminated to other managers through the company's **management information system (MIS)**.

When it comes to investment decisions, the CFO is in charge of the process by which the use of financial resources can maximise the returns to the company owners, the shareholders. This will involve comparing the various possible revenue streams and making assumptions about the financial costs of each opportunity. Even if there is only one investment opportunity under consideration this still needs to be compared to the opportunity cost of holding onto the cash. It can be a brave CFO who advises that doing nothing is the best course of action.

Indeed, courage has often been the hallmark of the best CFOs. They make objective decisions based only on the financial data they have available. It is not for them to speculate on future product developments or promising new markets. This means that CFOs are often derided as the head 'bean counter', a sub-species of business personnel whose role seems to be to eradicate all sense of fun from corporate life by focusing only on the numbers. This is nonsense, of course, but the financial managers who have the power to close down an exciting project due to its poor projected financial returns are often used as scapegoats when a company fails to release exciting new products. Some researchers deride the parsimonious bureaucrats for withholding investment funds and allowing products to lose competitiveness, when in fact it was the market itself that was changing (Olson and Mathias Thjømøe, 2010). It is often these very bean counters that save companies from their worst excesses and ensure that they are financially sustainable.

 MYTH BUSTER: BEAN COUNTER HEROES

Perhaps accountants and financial managers have only themselves to blame. Theirs is a discipline that demands meticulous attention to detail and sober interpretation of the data. They are tasked with uncovering the facts of the business, in its operations and in its future investments. To do this they must insulate themselves from the wilder aspects of the company's activities. They must avoid being seduced by dazzling new products or the chance to diversify the company into dynamic new industries. Every proposal put to them has to survive the test of their calculators. No wonder they are characterised as emotionally frozen!

It is just as well that they are able to exercise their powers. Companies are often driven by the passion and vision of their staff, but for the company to be sustainable in the long term somebody needs to make sure that the numbers are stacking up correctly. That somebody is the CFO. In some ways theirs is a thankless task, unnoticed until the company suffers a financial cataclysm. One rogue trader, Nick Leeson, brought down the venerable British bank Barings after a series of disastrous financial trades. He was found guilty, but it was the lack of management oversight that allowed him to operate with impunity for so long (Leeson, 1996).

Perceptions of the cold-hearted bean counter may be changing, though. The profession itself is increasingly advertising for more daring individuals, ones prepared to take risks. This may fit with global corporations that like to project a dynamic view of themselves but, as Baldvinsdottir et al. (2009) warn, it also raises the risk that the bean counters will lose their hard won trustworthiness.

Point of consideration: How can senior managers find the right balance between financial caution and business dynamism?

Sources: Leeson, 1996; Baldvinsdottir et al. (2009)

Increasingly, the role of the CFO is being seen as less tactical, reacting to financial data as it is presented, and being more strategic. This means that an effective CFO is an asset to the firm, actively seeking out the best financial opportunities. The opportunities for doing this are expanding in step with the steady globalisation of the world's financial markets. It also means that funding decisions are becoming more complex as the CFO has to balance risk and financial returns across national boundaries.

BALANCING RISK AND RETURN

A popular image of the most successful business person, so often a man, is that of a tough individual who is a risk taker. When a business opportunity has frightened away those with weaker constitutions only they have the nerve to put money on the table. The impression they like to portray is of a physically impressive business operator, with a firm handshake and steely eyes. We should make it quite clear that these corporate myths have no place in the modern world. Business decisions are made on an assessment of the available data, and this can be done by anyone regardless of race, colour, creed or gender. All that are needed are powers of critical analysis and the courage of one's own conviction.

The prevailing belief that the most successful business person is the one who has the iron will to take on the toughest challenges is entirely misplaced. In fact, a business should be **risk neutral**. It is immaterial to the investment opportunity that it is high, medium or low risk. This is because risk is only half of the financial equation; the other half is that of the financial returns. Financial management is about balancing the risk with a matching rate of return.

One of the highest risk industries is that of drilling for oil in the seabed. Not only is it technically and physically challenging to look for oil underneath some of the most dangerous seas in the world, the chances of actually finding sufficient oil down there are rather low. The **oil industry** would appear to be a classic high-risk activity where only the brave survive. However, when oil is found in sufficient quantities the company may enjoy a financial bonanza. So the risks are high, but so are the financial returns.

At the other end of the scale we have the low-risk investment opportunities, such as **government bonds**. These are considered amongst the very safest of investments and as such offer low rates of return. It would be wrong, though, to simply assume they are intended only for the risk averse. Instead they are ideally suited to investment strategies that demand a guaranteed return. Pension funds are therefore a big buyer of bonds.

Of course, the perfect strategy would be to find a low-risk opportunity that rewards the investor with a high rate of return as if it were risky. This is the area in which **entrepreneurs** operate. They may appear to be the toughest of risk takers but the reason why they are successful is that they have found a way to reduce the risk in a way rivals have been unable. So whilst the rival investors demand the highest rate of return to match the perceived high risk, the entrepreneur will accept only a slightly lower rate of return knowing that the actual risk is much lower still. The rival investors are scared away and the entrepreneur reaps the benefits.

It is this gap between the actual low risk and the high rate of return where the entrepreneur is able to make a financial killing. This cannot last and once rival investors have been able to replicate the entrepreneur's approach then the entrepreneur must move on to find another opportunity. Thus the entrepreneur is doomed to a restless life of searching for overrated risks offering relatively high returns.

FUNDING SOURCES

While other parts of a company may identify any number of new business opportunities, it is down to the CFO's team to quantify them in such a way that they can be directly compared for the level of risk and the expected rate of return. In the case of a domestic firm many systemic factors, such as political risk, are the same for all firms so do not require detailed analysis.

This is not the case for firms that are looking to compare international business opportunities. For the multinational corporation (MNC), it is necessary to include the full range of factors that impact on the risk and expected return. For example, if the investment opportunities are occurring in two different countries then it would be vital to quantify both the political risks in full. There is also the matter of exchange rate risk, not only its impact on sums of money being moved across national borders but also money that is only being reported in another currency.

Management investing for shareholders

As we have seen before, in private life debts are taken on as a method of acquiring ownership of an item by bringing spending from the future into the present. The price of doing this is the payment of interest, and as a consequence it is often prudent to draw on one's own savings rather than take on the burden of regular loan repayments. This does not have to be the same for commercial corporations.

It is certainly the case that corporations will often invest in projects using funds derived from their profits. In this way, like the private consumer, it is seen to avoid the costs of paying interest. Yet there is another view that the corporation is spending money that does not belong to it. Instead, the cash belongs to the owners of the firm, the shareholders. Any surplus funds for which the company has no immediate need should be distributed amongst the shareholders.

This is one example of the principal agent problem that is the source of so much conflict between senior managers who run the firm and the shareholders who own it. When the new business opportunity comes along it will change the original nature of the firm so the shareholders should reserve the right to decide whether to invest or not. When a company invests internal funds in a new project it is beholden on the senior management to achieve a better rate of return than the shareholder could do on their own. If this is not the case then the managers are running the firm for their own benefit, not the shareholders'.

Generally the company's senior management are investment specialists which the shareholders generally are probably not. If shareholders were they would be in management themselves. Nevertheless, the rate of return on the new project should meet or exceed the rate of return sought by the shareholders. As Quinn and Jones (1995) argue, the managers have a fiduciary duty to maximise the rates of return for the shareholder as well as a moral duty to act in the best interests of their clients. It is the fiduciary aspect that demands the financial analytical skills of the management team.

When is the money coming from?

It may seem bizarre to ask *when* rather than *where* the funds are being sourced but this is the basis of borrowing to invest. In essence, a company borrows from its future increased revenues in order to fund the investment that makes those higher revenues possible. The price for doing this is the **interest rate** on the loan.

Another personal example might help to understand this point. In order to join an educational course it is often necessary for less well-off students to take out a loan. This creates a financial burden over future years. However, it is assumed that in the future, with the new qualification safely awarded, a better paid job will ensue. Even after the payment of the loan, the future graduate should be better off financially. It is true that a wealthy student is in an even better situation since they do not have to pay interest on a debt, although there are **opportunity costs** for them in withdrawing their savings. Yet for both types of student the debt burden and the loss of savings are a wise investment since they benefit them financially in the future.

When companies borrow money they are also drawing on future financial resources. These anticipated resources are partly in the form of the future profits of the new investment. On the negative side there is the loss of future resources or the opportunity costs of using cash that they have on account in the present but will no longer have access to in the future. As long as the benefits of the investment exceed the costs of drawing on their sources of funding then the decision is a wise one.

The unwise decision is to pull forward future use of money for it to be spent in the present but with fewer benefits. Consumers are most vulnerable to this in their personal spending: perhaps they will take the wise decision of using a mortgage to buy a house only to take the less wise decision of adding to the mortgage with the purchase of an expensive car. They may find they are still paying for the car years after it has been scrapped!

It would be good to think that managers are rather better at organising their financial resources. It is the CFO's job to match the cost of the debt (or the opportunity costs of spending cash) with the future value of the investment. They will also organise current financial resources so that they are managed most efficiently in the interests of all the stakeholders.

Hierarchy of investors

The rate of return on an investment should satisfy more than just the shareholders; other sources of funding have their own particular desired rates of return. As we saw before, the rate of return should be appropriate for the risk. This risk to the investor is not always directly related to the nature of the new project itself but to the seniority of the lender. This means that if the project did not succeed and had to be wound up then the most **senior debt** holder would be paid off first, rendering their investment relatively low risk. This process would continue down the hierarchy of lenders, the most **junior debt** being paid last. Given that this is happening because the project failed the likelihood is that the junior creditors would receive little or nothing. Since their investment is higher risk they would seek compensation in a higher rate of return, while the senior creditors would require a much lower rate of return.

The most **senior creditor** is usually a bank or similar financial institution. They will have conducted due diligence studies in order to ascertain as closely as possible the risk attached to their investment. Only if they were they sole source of funding for the project would the risk attached to their involvement be the same as that for the project itself. Once there are other, higher risk, investors on board then the risk for the senior creditors goes down. Each lender has their own measure of risk and return but the overall risk for the project remains the same since there has been no material impact on it from the mix of financial backers.

Junior creditors are usually made up of individual shareholders. They would not have the resources to conduct due diligence and so, along with their junior status, they accept they are taking on a higher risk. Why are they happy to do this? Because they know that the banks are repaid in fixed amounts for a fixed term and then the debt is cleared. Anything above those fixed repayments is free to be distributed amongst the shareholders. If the project turns out to be more successful than originally thought then the additional profits accrue entirely to the shareholders. The shareholders may find that the pay out to them rises rapidly as the project succeeds.

Steinkamp and Westermann (2014) found, though, that during the financial crisis in Europe, which gained momentum from around 2010 onwards, the rescue by senior creditors like the IMF pushed the original creditors further down the hierarchy. In this way the junior debtors, private institutions and individuals, found themselves in invidious positions. Over the long term this may have the effect of inhibiting further private investment funds in those locations that have had bail-out funds from international institutions. The very rescue is therefore seen to increase the risk and, as a result, the interest rates.

One other source of funding has a more variable attitude to risk. This is government funding. It is often the most junior creditor because it is seen as a tool for encouraging the establishment and growth of new industries or the survival of old industries. When the global financial crisis that swept the world from 2008 threatened the existence of strategically important companies their national governments felt obliged to step in. In truth it was not the governments that took on this high risk, low return investment but the taxpayers. This is probably why governments can be so profligate with their cash.

The US government lent a little over $51 billion to GM to maintain its operations and keep its workers employed. The rescue mission lost the government around $11.2 billion but the overall bailout of the industry saved around 1.5 million jobs (Reuters, 2014). During the same period the US government also lent $168.5 million to electric car manufacturer Fisker Automotive to help establish the new automotive technology. When the firm collapsed the government was forced to find a buyer for the loan, accepting a bid of $25 million (Reuters, 2013). Other junior creditors included the unpaid workforce and customers who had put down deposits on undelivered cars.

Debt versus equity

The two main sources of funding, debtors and shareholders, have their own peculiar characteristics which are attracted to certain investment opportunities. Tax considerations are one of the most important but there may be historical reasons for the company choosing one over the other (Hovakimian et al., 2001). The differences need to be taken into account when a funding package is put together by the CFO.

Debt is raised from a financial institution, such as a bank, and **interest** is the price paid for the loan. The institution has expert personnel who will conduct a thorough analysis of the proposal, including due diligence. They are not infallible, of course, but they will secure the loan against some asset belonging to the company or its owners. Since the risk of the loan to the institution is reduced by the security the funders are able to charge a relatively lower rate of interest. The loan will be repaid in agreed amounts over a fixed period of time.

An advantage of debt is said to be that it leaves the current ownership structure and management of the firm untouched. It is certainly the case that the fixed nature of the repayments means that any profits left over are available to be distributed to the owners of the firm. However, if the company fails then the financial institution effectively becomes the owner and will sell those assets against which the loan was originally secured. If the firm enters formal bankruptcy proceedings then the management team will also find themselves supplanted by an administrative team appointed by the court.

Equity is raised from individual shareholders who buy shares, or stock, and then become part owners of the firm proportionate to the number of shares they own. The shares may be publicly traded in the exchange markets and **dividends** are the price paid by companies for raising investment funds from the shareholders. How much a company pays out in dividends is not a simple matter of higher dividends coming from higher profits, it is seen as a mechanism for communicating with the market. There are a number of different possible scenarios, as listed in Table 15.1:

Table 15.1 *Dividend communication*

Dividend	Communication to the Market
Reduced payment	– Company has come under financial pressure and profits will fall – The cash is required for a new investment opportunity
Stable payment	– Business as normal – Any recent rise or fall in profits is short-term and the underlying business is stable – No fundamental changes to the business are expected
Increased payment	– Recent investments are paying off – Profits are expected to rise and this is the share of it – Profits are expected to fall so the shareholders need to be kept loyal

In theory, any change in the dividend payment can be compensated for by trading shares, selling them to make up a fall in income or buying them to reduce an increase in income. Generally, though, shareholders prefer to maintain a stable income stream by diversifying their investment across a financial portfolio. A fully diversified portfolio will have as many dividends falling as there are rising, assuring a steady income stream overall.

Many shareholders will consider their investment carefully, and may have experts advising them, but everyone in the market should have access to the same information. Nevertheless, many investors like to think they have a mysterious talent for forecasting the equity markets. For this reason a lot of share buying is done on the subjective basis of gut-feeling, fashion and even a herd instinct in the market. The final arbiter of a company's success is the financial data that it releases, cutting short the reign of the stock market mystics.

Although shareholders are under no obligation to sell their shares at any point the pressure of time is still very much an issue. Unlike banks, shareholders are mortal beings and will eventually die. Knowing this the shareholders are very keen to see the share price rise, or the dividend increase, while they are still around to enjoy the money. Corporate staff are often rewarded with special issues of shares, or stock, so they too are looking for a rise in the share price.

With so many incentives to inflate financial results, publicly traded companies often resort to dramatic and short-term cost-cutting measures, such as reducing staff levels or other forms of spending. These measures will inevitably undermine the company's long-term sustainability, perhaps by the cancellation of marketing campaigns or the cancellation of new product development. As a consequence, the company will later find it has to take corrective action and spend vast sums on new marketing campaigns and new product development. This is one of the reasons why publicly traded firms can suffer from **boom and bust** volatility, swinging from cost cuts to fresh investments. The boom and bust attitude encouraged by the equity funding structure can be particularly damaging for firms with very long-term planning horizons, such as utility companies and power suppliers.

National differences in funding sources

The mix of funding sources varies from country to country, depending on the structure of industry, the political framework and even the social culture. The resultant capital structure, which is the relative proportions of equity and debt, should not have any effect on the overall value of the firm. This is known as the **Irrelevance Theorem** (Modigliani F and Miller M, 1958). However, there are known to be a number of factors that mean in practice there are considerations to make concerning the capital structure, particularly with regard to **tax**.

There is some evidence that tax regimes have an influence on the capital structure: tax relief on debt for corporations should encourage funding from loans, while lower tax rates on equity should encourage funding from shareholders. There is no clear resolution of these two alternative capital structures, so most companies are funded by a mix of debt and equity. Governments often construct tax systems that encourage a balance of the two funding sources.

In Germany corporations are permitted to deduct tax payments from taxable income, and this has led to a weighting towards debt funding. This kind of funding also suits German companies which are heavily involved in manufacturing. The stability of their sales lends itself to the regular payments that are made on debt. The banks in that country also take a close interest in the operations of the companies they invest in, almost acting like quasi-shareholders (Hartmann-Wendels et al., 2012).

The US economy is more volatile than Germany's and this suits the raising of capital through equity. We have seen that the United States is the birthplace of many corporations founded on new technologies, such as Google and Facebook. In the early years the income for these companies would have been variable and unpredictable. Their rapidly changing fortunes would not have suited the steady demands of debt repayment. As a result corporations such as these tend to be funded from equity. However, the volatility is further fuelled by the demand from large numbers of investors to buy, or sell, the equity in reaction to the latest share price forecasts and this exacerbates the boom-bust tradition in the industry.

Japan has a strong leaning towards equity capital structures, but in their case the equity is owned by banks or other companies in their group. The largest Japanese companies are known as *keiretsu*, modern descendants of the historic family-owned *zaibatsu*. *Keiretsu* are conglomerates that often centre on a founding company or bank. Mitsubishi is one such group, and it has been said that it is possible to work for the group and never come into contact with products from another group during one's life: the worker might drive home in a Mitsubishi car to a Mitsubishi apartment and relax in front of a Mitsubishi television.

In a Japanese *keiretsu* the constituent companies provide each other with a great deal of support. They are able to work very closely with each other and this helps the *keiretsu* to bid for large contracts. There is often a suspicion that the constituent companies can do cut-price deals with each other but in fact this would be counter-productive. The opportunity cost for the *keiretsu* supplier is that they are missing out on revenues that they might have invested in new projects. The group as a whole also misses out on the revenues that could have been earned by selling components at the full price outside the group. The main advantage of the *keiretsu* is that the cross-holding of equity secures stable business relationships for the long term so that the constituent companies can work closely together. In this way complex joint venture contracts do not need to be negotiated.

COSTS OF CAPITAL

When evaluating new projects the CFO and the rest of the finance team will be aware that the different funding sources will require different rates of return according to their measurement of risk. If the investors do not receive at least their target rate of return for the project then they will not be willing to invest. The CFO's task is therefore to evaluate the investment project in terms of those rates of return.

For any given project the two types of financial backer, creditor and shareholder, will provide funds according to the capital structure proportions deemed most suitable by the CFO. As we have seen, in Germany the banks would fund the majority, while an American corporation might rely mostly on shareholder funding. This means that we have two groups of backers each demanding different rates of return on the same investment.

WEIGHTED AVERAGE COST OF CAPITAL (WACC)

Fortunately, it is not necessary to do the investment evaluation from the point of view of each individual investor but only as a single group. This means calculating the average cost of capital for all the investors and weighting it according to the proportions of each type of investor. This is the weighted average cost of capital (WACC). Conceptually, at least, WACC is not a difficult calculation to understand:

WACC = (Cost of debt × proportion of debt funding) + (Cost of equity × proportion of equity funding)

To make things simple for us, let's imagine that a company is funded by a mix of bank debt and shareholder funding in the proportions 25:75. We know that the bank will require a relatively low rate of return, payable as interest, because the loan will be secured against the assets of the firm. Let's say the interest rate will be 5% per annum.

The shareholders are junior creditors, so they will require a higher rate of return, usually payable as dividends, but they will also look for a rising share price. They know that any free profits available after the interest has been paid will be available to them. The more lucrative the project the more they stand to gain, while the banks will only receive the payments they were contracted to. Let's say that the shareholders are looking for a return of around 10%.

Putting these figures into the equation will provide us with the overall result:

WACC = (5% × 25%) + (10% × 75%)
WACC = (1.25%) + (7.5%)
WACC = 8.75%

It is important to realise that 8.75% is not a rate of return that applies to either group of financial backers. In the case of the bank it would be a nice surprise for them if they could get away with charging such a high figure but presumably the company would simply go to a rival bank for the market rate of 5%. For the shareholders 8.75% is much too low; they would sell their shares and buy into a company that could deliver the 10% that they need. However, 8.75% is the average across the two groups, weighted according to the proportion of their funding.

The CFO can use this figure to evaluate the viability of an investment opportunity. All they need to know is that if the project will provide a return of at least 8.75% then both types of financial backer will be satisfied. Of course, the real intention is to exceed this figure. To understand how WACC is useful let's compare four basic ways of evaluating investment opportunities, in only two of which is WACC used:

1. Payback Period
2. Cost Benefit Analysis (CBA)
3. Net Present Value (NPV)
4. Internal Rate of Return (IRR).

1. Payback period

This is a highly intuitive method for evaluating projects by simply counting the number of years of income before the initial cost of the investment is paid off. This intuitiveness makes it popular in political circles when justifying instances of high public spending to the voting public. The formula for it is very simple:

Payback Period = Initial Expenditure/Average income per year

The new Port Mann Bridge near Vancouver, Canada, cost an estimated $2.46 billion and by charging tolls to vehicle drivers the payback period has been estimated at 40 years. Using the formula we can then calculate a steady annual revenue of around $62 million (Vancouver Sun, 2012). With the tolls and expected bridge usage figures publicised it is easy for the taxpayers to see how successful the project has been. The known usage of the previous bridge helps to provide a credible forecast for the new bridge.

There are, though, significant problems with this approach. The first is that the new bridge is a ten-lane highway with greatly improved access infrastructure, so we can expect usage to rise over the coming years. Having said that, usage will inevitably vary in line with fluctuations in the economy. The formula should therefore be adjusted to take account of each annual forecast income, not simply the same income each year. We can do this by looking at the cumulative revenue flow, adding up each period until we get to an amount that equals the initial investment cost:

Payback Period = Year of last negative cumulative revenue + (Amount of last negative revenue/revenue of following year)

Another problem with the payback period approach is that it only includes the initial cost of the investment. There are a number of other matters that need to be taken into consideration, such as routine costs (e.g. operational costs) and the **time value of money** (e.g. inflation rates, interest rates).

The Port Mann Bridge project does include some of these factors by stating a total cost of the project at $3.3 billion. Nevertheless, the bridge will continue to require regular maintenance through its life, which should also be compared with the long-term benefits to the local economy. This broader argument can be covered by the cost benefit analysis approach (CBA).

2. Cost Benefit Analysis (CBA)

Some very large projects are intended to bring benefits beyond their narrow definition. This often includes national infrastructure projects that will be paid for by the country as a whole while also impacting on those who appear at first glance to be unconnected to it. Many of these costs are not financial, so before they can be included in the analysis a reasonable attempt needs to be made at quantification.

Many countries around the world have constructed high-speed rail networks and the United States is, rather belatedly it has to be said, looking into building a network themselves. There are a number of proposals on the table and only a few of them would result in true high speed rail travel. The North East Corridor (NEC) route connecting New York and Washington DC will cost up to $151 billion and take until 2040 to complete, but the benefits include lower greenhouse gas emissions, less traffic congestion, fewer road related deaths and higher productivity (USHSR, 2014).

CBA is particularly useful when assessing aid projects in developing countries where the benefits may not be restricted to quantifiable economic expansion. There are lot of challenges in doing this, though, since the investments often have no precedent in the country. The **Little-Mirrlees** method of CBA makes allowances for foreign exchange rates and government involvement. However, in such impoverished countries large infrastructure projects can distort the economy in ways that are almost impossible to foresee (Boadway, 2006).

⊙ CASE STUDY – AMERICA LEARNS TO LOVE THE TRAIN

An historic land of opportunity and vast open spaces, the emerging United States of America seemed the perfect country for a comprehensive rail network. The drive to link the numerous markets and industrial centres, as well as the desire to promote unification after the civil war, led to the rapid growth of railways in the nineteenth century. By the end of the period there were around 130,000 miles of rail in place. According to economist Robert Fogel (1962), the railways made the most significant contribution to national GNP of any single innovation prior to 1900. Other economists have pointed out that there were also many positive externalities or spill over effects, the secondary consequences of improved communications and capital flows.

Then, in the twentieth century Americans fell in love with the car. The urban sprawl of the growing cities was better served by more flexible road transport. One of the most famous conspiracy theories, perpetuated by the attorney Bradford Snell, is that GM bought up urban tram systems only to close them down in order to force people into cars and buses. However, Cliff Slater (1997) found that there were many other factors involved. Whatever the causes, once urban areas were dedicated to road transport the railways began to be starved of investment.

There is now a growing movement to resurrect rail travel in the United States. Taking passengers directly from city to city over some routes can be faster than air travel, if time spent getting to and through airports is included. The new national plan is for 17,000 miles of track that would put 80% of the population within reach of a high-speed rail connection. Powered by electricity, the system would be environmentally clean and bring economic stimulus throughout the country. All for a mere US$500 billion. After years of low investment such a sum is necessary to bring the United States somewhere near European and Asian standards. The US High Speed Rail Association is hoping, perhaps optimistically, to have the planned network in place by 2030.

Point of consideration: San Francisco is a compact city with a public transport system on the European model, while Los Angeles is an urban sprawl served by the car. Which one offers the better quality of life?

Sources: Fogel, 1962; Slater, 1997; USHSR, 2014

3. Net present value

The broad brush evaluations of Payback and CBA are the preserve of national governments and other organisations that are taking a macroeconomic perspective. Companies will be involved in the projects but mainly as hired contractors on a contractual payment. When they are responsible for the investment project in its entirety then the companies need to conduct methods of analysis that provide exact details of what the company, and its financial backers, stand to gain. Net present value (NPV) does this by revealing how their wealth will change due to the investment.

NPV is one of those business concepts that seems, at first sight, to be more magical than mathematical. It involves taking all the costs and revenues of a project and converting the monetary quantities into a single sum expressed in terms of today's monetary value. It includes all the opportunity costs and the time value of money so if it returns a positive figure, whatever it is, then the project should be initiated since it indicates an increase in wealth. If the result is negative then the project should be abandoned, as it will lead to a decrease in wealth. What is particularly exciting about NPV is that it hopes to provide an incontrovertible result and gives the lie to the idea that success in business belongs to the tough, macho risk taker. All that is necessary with NPV is to have the resolve to act on its result.

It is perhaps easier to understand NPV if we first look at how money changes value over time. Let us look at a simple example. Imagine you have $100; you can either spend it or you can invest it. If you decide to invest then your opportunity cost is the value of the item you could have bought but decided to forgo. If you invested for one year and then received back $100 then the year you waited for your money was wasted. This would be irrational since you could have spent it and enjoyed it rather than waiting for a year and then spending it. Instead, you would expect to be compensated with some kind of interest rate the money earned over the period.

For the sake of argument let us say that the interest rate is 10% per annum. This means that the $100 you currently hold will be worth $110 in a year's time. In other words, $100 now has a future value (FV) in one year of $110. Conversely, that FV of $110 has a present value (PV) of $100. The formula for this is quite easy:

$$PV = FV/(1+\text{interest rate})$$
$$PV = FV/(1+i)$$

In our example, then:

$$PV = 110/(1+0.1)$$
$$PV = 100$$

Effectively, we are saying that $100 of pleasure now is worth $110 next year, or alternatively that the $110 of joy we will have to wait a year for is worth $100 right now. If we are undecided about the pleasure of $100 now or $110 next year then the 10% annual rate of interest is something of a watershed for us. If the actual rate of interest on our investment is less than 10% we would prefer to spend the $100 now because to invest would reduce our pleasure. If we can find a rate of return that is greater than 10% then we would much prefer to invest since it would lead to an overall increase in our pleasure. In that sense the higher return makes us wealthier.

This 10% is therefore our benchmark for evaluating investment opportunities. We use it as the discount rate to calculate the present value of our future returns. Mind you, if all we could find was a 10% rate of return then we would be ambivalent as to which course of action to take; we might as well simply toss a coin because we have already decided that $100 now has the same value as $110 in the future.

The point about the benchmark, or watershed, rate of 10% is that to take that investment opportunity we would not feel any better off next year than if we had spent it for pleasure right now. All things considered, there is for us no net gain or loss to investing the $100 for one year at 10%. The net change in our wealth will be zero so we say it has a net present value (NPV) of zero. The formula for NPV is therefore an extension of that for PV:

$$NPV = [\text{Cash inflow}/(1+i)] - \text{original investment}$$
$$NPV = [R/1+i] - \text{original investment}$$

The cash inflow is the money that will be returned to us at the end of the investment. We know that we are gaining an extra $10 but we have to wait a year to get it, so the formula subjects it to the interest rate that is being paid. Putting the numbers into the equation:

$$NPV = 110/(1+0.1) - 100$$
$$NPV = 0$$

As we can see, this puts us in an impossible dilemma. You might be tempted to claim that you would still wish to go ahead with the investment because you will be better off by $10 but this is quite incorrect: you came into this process with a 10% return as your target. If the NPV calculation is stating that the investment provides no advantage over that, having taken everything into consideration, then there is no purpose to pressing ahead.

The great advantage of NPV is that it can accommodate variations in the discount rate to reflect how interest rates change over time. It is therefore a highly sophisticated tool in revealing the wealth benefits of a prospective investment. It should be noted though that the result that NPV provides is a measure of the increase in wealth after all opportunity costs have been taken into account; it does not represent an actual sum of money.

WACC and NPV So far we have discounted our investment examples using the interest rate we might have got on deposit at a bank or other savings institution. This is not, though, acceptable for the riskier investment proposal connected to a business opportunity. This is where the WACC comes in. As we know, WACC is the average return that the financial backers, shareholders and creditors, would expect. If we use WACC as the discount rate for calculating NPV then it will tell us whether the proposed investment opportunity will be acceptable to them.

Any positive value of NPV that results from the calculation means that the project will lead to an increase in wealth. If there are competing projects then the one with the highest NPV is the winner. Any negative results are rejected, as the financial backers could find a better rate elsewhere in the market.

4. Internal Rate of Return (IRR)

The internal rate of return (IRR) is related to NPV and is simply the discount rate necessary to reduce the NPV to zero. If a proposal offers a high return then it will also take a high IRR to bring the NPV down to zero. In effect the IRR provides a benchmark rate against which the financial backers can compare the rate of return that they desire, e.g. WACC.

It is useful to have a rate for the IRR because many investors have little understanding of NPV, but they are able to compare rates of return. If a bank is offering savers an interest rate of 5% per annum while an investment opportunity is offering an IRR of 10% then the two can be ranked and the investor readily identify the investment as the better option. The NPV method would have delivered the same answer but in terms of a monetary wealth increase which can seem obtuse because it is not the actual monetary value that will be ultimately delivered.

 MANAGEMENT SPOTLIGHT: SELECTING INVESTMENT RETURNS

The four methods for evaluating investment opportunities given above have their own advantages. The payback period is one that the general population can readily visualise because it echoes their own approach to private budgeting. For corporations involved in national projects this is the kind of calculation that politicians would appreciate, even if it takes little account of the time value of money. Most large projects are designed to last, and earn revenues, for many years, but the break-even point at the end of the payback period signals the moment when any uncertainty over its financial viability is finally resolved (Weingartner, 1969).

For truly massive projects, the impact can be felt far beyond the confines of the project itself. National infrastructure and strategic industries would be examples of the kind of investment that has ramifications for a broad number of stakeholders, maybe even the whole country. This becomes doubly important when it is the general public, through taxation, that is paying for it. CBA is the method used to make such an inclusive evaluation. However, the calculations can be highly contentious because they need to identify the multitude of costs and benefits, and then attempt to monetise them (Layard and Glaister, 1994). Arguments over what should be included and their monetary values can delay the project for many years.

NPV is the preferred method for strictly defined commercial investments. At its simplest the discount rate is the one that the financial backers are demanding. Forecasting future revenues is never an exact science but it should not suffer from the same flights of fancy as those used in CBA. The NPV discount rate can be challenging when a multinational needs to define its own required rate of return for an investment because this involves some detailed risk analysis and exchange rate considerations. When the NPV comes out as a negative number, it can be tempting to revisit the risk assessments with the intention of producing a positive NPV, but this should be resisted at all times. If the corporation stands by the figures that are put into the NPV formula then it must abide by the result.

IRR is really just NPV from another perspective. If there is a problem with NPV it is that it is difficult to visualise when the monetary figure that denotes a change in wealth does not relate to a sum that will actually be received. Indeed, it is possible that profits may not emerge for many years and by then the effects of time will result in a very different set of nominal amounts from the NPV figure. IRR presents a basic rate of return figure that allows a straightforward comparison of rates without having to interpret monetary results. Managers may find that investors are persuaded more easily by the IRR than NPV, even though both are essentially the same calculation.

Point of consideration: Large projects, which were once publicly funded, are increasingly bringing together public and private partnerships (PPP) using private finance initiatives (PFI). What is the appropriate method of evaluating the viability of a large public project that is dependent on private investment funding? You might also want to consider government promises to underwrite the project.

Sources: Layard and Glaister, 1994; Weingartner, 1969

ALTERNATIVE SOURCES OF FINANCE

There have always been alternative routes to financing that are quite separate to the conventional debt or equity options. Many businesses are started on family loans, repayable under easy terms or not at all. At the other extreme are the unregulated loan sharks, predatory lenders who will accept the creditor's lack of security by charging high rates of interest on the loan. These rates are considered extortionate, and as the loan sharks operate outside the law they often obtain payments through the threat of violence. They should not be confused with payday lenders who offer unsecured loans at very high rates of interest (e.g. 4000% at an annualised rate) so the borrower is provided with sufficient funds until their next wage payment; payday lenders are regulated.

Business funding can also come from a variety of sources. It is common for suppliers to offer credit to their retailers of 30 days or more, often giving the retailer time to sell the product on to the consumer and use the revenue to pay the supplier. In this way the retailer may never have to own its stock. Other forms of funding may come from within a diversified conglomerate, such as the Japanese *keiretsu* structure. In China there are **shadow banks** that provide business loans outside the formal banking system (Krugman, 2011).

Modern finance has advanced to a point where whole new sources of funding have become available. Facilitated by new technologies and exposure to different cultures there is a degree of greater sophistication to the financial markets, allowing far higher numbers of projects to find suitable investors like never before. These new funding sources offer the possibility of increased economic development for individuals and whole communities.

CROWD-SOURCE FUNDING

Having gone to all the trouble of defining the rates of return required for a project and then using it to discount future revenue flows, there is a new source of funding that apparently eschews all such financial discipline. Crowd-source funding, or simply **crowdfunding**, is a method for attracting funding from financial backers *en masse* and in a very short space of time. The evaluation of the proposal by the interested backers is often cursory and dependent on the information provided by the proposers. It is particularly suited to online applications, although it is not absolutely necessary. The Statue of Liberty in New York was partly funded by this method back in 1885 (BBC, 2013).

The internet has promoted the rise of crowdfunding because it facilities the communication of information through the mass of potential backers. This raises the public profile of the proposer and provides an opportunity for instant market research. It also cuts out many of the intermediaries that are usual in funding situations, such as banks and advisors, and so reduces the cost of the transaction. Without adjusting the risk of the project the cost reduction means that the required rate of return for the project can also be reduced. This has the effect of raising the viability of more marginal opportunities and making them eligible for rational funding.

There is also evidence that the required rates of return may be even lower due to a kind of herd instinct amongst the financial backers. It is rare that financial investments can be emotionally exciting but crowdfunding seems to offer just such a sentiment. This does not necessarily mean that investors are taking leave of their senses, although there may be an element of that, and it may be that part of the return being demanded is not just financial. If this is the case then it should be possible to calculate the monetary value of financial excitement since it will be the difference between the crowdfunding rate and the more orthodox market rate.

Crowdfunding has many applications, being especially suited to charitable and other humanitarian causes where the personal satisfaction in supporting a 'good cause' is part of the return to the investor. In the entertainments industry, crowdfunding is becoming ever more popular. Lesser known pop artists will often fund tours, or the recording of new albums, based on crowdfunding. Not only do the investors help to bring about the creative output they enjoy but they also get to feel part of the process.

In more traditional business situations there are worries that crowdfunding exposes the project to theft of intellectual property due to the open nature of the online platform. There is also a cynical belief that the fashion for crowdfunding will simply die out. This is probably as likely as social media losing its appeal amongst the young.

CASE STUDY – CROWDFUNDING FOR ENTREPRENEURS

One of the myths of online business is that it brings the buyer and seller into direct contact without intermediaries. This is not quite true, as services like eBay and PayPal demonstrate. Similarly, it is not correct to say that crowdfunding brings the project proposer and potential investor into direct contact. As always there needs to be some kind of intermediary, even if that is nothing more than a platform, or website, listing different projects. There are as many kinds of platform as there are types of projects. Platforms will specialise in philanthropic causes, art events and appeals for charitable sponsorship.

Seedrs is a London-based, Europe-wide platform bringing together business start-ups and potential investors. It is regulated by the Bank of England's Financial Conduct Authority (FCA). The start-up issues shares to Seedrs which continues to hold them as a nominee of the investors. Seedrs works by offering a platform for entrepreneurs, the project proposers, to advertise their projects in the form of campaigns. Investors register with the site and then browse the various projects. They can invest from as little as £10 up to whatever sum the entrepreneur is seeking. Once the project receives the targeted funding necessary for it to commence operations the investor receives ordinary shares in line with the value of the investment. Dividends and share sale income is earned in the usual way, 7.5% of the profits going to Seedrs.

Point of consideration: To what extent could governments use crowdfunding to finance national projects? Would this be fairer than taxation?

Source: Seedrs, 2014

MICRO-FINANCE

For developing countries, any kind of charge for borrowing money can prove to be a heavy burden. In conventional banking terms this can be because a project backed with little security and offering low rates of future profitability would be high risk. It should therefore require a high rate of interest. In many cases, even the option of finance may not exist because the fixed costs of administering a small loan are relatively large and therefore uneconomic. The consequence of this is that poorer people are doomed to a poverty trap, where they cannot afford the loans that they so desperately need to lift themselves out of penury.

The World Bank Group has been instrumental in extending loans to poorer communities but the projects tend to be at the national level. Micro-finance is an alternative funding source that bridges the gap between conventional banking and poorer borrowers at the local level. To some extent, the gap can be narrowed by reducing the risk of the loan. This may involve diversifying the loan across a group of borrowers or even an entire community. The loans themselves are small in absolute terms but relative to the debtors assets they are still a major financial commitment. In practice, financial logic cannot be denied and the high risk of the loans, plus the relatively high administrative costs, means that even microfinance interest rates can be unbearably high.

There are a number of organisations that offer micro-finance. The Grameen Bank, whose Bengali name means 'bank of the villages', was founded in 1976 by Professor Muhammad Yunus (Grameen Bank, 2014). The ethos of the bank is that a debt is preferable to charity since the loan is provided for a specific project and thus encourages business initiatives. The bank targets the poorest in Bangladesh, particularly women. There has been criticism that the bank is too compromised in its approach, lacking enough of a business foundation to be self-sustaining, while putting the poor under the same stresses they would suffer with a commercial loan from a conventional bank. Ultimately, the dilemma between charity and debt for eliminating the poverty trap may be impossible to resolve.

RAISING EMPLOYABILITY: FROM ACCOUNTANT TO CFO

In 2010 Ernst & Young conducted research on CFOs and the growing importance of these financial experts to modern corporations (EY, 2013). As befits their new-found status as leaders of strategy there has been a shift away from narrow accounting backgrounds. Of the CFOs surveyed only 27% were qualified accountants, while an equally large proportion claimed an MBA as their highest qualification. The biggest group, at 29% of the total, had a degree in general finance.

More important than qualifications, the research found that it was vital that the character of the manager fitted the unique role of the CFO. Positioned on the right hand, as it were, of the CEO it was the job of the CFO to defend the truth of the financial analysis in the face of challenges from other managers. The CFO may not formulate the strategy but their support was critical to its adoption. So powerful has the CFO's position become in the organisation that many have come to see it as the ultimate ambition, even in preference to that of becoming CEO. The report's conclusion on the qualities of the perfect CFO can be summarised as follows:

- Financial skills
- Business acumen
- Good communicator
- Able to handle conflict
- International experience.

It is notable that the globalisation of business has pushed business accountants from the backroom to the boardroom. As CFOs this has meant a dramatic increase in the scope of their responsibilities, encompassing the strategic sourcing and allocation of financial resources across international operations. The International Federation of Accountants (2013) published a discussion paper laying out the five principles of the CFO's role:

1. A key leader in the senior management team
2. Able to combine stewardship with business partnership
3. An integrator and navigator for the organisation
4. Responsibility for the organisation's accounting and finance division
5. Upholding a professional attitude to finance.

It is because of the complexity of the CFO's role that it means it is no longer reserved for financial specialists, hence why MBA graduates have just as much chance of achieving the post of head financier within the corporations. It is vital that those who are ambitious for the position gain the soft skills necessary for communicating with a wide variety of stakeholders, sometimes conveying the kind of information that is guaranteed to make them unpopular. Ironically, CGMA Magazine (2013) found that CFOs recognised the importance of soft skill training yet were failing to provide it. Curiously, this ensures that the highest position of specialisation in the organisation is still open to ambitious executives who are willing to put the effort into accumulating the right skill set.

THE STORY SO FAR: CFO AS CORPORATE NAVIGATOR

If the CEO is the captain of the corporate ship then the CFO is its navigator. While the CEO sets the strategic objectives, the CFO is responsible for charting the course using in-depth quantitative analysis just as a navigator uses a sextant and slide rule. It is the job of the CFO to make the figures as accurate as possible and demonstrate the courage to stand by the objective analysis. They have a wide variety of tools at their disposal, but ultimately they have to please the financial backers in order to secure the long-term viability of the business. Fortunately, the diversity of potential sources of funding is broadening almost by the day, online sources in particular revealing new pools of finance to dip into.

 WEB SUPPORT

1. CFO Magazine www.ww2.cfo.com/source/cfo-magazine/

   A free publication with a wide variety of articles shedding light on the life and work of the modern CFO.

2. Net Present Value from Maths Is Fun www.mathsisfun.com/money/net-present-value.html

   A beautifully clear flow diagram that explains net present value step-by-step. Includes a handy link to internal rate of return (IRR) as well.

3. Microfinance from the Microfinance Gateway www.microfinancegateway.org/

   Although the website provides only a basic introduction to microfinance it also acts as a conduit for information from many other sources. As the title says, it is a gateway.

Research Projects

1. If you were to propose a high-speed rail network to connect north and south Africa, how would you calculate its financial viability: payback period, cost-benefit-analysis or net present value?
2. What lessons can Western banking systems learn from sharia-compliant Islamic banking?
3. Is micro-finance just charity with strings attached?
4. Does crowd-source funding unlock new sources of finance from sophisticated backers or simply unleash the chaos of mob finance?

 CASE STUDY – ISLAMIC FINANCE

Rates of return and interest are standard features of finance around the world. They put a price on the time value of money in a way that is often taken for granted. In some cultures, though, the charging of interest is seen as **usury** and therefore immoral.

Strictly speaking, usury is a charge levied in excess of reasonable compensation. In a standard business relationship the seller needs compensating for cost of the raw materials and the time spent working. After all, the seller could have spent the time working for their own benefit. It is difficult to be precise in valuing the compensation but we would understand it as the market or 'going' rate. If the seller charges a higher rate when they have put in no additional work then it is usury. In financial terms, interest charges are seen as usury because the amount lent, or the time period, has no relation to the work put in by the lender.

The view that interest is usury has been a commonly held view throughout history. In the Western business world it is seen as a little anachronistic to take a moral view of free market transactions. However, under the rules of Islamic sharia law, interest charges are still seen as usury. This does not mean that sharia-compliant loans are free of any charges but that the charges are calculated according to principles of fair compensation.

As an example, let us take the case of a house purchase. Most of us will be familiar with the concept of a mortgage: the bank pays for the house and then we pay them back the price of the house (capital) plus the interest due at the agreed rate. These payments are spread out over a number of years, often 25 or even more. As a result, the total sum of money spent on buying the house can be double the original price.

We accept this because the alternative would be to rent a house and save for house purchase simultaneously. This would take so long that by the time we could buy we would be so old we would not live long enough to enjoy it! Relatively speaking the mortgage is cheap because it takes into account the time value of money.

In **sharia-compliant banking**, usually known as **Islamic banking**, money has no intrinsic value and therefore a charge for its use would be usury. Instead, wealth is created through trade and investment in assets. Islamic banking is based on the idea of sharing risk between the borrower and the lender.

In our house buying example, the Islamic bank would buy the house and the borrower would rent the house from the bank (IBB, 2014). The cost of the rent is related to the price of the house and the payments are made over a period of years. At the end of the period ownership is transferred to the borrower.

Businesses can also access sharia-compliant bank loans. Islamic finance is based on risk sharing, this time between the bank and the entrepreneur. Here, the entrepreneur provides the expertise and the bank provides the capital. The end result should be that both profit from the deal.

In practice Islamic banking only differs in philosophy from conventional banking; the financial terms may be very similar or identical. This should not be taken to mean that Islamic banking is the same as conventional banking only hidden behind a veil of sharia respectability. Indeed, in the wake of the financial scandals that have swept conventional banking in recent years it might even be argued that banking based on a coherent set of principles can only be a good thing.

The government's slice of economic profit, taxation, is less clear under the rules of sharia compliance. Zakat is a specifically Islamic form of payment, somewhere between a religious tax and a voluntary donation. Its purpose is to redistribute money from wealthy Muslims to the less well off and to be put to the service of the religion itself. Zakat is raised in an equitable fashion and should be spent in accordance with sharia principles of morality and modesty. It is not intended for extravagant projects or the personal spending of the ruler. However, zakat does not preclude the raising of other taxes for non-sharia-compliant spending (Bakar and Rahman, 2007).

Critics of Islamic finance point out that the rulings of ancient texts are not appropriate to the environment of modern international finance. Even supporters of sharia compliance struggle to impose the principles on a system that could never have been imagined when the rules were compiled (Visser, 2013). Nevertheless, the high moral stance is one that can be learned from in the wake of the financial scandals that have beset conventional banking in recent years.

Point of consideration: To what extent can the principles of Islamic finance be incorporated into conventional finance? Are there other faiths and philosophies that offer lessons to financiers?

Sources: Bakar and Rahman, 2007; IBB, 2014; Visser, 2013

? MULTIPLE CHOICE QUESTIONS

Choose the response that most effectively answers the question:

1. Which senior executive is usually considered to be one below the CEO in the corporate hierarchy?
   a. Director of human resources.
   b. Chairman of the board.
   c. Chief financial officer (CFO).

2. Should a company accept a high-risk investment opportunity?
   a. Yes, but only if it is balanced by a high rate of return.
   b. No, risk should always be minimised.
   c. Yes, because only the brave win at business.

3. Under what circumstances is uncertainty acceptable in an investment opportunity?
   a. Never – it cannot be calculated so the appropriate rate of return cannot be identified.
   b. Sometimes – but only if it can be diversified by other uncertainties or if there is a company specific method for reducing it to a known risk.
   c. Always – it is a standard feature of business activities.

4. Which stakeholder will tolerate the higher risk, a bank or a shareholder?
   a. Bank – because it has a senior claim on the assets.
   b. Shareholder – because variable rates of return mean that they can enjoy increasing benefits as the investment succeeds.

5. For what kind of investment is cost benefit analysis (CBA) suited?
   a. Opening a high street coffee shop.
   b. Starting a charity.
   c. Building a national rail network.

6. Under what circumstances would a CFO find a pay-back-period analysis useful?
   a. Promoting an investment to gain public support.
   b. An investment with a limited time period.

7. Which is better for analysing investment opportunities: net present value (NPV) or internal rate of return (IRR)?
   a. NPV – because it shows the increase in wealth.
   b. IRR – because it gives a rate that can be readily compared.
   c. Neither – because they are both essentially the same analysis but from different perspectives.

8. What are the advantages of crowd-source funding for businesses?
   a. It taps into a new source of funding.
   b. The funding is guaranteed.

9. What does micro-finance offer that other sources of finance do not?
   a. Low rates of interest for investment opportunities that lack assets.
   b. Very small funds for very small investment opportunities.

10. What rate of interest would be charged by an Islamic sharia-compliant bank in comparison to conventional bank?
    a. Higher – there is an additional payment as a religious donation.
    b. Lower – interest is usury and cannot be charged.
    c. Same – but it is considered to be a service fee, not interest.

Answers

1c, 2a, 3c, 4b, 5c, 6a, 7c, 8a, 9a, 10c

REFERENCES

Bakar N B A and Rahman R A (2007) 'A comparative study of zakah and modern taxation' *J. KAU: Islamic Economics* 20(1), pp. 25–40

Baldvinsdottir G, Burns J, Nørreklit H and Scapens R W (2009) 'The image of accountants: from bean counters to extreme accountants' *Accounting, Auditing & Accountability Journal* 22(6), pp. 858–882

BBC (2013) 'The Statue of Liberty and America's crowdfunding pioneer' 25 April 2014 from www.bbc.co.uk/news/magazine-21932675 accessed 8 November 2014

Boadway R (2006) 'Principles of cost benefit analysis' *Public Policy Review* 2(1)

CGMA Magazine (2013) 'CFOs say soft skills are needed, but many aren't offering training in them' 1 July 2013 from www.cgma.org/magazine/news/pages/20138259.aspx?TestCookiesEnabled=redirect accessed 5 April 2015

EY (2013) 'A study of what makes a chief financial officer' from www.ey.com/Publication/vwLUAssets/The-DNA-of-the-CFO-2010/$FILE/The-DNA-of-the-CFO-2010.pdf accessed 5 April 2015

Fogel R W (1962) 'A quantitative approach to the study of railroads in American economic growth: a report of some preliminary findings' *The Journal of Economic History* 22(2), (Jun 1962), pp. 163–197

Foreman-Peck J, Makepeace G and Morgan B (2006) 'Growth and profitability of small and medium-sized enterprises: some Welsh evidence' *Regional Studies* 40(4), pp. 307–319

Grameen Bank (2014) Homepage from www.grameen-info.org/ accessed 8 November 2014

Hartmann-Wendels T, Stein I and Stöter A (2012) 'Tax incentives and capital structure choice: evidence from Germany'. Deutsche Bundesbank Discussion Paper No 18/2012 from www.bundesbank.de/Redaktion/EN/Downloads/Publications/Discussion_Paper_1/2012/2012_08_27_dkp_18.pdf?__blob=publicationFile accessed 8 November 2014

Hovakimian A, Opler T and Titman S (2001) 'The debt-equity choice' *Journal of Financial and Quantitative analysis* 36(01), pp. 1–24

IBB (Islamic Bank of Britain)(2014) 'Home purchase plan' from www.islamic-bank.com/home-finance/home-purchase-plan/ accessed 8 November 2014

International Federation of Accountants (IFAC)(2013) 'The role and expectations of an accountant' from www.ifac.org/sites/default/files/publications/files/Role%20of%20the%20CFO.pdf accessed 5 April 2015

Krugman P (2011) 'Will China break?' *New York Times* 18 December 2011 from www.jordipujol.cat/files/articles/xina19.pdf accessed 14 November 2014

Layard R and Glaister S (1994) *Cost-benefit analysis.* Cambridge: Cambridge University Press

Leeson, N (1996) *Rogue trader*. London: Warner Books

Modigliani F and Miller M (1958) 'The cost of capital, corporation finance and the theory of investment' *American Economic Review* 48 (3) pp. 261–297

Olson E L and Mathias Thjømøe H (2010) 'How bureaucrats and bean counters strangled General Motors by killing its brands' *Journal of Product & Brand Management* 19(2), pp. 103–113

Quinn D P and Jones T M (1995) 'An agent morality view of business policy' *Academy of Management Review* 20(1), pp. 22–42

Reuters (2013) 'Judge raises concerns about Fisker's race through bankruptcy' *Reuters* 10 December 2013 by Tom Hals from www.reuters.com/article/2013/12/10/us-fisker-bankruptcy-judge-idUS-BRE9B917P20131210 accessed 7 November 2014

——— (2014) 'U.S. government says it lost $11.2 billion on GM bailout' Reuters 30 April 2014 from www.reuters.com/article/2014/04/30/us-autos-gm-treasury-idUSBREA3T0MR20140430 accessed 3 April 2014

Seedrs (2014) Homepage from www.seedrs.com/ accessed 8 November 2014

Slater C (1997) 'General Motors and the demise of streetcars' *Transportation Quarterly* 51(3), Summer 1997, pp. 45–66

Steinkamp S and Westermann F (2014) 'The role of creditor seniority in Europe's sovereign debt crisis' *Economic Policy* 29(79), pp. 495–552

USHSR (United States High Speed Rail Association) (2014) US High Speed Rail Network Map from www.ushsr.com/ushsrmap.html accessed 8 November 2014

Vancouver Sun (2012) 'Port Mann Bridge tolls to start at $1.50 as incentive for drivers' *Vancouver Sun*, 12 September 2012 by Kelly Sinoski from www2.canada.com/story.html?id=7232152 accessed 8 November 2014

Visser H (2013) *Islamic finance: Principles and practice*. Cheltenham, Glos.: Edward Elgar Publishing

Weingartner H M (1969) Some new views on the payback period and capital budgeting decisions *Management Science* 15(12), pp. 594–607

Zorn D M (2004) Here a chief, there a chief: the rise of the CFO in the American firm *American Sociological Review* 69(3), pp. 345–364

Part VI Global Management of People

What makes global management international is coming face-to-face with other cultures; without that, international business is just business. Yet what makes these seemingly exotic lands so beguiling and mysterious is also what makes them so risky for business; in being unfamiliar they are also unpredictable, and this is not what a sound business plan is based upon.

Culture is the artefact of human society that gives rise to perhaps the greatest disagreements. In the rush to distinguish ourselves from each other we like to claim the best attributes for ourselves and consign the worst to our neighbours. Obviously 'we' cannot be noble in all respects any more than 'they' can be despicable in all other respects. Yet if there is one thing all humans have in common it is that they give this cultural prejudice a pretty good try.

In the narrower business sense this can give rise to concerns about overseas operations, where productivity and quality might be vulnerable to lower standards. There are also concerns that different working patterns will lead to meetings being missed or communications misunderstood. Attempts have been made to bring coherence to the anxieties by analysing culture objectively. Two of the leading proponents are, respectively, Hofstede and Trompenaars who, along with their co-researchers, formulated dimensional measures of culture.

These theories have excited a high volume of debate on their validity. Not only has empirical support been patchy but they have all the while been subtly undermined by MNEs who have quietly gone about the business of establishing operations overseas anyway. Despite these criticisms the theories of cultural differences have at least been successful in encouraging some sort of objective analysis in place of the emotive arguments that preceded them.

A deeper understanding of how people work is becoming increasingly valued in business, as they are found to be the source of many competitive advantages. A company may enjoy the advantages of many physical assets but these can be bought in from outside and periodically upgraded. Company personnel departments used to treat workers in a similar fashion to physical assets but this has been replaced by the more enlightened human resources (HR) function. Human resources are unique in that they may be hired for a known set of attributes and then further developed to reveal new attributes. The purpose of the HR function is to continually review how the requirement for new attributes fits with the latest corporate strategy.

It is the link with the corporate strategy that has raised HR to the level of a strategic function within the company. Once the overall corporate strategy has been decided then the HR strategy needs to serve it through recruitment, training and incentives. This is further complicated at the international level, where decisions need to be made on the relocation of staff according to where the most valued human assets lie: in the domestic location, at the new overseas location or globally.

The recognition that people matter is not just confined to the internal workings of the firm. There is a growing realisation that firms are responsible, to varying degrees, for all the stakeholders, i.e. anyone who has an interest in the company. In short, this is just about everyone on the planet. If companies are to take their place alongside the rest of the world then the understanding is that they need to demonstrate corporate social responsibility (CSR).

CSR can take many forms depending on the stakeholders being targeted. If it is the shareholders and other providers of funds then it is the governance of the firm that needs to be equitable and transparent. When it is the employees that are being considered then subjects like health and safety come to mind. Then there is the wider community, beyond the factory gates, for which the company has some responsibility.

Clearly, the challenges facing global managers extend far beyond the company boundary. The basic purpose of a business can still be expressed in the mission to maximise value to the customer at minimum cost to itself. Globalisation does not contradict this but introduces new complications for the global manager of which CSR is just the latest. The only thing we can be sure of is that in the dynamic world of global management new challenges are only just around the corner.

16 International Culture and Business

Chapter Objectives

As companies explore new markets and locations they must move beyond the technicalities of business models and strategies to confront the mysteries of international culture. Usually perplexing, sometimes unfathomable but always fascinating, unfamiliar cultures around the world present a whole set of seemingly random challenges to the uninitiated. In this chapter, we will see how managers can understand the peculiarities of cultural differences:

- The roots of culture and its impact on business.
- Analysing culture for business strategies.
- Prejudice and the darker side of culture.

ONE HUMANITY, MANY CULTURES

One of the most fascinating aspects of being an international manager is the opportunity to meet people from other cultures. There are few things more delightful than experiencing at first hand different ways of living and working. Despite the various boundaries of language and customs somehow we seem to muddle through, coming out of it enriched and inspired. Some even believe that business is a tool for international understanding, ultimately promising worldwide peaceful coexistence. Maybe there is something in this; despite the dramatic spread of globalisation and the expansion in the human population it is salutary to note that armed conflicts are generally localised. It has been nearly seventy years since the end of World War II, and perhaps business can take some of the credit for bringing us all closer together.

International managers are constantly exposed to unfamiliar cultures in a way that the final consumers are not. True though it is that consumers can choose from global sets of products, thereby accessing the best products at the lowest prices, their only real concern is product, not the place of origin. The consumer does not have to deal with unfamiliar languages or product specifications because the product must meet the consumer's requirements; it is the product that must compromise, not the consumer. In contrast, it is the international manager who must deal with the cultural challenges in order that the consumer does not have to.

If culture was simply about language then there would not be such a problem. All a manager would have to do is learn the local language in order to conduct business in the country. Alternatively, both sides could settle on a common international language, like the artificially constructed language Esperanto. But of course culture is much more complicated than that and this is just as well; without all those cultural complications international business would not be so beguiling.

Nature or nurture

Culture is an integral part of what being a human being is all about. Some would even claim that it is what marks us out as different from the rest of the animal kingdom. It provides us with a concept of communities and societies along with a sense of belonging to these groups. How we become members of such of groups is part of the **nature–nurture** debate: the argument whether nature has pre-programmed us with our various characteristics or we have learnt them from those around us (Rutter, 2006).

There is no definitive answer to the nature–nurture question, although we are undoubtedly born with certain instincts that would have served us well in a purely natural habitat. The real argument concerns the extent to which we can extend these natural instincts to other attributes, such as abilities for scientific thought or artistic creativity, personal achievement or community service. The nature–nurture debate even encompasses whether we believe in a justice system based on rational debate or on religious ideology. If culture is determined by nurture then we can educate ourselves to change that culture. However, if nature is the determinant of culture then we are slaves to our unchanging instincts.

Most people like to believe that to some extent their culture is as deeply rooted as their natural instincts but this is also the more dangerous route to take. Not only does it allow certain characteristics, attitudes and moral beliefs to be claimed as innately cultural and therefore excused from explanation or justification, this view also allows another set of characteristics, attitudes and morals to be attributed to those outside one's social group. You can bet that the attributes claimed for one's own group are generally positive and those for the other group are generally negative.

If these cultural judgements were made at random it might not be so bad but they become systemised into stereotypes and even outright prejudice. At their mildest they accord qualities such as 'ruthless efficiency', 'group loyalty', 'creativeness', 'inscrutability' and 'mathematical ability' to particular national groups. Never mind that these nations are so often made up of further disparate national sub-groups that acknowledge little common ground between them: from China to Spain the nation state as a vessel for a unified culture is one that is recognised more by outsiders than those on the inside.

At the most extreme, the belief in the innateness of culture can lead to the most negative of prejudices. Most infamously it leads to racism and the ill-conceived idea that there is such a thing as a pure human being of a particular type. In fact, DNA research has found that all races share common ancestors. However, prejudice has deep roots in societies and gives rise to classism, ageism, sexism and so on. In fact, the us-and-them attitude pervades every corner of every society.

In international business it is important to acknowledge as a fact that the individuals with whom we interact will have their own cultural identities and allegiances. Yet whilst being sensitive to these differences on a practical level it is surely vital that we recognise the common human bond that joins us all, regardless of race, colour, gender or creed. Whatever the truth about the nature–nurture debate, holding to the principle that we are all the same under the skin is the only defensible course to take in an inclusive human society.

The basis of culture

Culture comprises the accepted forms of values and behaviours that allow us to identify with particular groups in society. As members of these groups we subscribe to their **norms** even though at times they may conflict with our own personal values and behaviours. To be a member of a group is to subsume the great part of our personalities into the culture. How the norms of the group tolerate individualism is itself another norm of the group.

We can share in as many cultures as there are groups of which we are members. These groups range in size and importance from the family unit to the **nation state**. In between there are a myriad of other groups, such as work colleagues we identify with, sports teams we support, political parties and so on. Our membership of each group may be temporary or tangential and the culture of the group may be weak or strong but it will be present nonetheless. Culture is an irrefutable part of human society.

The great challenge with culture is that because it provides a sense of identity it tends to be laden with value. To come into conflict with an aspect of culture is often to conflict with the very sense of identity held by the members of that culture. The weight that people put on these aspects of culture means that some of them have more value than others. This gives rise to the idea of high and low culture, high culture being that which sits at the very summit of the sense of identity. Figure 16.1 depicts national culture as an iceberg, high cultural items being conspicuous features of the nation with the bottom made up of more general characteristics.

The **cultural iceberg** depicts national culture as being made up of the few visible aspects, as would be observable by outsiders, underpinned by many more cultural aspects that are mainly intangible and difficult to define. As a consequence, nations will often take overt pride in having a national language, their own traditions and perhaps a religion too, although this is often regional rather than national. Art is also seen as symbolic of culture, and nations will maintain large public collections of art in magnificent museums. It is all these conspicuous symbols that mark a culture out as obviously different and which we find so beguiling as a visitor.

Below the waterline of the cultural iceberg are those aspects of culture that are much less obvious. In some ways these are the foundations of a culture because they set the general tone and give direction to the society. If we think of the culture's behaviour as being above the iceberg's waterline then the culture's personality lies below it. Here we find the belief systems, the folklore and the attitudes of the culture. As tourists we would only be vaguely aware of these traits but for international business managers they are the major challenge. It is these fundamental aspects of culture that decide how people work, how they negotiate business deals and how they engage in the market. Also included are attitudes to the law, rules, welfare and taxation. Without understanding the foundations of a culture then business in that place becomes risky, even uncertain, because behavioural outcomes will be difficult to predict.

Yet this analysis of culture is as value-laden as culture itself. An interesting exercise is to complete a cultural iceberg with aspects of one's own culture. If we were Spanish we would put the Spanish language, dishes like paella and flamenco music above the waterline. Below the waterline we might put traditions

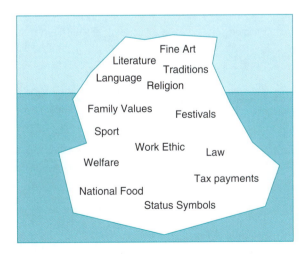

Figure 16.1 Cultural iceberg

such as bull-fighting, beliefs derived from the Roman Catholic religion and the heritage of the empire years. Although the result might be a fair illustration of Spanish culture, at the same time many of these aspects are shared by other countries. Spanish is spoken more widely in South America than it is in Spain and bullfighting is also far from unique to Spain. Indeed, sports involving some sort of duel to the death with an animal are a common feature of most human societies at some point in their history. Flamenco music is certainly a unique feature of Spain but one that is also enjoyed beyond the nation's borders; you do not have to be Spanish to practise flamenco.

The cultural iceberg, then, illustrates perceptions of culture rather than the structure. For example, to be culturally sensitive is to be aware that the French place a high value on the culinary arts or that Americans extol the virtues of individualism. To accept these characteristics as unique and factual, though, would be to believe that one culture can never truly understand another. If this were the case then international business would never flourish.

Shaping the culture of the nation state

The most conspicuous cultural identity is with the nation state. People will frequently state their **nationality** as if their place of origin explains who they are. Each nationality likes to claim for itself a set of cultural characteristics, only some of which coincide with the impression outsiders have. Americans, for example, see themselves as standard bearers for freedom, while a number of nations see the United States as oppressive. Indeed, there is a prevailing fear that American culture is overpowering other cultures around the world to the extent that we are all converging on a unified international culture derived from the American.

In Figure 16.2 we can see the main **determinants of national culture**. These include the dominant religion, particularly as sanctioned by the government, the educational system, how society is structured in terms of perceived classes and so on.

What is interesting about Figure 16.2 is how many of the cultural characteristics for a country may actually be imported from outside. Three of the biggest **religions** in the world, Judaism, Christianity and Islam all originated in the Middle East. Christianity spread to Europe and from there to the European

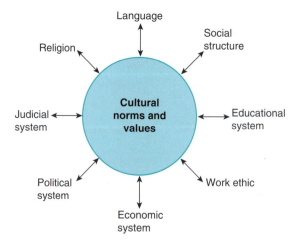

Figure 16.2 *Determinants of national culture*

colonies in North and South America but has only a minor presence in its place of origin. Islam has remained strong in its place of origin but has spread through Muslim trade throughout the Asia-Pacific region, where around 60% of Muslims now live; the largest Muslim country is Indonesia (Pew Research, 2011). Judaism is unique in suffering an enforced exile from its birthplace only to return to the sovereign nation of Israel in the mid-twentieth century.

There are a multitude of other religions and faiths around the world, occasionally coming into conflict with each other as they defend their values to the death. Despite this, not only are these belief systems frequently transferred between peoples but they are themselves subject to evolutionary changes over time. This has knock-on effects for other determinants of culture, such as the **educational** and **political systems**, which may be partly or wholly founded on a religious base. Some countries have a more philosophical foundation to their culture, notably China and **Confucianism**, particularly its impact on the educational system. Although the brutal rise of communism, and the more recent economic renaissance incorporating some capitalist principles, seems to have consigned Confucianism to history, there are still those who consider the Chinese culture to retain significant Confucian ideals (Paradise, 2009).

It is because the determinants of culture shown in Figure 16.2 wax and wane in the power of their influence that it is not possible to precisely state how the culture has come to be shaped by them. Furthermore, the culture has a reflexive impact on those determinants, leading to changes in them as well. The political and judicial systems may enforce the values of a culture but then they are subject to changes when they are considered to be out of step with the times. The economic system may even vary with the business cycle, socialist tendencies rising and falling with the perceived need for welfare. In a similar way, the work ethic may evolve, Germany and Japan being famous for the way their attitudes to work brought about their economic recoveries after the end of World War II.

Culture is perceived as being at the core of a society's identity but, as we have seen, the forces that mould the culture are continually shifting. As a result, the culture itself is in a constant state of flux. This lack of permanence extends even to language, so often considered to be the most dependable feature of a culture.

Language as the totem of culture

Leaving aside the inconvenient fact that languages migrate, merge and evolve as much as any other aspect of culture they are nevertheless often perceived as being a core feature of the culture. Countries will even attempt to hold back the dynamic changes in the language when they are seen as threats to the culture.

Where the local language is being superseded by another there may be attempts to fund its preservation through the creation of schools and media outlets that promote use of the original language. The UK is not unique in actively supporting the continued use of Welsh, Gaelic and Cornish, native languages that were either on the point of extinction or already dead. In France the Académie Française, an almost 400-year-old institution, is charged with protecting the national language from foreign contamination; its website is available only in French (Académie Française, 2014).

Philosophers like Noam Chomsky (2002) have put forward the idea that all languages have some common form buried deep within the human psyche. This is in contrast to the generally held belief that each language indicates an entirely unique way of thinking. It is sometimes claimed that some languages do not have a future tense, or numbers that go beyond what you can count on your fingers. These features are said to weigh heavily on the development of the nation. Oddly enough, English, like Japanese, does not have a proper future tense but we seem to get around the problem just fine.

Figure 16.3 *Japanese Kanji*

For outsiders, Japanese is a most curious language because the written form contains pictographs, or logograms, known as kanji. These are highly stylised representations of the physical object. Originating in China, over the centuries many of these kanji have been highly abstracted from the historic form but the meaning can still sometimes be guessed. Take a look at Figure 16.3 and, assuming you are not familiar with the Japanese or Chinese languages, see if you can make out their meaning.

Reading the kanji in the Japanese style, that is from top right down, finishing in the bottom left, these are the respective meanings:

- Person – body and legs spread apart
- Child – head at the top, arms stretched out
- Tree – trunk and roots spreading out below, branches above
- Woman – seated cross-legged.

Sadly, only a few Japanese and Chinese characters can be guessed so easily, but all written words in the languages contain some sort of graphic image, no matter how obscure. The official list of Japanese kanji runs to 2136 characters, supplemented by two additional syllabic scripts which are used to spell out words phonetically. The Chinese language has only the pictographs, of which there are in excess of 50,000 characters, although a mere 4000 are necessary in daily life. In languages that use the Roman alphabet, like English, the letters are purely abstract and have no visual relationship with the object they represent. Well, perhaps there is just one: 'bed', the word looking a bit like a bed if you squint hard enough.

If the Japanese language is so visual, so graphic, then we would expect the Japanese themselves to be very visual people. For example, we might expect them to be highly advanced in the visual arts, such as painting, photography and film-making. There are, of course, well known Japanese practitioners of the visual arts, the film director Akira Kurosawa, comes to mind, but no more so than any other culture. Research has found only weak evidence for Japanese kanji being processed in the brain as if it were graphic rather than linguistic (Hanavan and Coney, 2005). If the Japanese have a visual approach to finance it is because they were taught that way: they use the *soroban* abacus to a very advanced level and thereby gain a feel for arithmetic that Westerners, with their abstract number system, almost completely lack.

MYTH BUSTER – CONFUSING JAPANESE

In the West the Japanese have a reputation for being highly ordered, even regimented people. Anyone who believes that should try learning the language; one of the most devilishly complex ever devised! The most curious feature of the Japanese writing system, though, is that it is not Japanese at all. As so often with languages it was imported from elsewhere, in this case China. The Chinese language is not related at all to Japanese, and while it is suited to the pictograph system this is not really so for Japanese. So awkward is the fit between the Japanese language and Chinese characters that two additional writing systems have had to be invented in order to achieve complete transcription of spoken Japanese. If the kanji system says anything about the Japanese psyche it is that the Japanese are obstinate in making something fit!

The role of Japanese kanji is to supply units of meaning. The fact that the written word is pronounced one way in Japanese and the other in Chinese should not, on the face of it, cause any problems. So the symbol for vehicle, 車 (which is a picture of a cart seen from above), is pronounced *kuruma* in Japanese and *chē* in Chinese. The problem is that the two languages quickly diverge in their usage. The Japanese word is used specifically to mean *car* in English, but the Chinese word for car is actually two characters, 汽車 (pronounced *qichē*). The Chinese build up their words in this modular way that is both surprisingly modern in conception and perfectly suited to the ideograph style.

The Japanese follow this modular construction but when they do they switch to Chinese pronunciation, or what they think they heard the Chinese saying at the time that they borrowed the word from them. This might have occurred several hundred years ago so not only will the Japanese pronunciation be quite different from the original Chinese the meaning may also have evolved over time. For example, the Japanese word 汽車 is the word the Chinese use for car but the Japanese pronunciation is *kisha* and it means train, specifically steam train. So that character we saw for car, 車, is pronounced in Japanese as *kuruma* when it is on its own and as the quasi-Chinese *sha* when it is joined with another word. The Japanese reading is known as *kun-yomi* and the Chinese derived reading as *on-yomi*. Since the original Chinese words may have been borrowed at various times in history and from different parts of China a single character can have several on-yomi readings. To make matters worse, there can be several *kun-yomi* readings for the character as well!

It might not be so bad if every Japanese word had a direct Chinese equivalent, but this is not the case. For words that exist only in Japanese there has to be another system that spells out the word. Sometimes erroneously known as a Japanese alphabet, the symbols are used to represent the syllables of a word phonetically. Of course the Japanese are not satisfied with using just one phonetic system so they have two, hiragana and katakana. The two systems are closely related but differ in their applications: hiragana is used for Japanese words and katakana for foreign words or for emphasis, the equivalent of putting a word into *italics*.

It has been suggested that the complexities of the Japanese written language are an impediment to education and a barrier to international trade. A number of attempts have been made to simplify the written language but to no avail. It remains maddeningly difficult for Westerners in particular to learn but a cause of deep fascination for the culture. The world would be a poorer place without it.

Point of consideration: For cultures that do not use the Roman alphabet in their languages, to what extent is this an impediment to international business? How can they reduce the disadvantages and heighten the advantages?

Source: Henshall, 1988

RELIGIOUS CULTURE, ETHICS AND BUSINESS

Religion has had an enormous impact on culture. If language is said to be a culturally sensitive topic then religion can prove positively inflammatory. Religious differences have brought many peoples to war, and as a source of friction their abrasive role has in no way diminished over the years. At the same time, though, it would be wrong to argue that religions cannot co-exist. Most religious practitioners respect each other's disagreements and live alongside one another in peace and harmony.

It could even be argued that religion preceded business as a globalising influence. It is quite common for religions to transcend nation states and create a sense of international community. Far from promoting social conflict, these shared religions can pull national cultures closer together. International business can act in a similar fashion, bringing groups of people together to their mutual benefit.

Religions have a key part in the definition of a culture because they tend to set out a framework for living, including prescribed rules and guidelines. Many of these overlap with business, and so the international manager needs to be sensitive to the religious norms in order to avoid appearing disrespectful. Although the religious rules can seem forbidding to an outsider it is often a simple matter of following one's hosts. For example, in some countries the consumption of alcohol is banned, which means that it is simply not offered; the danger of committing a *faux pas* in such a country should therefore never arise.

Beyond the explicit religious rules are the ethical codes, though they often have a religious base. These may occur where religion meets the national or political culture. The codes of practice are derived from religious dictates but are not necessarily religious in themselves. Countries that share the same religious beliefs can have widely contrasting views on such topics such as **gender equality**, **social mobility**, **corruption** and so on. These codes of practice are specific to the country and so can be impossible to predict even for those international managers who share the same religion.

 ## CASE STUDY – PROTESTANT WORK ETHIC

The Protestant work ethic is characterised as an almost religious devotion to hard work which is found in the countries that turned away from Roman Catholascism in the early sixteenth century. Influenced by the doctrines of Martin Luther, first Germany and then neighbouring countries rejected the excesses of the Roman Catholic Church and embraced the reformation. England's protest against the Catholic Church was driven by a power struggle between King Henry VIII and the Pope, but the result was the emergence of a Protestant Church in parallel with that in Europe. In subsequent centuries immigrants from these regions brought their religious beliefs with them to North America.

According to the the philosopher Max Weber, the Protestant work ethic is one that reclaims from religious clerics the right by an individual to find favour with God. It is no longer work for the church that earns a place in heaven but application to one's own career, putting to use ones own talents and skills. By this principle even the most humble of work is equal to that of an officer of the church. Individuals thereby had a duty to themselves to maximise their efforts with the inevitable result that they accumulated wealth on their own account. However, this wealth was not to be wasted on a luxurious lifestyle or charitable donations, which were considered to inspire indolence in their recipients, so the Protestant work ethic gained a reputation for being austere and even cruel.

Weber's argument links the economic efficiency of the Protestant work ethic with the dominance of industrial societies across Northern Europe and North America. On the positive side it is typified by hard work for personal gain, a self-help attitude and capitalist business practices. On the negative side it is often seen as selfish and unsympathetic to those who are disadvantaged. In its more extreme form it is known as Anglo-Saxon capitalism, specific to the UK and United States. A belief in the Protestant work ethic is, by implication, a sly dig at attitudes to work in Southern European and South American cultures, which are often stereotyped as more socially minded but also, dare one say, lazy.

Like all attempts to pigeon-hole people there may once have been a grain of truth in the idea of a religious basis to work, and it is true that the industrial revolution took hold first in the Protestant countries. Yet those countries were also endowed with the factors of production, and markets, that could support industrialisation. More importantly, once other countries also gained the appropriate factors of production they too joined the global industrial revolution. Not just the countries of Southern Europe but also South America and, of course, South East Asia, have come to economic prominence. A glance at working hours around the world will show there is nothing Protestant about the work ethic.

Point of consideration: For a religion, faith or philosophy of your choice discuss how its ideology impacts on attitudes to work. Then compare this analysis with the actual employment and economic conditions apparent in a country that is dominated by the ideology.

Sources: Becker and Wossmann, 2007; Lee et al., 2007

CULTURAL CONVERGENCE

A force pulling on the roots of culture is the internationalisation of human society. There is a general feeling that the deep sense of identity people have with their immediate communities is disappearing and being usurped by a unified international culture (Leung et al., 2005). Blame for this is being levelled at the globalisation of business. Since the greatest concentration of successful commercial enterprises is, by definition, in the developed world this means that Western MNEs stand accused. Prominent amongst them are the US corporations.

There is evidence that cultures around the world are rapidly evolving, but equally it could be argued that this is a normal part of human society. A static culture is one that has made no developments, or else forces for change have been suppressed politically. Where political forces attempt to hold back cultural change they tend to do little more than delay a rising tide of public sentiment. As the pressure for change increases so does the repressive political bulwark until eventually one or other gives way. This can occur in an explosion of revolutionary fervour.

Even in political systems that are designed to channel forces for change in a socially agreeable direction, as democracy is intended to do, there can still be a minority backlash against the erosion of established culture as an apparently foreign culture sweeps in. This is particularly the case when the imported culture is being introduced by immigrants, giving rise to local resentment.

Many MNEs find themselves exposed, as they are perceived to be in the vanguard of these cultural conflicts, local enmity boiling over when a local firm is portrayed as a victim. One corporation that is commonly attacked in the local media is McDonalds, the US-based fast food chain. Yet the international spread of a restaurant chain with a Scottish name serving a vaguely German-style meat (hamburger) and Belgian vegetables ('French' fries) is perhaps more a symbol of cultural synergy than cultural imperialism.

ANALYSING CULTURE FOR INTERNATIONAL BUSINESS

For the international manager, cultural differences are something of a social and commercial minefield. There seem to be an infinite number of rules, taboos and guidelines that need adhering to or else potential customers will be offended and business prospects damaged. Some of the guidance offered can be an insult to the intelligence: in Thailand it is considered an offence to touch someone's head but then it is difficult to think of any culture where one might pat one's opposite number on the head.

In practice, international business people are fairly forgiving of each other's cultural peculiarities. If a western business person does not perform a flawless bow to a Japanese counterpart it is not usually the end of the world. It is a different matter when committing to a new investment project that will be employing armies of local recruits and working with scores of local suppliers. It then becomes important to have a solid understanding of local attitudes to work and business relationships in order to avoid costly misunderstandings.

As when analysing any business opportunity, the manager needs a framework in order to make a systematic investigation. Fortunately, there are a number of these for analysing cultures, the most well-known of which are the two cultural dimension theories of Hofstede and Trompennars.

1. Hofstede's theory of cultural dimensions

Geert Hofstede is a social psychologist who first became interested in cultural differences when he discovered that two geographically close countries, the Netherlands and UK, were culturally highly distinct. He developed this interest while working for IBM, the international computer giant based in the United States (Hofstede, 2001). From his research he developed a theory of culture based around four, eventually six, dimensions. Each of these dimensions describes how a national characteristic might rate for a particular attitudinal aspect of culture relevant to business. Using numerical scores, each of these dimensions then delivers a measure of how people within the national group share values that then shape their approach to business. An outsider can use the dimensions to analyse the best approach to doing business with people in that country.

The original four dimensions were as follows:

- Power distance – attitudes to the uneven distribution of power
- Individualism – the relationship between the individual and their identified group
- Uncertainty – the degree to which uncertainty is managed
- Masculinity – the relative dominance of gender values, male or female.

To these dimensions were subsequently added two more, at different stages in the theory's development:

- Long-term orientation – the ability to cope with long-range strategies that deliver their returns in the distant future.
- Indulgence versus restraint – the extent to which self-restraint is a feature of the culture.

Taken as a complete set it should be possible for a manager to analyse any national culture and so formulate a corporate entry strategy, or even avoid the country altogether. Certainly the dimensions have a strong intuitive attraction since all communities have a psychological need to assign to themselves to cultural characteristics. They then contrast themselves with other communities on these characteristics. Hofstede's purpose is to systemise the multitude of differences into the core dimensions and measure them quantitatively. While superficially reasonable, on closer inspection each dimension is fraught with inconsistencies. Let's delve into each of these dimensions in more depth.

1. **Power distance index (PDI)** – in some countries the citizens are able to tolerate a wide gap in political influence between themselves, with little power to change the world they live in, and those at the top of the social pyramid that wield all the power. This is high power distance because there is a big difference between those that have power and those that do not, dictatorships being the most extreme example. At the other end of the scale are the lower power distance politics of democracies, where the citizens retain ultimate power but delegate it, regularly and temporarily, to their political representatives.

   One of the most hackneyed examples of a high power distance country is North Korea, where the ruling dynasty wields total power, the general populace being cowed and subjugated. The problem with this view is that the citizens may have had this situation imposed upon them. The neighbouring country of South Korea shared broadly the same history and culture up until the division of Korea in 1945. After years of autocratic rule South Korea was transformed into a democracy, becoming a highly successful economy from the late 1980s (Rodrik, 1995). This gives us two contrasting PDI measures for twin countries that share a culture but have vastly different economic and political systems.

2. **Individualism versus collectivism (IDV)** – in some cultures there seems to be a great emphasis placed on individuals expressing themselves and asserting their independence. This is in contrast to collectivist societies, where members are expected to subsume themselves into the group and work for the benefit of everyone, not just themselves.

   An example of a proudly individualistic society is said to be that of the United States. It is also one of the most culturally diverse countries in the world, which would seem to support the IDV score. Yet the country is also one of the largest in the world, both in terms of population and land area, supported by a vibrant and successful economy. For such a mixture of individuals to hold together as a single nation, there must be some cohesive force creating a sense of unity. Indeed, another characteristic of the United States is the open display of patriotism that denotes a strong group identity overlaying the professed belief in individualism. This was particularly noticeable in the widespread flag-display behaviour observed after the terrorist attacks on New York in 2001 (Skitka, 2005). On this basis, the United States might be said to be an individualistic society but only at one level, a sense of collectivism binding the people together in the national identity at the highest level.

3. **Uncertainty avoidance index (UAI)** – a high score here indicates a culture that will attempt to minimise uncertainty wherever they can, perhaps because they are emotionally sensitive. This group needs strong social rules and norms in order to maintain order within the group. By contrast, a group that can tolerate uncertainty will be able to cope with the unsure element in any new situation as it occurs. These people will have a low score on the index.

   Businesses with their roots in a high uncertainty avoidance culture will themselves tend to be risk averse. Although risk aversion is a term often applied to companies that tend to be cautious it is not a phrase that has any place in business management studies. Just as a medical doctor needs to act in accordance with their diagnosis, any risk being neither avoided nor welcomed but rather minimised, so a professional manager should make an objective analysis and then act on it. A risk-averse company is simply one that is too timid to take the action that its own analysis has recommended. A risk-averse culture is therefore one comprising companies that are incapable of taking what is essentially the correct course of action. Japan is often put forward as an example of a risk-averse culture; quite how the country could be home to innovations like the Sony Walkman or the Toyota Prius hybrid car is difficult to explain.

4. **Masculinity versus femininity (MAS)** – one of the more value laden dimensions since it applies gender clichés to the business environment. The masculine values are said to comprise a highly developed sense of competition, assertiveness and hierarchies based on power. Feminine values, meanwhile, are said to include an emphasis on relationships and a broad regard for the quality of life.

    Scandinavian countries are often claimed to be more feminine because of the comprehensive, and expensive, welfare programmes operated by the governments. Corporations in Scandinavia follow this approach with generous provisions for parental leave, although they are required to do this by law. While such government intervention is quantifiable, it may not be symbolic of a caring society but one that is prepared to trust the government to make the provisions (Pfau-Effinger, 2005). In wealthy countries that have less pervasive welfare systems, provisions are still made but by individuals or groups of individuals, such as families. In the least wealthy countries of the world a welfare system is a distant dream. In either case the values of the corporation are decided by government policy and economic wealth.

5. **Pragmatic versus normative (PRA)** – this dimension relates to the need people have to explain the mysteries of the world around them. A pragmatic person would concede that it is impossible to know everything and so would develop strategies for working with what limited knowledge they have. They are able to cope with apparent contradictions and are happy to let conditions develop over the long term. These people tend to display strong perseverance and will save for the future. At the other end of the dimension normative people believe that everything can be explained and put greater faith in a world governed by fundamental rules. They put a high value on social conventions and have a short-term view with less need to save for the future.

    As happens with the other dimensions, it is difficult to see how pragmatism can be translated into the complexities of the business environment. The Japanese culture is one that is thought to embody the Confucian ethos of a rigid respect for history and one's seniors, although Confucius never set foot outside his native China. Though the Confucian connection is often oversimplified (Chung et al., 2008) Japanese companies seem to have absorbed some of this attitude and famously promote workers on years of service rather than merit. At the same time this is balanced by a more pragmatic, team-working approach that means high-achieving juniors still have a voice within the group. Japan also has one of the highest savings rates in the world.

6. **Indulgence versus restraint (IND)** – this dimension measures the degree to which those in a culture demand instant gratification as opposed to restraining themselves. An indulgent culture would be one where rewards must be immediate and public, with conspicuous displays of wealth. A culture with restraint would be more conservative in its tastes and prepared to delay rewards.

    Indulgence and restraint may have more to do with the presentation of behaviour than the underlying attitudes. British culture tends to promote restraint but there are numerous examples of conspicuous materialism such as the historic stately homes, so popular with tourists. Equally, Italian culture is known for flamboyance, while the Roman Catholic religion preaches restraint.

MYTH BUSTER – SWEDEN AND THE 'CARING' WELFARE STATE

In the mid-eighteenth century, Sweden was a major political power in Europe but was concerned that its population had been seriously diminished by war and disease. If the population had shrunk to a dangerously low level then government tax receipts would fall and the country would be unable to defend itself, either against external invasion or internal insurrection. The first national population census, the Tabellverket, was therefore instigated in 1749.

The Tabellverket was compiled by Lutheran priests as a record of all the births, deaths and demographics in each parish. Understandably, given the era, there were a number of practical challenges in gathering the data but to have such pillars of the local community responsible for surveys was the masterstroke of the Tabellverket. The final results were remarkably accurate, and worrying for the Swedish government.

The first Tabellverket showed that the population of the country at that time, including non-Swedes, was around 1.78 million. By comparison, the population in Great Britain was estimated at around 6.5 million and France at almost 25 million people. This was alarming news to the Swedish government, which then realised that far from being in the front rank of European nations it was in fact a minor player.

Today, Sweden is said to have one of the most supportive and caring societies anywhere. Yet the roots of the current Swedish welfare system, one of the most extensive in the world, are in the eighteenth-century requirement to expand the population and strengthen national security. Furthermore, the reliability and detail of the data, along with the need to project into the future, stimulated the development of advanced statistical analysis. From the first national census was created the reputation for a caring society and the scientific rigour of statistics. From these twin outcomes the question then arises: is Sweden a caring, feminine culture or a calculating and controlling masculine culture?

Point of consideration: Do you consider taxpayer-funded welfare to be symbolic of a caring society or a government intent on population control?

Source: Sköld, 2004

2. Trompenaars' theory of cultural dimensions

Fons Trompenaars developed his theory of cultural dimensions in partnership with Charles Hampden-Turner (Trompenaars and Hampden-Turner, 1998). Like Hofstede, Trompenaars is Dutch, and the two sets of dimensions have a passing similarity. However, where Hofstede's theory is based on psychology and purports to explain how cultural differences spring out of unique ways of thinking, Trompenaars' theory is behavioural. Trompenaars' approach does not, therefore, explain how cultures think differently, only how they behave differently.

In Trompenaars' theory there are seven dimensions, some coinciding with Hofstede's but others specific to Trompenaars.

1. **Universalism versus particularism** – the extent to which cultural behaviour is conducted according to universal rules or each situation is dealt with on its own merits. In workplaces such as the emergency services or military this can create a dilemma between the need for a robust decision-making framework alongside flexibility in a highly dynamic, uncertain environment.

2. **Individualism versus collectivism** – coincides with Hofstede's dimension of the same name but from a behavioural point of view. In the workplace many tasks can only be completed by a team, so measurement on this dimension needs to take this into account. It might even be argued that individualism is a luxury that is not welcome in low-skill jobs like assembly work.

3. **Neutral versus emotion** – this dimension is based on observation of how emotion is expressed. Although these differences are often apparent when comparing one culture with another it could be a presentational issue. It may not be that emotionally neutral cultures do not show emotion, only that they are subtle about it. For outsiders it is necessary to learn how to recognise the emotional cues; it is not that the cues do not exist. Measurement on this dimension is therefore vulnerable to subjective judgements, depending on whether the observer empathises with the culture or not.

4. **Specific versus diffuse** – the separation of work life from home life. Some cultures have specific behaviours for each, which means they are kept separate. This dimension is complicated by the difficulty in precisely drawing the work–home boundary. In China and Japan it is often culturally necessary for senior and junior colleagues to socialise outside work. However, these occasions are still work-related and the work–home boundary is shifted to a time after the event. Just because the company has organised a social activity does not mean that work and family has merged.

5. **Achievement versus ascription** – the dimension measures whether status comes from personal merit or is ascribed by the system. There is some analogous connection with Hofstede's long-term orientation metric but with less emphasis on the time element. An ascription culture could still reward behaviour within a short time-span but the reward would go to a representative of the team rather than identifying the individual solely responsible. National public service prizes are often awarded on this basis.

6. **Sequential versus synchronic** – a dimension that has no equivalent in Hofstede's theory. The dimension measures whether tasks are conducted in a set order, starting one task when the other is finished, or they are conducted all at the same time. This utility of this dimension is difficult to support since it is shaped by competitive forces. A sequential approach is likely to delay the outcome: a process that could be disastrous when developing a new product in competition with a company that is using a synchronic approach. Equally, agricultural work has always been sequential and that is unlikely to change.

7. **Internal versus external control** – the degree to which the group or culture has control over its environment or the environment controls the group. This dimension might find some echoes in Hofstede's power distance index; a culture that enjoys internal control might also be considered low power distance. Trompenaars, though, is interested in observable behaviour.

The main problem with the theories of Hofstede and Trompenaars is that both of them are based on the observable aspects of culture, and so the apparently unique aspects of cultures may actually be presentation issues. For example, Trompenaars noted that in the west a person's name is shown in the order of given (first or Christian) name then family name; in Japan the order is the reverse. In practice, Western names are often shown with the given names initialised and only the family name in full. In effect, when addressing someone in either culture the family name takes precedence. We could argue that such features of culture are really only artefacts; they have no deeper meaning. As such we only need to know that they exist for procedural reasons, e.g. when addressing a letter to a Japanese person it is important to get name order correct simply to ensure it gets there!

EMPIRICAL SUPPORT FOR HOFSTEDE AND TROMPENAARS

The theories by Hofstede and Trompenaars offer an enticing opportunity to bolster entrenched opinion on cultural characteristics. This is considerably supported by a basic psychological desire of identifiable social groups to distance themselves from other groups by accentuating their differences. Theories of cultural dimensions help to express, in an apparently scientific form, observable features of other social groups. In reality, the differences may be small, presentational or simply procedural.

A major problem with the cultural dimensions is that they presuppose that a culture exists and then attempt to measure it on a characteristic. If we conclude, inductively, from our observations that individualism and collectivism are at opposite ends of a single dimension then it is a simple matter to work back through our observations and assign scores according to our spectrum of measures.

Empirical tests of the two theories are not supportive. Kirkman et al. (2006) reviewed 180 examples of research into Hofstede's theory and found that there was empirical evidence for cultural differences but it was often inconsistent with the theory, such as being company- rather than nation-specific. It was also noted that the dimensional scores are frequently unstable, changing over time as the underlying culture evolved. We have already seen the example of North and South Korea, one country that has rapidly diverged into two cultures. A similar observation might be made of Germany, which was divided into two distinct entities, with apparently separate cultures, only to be successfully reunited.

Cultural groups exist at many different levels, from family to the national via the workplace, and sometimes come into conflict. Hofstede restricts his theory to the nation, but in some societies it is the family unit that is stronger. In any case, nations are a rather arbitrary concept. Some, like Japan, are relatively unified with only small regional variations. Others, like Spain, Italy or the UK, appear unified to outsiders, while insiders claim huge internal differences; the truth may lie somewhere in the middle. Then there are nations like the United States and China that are able to unite multi-cultural societies under a common national view.

 ## MANAGEMENT SPOTLIGHT: CULTURAL DIVERSITY IN ALL WORKPLACES

That international managers will be challenged by issues of cultural diversity in overseas workplaces is to be expected, but globalisation means that cultural diversity can be present in *all* workplaces. Whereas theories of cultural dimensions are designed to help managers comprehend working practices in new locations, assuming that a unified culture reigns there, this is of little help when a multitude of cultures is gathered in a single location and one that is not necessarily overseas. Indeed, cultural diversity is a challenge confronting many managers who never leave their home location.

When the workforce is populated by a variety of cultures, it is no longer feasible to adapt working practices to the corporation, or even the corporation to the working practices. Instead, the cultures must be accommodated within a single workplace community. This places a heavy burden on managers since they will be required to take a vast array of cultural factors into consideration as they strive to help them co-exist. For example, the University of California in San Francisco (UCSF, 2015) poses twelve questions as a checklist of management competency in cultural diversity. These can be summarised as follows:

- Do you test your assumptions before acting on them?
- Is there more than one way of achieving goals?
- Are your relationships with staff honest?
- Are you comfortable criticising staff from other cultures?
- Do you insist on cultural diversity amongst candidates for a job?
- Is the teaching of cultural sensitivity part of your staff induction procedure?
- Do you review your processes and policies for cultural sensitivity?
- Are you open to suggestions for improvements from any staff member?

- Do you act promptly against those who act with cultural insensitivity?
- Do you aim for affirmative action i.e. supporting minority groups?
- Are you vigilant for instances of racism, sexism and other forms of prejudice?
- Are opportunities accessible to everyone?

Compliance with the checklist will help to avoid many of the problems that come with cultural friction, such as falling productivity and the inability to attract or retain staff. Nevertheless, it is clear that the management of cultural diversity is time-consuming at best and can test even the most skilled of managers.

The costs of cultural sensitivity can be offset when diversity is perceived as a source of competitive advantage. Cox and Blake (1991) argued that diversity in the workforce is increasingly unavoidable, so the real costs were in failing to grasp the challenges. Once diversity has become established in the organisation then managers would find a greater ability amongst the workers to problem-solve and innovate, as well as a broadening of empathy by the organisation with minority groups in the target markets. The diversity will also impact on the organisational structure, embedding a deeper acceptance of flexibility.

Yet more competitive advantages can be discovered by digging deeper into the many characteristics of the workforce. Diversity, by its nature, has no limits and is not restricted to culture alone. Ethnicity and race are obvious social groupings but there are also more subtle divisions along the lines of gender, age, social class and so on. Managers that recognise the value in all diversity will understand that the more groups that are made to feel they have a stake in the organisation the more value will be received from them. In global management it is diversity that gives the organisation the ability to evolve.

Point of consideration: The fashion industry is often accused of using female models whose physical appearance bears little resemblance to real people. How could an increase in diversity bring benefits to the industry?

Sources: Cox and Blake, 1991; UCSF, 2015

NORMATIVE USE OF CULTURAL THEORY

If there is so little evidence to support the dimension theories of culture the question then arises as to why managers should pay any head to them at all. There are two reasons why they have continuing utility.

First, it is that they provide some sort of analytical framework, albeit an incomplete one, for evaluating unfamiliar communities. The alternative is for managers to become caught up in a web of anecdotes and propaganda about cultures which may be amusing at best, or misleading at worst. A well-known piece of advice to managers dealing with Chinese companies is that the Chinese culture places a high value on maintaining 'face', i.e. not being publicly revealed as losers in a negotiation. The advice then is that if the overseas manager should get the better of their Chinese counterpart the overseas manager should not openly gloat over their success. Then again, should that manager try gloating when getting the better of a manager from Glasgow they would soon find that Scottish managers do not much like losing face either. Fortunately, neither Hofstede nor Trompenaars would be caught out by such a trivial piece of guidance.

Second, the two theories may also be useful in an unintended way. Instead of explaining how a culture works at the national level they may instead be normative theories of culture at the corporate level. Such cultures evolve in response to the immediate business environment, so if a manager has an understanding of the kind of culture demanded by the conditions then human resource (HR) planning can help to create the desired culture. We would typically see such an approach in the armed forces, where conditions of extreme danger require high levels of discipline and aggressive action. It would be quite usual for an army to train recruits for the culture demanded by the tasks, so it is hardly surprising that armed forces around the world share similar internal cultures.

Similarly, in business we can use theories of culture to assess the demands of the environment and then define the most suitable culture in terms of its dimensions. The company would then delegate to the HR department the task of recruiting and training personnel that best suited the target culture. Table 16.1 shows how different business activities demand a suitable set of measures on Hofstede's dimensions.

From Table 16.1 we can see that a sales team would need recruits that can work in a business with clear cultural expectations:

1. Ability to follow orders (high PDI)
2. Strong team spirit (low IDV)
3. Little need to avoid uncertainty (low UAI)
4. Aggressive attitude to achieving sales (high MAS)
5. Pragmatic attitude when prospecting for new business and setting targets (high PRA)
6. A need for instant rewards when making sales (high IND).

As the business environment changes then the required corporate culture will have to be reformed in order to keep pace. For a sales team selling a product that has achieved maturity in the market then the customer relationship will come to prominence. This will involve higher uncertainty avoidance and less aggression when making a sale. The reward structure may also have to change, implementing one that encourages the nurturing of a long-term customer relationship rather than instant sales.

Since different corporate functions have different roles we would expect that each would have its own culture and, therefore, a unique HR requirement. R&D should promote a strong team spirit or, if the project demands it, high individualism. In finance we would expect a culture that promoted a team spirit in pursuit of strictly prescribed outcomes. The culture in production should also be one that can sustain repetitive work cycles according to a set of rules, but there may be less need for teamwork. Overarching all them would be a general corporate culture according to the context in which it is situated. Both Hofstede's and Trompenaars' theories can be used to assess the corporate demand for a particular culture and then devise an HR strategy.

Table 16.1 *Corporate functional requirements for Hofstede's cultural dimensions*

	Hofstede's Cultural Dimensions					
	PDI	IDV	UAI	MAS	PRA	IND
Sales	High	Low	Low	High	High	High
R&D	Low	High	Low	Low	High	Low
Finance	High	Low	High	Low	Low	Low
Production	High	Low	High	Low	Low	Low

CULTURES OF YOUTH

If there is one thing we can be sure of with human beings it is that they are not produced in batches. There can be a tendency for particular months to be a little more popular than others. The New York Times (2006) found that 16 September was the most popular birthday in the United States for the period 1973 to 1999, but it is not as if human breeding is seasonal. Many other factors can influence birth rates. If we count back nine months, the human gestation period, from 16 September we find ourselves somewhere around the Christmas holidays. Make of that what you will.

It is due to the fact that baby humans appear as if from a continuous assembly line that the concept of generations is an artificial one. While we can say that grandparents, parents and children comprise three distinct generations, each one probably separated by a couple of decades, it is not as if each generation is defined by a specific age.

We would naturally expect each generation to have their own characteristics, which we might call a culture. If it is not too facetious to say so, the grandparents would probably be concerned with healthcare issues, the parents with daily living costs and the children with fashion. However, it is another matter altogether whether we can extend these generational differences horizontally across other people of a similar age around the world. Are all young people interested in fashion as a phase they go through, or is it a characteristic specific to the current generational 'batch', the following generation having a new characteristic of their own?

There are occasions where environmental factors converge to create a generation that, perhaps, can be considered to represent a distinct social group with its own set of characteristics. It may even be said to have a specific culture. One such would be the **baby boomers**, the generation that was born after World War II. Most famous in reference to the United States, the baby boom is generally considered to have occurred between 1946 and 1964. There are a range of factors that brought about this boom in the birth rate, from the provision of affordable housing to the desire of returning soldiers to make families with indecent haste. Figure 16.4 shows the baby boom period in red (CDC, 2015).

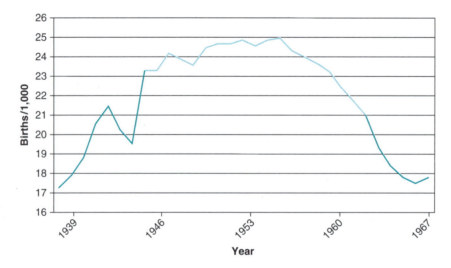

Figure 16.4 *The baby boomers – births per 1000 population in the US, 1939–1969*
Source: CDC, 2015

Although the baby boomers are often spoken of as if they were a single group, as it spans twenty years the boom contains within it enough time for the earliest baby boomers to give birth to the next generation still within the same baby boom. You might also argue about the arbitrary definition of the boom, preferring from the data to anchor it in 1940 when growth first started, excusing the understandable setback in the closing two years of the war, and then having the boom finally peter out in the late 1960s. Although this view probably fits the data better it is just too long a period for it to be perceived as a unified generation.

This is important because it is convenient to ascribe a distinct culture to the baby boomers. Growing up during a period of rapid economic growth in the United States, the boomers are said to be the type of people who live to work. They are generally considered self-obsessed, although their experience of the changing gender roles in society and racial conflict has engendered in them a concern for social causes. Boomers have grown up with so much turmoil in their lives that they find it difficult to achieve a sense of balance in their professional and family lives (Beutell and Wittig-Berman, 2008).

Following the boomers came **Generation X**, so named because they seemed to be an unknown quantity. Confusingly, the term was originally applied to those born immediately after World War II and was only later used to describe the post-boomers. The 2011 Generation X Report from the University of Michigan (Miller, 2011) described the Xers as 'active, balanced and healthy', with ambitions to extend their educations while remaining stoutly family orientated.

First appearing in 1961, the immaculate Generation X came to a close in 1981. The mantle was then taken up by **Generation Y**, identified by Strauss and Howe (2000) as the great hope for humanity's future. They are more educated, motivated and ethnically diverse than their ancestors. Not only are they high achievers but they are modest with it, love working in teams and place a high importance on good conduct. This is a generation so coated in sugar it can cause toothache just thinking about them.

Dividing culture across time in this way, from the baby boomers to Generation Y, is an expedient way of segmenting the market for business purposes. For example, Littrell et al. (2005) looked at attitudes to Fair Trade clothing. Baby boomers were interested in the authenticity of the products and the real impact of Fair Trade on the producers. Greater, though, was the emphasis they placed on the value and comfort of the clothing. The Generation X consumers, meanwhile, were focused a little more on fashion. It is worth thinking about this for a moment: an older generation that seeks value and comfort in its clothing, a younger generation that seeks fashion. Who would have guessed that?

The problem here is that the generations may not actually be exhibiting distinct cultures at all, instead, they are being defined by their situations. When the situation changes then the generational characteristics change with it. The conscientious, fashion seeking 'can-do' Generation X will, in time, mature into the self-absorbed, comfort seeking 'been-there-done-that' culture of the baby boomer generation. In this way, it is the context that defines the culture. If this neatly side-steps the whole nature–nurture debate then so much the better: when context makes culture it brings culture under the control of those that wish to redesign it, and that means business.

RAISING EMPLOYABILITY: GUIDES FOR THE INTERNATIONAL BUSINESS TRAVELLER

Overseas travel is an indispensable feature of an international manager's life. Those that have long experience of visiting other cultures have a significant advantage when it comes to business negotiations so it behoves the less well travelled to bring themselves up to speed as soon as possible. As with all training, an effective means of transferring experience and knowledge will enhance the employability of the aspiring international manager.

Theories on culture are all very well but whatever the academic arguments the international manager still needs to get out there and deal with the differences face-to-face. There are a broad number of guides available to help the manager avoid the pitfalls and embrace the diversity. International Business Center (2015) offers guides for around thirty countries which have been assessed using Hofstede's dimensions. Here is a selection of some precious advice for business travellers to Indonesia:

- Do not put your hands in your pockets when talking to someone
- Do not touch anything with your foot
- Never touch another person's head
- Never write on a business card.

It is, perhaps, a little unfair to selectively criticise a guide that also contains practical information on business relationships and negotiation customs. It can certainly be tempting to write notes on business cards, so it is useful to know it is not acceptable to do so in Indonesia. Nevertheless, there are few countries in the world where having your hands in your pockets is anything other than slovenly or where you might want to touch anything with your foot. And what would possess any business person to touch another's head?

In practice, managers do not need to heed a long list of etiquette rules in order to project a professional impression of themselves. The UK Government's (2015) advice is brief and easily remembered, focusing on the crucial matters of the law. For Indonesia, it points out that gambling is illegal and that there is a zero tolerance attitude to illegal drugs. Advice on Japan makes a general reference to strict enforcement of laws and a tendency to be undemonstrative in public.

Hurn (2007) notes that there has been very little research of an academic standard on the impact of cultural differences on business relations. He recommends cultural sensitivity training for managers before they embark on cross-cultural business negotiations. Rather than attempting to learn about the many delightful, but commercially irrelevant, artefacts of culture the emphasis of the training should be on attitudes, values and perceptions, as these are the foundations of the other party's business philosophy. The author provides six basic guidelines for international negotiations:

1. Prepare for negotiations using a cultural review
2. Adapt the negotiating style to the cultural conditions
3. Build trust
4. Be patient
5. Access the best translators and interpreters
6. Be prepared for negotiations to continue after the 'agreement'.

Sometimes, though, detailed preparation is not possible. Fortunately, mistakes should be rare because of two major considerations: first, both sides in a business negotiation will already be aware that cultural differences exist. Second, both sides want any negotiations to be a success. It would be unusual, then, for either side to be insensitive to the cultural habits and attitudes of the other party or want to exploit misunderstandings. We can perhaps condense the advice into four simple principles:

- As a host, put your guests at ease by giving explicit directions on etiquette and demonstrate by example
- As a guest, ask for directions and follow the example of your host
- Eat and drink a little of everything that is put in front of you
- Dress like the country's national TV news presenters.

And of course, if you do not know what to do, just ask; people are usually delighted to have the chance to explain their culture!

THE STORY SO FAR: A CONFUSION OF CULTURES

If there were no cultural differences then international business would be a simple matter of geography and nothing like as interesting as it is. With the march of globalisation these differences are becoming more pertinent but also better known. In an attempt to untangle the mass of details, cultural theories, such as those by Hofstede and Trompenaars, have tried to simplify our analytical approaches. However, these theories seem to be trying too hard to bring coherence to what might be random or context-specific artefacts of human society. The international manager first needs to assess how relevant culture is to the business and then identify the aspects of culture that need accommodating, adapting or even rejecting. Above all cultural sensitivity is more important than formulaic analysis.

 WEB SUPPORT

1. Hofstede www.geert-hofstede.com/ original website:

   Information from the man himself, including assessments of national cultures. Obviously lacks critical perspectives on the theory, and the website is a shop window for the consultancy business. Trompenaars and Hampden-Turner's consultancy business is now part of KPMG.

2. CDC (Centres for Disease Control) www.cdc.gov/nchs/products/vsus.htm

   Not a place you would normally expect to go for data on the United States but surprisingly useful all the same. Data on population and health going back to 1890.

3. International Business Center www.internationalbusinesscenter.org/

   Both fascinating and delightfully silly. Apparently, in Argentina a pat on the shoulder is a sign of friendship: who would have guessed? Most fun is to look at your own country and find out how others perceive it. Still, there is the odd nugget of golden advice.

Project Topics

1. Some industries are more sensitive to cultural issues than others. Compare and contrast two examples, one that is culturally sensitive and another that is not.
2. For a country of your choice, list the social taboos that a visiting foreign business person should avoid. To what extent are these taboos unique to the country?
3. When emigrating to a new country, is it possible to learn and internalise the culture or will it always remain foreign?
4. What new dimensions would you add to the theories of Hofstede or Trompenaars? What does this mean for the validity and reliability of the theories?

CASE STUDY – SOUTH AFRICA AND THE DARK SIDE OF CULTURE

A notable deficiency in both Hofstede's and Trompenaars' theories is their inability to account for the uglier aspects of culture. These include prejudicial attitudes such as racism, sexism and so on, as well as aggressive intolerance of other cultures.

South Africa practised apartheid, the division of society into the arbitrary racial groups 'white', 'black', 'coloured' and 'Indian'. They lasted until full democratic elections took place in 1994. The segregation of society had long been in existence in the British colony but it was formalised in 1948 on independence by the white Afrikaans government. Although the purpose of the policy was to separate social groups in its implementation the policy meant that non-whites were severely disadvantaged. With most government resources directed towards whites, the other groups were consigned to an impoverished underclass.

The policy was the cause of particular embarrassment for the white government when Japanese companies were invited to invest. The economy desperately needed the injection of funds but the visiting Japanese were officially non-white. This meant that they would have to be denied entry into hotels, restaurants and other places designated for whites. In order to resolve this predicament the Japanese were re-categorised as honorary whites.

Even investors from majority white countries had difficulties investing in South Africa due to social pressure back in their home countries. Barclays Bank of the UK, for example, became a target of anti-apartheid student protestors, who were determined to have the company pull out of South Africa unless the apartheid laws were repealed. The bank even earned the nickname 'Boerclaysbank'.

Although apartheid is the most infamous example of national racism there are few countries in the world that can truly claim to be free of racist or other prejudicial attitudes. The southern states of the United States practised racial segregation until the mid-1960s and other countries deny equal rights to women. With investors and companies increasingly obliged to include these darker aspects of culture in their assessments, perhaps cultural theories too should be more explicit in recognising them.

Point of consideration: Compare the abilities of Hofstede's and Trompenaars' theories in accounting for prejudice in a culture. How relevant are these issues when analysing a culture for a business investment?

Source: Osada, 2002

MULTIPLE CHOICE QUESTIONS

1. Which country is the most cultured?
   a. France, because of artists like Monet and Van Gogh.
   b. Germany, because of composers like Beethoven and Mozart.
   c. Neither; culture cannot be measured, it is a set of characteristics.

2. How is Japan said to have a Confucianist culture?
   a. The people are very hard working.
   b. Teachers teach, students listen.
   c. They devote their work to religion.

3. What does a strong welfare state tell you about a country?
   a. It is a wealthy country that can afford to provide for the less fortunate.
   b. The culture scores high on Hofstede's masculinity (MAS) dimension.
   c. The country suffers from high unemployment.

4. For a country with a low score on Hofstede's power distance index (PDI), how would you expect the police force to be structured?
   a. There would be a democratically elected chief-of-police.
   b. Low ranked police officers would not be able to exercise their initiative.
   c. The police force would have significant political influence over the government.

5. According to the dimensions by Trompenaars and Hampden-Turner, what kind of culture would be most suited to a complex process such as shipbuilding?
   a. Sequential – it makes sense to put the ship together in a logical order before launching it in the water.
   b. Synchronic – most tasks can be done simultaneously on dry land as sub-assemblies, being brought together for final assembly and launching only in the final stage.
   c. Individualistic – there needs to be one person in charge to oversee the multitude of tasks.

6. For what kind of industry are cultural considerations most important?
   a. Oil exploration – the workers must operate in a familiar culture otherwise dangerous misunderstandings can occur.
   b. Medical care – patients are not just a collection of diseases, they need to be treated as people first.
   c. Retail – consumers shop in their own peculiar ways; you need to understand them to sell to them.

7. Would the industrial revolution have started in Italy if the religion had been Protestant and not Roman Catholic?
   a. Yes – the Protestant religion glories in productive work.
   b. No – the Protestant religion is selfish and industry requires teamwork.
   c. Neither – the industrial revolution started in the UK for complex contextual reasons, Italy just industrialised later.

8. For what kind of career are Generation X people suited to?
   a. Teachers – sharing education with the rest of humanity.
   b. Bond traders – gambling other people's money to make a fortune for themselves.
   c. Social workers – bringing ethnic communities together in harmony.

9. When did segregation by race end in the United States?
   a. 1776.
   b. 1954.
   c. Still exists.

10. If the first person on the moon had been Swedish, what kind of flag would they have planted in the ground?
    a. Swedish – he would have claimed it for his country.
    b. United Nations – she would have claimed it for the world.
    c. IKEA – business comes first.

Answers
1c, 2b, 3a, 4a, 5b, 6c, 7c, 8a, 9b, 10b

REFERENCES

Académie Française (2014) Homepage from www.academie-francaise.fr/ accessed 31 December 2014

Becker S O and Wossmann L (2007) 'Was Weber wrong? A human capital theory of Protestant economics history' *Munich Discussion Paper No. 2007–7, 22 January 2007* from www.epub.ub.uni-muenchen. de/1366/1/weberLMU.pdf accessed 1 January 2015

Beutell N J and Wittig-Berman U (2008) 'Work-family conflict and work-family synergy for generation X, baby boomers, and matures: generational differences, predictors, and satisfaction outcomes' *Journal of Managerial Psychology* 23(5), pp. 507–523

CDC (2015) 'Vital Statistics of the United States' from Centers for Disease Control and Prevention 1890–2003 from www.cdc.gov/nchs/products/vsus.htm accessed 9 May 2015

Chomsky N (2002) *Syntactic structures* (2nd edition). Berlin: Walter de Gruyter

Chung K Y, Eichenseher J W and Taniguchi T (2008) 'Ethical perceptions of business students: differences between East Asia and the USA and among "Confucian" cultures' *Journal of Business Ethics* 79(1–2), pp. 121–132

Cox T H and Blake S (1991) 'Managing cultural diversity: implications for organizational competitiveness' *The Executive* 5(3), pp. 45–56

Hanavan K and Coney J (2005) 'Hemispheric asymmetry in the processing of Japanese script' *Laterality: Asymmetries of Body, Brain, and Cognition* 10(5), pp. 413–428

Henshall K G (1988) *A guide to remembering Japanese characters*. Boston, MA: Tuttle Publishing

Hofstede G (2001) *Culture's consequences: comparing values, behaviours, institutions and organizations across nations* (2nd Edition). Thousand Oaks CA: Sage Publications

Hurn B J (2007) 'The influence of culture on international business negotiations' *Industrial and Commercial Training* 39(7), pp. 354–360

International Business Center (2015) Homepage from www.internationalbusinesscenter.org/ accessed 13 May 2015

Kirkman B L, Kevin B Lowe K B and Gibson C B (2006) 'A quarter century of culture's consequences: a review of empirical research incorporating Hofstede's cultural values framework' *Journal of International Business Studies* 37, pp. 285–320

Lee S, McCann D and Messenger J C (2007) *Working time around the world*. Geneva: ILO

Leung K, Bhagat R S, Buchan N R, Erez M and Gibson C B (2005) 'Culture and international business: recent advances and their implications for future research' *Journal of International Business Studies* 36(4), pp. 357–378

Littrell M A, Jin Ma, Y and Halepete J (2005) 'Generation X, baby boomers, and swing: Marketing fair trade apparel' *Journal of Fashion Marketing and Management: An International Journal* 9(4), pp. 407–419

Miller J D (2011) *The Generation X Report Vol.1, Iss.1, Fall 2011* from www.home.isr.umich.edu/ files/2011/10/GenX_Report_Fall2011.pdf accessed 11 May 2015

New York Times (2006) 'How Common Is Your Birthday?' *New York Times* 19 December 2006 by Amitabh Chandra, Harvard University from www.nytimes.com/2006/12/19/business/20leonhardt-table. html?adxnnl=1&adxnnlx=1431186836-iJnU20y6OKoMgp61pesl0w accessed 9 May 2015

Osada M (2002) *Sanctions and honorary whites: Diplomatic policies and economic realities in relations between Japan and South Africa* (Vol. 93). Westport, CT: Greenwood Publishing Group

Paradise J F (2009) 'China and international harmony: the role of Confucius institutes in bolstering Beijing's soft power' *Asian Survey* 49(4) (July/August 2009), pp. 647–669

Pew Research (2011) *The Future Global Muslim Population: Projections for 2010–2030*. Pew Research Centre, January 2011 available www.pewforum.org/files/2011/01/FutureGlobalMuslimPopulation-WebPDF-Feb10.pdf accessed 31 December 2014

Pfau-Effinger B (2005) 'Culture and welfare state policies: reflections on a complex interrelation' *Journal of Social Policy* 34(01), pp. 3–20

Rodrik D (1995) 'Getting interventions right: how South Korea and Taiwan grew rich' *Economic Policy* 10(20), pp. 53–107

Rutter M (2006) *Genes and behavior: Nature-nurture interplay explained*. Oxford: Blackwell

Skitka L J (2005) 'Patriotism or nationalism? Understanding post-September 11, 2001, flag-display behavior' *Journal of Applied Social Psychology* 35(10), pp. 1995–2011

Sköld P (2004) 'The birth of population statistics in Sweden' *The History of the Family* 9(1), pp. 5–21

Strauss W and Howe N (2000) *Millennials rising: The next great generation*. New York: Vintage

Trompenaars F and Hampden-Turner C (1998) *Riding the waves of culture*. New York: McGraw-Hill

UCSF (2015) *Guide to Managing Human Resources. Chapter 12: Managing Diversity in the Workplace* from www.ucsfhr.ucsf.edu/index.php/pubs/hrguidearticle/chapter-12-managing-diversity-in-the-workplace/ accessed 21 October 2015

UK Government (2015) *Foreign travel advice* from www.gov.uk/foreign-travel-advice accessed 13 May 2015

17 International Human Resource Management

Chapter Objectives

The most important asset that any company has is its staff, the humans that create and develop the ideas that push the business forward. While much of the manual work has been passed to machines, it is still the people that are the source of the competitive advantage for the company. Responsibility for extracting the maximum benefit from the people is down to the human resources (HR) function. In this chapter, we will consider the growing strategic role of HR:

- Humans as a competitive resource.
- Further development of human resources.
- HR and strategic alignment.
- HR for international managers.

HUMANS: THE FIRST CORPORATE ASSET

Over the past few decades, there has been a steady realisation that industry is not just about machines but also about people. In fact, for a long time it was as if workers *were* machines, at least as far as management were concerned. The industrial revolution heralded the era of mechanisation, when hand crafted production was replaced by long production runs of identical products produced on a massive scale; mass production, in other words.

Since machines need to be run at a constant rate in order to achieve their optimum efficiency people then became extensions of the machines. They were there only to monitor, maintain and feed the production system. As the technical capability of machines advanced, so the skills required to operate them declined. It seemed as if we were heading for a dystopia of low-paid, unskilled workers toiling as servants of the machines. The hiring and firing of workers would become a routine process.

That this gloomy prophecy has never come to pass is due to the fickle nature of the customer. If the great advantage of machines is their ability to relentlessly churn out identical products, it is also their fatal flaw. Customers demand change, either due to fashion or technical **innovation**. Many manufacturers and service providers learn to rue the day they neglected to update their products, erroneously preferring to produce the same thing in the same way. Such dinosaurs of the industry are soon overtaken by young upstarts that have new products and innovative production systems to match.

Change is a normal part of any sustainable industry. Humans are the source of this change, both as customers and as inventors. Within a company this means even if the efficiencies are mainly machine based, the unique aspect of any competitive advantage is sourced from the human beings. As a consequence, humans are as much a benefit to the company as are the physical resources. These **human assets** require as much care as the **physical assets**.

Taylorism: humans as machines

Frederick Taylor was a pioneer of management as a science (Taylor, 1911), often known now as **Taylorism** in his honour. Living in the United States in the later part of the eighteenth century, Taylor would have seen the extraordinary rise of his country as the world's foremost industrial nation. He also lived in an age when science was increasingly illuminating human existence, bringing order and rationality where once there had been chaos and superstition. Science had put the chemical elements into their proper order, tamed electricity and harnessed the power of steam. Taylor wanted to bring the same scientific rationality to the way people worked.

Taylor took the view that there was no mystery to the way craftwork was conducted and that all work could be broken down into discreet activities. This was later developed into '**time and motion** studies' that measured these activities against a stopwatch. Although Taylor may not have fully understood the implications of his perspective, the consequences were that it meant treating humans as if they were without humanity. The approach may have taken into account the role of incentives for workers, that they will work faster and better for a promised reward, but then the same approach is also used for draft animals.

Perhaps workers were not even considered to be living creatures under Taylor's style of scientific management. It reduced workers to the status of inanimate objects in a vast corporate machine, almost as if they were robots. If they needed time for rest it was the equivalent of maintenance time for machines. Workers received training but it was directed towards the job demanded of them, it was not intended to develop them as human beings. Individuality was not suppressed; it was simply ignored. Taylor is credited with the statement:

> In the past the man has been first; in the future the system must be first.
>
> (Taylor, 1911, p. 2)

When workers are treated in this way the best that can be achieved is that they slot into the production process and work efficiently. At worst they come to resent being treated as tools of a management with whom they share little or no common purpose. This can be one of the underlying causes of industrial action as the workers fight to extract concessions even if it threatens the very existence of the firm. There has been a move in recent years to structuring work teams along more democratic lines, empowering individual workers. However attractive this sounds in theory, researchers like Pruijt (2003) have found that the simple and rigid structure of the Taylorist approach is very effective within the predictable constraints of mass production, as observed in the automotive industry.

 ## CASE STUDY – TAYLORISM AND THE GOOD SOLDIER SCHMIDT

One of Frederick Taylor's most famous case studies was on the movement of pig iron. It is an intermediate form of iron which has been smelted from ore and can be stored before being melted again to form purer types of iron for use in final products. At the time Taylor was working for the Bethlehem Steel Company, which had suffered a temporary collapse in demand for iron. It being far too costly to adjust the output of pig iron from the blast furnaces, the company had instead accumulated 80,000 tons in storage. The start of the Spanish–American War in 1898 had revived demand and prices, so the company was ready to start selling the stored pig iron once more.

Taylor calculated that pig iron could be loaded at the rate of around 47 to 48 tons per man per day. He was astounded to discover that a particular team of 75 men, thought to be a representative sample with an experienced supervisor, were actually moving an average of 12.5 tons per man per day. This low rate of work was known as 'soldiering'. In order to uncover the inefficiencies in the team Taylor conducted a series of interviews before selecting the best candidate, a man he nicknamed 'Schmidt'. This character was a Dutch immigrant of boundless energy who, despite the hard physical labour, found the energy to fit in some construction of his own home before and after work. At Bethlehem Steel he was earning US$1.15 per day.

To find out more about Schmidt's attitude to work Taylor questioned him closely in a manner that we would now consider demeaning and patronising. Taylor's excuse was that Schmidt was 'mentally sluggish' and that if he were asked to raise his productivity for the same rate of pay he would refuse, for reasons that seem to escape Taylor. The alternative was to lead Schmidt through the day's task under the direction of a time-and-motion man, telling Schmidt when to work and when to rest. Again, having a highly paid management consultant teaching a low-paid manual worker how to be more cost effective in their work is an irony that seems to have eluded Taylor. At least the result was that Schmidt's output rose to 47.5 tons for the day and his pay was increased by 60% to US$1.85.

Leaving aside Taylor's derogatory attitude to manual work there were some aspects of the exercise that were surprisingly enlightened. For example, Taylor understood that selection of the most suitable worker was vital and that appropriate training should be given. Furthermore, that periods of rest were an important feature of efficient work practices. Taylor also argued that the workers should be complicit in the organisation of their work in order to avoid antagonising them and causing industrial unrest. What we have in scientific management, then, foreshadows the modern approaches of human resource management but without yet perceiving the strategic opportunities inherent in the workforce.

Point of consideration: Although Taylor's scientific management is considered to be the first attempt at management for efficiency it had little influence on Henry Ford's parallel development of mass production in the automobile industry. According to your own research, how was Fordism different to scientific management and which do you think was the most enlightened?

Source: Taylor, 1911

DEVELOPING THE WORKFORCE

In the ages before the industrial revolution, workers gained skills by attaching themselves to a master craftsman, learning by observation and practice over many years. Although this meant following a strict set of rules, often laid down by a guild, the progress of the individual worker was their own responsibility. There was no grand strategy to develop skills, either at the national or corporate level. In those days labour was organised on an *ad hoc* basis.

The industrial revolution, which emerged in the middle of the eighteenth century, brought workers together into teams organised around production systems (Monteux, 1961). Although this reduced the skill requirement it also meant that the division of labour and the specification of work had to be made explicit. It was no longer sufficient for workers to produce to their own standard and pace since the production system was structured around the team, not the individual. Industrial luminaries such as Frederick Taylor and Henry Ford introduced the concept of labour being as much a part of a production system as the capital invested. To get the best out of the system the workers needed to be managed in much the same way as the machinery.

In recent times a more enlightened approach has emerged. Recruitment has become more sophisticated, training provides skills for the future as much as the present and governments have taken an interest in the long-term national skill requirements. There is even a view that a company's competitive advantage is rooted in the people it employs, namely that they are a resource.

Personnel management

The scientific management approach leads managers to think of workers as being essentially passive elements in the production process. They are commanded to follow the edicts of the company, and they are not expected to have much control over shaping their work. Depending on the job, the worker might have some control over the schedule and pace of the work but they are not asked to innovate in a way that may impact on the company strategy.

Recruiting and retaining staff in a scientifically managed organisation has been the responsibility of the **personnel department**. Historically, this department did not used to have much strategic importance with firms, as it concerned itself with fairly routine tasks, and was a kind of service function with a low status within the organisation (Malm, 1960). Its duties included:

- **Recruitment of suitable staff** – the job description demands a specific type of worker; recruitment is the process of attracting and selecting the most suitable person. It has become increasingly sophisticated, with psychometric testing, batteries of tasks and multiple-interviews. The Myers-Briggs Type Indicator test is one of the most popular, yet controversial, techniques.
- **Remuneration** – administration of pay scales, salary payments and entitlements for time-off. However, strategic matters such as collective bargaining are usually in the hands of the corporate management.
- **Training** – as the company develops its products and production methods so the nature of the jobs will change. Training identifies the new skills that are required and puts in place the training programmes. The programmes are often out-sourced to external providers.
- **Redundancy** – the company may develop in a way that is beyond the scope of current staff skills, or where additional training programmes are uneconomic. The affected positions within the firm then have to be eliminated, as they are not part of the new corporate strategy and the workers in those positions lose their jobs. The personnel department will coordinate the process, but, again, the strategy will be the responsibility of the corporate management.
- **Disciplinary procedures** – the personnel department is charged with ensuring any disciplinary actions are conducted within the law and the company's own guidelines.

The personnel department's view of labour is that it is an asset of a human kind. Just as **physical assets** need to be acquired and maintained so **human assets** need to be recruited and supported. Each of the personnel tasks therefore tend to be administrative and underpin the operations of the firm. If the tasks are being conducted effectively then the firm should be able to continue with its other roles, from strategic planning to product R&D, in a smooth and efficient manner. However, when the role of the personnel department is narrowly defined in this way it cannot contribute to developing the strategic purpose of the firm.

The role of the personnel department is static, not dynamic. It takes the classical economic view that employment is a market-based relationship between the employer and the employee. From a transactional position this can be economically efficient, particularly when there is a free market in labour. However, by using labour for the skillset it brings with it, or can be trained for, the employer misses out on the ability of labour to innovate in its own way. When this is allowed to happen the employees become a resource in their own right, one that can be used to push forward the company's competitive advantage.

Human resources (HR)

If the personnel department typically treats workers as assets then the firm can only benefit from their skills within the current corporate strategy as defined by the senior management. If the corporate strategy changes then it instantly renders the personnel department out of date. A more dynamic approach is to treat the workers as a source of additional and new competitive advantages. In this way the staff across the entire firm can be a resource as much as the marketing or product design functions. HR is therefore part of the shift from the old strategy to the new one.

HR has a high-status strategic purpose (Tsui and Milkovich, 1987) and is charged with ensuring that the staff of the company are an integral part of the overall corporate strategy. The HR function therefore includes all the activities of the personnel department and in addition takes a number of proactive roles in shaping the future of the company. These roles include:

1. HR strategy aligned with corporate strategy
2. Staff as strategic assets
3. HR as a source of competitive advantage
4. Staff motivation.

1. *HR and corporate strategy alignment* The strategy of a firm sets out its course for the foreseeable future. The HR function needs to go beyond the day-to-day administration of personnel matters and identify what the labour requirements of the firm will be in the future. For example, if the firm was investigating the outsourcing of certain functions to international locations then HR would need its own strategy that could support the new direction. It can then play a part in creating a corporate culture that is conducive to achieving the overall corporate aims.

In the pharmaceutical industry the key activity of companies is not the current range of medical products being manufactured but the next generation of products being developed. It is therefore possible to perceive the future shape of the company from its R&D activities. There is also great pressure on the companies to reduce the cost of production so that they can compete against the producer of low-price generic products. This corporate strategy needs to be supported by hiring people who can innovate and pursue the lowest cost solutions (John, 2006).

2. *Staff as strategic assets* The core role of the HR function is that it challenges the notion that workers are little more than employees passing through the company, hired and fired out of expediency. If not exactly indispensable, HR views staff as a key strategic asset. However, their importance to the corporate strategy varies according to their position in the corporation and the nature of the industry.

Modern manufacturing industries are generally highly automated but these machines are usually available in the open market. As a consequence, it is relatively easy to replicate the work of one plant almost anywhere else in the world and have it produce a similar range of products. Where the two plants will differ is in the **human capital**, the workers who labour in the plants. Manufacturers strive to inculcate production staff with the corporate culture and the overall strategic thrust of the company. This may have some impact on product quality and lowering rates of absenteeism.

Service industries are far more labour intensive and although they may have codes of practice an effective HR function will also encourage workers to have some input into the nature of their work. In particular, this often concerns how the member of staff relates on a personal level with customers. This can increase the rate of sales made to the customer, but it also improves the opportunities for gaining feedback and intelligence from the customer. This is then managed through a **customer relations management (CRM)** system (Kotorov, 2003).

3. *HR as a source of competitive advantage* The HR function can contribute to the competitive advantage of the firm when it nurtures a workforce that can innovate at all levels. Instead of being extensions of the machines they operate workers develop new methods and techniques.

In the service industry it has become an article of faith that staff are the main source of competitive advantage. In a car dealership the sales staff are the most prominent customer-facing workers, but it is also important that the mechanics working on the cars also understand how they can maximise the customer experience. Where a personnel department would provide a customer care training programme for sales staff alone, an HR function would extend this to all members of the dealership, whatever their role.

The ability of HR to extract the greater benefits from the staff can be extended even to the senior management team. Collins and Clark (2003) found that HR could be instrumental in nurturing the social networks connecting managers. The formation and strengthening of the network can be achieved through mentoring, incentives and performance appraisals.

4. *Staff motivation* An HR function would go further than the basic remuneration packages that a personnel department would put together and take a closer interest in the desires and needs of each worker. This can involve a wide range of issues, from flexible working hours to parental leave. The HR function may also implement or subsidise educational classes. Mathauer and Imhoff (2006) found that medical staff, both doctors and nurses, could be motivated by recognising their sense of professionalism and desire to further their careers with additional qualifications. This has implications for non-governmental organisations (NGOs) that may be dependent on medics giving their time cheaply or freely in the name of charity, an act which can be inherently rewarding.

Few corporations see themselves as charitable organisations serving the needs of their workers, as if they were a kind of vocational university. Most firms need to benefit from some sort of return for motivating workers. Those that subsidise educational courses will only do so if there is common ground with the business of the firm. For example, if the firm is looking to expand overseas then it may sponsor language courses appropriate to the target countries. By the same token, travel companies will provide substantial discounts for employees to visit tourist areas but only on the assumption that they can then recommend the trips to clients.

CASE STUDY – GOOGLE DOES GOOD FOR ITS EMPLOYEES

Not only has Google pledged 'Don't be evil', it has also put in place a structure for doing good for its employees. It has a broad range of opportunities and facilities to support workers, its ultimate hope for them being that 'you become a better person by working here'. Such ingratiating speciousness from a global corporation would normally trigger alarm bells of cynicism, but Google does indeed have a comprehensive set of benefits and perks in place. Perhaps it really does care.

The sorts of offers it has for employees are not necessarily unique but they are well chosen considering the type of person who works at the company. With a young workforce Google's offer of financial support for those blessed with newborn children will be highly attractive. Family holidays are covered by travel insurance even when unrelated to company business. Older workers may be more interested in the on-site medical provision and healthcare coverage, plus access to discounts on legal advice.

For workers who are ambitious to get further in life, Google will pay for adult learning classes and even degree courses. In countries where students must pay for their college education this is excellent news, but it is also at this point that Google reveals a colder, more rational side: the course should be directly related to the work at Google.

It is not that Google is being suddenly parsimonious with its educational stipends, simply that it is revealing the kind of human resource strategy any forward-thinking corporation should have. Google is not a charity for its employees and, financially successful though it is at the moment, dolling out cash indiscriminately would put it on the short road to bankruptcy. Indeed, on second viewing we can see that all the benefits and perks offered by Google are intended for the mutual benefit of corporation and employee. Healthcare is necessary to keep workers in their jobs, and the same could be said of travel insurance. Legal advice, too, sounds attractive but it is offered at a discount, not free. Finally, payment of college expenses for work-related courses is an investment by Google, not a gift.

Whatever Google may be offering its employees it is important to judge the HR strategy as a whole. It is clearly designed to attract the right people by offering them the kind of things that concern them. Furthermore, the strategy seeks to develop their skills further to the future benefit of the company. It is with this HR strategy that Google is signalling its intention to remain at the top of a highly dynamic industry while keeping total employee costs under control.

Point of consideration: Select a company from a much less dynamic industry than Google's, such as mining or steel production. What kind of HR strategy should the company put in place to attract, retain and develop the best employees at a reasonable cost?

Source: Google, 2015

MASLOW'S HIERARCHY OF NEEDS AND JOB ENRICHMENT

Abraham Maslow put forward his ideas about human motivation towards the end of World War II and consolidated them in his book *Motivation and Personality* (1954). His theory argued that workers are motivated by their desire to satisfy their needs, and that these needs are ranked in an order or hierarchy. Maslow stated that there were five basic needs and they are commonly illustrated in a pyramid structure, as shown in Figure 17.1.

The base of the pyramid is made of the physiological needs, such as the basic human requirements for food and water. At the very least a job must offer these or the worker has no motivation at all: even the worst kind of slave labour must at least feed the workers. The next level up is safety, which will motivate the workers further, assuming that the physiological needs are also being met. In modern industrial environments these first two levels in the hierarchy are usually legal requirements.

After that are the social needs for being loved and belonging to social groups. An unskilled worker should enjoy the first three levels of Maslow's hierarchy but it is the skilled worker, or the middle

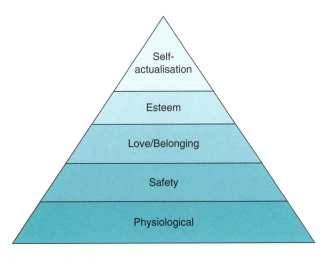

Figure 17.1 *Maslow's hierarchy of needs*

manager, that will be motivated by a sense of esteem. The highest level is self-actualisation, the ability to act on one's own decisions; it can only occur when all the other lower needs have been met, and it is the most powerful motivator. Generally, only senior managers or creative types, such as artists, get to complete their hierarchy of needs.

Maslow's hierarchy approaches the subject of motivation from the opposite side of Taylorism. Where Taylor advocates scientific study to define the minimum level of input necessary to maximise a worker's productivity, Maslow is suggesting that the incentives should be maximised in order to optimise worker motivation. Where Taylor would have no regard for a worker's spiritual well-being, Maslow sees the satisfaction of physical and spiritual needs as the highest purpose of the workplace (Gutenschwager, 2013).

Based on Maslow's idea a popular movement that emerged during the 1970s was a push towards making the workplace a more interesting and stimulating place to be. Studies have shown that a job redesign that gives workers a sense of empowerment, competence and self-determination can raise employee commitment (Ugboro, 2006). A particularly famous case was the way Volvo Truck organised its assembly workers into teams, each member of the team learning the skills of their colleagues so that they could readily transfer within the team as necessary. This gave the workers greater competency, a wider variety of tasks and a sense of autonomy. However, the system was also less efficient than the intensive work practices found in countries like Japan (Erez, 2010).

JAPAN PUTS QUALITY FIRST

Superficially, the approach taken in Japan had some of the appearance of job enrichment. It was here that **total quality management (TQM)** took root, based in part on the work of the American academic **W Edwards Deming**. Indeed, Deming has become more famous in Japan than in his home country. Deming devised a set of **fourteen principles** (W Edwards Deming Institute, 2015) for management to follow in order to get the best out of the workforce:

1. Continuous improvement of product and service to remain competitive
2. Management should be ready to adopt new philosophies

3. Post-production quality inspection should be replaced by quality in production – getting it right first time
4. Adopt long-term relationships with suppliers and focus on the total costs
5. Continuous improvement of product and service to reduce costs
6. Provide on the job training
7. Manage by leadership
8. Give workers a sense of job security
9. Promote a sense of corporate teamwork by breaking down barriers between departments
10. Eliminate corporate slogans, targets, quotas and objectives that create adversarial work relationships or wasteful practices
11. Promote a sense of pride in workmanship and quality in unskilled work
12. Promote a sense of pride in workmanship and quality in skilled work
13. Promote education and self-improvement
14. Promote a sense of common destiny for the entire company.

Given Deming's unfashionably long list we can perhaps summarise it into six underlying principles:

1. Continuous improvement of products and services
2. Get quality right first time
3. Minimise costs continuously
4. Encourage worker training
5. Promote a sense of pride in the job
6. Promote a sense of common purpose throughout the company.

The Japanese embraced Deming's principles and incorporated them into their broader corporate philosophies, like the **Toyota Production System (TPS)** described by Mehri (2006). **Employee circles** became a common feature of the workplace, employees of all ranks gathering in their teams to discuss their work and put forward improvements. Employee suggestion schemes go to the very heart of human resource management, treating all workers as possible sources of competitive advantage, and ideas that reduced costs or raised productivity were financially rewarded. Other schemes include **Six Sigma**, devised by Motorola to focus specifically on quality (Andersson et al., 2006).

Job enrichment and worker empowerment are attractive concepts, particularly to academics, and in 1944 the International Labour Organisation (ILO) released its Philadelphia Declaration, stating that labour is not a commodity and seeking to enshrine a wide range or employment rights (ILO, 2015). However, managers find that the pressures of the commercial environment make implementation very challenging. Modern production systems are often highly automated and the work is machine paced, so there are limitations on the amount of freedom that can be given to workers. Even the service sector, which is more labour intensive, has its own work flow systems that require adherence to set standards and deadlines.

APPRENTICESHIP TRAINING PROGRAMMES

As a sign, if it were needed, that there are few things in business that are truly new there has been a resurgence of interest in apprenticeship schemes. This type of master–disciple relationship is almost as old as business itself and certainly predates the foundation of technical training colleges and even compulsory school education. Traditionally, apprenticeships involved a master craftsman passing skills on to an apprentice over a number of years according to their contract. During that time the apprentice learned by mimicking the work of their master, earning their right to work as an independent craftsman once the contracted period of indenture was over.

Although the traditional style of apprenticeship allowed for the transfer of knowledge from one generation to the next it was also inflexible and resistant to innovation. By the time of the industrial revolution new skills were required in some processes, while in others there was extensive de-skilling as the principles of mass production took hold. The apprenticeship scheme then went into decline, replaced by unskilled labour at one end of the scale and college-trained workers at the other.

More recently there has been a recovery in apprenticeship schemes, most notably in the UK (Gov.uk, 2015). In combination with academic studies, apprenticeships are seen as an effective method of knowledge transfer for practical skills. In addition to receiving national qualifications apprentices are also encouraged to gain broader life skills. During the apprenticeship a number of working hours is guaranteed along with a wage. The apprenticeship should last at least a year, although the degree standard ones last longer.

At the end of the training period the majority of qualified apprentices tend to stay with the company that trained them. From the company's point of view this means a new generation of workers who hold exactly the qualifications needed and who are already accustomed to the work culture. Some companies view apprenticeships as being a blend of recruitment and on the job training. Even those apprentices who leave at the end of their training take with them nationally recognised and readily transferable skills.

Other countries take a less organised view of apprenticeships, though they still encourage on the job training, often through time release programmes that allows employees to use part of their working hours to attend college. The company will pay for the training if it is aligned with their skill requirements and the employee is contracted to return to the workplace for a specified period after training is complete. In the United States there is the Electrical Training Alliance scheme organised by two unions, but it is specific to the electrical industry (Electrical Training Alliance, 2015).

MANAGEMENT INTERNSHIP TRAINING

At the management level it is common for university students and graduates to join **internship** programmes at companies. For the intern, these schemes help to overcome the experience trap, the vicious circle where experience is required for the first job but, of course, prior to the first job the applicant has no experience. The internship fills the gap by providing the experience. The company also gains because the internship can be treated like an extended recruitment process; if the intern proves themselves on the job then they will be offered a full-time position.

However, since internship programmes are unregulated there is no guarantee of quality. In some cases companies have been accused of using interns as cheap labour. The interns often receive no pay, despite doing valuable work, and they may not receive the experience they need either. That said, in some countries the programmes are regulated and at UK universities they are incorporated into the degree. Known as sandwich courses, the **work placement** takes place before the final year of studies, they are validated by the university and the student gains an additional qualification from the placement. Generally, students return from placements with a greater sense of professionalism and a keener aptitude for learning, although it should be noted that the scheme tends to attract the better students in the first place (Bullock et al., 2009).

MYTH BUSTER – BURGER-FLIPPING GRADUATES

The fast-food industry is notorious for being the last refuge of those with the lowest employability. From high school dropouts to PhD graduates, if they don't have what the job market wants then they end up flipping burgers for a mass of humanity. Yet if these career rejects are failing at anything it is to see the opportunities that are right in front of them. The largest corporations usually have their own training facilities and it is here that lives can be turned around.

One of the most famous training facilities is the Hamburger University, the creation of the fast food company McDonald's. The facility is adjacent to the corporate offices in Illinois, United States, and trains managers who have already achieved some company qualifications in their work places or at regional training centres around the world. The university then takes over training for mid-managers and potential senior executives.

The various training schemes and the university play three important roles in the corporation:

1. The staff are trained in techniques specific to the organisation
2. The offer of training acts as a staff incentive and motivator
3. The quality of the training programme acts as a promotional tool, countering some of the negative publicity directed at the fast food industry.

A traditional personnel department would have devoted itself to delivering on the first role only. The HR function goes one step further to look beyond the immediate, task-oriented training programmes and seek to support the corporate strategy. The McDonald's HR approach to training is closely aligned with the corporate strategy and will help to develop the strategy further. The training provides personnel who are skilled in restaurant management, customer relations and hygiene. In training future senior managers it prepares them to take the corporate strategy into the future.

The danger is that the Hamburger University training is too company specific and that the trainee senior managers will have a narrow knowledge base. No matter how effective the training programmes, it is still important to recruit some managers outside the organisation.

Point of consideration: For a large retail chain of your choice, what purpose would a company university serve? Should it offer internal company specific qualifications or nationally accredited ones?

Source: McDonald's, 2015

HR AND INTERNATIONAL MANAGERS

The growth of multinational enterprises (MNEs) has inevitably meant that managers are needed who can work on an international scale. HR activities need to be able to recruit and retain such managers and ensure that their skills are aligned with the corporate strategy. It is expedient to relate HR approaches to the four generic international business strategies of Bartlett and Ghoshal (2002):

1. International – home strategy extended to overseas markets, e.g. exporting
2. Multi-domestic – semi-autonomous overseas locations
3. Global – integration of worldwide operations
4. Transnational – multi-domestic business units working as part of a wider global strategy.

The HR function's task is to place managers appropriate to the selected international business strategy. The managers may be recruited externally or nurtured internally.

1. International strategy

As the home operations dominate this strategy the managers based there will be the prominent ones in the organisation. To enforce the company's will these managers will have to travel frequently, or be based at those overseas locations for given periods. They will be very familiar with the company's home operation, so it is likely that they will have some years' experience. This suggests managers who may lack the vital knowledge of the overseas operations, perhaps not even speaking the local language. In combination with the strong central strategic control such a corporation can be inflexible and exacerbate an unresponsive attitude to local market developments.

The HR function will recruit locally for lower level jobs or specific managerial roles. The main focus of manager recruitment and retention will be in the home location. Internal appointments will have poor local knowledge of each overseas location and they will require extensive training, particularly with regard to language and culture. The relocation costs will also be significant. Externally appointed managers will bring their skills with them, reducing the training needs but raising concerns about their detailed knowledge of the corporation.

The bias towards home managers can lead to the demotivation of local staff as their opportunities for advancement will be capped and so may be a cause of some resentment. Although the corporate strategy is designed for strong coordination and control it puts the HR function in the invidious position of resolving local and international frictions within the management.

2. Multi-domestic strategy

The local business units are granted extensive powers for developing their own strategies and responding to local market developments. Along with their associated business units the HR functions will have a local focus. The managers will be recruited and trained locally, so they will have detailed knowledge of the local business conditions. There will be few training requirements for international managers, if any, and no relocation costs. If the local managers are competent then the business unit will grow and the corporate multi-domestic strategy will be validated. However, the corporate strategy by its nature raises control and coordination questions which are compounded by local management teams that develop independent strategies. The lack of a strong central HR function only heightens the problems.

Where the local strategy is successful the financial returns will be positive but the business unit may grow beyond the central corporate strategy. This further reduces what few synergies are available to other business units under this corporate strategy. At the other extreme, when a business unit fails it is difficult for the central headquarters to send another management team since that capability is against the remit of the multi-domestic strategy. Indeed, the arrival of a management team from HQ is often the surest evidence that the multi-domestic strategy has failed.

3. Global strategy

The global strategy treats the world as a single, unified location. Functions in R&D, marketing, production and so on may be located in particular regions, but the integrated structure of the corporation means that they are all working together. This takes meticulous coordination from the global headquarters. However, the managers will not be from the home location but, like the spread of operations, they will be sourced from the various corporate locations around the world. This brings the HR and corporate strategies into close alignment.

Internal appointments to the international team will be from a pool of managers who have gained experience at the local business units. This creates a team of international managers who have built up their experience at a number of locations over the years. They are intimate with the overarching corporate culture and strategy, while able to apply themselves at the local level. External appointments will be drawn from similarly diverse MNEs, although they will lack specific corporate knowledge and may even come from other industries.

International managers of this calibre are highly effective but they need to be, as they command high salaries and substantial relocation costs. A weakness in this style of management is that it can lead to an elite class of super-managers who appear remote from local operations. It can also be difficult for less experienced local managers to break into this class, which can be demotivating for them.

4. Transnational strategy

As befits a strategy that is attempting to cover all eventualities the management team needs to be able to resolve the tensions that will arise between the market need for local responsiveness and the corporate need for integration. Local managers will be delegated the kind of power enjoyed by managers in the multi-domestic strategy but overseen by the international management team of the global strategy.

The HR function, in alignment with the corporate strategy, will itself have both local responsiveness and central coordination powers. This apparent contradiction means that it will be difficult for the HR function to have a unified approach to recruiting and retaining staff, instead having to operate in two spheres simultaneously. For internal appointments this can lead to two classes of management, one that is making their name locally and one that is enjoying a more international career. In practice, there may not be as much friction in the boundary between the two management approaches as implied by the corporate strategy. It is likely that managers will be recruited and trained locally as per the multi-domestic strategy, using the experience as a base for promotion to the international league.

For external appointments the split nature of the HR strategy is more apparent. Managers may be recruited locally or internationally according to their intended role but both can be handicapped by a lack of knowledge about the other's responsibilities. They will lack the broad experience of the corporation that internally appointed managers will have accumulated through years of learning from their colleagues by osmosis.

CREATING THE INTERNATIONAL MANAGEMENT TEAM

Depending on the multinational business strategy in place, the management team may be recruited internally or externally, locally or internationally. The policy on assembling the management team will have a direct effect on the culture and working practices of the team. At one extreme we might have a team made up of internally appointed local managers who are steeped in the traditions of the corporation as well as their own national cultural identity, at the other we might have an externally recruited and multicultural team, each contributing from the wealth and variety of their experiences. The spectrum of options can then be consolidated into the three distinct management team structures derived from Heenan and Perlmutter (1979):

1. **Ethnocentric** – the focus of the team structure is on the home management. This is not ethnicity in terms of human race or culture but the dominance of home managers in the multinational team. Of course, if the home country is a racially diverse one then the team structure will reflect that, but it will still include a home bias. The most senior management positions will be filled by executives from the home country, and this will facilitate a singular approach to the running of the global corporation.

However, the ethnocentric HR strategy can demotivate local executives around the world, who will perceive obstacles to their further advancement, particularly to the senior team. This will have the effect of suppressing innovation at overseas business units. Caligiuri and Stroh (1995) found that lack of local responsiveness made this the least successful of the three staffing strategies.

The ethnocentric senior management team structure is most commonly seen in the international business strategy.

2. **Polycentric/Regiocentric** – the local or regional management teams hold sway within their own dominions. It can be seen as a localised version of the ethnocentric approach, the management teams in each location having power delegated to them. The structure of the team should reflect the working practices of that business unit and the national cultural environment. The intention is that the team will have a visceral understanding of how the business should respond to local changes. This will create a flexible business unit that can make faster and more appropriate decisions than one being controlled from a remote central head office.

The local management team will feel highly motivated since they are able to make and act on their own decisions for their location, although they may feel there are obstacles to gaining international advancement. There is also the problem that the polycentric/regiocentric structure accelerates the drift away from a common global management style for the corporation, heightening problems of group control and reducing the ability to transfer knowledge between the business units.

The polycentric/regiocentric structure is most commonly observed in the multidomestic business strategy.

3. **Geocentric** – it could be argued that this structure is not centric at all since it appoints managers on merit alone, their nationality being entirely coincidental. This creates a class of stateless executives who may be stationed anywhere in the world. Not only does this make the best of the available managerial skills in the organisation but it also opens any location to external recruitment.

It is, though, a costly procedure because the HR function also needs to have a global reach in order to recruit and retain the best executives. When appointed, these executives will often require relocation and training, itself an expensive process. This can be counterproductive if it creates an elite senior management team that is expert at macro-business factors, like international finance, but remote from the grassroots operational matters. In some cases an elite management can become self-serving, more concerned with boosting short-term financial results because of the impact on their bonuses instead of growing a solid, sustainable business.

The geocentric structure is closely associated with the transnational business strategy but it also suits the global strategy.

LIVING OVERSEAS

Without doubt one of the most exciting aspects of international business is the opportunity of living overseas. Sometimes frustrating but always fascinating, life in a foreign country is a constant professional and personal challenge that shapes one into an entirely new kind of person. Of course, it does not suit everyone, and an effective HR process needs to ensure that only the right candidates are selected.

The character of the international manager

It is an old fashioned cliché of the business world that managers need to be tough and decisive leaders, extroverts driven by a thirst for financial gain. In more enlightened times we realise that there are as many types of managers as there are types of business; infinite, in other words. Despite this, there is still a sense that international business is a specialism that suits only certain kinds of personalities.

When it comes to working internationally there are a number of constraints on the kinds of managers who might be able to take up a position. They need to be ready to uproot themselves from their familiar home environment, mentally prepared for a life of seemingly endless challenges. Furthermore, they need to make a commitment to staying in the location for the required length of time. The relocation will not only affect themselves but also the family and friends who support them. As a consequence, international managers conform to a prescribed type more than managers in their home location.

As for most workers, the most important restriction on movement is the family, particularly when children are involved. International managers tend, therefore, to fall into one of three groups:

- **Young managers** – single and ambitious to improve their promotion prospects by gaining some early international experience. Both genders are generally available at this stage in their lives. Some companies will even routinely assign young managers to overseas business units as an obligatory part of their early career. For HR, the relocation expenses are reasonable as there are no implications for moving the family and there are few constraints on recruitment. Younger managers are more willing to accept accommodation in company apartment blocks and may relish the cultural challenges. They will have a higher tolerance for being sent to some of the less attractive parts of the world.
- **Mid-career managers** – experienced managers with clear prospects for gaining senior executive positions in the future. They need to have been identified as high-fliers within the firm because they are the toughest to relocate. There are often family ties, such as children, who need to have suitable schools to attend; this may mean private education. Since it is rare for a female manager to relocate and bring her husband it is more common to see male mid-career managers being transferred, the accompanying wife then taking a part-time job or having no job at all. This can be a source of considerable pressure on the family, so it is imperative that the decision to move is a family one, thereby complicating the HR issues for the company. Living conditions will become critical to the transfer decision.
- **Older managers** – career tail-end managers with reduced family ties. The company will see this as an opportunity to disseminate the corporate culture to the far-flung business units and pass on the experience of the manager. There is more likelihood of recruiting male and female managers but the majority will still be male. Though the relocation costs will not be as high as for mid-career managers with families the older managers will still require a higher standard of living than the young, single managers. Promotional prospects will be largely irrelevant, but it is often expected that transfer to a highly attractive location will count as a reward for years of service.

Since the HR function will find that there are limitations on which managers will agree to be relocated the pool of potential recruits needs to be widened in other ways. HR may be obliged to recruit internationally and find managers from third party countries, i.e. from countries other than the home and overseas locations.

A final alternative evades the HR issues altogether: simply fly executives around the world from the home location. There are no relocation costs and training can be minimised. The pool of available executives is much wider because few can refuse to go on temporary missions, even if they would rather stay at home. Naturally, travel and hotel costs will rise but the annual total should still be less than providing permanent accommodation. A further advantage is that there will be greater control and co-ordination from the centre and some possibility of return knowledge being rapidly transferred from the overseas unit. However, such knowledge will lack the depth of information that comes from working in the location over an extended period. Long travel times are also an inefficient use of an executive's time and they may personally resent the frequent trips.

MANAGEMENT SPOTLIGHT: SHOCKING LIFE OF THE EXPATRIATE

The accelerated adjustment period that a manager undergoes on being relocated overseas is known as **culture shock** (Xia, 2009). This is the effect of having to deal with differences in working practices, behaviour, etiquette, language and customs all at the same time. The severity of culture shock depends on the psychic distance of the new location from the home location. Two countries that are geographically distant but psychically close would be the UK and New Zealand, while Japan and Australia are relatively close geographically but far apart in psychic distance.

For an Australian manager, to take one hypothetical example, to be relocated to Japan they would be confronted by a bewildering array of differences that include, but are certainly not restricted to:

- **Language** – spoken and written Japanese is totally alien to English speakers
- **Business etiquette** – increased use of business cards, attitudes to seniority
- **Working hours** – much longer working day, weekends included
- **Food** – huge variety of fish, cooked and raw
- **Travel** – greater dependence on public transport
- **Accommodation** – much smaller apartments, particularly bathrooms, and primitive looking kitchens.

From the HR perspective this can create a lot of challenges in terms of recruiting the most suitable managers, devising sufficient training and arranging acceptable living conditions. Many HR functions, faced with a wide psychic distance, prefer to recruit locally but this only exacerbates the psychic distance problem within the corporation.

Remuneration is another problem for HR. In countries with very different levels of pay, where perhaps low labour rates may have been the original motivation for investing there, the higher pay of an incoming manager can be the cause of local friction. HR can avoid this by giving the manager a unique position with no local equivalent, or paying a low salary but loading it up with various relocation benefits and expense allowances. If the position does not at least allow the manager to maintain the same lifestyle as previously then it is unlikely there will be any applicants, unless they are young managers being assigned as part of stated company policy.

On returning home the expatriate manager can suffer **reverse culture shock**, the curious challenges of readjusting to the home environment. This period of time can last for over a year. From business practices to leisure time, behaviour that was once so familiar has to be relearned.

For the MNE, the returning managers represent a significant source of international experience. However, it is often difficult to find a position for them. The repatriated executive will have career expectations which may conflict with the opportunities available back home, particularly if the skills learned are only relevant in the overseas location. They may then feel that their experience is not being fully recognised and this sense of disaffection leads them to seek employment with another company. Cox et al. (2013) argue that the HR function needs to take a strategic view of repatriates, offering training and career opportunities that build on the international experience. However, this has so far been an underdeveloped opportunity.

Point of consideration: When managers return from service overseas how should their experience and knowledge be disseminated throughout the organisation? You might want to consider anything from inclusion in formal cultural awareness training programmes to strategic placement of returning managers within teams requiring their experience.

Sources: Cox et al., 2013; Xia, 2009

INTERNATIONAL HR AS SOCIAL CHANGE

As HR has moved on from the passive, administrative role of the personnel department to take a proactive role in business strategies, so it has also been confronted with some awkward issues. In all locations there are the challenges of accommodating increasingly diverse workforces, in extreme cases taking **affirmative action** to positively promote particular ethnic and social groups (Kalev et al., 2006).

HR-led programmes for social improvement are more complicated for the MNE that has moved into an overseas location that offers low labour costs and little regulatory interference. While such a location is attractive from a business point of view, it can bring the corporation into contact with some unpalatable local business practices. These can range from the use of child labour to harsh working conditions and even substandard safety. Research by Edmonds (2005) found that in Vietnam working conditions improved in step with the growing economy, so the temptation of MNEs must be to let external forces push through the improvements, particularly as these will then impact on all firms equally. Nevertheless, if issues are not addressed directly, and the company is exposed in the international media, the negative publicity can be very damaging to the business.

Some HR issues relate to simple differences in working and living practices. Clearly, safety issues are entirely non-negotiable. When the differences pertain to religion it will be necessary to allow observance of religious holidays, prayer breaks and styles of clothing. However, HR managers may find that when the allowances for religion are extensive this too can attract negative publicity if it can be made to look like preferential treatment or collusion with a religious bias. This may even lead the company into appearing racist or sexist, so HR policies need to be implemented to avoid these accusations.

Training is a normal part of HR in the domestic setting and it can be even more powerful when applied in less developed overseas locations. Training in new technology is advantageous to the company, it is culturally neutral and will be welcomed politically. It leads to a more highly skilled workforce who can then help to develop the company. However, improving skills means rising wages and the company may, in any case, have no intention to develop the local operation beyond its original strategic purpose. If a plant was established as a source of cheap production then it might seem to the corporation inconvenient to progress beyond that. This would be a short-sighted view, as it ignores the role of innovation within the existing operations.

Incoming foreign firms can take a leading role in offering positions to members of society that may have previously been overlooked. For example, in some cultures there may be resistance to female, ethnic minority or other disadvantaged groups taking managerial appointments; an enlightened HR function can be inspirational in its **inclusive recruitment strategy**. This, after all, is what human resource management means.

RAISING EMPLOYABILITY: FROM SHARING TO BRAIN DRAIN

As companies have steadily globalised their operations there has been increasing pressure on HR to deliver managerial talent where it is needed. In the beginning this has meant taking the ethnocentric approach and sending managers from the domestic headquarters to the far-flung international business units. While this is expedient for the company, it can suppress managerial skills and reduce motivation in the locality.

Japanese firms are particularly notorious for sending their own managers to take charge of their overseas operations. Beamish and Inkpen (1998) found that in a typical joint venture manufacturing situation the Japanese management held the top positions as chairman, head of production and head of sales, as well as significant engineering posts. The accusation is that this creates a 'rice paper ceiling', a limit beyond which local managers cannot be promoted.

This Japanese expatriate dominance has brought the companies international experience, invaluable given that Japan is one of the leading foreign direct investment (FDI) countries in the world, but it also meant that knowledge transfers could take place. Over time we would expect the local managers to absorb knowledge from their expatriate colleagues. More recent trends have shown that Japanese firms are increasingly willing to recruit local managers. This may be a circumstance that is forced on them, perhaps because of a shortage of Japanese managers at home or because local governments demand local managers, but the change in HR strategy does not appear to have had a damaging effect.

In China the government has been actively encouraging a polycentric HR strategy alongside the vast inflows of FDI, sometimes requiring local management quotas be fulfilled (Gamble, 2000). However, desperate shortages of suitably qualified local managers have meant that expatriate managers still tend to hold the 'watch dog' positions of highest influence. This is balanced by the equally desperate need for foreign firms to plug into the mysterious *guanxi* social network, the web of connections that some argue is a unique feature of Chinese business life. Yet despite a general agreement that local managers need to be recruited in higher numbers, it is not enough that management knowledge be transferred tacitly; it also requires specific HR strategies of training and seminars (Kühlmann and Hutchings, 2010). For this reason FDI has meant significant investment in local management skills in parallel with the production investment.

Where the polycentric approach is successful in raising local managerial talent it should then support a geocentric HR strategy that can draw on human resources around the world. This, though, is a controversial issue when it leads to **'brain drain'**, the leaking away of talent from poorer countries to the more lucrative opportunities found in the wealthier countries. This effect has been most pernicious in medical services, with nurses and doctors being enticed away, leaving their home countries starved of their skills. When it comes to the business arena, though, the dangers might have been overstated. Glāvan (2008) argues that there are three main advantages to the home country giving up its managers:

1. The home country receives a share of the income in the form of foreign exchange remittances
2. The opportunities revealed by the freedom to travel encourage investment in education
3. The expatriate managers contribute to the development of international trade, benefiting all parties including the home country.

Whatever the dangers of brain drain are it is extraordinary to note that the main force holding it back is the political policies of the target countries. Most wealthy countries actually fear the influx of talent, even restricting the ability of foreign students to gain work experience in the country after their studies have ended. As a result one of the least globalised parts of an MNE may be the very management that controls it.

THE STORY SO FAR

In amongst all the analysis and planning that goes on in business we tend to lose sight of the most important aspect: businesses are about people. It is people who start the companies, work for them, manage them and design the products. The realisation that the most important asset is the human one has been late coming but now most organisations have a human resource function to take a strategic view of the people involved. The purpose of HR is to realise the strategic advantages of the people in alignment with the corporate strategy. This has meant far-reaching developments in recruitment and training. For MNEs, additional consideration must be given to how the international corporate strategy can be best served by managers drawn domestically, locally or anywhere across the world. Not only does this represent a revolutionary change to the way corporations are managed; it can also create subtle but fundamental shifts in the societies within which they operate.

WEB SUPPORT

1. Myers-Briggs Test critique www.vox.com/2014/7/15/5881947/myers-briggs-personality-test-meaningless

   HR departments frequently make use of psychometric tests to evaluate recruits. They may be popular but their quality is variable to say the least. The article on Vox.com shows how one of the most popular tests is also the target of vehement criticism. Do you think a psychometric test should decide whether you get a job or not?

2. Corporate religion www.articles.latimes.com/1991-06-17/business/fi-652_1_hong-kong/2

   Part of the job of HR is to help nurture and protect the corporate culture. Rarely, though, does it promote a corporate religion but that is what the Japanese Yaohan retail group seemed to have had in the Seicho no Ie faith.

3. Strategic HRM models www.youtube.com/watch?v=ZMnJc_XKlwE

   A publicly accessible video from the Westminster University course on Human Resource Management. A very concentrated overview of the various strategic human resource management (SHRM) models. Recommended viewing.

Project Topics

1. What additional value is to be found in human capital? You should make a comparison between human and physical assets.
2. How do you think Frederick Taylor would have reacted to the emergence of job enrichment programmes? Should such programmes serve a social purpose beyond that of the corporation?
3. Generally, domestic firms recruit their managers from the home location. What advantages are there to recruiting managers internationally even for companies that restrict their operations to the domestic market?
4. It is costly to station expatriate managers overseas. Suggest ways in which an MNE can minimise these costs. Indicate where savings would be counter-productive and lead to long-term higher costs or a loss of competitive advantage.

CASE STUDY – OLYMPUS APPOINTS FOREIGN CHIEF FOR TWO WEEKS

Japanese corporations were highly successful in entering foreign markets in the decades after World War II. In particular, from the 1960s the country came to prominence in industries like car manufacturing and consumer electronics. In the camera industry brands like Nikon, Canon, Panasonic and Fujifilm now dominate. They did this from a strong home position with a highly motivated workforce and a large, increasingly wealthy, domestic market.

Yet as the corporations invaded, and defeated, markets around the world the corporations continued to be ruled by Japanese senior management teams based in the home location. Oversight came from the banks that traditionally have a close involvement in the corporations they fund. This governance structure is unique to Japan and creates a kind of insider-type governance structure.

This robust management style was severely undermined by the bursting of the bubble economy in the early 1990s. The subsequent slump in asset prices was partially offset by injections of funds from foreign investors. This required a loosening of the Japan-centric management structures and some corporations began to hire foreign executives. Welsh-born American executive Howard Stringer became the first foreign CEO of a major Japanese corporation when he was appointed head of Sony in 2005.

In 2011 the famous camera manufacturer Olympus installed the British businessman Michael Woodford as president and chief operating officer. He was the first foreigner to achieve such a position. It was an internal appointment, he had been with the company for 30 years, but within two weeks the senior management structure began to unravel as Woodford uncovered alarming practices at the top of the company.

The Olympus board had made some disastrous investments in financial derivatives in the early 1990s. Then in 2008 the company purchased some overseas companies for vastly inflated sums. One of these was the British medical equipment company Gyrus, acquired for US$2 billion. Although Woodford was then head of the European operations the acquisition of Gyrus was handled centrally from Japan.

In April 2011 Woodford attained his position at the head of the company. At the same time he learned of stories being circulated by the minor Japanese business publication FACTA about the company's purchases. There were allegations of tobashi, the practice of acquiring assets as a way of hiding losses suffered elsewhere, and also of involvement by the yakuza, the Japanese organised crime groups.

As Woodford dug deeper into the scandal he was dismissed by the very man that he had replaced just two weeks before, Tsuyoshi Kikukawa. It was clear to Woodford that he had been Kikukawa's puppet and that the real power had remained with the Japanese senior management team all along. However, even the senior board could not resist the official investigations and in the subsequent court case Kikukawa was sentenced to three years in prison, suspended for five years.

Point of consideration: Identify the critical point at which the traditional style of Japanese management structure was no longer effective and needed reforming for the international business environment.

Sources: Bloomberg, 2012; Tetsuhiro, 2013

❓ MULTIPLE CHOICE QUESTIONS

1. Which role is traditionally part of the personnel function?
   a. Payroll.
   b. Customer service.
   c. Corporate sponsorship.

2. Why are personnel functions being phased out?
   a. Modern companies employ fewer people.
   b. Employees need to be managed strategically.
   c. Recruitment is increasingly outsourced.

3. What new role comes within HR and not personnel?
   a. Psychometric testing.
   b. Customer relation management (CRM) training.
   c. Job description specification.

4. Which theory fits the HR model of strategic human assets?
   a. Taylorism – scientific analysis of work.
   b. Fordism – the five dollar workday.

5. Which industry is best suited to the ethnocentric strategy for placing managers?
   a. Coal mining.
   b. Pharmaceutical.
   c. Fashion.

6. Which industry is best suited to the polycentric strategy for placing managers?
   a. Coal mining.
   b. Pharmaceutical.
   c. Fashion.

7. Which industry is best suited to the geocentric strategy for placing managers?
   a. Coal mining.
   b. Pharmaceutical.
   c. Fashion.

8. How can culture shock be reduced?
   a. Cultural awareness training.
   b. Local rates of pay.
   c. Employ local managers.

9. How can HR be a force for social change?
   a. Using local employment practices.
   b. Introducing internationally recognised employment practices.
   c. Outsourcing operations to low labour cost locations.

10. What can HR do to reduce brain drain?
   a. Nothing, free movement is a human right.
   b. Provide training that is company specific.
   c. Link training to fixed term employment contracts.

Answers
1a, 2b, 3b, 4b, 5a, 6c, 7b, 8a, 9b, 10c

REFERENCES

Andersson R, Eriksson, H and Torstensson H (2006) 'Similarities and differences between TQM, six sigma and lean' *The TQM Magazine* 18(3), pp. 282–296

Bartlett C A and Ghosal S (2002) *Managing across borders: The transnational solution* (2nd edn.). Boston, MA: Harvard Business School Press

Beamish P W and Inkpen A C (1998) 'Japanese firms and the decline of the Japanese expatriate' *Journal of World Business* 33(1), pp. 35–50

Bloomberg (2012) 'The Story Behind the Olympus Scandal' *Bloomberg* 16 February 2012 by Karl Taro Greenfeld from www.businessweek.com/articles/2012-02-16/the-story-behind-the-olympus-scandal#p1 accessed 4 May 2016

Bullock K, Gould V, Hejmadi M and Lock G (2009) 'Work placement experience: should I stay or should I go?' *Higher Education Research & Development* 28(5), pp. 481–494

Caligiuri P M and Stroh L K (1995) 'Multinational corporation management strategies and international human resources practices: bringing IHRM to the bottom line' *International Journal of Human Resource Management* 6(3), pp. 494–507

Collins C J and Clark K D (2003) 'Strategic human resource practices, top management team social networks, and firm performance: the role of human resource practices in creating organizational competitive advantage' *Academy of Management Journal* 46(6), pp. 740–751

Cox P L, Khan R H and Armani K A (2013) 'Repatriate adjustment and turnover: the role of expectations and perceptions' *Review of Business & Finance Studies* 4(1), pp. 1–15

Edmonds E V (2005) 'Does child labor decline with improving economic status?' *Journal of Human Resources* 40(1), pp. 77–99

W Edwards Deming Institute (2015) The fourteen principles for management from www.deming.org/theman/theories/fourteenpoints accessed 4 January 2015

Erez M (2010) 'Culture and job design' *Journal of Organizational Behavior* 31 (2010), pp. 389–400

Gamble J (2000) 'Localizing management in foreign-invested enterprises in China: practical, cultural, and strategic perspectives' *International Journal of Human Resource Management* 11(5), pp. 883–903

Glăvan B (2008) 'Brain drain: a management or a property problem?' *American Journal of Economics and Sociology* 67(4), pp. 719–737

Google (2015) Careers: Benefits available from www.google.co.uk/about/careers/lifeatgoogle/benefits/ accessed 3 January 2015

Gov.uk (2015) Become an apprentice from www.gov.uk/apprenticeships-guide accessed 5 January 2015

Electrical Training Alliance (2015) Homepage from www.electricaltrainingalliance.org/ accessed 5 January 2015

Gutenschwager G (2013) 'From Epicurus to Maslow: happiness then and now and the place of the human being in social theory' *Cadmus* 1(6), May 2013, pp. 66–90

Heenan D A and Perlmutter H V (1979) *Multinational organizational development: A social architectural approach.* Reading, MA: Addison-Wesley

International Labour Organisation (ILO) (2015) ILO Constitution. Annex: Declaration concerning the aims and purposes of the International Labour Organisation (Declaration of Philadelphia) from www.ilo.org/dyn/normlex/en/f?p=1000:62:0::NO:62:P62_LIST_ENTRIE_ID:2453907:NO#declaration accessed 4 January 2015

John S (2006) 'Leadership and strategic change in outsourcing core competencies: lessons from the pharmaceutical industry' *Human Systems Management* 25(2), pp. 135–143

Kalev A, Dobbin F and Kelly E (2006) 'Best practices or best guesses? Assessing the efficacy of corporate affirmative action and diversity policies' *American Sociological Review* 71(4), pp. 589–617

Kotorov R (2003) 'Customer relationship management: strategic lessons and future directions' *Business Process Management Journal* 9(5), pp. 566–571

Kühlmann T and Hutchings K (2010) 'Expatriate assignments vs localization of management in China: staffing choices of Australian and German companies' *Career Development International* 15(1), pp. 20–38

Maslow A (1954) *Motivation and personality*. New York: Harper

Malm F T (1960) 'The development of personnel administration in Western Europe' *California Management Review* 3(1), pp. 69–83

Mantoux P (1961) *The industrial revolution in the eighteenth century: An outline of the beginnings of the modern factory system in England*. London: Jonathan Cape

Mathauer I and Imhoff I (2006) 'Health worker motivation in Africa: the role of non-financial incentives and human resource management tools' *Human Resources for Health* 4(1), 24 from www.human-resources-health.com/content/pdf/1478-4491-4-24.pdf accessed 23 October 2015

McDonald's (2015) Hamburger University from www.aboutmcdonalds.com/mcd/corporate_careers/training_and_development/hamburger_university.html accessed 5 January 2015

Mehri D (2006) 'The darker side of lean: an insider's perspective on the realities of the Toyota production system' *The Academy of Management Perspectives* 20(2), pp. 21–42

Pruijt H (2003) 'Teams between neo-Taylorism and anti-Taylorism' *Economic and Industrial Democracy* 24(1), pp. 77–101

Taylor F W (1911) *The principles of scientific management*. New York: Harper and Brothers

Tetsuhiro K (2013) 'Corporate governance in established Japanese firms: will the Olympus scandal happen again?' *Journal of Enterprising Culture* 21 (2013), pp. 421–446

Tsui A S and Milkovich G T (1987) 'Personnel department activities: constituency perspectives and preferences' *Personnel Psychology* 40(3), pp. 519–537

Ugboro I O (2006) 'Organizational commitment, job redesign, employee empowerment and intent to quit among survivors of restructuring and downsizing' *Journal of Behavioral and Applied Management* 7(3), pp. 232–257

Xia J (2009) 'Analysis of impact of culture shock on individual psychology' *International Journal of Psychological Studies* 1(2), pp. 97–101

18 Corporate Social Responsibility

Chapter Objectives

In a crowded world of overstretched resources and saturated environment companies, are coming under increasing pressure to take responsibility for their impact. This means accounting for the effects on all stakeholders, from the workers to the local communities, from the suppliers to the customers. While there is general agreement that companies need to play an active role in making the world a better place for all of us, the lofty ideals do not translate easily into regulated policies. In this chapter, we will be considering the various calls on companies to behave more responsibly. The areas of responsibility include:

- Taking an inclusive and holistic approach to costs.
- Protecting the people that depend on the company.
- Minimising the environmental impact.

CORPORATIONS IN HUMAN SOCIETY

When asked why they work, people will often reply that they do it to earn money. Yet if you ask them why they do a specific job they will give a range of reasons, from the satisfaction of helping clients to the enjoyment of socialising with colleagues. Indeed, there may be a myriad of motivations for working for a particular organisation, such as family connections, personal development or even a belief in a greater social purpose. Clearly, people go to work for more than just the paycheck at the end of it.

It is a similar story with corporations. Once, it would have been easy to simply state that the purpose was to earn a profit for the shareholders. This dehumanises corporations and the managers who lead them to the level of money-making machines. More recently, we have begun to recognise that corporations have a role to play in our societies and as such carry with them responsibilities. There are four main areas that we are concerned with:

1. Accounting for externalities
2. Protecting the employees
3. Protecting the suppliers
4. Protecting the environment.

We will look at each of these major areas of responsibility in turn.

1. ACCOUNTING FOR EXTERNALITIES: THE CORPORATION AS A SOCIETY MEMBER

A corporation is more than just a device for making money: it impacts on the lives of multitudes of people, both inside and outside the company. We can think of these people as **stakeholders**, those that have a vested interest in the operations of the company. Figure 18.1 is a sample of the range of stakeholders that a typical company might have.

On the input side, we have a relatively small range of stakeholders who provide the firm with goods, services and other items. Clearly, among them are the component and raw material **suppliers** as well as the utility companies, providing water and electricity. We should also include the sources of finance, ranging from banks to the equity provided by **shareholders**. Then there are the stakeholders that might have a relatively minor role such as **information technology (IT)**, **legal advisors** and **government agencies**. Each of the stakeholders on the input side is dependent on the firm to take their outputs but they may reappear on the output side as recipients of the firm's activities.

The government is a major beneficiary of the firm since it receives taxes on the firm's profits and various business activities. The taxes will then fund government expenditure, part of which may return to the firm as inputs in the form of grants, investments and purchases. Suppliers, too, are dependent on the output side; a rise in final sales for the firm will inevitably boost the demand for supplies.

Stakeholders on the output side that would be most closely involved include the **employees** and **shareholders** since they are financially affected by any actions made by the company. Their earnings then feed directly into **household expenditure**. There are also the small businesses in the locality that may not supply the firm directly but do sell retail products to the employees. Some of these businesses may benefit indirectly from the training that employees undergo at the firm, raising their skill levels, which they take with them if they transfer their employment to other businesses. It is through this network of stakeholders that the wider economy can enjoy **trickle-down** effects, the secondary knock-on benefits of the firm's activities.

If the range of financial stakeholders looks wide, the total number of stakeholders is wider still if we include the impact of the company on its **ecological environment**. We can immediately think of the

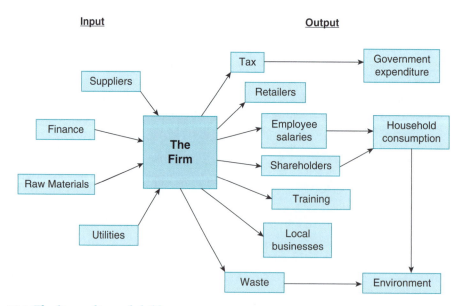

Figure 18.1 *The firm and its stakeholders*

polluting effects of waste products in their various forms and sometimes these effects lie undetected for many years. For example, when industrial land becomes vacant it is often an expensive process to prepare it for other uses, such as for housing, due to the seepage of toxic substances into the soil. These substances need treating or removing before people can live there.

There is also the long-term impact that a firm can have on the **social environment**. Generally, we would hope that the firm is making a positive contribution through the earnings of its employees, and if it were not we can assume that people would take their skills to alternative employment. Nevertheless, where firms are the dominant local employers they may abuse their monopoly power by exploiting the workers with low labour rates, poor working conditions and low investment in skills development. The firm may also decide to make employees redundant, which can have a devastating impact on the local community when there are few alternative jobs.

Some of this power that firms have over the social environment may be balanced by labour being organised into **trade unions**. Through collective action, they can have some influence over the way the decisions of the management impact on local communities. In developing economies, though, there may be little appetite for challenging the power of employers when the jobs are so desperately needed.

Paying for the externalities

As Figure 18.1 indicates, the complex network of stakeholders is almost impossible to quantify precisely but this does not mean the impact of a corporation on stakeholders is not measurable at all, only that we may have to settle for estimates and approximations. As tools for financial analysis become more sophisticated we are gaining an ever clearer idea of the wider costs on the stakeholders of corporate activities. These consequences have not traditionally been included in the narrow view of corporate accounting which tends to serve the purposes of the financially interested parties i.e. shareholders, creditors and government. More recently there has been an increasing move to attempt some kind of broader measurement of factors as they impact on all stakeholders. These factors that lie beyond the normal scope of financial accounting are known as **externalities**.

We are accustomed to firms incurring costs as part of their formally defined operations. We know that a steel mill has to pay for iron ore, fuel, employee wages and various other financial costs. These are accounted for in the accepted manner and ultimately charged to the customer. However, once you look beyond the immediate stakeholders that have a direct financial interest in the company, then further unaccounted costs come into focus. These costs are real but not borne by the company or, by extension, their customers. Instead, it is the government or society in general that ultimately pays.

Figure 18.1 can be restated therefore to show how the economic, social and environmental responsibilities of the firm are disseminated through the various stakeholders. In Figure 18.2 the inner rings are directly affected by the firm, incorporating the legal and financial implications. The closest ring is made up of those that have a formal financial interest, regulated by contracts and secured by assets. Indeed, they may have their own assets committed to the relationship, putting their operations at risk. Strict rules of accounting allocate financial responsibilities across the parties.

Employees and retailers are also directly impacted by the firm but with less commitment on their side. Local businesses also enjoy the wider benefits of having a financially healthy firm in their midst, as do households throughout the community, but the financial quantification of the effects is difficult to calculate. Depending on the political environment most governments would have their interests at this level, extracting their taxes some of which would be spent on general education and training that should be useful to the firm. Finally, there is the ecological environment, certainly affected by business activities in general but often in ways that are difficult to attribute to one particular firm or industry.

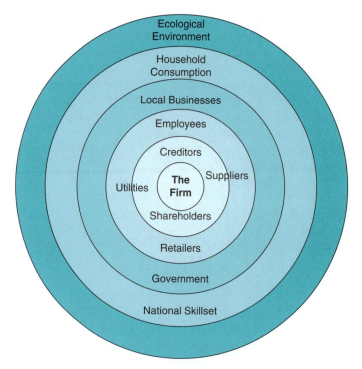

Figure 18.2 *Stakeholder layers*

It is this outer ring of externalities that impact on the locality but have been historically overlooked. These can range from traffic congestion around a plant, which raises road safety issues and delays people in the area when they are driving. Other inconveniences may include air and noise pollution as well as the negative impact on the beauty of the area. Managers of the company may find they are confronted by a united local opposition that is in conflict with the strategic intentions of the company. The managers may have to change the corporate strategy to take account of local demands. They may consider making compensation payments or playing a more active role in the social aspects of the community. All of these are likely to increase overall costs but not in a way that is easy to record in the company accounts.

Beyond these externalities are those that have more long-term consequences. These are difficult to predict and may even arise after the company has ceased operations. The corrosive effects of air pollution have become increasingly apparent in recent years, physically visible in the deterioration of ancient stone buildings. The accumulation of toxins can often be traced back over many decades, even a century of more. The effect on the fabric of buildings means that regular and expensive repairs are necessary.

MYTH BUSTER: DEADLY RAIN

Whatever filth the modern world may throw into the environment we like to think that eventually the rain will come and wash the land clean again. The last thing we expect is that the rain will bring even more toxins to attack our property, poison our food and threaten our health. What we forget is that the water falling from the heavens has to descend through layers of atmospheric dirt. By the time it gets to us it can be substantially contaminated, even acidic.

Acid rain is any kind of precipitation (rain, snow, fog, etc.) that contains unusually high levels of sulphur and nitrogen compounds which lower its pH value into the acid range. Pure water has a neutral acidity of pH7 but acid rain has been measured at almost pH4. Fish cannot live at this level of acidity, so clearly a fishing industry would not be sustainable. On land, vegetation is also affected by the acidification of soil.

Humans are not directly affected by acid rain, although it can lead to various health problems. Acid rain will also corrode buildings made from rock such as marble and limestone. Many ancient buildings, having survived wars and declining use, are dissolving before our very eyes.

Acid rain can occur naturally, such as from volcanoes and electric storms, but the vast majority of the blame lies with human industrial activity. Emissions from power stations, cars and fuel-burning factories can significantly raise acid levels in airborne moisture. The vapour can then drift large distances into other regions, countries and even continents.

Various technologies are used to reduce the sulphur and nitrogen compounds being released into the atmosphere. On coal-fired power stations, for example, 'scrubbers' are used to remove sulphur dioxide from the exhaust gases and turn it into calcium sulphate. If the quality of the calcium sulphate is high enough it can be sold for industrial uses.

In the United States, the Environmental Protection Agency (EPA) has implemented Title IV of the Clean Air Act Amendments of 1990. The agency has calculated that the programme's cost of cleaning acid rain emissions was around US$3 billion in 2010. However, the savings on health costs were US$119 billion and environmental cost savings were US$2.6 billion. The agency estimates that the programme has saved the lives of 17,000 people in the United States alone.

Point of consideration: In what sense has the EPA's programme internalised the externalities of acid rain damage? Do you think the programme is fair to stakeholders?

Source: Environmental Protection Agency (2010)

Sometimes the damage is beyond mere repair and complete rebuilding is necessary. The mining indus-try, even where the mines are long disused, is often the cause of ground subsidence problems at the surface. The effects range from cracks in walls to total destruction of buildings and loss of life. In cases where the original mining company is no longer in existence then it is the government that will pay out compensation. However, accusations can be levelled against mining companies that they must be aware of the likely effects of their activities, and so should include the costs in their strategic planning. Ultimately, this shifts the remedial costs onto the customers of the mining company who pay through higher prices.

Figure 18.2 shows that a major weakness with traditional forms of financial accounting is that they are disconnected from many of the stakeholders and externalities related to the firm. Financial protocols take a short-term view, perhaps just a single year when it comes to the annual report, and they only include those items that can be readily measured in financial terms. This means that the final customer is being charged only for the direct costs of labour, materials, production, invest-ment and IPR. Indirect costs related to the environment, which are not immediately pressing but must be met at some point, are not factored into the price paid by the customer. This is considered economically inefficient and in extreme cases can mean that the benefits of economic benefits are unwound by the later need to restore the damage done to the environment. In the longer term, then, the twin challenges are to include all monetary and non-monetary costs by taking a holistic view of commercial activities.

There are a number of suggested ways in which conventional accounting methods can be reformed to take an inclusive approach to the allocation of costs. The three major ones are:

- Triple bottom line
- Social accounting
- Principles for Responsible Investing (PRI).

Triple bottom line accounting

Triple bottom line (**TBL** or **3BL**) was developed for public sector organisations, and it measures the progress of the organisation on economic, ecological and social scales. The phrase itself was first put forward by John Elkington (1997), and it builds on standard accounting practices to provide a more complete picture of the effects of the organisation's activities. The purpose of the approach is to promote concepts of fairness by encompassing the costs and benefits for all the stakeholders. It covers three broad areas:

- **People** – employees, local community and others affected by the organisation. All groups should benefit without any being exploited.
- **Planet** – a long-term life cycle assessment is taken to ensure that all environmental costs are accounted for. The ecological relationship should be low-cost and sustainable. This means minimising use of natural resources.
- **Profit** – includes conventional accounting views but widens this to the economic profit being made by all stakeholders. The economic benefits to the wider community should outweigh the costs.

TBL is most suited to **public organisations** since they do not have the same singular profit-making purpose of private corporations. Public organisations have a wider implied agenda to serve the citizens of their communities. A local government waste service not only disposes of the refuse in a cost-effective manner it is also expected to show leadership in recycling and public education. In certain cases the local government may use the service to provide employment and training opportunities; for example, the city of San Francisco runs a Green Careers programme (San Francisco, 2015). However, the broad scope of the social ambition can make the formulation of a TBL-based strategy open to misinterpretation. For example, the organisation may decide that only its national citizens should be the beneficiaries of the employment policies.

Private organisations are less suited to TBL, as the basic tenet is for a commercial company to make an attractive financial return for its investors. TBL suggests that the company should diversify away from its core competencies to an extent where it could stray into unprofitability. It is for this reason that public goods, like street lighting, are funded by government; a private company could only justify providing lighting in areas where there were residents prepared to pay for it.

Despite the good intentions of TBL, the main flaw lies in the difficulty of objectively quantifying the various targets. The great strength of conventional financial accounting is that it is transparent; all the monetary amounts are backed up by broadly objective evidence. TBL is based on subjective interpretation of the available information, sometimes of a nature that is impossible to quantify.

SOCIAL ACCOUNTING

The advantage of financial accounting is that it brings rigour to the reporting of a company's progress, even if the one standardised approach may not be suited to all organisation types. The purpose of social accounting is to align the measures of company performance with the broader needs of all the stakeholders to whom it is accountable, not just those with a financial interest in the company.

There are a number of different approaches being taken, some offered as business services by private consultancies:

1. The approach put forward by David Crowther (2000) includes social and environmental accountability. The **Social Responsibility Research Network (SSRN)** is a related organisation that promotes scholarly research in the subject area.
2. The **Accountability AA1000** (Accountability, 2011) is intended to provide a benchmark standard for engagement with stakeholders of an organisation. As part of this process the organisation should recognise the demands of the stakeholders and be answerable to them. Communication is the catalyst to this relationship, and the organisation needs to be transparent in its dealings with the stakeholders. While this might be feasible for public organisations, for private companies there is the danger of losing commercial focus and falling into less profitable but socially beneficial activities.

    Transparent communications can make it difficult to defend the intellectual property rights (IPRs) that underpin the competitive advantage of the company. This vulnerability can be balanced, though, by the increased market intelligence that can come from greater engagement with stakeholders. The stakeholders can even be thought of as an additional resource, forewarning the changing demand patterns in the market and generating new solutions.
3. **Global Reporting Initiative (GRI)** is a non-profit organisation that provides a set of guidelines for reporting on economic, environmental, social and governance matters (GRI, 2014). It is sector specific, so reports prepared by firms are not expected to cover every eventuality, only those that are relevant to the firm's activities. GRI is a supporter of integrated accounting, a system that allows a company to report on all value creation activities, not just those that are measured in financial terms. It is supported by the **International Integrated Reporting Council (IIRC)**.
4. The United Nations Department of Economic and Social Affairs has its own recommended approach, devised by the Division for Sustainable Development. **Environmental Management Accounting (EMA)** tries to address the problem of so many social accounting approaches, which is that they depend on appealing to the good intentions of corporations. EMA appeals to their profit-seeking tendencies by providing a system that allows corporations to discover the commercial benefits of acting sustainably (United Nations, 2001).

There is a wide variety of alternative accounting systems that attempt to resolve the same issues of corporate profitability and environmental sustainability. The number of approaches being offered is itself a problem since their very diversity defeats the objective of providing a standardised approach to rival that of conventional financial accounting.

Principles for responsible investment

As we have seen, the United Nations has developed the EMA system and it also has the overarching **Principles for Responsible Investment (PRI)** for more general guidance. The principles were first tabled in 2005 and launched in early 2006 under the sponsorship of some of the world's largest institutional investors. PRI targets the users of the kind of social accounting reports listed above, encouraging them to base their investment decisions on the new information that these reports offer. Investors that support PRI declare their commitment through six principles of **environmental, social and corporate governance (ESG)**:

Principle 1: We will incorporate ESG issues into investment analysis and decision-making processes

Principle 2: We will be active owners and incorporate ESG issues into our ownership policies and practices

Principle 3: We will seek appropriate disclosure on ESG issues by the entities in which we invest

Principle 4: We will promote acceptance and implementation of the Principles within the investment industry

Principle 5: We will work together to enhance our effectiveness in implementing the Principles

Principle 6: We will each report on our activities and progress towards implementing the Principles.

Source: PRI, 2014

Like all social accounting, PRI is probably most effective in creating a cultural shift in the corporate world towards a sense of responsibility beyond the basic financial stake. A single, unified approach along the lines of the **Generally Accepted Accounting Principles (GAAP)** that govern financial accounting is still some way into the future. Until then, social accounting will be more of a statement of intention rather than a system for transparent and comprehensive reporting.

MANAGEMENT SPOTLIGHT: ETHICS AND MORALS IN THE WORKPLACE

The modern international manager may be willing to embrace ethics and morality in the workplace but the first step is to tell them apart. Both mean 'doing the right thing' but they approach the solutions from entirely different viewpoints. Even so, clear definitions are elusive. According to Kelemen and Peltonen (2001), Michael Foucault distinguishes between the personal construction of ethics and the external imposition of morality. Business, though, is rarely personal, and so Zygmunt Bauman's definition is perhaps more apposite: ethics are normative and morals are descriptive.

Morality, then, is handed down from outside sources and often has a religious provenance. If we accept its edicts then we do so on faith, a decision which is personal. As a complete set, a moral system should be internally coherent but its foundation is unlikely to be related to rational argument. The Ten Commandments delivered by Moses are, in the main, pretty agreeable even to those outside the relevant religions. Nevertheless, the prohibition of idol worship is not one that fits well with the modern materialist world. Ethics, on the other hand, are rigorously internally consistent because each element is part of a broader rational argument. An ethical system may still have its roots in a historic religious morality but the connection will be distant and often unacknowledged.

Businesses identify with ethical codes because these, being rational, are assumed to be common to all businesses and markets. Within its domestic setting, and with reference to the legal framework, companies will have ethical policies on recruitment, confidentiality, sexual harassment and so on. However, as Asgary and Mitschow (2002) point out, extending the business into international operations means that the company will come face-to-face with locations where the legal framework is different or completely absent. The authors concede that a universal code is therefore difficult to achieve, given the complexity of international business.

A major problem is that even if a universal ethical code for international business could be proposed, there will always be problems with incorporating the demands of those countries that base their codes on morality, particularly religious. Wilson (2006) reported that Muslim countries are perceived to be anti-business, with decisions being made in compliance with sharia law. As a consequence, great importance is placed on having a company head who is religiously pious, a phenomenon much less likely in a western firm.

Strategic alliances offer an expedient method for resolving these moral issues because the local management understand and incorporate the moral systems into the corporate ethical codes. However, international managers should be aware that their stakeholders will still hold them partly responsible for any corporate social responsibility issues that arise. It is for this reason that international ethical codes are slowly emerging but only after a trial and error process fraught with high profile mishaps.

Point of consideration: When doing business with a supplier in a country with sharply different ethical standards, what measures can an international manager take to bring the supplier to a more generally acceptable standard of behaviour?

Sources: Asgary and Mitschow, 2002; Kelemen and Peltonen, 2001; Wilson, 2006

2. PROTECTING THE EMPLOYEES

Historically, employers took little responsibility for the protection of their workers and there was not much recognition for employee rights. More recently, working people have gained in political influence and there has been a growing acceptance that they represent an economic asset. If only for that reason it makes business sense to look after the workers. Progress has been supported by increasing mechanisation, which has removed people from the more dangerous aspects of the working environment.

During the first part of the industrial revolution, the eighteenth and nineteenth centuries, adults worked alongside their children in mines and factories. This was not considered unusual at the time, as this was how families had worked in the preceding agrarian societies, and they continued to work this way even when industrial work came to their homesteads and cottages. As factories began to replace cottage industries, the workforce simply transferred. The principle of children working around textile machinery in a factory was little different to working with a parent operating a machine at home, although it was more dangerous.

Historically, all industries were labour intensive and the more hands that were employed the higher was the family's income. In any case, societies were accustomed to high death rates through illness. Without compulsory education there was no concept of developing children for more highly skilled work. Although many countries have attempted to outlaw child labour, the main force for change has been the use of technology in production and the falling birth rate (Doepke and Zilibotti, 2005).

As part of a move towards greater democracy, the twentieth century has also hosted the rise of worker power in the form of trade, or labour, unions. Trade unions are rooted in the guilds that arose in medieval Europe, although guilds were formed exclusively by skilled master craftsmen and not unskilled workers. The purpose of a trade union is to claim power for the least skilled workers by uniting them into a collective force. In large groups they can influence the corporate and political authorities by the simple threat of withdrawing their labour. The relationship between unions and authorities can be antagonistic, leading to genuine battles and loss of life, though equally the relationship can be mutually supportive.

Trade union power

Even as far back as Adam Smith's treatise, *The Wealth of Nations*, it was recognised that it was economically inefficient to allow employers the sole power to fix wages for employees. The modern trade unions movement may not have coalesced in the interests of economic efficiency but they were a necessary counter-balance to the power of the employers. Through a process of dialectic negotiation the two sides can hammer out an agreement based on the supply and demand of labour.

In the first half of the twentieth century unions and employers tended to be in conflict with one another. The unions may have been struggling to end exploitation of the workers but they could themselves use their power to exploit the employers. In some cases unions have been blamed for extracting unaffordable concessions from the employers that render the corporation uncompetitive. Union power may be the antidote to employer power, but it can still lead to a distortion in the labour market (Friedman, 2007).

Latterly unions and employers have developed a much less adversarial style and they have shown they can work together towards a mutually beneficial goal. In Germany, companies with more than five employees must allow the workers to elect a works council to represent their interests at board level. The council has the right to co-determine policies that directly impact on the employees, although they are not permitted a voice on matters relating to corporate strategy, product planning and other business-related activities (Seifert and Massa-Wirth, 2005). Managers need to understand the legal status of workers' councils because they wield influence on behalf of the employees, and the council members themselves have a special status within the firm.

In some cases the union is formed by the firm itself, in which case it is an **enterprise union**. Like workers' councils they represent the interests of their members but they work even more closely with the management. Indeed, the union may include junior management among its members. Enterprise unions are common in Japan, and the relationship between union and management is usually quite amicable, disturbed only during the annual 'spring offensive' *shuntō* wage negotiations (Nakamura, 2007). Management find it much easier to work with enterprise unions, but there are often suspicions of collusion between the union and management, with workers' rights suffering as a consequence.

International Labour Organisation (ILO)

As corporations have extended their operations overseas, they have also enjoyed an increase in their bargaining power with workers. Whereas domestic firms are vulnerable to the threat of collective action by trade unions, multinationals can counter this with the threat of moving their activities to another country.

The International Labour Organisation (ILO) was founded after World War I to promote social justice through workers' rights and opportunities. It became an agency within the United Nations in 1946. It has four key aims (ILO, 2014):

- Promote working standards and rights
- Create opportunities for decent incomes and employment for men and women
- Support social protection
- Encourage communication between governments, employers and workers.

The ILO is not some kind of multinational trade union to balance the multinational corporations but like the rest of the United Nations it seeks to facilitate dialogue and research in order to bring about shared benefits. It has no power to make collective demands on behalf of member workers like a union might. It is unusual, though, in having worker representatives taking their place alongside government and corporate representatives from its 185 member countries.

Among the issues that the ILO must deal with are

- A balance between flexible employment contracts and job security
- Minimum wages and competitive labour costs

- The improvement of worker skill levels in order to advance economic development
- Equal opportunities.

Managers at multinationals are not directly affected by ILO but the guidelines set a common global standard that can, on occasion, cause embarrassment for corporations that contravene them. This exerts a subtle pressure on management to include the guidelines in their ethical practices.

3. PROTECTING THE SUPPLIERS

In a monopsony, dominant buyers have powers in the market similar to monopolies except that this time the pressure is from the buyer to the supplier. Rather than the **rent-seeking** behaviour that is observed in higher prices which then undermine consumer welfare, a monopsony inflicts the pain on the supplier and inhibits them from making normal profits.

When this occurs in developed markets the more inefficient suppliers may be driven out of the industry, but those that remain have the opportunity to consolidate and reach for economies of scale. Indeed, it is this cost reduction that is often the unconscious aim of the buyer when exerting their monopsony power. Japanese corporations have made this an integral part of their strategies, identifying favoured suppliers and encouraging them to continually search for lower costs through innovation, investment and expansion. In a sense, the management of the corporation is managing its supplier by proxy. This means a strong strategic and cultural fit between the two management groups but it also supports a sense of common purpose and stability.

In such an arrangement the power is balanced by the ability of the supplier to innovate. In developed economies the industry actors are often engaged in complex processes that result in sophisticated products. Innovation can occur at any point in the production system or in the components that make up the final product. It is therefore in the interests of all the suppliers and buyers to work together to their mutual benefit. As a consequence, there is no reason for an external body to referee.

Monopsony power in developing economies

In developing economies the products being traded in the supply and production system are generally less complex. They tend to include raw materials or agricultural goods of a generic nature. It is by the nature of less developed economies that the processes will be less complex. It should be stated that this is not because the need or the capability to operate more advanced processes is lacking but that investment has not been forthcoming, for whatever reason.

Multinational corporations have earned something of a poor reputation when dealing with suppliers in developing economies. This may be unfair since they are simply behaving in a rational commercial manner, the same one that underpinned their earlier success and rise to dominance. They are seeking the most appropriate supplies at the best prices, and they will exert whatever pressure they are able to. When there is a **global commodity chain (GCC)** that is dominated by the MNE buyer the result is that the MNE is able to dictate market prices and product specification (Buckley and Ghauri, 2004). The developing economy suppliers have very little market power of their own with which to defend themselves.

Just as suppliers and buyers in developed economies are able to build a mutually beneficial co-operative relationship on the foundation of adversarial competition, so multinationals would benefit if their developing economy suppliers could raise their technical capabilities. It is not just out of moral duty that the suppliers need help from wealthy multinationals, valid though that argument may be, but also for reasons of common economic purpose.

Free trade and Fair Trade

From a moral point of view, Fair Trade is very attractive since it appears to rebalance the power relationship between the omnipotent multinational corporations and their downtrodden suppliers. Some commentators portray the multinationals as neo-imperialists, not exactly seeking territorial expansion but certainly dominating local markets without regard to community or economic development. Their buyer power allows them to exploit the vulnerable suppliers and perpetuate the mercantilist trade theory approach of using colonies as a source of raw materials to feed a production system based in the home country. The basis of the exploitation was the dependency of the suppliers in the developing economies on the buyers in the developed world (Green, 2007).

Against this argument are the theories of international trade based on the principles of comparative advantage. Here, the two sides trade as partners, each specialising in the area where they hold a comparative advantage. The concept of 'fairness' is inherent in the deal since each side is free to trade, prices are set by the market and both sides benefit (Maseland and De Vaal, 2002). In this interpretation free trade *is* fair trade, at least when considering developed country trading partners. However, this may not hold for developing economies.

When it comes to trade between developed and developing economies, the benefits of free trade due to comparative advantage should, in theory, still hold true. Unlike some empires in history, the two sides are not being forced to trade and nothing is being stolen from the developing nation. Since the trade is rational the developing nation must be benefiting, at least in the sense that it is better off than it would otherwise be. It is at this point that the moral and economic arguments converge.

Although developing nations should be ultimately better off under free trade conditions they can still be considered to be suffering an unfair disadvantage relative to developed nations. There are a number of reasons for this:

- They have a comparative advantage in just one of an extremely limited range of outputs, so there is very little opportunity to switch between commercial activities as conditions change.
- They produce unprocessed raw materials and agricultural goods with little added value – there are fewer opportunities for learning, innovation and investment.
- Agricultural goods are often perishable and have to be sold whatever the market conditions at the time.
- The generic nature of the goods means supplier power is low.
- The first mover advantages are already with the incumbent industries of the developed economies.
- Barriers to entry, such as economies of scale, are a major obstacle to developing industries.
- Developing economies are caught in a poverty trap – they need loans to develop their industries but they cannot afford the high rates of interest on the loans.

In addition to the economic disadvantages, developing countries often suffer from ineffective political systems that hold back development or waste opportunities when they appear. This can politicise the trade argument, with opposing views both claiming that theirs represents true Fair Trade. With a broad range of views emerging on the precise nature of Fair Trade as it relates to developing economies, it is no longer possible to have recourse to a single basic theory of trade. Strictly speaking, then, when we talk about Fair Trade we are specifically referring to the Fair Trade Movement, not a unified theoretical concept.

Fair Trade movement

As a concept, Fair Trade does not come with a fixed definition of what it should involve and who it should apply to. Obviously, it is targeted at less developed producers who are caught in a poverty trap, but there are no objective and quantifiable metrics to provide a standard. As a consequence, the Fair Trade Movement is made up of a number of organisations all attempting the same kind of work but differing in detail. An informal association, FINE, is made up of four separate organisations:

- Fairtrade Labelling Organisations International (FLO) – Founded in 1997 to bring together various initiatives that promoted Fair Trade through labelling of approved products with the Fairtrade logo (Fairtrade International, 2014). The organisation split in 2004 into:
  - FLO with responsibility for standards and support of producers.
  - FLO-CERT with responsibility for inspecting and auditing producers.
- International Fair Trade Association (IFTA), now the World Fair Trade Organisation (WFTO) – made up of 450 members across 75 countries committed to the organisation's ten Principles of Fair Trade (WFTO, 2014).
- Network of European Worldshops (NEWS!) – represented worldshops (shops selling Fair Trade products) in Europe. Absorbed by WFTO in 2008.
- European Fair Trade Association (EFTA) – founded in 1987, it brings together ten Fair Trade importers across nine European countries. It facilitates communication between its members and acts as a store of information (EFTA, 2014).

There are a number of other organisations that have similar aims to those listed above, often overlapping in their activities but sharing a common ethos. As an example, the ten Principles of Fair Trade stated by WFTO (2014) are representative of the common purpose:

1. Creating opportunities for economically disadvantaged producers – allows producers to progress towards sustainability.
2. Transparency and accountability – WFTO is accountable to its members.
3. Fair trading practices – early payment to producers, stable trading relationships and respect for cultural identity.
4. Payment of a fair price – mutually agreed price that permits future investment.
5. Ensuring no child labour and forced labour.
6. Commitment to non-discrimination, gender equity, women's economic empowerment and freedom of association (i.e. unionisation).
7. Ensuring good working conditions – in accordance with ILO conventions.
8. Providing capacity building – buyers assist producers with training and other needs.
9. Promoting Fair Trade – WFTO promotes Fair Trade and raises awareness.
10. Respect for the environment – sustainable use of resources.

Although the list strays beyond any economic trade theory, from a moral point of view it is difficult to disagree with the good intentions of the ten Principles. They place the onus on managers at buyer companies and provide them with a set of guidelines, even if they stop short of the kind of numerical targets that organisations like when formulating strategies. The principles do not, though, provide a business rationale for following them. The benefits to the producer are set out but not the benefits to the buyer, so managers of multinationals may struggle to include the ten Principles of Fair Trade in their business planning.

Criticisms of Fair Trade

Supporters of Fair Trade believe that market imperfections mean producers in developing economies are at an unfair disadvantage when exposed to free trade. It is not that they advocate intervention in the market *per se* but that intervention should be used to correct for the imperfections in the system (Becchetti and Huybrechts, 2008). In short, they believe that market intervention is necessary just as spectacles are necessary for correcting imperfect sight.

However, it is this intervention that critics say distorts the market and creates even more imperfections. Fair Trade may have the best intentions in attempting to counter the power of multinationals but in the process they wield great power themselves. Producers find it difficult to reach their high standards on such laudable ideals as equality and good working conditions. Once they are within the Fair Trade fold they enjoy heightened security through reliable contracts and pricing but this means that producers that fail to attain Fair Trade status must suffer all the volatility of the rest of the market. If the world price of coffee falls, for example, instead of the pain being distributed across the entire market it is focused on the very weakest farmers, while the Fair Trade farmers are protected (Calo and Wise, 2005). In such a way Fair Trade can hasten the most pernicious consequences of free trade rather than acting as a cushion.

Other critics point out that Fair Trade acts as a subsidy by guaranteeing higher prices which are paid for by the consumers. An indirect result of this is that consumers then have less to spend on other items, shifting income away from other producers to benefit those in Fair Trade. This can also mean that Fair Trade producers are inhibited from switching to alternative forms of production, and so overall economic development is held back. A Fair Trade banana grower would have little incentive to move into dairy farming even though this might be a better use of the nation's natural resources. Globally, it might also mean over-production of bananas at the expense of dairy products.

Defenders of Fair Trade counter this argument by stating that the apparent subsidies are only lifting the prices to where they should be if developing economies were able to trade on fair terms. Under the WTO rules protecting infant industries it is accepted that economies need to be allowed an adjustment period when they are exposed to free trade for the first time. The Fair Trade Movement can be seen to be part of this yet there are no indications on how it might reduce its protective policies. For Fair Trade to mean fair trade, it should have in place a mechanism for retiring once its targets have been met, otherwise it will be the multinationals and their customers who will find themselves ultimately disadvantaged, even exploited, by trade.

 ## CASE STUDY: ADAM SMITH INSTITUTE AND FAIR TRADE

One of the most forthright criticisms of Fair Trade comes from the Adam Smith Institute, an economic think tank that promotes libertarian free market ideas. Politically, it has a reputation for being right-wing and is associated with the privatisation of state-owned industries. It is therefore philosophically opposed to the kind of market intervention practised by the Fair Trade institutions.

In an article published in 2007, the author, Marc Sidwell, attacks Fair Trade for enriching retailers and a select group of producers, while poorer ones are left even worse off. He also argues that Fair Trade prevents economic development because it raises exit barriers – there is little reason to move into new industries when the current industry is enjoying artificially low risks. Perhaps most cynically, he believes that Fair Trade is little more than a successful marketing strategy to raise the Fair Trade brand to a position of dominance in a crowded market.

The report suggests that there are other approaches that better reward producers in developing economies. These include measures like long-term contracts, conditions of employment and training. Such close business working replicates the kind of mutually beneficial relationship nurtured in developed economies between manufacturers and their suppliers, an approach often practised in Japan. This leads to sustainable and broad-based economic development rather than the highly selective benefits of Fair Trade.

The argument is compelling but it is also an extreme form of 'tough love'. In the long run it may be free trade that 'makes you rich' (p. 3) but this comes after years of economic restructuring. Such a process is painful enough in a developed economy with funds to smooth the transition, most notably with welfare payments, but it can be devastating for a poorer nation. It is for this reason that the WTO allows a temporary period of infant industry support. Perhaps the real flaw in Fair Trade is that it has no exit strategy when it succeeds.

Point of consideration: Select an example of Fair Trade in practice and indicate what its ultimate purpose might be. Then suggest what the organisation should do once this end point has been reached.

Source: Sidwell/The Adam Smith Institute (2008)

4. CARING FOR THE ECOLOGICAL ENVIRONMENT

It has been some 250 years since the start of the industrial revolution, and over the centuries, starting in Europe and then spreading to the rest of the world, factories and workshops have disposed of their waste products into the environment almost unchecked. Liquid toxins have been poured into the rivers and seas, solid waste has been dumped on green fields and exhaust gases vented into the air.

Even as long ago as 1858 London was debilitated by 'The Great Stink', an overpowering stench of raw sewage rotting in the Thames during an especially hot summer. Nearly one hundred years later, in 1952, air pollution in the city mixed with damp air to create the Great Smog, a combination of smoke and fog, which was so thick in places that people could not see their feet. At least 4000 people died (Met Office, 2014).

While London has cleaned up its act, newer industrialised cities have inherited the same problems but this time it is the motor car that must carry some of the blame. According to the World Bank (2007) air and water pollution in China could be costing it up to 5.8% of GDP each year. Some estimates put the cost of the damage even higher. In effect, China is storing up environmental problems of such magnitude that the costs of rectifying them will unwind much of the economic growth the country has been enjoying.

Although the effects of pollution are becoming plain, among the externalities that result from business activities they are the most difficult to cost and pay for. The results may be subtle, a long time in emerging and far from the location where they originated. The exact causality can be open to question and in some notorious cases there can be significant reluctance to admitting that the damage is even occurring. Other forms of pollution, such as urban lighting and noise also reduce human welfare but are almost impossible to cost in economic terms.

Land and social pollution

Of all the forms of pollution, land pollution is the most visible. It is distinct from air and water pollution, although both of these may be associated effects of polluting the land. Environmental damage to the land should also be the most straightforward to put right, if expensive. For example, a disused and derelict factory renders the land it is on both economically and ecologically useless. The cost of returning the land to some kind of value would involve demolishing and clearing the buildings. Financially, the costs of land clearance can be readily accounted for.

Secondary effects of land pollution are often more difficult to eradicate. There may have been seepage of chemicals into the ground, threatening the water supplies, during the period the factory was operating. This is water pollution, which then goes on to impact a broad range of stakeholders, from farmers to families. In many cases these costly but hidden externalities will not have been accounted for and this is why disused industrial land is often left abandoned.

Waste from mining is another form of land pollution. The material itself, in the same state as when it was deep in the ground, is usually environmentally inert. Piled in heaps it serves no economic function but its presence can still represent a serious threat to safety. In 2008, a landslide of waste from an iron ore mine sent hundreds of tons of debris into the village of Taoshi. Almost the entire community was wiped out (Asia News, 2008).

 ## CASE STUDY: ABERFAN MINING DISASTER

The morning of 21 October 1966 should have been the start of another ordinary day in the unremarkable South Wales mining community of Aberfan. It was 9.15am and the children of the local Pantglas Junior School had made their way back to their classrooms from morning assembly. They had been singing the hymn 'All Things Bright and Beautiful', but outside it was foggy after days of rain.

Overlooking the school was a pile of unprocessed waste, or spoil, from the local mine. Undercutting the spoil heap was a small stream which had become swollen from the days of rainwater. There was little between the spoil heap and solid ground but a thin film of water. The pile itself was saturated and that morning it liquefied into a slurry of water and debris. The resultant cocktail of death was as tragic as it was inevitable. Eyewitnesses described the sound as being like that of a jet engine as 150,000 cubic metres of spoil broke away and roared down the hillside.

The tidal wave of slurry smashed into the side of the school where the classrooms were. Many of the children had time to take refuge under their desks where they thought they would be safe; they were buried under 10 metres of mining debris. 116 schoolchildren died that morning, along with 5 teachers and other members of the village.

If the human cost is incalculable, the attempts to meet the economic costs have been controversial and even shameful. The company that had originally owned the colliery had been absorbed into the state-owned National Coal Board (NCB). The Aberfan Disaster Fund attracted over £1.75 million, but there were heated debates over who should be given financial assistance and how much. When the National Coal Board and the government refused to pay to have the remaining tips removed the Disaster Fund had to foot the £150,000 bill. No member of the NCB or government has ever been held to account.

Point of consideration: If the externalities of the mining had been fully understood and accounted for prior to the disaster how might this have changed the outcome?

Source: Johnes and McLean, 2014

Social pollution is a degradation of the environment that is felt emotionally rather than physically. The effect is often on human welfare and happiness. This would include the light and noise pollution that blight urban living. There is also the desecration of sites of natural beauty. In California it is estimated that the Bay Area is losing 30,000 acres of farmland per year under house building initiatives, a clear economic loss (Greenbelt Alliance, 2013). Many other urban centres have reacted to this pressure by creating greenbelts, land circling the city where new construction is restricted. Critics argue that this simply displaces the urban spread to other locations.

Water pollution

Historically, water pollution has been the most prominent form of environmental concern. Even before the mechanism of diseases was fully known people were aware that there were risks to drinking dirty water. By trial and error it was found that drinks containing alcohol were generally safer. Initially, the sugars in vegetable matter were fermented to create wines in warm climates where grapes could be grown, or beer from grain in colder climates. The safety of beer was further improved by boiling the water as part of the process, and being made in high quantities it could be made available to the general population. In medieval periods even young children were known to drink it. Nevertheless, water was still a vital element in people's lives.

The urbanisation caused by the industrial revolution concentrated the problems of providing clean water. Before microbiology was understood the only test for dirty water was its foul smell. Early sewage systems were a way of keeping the stench down and washing refuse out of the city, disease control being a happy coincidence. Even when early use of statistical analysis in the mid-nineteenth century demonstrated that cholera was a water-borne disease the precise mechanism was unknown, so only vague preventative methods were possible.

 MYTH BUSTER: DR JOHN SNOW AND STATISTICAL MEDICINE

Generally, if there is an epidemic of a deadly disease you would be advised to call a medical doctor, not a statistician. However, Dr John Snow was a Victorian physician who enjoys the curious reputation of being a major influence on two distinct scientific approaches simultaneously: epidemiology, the study of epidemics, and statistics.

In 1854 there was a cholera outbreak in the Soho district of London, an area not yet connected to even the rudimentary sewage system that was then struggling to serve the city. In poor areas like Soho, waste collected in cesspools under the houses and was then transported to the Thames at night to be dumped in the river. Since the Thames was also the source of drinking water for the city any diseases were quickly recycled into the population.

With no knowledge of germ diseases, Dr John Snow found that the cholera outbreak was concentrated around a water pump in Broad Street. Snow was surprised to find that monks in a local monastery were apparently immune from the disease. Then he discovered they drank beer, not water. Convinced that the disease was linked to the water supply, he persuaded the local authority to decommission the water pump in Broad Street by removing the handle.

The local death rate rapidly declined but Snow realised that this could equally be explained by the evacuation of residents from the area. He then conducted a statistical analysis of cholera incidences in the city and was able to link them to the public water pumps. He thereby demonstrated a link between cholera and water quality without any understanding of how the link worked.

Point of consideration: discuss how statistical methods can be used to assess business opportunities without any knowledge of the market characteristics or even the product.

Source: Johnson (2006)

Air pollution

Over the centuries people have tended to assume that diseases were airborne and so, again, with poor scientific understanding corrective actions have been random at best. For example, factories vented exhaust gases through high chimneys which dispersed the fumes at higher altitudes. This reduced the toxins in the area where they were produced but spread the problem to other areas. This made the accounting for externalities very difficult and so the individuals responsible could not be identified.

More recently, scientific studies have brought a much more sophisticated view of how the air is a resource and a depository for waste. Acid rain has been known about since the middle of the nineteenth century, and organisations such as the Environmental Protection Agency (EPA) in the United States have made cost-benefit analyses of the various preventative measures in order to monitor the rate of progress.

The current global concern is that of **global warming**, or more properly, **climate change**. There is a degree of controversy attached to the phenomenon since the expected change in the climate is difficult to measure in the short term because the temperature shift is occurring over a long period of time. If we focus purely on the expected rise in temperature there are a number of different scenarios. Projections from the Intergovernmental Panel on Climate Change (IPCC, 2014) suggest a range of outcomes for the end of this century of surface temperature increases between 3.7°C and 4.8°C. While the lower estimate would be fairly unremarkable, on a day-to-day basis it should be noted that this is the increase in the mean temperature. Remember, ice both freezes and melts at 0°C so an increase of 3.7°C could have a devastating impact on ice and water levels. The rise in mean temperature is theorised to set off a chain of events that would lead to extreme climatic conditions, known as climate change.

Climate change is said to be caused by a build-up of **greenhouse gases (GHG)**, which are those gases that blanket the earth's atmosphere and radiate heat back to the surface, causing it to warm. There are a number of different gases contributing to this effect, the dominant one, most surprisingly, being water vapour. However, given that climate change is a natural part of the planet's ecological rhythm, the main controversy concerns the **anthropogenic greenhouse gases**, those that result from human activities. These GHG are dominated by **CO_2 emissions**, particularly those that are a by-product of fossil fuel combustion.

Kyoto protocol

The United Nations Framework Convention on Climate Change (UNFCCC, 2014) is a treaty intended to stabilise levels of CO_2 in the atmosphere. As part of this, the Kyoto protocol was signed in 1997 to set binding agreements, in many cases including target reductions.

There is a curious commercial basis to the different approaches that are available for countries in achieving their GHG aims. Those countries that undershoot their targets, perhaps because they are de-industrialising, can trade their surplus with countries that are failing to reach their targets. It is also possible to earn credits by assisting developing nations or investing in GHG reductions in other countries. In effect the programme is harnessing the mechanisms of the market to achieve its environmental aim. A criticism of the approach is that it simply shifts the problem from high-polluting countries to low-polluting countries and thereby maintains average global pollution rather than reducing it. Matters are hardly helped by the reluctance of the United States to join in (Eckersley, 2007).

At the corporate level managers will need to be aware of the policies and regulations that will increase their cost base. Fortunately, government regulations hit all companies working in the targeted sector so they should be impacted equally. Nevertheless, the policies can be enough to render the worst offending companies, perhaps those that have been neglected by investors, commercially unviable, with the result that they exit the industry.

RAISING EMPLOYABILITY: THE MORAL EXECUTIVE

Business leaders often like to attribute their success to their ruthless pursuit of profit, completely unencumbered by sentimental baggage. These are the executives who pressure suppliers to reduce prices without regard for the consequences and they are remorseless in the consumption of earthly resources for the advantage of the corporation. They are tough, they are conceited and they are, fortunately, a dying breed.

We are possibly entering a new business paradigm, one where commercial organisations need to take their place in society by being responsible for their actions. This requires a new kind of manager, one that is rational in analysing and implementing corporate social responsibility. Future employability depends on being able to comprehend what it means to be a responsible manager. This means more than being a consciously nicer person since under the surface are all the usual human frailties that unconsciously hold us back. Banaji et al. (2003) warn us that there are four areas of weakness:

- Implicit prejudice – not to be confused with explicit bias like racism, implicit prejudice means judging people against an erroneous stereotype, e.g. females are better suited to the caring professions, males are not.
- Bias towards one's own group – a loyalty towards friends and acquaintances. Can result in a powerful and exclusive social network, e.g. Chinese *guanxi* network.
- Conflict of interest – confusing the common good with personal gain, e.g. earning a commission on referring clients to another business.
- Claiming undue credit – the natural and insidious effect of believing one's own contribution is more important than it is. This can have a corrosive influence on teamwork and alliances.

It is because these are inherent weaknesses that it is not enough for a manager to simply aim to be nicer; a rigorous and systematic programme needs to be put in place to encourage genuinely ethical behaviour. Ghoshal (2005) argues that the problems are introduced at the beginning of executive training with the wrong emphasis being put on management theories. These theories accept a rather pessimistic attitude to human vices, such as opportunism, and then promote management practices to counter them. This then frees managers from making their own moral decisions, trusting instead the system to put in place structures, such as legal frameworks, that provide protection.

Liberated from their obligations, managers then pursue profit for its own sake, incorrectly identifying the shareholders as the sole owners of the company when in fact they only have a claim on a share of the profits. In this narrow view the principals and agents are united in profit. However, in order to act ethically, managers need to recognise that all the stakeholders are, in the broadest sense, owners of the company. In doing so managers should then practise moral awareness, a skill that formal business theories usually eschew altogether. Given that the moral angle is not always obvious, Geva (2006) proposes a typology of moral situations dependent on management motivation and the clarity of the moral question:

- Laxity – low motivation to act when faced with a poorly defined moral situation.
- Compliance – low motivation despite the clearly defined moral issues.
- Dilemma – high motivation to act but the moral question itself is poorly defined.
- Non-problem – high motivation to act and a well defined moral situation.

According to Geva's model of business ethics the twin challenges are to clarify the moral factors and to increase the motivation to deal with them. Accountability goes some way towards a resolution because it highlights the moral issues and then indicates those that are responsible. However, as we have seen previously with techniques like TBL accounting, the process can be a heavy consumer of management resources. Furthermore, without agreed targets to act as the alternative bottom lines, there are no guarantees that the management will pursue the most ethical path.

Ethical codes are an effective way of streamlining decisions about moral issues and allocating responsibilities by incorporating them into a systematic approach. Many companies now like to boast of their ethical codes and proudly publish them for public approval. Yet with the company risking only its reputational, not financial, capital there is plenty of scope for moral hazard; even Enron had a 64-page ethical codes document (Norman and MacDonald, 2004).

For Clegg et al. (2007), business ethics are about practice, not prescribed rules and codes. In this way the demands of each context can be recognised and resolved uniquely. Ironically, though, this call for case-by-case ethical decisions brings us full circle; we are no closer to providing a model of the perfect ethical manager. The key, though, may lie in the variety of stakeholders who make up the unique context. Just as managers need to take responsibility for their actions so should all of the stakeholders in their own ways. This means government through legislation, customers through their buying power, workers through their labour provision and investors through their financial resources. Each of them has their own leverage over the company and if they believe in ethical business then it is their duty to use it.

THE STORY SO FAR: THE CITIZEN CORPORATION

There is a growing consensus that corporations are as much members of human society as people, so it falls on the managers that lead them to ensure they operate ethically. This means being responsible for the impact on the many stakeholders, from the investors to the workers, the suppliers to the buyers, the local communities and the ecological environment. Incorporating all these externalities into the corporate operations is economically efficient but it is also a complex and often contentious process. Even apparently simple ethical considerations, such as Fair Trade or care of the environment, are replete with counter arguments. This may be the nub of the problem and, in the end, managers are just one of the many stakeholders responsible for running the firm.

 WEB SUPPORT

1. Radio Labour. A mass of resources on international labour rights and more:
   www.radiolabour.net/

2. Fair Trade USA. Information on the Fair Trade movement and how to register products:
   www.fairtradeusa.org/?gclid=CM-Pkrew2MUCFYPHtAodTXoAGA

3. CO2 Science provides the counter argument to climate change. Derided by many as climate change deniers and practisers of pseudoscience:
   www.co2science.org/index.php

4. The Royal Society hits back at the more nagging criticisms of climate change theory:
   www.royalsociety.org/~/media/Royal_Society_Content/policy/publications/2007/8031.pdf

Project Topics

1. There are a multitude of approaches for incorporating externalities into accounting reports. What sorts of problems does it cause for stakeholders in their being such a wide variety?
2. The Chinese government is aware that alongside meteoric economic growth there are substantial environmental problems. If the costs of correcting the ecological damage are included in the economic growth figures, what will the final result be?
3. Under what conditions would developing economies be advised to abandon Fair Trade policies?

CASE STUDY: UNION CARBIDE AND THE BHOPAL DISASTER

Bhopal is the capital city of Madhya Pradesh in central India. It is a vibrant city of around 2.5m people, and it is famous for the ring of lakes that circle it. Its convenient location had attracted a number of different industries, including Union Carbide India Ltd (UCIL), a chemical company under joint US and Indian ownership. At its peak it employed around 9000 people across 14 plants.

The plant in Bhopal had been established in 1970 to produce pesticides but it was ill-fated right from the start. It was designed to produce carbaryl (sold under the Sevin brand name), which uses methyl isocyanate (MIC) in the production process. It is a highly toxic substance, even in minute quantities. At that time few Indian farmers could afford pesticides, despite the obvious benefits to harvest yields, and so output at the plant never reached the projected quantities. By the early 1980s sales had dwindled and investment had dried up. The maintenance of the plant was in a very poor state despite the large surplus volumes of MIC remaining on site.

On the night of 2 December 1984 water leaked into an overloaded MIC storage tank. Along with the presence of other contaminants this led to an uncontrollable runaway reaction and temperatures inside the tank rocketed to around 200°C. With the tank unable to contain the pressure or release it safely, over 30 tons of MIC escaped into the atmosphere in the ensuing hour. The wind blew the gas cloud to the south-west, in the very direction of the surrounding shanty town.

The effect that night on the population was devastating. Contact with MIC causes severe irritation to the eyes and throat, leading to coughing and vomiting. As a heavy gas it tends to sink to the ground, so children and the elderly were the most affected. Within hours there were dead littering the streets, nearly 4000 by some estimates. Eight thousand people were dead after two weeks and another 8000 have died since. It is thought that 50,000 people are unable to work due to their injuries. The area remains contaminated to this day, and in 2009 the Centre for Science and Environment (CSE) found affected groundwater up to 3km from the plant.

The Indian legal system has attempted to confront the company with the costs of these externalities. Five years after the disaster, Union Carbide agreed to a partial payout of US$470 million, providing victims with just US$300–500 or the value of around five years of medical treatment. Seven employees of UCIL were given two-year suspended prison sentences and fined a little over US$2000 each.

Point of consideration: The disaster at Bhopal is an example of externalities at their most cruel and tragic. How could these externalities have been internalised and would it have made any difference to the outcome?

Sources: Bhopal Medical Appeal, 2014; Centre for Science and Environment, 2014

? MULTIPLE CHOICE QUESTIONS

1. Corporations need to accept their responsibilities to human society because:
   a. Under US law they are classified as people.
   b. They are operated by people for the benefit of people.
   c. They make profits from people.

2. For an atomic power station in Japan, which of these are stakeholders:
   a. The owners of the power station.
   b. The paying customers.
   c. The entire world.
   d. All of the above.

3. If the externalities for a coal-burning plant are accounted for by the company, who pays for the clean-up?
   a. The paying customers.
   b. The management.
   c. The government.

4. In which region is there free movement of labour?
   a. The World – it is a basic human right.
   b. The EU – enshrined in law.
   c. NAFTA – it is a free trade area.

5. Electric vehicles are often subsidised by governments. Does this mean the externalities are being internalised?
   a. Yes – all of society benefits so all of society should pay.
   b. Not quite – all of society benefits but only the taxpayers fund the subsidies.
   c. No – the customers should pay the full price as they are the only beneficiaries.

6. Why are public organisations more environmentally responsible than private organisations?
   a. They are not required to make a profit.
   b. They have higher standards.
   c. They are owned by the public.

7. When is free trade not fair?
   a. When it involves deception by one of the parties.
   b. When it is not governed by a Fair Trade body.
   c. When the poorest party has little to no bargaining power.

8. Should producers in developed economies be allowed to form their own Fair Trade organisations?
   a. Yes, because they need to uphold high standards.
   b. No, because they already wield sufficient power in the market.

9. Which country has not ratified the Kyoto Protocol?
   a. China.
   b. United States.
   c. Switzerland.

10. Who has most control over the corporate social responsibility (CSR) policies of a company?
    a. Senior management.
    b. Shareholders.
    c. Government.
    d. Workers.

Answers
1b, 2d, 3a, 4b, 5b, 6a, 7c, 8b, 9b, 10a

REFERENCES

Accountability (2011) AA1000 Stakeholder Engagement Standard 2011 from www.accountability.org/images/content/5/4/542/AA1000SES%202010%20PRINT.pdf Accessed 11 October 2014

Asgary N and Mitschow M C (2002) 'Toward a model for international business ethics' *Journal of Business Ethics* 36(3), pp. 239–246

Asia News (2008) 'Taoshi landslide: hundreds dead, mine owner and government accused' from www.asianews.it/news-en/Taoshi-landslide:-hundreds-dead,-mine-owner-and-government-accused-13188.html 9 November 2008 accessed 11 October 2014

Banaji M R, Bazerman M H and Chugh D (2003) 'How (un) ethical are you?' *Harvard Business Review* 81(12), pp. 56–65

Becchetti L and Huybrechts B (2008) 'The dynamics of fair trade as a mixed-form market' *Journal of Business Ethics* 81(4), pp. 733–750

Bhopal Medical Appeal (2014) What happened? from www.bhopal.org/what-happened/ accessed 9 October 2014

Buckley P J and Ghauri P N (2004) 'Globalisation, economic geography and the strategy of multinational enterprises' *Journal of International Business Studies* 35(2), pp. 81–98

Calo M and Wise T A (2005) *Revaluing peasant coffee production: Organic and fair trade markets in Mexico.* Global Development and Environment Institute, Tufts University from www.ase.tufts.edu/gdae/pubs/rp/RevaluingCoffee05.pdf accessed 19 May 2015

Centre for Science and Environment (2014) *Bhopal: the way ahead* from www.cseindia.org/content/bhopal-toxic-legacy-0 accessed 9 October 2014

Clegg S, Kornberger M and Rhodes C (2007) 'Business ethics as practice' *British Journal of Management* 18(2), pp. 107–122

Crowther D (2000) *Social and environmental accounting.* London: Financial Times Prentice Hall

Doepke M and Zilibotti F (2005) 'The macroeconomics of child labor regulation' *The American Economic Review* 95(5), (Dec., 2005), pp. 1492–1524

Eckersley R (2007) 'Ambushed: the Kyoto Protocol, the Bush administration's climate policy and the erosion of legitimacy' *International Politics* 44(2), pp. 306–324

European Fair Trade Association (EFTA)(2014) Homepage from www.european-fair-trade-association.org/efta/index.php accessed 11 October 2014

Elkington J (1997) *Cannibals with forks: The triple bottom line of 21st Century business.* New Society Publishers.

Environmental Protection Agency (2010) 'Acid rain program benefits exceed expectations' from www.epa.gov/capandtrade/documents/benefits.pdf accessed 9 October 2014

Fairtrade International (2014) Homepage from www.fairtrade.net/361.html accessed 11 October 2014

Friedman M (2007) *Price theory*. New Brunswick, NJ: Transaction Publishers

Ghoshal S (2005) 'Bad management theories are destroying good management practices' *Academy of Management Learning & Education* 4(1), pp. 75–91

Global Reporting Initiative (GRI)(2014) Homepage from www.globalreporting.org/Pages/default.aspx accessed 11 October 2014

Green C A (2007) 'Between the devil and the deep blue sea: mercantilism and free trade' *Race & Class* 49(2), pp. 41–56

Greenbelt Alliance (2013) *Can California farmland be saved?* from www.greenbelt.org/general/can-california-farmland-be-saved/ 15 August 2013 accessed 11 October 2014

Intergovernmental Panel on Climate Change (IPCC, 2014) *Climate change 2014: Mitigation of climate change*. Cambridge, UK and New York, NY, USA: Cambridge University Press. Available from www.mitigation2014.org/report/final-draft/ accessed 11 October 2014

International Labour Organisation (2014) About ILO from www.ilo.org/global/about-the-ilo/lang--en/index.htm accessed 11 October 2014

Johnes M and McLean I (2014) *The Aberfan disaster* from www.nuffield.ox.ac.uk/politics/aberfan/home.htm accessed 11 October 2014

Johnson S (2006) *The ghost map*. New York, NY: Riverhead Trade

Kelemen M and Peltonen T (2001) 'Ethics, morality and the subject: the contribution of Zygmunt Bauman and Michel Foucault to postmodern business ethics' *Scandinavian Journal of Management* 17(2), pp. 151–166

Maseland R and De Vaal A (2002) 'How fair is fair trade?' *De Economist* 150(3), pp. 251–272

Met Office (2014) The Great Smog of 1952 from www.metoffice.gov.uk/education/teens/case-studies/great-smog accessed 11 October 2014

Nakamura K (2007) 'Decline or revival?: Japanese labor unions' *Japan Labor Review* 4(1), pp. 7–22.

Norman W and MacDonald C (2004) 'Getting to the bottom of "triple bottom line"' *Business Ethics Quarterly* pp. 243–262

Principles for Responsible Investment (PRI) (2014) Homepage from www.unpri.org/ accessed 9 October 2014

San Francisco (2015) *Environment now: green careers* from www.sfenvironment.org/education-equity/green-jobs/environment-now-green-careers accessed 18 May 2015

Seifert H and Massa-Wirth H (2005) 'Pacts for employment and competitiveness in Germany' *Industrial Relations Journal* 36(3), pp. 217–240

Sidwell M (2008) *Unfair trade*. London: The Adam Smith Institute from www.adamsmith.org/sites/default/files/images/pdf/unfair_trade.pdf accessed 11 October 2014

SSD (2014) 'The 10 Most Important Facts for Employers About Works Councils and Their Rights in Germany' from www.squiresanders.com/files/Event/110cb877-897f-43b8-a30f-142a6bf00538/Presentation/EventAttachment/c82733b3-8d42-4feb-b7bb-ad5a397dbf0e/Dealing_With_German_Works_Councils.pdf accessed 11 October 2014

United Nations Department of Economic and Social Affairs (2001) *Environmental Management Accounting: Policies and Linkages* from www.sustainabledevelopment.un.org/content/documents/policiesandlinkages.pdf accessed 11 October 2014

United Nations Framework Convention on Climate Change (UNFCC)(2014) UN climate change newsroom from www.newsroom.unfccc.int/about/ accessed 11 October 2014

United Nations (2001) *Environmental managing accounting procedures and principles* May 2001 from www.un.org/esa/sustdev/publications/proceduresandprinciples.pdf accessed 14 November 2014

Wilson R (2006) 'Islam and business' *Thunderbird International Business Review* 48(1), pp. 109–123

World Fair Trade Organisation (WFTO) (2014) *10 Principles of Fair Trade* from www.wfto.com/index.php?option=com_content&task=view&id=2&Itemid=14 accessed 11 October 2014

World Bank (2007) *Cost of pollution in China: economic estimates of physical damages* from www.siteresources.worldbank.org/INTEAPREGTOPENVIRONMENT/Resources/China_Cost_of_Pollution.pdf accessed 11 October 2014

Index